A Constructed Peace

PRINCETON STUDIES IN INTERNATIONAL HISTORY AND POLITICS

SERIES EDITORS
Jack L. Snyder and Richard H. Ullman

A Constructed Peace

THE MAKING OF
THE EUROPEAN SETTLEMENT,
1945 – 1963

· *MARC TRACHTENBERG* ·

PRINCETON UNIVERSITY PRESS

PRINCETON, NEW JERSEY

Library of Congress Cataloging-in-Publication Data

Trachtenberg, Marc, 1946–
A constructed peace : the making of the European
settlement, 1945–1963 / Marc Trachtenberg.
p.   cm. — (Princeton studies in international
history and politics)
Includes bibliographical references and index.
ISBN 0-691-00183-9 (cloth : alk. paper). — ISBN
0-691-00273-8 (pbk. : alk. paper)
1. Europe—Politics and government—1945–
2. Europe—Foreign relations—United States.
3. United States—Foreign relations—Europe.
4. Peace.   5. North Atlantic Treaty Organization.
6. Nuclear weapons—International cooperation.
I. Title.   II. Series.
D1058.T718   1999   327'.094'09045—dc21   98-34874   cip

This book has been composed in Berkeley

The paper used in this publication meets the minimum requirements of
ANSI/NISO Z39.48-1992 (R1997) (*Permanence of Paper*)

http://pup.princeton.edu

Printed in the United States of America

1   3   5   7   9   10   8   6   4   2

1   3   5   7   9   10   8   6   4   2
(Pbk.)

• C O N T E N T S •

THIS BOOK has a simple goal: the basic aim here is to tell the story of how peace came to the world of the great powers during the Cold War period—or, more precisely, during the period from 1945 to 1963. The basic argument is also quite simple: the claim is that the problem of German power lay at the heart of the Cold War; a resolution of that problem was therefore the key to the establishment of a stable international system in Europe, and ultimately in the world as a whole.

Why was the German question so important? After World War II, Europe was divided between east and west, and the division of Europe, broadly speaking, provided an answer to the fundamental political question of how the two sides, the Soviet Union and the western powers, could get along: each would have a free hand on its side of the line of demarcation. But there was one great exception to that general rule, and this had to do with Germany. The Soviets would not stand idly by if their former allies allowed West Germany to become too strong or too independent. A strong Germany would not be dependent on the western allies for protection and would thus not be locked into a purely defensive policy; a resurgent West German state might intervene in the event of an uprising in the east; as the Soviets saw it, a powerful Germany meant a greatly increased risk of war. To head off these dangers, decisive action might well be warranted; matters might have to be brought to a head before it was too late.

The problem of German power was thus fundamental, and it was for this reason that the arrangements the western countries worked out among themselves were of such enormous political importance. It was not as though there were NATO questions and questions of east-west relations, with the two sets of issues only marginally related to each other; these problems were all tightly intertwined. If the western countries could create a political system of their own in which German power was limited, this was something the USSR could live with; if they were unable to do so, there might be very serious trouble indeed.

And it was not as though the problem of how the West was to organize itself had a simple and obvious solution that was worked out relatively early on. No one thought it would be easy to construct a system in which West Germany would not be free to act independently and would thus have no choice but to accept the status quo in Europe. After all, the western powers were determined to make West Germany an integral part of the western world. Didn't that mean that sooner or later Germany would have to be made a full partner, with the same rights as the other western countries? Wouldn't Germany therefore have to be allowed to build a nuclear force under her own control? Wouldn't the Federal Republic, exposed to Soviet power as she was, more or less have to build such a force if she could not count on America to defend her? And with the growth of Soviet nuclear capabilities, how could anyone think that the United States would forever remain willing to go to war for the sake of western Europe—a war that might well mean the total destruction of American society? On the other hand, to remove the constraints on German power entirely, and above all to permit Germany to acquire a nuclear force of her own, might lead directly to a clash with Russia, and then what would the western powers do? And quite apart from the Soviet reaction, could Germany be trusted to respect the status quo once she had become a strong nuclear power? These were all very difficult issues; no one could tell for sure how they would be worked out; and, indeed, things ran their course in a way few would have predicted in 1945, or 1949, or even 1954.

People still think of the Cold War as a simple two-sided conflict, a kind of gigantic arm wrestle on a global scale. But this view, I believe, is profoundly mistaken. A purely bipolar system would have been quite stable: Soviet power and American power would have balanced each other so completely that the risk of general war would have been minimal. But we know the Cold War was a serious conflict. We know that the risk of war was at times very real indeed. The problem, therefore, is to understand where the clash was coming from. To do that, the story has to be reconstructed in a way that brings out in some detail what was actually going on.

And there is a real story here. All kinds of issues were involved. There was the central problem of German power; this was bound up with a whole cluster of questions relating to America's role in Europe—questions about the American military presence in Europe, about the meaning of NATO and the nature of the relationship between the United States and the major European allies, especially in the key nuclear area. These questions were in turn closely related to a number of very basic military issues—problems having to do with the role of nuclear weapons in the defense of western Europe, with the control of nuclear forces, and with the course that a military confrontation with the USSR would, or, in some sense, should, take. And these intra-alliance questions were all linked to the most fundamental problems of international politics: could a basic political understanding with the Russians ever be worked out? If so, on what terms? If, on the other hand, it turned out that no understanding was possible, should the western side, in the final analysis, be prepared to accept a military showdown with the Soviets in central Europe?

All this makes for a rather complex story. To understand why things took the course they did—why the central problems were resolved the way they were, and thus how it was that a stable peace took shape—a whole series of issues has to be explored in some depth. This is a long book, much longer than I would have liked, but this is not because I had done a lot of work and wanted to include everything I had found. This book lays out an argument; that argument has to be fleshed out. It involves elements which are not well understood; those elements have to be explained and their importance made clear. Thus MC 48, the strategy for the defense of western Europe adopted in December 1954, is a very important part of the story here: it was one of the three great taproots of the Eisenhower nuclear sharing policy, something which in turn was of basic importance because of its bearing on the question of Germany's nuclear status. But how many people have even heard of MC 48, let alone understand its importance? So this is the sort of thing that needs to be discussed in some detail.

Many readers, moreover, are going to find some of the central claims advanced here hard to accept; this again means that the evidence has to be massive. The argument, for example, that Eisenhower wanted the United States to withdraw from Europe in the not too distant future, and that he therefore wanted the major NATO allies, including West Germany, to have nuclear forces under their own control, is often rejected out of hand: it is taken practically as an article of faith, both in America and in Europe, that no U.S. government could possibly have had such a policy. I remember McGeorge Bundy's reaction, a few years ago, when I made that argument about Eisenhower: "Do you really believe that Ike would ever have let the Germans get their hands on nuclear weapons?" The only way to overcome this kind of resistance is to present a mass of evidence, organized into a structured argument; isolated quotations are never taken as compelling.

So some issues are treated at great length, but other subjects are more or less ignored. The Suez affair is treated as a kind of sideshow; Sputnik is scarcely mentioned; events in East Asia, even the Korean War, do not play a major role here, at least not until the final chapter. The focus of the book is unrelentingly Eurocentric, but even major European events—the East German uprising of 1953, for example, or the Hungarian revolt of 1956—are passed over in silence. How can a book that purports to be about the Cold War ignore events that received so much attention at the time and that most people still think are of fundamental importance?

But there are reasons why I took this kind of approach. First of all, it seemed to me that the argument was complex enough, and the text massive enough, as it is. It was important not to add to the burden placed on the reader by straying from the central thrust of the argument; it was important to keep the text as lean, as sharp, and as easy to follow as possible. This book, moreover, was not meant to be an encyclopedia. The aim was not to cover every issue, but rather to get at the heart of the story. If the goal, however, was to bring out what was driving things, the text had to make it clear what was important, and, implicitly, what was not. To dwell on an issue was a way of saying that it was important; to ignore it was a way of saying that no matter how much attention it got at the time and still gets in standard historical accounts, it did not play an important role in the central story.

What this meant, however, was that the interpretation was going to have loose ends. To explain is to focus on fundamentals—that is, to give a relatively simple picture of what was going on. But historical reality is complex; there was thus bound to be a certain gap between what the interpretation explained and what the evidence showed. And in fact there are elements of the story which are hard to account for—indeed, which in some cases run counter to the basic thrust of the interpretation. Were these to be swept under the rug and just explained away with ad hoc arguments? I thought it best not to go that route. If I myself did not understand something, why should I pretend to have the answer? And why shouldn't the reader get to see that the interpretation does not explain everything—indeed, that there are important aspects of the story which it does not account for at all?

One of the basic arguments here, for example, is that the USSR was deeply concerned, in the late 1950s and early 1960s especially, with the question of a German nuclear capability, and that this concern was a key factor shaping Soviet policy during the whole Berlin Crisis period. But there is a major problem with this argument: if the German nuclear issue was as important as I say, why didn't the Soviets settle the crisis in late 1961 and early 1962 when the Americans offered a non-nuclear Germany as part of a deal for a settlement? This problem is not fatal for my purposes. The fact that the American terms were not accepted only shows that by the early 1960s additional factors must have come into play, not that the German nuclear issue had faded away. But there is no getting around the fact that it would have been nicer, from the point of view of the argument in this book, if the Soviets had closed the deal with the Americans as soon as the new terms were put on the table in late 1961. Should I have tried to deal with this issue by speculating about what those additional factors might have been? The problem was that I had no really adequate evidence from Soviet sources to work with, so it seemed best to just let it be. Soviet policy at this point had to be accepted as lying somewhat beyond the reach of the basic interpretation in the book. What this meant was not that the argument as a whole was worthless, but simply that it had its limits—indeed, limits that had to be accepted philosophically.

Finally, let me say a word about some technical matters. To keep the baggage of source citation as light as possible, abbreviations have been used extensively. Those abbreviations appear in brackets the first time a source is cited in the footnotes, and again in the bibliography; in addition they appear in the list of abbreviations on pp. xv–xvi. In order to keep the argument in the text on track, various ancillary issues are dealt with in the footnotes. Some of these became so long and unwieldy that they were made into appendices, which appear not in this book, but in an internet supplement: http://www.history.upenn.edu/trachtenberg. The internet supplement contains other material as well; the contents are described in a note at the beginning of the bibliography.

A book of this sort is not something I could have done entirely on my own. A number of political scientists—above all Robert Jervis, John Mearsheimer, and Stephen Van Evera—had an enormous impact on the way I have come to think about these issues; what I owe them is difficult to put into words, but the debt is very real. I also feel deeply indebted to a number of historians—and to four in particular who played a key role in shaping my understanding of the issues discussed here, not just through their written work, but through extensive personal contact as well. David Rosenberg, whose work revolutionized the study of nuclear issues, had a profound impact on the way I deal with the nuclear side of the story. Robert Wampler opened my eyes to what was going on in NATO in the 1950s—to the meaning of MC 48, for example, and to the course of American policy for the defense of Europe in the latter part of the decade—and was also extremely generous in sharing documents with me. I also owe a great deal to two French scholars: to Cyril Buffet, whose work on the German question in the late 1940s, especially his doctoral thesis, played a key role in shaping my understanding of the subject; and to Georges-Henri Soutou, who was the first to explain to me the importance of the Paris accords, and whose work in general has had a profound influence on practically every chapter in this book. There were a number of people—Aaron Friedberg, Bob Jervis, John Mearsheimer, Bill Stueck, Walter McDougall, and Bruce Kuklick—who commented on an earlier draft of the manuscript; it is hard to exaggerate how valuable that sort of feedback is, and I very much want to thank all of them. I am particularly grateful to Gavin Lewis; he and I both know how extraordinary his contribution was. I also owe a very special debt of gratitude to Carl Kaysen for all the help he has given me over the years. And, finally, I want to express my appreciation to the Guggenheim Foundation, the MacArthur Foundation, and the German Marshall Fund for making it possible for me to do the work that led to this book.

GENERAL ABBREVIATIONS

ABC	Atomic, Biological, and Chemical (weapons)
AEC	Atomic Energy Commission (US)
BNSP	Basic National Security Policy (US)
CDU	Christian Democratic Union (FRG)
CINCEUR	Commander in Chief, Europe (US)
CSU	Christian Social Union (FRG)
DDR	German Democratic Republic
DOD	Department of Defense (US)
DPM	Draft Presidential Memorandum
EDC	European Defense Community
EEC	European Economic Community
FIG	France-Italy-Germany (nuclear cooperation agreement)
FRG	Federal Republic of Germany
GDR	German Democratic Republic
ICBM	Intercontinental Ballistic Missile
IRBM	Intermediate Range Ballistic Missile
JCAE	Joint Committee on Atomic Energy (US)
JCS	Joint Chiefs of Staff (US)
MLF	Multilateral Force
MRBM	Medium Range Ballistic Missile
NATO	North Atlantic Treaty Organization
NESC	Net Evaluation Subcommittee
NIE	National Intelligence Estimate (US)
NSAM	National Security Action Memorandum
NSC	National Security Council (US)
PAL	Permissive Action Link
SAC	Strategic Air Command (US)
SACEUR	Supreme Allied Commander, Europe
SHAPE	Supreme Headquarters, Allied Powers, Europe
SIOP	Single Integrated Operational Plan (US)
SPD	Social Democratic Party (FRG)
USAF	United States Air Force
WEU	Western European Union

SOURCE ABBREVIATIONS

Explanations of abbreviations are not complete citations, but provide enough information to enable the source concerned to be located in the bibliography. Abbreviations used in the explanations themselves will also be found in this list.

A	Administration Series, AWF
A	Alphabetical subseries, in Subject Series, SS
AAPBD	Federal Republic of Germany, Auswärtiges Amt, *Akten zur auswärtigen Politik der Bundesrepublik Deutschland*

AP	Dean Acheson Papers
AWD	Ann Whitman Diary Series
AWF	Papers of Dwight D. Eisenhower as President (Ann Whitman File)
Bowie Report	Robert Bowie, "The North Atlantic Nations: Tasks for the 1960's"
BP	Bonnet Papers
CF	Conference Files, RG 59, USNA
CJCS	Chairman's Files, RG 218: Joint Chiefs of Staff, USNA
CWIHP	Cold War International History Project
DBPO	*Documents on British Policy Overseas*
DDED	Dwight D. Eisenhower Diary Series
DDEL	Dwight D. Eisenhower Library, Abilene, Kansas
DDF	France, Ministère des Affaires Etrangères, Commission de Publication des Documents Diplomatiques Français, *Documents Diplomatiques Français*
DDRS	Declassified Documents Reference System
DH	Dulles-Herter Series
DoD	Department of Defense subseries, in Subject Series, SS
DOD-FOIA	Department of Defense, Freedom of Information Office
DoS	Department of State subseries, in Subject Series, SS
DOSCF	Department of State, Central Files
DOSB	*Department of State Bulletin*
DOS Berlin History	United States, Department of State, Historical Office, "Crisis over Berlin: American Policy Concerning the Soviet Threats to Berlin, November 1958–December 1962"
DOS-FOIA	Department of State, Freedom of Information Office
DP	John Foster Dulles Papers, DDEL and ML
DSP	Dulles State Papers, ML
FD	Forrestal Diaries, ML
FFMA	French Foreign Ministry Archives, Paris
FO 371	Foreign Office, Political Correspondence, PRO
FOIA	Freedom of Information Act
FP	James Forrestal Papers, ML
FRUS	United States, State Department, *Foreign Relations of the United States*
GCM	General Correspondence and Memoranda Series, DP
Holifield Report	U.S. Congress, Joint Committee on Atomic Energy, Report of Ad Hoc Subcommittee on the Assignment of Nuclear Weapons to NATO
HP	Averell Harriman Papers, LOC
HSTL	Harry S Truman Library, Independence, Missouri
I	International Series
IS	Internet Supplement to this work
ITM	International Trips and Meetings Series, SS
JCS History	Joint Chiefs of Staff, Historical Office, *History of the Joint Chiefs of Staff*
JFKL	John F. Kennedy Library, Boston, Massachusetts
KP	Arthur Krock Papers, ML
Krone Diary	Heinrich Krone, "Aufzeichnungen zur Deutschland- und Ostpolitik 1954–1969"
LHCMA	Liddell Hart Centre for Military Archives, King's College, London

LNC	Charles de Gaulle, *Lettres, notes et carnets*
LOC	Library of Congress, Washington, D.C.
ML	Seeley Mudd Library, Princeton, New Jersey
MP	Massigli Papers, FFMA
NDU	National Defense University, Washington, D.C.
Neustadt Report	Richard Neustadt, "Skybolt and Nassau: American Policy-Making and Anglo-American Relations"
NP	Norstad Papers, DDEL
NSA	National Security Archive, Washington, D.C.
NSABF	Berlin Crisis File, NSA
NSF	National Security Files, JFKL
OSANSA	Office of the Special Assistant for National Security Affairs Files, DDEL
P	Presidential subseries, SA
POF	President's Office Files, JFKL
PP	Policy Papers subseries, in NSC, OSANSA
PPP	*Public Papers of the Presidents*
PPS	Policy Planning Staff records, RG 59, USNA
Prem 11	Prime Minister's Office files, PRO
PRO	Public Record Office, Kew
PSF	President's Secretary's Files, HSTL
RG	Record Group, USNA
S	Subject Series or subseries
SA	Special Assistant's Series, OSANSA
SACS	Special Assistant's Chronological Series, DP
SDWHA	State Department and White House Advisor, AP
SHAT	Service Historique de l'Armée de Terre, Vincennes
SS	White House Office, Office of the Staff Secretary Files, DDEL
SSMC	United States, Department of State, *Secretary of State's Memoranda of Conversation*
SWNCC	State, War, Navy Coordinating Committee
TC	Telephone Conversation Series, DP
TP	Maxwell Taylor Papers, NDU
USNA	United States National Archives, College Park, Maryland
WH	White House subseries, in Subject Series, SS
WHM	White House Memoranda Series, DP

PART I

The Division of Europe

A Spheres of Influence Peace?

THE UNITED STATES, the Soviet Union, and Great Britain were allies in 1945. To-gether they had defeated Nazi Germany so thoroughly that by May the Germans had been forced to capitulate. Japan, the other major enemy power, surrendered a few months later. But victory did not mean peace. Even before the war ended, the USSR and the western allies had started to quarrel with each other, and by early 1946 many people were beginning to think that a third world war might well be unavoidable.

The Soviet Union and the western powers of course never did go to war with each other, but the great conflict they engaged in—what came to be called the Cold War—dominated international politics for almost half a century. In the 1950s and early 1960s especially, a global war was not just a theoretical possibil-ity. The threat of armed conflict was real, and at times it seemed that a new war might be just months—perhaps even just days—away. And war at this time meant general nuclear war. The feeling was that the survival of civilization, perhaps even of the human race itself, might well be hanging in the balance.

How is the Cold War to be understood? It is often taken for granted that the conflict was ideological at its core—that the Soviets wanted to dominate Europe and impose Communist regimes on the continent as a whole, while the U.S. gov-ernment, at any rate after President Franklin Roosevelt's death in April 1945, was incapable of thinking in "spheres of influence" terms and of accepting the division of Europe. The Americans, the argument runs, could not abandon their principles and had to support the independence of Poland and other countries in eastern Eu-rope, and this was what led to the first great clash between the United States and the Soviet Union at the beginning of the Truman period, the quarrel over Poland. And this dispute, it is commonly assumed, played a key role in getting the Cold War started: once the ball had started rolling, there was just no way to stop it.[1]

It was certainly natural that Stalinist Russia and democratic America were un-able to work together intimately in the postwar period, but does this mean that they were bound to get involved in a dispute that could conceivably have led to war? Maybe the Americans would have liked to see their kind of system spread throughout Europe, and perhaps the Soviets would have liked to communize the entire continent. But given power realities and both sides' aversion to war, what bearing did those wishes have on effective policy? The United States was not going to use force to try to expel the Russians from eastern Europe, nor was the USSR going to provoke a third world war in order to push the Americans out of western Europe. Didn't both sides, therefore, regardless of what they said, more or less have

---

[1] See, for example, the passages cited in Lynn Davis, *The Cold War Begins: Soviet-American Conflict over Eastern Europe* (Princeton, N.J.: Princeton University Press, 1974), pp. 3–4.

to accept things as they were in Europe? Didn't American power and Soviet power balance each other so completely that neither side was really able to challenge the status quo there? If so, where was the problem?

Indeed, looking back, it is hard to understand why there was a serious risk of armed conflict during that period. American policymakers, and Soviet leaders as well, were not prisoners of their own ideologies, and were perfectly capable of recognizing power realities and constructing their policies accordingly. American policy in fact became more "realistic"—that is, more attuned to power realities and thus more willing to accept the Soviet domination of eastern Europe—under President Harry Truman in the second half of 1945 than it had been under Roosevelt at the beginning of the year. The United States, under the guidance of Secretary of State James Byrnes, the real maker of American foreign policy during the early Truman period, took the lead, especially at the Potsdam Conference in July 1945, in pressing for what amounted to a spheres of influence settlement in Europe: the western powers would accept, in fact if not in words, the Soviet sphere in the east; in exchange, the Russians would respect western domination of the areas Britain and America controlled. There were strong indications that the Soviets would go along with an arrangement of this sort. And so, by late 1945, it might have seemed that a more or less permanent settlement was taking shape: each side would have a free hand in the area it dominated, and on that basis the two sides would be able to get along with each other in the future.

But a settlement of this sort did not come into being, not until 1963 at any rate. Why was it so long in coming? Why did the division of Europe not lead directly to a stable international order? To answer those questions is to understand what the Cold War was about.

THE CONFLICT OVER EASTERN EUROPE

As the war in Europe drew to a close in early 1945, the Soviet Union and the western powers quarreled over eastern Europe. The Red Army occupied most of the region, and there were many signs the USSR wanted to dominate that area on a more permanent basis. Britain and America, on the other hand, favored arrangements that would allow the east Europeans to play a much greater role in shaping their own destinies.

The most important issue here was the fate of Poland, and indeed the Polish question dominated relations between the Soviet Union and the western powers at the beginning of 1945. This was no accident: Poland was far more important for both sides than any other east European country. It is not hard to see why the Soviets wanted a "friendly" Poland: the country lay astride the great invasion path between Germany and Russia. Poland was important not just as a buffer area in the event Germany recovered her power and threatened to invade Russia again; it was also important that the Red Army be able to march through Poland so that Soviet power could be brought to bear on Germany and the Germans could be kept in line. The USSR needed both the right of free passage and secure lines of communication. The problem was that if Poland were truly independent, these rights might not be secure. The Poles had long feared and distrusted their great neighbor to the east. The war, which had begun with the USSR carving up Poland with Nazi Germany, had led to a number of episodes which had intensified Polish hatred, especially the murder in the Katyn Forest of Polish officers who had fallen into Soviet hands in 1939, and the crushing of the Warsaw Uprising by the Germans in August and September 1944 while the Red Army stood by and did nothing. Could a truly independent Poland accept the presence of Soviet troops on her territory? The USSR wanted a Poland she could depend on, which meant in the circumstances of 1945 a Poland she could control—a country ruled by Communists and run as a police state.[2]

By the start of 1945, the thrust of Soviet policy was clear. The USSR, over the objections of her western allies, had just recognized the Communist-dominated Lublin Committee as the provisional government of Poland. How were Britain and America to react? Neither government insisted that the principle of self-determination was the only acceptable basis for ordering international affairs, nor was either government dogmatically opposed to arrangements based on spheres of influence. President Roosevelt was willing, for example, to recognize Soviet predominance in Manchuria as part of the deal for getting the Russians to come into the war against Japan.[3] In October 1944, he endorsed the famous "percentage agreement" in which Winston Churchill and Joseph Stalin, the British and Soviet leaders, had divided southeastern Europe into spheres of influence: British predominance was recognized in Greece, and Soviet predominance in Bulgaria and Rumania.[4] It is clear, more generally, that Roosevelt was willing to accept Soviet control over certain areas—the Baltic republics and the eastern part of prewar Poland—no matter how the populations in question felt about rule by the USSR.[5] And he also accepted, as a simple fact of political life, that Soviet power would cast a deep shadow over all of eastern Europe.

But this does not mean that Roosevelt had come to view the whole region as an area in which the Russians could exercise a free hand. The one country that Roosevelt, and Churchill as well, were particularly interested in was Poland, or more

[2] The Katyn Forest and Warsaw Uprising episodes were just the best-known incidents in what was, from the start, an extraordinarily brutal process. See Jan T. Gross, *Revolution from Abroad: The Soviet Conquest of Poland's Western Ukraine and Western Belorussia* (Princeton, N.J.: Princeton University Press, 1988).

[3] "Agreement Regarding Entry of the Soviet Union into the War against Japan, February 11, 1945," in United States, Department of State, *Foreign Relations of the United States, The Conferences at Malta and Yalta, 1945* (Washington, D.C.: GPO, 1955) [FRUS Yalta], p. 984.

[4] Robert Dallek, *Franklin D. Roosevelt and American Foreign Policy, 1932–1945* (Oxford: Oxford University Press, 1981), pp. 479–480. For an account that takes the opposite line on this point, see Albert Resis, "The Churchill-Stalin Secret 'Percentages' Agreement on the Balkans, Moscow, October, 1944," *American Historical Review* 83 (1978): 368–387. See also Warren Kimball, *The Juggler: Franklin Roosevelt as Wartime Statesman* (Princeton, N.J.: Princeton University Press, 1991), chap. 8, and the other writings cited there (n. 44). For some key British documents, see Joseph M. Siracusa, "The Meaning of TOLSTOY: Churchill, Stalin and the Balkans, Moscow, October 1944," *Diplomatic History* 3 (1979): 443–463.

[5] See, for example, the minutes of Roosevelt's meeting with Stalin, December 1, 1943, FRUS Cairo and Teheran, pp. 594–595; and also Gar Alperovitz, *Atomic Diplomacy: Hiroshima and Potsdam* (New York: Simon and Schuster, 1965), pp. 134–136.

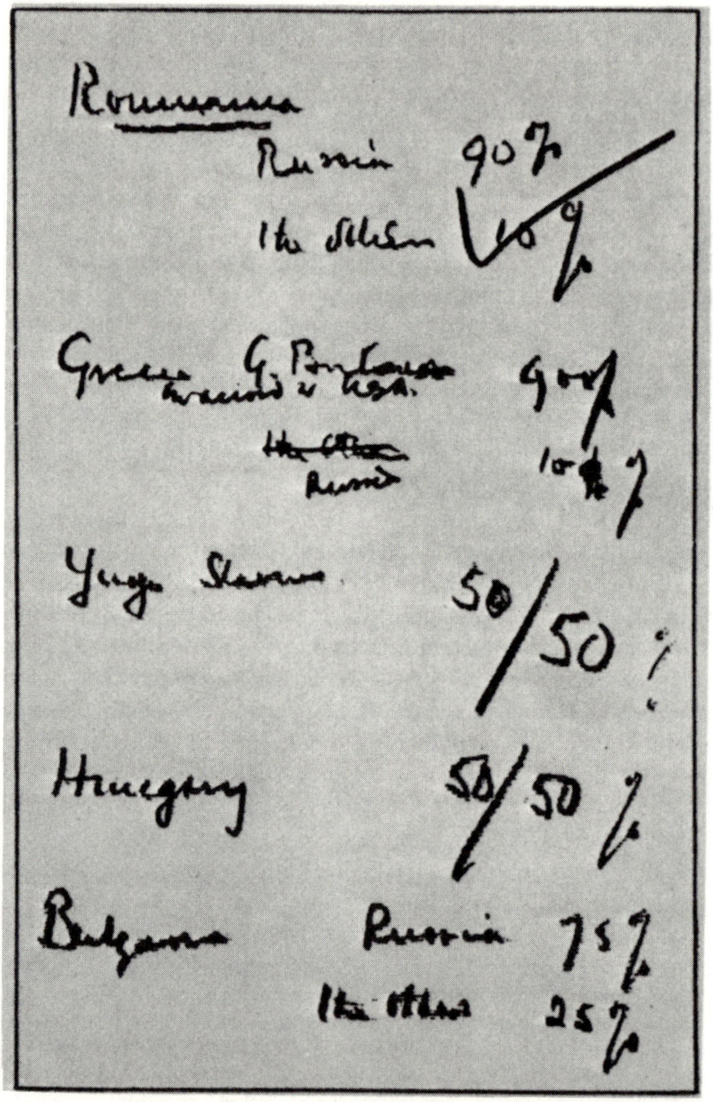
Roumania
Russia 90%
The others 10%

Greece G. Britain 90%
(in accord with U.S.A.)
Russia 10%

Yugoslavia 50/50%

Hungary 50/50%

Bulgaria Russia 75%
The others 25%

Figure 1. The Percentage Agreement. After explaining what he had in mind, Churchill (as he later told the story) pushed this document across to Stalin. "There was a slight pause. Then he took his blue pencil and made a large tick upon it, and passed it back to us. It was all settled in no more time than it takes to set down." Winston Churchill, *Triumph and Tragedy* (Boston: Houghton Mifflin, 1953), p. 227. The document itself is reproduced from the copy published in C. L. Sulzberger, *Such a Peace: The Roots and Ashes of Yalta* (New York: Continuum, 1982).

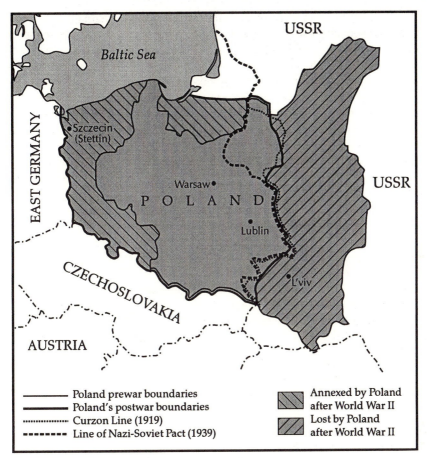

Figure 2. The Borders of Poland.

precisely Poland west of the Curzon Line (see Figure 2). Rumania and Bulgaria had not been on the allied side during the war, but Poland was different. It was to defend Polish independence that Britain had gone to war in the first place in 1939; the Poles had fought bravely against Germany; and a Polish army was still fighting side by side with the western allies in the war. Moreover, while there were not many Americans of Bulgarian or Rumanian descent, there was a fairly large Polish-American community, concentrated in some key industrial states in the midwest.

Both sides therefore had a great interest in Poland, and by the beginning of 1945, the problem had become a serious threat to allied unity—and the maintenance of unity was one of Roosevelt's fundamental goals. What was to be done? When the allied leaders met at Yalta in February, their main purpose was to deal with the Polish problem.

The agreement worked out at Yalta called for the Communist-dominated provisional government in Poland to be "reorganized on a broader democratic basis with the inclusion of democratic leaders from Poland itself and from Poles abroad."

Soviet Foreign Minister Molotov and the American and British ambassadors in Moscow were to help bring this new government into being, and that government would be "pledged to the holding of free and unfettered elections as soon as possible on the basis of universal suffrage and secret ballot."[6] The agreement, as Roosevelt later wrote, represented a compromise between the western view that an "entirely new" Polish government be formed, and the initial Soviet view that the Lublin government "should merely be 'enlarged.'" As such, it clearly placed "more emphasis on the Lublin Poles than on the other two groups from which the new government is to be drawn."[7]

Did this mean, however, that the western powers had agreed to give the USSR a free hand in Poland, and implicitly in all of eastern Europe? It is often argued that all the talk about free elections and non-Communist representation in the provisional government was mere window-dressing, designed essentially for domestic consumption. Roosevelt, the argument goes, knew that "the Russians had the power in eastern Europe," that the West's bargaining position was therefore weak, and that the best he could hope for was a deal that would save appearances while conceding to the Soviets effective control of the area.[8]

But does this interpretation really hold up to analysis? Roosevelt certainly knew that the Soviets had the power to impose a communist regime on Poland, but this fact did not in itself oblige him to put an official seal of approval on such an arrangement. There would be no point to an agreement if it did not provide ben-

[6] For the texts, see FRUS Yalta, pp. 968–984.

[7] Roosevelt to Churchill, March 29, 1945, Francis Loewenheim et al., eds., *Roosevelt and Churchill: Their Secret Wartime Correspondence* (New York: Dutton, 1975), p. 690.

[8] This is one of a number of key areas in the interpretation of Cold War history where Left and Right join hands in misconception. On the left, it is commonly assumed that at Yalta Poland, and a fortiori the rest of eastern Europe, were accepted as part of the Soviet sphere of influence. The "Yalta policy" is seen in this quarter as a realistic accommodation to Soviet power in this part of the world, a sensible recognition of Soviet security requirements, and an essential part of a policy of postwar allied cooperation. The West is condemned, not for accepting the Soviet domination of eastern Europe, but for trying to "undo" the Yalta agreement, especially after Roosevelt died and Harry Truman took over as president. For some representative examples: Athan Theoharis, "Roosevelt and Truman on Yalta: The Origins of the Cold War," *Political Science Quarterly* 87 (1972): 220–221; Diane Clemens, *Yalta* (New York: Oxford University Press, 1970), pp. 215, 269, 279; Robert Messer, *The End of an Alliance: James F. Byrnes, Roosevelt, Truman, and the Origins of the Cold War* (Chapel Hill: University of North Carolina Press, 1982), pp. 42, 50–51, 56–58. On the right, it is also commonly assumed that Yalta represented the West's acceptance of a Soviet free hand in eastern Europe, only this time the policy itself is condemned. See especially Edward Rozek, *Allied Wartime Diplomacy: A Pattern in Poland* (New York: Wiley, 1958), pp. 350–351, 442–444. The argument is still very much alive in Europe today. The idea that at Yalta the "Anglo-Saxons" divided up Europe with Russia has long been a common view, especially among French Gaullists; see, for example, Charles de Gaulle's own *Mémoires d'espoir: Le renouveau* (Paris: Plon, 1970), p. 239. The myth plays an even more important role today in eastern Europe. In the early 1990s, this interpretation of Yalta as a betrayal of eastern Europe was used, particularly by the Czech president, Václav Havel, but by other eastern European leaders as well, to shame the West into extending NATO security guarantees eastward. See "Czech Leader Pushes for Open NATO," *New York Times,* October 22, 1993, and especially the references to Havel's speech on the "third betrayal of the West," Munich and Yalta being the first two "betrayals" and the refusal to expand NATO being the third. For the use of the argument by other countries in the region, see "NATO Commitment Sought by Poland," ibid., December 12, 1993; "Hungary Is First Nation to Accept NATO Membership Compromise," ibid., January 9, 1994.

efits for both sides. If all the Americans could hope for was a façade of democratic respectability, then this would be no gain at all. On the contrary, it would be worse than useless. The truth could not long be hidden; as soon as the real situation became clear, there was bound to be a sense of betrayal. The makers of the agreement would be revealed as fools, or worse.

The fact that the Soviets controlled Poland militarily did not mean that the U.S. government was totally powerless on this issue. If Roosevelt had felt that he had no chance of getting anything real out of Stalin, why would he have opposed him on the issue in the first place, and why—especially given his physical condition—would he have traveled halfway around the world to try to work the problem out? The Americans, after all, had certain obvious sources of leverage in the dispute. Above all, American power might well play a key role in the postwar world, especially in keeping Germany under control. This fact alone meant that the Soviets had a strong interest in staying on good terms with the United States. Moreover, the Soviets would very much want to receive economic help from America, and from other sources under U.S. control, given the enormous devastation they had suffered and the consequent priority they would have to place on reconstruction. This was another major source of leverage: the top American leadership took it for granted that the Russians knew they had a great interest in not antagonizing American opinion.[9]

The Americans therefore had reason to hope for something of substance at Yalta. In fact, they came back with more than they had expected, for why else would they have been so pleased with the results of the conference, even in private?[10] British officials from Churchill on down, including even the top professionals in the Foreign Office, were also quite satisfied with what had been achieved at Yalta.[11] If Poland had indeed been written off, it is scarcely conceivable that the leaders of either government would have left the conference in this mood. And Roosevelt's attitude after Yalta—his refusal to accept a "whitewash" of the Lublin regime, his "anxiety and concern" over the Soviet attitude on the Polish issue at that time—is incomprehensible if one believes that his goal at Yalta had merely been to provide "face-saving formulas for the West."[12]

What Roosevelt and his chief advisers were aiming at was a Poland closely aligned with Russia on matters of foreign and military policy, but with a large mea-

[9] See Bruce Kuklick, *American Policy and the Division of Germany: The Clash with Russia over Reparations* (Ithaca, N.Y.: Cornell University Press, 1972), pp. 103–113; John Lewis Gaddis, *The United States and the Origins of the Cold War, 1941–1947* (New York: Columbia University Press, 1972), pp. 189–197.

[10] William Leahy, *I Was There* (New York: Whittlesey House, 1950), p. 323; Robert Sherwood, *Roosevelt and Hopkins: An Intimate History* (New York: Harper, 1950), p. 869.

[11] See, for example, Cadogan diary, February 10 and 11, 1945, and Cadogan to Halifax, February 20, 1945, in David Dilks, ed., *The Diaries of Sir Alexander Cadogan* (New York: Putnam, 1972), pp. 707, 709, 717. See also Roy Douglas, *From War to Cold War, 1942–1948* (New York: St. Martin's, 1981), pp. 71, 73. Churchill's reaction was typical. "I am profoundly impressed with the friendly attitude of Stalin and Molotov," he wrote Attlee on February 17. "It is a different Russian world to any I have seen hitherto." Quoted in Joseph Foschepoth, "Britische Deutschlandpolitik zwischen Jalta und Potsdam," *Vierteljahrshefte für Zeitgeschichte* 30 (1982): 675 n. 2.

[12] Roosevelt to Churchill, March 11 and March 29, 1945, in *Roosevelt and Churchill*, pp. 668, 689. "Face-saving formulas": Theoharis, "Roosevelt and Truman on Yalta," p. 221.

sure of autonomy on domestic issues. This, in fact, was the American dream for eastern Europe as a whole, a dream which persisted throughout the entire Cold War period.[13] It was not absurd to think that arrangements of this sort could be worked out. Poland herself could not be much of an obstacle: even a free and democratically governed Poland would have little choice but to accept this kind of relationship. Power realities were bound to dominate the situation, and no matter how they felt about the Russians, the Poles had little room for maneuver. If they were obstinate and refused to accommodate the Soviets on matters relating to vital Soviet security interests, the western powers would wash their hands of any responsibility and leave Poland to her fate. But faced with that prospect, the Poles could almost certainly be brought to heel. The attitude of the three great allies, acting as a bloc, would in the final analysis be controlling. This was especially true since Poland was about to be compensated for her losses in the east with a good deal of German territory; this, it was assumed, would inevitably lead to German resentment, and thus to increased Polish dependence on the allies.[14]

Thus, there was some hope after Yalta that a satisfactory settlement of the Polish problem could be worked out. But the Soviet government had no intention of taking the Yalta texts as binding. When Molotov, for example, pointed out that an American draft of one of the main Yalta documents went too far, Stalin dismissed his concerns: "Never mind. . .we'll work on it . . .do it our own way later."[15] And

---

[13] Note, for example, the tone of Byrnes's comments in a meeting with Molotov on September 16, 1945, FRUS 1945, 2:196–197, and also Harriman's views, cited in John Lewis Gaddis, *We Now Know: Rethinking Cold War History* (Oxford: Clarendon, 1997), p. 17. Even at the height of the Cold War, American leaders were very much in favor of a solution of this sort. Secretary of State Dulles, for example, told the Soviet foreign minister in October 1957 that the USSR was "entitled to a sense of security," and that "if a relationship could be developed with other bordering countries similar to that between Finland and the Soviet Union and Yugoslavia and the Soviet Union, with a sense of independence and yet close relations, this would be a very acceptable solution." Dulles-Gromyko meeting, October 5, 1957, Declassified Documents Reference System [DDRS] 1991/925. Dulles in fact had long favored a solution whereby Soviet relations with the eastern European countries would evolve into "something like a Finnish relationship." Dulles-Churchill meeting, April 12, 1954, Dulles Papers [DP], White House Memoranda series [WHM], box 1, Meetings with the President, Eisenhower Library [DDEL], Abilene, Kansas. See also Dulles memorandum (for Eisenhower), September 6, 1953, FRUS 1952–54, 2:460; and Dulles at Chiefs of Mission meeting, May 7, 1957, FRUS 1955–57, 4:597. Note also Dulles's evident approval in 1947 of the idea of a "spheres of influence" arrangement for Europe; see below, note 30. On this issue, see also Eduard Mark, "American Policy toward Eastern Europe and the Origins of the Cold War, 1941–1946: An Alternative Interpretation," *Journal of American History* 68 (September 1981): 313–336, and Fraser Harbutt, *The Iron Curtain: Churchill, America, and the Origins of the Cold War* (New York: Oxford, 1986), p. 131.

[14] In November 1944, Roosevelt told Arthur Bliss Lane, a career diplomat who had just been named ambassador to Poland, that Stalin's idea of a "Poland under Russian influence," which could serve "as a bulwark to protect the Soviet Union against further aggression," was "understandable." In June of that year (according to Polish ambassador Ciechanowski's memoirs), the president had told the non-Communist Polish leader Mikolajcyzk that Russia could "swallow up Poland if she could not reach an understanding on her terms," and that "when a thing becomes unavoidable, one should adapt oneself to it." A few days later, he reminded the Polish representatives that "you cannot risk war with Russia. What alternative remains? Only to reach agreement." Arthur Bliss Lane, *I Saw Poland Betrayed: An American Ambassador Reports to the American People* (Indianapolis: Bobbs-Merrill, 1948), pp. 58 (quoting Ciechanowski's account), 67.

[15] *Sto sorok besed s Molotovym: Iz dnevnika F. Chueva* [One Hundred Forty Conversations with Molo-

in fact, in the Moscow negotiations on the reorganization of the provisional Polish government, the Soviets took a hard line and sought to give the Communist authorities in Warsaw—what was still called the Lublin government—a veto over which Poles would even be invited in for consultations.[16] Soviet intransigence looked particularly ominous in the light of what was going on inside Poland. The Russians, by all indications, were in the process of imposing a Communist police state on the country, and to Roosevelt this meant that the Soviets were not living up to the Yalta agreement. "Neither the Government nor the people of this country," he wrote Churchill, "will support participation in a fraud or a mere whitewash of the Lublin government, and the solution must be as we envisaged it at Yalta."[17]

Churchill wanted to confront the Soviets directly on the issue, but Roosevelt disagreed.[18] If he really had to, the president was prepared to "bring the matter to a head" with Stalin,[19] but he preferred to deal with the problem in a more indirect way. American opinion was manipulated so as to generate public expectations that would place considerable pressure on the Soviets. James F. Byrnes, "assistant president" during the war and one of the leading figures in American political life at the time, was the chief vehicle Roosevelt used for this purpose. Byrnes had accompanied the president to Yalta, and upon his return from Russia, he gave the American public its first authoritative account of what the Yalta agreement meant. The Declaration on Liberated Europe adopted at the conference, a document full of Wilsonian pieties about democracy and self-determination, had not been meant to be taken at face value.[20] But Byrnes—although his real view was rather different—declared this to be a document "of the greatest importance": it marked the end of spheres of influence. With regard to Poland, he said, the three main allies would run things there "until the provisional government is established and elections held." This was highly misleading, but Roosevelt fully approved of what he called Byrnes's "magnificent" performance, and he himself went on to report to the nation on Yalta in a similar vein.[21]

---

tov: From the Diary of F. Chuev] (Moscow: Terra, 1991), p. 76, extracts translated in Woodford McClellan, "Molotov Remembers," Cold War International History Project [CWIHP] *Bulletin*, no. 1 (Spring 1992): 19. For a full translation, see Felix Chuev, *Molotov Remembers: Inside Kremlin Politics, Conversations with Felix Chuev*, ed. Albert Resis (Chicago: Dee, 1993).

[16] For the negotiations, see FRUS 1945, 5:110–210.

[17] Roosevelt to Churchill, March 11, 1945, in *Roosevelt and Churchill*, p. 668. See also ibid., pp. 674, 690.

[18] See ibid., documents 510, 512, 513, 515, 517, 518, 528, 529 and 534.

[19] Roosevelt to Churchill, March 29, 1945, ibid., p. 690.

[20] The declaration is to be understood as a gesture which, as Secretary of State Stettinius said at the time, would serve "to reassure public opinion in the United States and elsewhere." Quoted in Alperovitz, *Atomic Diplomacy*, p. 136n. Alperovitz's general argument about the declaration (pp. 135–136) is quite persuasive.

[21] For the basic story, see Messer, *End of an Alliance*, chaps. 3 and 4, and esp. pp. 52, 56–58. Messer says that what Byrnes was doing was at variance with Roosevelt's Yalta policy of simply trying "to put a good face on the division of Europe" (p. 57), although much of his argument is to the effect that Roosevelt was still pulling the strings. See esp. p. 60, where he comments on FDR's approval of "his salesman's" performance. The point that the manipulation of American public opinion via Byrnes was meant to put pressure on Russia was developed explicitly by Harbutt, *Iron Curtain*, pp. 86–92. For Roosevelt's

But Roosevelt's tactics did not have the desired effect, and relations between the Soviet Union and the western allies now quickly deteriorated. In the Moscow talks, Soviet intransigence was met by a toughening of the western line. Even before Roosevelt's death in April, the American representative in the Moscow talks sought to place the non-Communist Poles on a "par" with the Lublin regime, leading Stalin to complain that the western powers were trying to undo the Yalta agreement.[22] When Harry Truman succeeded to the presidency after Roosevelt's death in April, the American government took a yet tougher line on the issue. The demand now was for a provisional government "genuinely representative of the democratic elements of the Polish people."[23] This corresponded to America's initial position at Yalta, but the final agreement had merely called, in less categorical terms, for the existing regime to be "reorganized on a broader democratic basis." For Truman at this point, the simple fact was that the Soviets, in violation of the Yalta agreement, were imposing a communist regime on Poland. This breach of faith was intolerable, and he immediately decided to deal with the issue head on.

On April 23, barely a week after succeeding to the presidency, Truman met with his top military and foreign policy advisers. "Our agreements with the Soviet Union so far," he said, "had been a one-way street and that could not continue; it was now or never." The Soviets had to keep their side of the Yalta bargain. It was clear to him from the meeting "that from a military point of view there was no reason why" America should not insist on its understanding of the agreement on Poland.[24] He confronted Molotov that very evening and demanded in extremely blunt terms that the Soviets keep their promises. "I have never been talked to like that in my life," Truman later reported Molotov as saying. "Carry out your agreements," the president quoted himself as replying, "and you won't get talked to like that."[25]

But this belligerent tone was quickly abandoned. Neither Truman nor Byrnes really wanted to break with the Russians, and the Yalta agreement, the new president soon realized, was not as unambiguous as he had initially thought.[26] Tru-

---

own speech on Yalta, see *Department of State Bulletin* [DOSB], March 4, 1945, pp. 321–326. Messer, moreover, implies that Byrnes was bamboozled by Roosevelt, but this was not the case: Byrnes clearly understood the heart of the Yalta agreement. See the notes of his meeting with Turner Catledge of the *New York Times*, Catledge to Krock, February 26, 1945, Krock Papers [KP], box 1, p. 153ff., Mudd Library [ML], Princeton.

[22] Harriman to Stettinius, March 25, 1945, and Stalin to Roosevelt, April 9, 1945, FRUS 1945, 5:180, 201–204.

[23] Truman to Stalin, April 23, 1945, FRUS 1945, 5:258–259; Harry Truman, *Memoirs: Year of Decisions* (Garden City, N.Y.: Doubleday, 1955), p. 81.

[24] White House meeting, April 23, 1945, FRUS 1945, 5:252–255. This did not mean that he was ready to face the possibility that a showdown with Russia might lead to armed conflict, but simply that the United States was not so dependent on Soviet military cooperation in the war that it could not afford to risk Russian displeasure.

[25] Truman, *Year of Decisions*, pp. 79–82.

[26] See Melvyn Leffler, *A Preponderance of Power: National Security, the Truman Administration, and the Cold War* (Stanford, Calif.: Stanford University Press, 1992), pp. 32–33. Note also Byrnes's views, cited in Lloyd Gardner, *Spheres of Influence: The Great Powers Partition Europe, from Munich to Yalta* (Chicago: Ivan Dee, 1993), pp. 242–243, and Truman's comment on May 25 that every time he read the Yalta agreements, "he found new meanings in them." Robert Ferrell, ed., *Truman in the White House: The Diary of Eben A. Ayers* (Columbia: University of Missouri Press, 1991), entry for May 25, 1945, p. 28.

man was willing to "have another go" at Stalin, and in May sent Roosevelt's close adviser Harry Hopkins to Moscow to work things out with the Soviet leader. An agreement was quickly reached on the shape of the Polish provisional government, and the reconstructed but still Communist-dominated government was then recognized by the United States.

This decision marked a turning point. The American government more or less gave up on trying to save democracy in Poland. Free elections had been repeatedly promised, and Stalin, in his meetings with Hopkins and on other occasions, had explicitly denied any "intention to Sovietize Poland." The goal, he said, was to set up a western-style parliamentary democracy like Holland.[27] But the U.S. government made little attempt to get the Communists to honor these commitments. At the Potsdam conference in July 1945, it was the British delegation that carried the ball on Poland. The Americans were passive. Diplomatic recognition had been extended after the Communists had made definite promises about free elections, but when those elections were not held, there was no thought, for example, of withdrawing recognition. In late 1945, the U.S. government was no longer very interested in what was going on in Poland. That country had come to be accepted, in fact if not in words, as an integral part of the Soviet sphere of influence.[28]

With Poland effectively written off in mid-1945, it was hardly likely that the United States would take a stand over democracy elsewhere in eastern Europe. The Poles were allies and had fought hard for their freedom against enormous odds. But Rumania, for example, had fought on the Nazi side, and Bulgaria had cooperated with Germany in lesser ways; both countries, moreover, had been consigned to the Soviet sphere by the percentage agreement. In late 1945, there was some halfhearted wrangling over the fate of those countries. But Byrnes, who had been made secretary of state just before Potsdam, disapproved of the tough line U.S. diplomatic representatives in Bulgaria and Rumania wanted to take.[29] Indeed, he quickly reached the conclusion that the time had come to settle with the Soviets on the basis of the status quo. During the London foreign ministers' meeting in September he met with John Foster Dulles, the top Republican in the U.S. delegation, to discuss the talks, which so far were getting nowhere. "Well, pardner," he said, "I think we pushed these babies about as far as they will go and I think that we better start thinking about a compromise."[30] By December the evolution

[27] Hopkins-Stalin meeting, May 27, 1945, FRUS Potsdam, 1:38–39. See also Douglas, *War to Cold War*, p. 96.

[28] On U.S. passivity on the Polish question at this time, see Davis, *The Cold War Begins*, pp. 237, 244–248, 251; Geir Lundestad, *The American Non-Policy towards Eastern Europe, 1943–1947: Universalism in an Area Not of Essential Interest to the United States* (New York: Humanities Press, 1975), pp. 111, 206–211; and Harbutt, *Iron Curtain*, p. 115. The U.S. ambassador to Poland, Arthur Bliss Lane, had made no secret of his view that the American government should take a tough line on the issue. But his advice was ignored, and (as he himself put it) "for some reason Mr. Byrnes did not consider my presence necessary" at Potsdam. Lane, *I Saw Poland Betrayed*, p. 128.

[29] Note especially his anger at actions taken by the U.S. representative in Bulgaria in August 1945, an attitude at variance with America's public stance at the time. Michael Boll, *Cold War in the Balkans: American Foreign Policy and the Emergence of Communist Bulgaria, 1943–1947* (Lexington: University Press of Kentucky, 1984), p. 150.

[30] Quoted in Daniel Yergin, *Shattered Peace: The Origins of the Cold War and the National Security State* (Boston: Houghton Mifflin, 1978), p. 129. Yergin has Dulles at this point blocking this policy by threatening "a public attack on Byrnes as an appeaser," and this is in line with a common interpretation which

of American policy was complete. Byrnes agreed at the Moscow foreign ministers' meeting that month to recognize the Communist regimes in Bulgaria and Rumania in exchange for cosmetic changes in the composition of those governments and what he certainly now knew were empty promises about free elections.[31]

The United States continued to pay occasional lip service to the ideal of democratic governments in eastern Europe, but in practice the entire region had by December 1945 been accepted as an area where the Soviets would run the show. The American government certainly did not like what the Russians were doing there. The gradual setting up of Communist police states—the intimidation, the arrests, the "liquidations"—had offended American sensibilities, and control had been imposed in a way that had left the Americans feeling cheated. Stalin's lies about not wanting to communize Poland, the many broken promises about free elections, the general contempt shown for American wishes—all this left a residue of bitterness that was not without political importance. The Soviet sphere in eastern Europe was nonetheless something the Americans felt they could live with. It was not just that, short of going to war, the United States had no choice but to accept Soviet control of the area. The American policy was more positive than that. The key indicator was diplomatic recognition, which was something the U.S. government was by no means forced to bestow. Conferring recognition meant that the division of Europe was accepted as the basis of the postwar international order.

And by late 1945 an arrangement of this sort had become the real goal of Byrnes's policy. After the Moscow conference, the secretary of state was accused of being an appeaser, of striving for agreement as an end in itself, of being overly accommodationist and too ready to make concessions. But Byrnes was not trying

---

holds that Byrnes was simply interested in avoiding trouble by accommodating Soviet demands, and that he changed course in early 1946 only because the domestic political climate within the United States had shifted sharply in an anti-Soviet direction. But a more recent study has shown that even at this time Byrnes was taking a *tougher* line on eastern Europe than Dulles, who, incidentally, was already thinking not in Wilsonian but rather in spheres of influence terms. See Ronald Pruessen, *John Foster Dulles: The Road to Power* (New York: Free Press, 1982), pp. 281–282, 314–321. Note also Dulles's reply to a suggestion in June 1947 that it might be "possible and desirable to reach an agreement dividing Europe at the Elbe." He by no means rejected the idea out of hand, but replied simply that "it would be quite impossible to attain this effectively by agreement until we have first attained it in fact." Council on Foreign Relations discussion, June 6, 1947, p. 10, Dulles Papers, 1947: Council of Foreign Ministers File, ML.

[31] On the Moscow agreement on Rumania and Bulgaria, see Davis, *Cold War Begins,* pp. 328–329, and Messer, *End of an Alliance,* pp. 153–154. The closest students of American policy in late 1945 present a good deal of evidence demonstrating U.S. passivity toward eastern Europe and the government's recognition of special Soviet interests there, but they are reluctant to come out and say directly that the United States was writing off the area. Lundestad, *American Non-Policy* (p. 102) even says explicitly that the Moscow agreement did not mean that America was "writing off" the region "as being completely within the Soviet sphere." Routine declarations about democracy and free elections are taken quite seriously, especially by Davis, even though it is hard to see what impact they had on anything that was actually done. Eduard Mark also thinks that Byrnes did not "abandon" Rumania and Bulgaria at Moscow. The secretary's aim, he says, was to institutionalize an "open" Soviet sphere where the local countries would have a good deal of domestic political autonomy, "in the hope of preventing its consolidation into an exclusive sphere" marked by tight control exercised through Communist police states. Mark, "American Policy," p. 329, esp. nn. 82 and 83. My own view is that while an "open sphere" was for Byrnes and most American policymakers the optimal solution, they did not really think that it was within reach; and that Byrnes, in particular, accepting realities for what they were, was willing in effect to accept total Soviet domination of the area.

to buy Soviet goodwill in the hope of propping up a regime of great power coop-eration. He had come to the conclusion very early on that Russia and America were too far apart on basics for the two sides to work hand in hand with each other.[32] The key to getting along with the Soviets was for each side to accept what the other was doing in the area it controlled, the area most vital to its security. And Byrnes was willing to accept eastern Europe as an area where Soviet interests were pre-dominant. In exchange, he expected the USSR to accept the predominance of the western powers in the areas they considered vital—above all western Europe and Japan, but also the Mediterranean and the Middle East. It was for this reason that he was ready even in late 1945—that is, well before the president and the rest of the administration adopted a tough anti-Soviet policy—to defend the Turkish Straits, something which certain later Cold Warriors (like Dulles) were at the time rather wary about doing.[33] And one of the things he got during this period was Soviet acceptance of American preeminence in Japan.[34]

There was nothing particularly arcane or subtle about such an approach. The term "spheres of influence" might evoke images of the highly professional diplo-macy of the late nineteenth century, but the basic concept is quite familiar from everyday life. Two boys are fighting in a schoolyard: the natural solution is to pull them apart. Or a husband and wife are always quarreling: an obvious answer is for them to get divorced and lead separate lives. This approach ran against the grain of the Wilsonian tradition—certainly one of the basic traditions in American for-eign policy, above all at the level of public rhetoric—and for that reason, a certain amount of discretion was always necessary. But the force of that tradition—the emphasis on democracy and self-determination, the distaste for thinking in terms of power, strategic interest and especially spheres of influence—is not to be exag-gerated. The makers of American policy, it has become increasingly clear from re-cent historical work, were not starry-eyed idealists, but rather by and large un-derstood that Wilsonian principles could not be applied dogmatically, and that political realities had to be taken into account.[35] Byrnes in particular did not care much for abstract principles in any case and had no problem basing his policy on those power realities. The division of Europe was a fact, and if both sides accepted it, an end could be put to the quarreling and the allies could go their separate ways in peace.

POTSDAM AND THE GERMAN QUESTION

The same philosophy lay at the heart of Byrnes's policy on the German question, and indeed his policy on this issue provides the most striking example of his gen-

---

[32] Byrnes remarks of July 24, 1945, quoted in Walter Brown diary, cited in Yergin, *Shattered Peace*, p. 118.

[33] See Pruessen, *Dulles,* p. 319.

[34] See William Taubman, *Stalin's American Policy: From Entente to Détente to Cold War* (New York: Norton, 1982), p. 124; Lundestad, *American Non-Policy,* p. 245; and Yergin, *Shattered Peace,* pp. 146, 150.

[35] See especially Leffler, *Preponderance of Power;* Lundestad, *American Non-Policy,* esp. pp. 73–106; and Mark, "American Policy."

eral approach in 1945 to international problems. Real cooperation with the Soviet Union was in his view just not in the cards. "There is too much difference in the ideologies of the U.S. and Russia," he noted on July 24, "to work out a long term program of cooperation."[36] The way to get along was for each side to run things in the area it occupied. This simple idea was the basis of Byrnes's policy at the Potsdam conference in late July and early August 1945, and it was an idea that Stalin was quite happy to accept.

How did an arrangement based on this concept come to be worked out? During the war, the allies had not agreed on a common policy for Germany, but this had been no mere oversight.[37] The simple fact was that there had been no obvious policy to pursue. A punitive approach might over the long run lead to such bitterness and hatred that the Germans would once again revolt against the status quo, but a soft peace seemed entirely inappropriate given the extraordinary crimes they had committed.

The Americans in particular were sharply divided on this issue during the war.[38] The State Department tended to think in terms of building democracy in Germany, and was thus inclined to favor a relatively mild peace. Treasury Secretary Morgenthau was enraged by this policy and pressed instead for a plan for "pastoralizing" Germany. "I don't care what happens to the population," he told his chief assistant. He would "take every mine, every mill and factory and wreck it."[39] Roosevelt embraced the Morgenthau Plan in late 1944. At one point he even remarked that he was unwilling "to say that we do not intend to destroy the German nation."[40] But no firm decision was ever made to implement the Morgenthau Plan, nor was any alternative policy ever adopted. Instead, the president put off all but the most urgent decisions. In 1918, at the end of the First World War, the Germans had entered into an agreement with their enemies before laying down their arms; the Germans later claimed that the allies had reneged on their part of the bargain, and that they therefore had the moral right to resist the peace settlement the western powers had so deceitfully imposed. So this time there would be no pre-armistice agreement. Germany was to surrender unconditionally; the allies' hands would not be tied.[41]

The basic question of the nature of the settlement with Germany thus remained

[36] Walter Brown diary entry, July 24, 1945, quoted in Yergin, *Shattered Peace*, p. 118.

[37] See Kuklick, *American Policy,* chapter 2, and Gaddis, *United States and the Origins of the Cold War,* chapter 4.

[38] See especially Paul Hammond, "Directives for the Occupation of Germany: The Washington Controversy," in *American Civil-Military Decisions: A Book of Case Studies,* ed. Harold Stein (University, Ala.: University of Alabama Press, 1963).

[39] John Morton Blum, ed., *From the Morgenthau Diaries: Years of War, 1941–1945* (Boston: Houghton Mifflin, 1967), p. 351. On the Morgenthau Plan, see especially Warren Kimball, ed., *Swords or Ploughshares? The Morgenthau Plan for Defeated Nazi Germany, 1943–1946* (Philadelphia: Lippincott, 1976).

[40] Quoted in Edward N. Peterson, *The American Occupation of Germany: Retreat to Victory* (Detroit: Wayne State University Press, 1977), p. 21.

[41] On the "unconditional surrender" policy, see Michael Balfour, "The Origins of the Formula 'Unconditional Surrender' in World War II," *Armed Forces and Society* 5 (1979): 281–301, and Raymond O'Connor, *Diplomacy for Victory: FDR and Unconditional Surrender* (New York: Norton, 1971).

in limbo until the very end of the war. The question, for example, of whether Germany would be dismembered was of fundamental importance. But on this issue Roosevelt laid down the line that "our attitude should be one of study and post-ponement of final decision"—and this was in April 1945, with the surrender of Germany just a month away.[42]

So only the most minimal agreements had been reached by the time the war in Europe was over. The allies had worked out terms of surrender for Germany (although through a foul-up on the American end, these were not the terms actually used).[43] There had also been an accord dividing Germany up into zones of occupation; zones were assigned not just to Britain, America and Russia, but eventually to France as well. This arrangement left Greater Berlin, itself divided into four sectors, well within the Soviet zone.[44] Finally an agreement on control machinery for Germany was signed in November 1944, and ratified just before the Yalta conference in early 1945. An Allied Control Council would be set up, composed of the allied commanders in chief, each of whom would exercise supreme authority in his own zone of occupation. The Control Council was to take action on "matters affecting Germany as a whole," but only when all four zonal commanders agreed on specific measures. This plan did not lay out how Germany was to be treated. It simply set up machinery through which a common policy could be implemented, assuming the allies were able to agree on one.[45]

The assumption, however, was that the allies really would be able to cooperate on German questions. For Roosevelt, the essential thing was to build a relationship of trust with Stalin. If this were done, he was confident, at least until the last month or so of his life, that the two countries would be able to work together. He and other key officials were therefore reluctant to do anything that would provoke Russian distrust. It was essentially for this reason, for example, that in drafting the

[42] Stettinius to Winant, April 10, 1945, FRUS 1945, 3:221. Note also the judgment of Emile Despres, the State Department's adviser on German economic affairs. Apart from the Yalta conference, Despres wrote, "the progress to date on economic planning for Germany has been slight. Not only has discussion at the intergovernmental level been meager, but divergences among government departments on basic issues have prevented the formulation of an agreed American position." Despres memorandum, February 15, 1945, ibid., p. 412. Roosevelt himself had instructed the State Department in September 1944 *not* to sound out the British or the Russians on the treatment of German industry after the war, and the following month he told the secretary that he disliked "making detailed plans for a country which we do not yet occupy." Roosevelt to Hull, September 29 and October 20, 1944, FRUS Yalta, pp. 155, 158. See also Gaddis, *United States and the Origins of the Cold War,* pp. 106–107; Robert Murphy, *Diplomat Among Warriors* (Garden City, N.Y.: Doubleday, 1964), chap. 16, esp. pp. 227–228; Clemens, *Yalta,* p. 38; and Hans-Peter Schwarz, *Vom Reich zur Bundesrepublik* (Neuwied: Luchterhand, 1966), pp. 105–119.

[43] Draft instrument for the unconditional surrender of Germany, July 25, 1944, FRUS Yalta, pp. 110–118; Grew to Truman and Matthews-McCloy telephone conversation, both May 12, 1945, and Matthews to Murphy, May 14, 1945, with Bedell Smith to Hull, May 10, 1945, in FRUS 1945, 3:289–90, 294–297.

[44] Protocol on zones of occupation and the administration of Greater Berlin, September 12, 1944, FRUS Yalta, pp. 118–121. On this issue, see especially William Franklin, "Zonal Boundaries and Access to Berlin," *World Politics* 16 (October 1963): 1–31.

[45] Stettinius to Roosevelt, January 19, 1945, and Roosevelt to Stettinius, January 23, 1945, FRUS 1945, 3:173, 173n. Note also the discussion in a high-level meeting, March 15, 1945, ibid., p. 454. For the text of the November 14, 1944, agreement, see FRUS Yalta, pp. 124–127.

Figure 3. The Zonal Division of Germany.

agreement on occupation zones, the Americans did not insist on an explicit guarantee of free access to Berlin.[46]

But by the time the Potsdam conference met in July, many top American and British officials had reached the conclusion that real cooperation with the Soviet Union was just not possible. The Soviets seemed to be pushing outward wherever they could, in northern Norway, in the Mediterranean, in the Middle East, and in the Far East as well.[47] The most menacing of the new claims was the demand for military bases on the Turkish Straits. This demand was backed up by troop move-

[46] Murphy, *Diplomat among Warriors*, pp. 231–233.

[47] See, for example, Anderson to Collier, July 16, 1945; Collier to Warner, July 30, 1945; Bullard to Eden, July 11, 1945, with Eden Minute; and especially Eden to Churchill, July 17, 1945; in *Documents on British Policy Overseas* [DBPO], ser. I, vol. 1, *The Conference at Potsdam, July–August 1945* (London: HMSO, 1984), pp. 322–323, 1201, 166, 168, 353.

ments in the Balkans and a strident press and radio campaign directed against the Turkish government.[48]

The USSR had evidently opted for a simple expansionist policy. The Soviets, as Molotov later recalled, had gone "on the offensive" in the early postwar period; the aim had been "to extend the frontier of our Fatherland to the maximum."[49] If there was a chance of making gains, why not make the attempt? Who was going to stop them? The United States did not seem committed to blocking an expansion of Soviet power, and the British were too weak to hold the Russians back without American support. If by some chance the Soviets encountered major resistance, they could always pull back, so what was there to lose? In any event, there was nothing really new about Russia's expansionist goals. The tsarist regime had long coveted the Straits, and before the First World War had been active in the Balkans, northern Iran, and Manchuria. Stalin saw himself as the rightful heir to those tsarist policies, and thus as entitled to claim for himself rights acquired by the imperial regime, including the right conceded by the western allies during the First World War to take control of the Straits.[50] How could Britain, for example, deny to the Soviets what she had been ready to give the tsars? Stalin insisted on being treated as an equal. Britain controlled Suez and America had the Panama Canal, so why shouldn't the USSR dominate the Straits?[51] This was her prerogative as one of the three great powers.

The western governments might talk a lot about the rights of small nations, but, as Stalin saw it, they certainly understood that in the final analysis the interests of countries like Panama, Egypt, and Turkey were of minor importance. The great powers would decide things as they always had. It was therefore an outrage, for example, that "a small State (Turkey)" held "a great State (Russia) by the throat."[52] International politics was the politics of power. Everyone understood that regardless of what was said in public the three great powers would run the show, and that they would relate to each other on the basis of their core strategic interests.

Stalin was not opting for a policy of confrontation with the west. What he wanted was to conduct foreign policy in classic pre–World War I fashion. He saw the USSR as a great imperial power that had to deal with a rival, although not necessarily hostile, bloc of powers. Disputes between the two sides would naturally arise, but international politics was no love feast, and conflict could be taken philosophically, as simply a normal part of the game. There was certainly no reason for Stalin to think that the policy he had chosen would put him on a collision course with his wartime allies.

The western governments, however, had been counting on the Soviets to cooperate with them in running the postwar world, and were profoundly disappointed

---

[48] See Bruce Kuniholm, *The Origins of the Cold War in the Near East* (Princeton, N.J.: Princeton University Press, 1980), pp. 255–270; for British views, see DBPO I, 1:10, 29–30, 171, 542, 544, 547.

[49] McClellan, "Molotov Remembers," pp. 17, 19.

[50] See especially the wording of the "Agreement Regarding Entry of the Soviet Union into the War Against Japan," February 11, 1945, FRUS Yalta, p. 984, and Molotov's remarks in a meeting with Bevin, September 23, 1945, DBPO I, 2:317–318.

[51] Potsdam conference, plenary meeting, July 23, 1945, FRUS Potsdam, 2:303, 313.

[52] Potsdam conference, plenary meeting, July 23, 1945, DPBO I, 1:585.

by the new thrust of Soviet policy. Averell Harriman, for example, the U.S. ambassador to the Soviet Union, complained about "expanding demands being made by the Russians." "They are throwing aside all their previous restraint as to being only a Continental power and not interested in further acquisitions," he told the top civilians in the War Department on July 23, "and are now apparently seeking to branch in all directions."[53] Anthony Eden, the British foreign secretary, was also disturbed by the emerging "pattern of Soviet policy." Eden, who during the war had tried hard to lay the basis for a cooperative relationship with the USSR, now felt that the Russians were becoming "more brazen every day."[54] Real cooperation of the sort people had hoped for during the war was evidently not possible. Churchill, on his return from Potsdam, summed up Soviet policy there in a nutshell: "'Everything I have is mine,' says the Russian; 'as for what you have, I demand a quarter.' On that basis, nothing can be done."[55]

This led to a fundamental change in American policy on Germany. Given the new thrust of Soviet policy, given in particular the way the Russians had acted in Poland and elsewhere in eastern Europe, was it still a good idea to try to govern Germany together with them? The western powers might be wise to think about running Germany on a somewhat different basis.[56] The Control Council regime might simply be unworkable. General Lucius Clay, who just two months earlier had been put in charge of the American military government in Germany, made the obvious point on June 6. The Control Council, he pointed out, might "become only a negotiating agency and in no sense an overall government for Germany." If the allies could not run Germany as a unit, maybe the western powers, he said, should think about running western Germany by themselves.[57]

So the great issue at Potsdam was whether Germany could be run as a unit, and if not, what alternative arrangements could be worked out. During the war there had been much talk of "dismembering" Germany—that is, of splitting her up into a number of smaller states—and at Yalta, as Churchill noted at the time, he and Roosevelt and Stalin were "all agreed on the principle of dismemberment." A committee was in fact set up to "study how to put dismemberment into effect." But interest in a formal partition of Germany soon waned, and by the time the Potsdam conference met, all three major allies had abandoned the idea. As one British official put it at the time, "whatever the *de facto* result of dividing Germany into zones

[53] Stimson diary for July 23, 1945, FRUS Potsdam, 2:260n.

[54] Eden to Churchill, July 17, 1945, DBPO I, 1:352–354; Victor Rothwell, *Britain and the Cold War, 1941–1947* (London: Jonathan Cape, 1982), pp. 89, 122, 124–125.

[55] Reported in Massigli to Bidault, July 30, 1945, Massigli Papers [MP], vol. 92, French Foreign Ministry Archives [FFMA], Paris, henceforth cited in the following form: MP/92/FFMA.

[56] See, for example, McCloy-Stimson phone conversation, May 19, 1945, Henry Stimson Papers, box 172, Sterling Library, Yale University, New Haven (reel 128 in the microfilm edition). Note especially the references to "the pattern which Russian policy was disclosing in the Balkans, Austria and in Poland" and the "growing feeling that we should be reluctant to break up SHAEF and institute the Control Council management of Germany." SHAEF—Supreme Headquarters, Allied Expeditionary Force—was the organization, commanded by General Eisenhower, that Britain and America had established to control military operations in western Europe.

[57] Clay (signed Eisenhower) to JCS, June 6, 1945, in Jean Smith, ed., *The Papers of General Lucius D. Clay: Germany 1945–1949*, 2 vols. (Bloomington: Indiana University Press, 1974), 1:18–20.

of occupation may be, the idea of planned and deliberate dismemberment is dead."[58] A unified Germany was by now in principle the preferred solution, especially in the U.S. State Department. The general sense was that a policy of repression—dividing Germany up, crippling her economy, and preventing her from governing herself—could not work over the long run.[59] And beyond that, many high officials in America, and in Britain as well, whatever their misgivings about Soviet policy, were reluctant to give up too quickly on a four-power solution. To abandon the goal of a unitary Germany would be tantamount to admitting that the allies could not cooperate even on this vital issue, and for many key policymakers wartime hopes died hard.[60]

But although a unified Germany run on a quadripartite basis was in theory the optimal solution, the prospect of a divided polity growing out of the zonal division was not viewed with anything like horror. A division of Germany between east and west in fact had a certain appeal, and there were three distinct reasons why people in the American government especially were attracted to the idea. First, a divided Germany would be weak. The goal of the dismemberment plans had been to punish the Germans and keep them down permanently, and at the end of the war anti-German sentiment still carried a good deal of weight. A formal policy of dismemberment might have been abandoned, but it was understood very early on that a permanent partition of Germany might grow out of the zonal division of the country, and that this might have the same political effect. Roosevelt,

---

[58] Churchill's comment at Yalta is quoted in Keith Sainsbury, "British Policy and German Unity at the End of the Second World War," *English Historical Review* 93 (October 1979): 798. For the British official's remark, see Harrison to Bevin, July 30, 1945, DBPO I, 1:1009. On this issue in general, see also Frank King, "Allied Negotiations and the Dismemberment of Germany," *Journal of Contemporary History* 16 (1981): esp. 589–592; Kuklick, *American Policy and the Division of Germany*, pp. 75–76, 164; Rothwell, *Britain and the Cold War*, p. 44; and Stettinius to Winant, April 10, 1945, Hopkins to Truman, May 30, 1945, and Balfour to Stettinius, August 18, 1945, in FRUS 1945, 3:221–222, 317–318, 367–368.

[59] For a typical State Department view, see the briefing paper on the "treatment of Germany," January 12, 1945, FRUS Yalta, pp. 185–186.

[60] See, for example, Stimson's views in a phone conversation with McCloy, May 19, 1945, Stimson Papers, box 172 (reel 128). Note also Clay's comments in a meeting with key U.S. officials in Washington. Germany, he said, was a kind of laboratory; if the United States and the Soviet Union could not cooperate effectively there, then "our entire foreign policy with respect to Russia would be in jeopardy." This belief led him to exaggerate how cooperative the Russians were in fact being—and some scholars have taken these remarks as proving that the Russians really were willing to go along with the "unitary" policy. "The entire record of the Control Council," Clay said at this meeting, "showed that the USSR was willing to cooperate with the other powers in operating Germany as a single political and economic unit." But a month earlier he had informed the War Department that the Soviets, who had "hitherto been cooperative with reference to uniform policies and to early establishment of central administrative machinery," seemed to be "laboring under instructions to be obstructive." Meeting at State Department, November 3, 1945, and Clay to War Department, October 4, 1945, *Clay Papers*, 1:113, 90. For another example of Clay misrepresenting the facts in order to promote his policy of trying to run Germany in cooperation with Russia, see B. U. Ratchford and W. D. Ross, *Berlin Reparations Assignment: Round One of the German Peace Settlement* (Chapel Hill: University of North Carolina Press, 1947), p. 129. In a January 1946 cable to the War Department, these two former officials wrote, Clay "made the generalization, startling to those familiar with negotiations at lower levels, that in most economic matters the U.S. position was about midway between the Soviet and British positions and that by slight compromises downward we were usually able to reach agreement with the Soviets."

for example, had noted this possibility at Yalta, and it was clear that the president did not view partition as an entirely undesirable result.[61]

The second factor had to do with the interest of the U.S. military authorities in making sure that they had the unobstructed power to run things as they saw fit in the American zone. War Department officials insisted in early 1945 on the need to safeguard the authority of the zonal commander and to make sure that it could not be undercut by a foreign majority on the Control Council. Indeed, American representatives at times defended the principle of zonal authority more zealously than their British or even French counterparts.[62] The Army would be responsible for administering the part of Germany occupied by the United States, and the zonal commander could not have his hands tied by a cumbersome and possibly unworkable quadripartite regime.

The third and by far the most important set of considerations had to do with the Soviet attitude. Events in eastern Europe and elsewhere had made it clear that the Russians were difficult to get along with, and in Germany itself it seemed that they were not really interested in governing the country as a unit, but rather would run their own zone as they pleased. As Field Marshal Montgomery, the British commander in Germany, reported on July 8, there was already "a complete 'wall'" between the Russian Zone and the Zones of the western allies."[63] But if the Russians were going to run the eastern zone as a sort of private fiefdom, why should they be allowed any influence in the western part of Germany? What was good for the goose was good for the gander: the western powers should also get to run their part of Germany as they saw fit.[64]

All of these considerations added up to one conclusion: in all likelihood, Germany was going to be divided. And while a division of Germany was not seen as the ideal solution, it was not viewed as a catastrophe either. Far from it: a weak Germany would pose no threat; the western powers would have a free hand in the

[61] Roosevelt-Churchill-Stalin meeting, February 5, 1945, FRUS Yalta, p. 612. Note also Roosevelt's remark in late 1944 that the Russians would do "more or less what they wish[ed]" in the eastern zone, which suggests a certain continuity between his thinking and the policy later pursued by Byrnes at Potsdam. Roosevelt to Hull, September 29, 1944, FRUS Yalta, p. 155.

[62] Draft directive, January 6, 1945; Winant to Dunn, January 26 and February 5, 1945; Mosely memorandum, February 3, 1945; Winant to McCloy, February 24, 1945; State-War-Navy meeting, March 14, 1945; high-level meeting, March 15, 1945; State Department memorandum, March 16, 1945; Winant to Stettinius, May 7, 1945; in FRUS 1945, 3:378–388, 396–403, 430, 451–457, and 504–505 (for somewhat less extreme British and even French views). For another example of a more moderate French view, see Gunter Mai, *Der Alliierte Kontrollrat in Deutschland 1945–1948: Alliierte Einheit—deutsche Teilung?* (Munich: Oldenbourg, 1995), p. 83.

[63] Montgomery notes, July 6, 1945, DBPO I, 1:71. On Soviet policy in Germany at this time, see Norman Naimark, *The Russians in Germany: A History of the Soviet Zone of Occupation, 1945–1949* (Cambridge, Mass.: Belknap Press, 1995).

[64] For examples of this sort of thinking, see Churchill's remark at the Potsdam Conference, July 25, 1945, FRUS Potsdam, 2:385, and Anne Deighton, *The Impossible Peace: Britain, the Division of Germany and the Origins of the Cold War* (Oxford: Clarendon, 1990), p. 72. These attitudes were embedded in a more general feeling that relations between the USSR and the western powers could not be conducted in the sort of one-sided way the Soviets evidently had in mind. Truman, for example, often insisted that relations with Russia could not be a "one way street," and that the same rules had to be applied to both sides. See, for instance, White House meeting and Truman-Molotov meeting, both April 23, 1945, FRUS 1945, 5:253, 258.

part of Germany they occupied, which was by far the most valuable part of the country; and—a point which was of considerable importance to Byrnes—a partition of the country along east-west lines might provide a framework for tolerable relations between the USSR and the western powers. Each side would do as it pleased in the part of Germany it occupied, and the two sides would be able to get along with each other on that basis.

An arrangement of this sort was in fact worked out as the three powers grappled with what turned out to be the central issue at Potsdam: German reparations. Byrnes pressed for an arrangement that would basically allow each power to take whatever it wanted from its own zone. This plan emerged at Potsdam in large part in reaction to what the Soviets were doing in eastern Germany. It was clear by the time the conference convened that the Soviets were stripping the eastern zone of everything of value that could be carted off. Whole factories were being dismantled and prepared for shipment back to Russia. The Soviet conception of "war booty" or "war trophies" was so broad that it allowed them to carry off practically everything they wanted from their zone.[65]

American and British officials disliked what the Soviets were doing. But the Americans, at least, came to wonder whether there was any point to arguing with them and trying to get them to limit their actions to what could be agreed to on a quadripartite basis. Instead of entering into endless quarrels about how much the removals were worth, about whether "war booty" should be counted as reparations, about how much Germany should be made to pay and about how exactly payment was to be made, wasn't it much better to opt for the extremely simple solution of letting each side draw off whatever it wanted from the areas it controlled? This was exactly what Byrnes now proposed.[66]

The reparation issue, however, could not be isolated from the broader question of how Germany was to be dealt with. Byrnes made it clear that there would be no limit to what the Soviets could take from eastern Germany. Even as late as July 29, Molotov, still thinking in terms of a four-power arrangement for Germany, could scarcely believe what Byrnes was now suggesting. If reparation were not dealt with on an all-German basis, the Soviet foreign minister wondered, how could Germany be treated "as an economic whole"? If Germany were to be run as a unit, the amount each power could take from its own zone would obviously have to be limited, and Molotov assumed that this must have been what Byrnes had in mind. As he understood the Byrnes plan, "the Soviet Union would look to its own zone for a *fixed amount* of reparations" and would in addition get a certain amount of the

---

[65] Kuklick, *American Policy and the Division of Germany,* pp. 143–144; U.S. Delegation working paper, July 23, 1945, Rubin to Oliver, July 25, 1945, and Pauley and Lubin to Truman, September 20, 1945, in FRUS Potsdam, 2:857, 871, 943.

[66] For the thinking behind the new U.S. plan, see especially Pauley to Maisky, July 27, 1945, FRUS Potsdam, 2:894–896. Pauley pointed out that it was obvious from the Soviet government's behavior that it had concluded that "the reparations program can best be conducted on a zonal basis" and not by "treating Germany as a single economic unit"; he argued that America, if she was not going to end up in effect paying Germany's reparations for her, would therefore have to "deal with reparations along the same lines." The zonal approach, he concluded, was a "regrettable but inescapable" consequence of the USSR's own unilateral actions. This letter had been approved in advance by Byrnes, Truman and Clayton; see ibid., p. 894n.

surplus industrial plant in the Ruhr. But Byrnes, who had insisted rather disingenuously that under his plan Germany would still be treated as an economic whole, was nevertheless quick to correct this misconception: Molotov's understanding was "not quite accurate," and in fact the idea was that "the Soviet Union would take what it wished from its own zone"—that is, without limit.[67]

In such circumstances, however, the western powers could hardly be expected to help finance the Soviet zone. If the Russians were intent on stripping the part of the country they controlled, there was no way to prevent them from doing so, but they and not the western powers would have to deal with the consequences. They and not the western powers, that is, would have to finance any deficit their zone would run. To help finance imports into the eastern zone, which America and Britain in effect would have to do if Germany were run on a unitary basis, would be tantamount to paying Germany's reparations for her. In a unitary system, the more thoroughly the Soviets stripped the east, the greater the burden on American and British taxpayers; the Soviets would thus be able to draw indirectly on western resources. As a British official later put it, they would in that case "simply milk the cow which the US and British are feeding."[68] Neither Byrnes nor Truman would have any part of it. "The American position is clear," the secretary of state declared at Potsdam, invoking what was called the "first charge principle," a long-standing American policy. The first claim on German resources had to be the financing of necessary imports; until the Germans could pay their own way, there would be no reparations—at least none from the American zone. "There can be no discussion of this matter," Byrnes said. "We do not intend, as we did after the last war, to provide the money for the payment of reparations."[69]

---

[67] Byrnes-Truman-Molotov meeting, July 29, 1945, FRUS Potsdam, 2:474–475 (emphasis added). Byrnes's statement here that "under his scheme nothing was changed in regard to overall treatment of German finance, transport, foreign trade, etc." could not have been meant seriously, since (as will become clear from the following discussion) Byrnes fully understood that foreign trade, and thus also the financing of German needs, could *not* under his plan be managed on an all-German basis. His claim that the principle of running Germany as a unit was not being sacrificed has to be seen instead as part of a policy of paying lip service to that principle, no matter what was really being done. One should also note that in the process of drafting the Potsdam agreement, various provisions which would have preserved the rudiments of the policy of treating Germany as a unit were simply dropped. The original American proposal, for example, had sought to reconcile the Byrnes plan with the basic policy of supporting German unity. The plan was to be an "interim" arrangement; it would "not preclude a coordinated administration of Germany"; and removals were not to be "inconsistent with the treatment of Germany as a single economic unit." But such attempts to square the circle were soon abandoned. These provisions were deleted from the revised version of the proposal, which emphasized the ultimate authority of the zonal commander to decide what could be removed from his zone, and which provided the basis for the final agreement. See FRUS Potsdam 2:867–869, 926–927, 1485–1487, for the initial U.S. proposal, the revised proposal, and the section of the Potsdam Protocol containing the final agreement. Note also the discussion in the foreign ministers' meeting, July 30, 1945, ibid., p. 488, for a striking example of Byrnes's insistence on the prerogatives of the zonal commander as opposed to the Control Council—something which strictly speaking was unnecessary since the Control Council could act in any event only on the basis of unanimity, but was important symbolically as an example of the U.S. government underscoring its preference for the zonal approach.

[68] Heath to Byrnes, December 11, 1946, FRUS 1946, 5:650–651.

[69] On the first charge principle, see, for example, Gaddis, *United States and the Origins of the Cold War*, pp. 127, 221–222; Kuklick, *American Policy and the Division of Germany*, pp. 123, 134, 135, 145.

The western powers would therefore under no circumstances help foot the bill for what the Soviets were doing in the east. But by the same token the USSR would not have to worry about financing essential imports into western Germany. If his reparation plan were adopted, Byrnes declared, the Soviet Union "would have no interest in exports and imports from our [i.e., the western] zone. Any difficulty in regard to imports and exports would have to be settled between the British and ourselves."[70]

It was thus clear, even at the time, that the Byrnes policy was by no means limited to the relatively narrow problem of German reparations. It was tied very explicitly to the assumption that Germany's foreign trade would also not be run on a four-power basis.[71] A decision had in fact been made, in the words of one internal American document from the period, to "give up" on a four-power arrangement not just for reparations but for imports as well.[72] But the management of foreign trade was the key to the overall economic treatment of Germany. If the country were to be run as a unit, exports and imports would obviously have to be managed on an all-German basis. If there were no common regime for foreign trade, normal commerce between eastern and western Germany would be impossible: the two parts of the country would have to relate to each other economically as though they were foreign countries.

This was not just some sort of arcane economic theory which Byrnes and the others were too obtuse to understand at the time. The secretary of state and other key American officials at Potsdam were fully aware of the implications of their new policy. Byrnes himself pointed out a few weeks after Potsdam that in the original American plan, "the German economy was regarded as forming a whole," and he implied that, given what the Soviets were doing in the eastern zone, this approach had had to be abandoned. His reparation plan, as one of the Americans involved with these issues pointed out, was in fact rooted in the assumption that the allies would probably not be able to "pull together in running Germany."[73] That plan, as a high State Department official noted after hearing Byrnes lay out his views, was based on the premise that the three western zones would constitute "a virtually self-contained economic area."[74] The top British official concerned with these matters at Potsdam, Sir David Waley, a man who had argued long and hard with

---

This insistence that the United States not, in effect, pay Germany's reparations for her is a very common theme in the documents. For various examples, see FRUS Yalta, p. 632; FRUS Potsdam, 1:470, 520; and FRUS Potsdam, 2:279 (for the quotation in the text), 896, 1558–1559.

[70] Foreign ministers' meeting, July 30, 1945, FRUS Potsdam, 2:491.

[71] See Collado to Thorp and Reinstein, July 23, 1945, ibid., p. 812.

[72] Memorandum for Clayton, July 23, 1945, ibid., p. 813.

[73] Byrnes-Bidault meeting, August 23, 1945, ibid., p. 1557; Rubin to Oliver, July 25, 1945, ibid., p. 871. The view that the initial goal of treating Germany as a unit had been abandoned was shared by many key officials back in Washington who were violently opposed to the new policy. One high-ranking State Department official, for example, wrote angrily that the Byrnes plan "virtually abandoned the whole concept of joint economic treatment of Germany in favor of splitting the country sharply between the Russian and the three western zones" and would "go very far toward a de facto division of Germany into two halves." Thorp memo, c. July 28, 1945, quoted in Kuklick, American Policy and the Division of Germany, pp. 161–162. See also Kindleberger to Lubin, July 28, 1945, quoted ibid., p. 162.

[74] The document is quoted in Carolyn Woods Eisenberg, Drawing the Line: The American Decision to Divide Germany, 1944–1949 (Cambridge: Cambridge University Press, 1996), p. 177n.

the Americans (including Byrnes himself) about their new policy and who was thus very familiar with the basic thinking that lay behind what the Americans were doing, made the same general point. "The American plan," he wrote, was "based on the belief that it will not be possible to administer Germany as a single economic whole with a common programme of exports and imports, a single Central Bank and the normal interchange of goods between one part of the country and another."[75] The British (and State Department) objection that the plan would lead to a division of Germany was not so much refuted as ignored. A British official who raised the point with the Americans at Potsdam noted in frustration that it was "quite obvious" that they considered him a "starry-eyed and wishful-thinking idealist" for still believing in a unitary solution for Germany.[76]

Byrnes's own views could scarcely have been clearer. When an incredulous Molotov asked him whether his plan really meant that "each country would have a free hand in their own zones and would act entirely independently of the others," the secretary of state confirmed that this was so, adding only that some arrangement for the exchange of goods between zones would probably also be necessary.[77] Byrnes certainly understood what he was doing. American officials at the time might have claimed, especially when confronted with the charge that their policy had the effect of dividing Germany, that they had not really given up on the quadripartite regime. But when one strips away the verbiage and reads the internal documents carefully, when one looks at what was actually done and the sort of thinking that real policy was based on, it is clear that the Americans at Potsdam had indeed essentially given up on the idea that Germany could be run on a four-power basis.

The basic idea of the Byrnes plan was thus for Germany to be split into two economic units which would exchange goods with each other as though they were separate countries engaged in international trade—or more precisely, international barter. And one should stress that under this plan, Germany was to be divided into *two* parts, not *four*. In the Potsdam discussions, and even in the Potsdam agreement itself, western Germany was treated as a bloc. There were in fact frequent references, in the singular, to the "western zone," and Byrnes in particular repeatedly referred to the western part of Germany as "our zone."[78] The assumption was that the three western powers—the Americans, the British, and even the French, who were not even present at the conference—would be able to work out a common policy among themselves, and that Germany would in all probability be divided along east-west lines.[79]

---

[75] Waley memorandum, August 2, 1945, DBPO I, 1:1258. See also Waley's comments in a staff meeting with Bevin and Attlee, July 31, 1945, and Cadogan note, July 28, 1945, ibid., pp. 948, 1053. For Waley's July 31 meeting with Byrnes—it was technically a Byrnes-Attlee meeting but the new prime minister let Waley do most of the talking—see Waley to Eady, July 31, 1945, ibid., pp. 1050–1051. Waley argued here that the Byrnes Plan, by drawing a "line across the middle of Europe," had an "importance far transcending reparations," but he could not convince the secretary to change course.

[76] Mark Turner to Treasury, July 28, 1945, quoted in Foschepoth, "Britische Deutschlandpolitik," p. 714 n. 162.

[77] Byrnes-Molotov meeting, July 27, 1945, FRUS Potsdam, 2:450.

[78] See, for example, Potsdam conference, foreign ministers' meeting, July 30, 1945, ibid., pp. 485, 487, 488, 491; and Clayton to Byrnes, July 29, 1945, ibid., p. 901.

[79] Collado to Thorp and Reinstein, July 23, 1945, and Clayton and Collado to Thorp, August 16,

What had led Byrnes to take this course? It was not just the fact that the Soviets were stripping the east and were in general acting unilaterally in the part of Germany they occupied that had given rise to the Byrnes plan. The more basic taproot was political in nature. In the secretary's view, what the Soviets were doing in their zone simply reflected the more fundamental fact that real cooperation with the USSR was just not possible. This was the lesson he and other top U.S. officials had drawn from America's dealings with the Soviets, especially on the Polish question, in the first half of 1945. And in fact it was on July 24—that is, the day after the new reparation plan was first proposed to the Soviets—that he made the comment quoted above about the two sides being too far apart on basics "to work out a long term program of cooperation."[80]

But that did not mean that serious tension was inevitable. The way to get along was to pull apart. The unitary approach, Byrnes argued over and over again, would lead in practice to "endless quarrels and disagreements" among the allies. The attempt to extract reparation on an all-German basis "would be a constant source of irritation between us, whereas the United States wanted its relations with the Soviet Union to be cordial and friendly as heretofore." If his plan were adopted, the West would not have to "interfere" in the determination of what was available for reparation from the Soviet zone, nor would the Soviets need to get involved in such matters in western Germany. The western powers would settle things among themselves. A clean separation was the best solution, the best way to put an end to the squabbling and lay the basis for decent relations among the allies.[81]

Here in a nutshell was Byrnes's basic thinking about how the two sides should relate to each other in the future. Let each side do what it wanted in its own part of Germany. This was the simplest formula for a settlement. The Soviets would almost certainly go on acting unilaterally in the eastern zone in any case. But if they ran eastern Germany as they pleased, they should not expect to have much influence in the western zones. The obvious solution was for each side to have a free hand in the part of Germany it controlled. The allies would go their separate ways, but there was no need for them to part in anger.

President Truman, although not deeply involved with these issues, agreed with Byrnes's general approach. He was determined not to pay Germany's reparations for her. The Russians were "naturally looters," he thought, but given what Germany had done to them, one could "hardly blame them for their attitude." The Americans, however, had "to keep our skirts clean" and avoid commitments. If the Soviets insisted on stripping the areas they occupied, they could not expect Amer-

---

1945, ibid., pp. 812, 829. The shift in the American approach is reflected in a memorandum Stimson sent to Truman on July 24. The secretary of war had earlier leaned toward a policy of trying to run Germany together with the Russians, but now he wrote the president that what the Soviets were doing in their zone was "bound to force us to preserve the economy in western Germany in close cooperation with the British." Ibid., pp. 808–809. For Stimson's earlier view, see the document cited above, note 60. One should also note that the French, at the time of Potsdam, were also considering the possibility of a tripartite system limited to the western zones in the event of a failure of the Control Council regime. See Mai, *Alliierte Kontrollrat*, p. 84.

[80] Walter Brown diary, July 24, 1945, quoted in Yergin, *Shattered Peace*, p. 118.

[81] Byrnes-Molotov meeting, July 23, 1945; foreign ministers' meetings, July 27 and 30, 1945; Byrnes-Truman-Molotov meeting, July 29, 1945; Rubin to Oliver, July 25, 1945; in FRUS Potsdam, 2:274, 430, 474, 487, 491, 871.

ica to foot the bill.[82] Truman had thus decided to take what he called a "very realistic" line at Potsdam. Soviet control over the areas the USSR now dominated was a fact of life, and if one accepted that, one could deal with Stalin in a straightforward way. People like Harriman might have been very upset about a new barbarian invasion of Europe, but Truman had no trouble adjusting to the new situation. Nazi aggression had opened up the floodgates, and Soviet power now dominated central Europe, but this was something the United States could easily live with: thanks to Hitler, the president said, "we shall have a Slav Europe for a long time to come. I don't think it is so bad."[83] He was not hostile to the USSR, but like Byrnes he felt that the Soviet Union and the western powers should go their separate ways in peace.

The American aim, therefore, was to reach an amicable understanding with the Soviets, and the U.S. government was willing to go quite far to achieve that objective. The reparation question was of fundamental importance at Potsdam and Byrnes knew in general how he wanted it settled. But he took care to make sure that his plan was not simply imposed on an unwilling Soviet Union that was left feeling cheated.[84] The original Byrnes proposal was that each country take reparations from its own zone. This of course was something each of those states would have been able to do even if no agreement had been reached, a point Molotov himself made during the Potsdam discussions: "if they failed to agree on reparations," he noted, "the result would be the same as under Mr. Byrnes' plan."[85] But to get the Soviets to accept this result more or less voluntarily—by their own admission, the same situation as that which would prevail in the absence of an agreement— Byrnes was willing to give the Russians two things that they valued highly.

First of all, he offered to accept the Oder-Neisse line as in effect the eastern border of Germany—that is, to accept the exact line that the Soviets had drawn as the border between Poland and eastern Germany—if the USSR agreed to his reparation plan. This was a major concession, as Truman was quick to point out.[86]

The Americans were also willing to give the Russians a substantial share of the industrial capital in the western zones that the allies could agree was "unnecessary for the German peace economy." Fifteen percent of this surplus capital would be sent east in exchange for food and certain other raw materials, and a further 10 percent would be transferred free and clear to the Soviets, with no return payment of any kind required.[87] Both parts of this arrangement were quite significant. The

[82] Truman diary entry for July 30, 1945, *Diplomatic History* 4 (1980): 325–326; Truman to Bess Truman, July 31, 1945, in Robert Ferrell, ed., *Dear Bess: The Letters from Harry to Bess Truman, 1910–1959* (New York: Norton, 1983), p. 522.

[83] James Forrestal diary entry for July 28, 1945, Forrestal Diaries [FD], vol. 2, Forrestal Papers [FP], ML. Only Truman's reference to his being "very realistic" appears in the version published at the height of the Cold War; the comment about a "Slav Europe" not being "so bad" was deleted from the published text. See Walter Millis, ed., *The Forrestal Diaries* (New York: Viking, 1951), p. 78.

[84] For the claim that the pushing through of the Byrnes plan reflected a new American toughness resulting from the first successful test of an atomic bomb, see Gar Alperovitz, *Atomic Diplomacy*, pp. 164–173, and, in milder form, Messer, *End of an Alliance*, pp. 94, 114, 131, 138, 139.

[85] Foreign ministers' meeting, July 27, 1945, FRUS Potsdam, 2:430.

[86] Truman-Byrnes-Molotov meeting, July 29, 1945, ibid., p. 472.

[87] For the bargaining, and evidence of the ever-rising Soviet share the Americans were willing to concede, see ibid., pp. 475, 481, 489, 932.

first part reflected the basic assumption, as a British official noted at the end of the year, "that Eastern and Western Germany are two separate economic units, run by Russia and the three Western Powers respectively."[88] A barter arrangement of this sort would scarcely make sense if Germany were in fact being thought of as a unit.

The second part of the plan—the part relating to the 10 percent of the surplus capital in the western zones that the Soviets would be getting free and clear—is worth noting for a different reason. The American goal here was to avoid slamming the door in the faces of the Russians. At Yalta, and in further discussions in Moscow, the U.S. government had recognized the right of the USSR to receive half of whatever could be gotten out of Germany as reparations, and although the USSR would have to "bow" to whatever the western powers decided about the Soviets' "right to receive reparations from the Western Zone," American officials did not want to renege on their commitment. The eastern zone would supply the USSR with something on the order of 40 to 45 percent of the total available for reparations in Germany as a whole, and the deliveries from western Germany—that is, the 10 percent of surplus capital that the Soviets would be getting outright— would approximately make up the difference between the eastern zone reparations and the 50 percent to which the Russians were entitled. This was "rough justice": the Soviets were still to be treated as allies whose interests were legitimate and whose goodwill was important.[89]

The American government, in other words, did not want to just impose the de facto arrangement that would exist in the absence of an agreement. The Americans worked for an agreement because they placed a certain premium on relatively friendly relations with the USSR, and to get an agreement the Soviets could accept, they were willing to sweeten the pot by making what they thought of as two major concessions. The two sides would go their separate ways, but the United States would try to be accommodating: the divorce need not be bitter.

And the Soviet government, after some initial hesitation, grasped the hand that the Americans had held out and accepted the sort of relationship Byrnes had in mind. To be sure, the Soviets had endorsed the principle that central administrations would be created to run the German economy, but this did not mean that they were not thinking primarily in zonal terms: the all-German administrations, in their conception at Potsdam, would just play a "coordinating" role, and real power in each zone would remain in the hands of the occupying power.[90] The Soviets were in fact determined to run the eastern zone as they saw fit, and Stalin was realistic enough to understand that the other side of this coin was that the western powers would dominate the part of the country they occupied—although that, of course, would not prevent him from asking for some say over what went on there.[91]

[88] G. D. A. MacDougall, "Some Random Notes on the Reparation Discussions in Berlin, September–November 1945," DBPO I, 5:520n.

[89] U.S. working paper, July 23, 1945, and Clayton to Byrnes, July 29, 1945, FRUS Potsdam, 2:857, 900–901. For various other documents bearing on this issue, see ibid., pp. 862, 871–872, 883–885, 897, 1557.

[90] See Mai, Alliierte Kontrollrat, pp. 82, 106–108, 218–219.

[91] See Jochen Laufer, "Konfrontation oder Kooperation? Zur sowjetischen Politik in Deutschland und im Alliierten Kontrollrat 1945–1948," in Studien zur Geschichte der SBZ/DDR, ed. Alexander Fischer (Berlin: Duncker and Humblot, 1993), p. 69, for a summary judgment very much in line with my

The sort of arrangement Byrnes was proposing was therefore in line with Stalin's own basic thinking. Even before Potsdam, the Soviet leader had come to the conclusion that there would be "two Germanies"; for him it was natural that each side would impose its kind of system on the part of country its armies occupied.[92] This of course did not mean that the rhetoric about four-power control, and institutions like the Control Council, would have to be abandoned. They symbolized the common interest of the four powers in keeping Germany in line. But in more concrete ways, Germany was not really to be run as a unit. From the very start, for example, the Soviets opposed the idea of managing German exports and imports on an all-German basis.[93] This was the touchstone issue, the great test of whether the allies really believed that the German economy, and thus ultimately the German polity, was to be managed as a single unit. The Soviets, moreover, were not at all upset when the French at the beginning of October vetoed the establishment of central administrations for Germany.[94] At the end of the year, the Soviets refused to go ahead with America and Britain in running the great bulk of the country without the French—something they would have been willing to do, of course, if they had been serious about circumventing French obstructionism.[95] And Soviet policy during the "level of industry" negotiations was cut from the same cloth. In late

own. On political developments in eastern Germany, see Jochen Laufer, "Die Ursprünge des Überwachungsstaates in Ostdeutschland: Zur Bildung der Deutschen Verwaltung des Innern in der Sowjetischen Besatzungszone (1946)," in *Die Ohnmacht der Allmächtigen: Geheimdienste und politische Polizei in der modernen Gesellschaft,* ed. Bernd Florath, Armin Mitter and Stefan Wolle (Berlin: Ch. Links, 1992), pp. 146–168, and Dietrich Staritz, "Das ganze oder das halbe Deutschland? Zur Deutschlandpolitik der Sowjetunion und der KPD/SED (1945–1955)," in *Die Republik der fünfziger Jahre: Adenauers Deutschlandpolitik auf dem Prüfstand,* ed. Jürgen Weber (Munich: Olzog, 1989).

[92] See especially the notes of a June 4, 1945, meeting in Moscow between German Communist leaders and top Soviet officials (including Stalin and Molotov). "'Es wird zwei Deutschlands geben': Entscheidung über die Zusammensetzung der Kader," *Frankfurter Allgemeine Zeitung,* March 30, 1991, p. 6; also in Rolf Badstübner and Wilfried Loth, eds., *Wilhelm Pieck: Aufzeichnungen zur Deutschlandpolitik, 1945–1963* (Berlin: Akademie Verlag, 1994), p. 50. To be sure, Stalin at this meeting called on the German Communists to champion the cause of a united Germany. But his instructions ("secure the unity of Germany through a unified Communist Party, a unified Central Committee, a unified working class party") had a certain sloganistic quality, and my own view is that he did not really take the prospect of a united Germany very seriously. The Soviet leader could scarcely have believed, especially given what he knew was going on in the Soviet zone, that the Communists could ever come to power in Germany except at the point of Soviet bayonets. The common view that the Soviets followed an inconsistent policy, subjecting the Germans in their zone to a "barrage of mistreatment and exploitation, while expecting not only them, but eventually their compatriots in the West, to choose socialism and an alliance with the Soviet Union," assumes that Stalin was unrealistic in the extreme—that in fact he was stupid. Given his overall behavior, and especially his respect for power realities, and given also his well-known distrust even of his own people, the assumption that he expected the Germans as a whole to opt for Communist rule more or less voluntarily is very hard to accept; it follows that his calls for German unity are to be understood in essentially tactical terms. The quotation is from Odd Arne Westad, "Secrets of the Second World: The Russian Archives and the Reinterpretation of Cold War History," *Diplomatic History* 21 (1997): 266, but one comes across this sort of argument in many discussions of the USSR's German policy at this time. For Stalin's assumption that military occupation would lead to political control, see the famous quotation in Milovan Djilas, *Conversations with Stalin* (New York: Harcourt Brace, 1962), p. 114.

[93] Laufer, "Konfrontation oder Kooperation," p. 70.

[94] See Mai, *Alliierte Kontrollrat,* pp. 91 and 91n.

[95] See below, chap. 2, n. 39.

1945 and early 1946, the Soviet Union and the three western powers negotiated an agreement to set the level at which German industry would be allowed to operate. But the Soviets made it abundantly clear that they did not take these "level of industry" negotiations seriously, even though these talks were supposed to be concerned with how the German economy was to be managed on a four-power basis.[96]

Given the basic Soviet approach, it is not surprising that Stalin at Potsdam embraced the new U.S. concept wholeheartedly. He in fact took the lead in extending the idea to cover the most liquid, and thus most readily transferable, German assets—gold, German holdings abroad, and shares in German firms. According to his plan, German gold, foreign assets, and shares of stock would *not* be pooled and apportioned on an all-German basis. Instead he proposed a simple rule for dividing those assets between east and west. The east-west line of demarcation, "the line running from the Baltic to the Adriatic," would be taken as a dividing line. Everything east of that line, assets in the eastern zone and German investments in eastern Europe, would go to Russia. Everything west of the line would go to the western powers. In particular, the Soviets would waive their claim to a share of the German gold that had fallen into the hands of their western allies. The whole plan was quickly accepted by Stalin's British and American partners.[97]

That this arrangement reflected a basic spheres of influence orientation is clear from its content and phrasing, and is also suggested by the fact that Stalin at first proposed that it be kept secret. But the most important point to note here is the Soviet leader's role in pressing for it. He was so taken with the basic idea of a spheres of influence solution for Germany, and implicitly for Europe as a whole, that he was even willing to abandon any claim to the German gold that had fallen into the hands of the western armies. A reasonable Soviet case could be made for at least a share of this all-German asset. A unilateral concession of this sort, which was not at all in keeping with the Russians' usual practice at Potsdam of presenting their allies with one demand after another, was thus a striking demonstration of Stalin's wholehearted acceptance of the basic Byrnes concept. And indeed at the very end of the conference, the Soviet leader took what was for him the unusual step of expressing his gratitude to Byrnes, "who has worked harder perhaps than any of us to make this conference a success." It was Byrnes, he said, who "brought us together in reaching so many important decisions." Byrnes had "worked hard"

---

[96] See MacDougall, "Random Notes," DBPO I, 5:527. The Soviets, MacDougall writes, often simply failed to turn up at meetings of the Level of Industry Committee in Berlin, without giving western representatives "any explanation before or after." "Towards the end," he writes, "their manners improved somewhat." They occasionally even told their western partners "at the time the meeting was due to begin that they could not come," and there was even "a notable occasion" when they informed the western officials the day before, and thus "saved us half an hour's car drive to and from the Allied Control Authority Building." See also Murphy to Byrnes, March 25, 1946, FRUS 1946, 5:533. The Soviets' real interest was to get as much by way of reparation from the western zones as they could, and that meant setting the "level of industry" as low as possible so that the surplus of plant and equipment available for reparation would be as high as possible. They rejected the western idea of approaching the problem in a more or less impartial way, and the negotiations ended up as a simple bargaining process. See Ratchford and Ross, *Berlin Reparations Assignment,* esp. pp. 89, 95, 97, 172–173.

[97] Potsdam conference, plenary session, August 1, 1945, FRUS Potsdam, 2:566–569.

and had "worked very well"; "those sentiments, Secretary Byrnes, come from my heart."[98]

So Stalin and Byrnes (supported in a very general way by Truman) had reached a real understanding at Potsdam. Each side was essentially to have a free hand in its part of Germany. To be sure, the Potsdam Protocol was full of passages that called for treating Germany as a unit.[99] Even foreign trade, according to the text, was supposed to be managed on an all-German basis. But the all-German language of the final agreement was simply a figleaf. The way the key foreign trade issue was handled again shows the real thrust of American and Soviet thinking at this time. It is clear from the drafting history that the unitary language of the official Potsdam Protocol was not meant to be taken seriously. Byrnes in fact had proposed dropping the provision in the draft agreement calling for the Control Council to formulate an import program for Germany as a whole soon after the new reparation plan was accepted.[100] Stalin agreed with Byrnes, and if it had just been up to the two of them the paragraph would have been completely dropped.

But Ernest Bevin objected. Bevin, foreign secretary in the new Labour government that had been swept into power in Britain in the middle of the Potsdam conference, was personally not a great supporter of German unity, but in his first days in office he did not want to take a line that diverged too radically from the views of his subordinates in the Foreign Office—or really of key Treasury officials—on this fundamental question. Byrnes, in keeping with his general philosophy, urged Bevin to deal with the problem of exports and imports and the financing of the German trade deficit on a zonal basis. Why couldn't the British, he asked, just "handle this in their own way since they were in control in their zone"? Because to do so would "cut across the agreement to treat Germany as a whole economy," Bevin rather innocently replied. "It would divide Germany into three zones."[101]

As a result of Bevin's resistance, a watered-down version of the provision on for-

[98] Potsdam conference, plenary meeting, August 1, 1945, ibid., p. 601; James F. Byrnes, *Speaking Frankly* (New York: Harper, 1947), p. 86. Note also the evidence of Stalin's and Molotov's satisfaction with Potsdam, and in particular with the reparation settlement, in Vladislav Zubok and Constantine Pleshakov, *Inside the Kremlin's Cold War: From Stalin to Khrushchev* (Cambridge, Mass.: Harvard University Press, 1996), pp. 37 and 40. Stalin, a document they cite shows, was also quite pleased that at Potsdam, Bulgaria was "recognized as within our sphere of influence." In fact, the Soviet leadership saw Potsdam as amounting to an acknowledgment by the western powers that they, the western countries, had "lost eastern Europe and the Balkans." Molotov as cited by the Yugoslav ambassador in Moscow, quoted in Vojtech Mastny, *The Cold War and Soviet Insecurity: The Stalin Years* (New York: Oxford University Press, 1996), p. 22.

[99] For the text, see FRUS Potsdam, 2:1477–1498.

[100] Potsdam conference, plenary meeting, July 31, 1945, ibid., p. 520.

[101] Potsdam conference, plenary meeting, July 31, 1945, ibid., p. 521. For Bevin's views on German unity, see Deighton, *Impossible Peace,* pp. 15, 21; and Rothwell, *Britain and the Cold War,* p. 225. For Foreign Office and especially Treasury opposition to the Byrnes plan and Bevin's reaction, see Troutbeck minute, July 26, 1945; Dent minute, July 27, 1945; staff conference with Attlee and Bevin, July 31, 1945; Waley note, July 31, 1945; Coulson to Cadogan, July 31, 1945, and enclosed memorandum; and Waley to Eady, August 1, 1945; in DBPO, I, 1:920n., 920–921, 1052–1054, 1068, 1069–1071, 1105–1106. One should note, however, that there was a certain degree of ambivalence in the British position, and that Waley, Eady, and even Churchill himself at first favored the American plan. See the evidence cited in Philip Baggaley, "Reparations, Security, and the Industrial Disarmament of Germany: Origins of the Potsdam Decisions" (Ph.D. diss., Yale University, 1980), pp. 534–535.

eign trade made it into the final agreement. This provision seemed to imply that Germany was to be treated as a unit: "in working out the economic balance of Germany the necessary means must be provided to pay for imports approved by the Control Council in Germany. The proceeds of exports from current production and stocks shall be available in the first place for payment for such imports."[102] But this changed nothing of substance, and the Americans who negotiated this part of the Potsdam agreement understood what the real situation was. The provisions calling for all-German arrangements in this area, they wrote, were subject to the already accepted principle that "if the Control Council failed to agree," policy would be managed on a zonal basis. And they thought it "quite likely" that the Control Council would deadlock on this issue. The control and financing of foreign trade would then "revert to the zone commanders," in which case the three western powers would probably be able to come up with a common import program for *western* Germany as a whole. So the all-German language of the agreement would probably have no substantive effect. Germany in all likelihood would still end up being divided between the Soviet Union and the western powers.[103]

Such assumptions formed the real basis of the Potsdam understanding. The formal agreement might have given a very different impression, but it was scarcely to be expected that a written accord would provide directly for an overt partition of Germany. And indeed what was the point of being too explicit about these matters? As long as the real issues had been settled with the agreement on the Byrnes plan, there was no harm in paying a little lip service to Wilsonian platitudes.

But if all this is true—if the western powers and the Soviets as well were prepared in late 1945 to accept a spheres of influence settlement in Europe—how, then, is the Cold War to be understood? Why was it that the sort of arrangement Byrnes and Stalin had agreed to at Potsdam failed to provide the basis for stable relations between the Soviet Union and her western allies? For by early 1946 things had moved off the track. By that point, a war of words had broken out between the western powers and the USSR; the German issue was the great focal point. What had gone wrong? The general problem of the origins of the Cold War turns on the answer to that question.

[102] For Paragraph 19 of part II of the Protocol, see FRUS Potsdam, 2:1485. This is to be compared with the pre–Byrnes plan draft, ibid., p. 799.

[103] Collado to Thorp and Reinstein, July 23, 1945; report to Byrnes, August 1, 1945; and Clayton and Collado to Thorp, August 16, 1945; ibid., pp. 812, 828, 829–830.

Toward the Rubicon

THE BYRNES POLICY of late 1945 was in essence aimed at bringing about an amicable divorce: the two sides, the Soviet Union and the western powers, would disengage from each other, and each would run things in the part of Germany—and implicitly in the part of Europe—its armies occupied. Stalin was willing to go along with this approach; it thus seemed that a way had been found for the two sides to coexist. But the Byrnes policy did not lead directly to a stable peace in Europe. Instead, east-west relations deteriorated dramatically, and by early 1946 the Cold War had begun.

What had happened to the Potsdam understanding? The conflict in 1946 was preeminently about Germany; if both sides had kept to the Potsdam understanding, no such conflict could have arisen. But the United States government had shifted its position: the Byrnes policy was abandoned by the American government itself.

At Potsdam, the division of Germany had been accepted as inevitable: the Americans had built their policy on the assumption that the Soviet Union and the western powers would not be able to "pull together in governing Germany."[1] In particular, Byrnes had made it quite clear that Germany's foreign trade would not be managed on an all-German basis. But by the spring of 1946, U.S. representatives were insisting with increasing stridency that Germany had to be treated as an economic unit. This, they stressed, meant above all that Germany's exports and imports had to be handled on an all-German basis. The Soviet preference for dealing with German foreign trade on a zonal basis was, in the new American view, "a complete negation of Potsdam." U.S. officials demanded, loudly and repeatedly, a common import-export policy. The claim now was that at Potsdam it had been agreed that Germany would be run as an economic unit, and that the Soviets were reneging on this agreement.[2]

America's German policy had been totally transformed, and this transformation was to play a fundamental role in setting the major powers at odds with each other. It meant that Germany, and implicitly Europe as a whole, was not going to be divided on a more or less friendly basis, as Byrnes and the others at Potsdam had intended. By mid-1946 the former allies were at each others' throats, each blaming the other for Germany's division. What the western powers were doing in Germany was coming to have a distinct anti-Soviet edge; the Soviets were coming to feel that they needed to deal with the situation before it got totally out of hand; soon it seemed that the two sides might be headed for a showdown.

But how is the shift in U.S. policy itself to be understood? The problem will be

[1] Rubin to Oliver, July 25, 1945, FRUS Potsdam, 2:871.

[2] For the quotation, see Acheson to Byrnes, May 9, 1946, FRUS 1946, 5:551. For other documents reflecting this aspect of American policy, see below, note 62.

approached here on two levels. First the general course of international politics in late 1945 and early 1946 will be examined; the focus will then shift to an analysis of the diplomacy of the German question during this period and beyond.

THE COMING OF THE COLD WAR

The Cold War did not develop out of the quarrel over eastern Europe. It was the dispute over Iran and Turkey that instead played the key role in triggering the conflict. This dispute led to a shift in America's general policy toward the Soviet Union, and that shift in turn led by early 1946 to a fundamental transformation of U.S. policy on the German question.

Both the British and the Americans had in effect accepted eastern Europe as a Soviet sphere of influence by December 1945. In late 1945, the U.S government, for example, went through the motions of standing up for the principle of self-determination as a basis for a political settlement in that part of the world, somewhat irritating the Soviets in the process. But by the end of the year even that policy had been effectively dropped: both Britain and America had for all intents and purposes accepted eastern Europe as an area that the USSR would control.

The question was whether Stalin would be willing in exchange to recognize that western interests were predominant in other key areas. If he were, the British certainly were ready to make a straightforward deal. If the Soviets were willing to recognize the Middle East and the Mediterranean as a western sphere of influence, Bevin for his part would be ready to accept the status quo in eastern Europe. He, and Prime Minister Attlee as well, might have disliked the idea of a spheres of influence settlement. But by the end of 1945 they had come to the conclusion that the alternative policy of working for the establishment of democratic governments in countries like Bulgaria and Rumania was bankrupt. And if, by recognizing political realities in eastern Europe, they could make the Middle East and the Mediterranean more secure, then this was a price they were quite willing to pay.[3]

Would the Soviets, however, go along with the idea? Given Stalin's general policy, a spheres of influence deal was by no means out of the question. The Soviet leader had readily accepted, and lived up to, the percentage agreement with Churchill, and that basic policy choice still seemed to guide his thinking at Potsdam.[4] On Germany, he had backed the Byrnes plan wholeheartedly, and his pol-

[3] For Bevin's dislike of the idea of spheres of influence, but also his growing sense that this kind of system was unavoidable, see Alan Bullock, *Ernest Bevin: Foreign Secretary, 1945–1951* (New York: Norton, 1983), pp. 134, 193–194, and also DBPO I, 2:15–18 and 565n. Note also the British ambassador's insistence in a May 1946 meeting with Stalin on the importance of the USSR accepting the Middle East as a British sphere of influence, in Rothwell, *Britain and the Cold War*, pp. 262–263. For Attlee's aversion to the idea of a spheres of influence system, see Bullock, *Bevin*, p. 117, and Attlee to Eden, July 18, 1945, DBPO I, 1:363–364.

[4] Note, for example, his comment at a private meeting with Churchill on July 18: "Marshal Stalin said that he had been hurt by the American demand for a change of Government in Roumania and Bulgaria. He was not meddling in Greek affairs, so he thought it was unjust of the Americans to make the present demand." DBPO I, 1:389. Note also Molotov's handwritten comments in February 1945 on a memorandum by Andrei Vyshinsky on the Polish question. The Soviet foreign minister sincerely re-

icy in Korea, the other divided country, was also inspired by the same general spheres of influence spirit.[5] It seemed in 1945 that Stalin was quite ready to accept the principle of a division of the world philosophically. "This war is not as in the past," he told the Yugoslav Communist leaders in April 1945. "Whoever occupies a territory also imposes on it his own social system. Everyone imposes his own system as far as his army can reach. It cannot be otherwise."[6]

But for Stalin to accept a spheres of influence settlement, how far would the Soviet sphere have to extend? Even in mid- and late 1945, the Soviets were pressing claims that had little to do with a security zone in eastern Europe. They asked for a trusteeship over one of the former Italian colonies in the Mediterranean and a zone of occupation in Japan. They sought control over northern Iran and demanded military bases on the Turkish Straits. In 1945, western leaders were not sure what to make of these claims. Perhaps the Soviets simply wanted to see what they could get on the cheap. Or perhaps these demands, or at least some of them, were not meant to be taken seriously at all. The Soviets might just be reacting, on a tit-for-tat basis, to western interference in the Soviet sphere, thus driving home to Britain and America the importance of adopting a consistent spheres of influence policy and granting the Soviets a free hand in eastern Europe as the price for operating freely in the areas the western powers controlled.[7]

But it soon became clear that Soviet goals were not merely tactical and that the Soviets were serious about expanding their power beyond eastern Europe. Indeed, Stalin in effect rejected the idea of a spheres of influence settlement on a status quo basis in a December 1945 meeting with Bevin. The Soviet leader was not happy with Soviet gains after the war; the status quo of a Soviet-dominated eastern Europe was obviously not good enough. The western allies each had their sphere but the Russians, he complained, "had nothing"—a stunning claim, given the obvious point, which Bevin was quick to make, "that the Soviet sphere extended from Lübeck to Port Arthur."[8]

The Soviets were pushing ahead in an area where the British were particularly sensitive: the eastern Mediterranean and the Middle East. In mid-1945, Stalin made it clear to Molotov that the south was the one area where he was dissatisfied with Russia's new frontiers.[9] By late 1945, the Russians were promoting leftist regimes in the area their armies occupied in northern Iran. According to their

sented western interference with what the USSR was doing in Poland, and his reasoning is quite revealing: "Poland—a big deal! But how governments are being organized in Belgium, France, Greece, etc., we do not know. We have not been asked, although we do not say that we like one or another of these governments. We have not interfered, because it is the Anglo-American zone of military action." Cited in Vladimir Pechatnov, "The Big Three after World War II: New Documents on Soviet Thinking about Post War Relations with the United States and Great Britain," Cold War International History Project [CWIHP] Working Paper no. 13 (Woodrow Wilson Center, Washington, D.C., 1995), p. 23.

[5] See Kathryn Weathersby, "Soviet Aims in Korea and the Origins of the Korean War, 1945–1950: New Evidence from Russian Archives," CWHIP Working Paper no. 8 (Woodrow Wilson Center, Washington, D.C., 1993).

[6] Djilas, *Conversations with Stalin,* p. 114.

[7] See, for example, Brimelow to Warner, September 6, 1945, DBPO I, 6:59; Bevin-Hall memorandum, August 25, 1945, ibid., 2:34.

[8] Bevin-Stalin meeting, December 24, 1945, ibid., p. 868.

[9] McClellan, "Molotov Remembers," p. 17.

wartime agreement with the western allies on Iran, the Soviets were to withdraw their forces from that country within six months after the end of the war. But although they repeatedly promised to be out by that deadline, it was becoming increasingly clear in early 1946 that they were not going to honor that commitment.[10]

The USSR also wanted to build military bases on the Turkish Straits. The issue had been raised with the Turks just before Potsdam, and at that conference Stalin pressed his allies to accept his right to control the Straits. America had the Panama Canal and Britain controlled Suez, so why shouldn't Russia control a waterway of equivalent strategic importance? The implication was that the USSR should have this right no matter how the Turks felt about the idea of Soviet bases on their territory. And when Turkey did resist their claims, the Soviets adopted tougher tactics. The press campaign against Turkey escalated, there were menacing troop movements in the Balkans, and diplomatic pressure on Turkey intensified.[11]

Stalin had taken his measure of the other great powers. The British were too weak to hold him back by themselves. With the United States it was a different story. In areas where the Americans had made their interests clear, and especially in key areas where U.S. troops were present—above all, western Germany and Japan—Stalin would not seriously challenge the status quo. What interest, however, did the Americans have in Iran or Turkey? There was no sign in late 1945 that they would use their power to block a Soviet advance. There was no reason, therefore, not to push ahead in that region.

But what the Soviets were doing in the Near East deeply alienated the American government. The top U.S. leadership was rapidly turning against Russia in late 1945 and early 1946. This was not because Byrnes and Truman now saw for the first time that the Soviet Union was an expansionist power: even in mid-1945, it had seemed that the Soviets were trying to push out wherever they could. But Byrnes, at that point, had thought he had found a way to deal with the problem. A sharp line would be drawn between east and west. The Soviets would have a free hand in eastern Europe, including eastern Germany; the hope was that in exchange for western acquiescence in the new status quo, the USSR, for her part, would also agree to live with things as they were, and that on that basis, relatively friendly relations would be possible. When it became clear, however, that the Soviets were not going to accept an arrangement of this sort, American attitudes shifted quite dramatically: there had to be some limit to Soviet expansionism, and if the soft line was not working, a tougher policy was called for.

In mid-1945, Truman, for example, had accepted the policy of the "amicable divorce." At Potsdam, as he later recalled, he had been a "Russophile as most of us were." He thought he could manage to live with Stalin, and in fact he "liked the little son of a bitch."[12] The Soviet leader, Truman said at the time, was "straightforward"; Stalin "knows what he wants and will compromise when he can't get

---

[10] See Kuniholm, *The Origins of the Cold War in the Near East,* pp. 270–286, 304–342.

[11] See ibid., pp. 255–270.

[12] Truman to Acheson (unsent), March 15, 1957, in *Strictly Personal and Confidential: The Letters Harry Truman Never Mailed,* ed. Monte Poen (Boston: Little Brown, 1982), p. 33.

it."[13] Truman might have disliked what the Soviets were doing in the areas they controlled, and he was certainly irritated with the way they had presented the United States with one fait accompli after another. But this did not lead him to embrace an anti-Soviet policy. Indeed, even as late as November 1945, he was still talking about how America had to get along with Russia.[14] The United States would therefore, he thought, have to stand aside if Russia tried to "grab control of the Black Sea straits." The Turks would fight, "but it would be like the Russian-Finnish war." America would not go to war with Russia over the issue.[15] A month later Truman was no longer sure what U.S. policy should be. The Soviets, he said, had presented America with a fait accompli in the case of Poland. They now had half a million men in Bulgaria and he was afraid that some day they were "going to move down and take the Black Sea straits" and confront America with another fait accompli. The only thing they understood was "divisions," but the U.S. government could not "send any divisions over to prevent them" from moving into Turkey: "I don't know what we're going to do."[16] And then, just three weeks after that, he opted for a hard line: "There isn't a doubt in my mind that Russia intends an invasion of Turkey and the seizure of the Black Sea Straits to the Mediterranean. Unless Russia is faced with an iron fist and strong language another war is in the making. Only one language do they understand—'How many divisions have you?'" With regard to Iran as well, Truman was by now beginning to take a hard line. Soviet policy in Iran, Truman now complained, was an "outrage if I ever saw one." Iran had been an ally during the war and the use of Iranian territory as a channel for millions of tons of supplies had been crucial to Russia's survival, "yet now Russia stirs up rebellion and keeps troops on the soil of her friend and ally, Iran."[17]

It was in the context of what was going on in Iran and Turkey that Truman now reinterpreted what had happened the previous year in eastern Europe. Everything, it seemed, was part of the same pattern. The Russians had been "high handed" and "arbitrary" in Poland and elsewhere in the region; their basic tactic was to confront the West with a fait accompli. Soviet policy in Poland, Rumania, and Bulgaria now became the first count in Truman's indictment of the USSR. Truman's attitude had shifted. At Potsdam, he had not liked the way Poland, with Soviet backing, had extended her frontier west to the Oder-Neisse line, but given what the Poles had suffered at German hands during the war, he could understand why they had annexed that territory. But now, in January 1946, the seizure of that part of Germany was a "high handed outrage," pure and simple.[18]

By early 1946, Byrnes had also turned against the Soviets. Was this simply because the political climate within the United States had shifted radically—because

[13] Truman to Bess Truman, July 29, 1945, *Dear Bess,* p. 522; *Ayers Diary,* entry for August 7, 1945, p. 59.

[14] *Ayers Diary,* entry for November 19, 1945, p. 97.

[15] *Ayers Diary,* entry for November 19, 1945, p. 97.

[16] Ibid., entry for December 17, 1945, p. 104.

[17] Truman to Byrnes (unsent), January 5, 1946, in Poen, *Strictly Personal,* p. 40.

[18] Truman to Byrnes (unsent), January 5, 1946, ibid., p. 40. Compare this with Truman to his wife, July 31, 1945, in *Dear Bess,* pp. 522–523.

Byrnes, who was personally inclined to pursue a policy of accommodation, had been forced by a sharp presidential intervention to change course and take a much tougher line? After the Moscow foreign ministers' meeting in December, where Byrnes had agreed to recognize the Communist governments in Bulgaria and Rumania, Truman in fact did write a letter to his secretary of state demanding that America stop "babying the Russians." America, he wrote, should not "play compromise any longer." In particular—and this was a direct slap at the policy Byrnes had pursued at Moscow in December—the U.S. government "should refuse to recognize Rumania and Bulgaria until they comply with our requirements."[19]

This letter was never sent, and it is highly unlikely that it was even read to Byrnes when he met with Truman on January 5.[20] Truman, as was his custom, was almost certainly just blowing off steam.[21] He was upset with Byrnes for not keeping him informed and for not respecting his authority as president. But their policy differences were not nearly as great as this letter might suggest. Truman had not been deeply involved with foreign policy in 1945, and had more or less let Byrnes run things. And Byrnes had not gone out of his way to consult with Truman. As a result, the president perhaps did not fully understand what Byrnes had been up to—that the recognition of Communist regimes in eastern Europe was not a simple act of appeasement, but was rather part of a policy of drawing a clear line between east and west. Byrnes was perhaps able to explain things to Truman, because the president soon reversed himself on the question of recognizing the communist regimes in the Balkans; Rumania was recognized the very next month.

Byrnes, in fact, had never taken what could be called a pro-Soviet line in late 1945. At that time, well before American opinion as a whole had shifted, the Secretary of State had taken a tougher line on a number of key issues than various individuals who would later become leading Cold Warriors. Dean Acheson, for example, then under secretary of state, was in favor of sharing America's nuclear secrets with the USSR. Acheson could not "conceive of a world," he said at a high level meeting on September 21, "in which we were hoarders of military secrets from our Allies, particularly this great Ally upon our cooperation with whom rests the future peace of the world." But Byrnes was dead set against the idea.[22] And in October 1945, Byrnes, came down hard on Joseph Davies, the pro-Soviet former ambassador to Moscow, who lectured him on the importance of seeing things from the Russian point of view. "Molotov was 'insufferable,'" he told Davies. He said that he was 'almost ashamed' of himself for having taken what he did from Molotov."[23]

In early 1946, Byrnes certainly did not give the impression of a man who had

---

[19] Truman to Byrnes (unsent), January 5, 1946, in Poen, *Strictly Personal,* p. 40.

[20] For the best analysis, see Messer, *End of an Alliance,* pp. 157–165.

[21] Poen, *Strictly Personal,* is essentially a collection of these unsent letters, some of which are quite extraordinary. Note especially a Truman desk note from June 1946, where he wrote about calling in trade union leaders, telling "them that patience is exhausted. Declare an emergency—call out the troops. Start industry and put anyone to work who wants to work. If any leader interferes, court-martial him. . . . Adjourn Congress and run the country. Get plenty of Atomic Bombs on hand—drop one on Stalin, put the United Nations to work and eventually set up a free world." Ibid., p. 31.

[22] Forrestal diary entries for September 21 and October 16, 1945, FD/3/FP/ML. Only the second of these was published, in part, in Millis, *Forrestal Diaries,* p. 102.

[23] Yergin, *Shattered Peace,* pp. 142–143.

adopted the new line reluctantly, solely for domestic political reasons. When Churchill came over in March to deliver his famous "Iron Curtain" speech, one of the opening shots in the Cold War, he showed Byrnes the text in advance. The secretary was pleased and "excited," and the two men had a long talk. Churchill for his part was delighted by what he had learned. There was "no doubt," he wrote Attlee, that the people at the top of the American government were "deeply distressed by the way they are being treated by Russia."[24]

The very same day that Churchill wrote that letter, Byrnes was up in arms over Soviet actions in Iran. After receiving some alarming reports about what the Soviets were doing there, Byrnes pounded one fist into the other and declared: "Now we'll give it to them with both barrels."[25] Truman at this point seemed ready to contemplate war over Iran.[26] But the USSR drew back and the crisis soon passed.

The Soviets also began to draw in their horns in the conflict with Turkey—again, as America deepened her involvement in that dispute. The Turkish affair climaxed in August 1946. Once again it was clear—indeed, even clearer than in March—that Truman was ultimately willing to risk war with Russia.[27] In January 1945, the U.S. Joint Chiefs of Staff had thought that it was "in the highest degree unlikely" that the United States and the Soviet Union would ever be aligned against each other.[28] Now war was accepted as a real possibility. America had come a long way in little more than a year.

The immediate effect of the Iranian and Turkish crises was to sharpen the line of demarcation between east and west. Each side had tested and was coming to terms with a new status quo. The western powers had written off eastern Europe. The Russians, for their part, withdrew from Iran, and their pressure on Turkey gradually subsided. Their less serious claims—about a trusteeship in Libya, for example, and a zone of occupation in Japan—were also dropped.

But if this was a spheres of influence settlement, it was very different from the sort of arrangement Byrnes and Stalin had contemplated in 1945. There was still no wish to commit American power in any serious way to the rolling back of Soviet influence over eastern Europe. America would never risk war, for example, to prevent the Communists from getting control over Czechoslovakia; even the threat of an American intervention would never be used to neutralize the threat of a Soviet intervention there. But the line would be drawn around the periphery of the area that had been consigned to the Soviets, and there was a growing willingness to defend that line if necessary with military force.[29]

[24] Churchill to Attlee, March 7, 1946, CHUR 2/4, Churchill Papers, Churchill Archives Centre, Churchill College, Cambridge University.

[25] Edwin Wright, "Events relative to the Azerbaijan Issue— March 1946," August 16, 1965, quoted in FRUS 1946, 7:347.

[26] See the president's comments reported in W. Averell Harriman and Elie Abel, *Special Envoy to Churchill and Stalin, 1941–1946* (New York: Random House, 1975), p. 550.

[27] Acheson to Byrnes, August 15, 1946, and Acheson-Inverchapel meeting, August 20, 1946, FRUS 1946, 7:840–842, 849–850. On the Turkish crisis, see especially Eduard Mark, "The War Scare of 1946 and its Consequences," *Diplomatic History* 21 (1997): 383–415.

[28] Leahy to Hull, May 16, 1944, FRUS Yalta, p. 107.

[29] For a typical example of this kind of thinking, see JCS to Byrnes, March 29, 1946, FRUS 1946, 1:1165–1166.

This policy of containment, as it came to be called, was adopted at the beginning of 1946. It was adopted even before the term was coined, certainly well before the rationale for the policy was developed by its chief theoretician, George Kennan.[30] This was a policy which rested on military power—on, as Kennan was to put it in a famous article, the "adroit and vigilant application of counter-force at a series of constantly shifting geographical and political points."[31] The Soviet Union was an expansionist power, and it was coming to be taken as axiomatic that only counter-vailing power could keep her in line. The world was obviously going to be divided. But that had been the assumption in late 1945 as well. The difference now was that this division was no longer seen as resting on mutual consent; it was no longer regarded as something both sides could accept in a relatively relaxed way. The Soviet Union posed a military threat, and only the power of the West kept her at bay. Power—the balance of power between east and west—was no longer something that loomed vaguely in the background of international politics. If force was the only language the Soviets understood, then the West had to be able to speak that same language and make it clear that it could only be pushed so far.

These new attitudes were to lead to a major shift in America's German policy in 1946.

THE TRANSFORMATION OF AMERICA'S GERMAN POLICY

At Potsdam, Byrnes had based his policy on the premise that Germany was going to be divided between east and west. But Byrnes's Potsdam policy was never actually implemented. Even during the period immediately after the conference, when U.S.–Soviet relations were relatively good, the United States did not press for the sort of zonally oriented policy Byrnes had had in mind. Instead, most American officials were not privy to the records of the top-level discussions at which the real Potsdam understandings were reached and took the Potsdam Protocol at face value. That formal agreement had specifically stated that Germany was to be "treated as an economic unit," and had called for "common policies" in seven specified areas including reparation and "import and export programs for Germany as a whole."

Thus the basic idea of the Byrnes plan was to put reparation squarely on a zonal basis. But as soon as the Potsdam conference was over, American officials took exactly the opposite line. Edwin Pauley, the top U.S. reparation official, for example, explained the meaning of the Potsdam reparation settlement to the American military authorities in Germany on August 11, 1945. The Allied Control Council, he said, was to "make every attempt to arrange for reparation removals throughout Germany on a uniform basis as to type, kind, and extent of such removals."[32] And the State Department in mid-August endorsed the "principle that proceeds of exports from all zones should be pooled to pay for imports"—even though the paragraph in the Potsdam Protocol it cited was one which Byrnes had wanted to drop

---

[30] On this point, see Leffler, *Preponderance of Power,* esp. pp. 60–61.

[31] "The Sources of Soviet Conduct," *Foreign Affairs* 25 (July 1947): 576.

[32] Pauley to Clay, August 11, 1945, FRUS 1945, 3:1251–1252.

entirely and which American representatives at Potsdam had succeeded in watering down precisely in order to avoid giving it this meaning.[33]

And then there was the question of whether there was to be any limit to what the Soviets could extract from their zone. It was obvious that if there were no ceiling, Germany could not be dealt with as a single economic area. At Potsdam, when Molotov had raised the point, Byrnes had answered that the Soviets could do as they pleased in eastern Germany. The clear implication then was that Germany would not be run as a unit, that each side would run things in its part of Germany and would not get involved in managing the economy of the other part. In early 1946, the basic point was the same, but the logic was rearranged: if there were no limit, Germany could not be run as a unit; the Potsdam agreement, however, provided that Germany was to be administered on a unitary basis; therefore, given the American insistence on minimizing the all-German deficit, a ceiling had to be placed on what the Soviets could take from their zone.[34] This amounted to a complete reversal of Byrnes's policy at Potsdam. American representatives even tried to back out of the arrangement dividing up Germany's foreign assets on an east-west basis. This idea, in fact, came from President Truman himself, which is another piece of evidence showing that he had not been very directly involved with what Byrnes had been doing at Potsdam. Even though the provision in the Protocol was unambiguous on this point, the U.S. government now wanted to vest "title to all German assets abroad in a quadripartite commission."[35]

Why did Byrnes allow this sort of thing to go on?[36] His basic views had obviously not changed overnight as a result of anything that the Soviets were doing. There had not been enough time for that. So if his thinking on the substantive issues had not changed, the main considerations shaping his policy after Potsdam must have been tactical in nature. And indeed it is not hard to imagine how the problem must have looked to Byrnes at the time. There were many people who disliked the idea of a spheres of influence policy. The Right objected to a policy that would consign millions of people to Communist rule. Maybe nothing could be done about it, but Soviet control of half of Europe should in the Right's view never be accepted as legitimate. The Left objected to a policy of giving up on four-power rule in Germany, which meant giving up on U.S.–Soviet cooperation in general, and perhaps also giving up on the one thing that might keep the Germans under control. And then there was the Wilsonian tradition, with its vision of a world made up of unified nation-states and its distaste for the very idea of the big

---

[33] Byrnes to Murphy, August 18, 1945, FRUS 1945, 3:1522. On this provision of the Potsdam agreement, see above, pp. 32–33.

[34] For an example of this type of thinking, see Clay to Eisenhower, May 26, 1946, *Clay Papers*, 1:214.

[35] Backer, *Winds of History*, p. 108.

[36] In September, when the State Department was pressing for a reparation plan based on the idea that Germany was to be treated as a unit, Byrnes objected from London, saying that he seriously doubted whether that approach "correctly reflects the spirit of the Potsdam Protocol or is likely to produce any tangible results." But that was just about as far as he went: he did not put his foot down and insist on a change in policy. Clayton to Harriman, September 6, 1945, and Byrnes to Acheson, September 28, 1945, FRUS 1945, 3:1284, 1319; the Byrnes letter is cited in an unpublished manuscript by James McAllister.

powers dividing up not just individual countries but even whole regions of the world in private deals.

So all sorts of arguments were mingled together. The "anti-Soviet" argument about the need to avoid an extension of Soviet power into the heart of Europe and the "pro-Soviet" argument that America should try hard to work together with the USSR both pointed toward the unitary policy. The "anti-German" argument about the need for a four-power regime to keep the Germans in line and the "pro-German" argument about the need to respect German national rights also pointed in that same direction. But the fact that the unitary policy was supported by such a hodgepodge of arguments meant that the forces arrayed behind that policy were an unstable mix. Every argument was balanced by a counterargument that pointed in the opposite direction. Yes, it was unfortunate that millions of east Germans were subjected to Soviet rule, but western Germany at least should not be allowed to fall into Communist hands. Yes, cooperation with the Russians might in theory be the ideal solution, but in practice the best way to get along with them might be to divide Germany and let each side run things in its part of the country. And of course, while it was important to keep Germany in line, four-power unity might not be the only way to achieve this goal. A divided Germany could pose no threat to world peace. A truncated Germany, in fact, could be treated gently: it would be easier to restore political rights to a western Germany threatened by Russia and thus dependent on the western powers for protection than to a unified German state, free of foreign military forces. But this situation, where every argument was balanced by a counterargument, meant that the unitary policy was built on sand and that in the long run it would probably collapse of its own weight.

For the time being, however, there was bound to be a good deal of opposition, from a wide variety of quarters, to a policy that explicitly looked toward a division of Germany. From Byrnes's point of view, the problems were obvious. Why confront all this opposition head on? Why run the risk of being blamed for a "defeatist" policy, for having given up on allied cooperation before he absolutely had to? As a skilled politician, Byrnes's instinct was to finesse the issue. The four-power rhetoric would not be abandoned, and the U.S. government would officially back the policy of running Germany on a unitary basis. The very realities that had convinced him that this was impractical would bring the others around soon enough, but in the meantime, as far as the world was concerned, the unitary policy would get its chance. American policy had earlier had a pronounced zonal emphasis, but from mid-August on, U.S. officials began to press very strongly—again, more strongly than anyone else—for a unitary solution to the German problem.

This certainly was the policy that General Clay now sought to implement. Clay was in charge of the American military government in Germany and he took the Potsdam Protocol as his charter. Germany, he thought, had to be run as a unit. Four-power cooperation was essential. To Clay, Germany was a kind of "laboratory": what was at stake here was the ability of the allies to work together in running world affairs in general.[37] He pushed hard in late 1945 for the establishment of centralized administrative machinery through which Germany could be run.

[37] Meeting at State Department, November 3, 1945, *Clay Papers,* 1:113.

Clay understood that the creation of an all-German administrative apparatus in such areas as transportation and finance was just a first step, and that the real test of "our ability to work effectively with the USSR" would only come later, when common policies had to be worked out for this machinery to implement.[38] But it was an essential first step, and he pressed energetically for the establishment of the central administrations.

The Control Council, however, was not able to move ahead in this area. Action required unanimity, and the French said they would not agree to the creation of the central administrations until they got their way on another issue: they wanted to split the Rhineland and the Ruhr off from the rest of Germany. But this the Americans would not accept. Clay then sought to go ahead without the French and set up the administrations in the American, British, and Soviet zones. But the Russians were not willing to go along with this idea, and even the British were cool to the plan. By late November 1945 it became clear that nothing would come of it.[39]

At the beginning of 1946 Clay, therefore, took another tack. The reparation arrangements worked out at Potsdam would provide him with the leverage he needed to press for an all-German solution. Under the Potsdam agreement, the Soviets were entitled to a quarter of the industrial equipment, judged unnecessary for the German peace economy, which could be removed from the western zones. Three-fifths of those deliveries—15 percent of the total earmarked for reparation from western Germany—were to be exchanged for food and raw materials from the east. The rest, amounting to 10 percent of the total, was to be given to the Soviets free and clear.

To determine what was available for reparation deliveries from western Germany—that is, how much *surplus* plant and equipment there was in the *western* zones—a plan for the German peacetime economy had to be worked out. Strictly speaking, for this purpose a level of industry plan needed to be worked out only for western Germany. If there was a political need for an all-German plan, it could have been a simple cobbling together of plans for western and eastern Germany, with only the first meant to be taken seriously. An arrangement of that sort would have been in keeping with the spirit of the Byrnes plan. In fact this kind of procedure was evidently considered, but ruled out, probably because of the implications about how Germany as a whole would be run.[40] So instead, and in a totally nonscientific way, the Control Council on March 26 reached agreement on a plan for Germany as a whole.[41]

[38] Ibid., p. 112.

[39] French memorandum, September 13, 1945; Murphy to Byrnes, September 29, October 2 and 18, 1945; Allied Coordinating Committee meeting, November 5, 1945; Byrnes–Couve de Murville meting, November 20, 1945; Byrnes to Caffery, December 6, 1945; in FRUS 1945, 3:869–871, 879, 844, 884, 888n, 907, 916. See also Clay to War Department, September 24, 1945, and Clay to Mc-Cloy, October 5, 1945, *Clay Papers*, 1:85, 92. For Soviet unwillingness to go along with the idea, see Murphy to Byrnes, November 24, 1945, and Caffery to Byrnes, December 11, 1945, FRUS 1945, 3:911, 918. For British coolness, see, for example, a French Foreign Ministry historical note of January 12, 1946, Y/284/FFMA.

[40] G. D. A. MacDougall, "Some Random Notes on the Reparation Discussions in Berlin, September–November 1945," DBPO I, 5:521.

[41] For the level of industry plan, see DOSB, April 14, 1946, pp. 636–639; for a discussion, see Ratchford and Ross, *Berlin Reparations Assignment*, chaps. 7–13.

Clay now argued that this plan for the overall German economy presupposed that Germany would be run as a unit, and that in particular there would have to be a "common import-export program" for the country as a whole. Officially, the Soviets, like everyone else, were in favor of treating Germany as a unit, but they were now taking "a very strong position against a common import-export program"—they had in fact opposed the idea from Potsdam on—and U.S. officials wondered what their attitude really was.[42] What would they do if the Americans held their feet to the fire?

Clay proposed to "smoke out" the Soviet position by threatening to cut off reparations, from the American zone at least, if they did not agree to a common policy on foreign trade. The Americans made what was to become their standard argument. The amount of reparation was determined by the level of industry plan; that plan presupposed that Germany would be treated as an economic unit, and in particular that a common program on exports and imports would be worked out. If the foreign trade program was blocked, therefore, the level of industry plan was no longer meaningful, and so the reparation agreements were no longer binding. On April 8, Clay informed the other occupying powers that unless a common import-export policy was worked out, the United States would "insist" on a revision of the reparation plan. The threat was soon carried out. At a four-power meeting on April 26, Clay insisted that Potsdam had to be taken as a whole. "A common import-export program," he said, "pooling all indigenous resources and the proceeds from all exports, was an essential part of Potsdam." The reparation program was "based on a common import-export program," so the failure of the Control Council to adopt a common program for German foreign trade meant that the Americans would have to suspend reparation deliveries.[43]

The State Department took the same basic line. The suspension of reparation deliveries was to be used as a lever. The aim was to get the other occupying powers to agree to run Germany as a unit. The point of proceeding along these lines was "above all, to put Soviet protestations of loyalty to Potsdam to [a] final test."[44] And indeed the decision to suspend reparations had been made at the top political level for reasons of high policy: this was not a case, as is often claimed, of Clay proceeding on his own, driven by essentially local considerations. The action, it is important to note, had been authorized in advance by Secretary Byrnes himself: Byrnes had just explained to Bevin why he was allowing Clay to suspend reparations "until the problem of Germany as a whole was settled." America, he told his British counterpart, was "going to have a show-down" with the Russians over the issue.[45]

The Soviet Union was thus the primary target of the American action, and not France, as a number of scholars have alleged. Indeed, the French representatives

[42] Clay to Echols, April 8, 1946, *Clay Papers,* 1:186–187.

[43] Clay statement in Allied Coordinating Committee, April 8, 1946, in Murphy to Byrnes, April 10, 1946; Murphy to Byrnes, May 2, 1946; and Acheson to Byrnes, May 9, 1946, in FRUS 1946, 5:538, 545–547, 551. Clay to Echols, April 8 and May 2, 1946, and Clay to Eisenhower, May 26, 1946, *Clay Papers,* 1:186–187, 203–204, 212–213; and Backer, *Winds of History,* pp. 122–123.

[44] Acheson and Hilldring to Byrnes (two documents), both May 9, 1946, FRUS 1946, 5:549–555.

[45] Bevin, "Anglo-American Discussions," May 5, 1946, FO 800/513, and Bevin-Byrnes "Discussion," April 26, 1946, FO 800/446, Public Record Office [PRO], Kew.

supported Clay at the crucial April 26 meeting. The three western powers backed a paper calling for foreign trade to be managed on an all-German basis. Only the Soviets were opposed. So Russian policy had been "flushed out": the USSR was not willing, it seemed, to honor the Potsdam agreement.[46]

This "fact" had major implications. If the Soviets would not permit foreign trade to be run on an all-German basis, that meant that the "Potsdam" policy of running Germany as a unit could not be effectively implemented. America could therefore no longer allow her hands to be tied by the Potsdam Protocol. If her partners were not living up to the agreement, then the United States should also have the right to a free hand in Germany.

This was the real meaning of the reparation stop. America was now reclaiming her freedom of action: she could no longer allow herself to be straitjacketed by arrangements which her partners were not respecting. If Germany was not to be run as a unit, then the U.S. government should be free to push ahead and get things moving in its own zone, together with any other zone that was willing to join up with it. In practice, this meant linking up with the British. The French, many U.S. officials hoped, might be brought in a bit later.

Clay, of course, would have liked to run Germany on a four power basis. But he understood from the outset that if this were not possible, then alternative arrangements, perhaps leading to a merger of the three western zones, would have to be worked out.[47] He wanted a unified Germany, but even more than that, he wanted the situation to be clear, so that he could move ahead and put the area he was responsible for back on its feet. Things certainly could not be allowed to go on as they were. Germany was in very bad shape. Her cities were in ruins, her industries were operating at just a fraction of the prewar level. Millions of refugees from the east had moved into the western zones and needed to be taken care of. It was obvious that in one way or another, the Germans had to be led out of economic limbo and put back to work. American and British taxpayers could not be expected to go on subsidizing their zones indefinitely. The U.S. Congress certainly would not stand for it, and Clay did not want the military government to be blamed for failing to put things on the right track.[48] The Germans would therefore soon have to pay their own way. Democracy, furthermore, could not take root in Germany unless the path to economic recovery was opened.[49] If this could not be

[46] Clay to Echols, May 2, 1946, *Clay Papers*, 1:203. The argument that the suspension of reparation deliveries was directed mainly at France was advanced by John Gimbel in his *The American Occupation of Germany: Politics and the Military, 1945–1949* (Stanford, Calif.: Stanford University Press, 1968), pp. 57–61. Evidence published the following year in FRUS 1946, vol. 5, cast doubt on this interpretation, as Gaddis pointed out in 1972; see his *United States and the Origins of the Cold War*, p. 330n. But Gimbel's views were unaffected. See his "On the Implementation of the Potsdam Agreement," *Political Science Quarterly* 87 (1972): 250–259. Many other scholars followed Gimbel's lead. See, for example, Yergin, *Shattered Peace*, p. 229 and p. 458 n. 21; Jean Smith, *Lucius D. Clay: An American Life* (New York: Holt, 1990), p. 350; and Leffler, *A Preponderance of Power*, p. 118.

[47] Clay to JCS, June 6, 1945, and Clay to McCloy, June 29, 1945, *Clay Papers*, 1:20, 38.

[48] The Army, moreover, had to finance German needs out of its own budget, and therefore had a certain incentive to put the part of Germany the United States was responsible for back on its feet as soon as possible. See Wolfgang Krieger, *General Lucius D. Clay und die amerikanische Deutschlandpolitik, 1945–1949*, 2d ed. (Stuttgart: Klett-Cotta, 1988), pp. 99–101.

[49] See, for example, Clay to Echols and Petersen, March 27, 1946; Clay to Eisenhower, May 26, 1946; and Clay to Echols, July 19, 1946; in *Clay Papers*, 1:184, 217, 243.

done on an all-German basis—if "Potsdam," for one reason or another, was unimplementable—then America and her friends would have to proceed on a west-only basis.[50]

The policymakers in Washington saw things in much the same light. Many State Department officials had in fact been quicker than Clay to give up on the possibility of four-power cooperation on Germany.[51] Secretary Byrnes himself had of course essentially abandoned that hope at Potsdam, although this was not generally known, even within the government. But now the U.S. authorities had formally reclaimed the freedom to move ahead without the Soviets.

So the reparation stop served to pave the way for what was called the "organization" of the western zones. This was made clear in an important State Department dispatch of May 9, 1946. The basic question was whether Germany was to be treated as a unit. The suspension of reparation deliveries, Acting Secretary Acheson wrote Byrnes, served to bring the issue of to a head with the Russians. He urged the secretary, then at a foreign ministers' meeting in Paris, to warn the Russians that if Germany could not be run as a unit, then America would have to consider the "disagreeable but inevitable alternative" of treating western Germany as an "economic unit and integrating this unit closely" with the west European economy.[52] A west-only solution was the obvious alternative to the failed "Potsdam" policy. Clay in fact was questioned on this point at a press conference on May 27.[53] It was still too early to deal with the issue in public, but in an important policy document that he had just written, Clay had already called for a merger of the British and American zones.[54]

Byrnes, for his part, agreed with Acheson and Clay. At the foreign ministers' meetings, he went through what had now become the Americans' standard arguments. The Potsdam agreement, he said, had provided that Germany was to be treated as a unit, but this agreement was not being carried out. The reparation level had been set on the assumption that Germany would be run as a unit; the failure of the Potsdam policy meant that that plan was no longer valid, and had thus led to the suspension of the deliveries. The American government still wanted the Potsdam arrangement to be put into effect, but if this turned out to be impossible, Byrnes announced in July, the United States would have no choice but to merge its zone with any other zone where the occupying power was willing to go along with the multizonal policy it had in mind.[55]

The offer to merge zones was quickly accepted by the British government.[56] As far as France was concerned, key foreign ministry officials, and above all the for-

---

[50] Note especially Clay's comment about the importance of "forcing the issue" in Clay to Dodge, July 31, 1946, quoted in Backer, *Winds of History*, p. 147.

[51] See especially Clay's exchange with Riddleberger (head of State Department Division of Central European Affairs), meeting at State Department, November 3, 1945, *Clay Papers*, 1:112–113. Note also Kennan to Byrnes, March 6, 1946, and Bedell Smith (now ambassador in Moscow) to Byrnes, April 2, 1946, FRUS 1946, 5:519, 535.

[52] Acheson to Byrnes, May 9, 1946, FRUS 1946, 5:551, 554.

[53] Clay press conference, May 27, 1946, *Clay Papers*, 1:221.

[54] Clay to Eisenhower, May 26, 1946, ibid., p. 217.

[55] Byrnes to Caffery, July 19, 1946, and Murphy to Byrnes, July 20, 1946, FRUS 1946, 5:578, 580. Note also the documents cited below, note 62.

[56] See Backer, *Winds of Change*, chap. 6, esp. p. 148.

eign minister himself, Georges Bidault, wanted to work with the Anglo-Saxons. But for a variety of reasons, the government could not openly take sides against the Soviet Union. These foreign ministry officials anticipated that France would naturally—but gradually, and through informal arrangements—gravitate to the Anglo-Saxon side.[57] For the time being, however, only the British and American zones were to be merged, and the Anglo-American bizone was soon officially brought into being.

It was clear from the start that this was a move of enormous political importance: the bizonal arrangements were not, as is sometimes said, a "temporary expedient" worked out for purely economic purposes.[58] An important step was being taken toward the establishment of a west German state. In public, the political significance of what was going on was played down, since neither America nor Britain wanted to be blamed for the division of Germany. But U.S. officials understood that their goal was the establishment of a German government. On April 2, for example, General Walter Bedell Smith, the ambassador to the USSR, wrote the State Department to convey impressions gathered during a brief trip to Germany. Everyone there agreed that a government should be formed in Germany "by organizing from the bottom up" in the western zones, with the "ultimate idea" of combining the western government with the Soviet-sponsored government in the east. His personal view, undoubtedly shared by many other officials, was that "this final step may never be taken."[59] Clay in particular was fully aware of what he referred to as the "political implications" of an Anglo-American zonal merger. He in fact called explicitly for the creation of a German government, a project which he thought might well be implemented only in the Anglo-American area.[60]

With the setting up of the bizone a major threshold had thus been crossed. The western powers were moving inexorably toward the establishment of a west German state. And American officials understood what they were doing. They may not have liked the term "state," since it implied too sharp a rupture with past policies, so they resorted to a variety of circumlocutions. Bedell Smith, for example, referred to "the integration of the western zones of Germany into a political unit oriented toward western Europe and western democracy."[61] But no matter how guarded the language, no one could doubt how events were moving.

This policy of "organizing" western Germany, moreover, was coming to have a distinct anti-Soviet coloration. America and Britain were forced to move ahead in the western zones, it was said over and over again, because the Russians had reneged on their promises and had sabotaged the Potsdam agreement. What the Soviets were doing in the eastern zone—running it as they saw fit, which at Potsdam the Americans had been willing to take philosophically—was now said to be totally unacceptable. If Germany was not being run as a unit, it was the Soviets who were to blame. What nerve they had blocking a common import-export program

---

[57] See, for example, Caffery to Byrnes, June 11, June 22, August 30, and September 18, 1946, FRUS 1946, 5:566–567, 567n., 596, 605.

[58] Backer, *Winds of History,* title of chap. 6, and pp. 129, 147–148.

[59] Bedell Smith to Byrnes, April 2, 1946, FRUS 1946, 5:535.

[60] Clay to Eisenhower, May 26, 1946, *Clay Papers,* 1:214–217.

[61] Bedell Smith to Byrnes, April 2, 1946, FRUS 1946, 5:536.

for all of Germany! This was in fact the key charge being leveled against them in early 1946. The implication was that the western powers were identifying themselves with German national aspirations, and were pointing to the Soviet Union as the great enemy of a unified German state.[62]

How is this change of course to be understood? Why had the Americans shifted away from Byrnes's spheres of influence approach at Potsdam to the policy of insisting on German unity and of blaming the Soviet Union for blocking it? Clay might not have understood the real Potsdam understanding, but Byrnes certainly did. And the secretary of state clearly knew what he was doing. He knew that American policy in 1946, especially on the question of the control of Germany's foreign trade, was totally at variance with the policy he had pursued at Potsdam, and that it was highly misleading for the American government to charge the Soviets with violating the Potsdam agreement.

Byrnes, moreover, was not the prisoner of his subordinates, and could have intervened at any point to restrain their "unitary" fervor. He could, in particular, have prevented American officials from insisting that Germany's foreign trade be managed on an all-German basis. He could at any point have put out the word about what the real Potsdam understanding was. In particular, he could have been much more open with General Clay, the strongest American personality pushing the unitary policy. Byrnes and Clay had worked together during the war and were on close personal terms. Indeed, Byrnes had been responsible for Clay's appointment as head of the military government, and it would have been easy for him to talk with Clay one-on-one and get him to pursue the policy he wanted him to follow.[63]

But Byrnes did none of these things, and the question is why. Evidence on this point is scarce, and the answer must remain somewhat speculative. But it does seem that Byrnes's motivation changed over time. Initially—that is, right after Potsdam—he was not looking for a quarrel with Russia, and thought that an amicable divorce was the key to tolerable U.S.–Soviet relations. But (as noted above) there were many people who felt, for a variety of reasons, that Germany should be run as a unit. Why not let them have their chance? If the attempt was not made, he would have to deal with criticism from a variety of quarters that he had been too quick to consign east Germany to Soviet rule, too willing to give up on four-power cooperation, too ready to accept a spheres of influence deal. Why not let the advocates of the quadripartite regime beat their heads for a while on the hard rock of political realities?

But if that was Byrnes's thinking in late 1945, by early 1946 his motivation was different. By now it was clear that the policy of insisting that Germany be treated as a unit was leading directly to a clash with the Soviets. If Byrnes chose to let this happen, then this could only be because by that point he wanted it to happen. American officials had tried hard to create a four-power regime in Germany and

---

[62] See, for example, Clay statement in Allied Coordinating Committee, April 8, 1946, in Murphy to Byrnes, April 10, 1946, and Acheson to Byrnes, May 9, 1946; ibid., pp. 538, 551–552; foreign ministers' meetings (and related U.S. memorandum), May 15 and July 9–12, 1946, ibid., 397–398, 400–402, 849, 873, 876, 884, 935; and Clay to Echols, April 8 and May 2, 1946, *Clay Papers*, 1:186–187, 203.

[63] Murphy, *Diplomat among Warriors*, pp. 248, 251.

Byrnes had given them free rein. The upshot was that by early 1946 a stick had fallen into his hands, and he was now ready to beat the Russians with it.

This new policy was clearly linked to the sharp deterioration of U.S.–Soviet relations at the beginning of 1946. But Byrnes was not simply getting back at the Russians for their brutish behavior in the Near East and elsewhere. Rather, the impression was taking hold that Soviet actions fell into a pattern. The USSR was an expansionist state and could only be contained if American power was brought to bear and if other countries could be brought to resist Soviet pressure.

American policy in 1946 was, in fact, directed above all at two audiences: the American public and the Germans in the western zones. If the Soviets were expansionist and could only be kept in check by countervailing power, then American power had to be committed to the defense of key areas on the Soviet periphery, and especially to the defense of western Germany. To commit power meant that the risk of war in certain contingencies would have to be accepted. And Byrnes certainly wanted to commit American power to Europe. Indeed, he had taken the lead in pressing for policies of this sort. This, he said in April 1946, was the point of his offer to the Soviets of a treaty of guarantee against a revival of German aggression.[64] And in September of that year, in a major address he gave at Stuttgart, Byrnes declared that American forces were not going to be withdrawn from Germany as long as any other power maintained a force of occupation there—a very important commitment which Byrnes made on his own, without first obtaining Truman's approval.[65]

For a policy of involvement to be sustained, however, the American people had to be behind it. Perhaps the nation was now in an anti-Soviet mood, but how long were such feelings likely to last? In high policymaking circles, there was a pervasive fear that the U.S. public might sooner or later turn away from world politics. After years of deprivation, after a long depression and then a long war, calls for further sacrifice might well fall on deaf ears. The country, secure within its own borders, might revert to isolationism: everyone remembered very clearly what had happened after the First World War.

The way to counteract this danger and to mobilize opinion in support of a policy of continued involvement—especially military involvement—was to present the international situation in stark and morally charged terms. America was engaged in a struggle for the future of civilization; the Soviets were solely responsible for the new threat to peace; the West now had to stand up and defend its liberty and the independence of other nations menaced by Soviet expansionism. This was the message of the Truman Doctrine speech of March 1947, and it was this message that sold the Marshall Plan to Congress that same year. Dean Acheson, the number two man in the State Department in 1946 and 1947, the same Acheson who as secretary of state in 1950 recognized the need to make things "clearer than truth" for political reasons, was the most fervent practitioner of this tactic.

---

[64] See, for example, his comments in a foreign ministers' meeting, April 28, 1946, FRUS 1946, 2:166–167. On the development of the proposal, see Byrnes's remarks in a foreign ministers' meeting, May 16, 1946, ibid., p. 431.

[65] For the text, see DOSB, September 15, 1946, pp. 496–501. See also Backer, *Winds of History,* p. 134, and Smith, *Clay,* p. 388.

But other top officials also understood the need to administer "necessary shocks to public opinion," and it can be taken for granted that Byrnes, consummate politician that he was, was not oblivious to considerations of this sort.[66]

On the central issue of Germany, what all this meant was that the Soviets had to be blamed in no uncertain terms for the breakdown of international cooperation. On May 9, Acheson and Assistant Secretary of State Hilldring wrote Byrnes that Soviet "loyalty to Potsdam" needed to be tested. The aim was to "fix blame" on them in the event they failed this test.[67] This was in fact the policy that Byrnes pursued at the Paris foreign ministers' meeting in mid-1946: the United States insisted that Russia comply with "Potsdam"; the Soviets failed the "test"; and the Americans then very publicly stressed Soviet responsibility for the collapse of the quadripartite regime. The British government also felt that it was "most important to ensure that responsibility for the break was put squarely on the Russians."[68]

The finger was being pointed at the USSR, but the goal was not simply to mobilize support for a firm policy within Britain and America. German opinion was the other major target of the policy. In "organizing" the western zones, the United States and Britain were admitting that Germany could not be run on a four-power basis. They were therefore running a risk that the German people would blame the western powers for writing off an all-German solution too quickly. By 1946 a divided Germany was coming to be seen as unavoidable, but as one British Foreign Office official put it, a division of the country could not be the "ostensible object of our policy since we have to make the Russians appear to the German public as the saboteurs of German unity."[69] The Germans were being told, in other words, that the USSR was their enemy, and that the western powers were basically in sympathy with German national rights.

To pull Germany toward the West, responsibility for the split thus had to be placed on Russia, and the deeper the split with Russia, the more important it was that western Germany be aligned with the western powers.[70] Increasingly in 1946 the German attitude was coming to be seen as crucial. The western governments had begun to see themselves as engaged in a struggle for Germany, and in their view the outcome of this struggle would be decided not by the presence of small armies of occupation in the western zones but ultimately by the sympathies of the Germans themselves. If matters continued to drift, the British military governor

---

[66] See Joseph Jones, *The Fifteen Weeks (February 21–June 5, 1947)* (New York: Viking, 1955), pp. 138–142; Dean Acheson, *Present at the Creation: My Years at the State Department* (New York: Norton, 1969), p. 375; Timothy Ireland, *Creating the Entangling Alliance: The Origins of the North Atlantic Treaty Organization* (Westport, Conn.: Greenwood, 1981), p. 30; Richard Freeland, *The Truman Doctrine and the Origins of McCarthyism: Foreign Policy, Domestic Politics, and Internal Security, 1946–1948* (New York: Knopf, 1972), esp. p. 89; and Leffler, *Preponderance of Power*, p. 145.

[67] Acheson to Byrnes, May 9, 1946, FRUS 1946, 5:549.

[68] Deighton, *Impossible Peace*, pp. 80 (for the quotation), 108–109, 125, 134; Rothwell, *Britain and the Cold War*, pp. 280, 321, 332.

[69] Hankey note, October 25, 1946, quoted in Deighton, *Impossible Peace*, p. 108.

[70] For the policy of saddling Russia with responsibility for the failure of the "Potsdam" policy of running Germany as a unit, see, for example, Acheson and Hilldring to Byrnes, and Acheson to Byrnes, both May 9, 1946, FRUS 1946, 5:549, 551–552. See also Murphy to Hickerson, October 26, 1947, FRUS 1947, 2:691, for an example of U.S. concern with German opinion.

warned in May 1946, the Germans would become "increasingly hostile" and "eventually begin to look east."[71] No one thought the Germans were such convinced democrats that the West could count on their loyalty no matter what policy it pursued.

And no one thought that the western powers were so strong that they could afford to ignore considerations of this sort. U.S. policy in particular in the early Cold War period in 1946 was not rooted in a sense of America's overwhelming strength. The American government did not feel that it was in control of so much power that it could do more or less whatever it wanted. Quite the contrary: the internal political situation placed limits on what the government could do, and especially on how much military strength could be generated. U.S. policymakers had to work within those constraints, but they were also looking for a way to increase their freedom of action.

So if American power was limited—if the United States could not do what it wanted in western Germany through brute force alone—and if that area could not be lost to the Soviets, then it was obvious that the west Germans somehow had to be won over to the western side. The Germans, long before they had a state of their own, were thus more than just a passive object of other countries' policies; their political sympathies, their political choices, were now of the utmost importance.

The most obvious implication was that the western zones had to be allowed to recover economically. The Germans in the eastern zone were better fed than those in the more heavily industrialized west. Unless this situation were reversed, and reversed quickly, all of Germany might soon be lost. There was little choice, Clay wrote in March, "between becoming a Communist on 1500 calories [a day] and a believer in democracy on 1000 calories. It is my sincere belief that our proposed ration allowance in Germany will not only defeat our objectives in middle Europe but will pave the road to a Communist Germany."[72] In May he pressed for a policy of economic and political reform—on a bizonal basis, if broader arrangements could not be worked out—with the argument that if the West failed to act, the Germans would turn toward communism.[73]

By July, America and Russia were competing openly for German favor. The Soviets were angered by the reparation stop, and concerned by what it implied. The United States was simply tearing up an important part of the Potsdam agreement. The Americans said that this was because the USSR refused to cooperate in running Germany as a unit. The Soviets could not answer this by pointing out that the real Potsdam understanding was based on the idea that Germany would in fact be divided between east and west, that foreign trade, in particular, would not be run on an all-German basis, and that the Americans were therefore reneging on the fundamental agreement that had been reached the previous year. The USSR, like the western powers, had a political interest in officially backing the principle of a unified Germany. But although they could not develop the point openly, the Soviets certainly understood that there had been a radical shift in American policy since Potsdam. There was no getting around the fact that the reparation stop, a

[71] Quoted in Deighton, *Impossible Peace,* p. 91.

[72] Clay to Echols and Petersen, March 27, 1946, *Clay Papers,* 1:184.

[73] Clay to Eisenhower, May 26, 1946, ibid., p. 217.

clear repudiation of what to the Russians was an unambiguous American promise, reflected a new American hostility toward the Soviet Union.

The Soviets were now worried about the whole thrust of America's new German policy. It seemed that western Germany was going to be "organized" not just without them, but quite possibly against them. They decided to try to counter that policy by appealing directly to the Germans. Molotov gave a major speech at the Paris Council of Foreign Ministers meeting on July 10 taking what was at that time a very soft line on the German question.

The American government, and Clay especially, felt that a strong response was in order.[74] On July 19, Clay drafted a summary of what he thought American policy should be. Some high officials thought that his draft tended "a bit in tone toward wooing the Germans."[75] But Byrnes agreed with Clay about what was necessary. At Stuttgart, on September 6, he laid out America's fundamental policy. The Stuttgart speech was in fact based on Clay's draft of July 19 and took the same moderate line.[76] "It is the view of the American government," Byrnes declared, "that the German people, throughout Germany and under proper safeguards, should now be given the primary responsibility for the running of their own affairs." The goal was to give the Germans some hope—some sense that they would eventually be given some control over their own destiny and that their future lay in partnership with the West.[77]

The importance of these developments can scarcely be exaggerated. The United States was blaming the USSR for the failure of the Potsdam agreement and thus for the division of Germany. The Americans were in effect saying that the division of Germany was illegitimate, and thus the Soviet policy of maintaining total control of their zone was also illegitimate. In order to win the Germans over to the West, the U.S. government seemed to be playing up to them, moving toward the creation of a German state, and endorsing German national goals. From the Soviet point of view, the dangers were obvious. In late 1946, Molotov brought together a group of advisers to analyze the Stuttgart speech. Byrnes's basic goal at Stuttgart, as that group saw it, was to "obtain for the United States support from German revanchist groups." The speech was "an attempt to convince the Germans that the United States is the only country which sympathizes with the German people and which is willing and able to help them."[78] The USSR's most fundamental security interests were at stake. Germany was on the road to independence, and the more independent she became, the more likely it was that she would be allowed once again to develop her power—that to keep western Germany on the American side, no matter what U.S. and British leaders now said, the controls on German power would have to be gradually dismantled. And this was a Germany that was being

---

[74] Lucius Clay, *Decision in Germany* (Westport, Conn.: Greenwood Press, 1950), p. 78; Smith, *Clay*, pp. 378–379.

[75] Clay to Echols, July 19, 1946, *Clay Papers*, 1:236–237; Assistant Secretary of War Petersen to Secretary of War Patterson, August 5, 1945, quoted ibid., 237n.

[76] Smith, *Clay*, pp. 378–389.

[77] DOSB, September 15, 1946, pp. 496–501.

[78] Soviet document quoted in Scott Parrish, "The USSR and the Security Dilemma: Explaining Soviet Self-Encirclement, 1945–1985" (Ph.D. diss., Columbia University, 1993), p. 177.

told that its most basic national goals were blocked by a Soviet policy which the western powers insisted was illegitimate. This, therefore, was a Germany which was being directed against Russia, a Germany which one day might pursue an active revisionist policy in central Europe aimed at the recovery of the eastern zone and perhaps even of the territories east of the Oder-Neisse line. And the United States might feel obliged to underwrite this irredentist policy as the price of keeping Germany in the western camp.

All these problems might take years to develop, but the ball had started to roll, and if nothing were done there was no reason to think that it would stop before it reached the bottom of the hill. Wasn't it best, therefore, to try to head off the danger before it was too late? Even in 1945, even as they tightened their grip on the eastern zone and embraced the Byrnes plan, the Soviets were not quite ready to give the western powers a completely free hand in the western part of Germany. They wanted total control in their own zone, but they also asked for some real say over developments in western Germany, especially in the Ruhr. This policy irritated the western powers. It was yet another example of the "one-way street," which Truman in particular complained about repeatedly. And this had fed into the growing sense that a relatively friendly settlement, based on a simple division of Europe where each side allowed the other a totally free hand on its side of the line of demaracation, was really not to be expected, and that the western powers therefore needed to take much stronger measures to defend their interests in Europe.

But if the Soviets, even in 1945, had not quite been ready to accept a clean spheres of influence arrangement for Germany, it was only to be expected that the new course of American policy in 1946 would greatly intensify their interest in having some control over developments in the western zones. The Russians understood what was at stake. They violently objected to the suspension of reparation deliveries and bitterly attacked the establishment of the bizone. But mere words would not prevent the western powers from pursuing their policy. The Soviets thus had to think about how their power could be brought to bear to prevent America and her friends from moving ahead with their new policy in western Germany.

The developing situation was very serious. The United States and the Soviet Union were embarked on a path that could lead to a third world war. The other disputes of the early Cold War period were of transient importance. The quarrels over eastern Europe and the Near East were in essence disputes about where precisely the line of demarcation between east and west was to be drawn. These conflicts ran their course, policies were tested, and the limits of each side's sphere of influence were clarified. Eastern Europe was effectively recognized as a Soviet sphere, and Turkey and Iran were seen as lying on the other side of the line.

But with Germany it was different. In the clash over Germany, the vital interests of both sides were now engaged. There was a good chance that the two blocs were set on a collision course. There was no longer any chance that the two sides would accept a settlement based on the simple idea that the Soviets could do what they wanted in the east, while America and her friends would have a free hand in the western zones. The clash over Germany was thus to be the mainspring of international conflict during the Cold War period.

THE END OF THE LINE

By the end of 1946, the course of western policy seemed set. In the immediate postwar period, Britain and America had been reluctant to move too quickly or too overtly toward the "organization" of the western zones—toward allowing them to recover economically and indeed politically as well. They had held back for a variety of reasons: a general desire to avoid a split with the Soviets; a sense that a breakdown of the alliance might well lead to a resurgence of German power, with the Germans playing off east against west; a certain fear that a divided Germany would never be acceptable to the Germans, whose efforts to recover their national unity would be a source of profound instability in Europe; and, above all, a strong wish to avoid blame for the division of Germany, especially in the eyes of the Germans themselves.

But with the passage of time, many of these concerns were losing their force. The split with the Soviets was coming to be taken as a basic fact of international political life. The division of Germany was coming to be seen as a natural, perhaps even as an inevitable, consequence of the collapse of the wartime alliance. And the more unavoidable it came to seem, the less the western powers had to worry about being blamed by the Germans for the division of their country if they took action to restore their economy and set up some kind of political system in the western zones.

With the passage of time, moreover, the arguments for action became more compelling. The Germans could not be kept in a state of limbo forever. They had to be allowed to get back on their feet. It was important, of course, that the burden on the British and American treasuries be reduced; for this reason alone, the economic recovery of western Germany was essential. But political aims were even more fundamental. The Germans needed to be given some hope that a way out of their present misery could be found; things had to start moving if democracy was ever to take root in Germany; and above all the Germans needed to be shown that their interests lay in close association with the western powers.

As it became clear that action was not possible on an all-German basis, it also became obvious that the western powers would have to act by themselves in the part of Germany they controlled. So what was called the "western strategy" was gradually embraced by high American and British officials, and, more discreetly, by leading French policymakers as well: western Germany would be "organized," both economically and politically; it would be protected by the western powers and tied to the western world in a whole variety of ways—economically, politically, and, ultimately, militarily.

By the end of 1946, this was the track that U.S. and British policy seemed to be moving along. And yet it would be a full year before the western governments took the plunge and embraced this strategy outright. In January 1947, General George

Marshall, the top American military officer in World War II, became secretary of state. Truman's relations with Byrnes had been cool throughout 1946—for personal reasons, and not because of any truly fundamental differences on policy. But the president, like most Americans, had enormous confidence in Marshall. And the new secretary wanted to make a fresh start: he wanted to see if U.S.–Soviet relations could be put on a new and more satisfactory footing.

Marshall understood that the German question was the central problem in international politics, but unlike many in high policymaking circles in the West, he still thought of four-power cooperation as the key to a solution. The Germans, in his view, were "indomitable"; they would play their former enemies off against each other if the allies failed to reach agreement among themselves; they would gradually recover their power and again pose a threat to the world. The Soviets, he thought, even in November 1947, needed to be brought into the system for the control of German power: "it would be difficult to conclude a definitive peace" without them.[79]

Marshall certainly understood the need for action in Germany and indeed in Europe as a whole. But he was very reluctant to break with the Russians. A good part of the reason was that he thought the American people could not be counted on to support a firm stance if the western strategy led to a prolonged confrontation with the USSR. The nation might currently be in an anti-Soviet mood, but that mood could change quickly. Even at the end of 1947, when by every indication the allies had reached the end of the road, he hesitated with this consideration in mind. The American people, he said, would applaud if the U.S. government told the Russians "to go to the devil," but when the implications became clear, that attitude would change soon enough.[80]

So Marshall was unwilling to move too forcefully toward the "organization" of the western zones. He very much wanted to see whether some arrangement could be worked out that would preserve German unity and avoid a sharp clash with the USSR. His tactic was to focus on finding practical and constructive solutions to concrete problems. Marshall disliked the increasingly ideological cast of American policy, and disapproved in particular of the Truman Doctrine speech: he "deplored the emotional anti-Russian attitude in the country and kept emphasizing the necessity to talk and write about Europe in terms of economics instead of ideologies."[81] The central political problems were to be put on the back burner. If the main goal had been simply to clarify the situation and thus provide a basis for independent action, Marshall could have focused on the fundamental political question of whether the Soviets would agree to abandon control of eastern Germany and allow the Germans to determine their own fate in truly free elections. But

[79] Marshall-Bidault meeting, March 13, 1947, and Marshall-Bonnet meeting, November 18, 1947, FRUS 1947, 2:247, 722; note also Marshall's remarks in a meeting with Stalin, April 15, 1947, ibid., p. 339.

[80] Marshall to Lovett, December 6 and 8, 1947, FRUS 1947, 2:752, 754. The problem of domestic political support had long been one of Marshall's basic concerns. Marshall's sensitivity to domestic politics is also a major theme in Charles F. Brower, "The Joint Chiefs of Staff and National Policy: American Strategy and the War with Japan" (Ph.D. diss., University of Pennsylvania, 1987).

[81] Reston memo, c. March 1947, KP/1/book 1/192ff/ML. See also Charles Bohlen, *Witness to History, 1929–1969* (New York: Norton, 1973), p. 261.

he did not want to bring matters to a head, and sought instead to focus on areas where agreement was possible—that is, on economic issues, and especially on reparation.

In early 1947, it seemed that some kind of deal with the Russians might actually be within reach. The key was a new approach to the reparation problem. The original Soviet policy of stripping the eastern zone—of dismantling factories and shipping them back to Russia for reassembly—was widely recognized as a failure. Railway sidings in eastern Germany were full of industrial equipment just rusting away. The Russians therefore wanted to change the system, and have the German economy, especially the west German economy, make reparation deliveries out of current production. Soviet officials suggested that if this arrangement were accepted, the USSR for its part would allow Germany to be run as an economic unit.

Clay and a number of his advisers thought that if the western powers were flexible, it was just possible that something could be worked out. Reparation deliveries out of current production might be bartered for Soviet acceptance of a Germany unified not just economically, but under a liberal democratic political system. Other high officials doubted whether the USSR would ever sacrifice political control over their own zone, but Soviet rhetoric in early 1947 suggested that there was some chance that they might actually agree to a unified and (in the western sense) democratic Germany. At the Moscow Conference of foreign ministers in March, the USSR called for the creation of a German republic with a popularly elected parliament, full "civil and religious guarantees," and a constitutional structure very much like the one that Germany had had in the 1920s.[82] On the surface, it seemed that the two sides might be able to work something out. Differences on the constitutional issue were not insurmountable. The Americans and the British wanted a somewhat more decentralized structure for the German state than the Soviets preferred. But Stalin was not intransigent. He was willing, he said, to accept the structure Marshall and Bevin had in mind if the Germans themselves agreed to go along with it.[83]

The reparation problem was ostensibly the sticking point. Marshall may have wanted to reach an understanding with the USSR, but there was not much flexibility in the official U.S. position in this area. Reparation out of current production might be permitted "within narrow limits" if the Soviets would in return agree to treat Germany as an economic unit.[84] But the key point even for Marshall was that an arrangement of this sort not increase the cost to America of financing essential imports into Germany.[85] Marshall's position was that the Potsdam agreement had ruled out reparations from current production. This, in fact, was not the case at all; the secretary of state had misunderstood what had been decided at Pots-

---

[82] On the possibility of a deal, see Caffery to Byrnes, August 24, 1946; Murphy to Matthews, October 14, 1946; Murphy to Byrnes, October 16, 1946; Durbrow to Byrnes, October 23, 1946; Murphy to Byrnes, October 25, 1946; in FRUS 1946, 5:593–594, 622–625, 628–629, 631–633. See also State Department briefing papers for Moscow conference, FRUS 1947, 2:215, 217; Backer, *Winds of History*, pp. 149–151; Eisenberg, *Drawing the Line*, pp. 242, 248–250, 288.

[83] Stalin-Marshall meeting, April 15, 1947, FRUS 1947, 2:342.

[84] State Department briefing paper on reparation, ibid., p. 218.

[85] Marshall-Bevin meeting, March 22, 1947, and Marshall to Truman, March 31, 1947, ibid., pp. 273–275, 298–299.

dam.[86] But given that misunderstanding, he felt justified in taking the line that the only way such reparations could ever be considered was as a substitute for the deliveries of plant and equipment which Potsdam had called for but which the western allies no longer wished to make.[87]

Neither the State Department nor Bevin wanted to go even this far. Before any production could be sent to Russia as reparation, the German economy, in their view, had to be made to pay its own way. As long as Germany was in deficit, and as long as the western powers had to bear the lion's share of covering that deficit, any increased production had to be sold abroad, the proceeds being used to pay for imports, cut the deficit, and thus relieve the burden on American and British taxpayers. Any arrangement that allowed goods to be sent east before imports and exports were in balance therefore meant that the economic burden on the western powers would be greater than it had to be, and thus that America and Britain would in effect be paying Germany's reparations for her. It was not good enough, therefore, to take Marshall's line and say simply that the burden would not increase; it was essential that it be decreased and indeed brought down to zero as quickly as possible. In fact, the previous advances that had been used to finance the German deficit needed to be repaid before any reparation from current production could be contemplated.[88]

Marshall did not end up taking quite so intransigent a line, but even his plan did not offer the Soviets very much, and it is clear that in 1947 the western powers in the final analysis took a fairly rigid line on the reparation issue. But it would be a mistake to assume that that attitude was the real cause of the failure of the four powers to work out an all-German settlement in 1947, and that if only the western governments had been more flexible, Germany could have been unified on a democratic basis in 1947. For behind their relatively inflexible stance lay judgments about what was really possible in the way of an all-German solution, judgments that reflected the way most key officials in Washington and London had by now come to see the problem.

What was the point, most officials were coming to think, of trying so hard to reach agreement on this issue? An agreement would simply reiterate the terms of Potsdam. One draft discussed at Moscow in fact called on the Control Council to set up central administrative agencies for the fields defined in the Potsdam Protocol.[89] But if the attempt at running Germany as a unit had failed in late 1945 and 1946, what basis was there for thinking that the same kind of policy would succeed now? East-west relations were certainly no better now than they had been right after Potsdam; in fact, they were a good deal worse. So how would it do any good, in effect, to simply reissue a slightly updated version of the Potsdam agree-

---

[86] See appendix 1, "The Potsdam Agreement and Reparations from Current Production," in the Internet Supplement [IS].

[87] Marshall to Truman, April 1, 1947, FRUS 1947, 2:303.

[88] Marshall to Truman and Acheson, March 17, 1947; Bevin to Marshall, March 23, 1947; Bevin-Stalin meeting, March 24, 1947; Truman to Marshall, April 1, 1947; ibid., pp. 256, 274n., 279, 302. For British views, see also Ernest Bevin, "Main Short-Term Problems Confronting Us in Moscow," February 20, 1947, CP(47)68, Cab 129/17, PRO, and the cabinet discussion of this issue on February 27, 1947, CM 25(47), Cab 128/9, PRO.

[89] Report of Coordinating Committee, April 11, 1947, FRUS 1947, 2:436–437.

ment? Robert Murphy, Clay's political advisor and thus the top State Department official in Germany, made the obvious point. The Allied Control authority was "a moribund organism incapable of withstanding the virus of Allied dissension."[90] What reason was there to think that this virus could be eliminated by a new agreement that simply repeated the terms of the old one?

How seriously, moreover, was all the talk about unifying Germany on a democratic basis to be taken? For the time being, the focus might be on economic issues, but economic unification was not an end in itself. The real goal, at least in principle, was German political unity. But was it reasonable to think, given their record in eastern Europe and in eastern Germany itself, that, no matter what texts were signed, the Soviets would agree to genuinely free elections in the eastern zone? Given what had happened in Poland two years earlier, Soviet promises about free elections were obviously to be taken with a grain of salt.

It just did not seem very likely that either the Soviets or the western powers would be willing to surrender control over their zones and risk seeing all of Germany end up on the opposite side.[91] This implied that a partition of Germany was inevitable. And this in turn meant that there was little point to holding off too long on the "organization" of the western zones. The Russians were certainly moving ahead unilaterally in "organizing" their own zone with the Communists in the driver's seat. And if the USSR was moving ahead unilaterally, why shouldn't the western powers be able to take action in their own area without first having to clear their policy with the Soviets?[92]

But even if, for the sake of argument, one assumed that a unified German state could be set up on the basis of truly free elections, one had to wonder whether this was the ideal outcome from the point of view of the western powers. The British, and to a certain extent the Americans as well, were reluctant to take their chances a second time with full democracy and self-determination in Germany—to see Germany resurrected as a strong and independent power, not aligned with either side and free once again to play them off against each other.[93] But if this was the western attitude, how could anyone expect the Soviets, whose ideology had a good

---

[90] Murphy to Byrnes, January 6, 1947, ibid., p. 846.

[91] See Michael Hogan, *The Marshall Plan: America, Britain, and the Reconstruction of Western Europe, 1947–1952* (Cambridge: Cambridge University Press, 1987), p. 44; John Lewis Gaddis, "Spheres of Influence; The United States and Europe, 1948–1949," in his *The Long Peace: Inquiries into the History of the Cold War* (New York: Oxford University Press, 1987), pp. 54–55. Note also the views of top British officials cited in Rothwell, *Britain and the Cold War,* pp. 308–309, 332.

[92] See, for example, Deighton, *Impossible Peace,* pp. 72–73; Rothwell, *Britain and the Cold War,* p. 310. See also Bevin's remarks in foreign ministers' meeting, April 11, 1947, summarized in Marshall to Truman et al., April 11, 1947, FRUS 1947, 2:327.

[93] The British especially were worried about losing Germany if the Germans were free to choose their own destiny. See Bevin's important analysis for the Cabinet of British policy toward Germany, CP(46)186, May 3, 1946, Cab 129/9, PRO: "If the German government in Berlin fairly reproduced the outlook of the country it would be neither wholly eastward looking nor wholly westward looking. The question would then turn on whether the western democracies or the Soviet Union would exercise the stronger pull. On the whole the balance of advantage seems to lie with the Russians." Note also Rothwell, *Britain and the Cold War,* pp. 311–312. Not everyone was so worried. See, for example, Strang's comments quoted ibid., p. 326, and the views of the American Joint Chiefs of Staff, in JCS to SWNCC, May 12, 1947, FRUS 1947, 1:741.

deal less appeal in Germany, to cooperate in setting up a unified German state over which they had little control? On the other hand, Germany might be unified but still kept weak—that is, subject to quadripartite controls, especially in the military area. From the standpoint of the western powers, there were two great arguments against this sort of solution. First of all, it had been tried after World War I, but the Versailles settlement had been a disaster; and it was commonly assumed that the post-Versailles period showed that this sort of arrangement was simply not viable. The second argument was that the Soviets could not be given the right to intervene in German affairs because they would not use that power in a way that America and Britain would find acceptable. The bottom line was that in neither case was a unified German state a particularly attractive outcome. If such a state were weak, it would be vulnerable to pressure from the east; if strong, it could play off east against west, develop its power, and thus once again pose a threat to the peace.[94]

All these considerations, although weighted differently by different people, pointed to one conclusion: the western powers should not pay much of a price to reach agreement with the USSR on the German question. The western governments did not set out to sabotage the Moscow conference. They had not decided on principle to turn down whatever offer the Soviets came up with, no matter how reasonable it was, out of a belief that a divided Germany was the best solution. This was certainly not Marshall's view; the conference for him was by no means a mere charade. But given the sort of thinking that had by this time taken hold in both Washington and London, neither America nor Britain was willing to go very far in these talks.

The British in particular had reached some major conclusions by early 1947. In 1946 Bevin had still not worked out a clear policy on the German question. On the one hand, he could not understand "why we could not proceed with our own policy in our own zone in the same way as the Russians were proceeding with their policy in their zone." But then, at that same April 1946 meeting, he went on to comment that setting up a government in western Germany and then partitioning the country "meant a policy of a Western Bloc and that meant war."[95] On May 3, he laid out for the Cabinet the pros and cons of a policy of moving toward the creation of a west German state. He recognized that feeling had evolved, that in recent months the Soviet threat had come to be seen as being "as great as, and possibly even greater than" the threat of a resurgent Germany. But on balance he, and with him the Cabinet as a whole, were unwilling to take the plunge: the "general dangers of splitting Germany" were too great.[96]

By early 1947, however, British policy had hardened. Foreign Office officials were now arguing explicitly that the West should be intransigent—that unless the Soviets accepted *all* the conditions the West wanted to impose, Britain and Amer-

---

[94] Marshall in meeting with Bidault, March 13, 1947, and in meeting with Bonnet, November 18, 1947, FRUS 1947, 2:247, 722. Note especially Dulles's views on these issues. See Backer, *Winds of History*, p. 173; Smith, *Clay*, pp. 415–416; and Pruessen, *Dulles*, pp. 335, 343–344.

[95] See Deighton, *Impossible Peace*, pp. 72–73.

[96] "Policy toward Germany," May 3, 1946, CP(46)186, Cab 129/9, PRO; CM(46)43rd Conclusions, Confidential Annex, May 7, 1946, Cab 128/7, PRO.

ica should begin building up western Germany.[97] Bevin was not quite willing to go that far, but in February 1947 he opted for a policy of insisting on conditions for a German settlement that the Russians were highly unlikely to accept—in particular, the ruling out of reparation from current production, at least for the time being, and the "establishment of genuine freedom of assembly and expression" throughout Germany. And he recognized that in the event no arrangement could be worked out, the western powers would continue their policy of "organizing" the part of Germany they controlled.[98] Indeed, at the Moscow conference in the spring, and even more at the London conference in December, Bevin placed a certain emphasis on these political conditions—that is, on the core political differences between the Soviet Union and the West.[99]

But this was precisely the sort of strategy that Marshall, in his search for an understanding, wanted to avoid.[100] He was of course very interested in finding out whether real cooperation with Russia was still possible. But instead of focusing on the core problems—especially the issue of the Soviets' willingness to accept a really free electoral process in Germany—Marshall preferred a more indirect and less confrontational approach. He wanted to take his own measure of Soviet policy, to deal with the Soviet leaders on a personal basis, and decide for himself whether the two sides could work together on Germany.

Marshall went to the Moscow foreign ministers' meeting looking for answers, and by the end of the conference, he had found them. On matters large and small, the Soviets were not friendly and not constructive. In an important meeting with Stalin on April 15, Marshall brought up the great problem of deteriorating U.S.–Soviet relations. His first complaint was that the Soviets often did not answer the communications the Americans sent them. The American people, he said, "simply could not understand such behavior." He complained about Soviet charges that the bizonal agreement was a violation of Potsdam, and that the United States wished to dismember Germany. He was particularly upset that the Soviets were not very interested in the American offer of a four-power treaty to guarantee the demilitarization of Germany. Even in the West, and in France especially, many people were skeptical about the value of such paper guarantees—a very understandable attitude, given the history of such promises in the interwar period.[101] But Marshall simply could not comprehend this sort of skepticism. If America gave her word, that was a fact of enormous political importance. To question the value

[97] Deighton, *Impossible Peace,* pp. 123–124, 134, 138, 148; and Rothwell, *Britain and the Cold War,* p. 341.

[98] Ernest Bevin, "Main Short-Term Problems Confronting Us in Moscow," February 20, 1947, CP(47)68, Cab 129/17, PRO.

[99] Marshall to Truman, March 31, 1947; U.S. Delegation to Truman, November 27 and 28, 1947; Marshall to Lovett, December 6, 1947; in FRUS 1947, 2:300, 735, 737, 752. See also Bevin to Attlee, April 16, 1947, FO 800/447, PRO.

[100] See, for example, Reston memo, c. March 1947, KP/1/192ff/ML.

[101] Georges Bidault, the French foreign minister, had told Marshall a month earlier that the French were cool to the idea of a demilitarization treaty because they were worried it might "be considered as a sort of 'substitute' for other guarantees"— namely, an American troop presence in Europe, especially in Germany—that his government believed to be necessary. Bidault-Marshall meeting, March 13, 1947, FRUS 1947, 2:247.

of such a promise, or to act as though a four-power treaty were not of central importance, was practically to accuse the United States of dishonesty. If the Soviets spurned even this American offer, then there was really very little hope that they would cooperate with the West on the German question as a whole.[102]

It is not hard to imagine how the Soviet dictator must have reacted to Marshall's litany of complaints. The U.S. president, in the Truman Doctrine speech, had just portrayed the conflict with Russia as a struggle of world-historical importance—as a titanic conflict between the forces of freedom and an aggressive totalitarian movement. And now Marshall's number one complaint was that the Soviets often did not answer their mail? The United States was of course a very strong country, but the people now running American foreign policy seemed a bit out of their depth. In any event, Stalin chose to humor Marshall and sought to smooth his ruffled feathers. The situation at the conference was not "so tragic," he said. Differences had occcured before, but after people had "exhausted themselves in dispute," they were generally able to reach compromises. Marshall should be patient and not become depressed.[103]

To Marshall, however, this was proof of Stalin's lack of seriousness. The Soviet leader acted as though the allies were engaged in some kind of game, and did not understand, or want to understand, that immediate action was essential. At Moscow, Marshall had told Stalin very directly that the Americans were "frankly determined to do what we can to assist those countries which are suffering from economic deterioration which, if unchecked, might lead to economic collapse and the consequent elimination of any chance of democratic survival."[104] And on his return to America, he gave a report to the nation, expressing his disappointment and stressing that matters could not be permitted to drift much longer: "the patient is sinking while the doctors deliberate."[105]

So Marshall was finally ready to move ahead without Russia. Europe, or at least western Europe, was going to be put back on its feet whether the Soviets were willing to cooperate or not. The failure of the Moscow conference thus led directly to the Marshall Plan, the great American program for the economic recovery of western Europe.[106]

In top American policymaking circles, a new and quite important idea was now taking hold: western Europe could be encouraged to pull together and develop a political personality of its own. Western Germany could be integrated into that western European community, which might in time develop into a "third force" capable of withstanding Soviet pressure without direct American involvement. Such a system would also help solve the German problem by limiting Germany's

[102] Marshall to Truman and Marshall-Stalin meeting, both April 15, 1947, ibid., pp. 335, 338. Note also Marshall's account of his interview with Stalin in Millis, *Forrestal Diaries*, pp. 266–268. Again, his emphasis on the USSR's failure to answer American communications is striking: "he said such conduct was not merely discourteous but that it amounted to an attitude of contemptuousness, and if their design was to earn our ill will they were going about it most successfully."

[103] Marshall-Stalin meeting, April 15, 1947, FRUS 1947, 2:343–344.

[104] Ibid., p. 340.

[105] Radio address of April 28, 1947, DOSB, May 11, 1947, p. 924.

[106] See John Gimbel, *The Origins of the Marshall Plan* (Stanford, Calif.: Stanford University Press, 1976), esp. pp. 15–17, 194, 254.

freedom of action and thus preventing her from once again posing a threat to international stability. If the west Germans were led to think of themselves as "west Europeans," their nationalist impulses might be tamed or deflected, and the division of their country might be made more tolerable for them. As Charles Bohlen, one of Marshall's chief advisers, put it at a high-level meeting in late August: "the three Western zones should be regarded not as part of Germany but as part of Western Europe." What an extraordinary comment! The fact that a top official would say that western Germany should not be regarded as part of Germany shows just how far U.S. policymakers had moved from traditional conceptions of how Europe was to be organized. And the assumption was taking hold that western Europe could come together politically only in a Cold War context. The Soviet threat on the Elbe would force the west Europeans to put aside their petty differences and unite behind a common policy of defending western civilization; the American presence in western Europe would reassure the west Europeans and allow them more easily to accept the west Germans as real partners.[107]

The Americans were now committing themselves to a policy of "building Europe"—meaning, of course, western Europe—as a political entity. Economic considerations merged easily into the new thinking. Western Europe could revive economically only if western Germany regained her economic health; and western Germany, for its part, could not recover in isolation from western Europe as a whole. The old national barriers had to be broken down. The region had to be thought of as a whole.

This whole way of thinking had a major impact on the shaping of the Marshall Plan. After the principle of a massive aid program to save Europe was accepted, the central question was whether the recovery program would be implemented on an all-European or a west European basis. Marshall wanted to "play it straight" and bring the Soviets in,[108] but his main advisers from the start thought in terms of a plan limited to western Europe.[109] Bevin and Bidault, for their part, also did not want the Soviets to participate in the recovery program.[110] And indeed the plan, as it was taking shape in the minds of American officials, would offer the Russians very little by way of aid, and might even threaten Soviet control over eastern Europe, if the countries in that area were allowed to participate.[111]

It was thus hardly surprising that the Soviets chose not to take part, or that they

[107] Interdepartmental meeting, August 30, 1947, FRUS 1947, 1:762–763. On "third force" thinking at this time, see Gaddis, *Long Peace*, pp. 57–60; Hogan, *Marshall Plan*, pp. 37–45, esp. pp. 39, 44–45, and also the quotation from an unpublished State Department history of the Marshall Plan in Max Beloff, *The United States and the Unity of Europe* (Washington, D.C.: The Brookings Institution, 1963), p. 28. The "third force" question will be discussed again in chapters 3 (pp. 67–68) and 4 (pp. 114–115).

[108] Hogan, *Marshall Plan*, p. 44.

[109] See, for example, Kennan and Policy Planning Staff memoranda, April 24, May 16, and May 23, 1947; Policy Planning Staff meeting, May 15, 1947; Clayton memorandum, May 27, 1947; in FRUS 1947, 3:220n, 220–232.

[110] Hogan, *Marshall Plan*, p. 52. For domestic political reasons, however, Bidault had to make it appear that he favored Soviet participation. See, for example, Caffery to Marshall, July 2, 1947, FRUS 1947, 3:305, cited, along with some other evidence supporting this interpretation, in chap. 3 of Will Hitchcock's *The Challenge of Recovery* (forthcoming).

[111] See Hogan, *Marshall Plan*, p. 52, and Leffler, *Preponderance of Power*, pp. 185–186.

prevented the east Europeans from accepting the American offer. The western countries, on the other hand, seemed to be organizing themselves into a bloc. The French in particular rallied quite openly to the Anglo-American side. The Communists had been dropped from the French government in May and Bidault was now freer to pursue a pro-western policy. This in turn made it easier for Britain and America to push ahead in western Germany.

More sharply than ever before, Europe was being divided between east and west. At the end of the war, Stalin had been ready to accept the division of Europe philosophically: "Everyone imposes his own system as far as his army can reach. It cannot be otherwise." But now Stalin reacted violently to the new thrust of American policy. The Cominform was set up in September. At its opening session Andrei Zhdanov, Stalin's heir apparent, proclaimed the new Soviet line: Europe was divided into two implacably hostile camps. Communist tactics became more openly confrontational, especially in France, where a wave of revolutionary strikes was instigated, but also in Italy and in Greece, where a Communist provisional government was set up in December.[112]

In this new and considerably chillier climate, it was clear that a German settlement was not in the cards. American policymakers thought in late 1947 that given the USSR's obvious hostility, any agreement would turn out to be a sham. A "bogus unity" would be of no interest to the West. It would bring the Russians into the Ruhr and give them a measure of control over the western zones. They would use that influence to sabotage European recovery or divert eastward the aid that western Germany would be getting.[113] In such circumstances an agreement on Germany could no longer be the main goal. By the time the foreign ministers met in London at the end of the year, the main western objective was to make the Soviets appear responsible for the breach and for the consequent division of Germany. Tactical considerations of this sort had been a major factor shaping policy all along, but by now they had assumed fundamental importance. As Bedell Smith put it on December 10, the American government really did not want a deal with Russia on German unification, since the Soviets had "declared war on European recovery" and an all-German arrangement would give them a way of sabotaging the recovery plan. But the western powers had constantly stressed the importance of German unity, and to block an apparently attractive unification plan would therefore "require careful maneuvering to avoid the appearance of inconsistency if not hypocrisy."[114] Marshall himself took a similar line.[115]

[112] See especially Lilly Marcou, *Le Kominform: Le communisme de guerre froide* (Paris: Presses de la FNSP, 1977), pp. 34–72. On France, see Georgette Elgey, *La république des illusions* (Paris: Fayard, 1993), pp. 405–470. On Greece, see Lawrence Wittner, *American Intervention in Greece, 1943–1949* (New York: Columbia University Press, 1982), p. 260. Note also the account, based on Czech archives, of the effect of the new policy on Communist tactics in Czechoslovakia in late 1947 in Karel Kaplan, *The Short March: The Communist Takeover in Czechoslovakia, 1945–1948* (New York: St. Martin's, 1987), pp. 75–77.

[113] Strang-Hickerson meeting, October 17, 1947, enclosed in Harvey to Massigli, October 21, 1947, MP/65/FFMA. See also Bedell Smith to Marshall, June 23, 1947, FRUS 1947, 3:266.

[114] Bedell Smith to Eisenhower, December 10, 1947, quoted in *Papers of Dwight David Eisenhower*, ed. L. Galambos, vol. 9 (Baltimore: Johns Hopkins University Press, 1978), p. 2130n.

[115] Marshall to Lovett, December 11, 1947, FRUS 1947, 2:765.

The Americans need not have worried about being embarrassed by a superficially moderate Soviet policy. By the time of the London conference in December, the Soviet position on Germany had hardened substantially.[116] There was clearly no way the new Soviet proposals could possibly be accepted. Molotov, moreover, accompanied these proposals with a bitter attack on the Marshall Plan and on western policy in general. The east-west split was so obvious that the hope of a four-power settlement in Germany could no longer be taken seriously. Marshall was personally enraged by the Soviet attitude.[117] There was no point in going on with what had become a charade, and on his initiative the conference was brusquely terminated.[118]

The Rubicon had now been crossed. The western powers had finally broken with Russia. It was now clear that America and her friends would move quickly toward the creation of a west German state.

[116] U.S. Delegation to Truman et al., December 8, 1947, ibid., p. 757.

[117] U.S. Delegation to Truman et al., and to State Department, both December 12, 1947, and Marshall to Lovett, December 13, 1947, ibid., pp. 767–770.

[118] U.S. Delegation to Truman et al., December 15, 1947, ibid., p. 771.

The Test of Strength

BY THE END of 1947, the three western powers had finally reached the conclusion that no settlement with Russia was possible and that they therefore would have to move ahead in western Germany on their own. In early 1948 it became clear that they intended to establish a west German state.[1] The Soviets, however, were deeply opposed to what the western powers were doing, and in June reacted by cutting off ground access to Berlin. Even in late 1947 it had seemed that the two sides might be headed for a showdown, and the risks were obviously much greater now. But if war was a distinct possibility, it was also true that there were no forces in place that could prevent western Europe from being overrun. It was only the American nuclear monopoly and the prospect of a one-sided air-atomic war that protected Europe from Soviet attack. It was therefore important to provide some real security for western Europe, or at least to lay the basis for a system that would in time provide an effective counterweight to Soviet power on the continent. And so events in 1948–49 proceeded along three closely related tracks: the process leading to the creation of a west German state; the clash with Russia centering on the struggle over Berlin; and the working out of a western security system, culminating in the signing of the North Atlantic Treaty in April 1949.

WESTERN CONSENSUS

At the London conference in December 1947, the three western powers had decided that no four-power arrangement for Germany could be worked out and that they themselves would therefore have to organize the western part of that country. It was Marshall who at London had put an end to the talks. The U.S. government had thus decided to press forward with the policy of building up western Germany, of establishing a west German state, and of tying that state closely to the West as a whole. Britain and France cooperated with that policy, but did they do so against their better judgment? Were they so dependent on the United States that they had little choice but to follow the American lead?

It was true, of course, that neither Britain nor France could do without American support. For both countries, American financial assistance was crucial. Both countries needed help getting their own economies back on their feet, and the British also needed American assistance in financing imports into their zone in

[1] Marshall to Lovett, December 8, 1947, and Bidault-Marshall and Bevin-Marshall meetings, December 17, 1947; FRUS 1947, 2:754–755, 814–816. The French account of the Bidault-Marshall meeting is in Y/297/FFMA. Bidault-Bevin meeting, December 17, 1947, FO 371/67674, PRO; a French translation is in Y/297/FFMA. Note also the Bidault-Marshall meeting, September 18, 1947, FRUS 1947, 2:681–684.

Germany. The British zone was the most heavily industrialized part of the country (it included the Ruhr basin, Germany's industrial heartland) and thus was for the time being the area least able to feed itself with its own resources. That in turn gave the United States a certain control over the Ruhr, and in particular over Ruhr coal, both matters of vital importance to France.[2]

And both Britain and France were dependent on American power to keep the Soviet Union at bay. During the war and in the late 1940s as well, there was a certain hope in Britain especially that a west European group—the term "bloc" was deliberately avoided—might in time be able to balance Soviet power on its own. As late as 1948, Bevin, for example, hoped that western Europe might eventually emerge as a "third force." A British-led grouping with a distinct social-democratic flavor would appeal to Europeans who both hated Soviet communism and "despised" American materialism, and would be able to steer a truly independent course in world affairs.[3] Britain therefore sought to work closely with France, traditionally the other major power in western Europe. In late 1945, the French government had called for the internationalization of the Ruhr and the political separation of the Rhineland from the rest of Germany, and it seemed in late 1945 that Bevin might be willing to go along with those ideas. "Our view," he told the French foreign minister, Georges Bidault, on September 16, "was favorable to the creation of a Rhenanian Republic."[4]

---

[2] Rothwell, *Britain and the Cold War*, p. 348. On the coal question, see Raymond Poidevin, "La France et le charbon allemand au lendemain de la deuxième guerre mondiale," *Relations internationales*, no. 44 (1985): 365–377, and John W. Young, *France, the Cold War and the Western Alliance, 1944–1949: French Foreign Policy and Post-War Europe* (New York: St. Martin's, 1990), p. 141. See also Clayton-Marshall meeting, June 20, 1947; Marshall to Clay, June 24, 1947; Clayton to Marshall, June 25, 1947; in FRUS 1947, 2:929, 931–932. On America's "predominant voice" on bizonal economic matters, see Royall to Marshall, May 18, 1948, FRUS 1948, 2:251–252. For an example of the way economic and financial issues were tied into the negotiations on general political issues, see Webb-Truman meeting, September 25, 1950. The French defense minister had said that if the U.S. government could see its way "to help on the financial and production problems, then the German matter will be much easier to handle. France needs about $100,000,000 of raw materials and has to find some way to finance a substantial budget deficit." FRUS 1950, 3:354. For another example, see Eisenhower-Ismay meeting, December 8, 1953, Policy Planning Staff [PPS] records, 1947–53, box 75, Bermuda Conference, Record Group [RG] 59, U.S. National Archives [USNA], College Park, Maryland. This shows how French support for the European Defense Community was tied to a U.S. grant of $385 million to support the French effort in Indochina.

[3] See CP(48)6, January 4, 1948, Cab 129/23, PRO. See also David Dilks, "Britain and Europe, 1948–1950: The Prime Minister, the Foreign Secretary and the Cabinet," in *Histoire des débuts de la construction européenne (mars 1948–mai 1950)*, ed. Raymond Poidevin (Brussels: Bruylant, 1986), p. 396, and Anthony Adamthwaite, "Britain and the World, 1945–9: The View from the Foreign Office," *International Affairs* 61 (1985): 226, 228. On the idea of a "western group," see Llewellyn Woodward, *British Foreign Policy in the Second World War*, vol. 5 (London: HMSO, 1976), 193 ff.; Bullock, *Bevin*, p. 242; Rothwell, *Britain and the Cold War*, chap. 8, esp. pp. 433, 435, 449. For a detailed official discussion, see the Foreign Office briefing paper, "Franco-German Treaty and Policy in Western Europe," July 12, 1945, DBPO I, 1:234–251.

[4] Bevin-Attlee-Bidault meeting, September 16, 1945, Prem 8/43, PRO. This document was also published in Rolf Steininger, ed., *Die Ruhrfrage 1945/46 und die Entstehung des Landes Nordrhein-Westfalen: Britische, Französiche und Amerikanische Akten* (Düsseldorf: Droste, 1988), pp. 331–332. This book, a massive collection of documents with a long introduction by the editor, is the best source of published material relating to the Ruhr-Rhineland question in the immediate postwar period. For an-

But gradually the British gave up on the possibility of a freestanding European bloc, even as a long-term goal. As early as 1946, Prime Minister Attlee had come to think of Britain, and even western Europe in general, not as an independent pole of power, but simply as America's eastern march. The British Isles, he said, might have to be considered "an easterly extension of a strategic area the centre of which is the American continent rather than as a power looking eastwards through the Mediterranean to India and the East." His great fear was that the United States might not go along with such an arrangement, and that America might instead try "to make a safety zone round herself while leaving us and Europe in No Man's Land."[5] Bevin was slower to abandon the idea of western Europe as an independent "third force" in world affairs. But even he, by 1949, had finally reached the conclusion that western Europe would never be strong enough to balance the Soviet Union by itself.[6] And however the long-term possibilities were assessed, it was universally taken for granted in the late 1940s that Britain could not for the time being contemplate a "show-down" with Russia unless she were sure of American support.[7] By 1947 many key French officials had also come to see that the security of the West, at least for the foreseeable future, had to rest primarily on American power.[8]

But these lopsided power relations did not mean that the U.S. government essentially imposed its will on America's allies, and that Britain and France only reluctantly followed the American lead. By December 1947, there was nothing grudging or forced about Bevin's or Bidault's cooperation with Marshall. At the

---

other example of Bevin's pro-French stance on this question, see Massigli to Bidault, October 26, 1945, MP/92/FFMA, discussed in Georges-Henri Soutou, "La politique française à l'égard de la Rhénanie, 1944–1947" in *Franzosen und Deutschen am Rhein: 1789, 1918, 1945,* ed. Peter Huttenberger and Hans-Georg Molitor (Essen: Klartext, 1989), pp. 53–54. See also Sean Greenwood, "Ernest Bevin, France and 'Western Union,' August 1945–February 1946," *European History Quarterly* 14 (1984):319–357, and Greenwood's "Bevin, the Ruhr and the Division of Germany: August 1945–December 1946," *Historical Journal* 29 (1986): 204.

[5] Bullock, *Bevin,* pp. 242, 340.

[6] See CP(48)6, January 4, 1948, Cab 129/23, and CP(49)208, October 18, 1949, Cab 129/37, PRO. See also Dilks, "Britain and Europe," p. 411; Adamthwaite, "Britain and the World," p. 228. The idea was ruled out again in early 1950 when Sir Stafford Cripps, the chancellor of the Exchequer, proposed it as an alternative to a policy that came "much nearer permanent subservience to the U.S.A. than anything else." There was a certain sense by this point that Britain could not take too independent a line even if she wanted to. As a Foreign Office official commented on Cripps's proposed policy, it was obvious that with Britain so dependent on American financial and military assistance and political support, "we cannot take up a completely intransigent attitude." See Cripps minute, May 2, 1950, and Makins to Bevin, May 7, 1950, DBPO II, 2:87 n. 4, 248. For other documents bearing on the issue, see DBPO II, 2:54–63, 214–215, 227–228. For Bevin's views on the issue in late 1950, see DBPO II, 3:290. For British policy on the "Third Force" question in 1945–48, see also Rothwell, *Britain and the Cold War,* pp. 414, 422, 435, 449, and Bullock, *Bevin,* p. 517.

[7] Jebb memorandum, July 29, 1945, DBPO, I, 1:993; Rothwell, *Britain and the Cold War,* p. 320. Note also the comment of a high Foreign Office official in early 1947 that "too great independence of the United States would be a dangerous luxury," quoted ibid., p. 270.

[8] See, for example, General Jean Humbert (temporary head of French General Staff) to prime minister, July 29, 1947, box 4Q2, Service Historique de l'Armée de Terre [SHAT], Vincennes; and General Pierre Billotte, *Le passé au futur* (Paris: Stock, 1979), pp. 33–52. Note also Bidault's remarks to the French parliament in February 1948, quoted in Cyril Buffet, *Mourir pour Berlin: La France et l'Allemagne, 1945–1949* (Paris: Colin, 1991), p. 79.

London conference, they in fact took if anything a somewhat firmer line than their American colleague, fully accepting the break, and not even caring much about how exactly it was to be stage-managed.[9] This was not the product of a sudden change on their part. Britain and America had in fact long seen eye-to-eye on fundamental issues. And even between the English-speaking countries and France, substantive differences were not nearly as great as they appeared at the time.

On the German question, the core issue in international politics, Britain and America pursued the same basic policy in the immediate postwar period. At Potsdam, Bevin did not really accept the philosophy behind the Byrnes plan. But he had never been a strong supporter of German unity, and he refused to take up the cudgels at that conference in support of the unitary policy. In late 1945, the British government had moved even closer to the Byrnes position. By that point, a united Germany was no longer a British goal: the British government, according to the minister responsible for German affairs, was willing to set up central administrations to run Germany on a unified basis, but not "effective ones, which indeed it would be one of its chief purposes to prevent."[10] This was, of course, at variance with what Clay was trying to do at the time, but was very much in line with Byrnes's policy. In 1946, the Americans took the lead in pressing for the western strategy, but many British Foreign Office officials wanted to move in that same direction. Bevin himself was somewhat reluctant to act. A partition of Germany, he said that spring, "meant a policy of a Western Bloc and that meant war."[11] Both he and the Cabinet as a whole felt "that the general dangers of splitting Germany now are greater than those of continuing our present policy."[12] But whatever his misgivings, he went along with the American plan to set up the bizone.[13]

In 1947, the situation was reversed. Now, with Marshall at the helm in Washington, the British took a somewhat firmer line than the Americans.[14] But Bevin, like Marshall, remained reluctant to embrace the western strategy wholeheartedly. The British foreign secretary, to be sure, now wanted to "organize" the western zones, but his goal in early 1947 was still to create a "stronger bargaining position" for dealing with the Russians and ultimately for working out with them a common policy on Germany.[15] And it was precisely because he still hoped to reach agree-

[9] Marshall to Lovett, December 8, 1947, FRUS 1947, 2:754–755. For the best window into Bevin's and Bidault's thinking at this point, see the fifteen-page account of their meeting of December 17, 1947, "Conversations anglo-françaises," Y/297/FFMA; or FO 371/67674, PRO, for the original English-language version.

[10] Quoted in Deighton, The Impossible Peace, p. 76. See also Elisabeth Kraus, Ministerien für das ganze Deutschland? Der Alliierte Kontrollrat und die Frage gesamtdeutscher Zentralverwaltungen (Munich: Oldenbourg, 1990), esp. pp. 103–104 (Sir Oliver Harvey's views) and pp. 112–113 (Bevin's support for Harvey's position).

[11] Quoted in Deighton, The Impossible Peace, p. 73.

[12] Ernest Bevin, "Policy towards Germany," May 3, 1946, CP(46)186, Cab 129/9, PRO; and CM(46)43rd meeting, Confidential Annex, May 7, 1946, Cab 128/7, PRO.

[13] For Bevin's reluctance to accept the American offer on the bizone, see Greenwood, "Bevin, the Ruhr and the Division of Germany," p. 209.

[14] This is one of the basic themes of Deighton's Impossible Peace: see, for example, pp. 124, 134, 136, 148, and esp. 163.

[15] Ernest Bevin, "Main Short-term Problems Confronting Us in Moscow," February 20, 1947, paragraph 14, CP(47)68, Cab 129/17, PRO.

ment with them that in late April he rejected Clay's proposal to create a real bizonal parliament. "Complete political fusion on this scale," he argued, "would in my view prejudice the chances of agreement with Russia when the Council of Foreign Ministers resumes discussion of the German question in November."[16] Bevin even now was reluctant to abandon what a year earlier he had called "the one factor which *might* hold us and the Russians together, viz., the existence of a single Germany which it would be in the interest of us both to hold down."[17] But like the Americans, by the end of the year he had come to the conclusion that the western powers had little choice but to act, and that meant to move ahead with the establishment of a west German state. So in both cases the basic picture is roughly the same: slow, halting, but inexorable movement toward full acceptance of the "western strategy" for Germany, and thus of a rupture with the Soviet Union.

With France, the story is more complex. France, of course, was fundamentally a western country, and the broad forces shaping British and American policy were bound to push French policy in the same general direction. From the outset, many French leaders were concerned about Soviet power and sought close relations with the United States. General Charles de Gaulle, head of the French government until January 1946, sometimes argued along very different lines, but even he made it clear to the Americans in November 1945 that he considered the Russian threat more important than the German problem and that he understood that France had to cooperate with America if she "wished to survive."[18]

This fear of Soviet power was a key factor shaping French policy on the German question. In late 1945, the French openly opposed the central administrations, enraging Clay by vetoing their establishment by the Control Council. Their ostensible goal was to put pressure on their allies to go along with their plans for the Ruhr, the Saar, and the Rhineland—that is, for the separation of these areas in varying degrees from the rest of Germany. The French said they would not support the central administrations until an acceptable arrangement for these areas was worked out.[19] Many French officials from de Gaulle on down took the Rhenish

---

[16] Ernest Bevin, "Implementation of the Fusion Arrangements in the British and United States Zones of Germany," April 30, 1947, CP(47)143, Cab 129/18, PRO. See also Rothwell, *Britain and the Cold War*, p. 328.

[17] Ernest Bevin, "Policy towards Germany," May 3, 1946, CP(46)186, Cab 129/9, PRO. Emphasis in original. Bevin's caution through mid-1947 is emphasized in John Baylis, *The Diplomacy of Pragmatism: Britain and the Formation of NATO, 1942–1949* (Kent, Ohio: Kent State University Press, 1993), pp. 42–48.

[18] On de Gaulle, see Georges-Henri Soutou, "Le Général de Gaulle et l'URSS, 1943–1945: Idéologie ou équilibre européen?" *Revue d'histoire diplomatique* 108 (1994): 347–353. As Soutou shows (p. 353), by late 1945 de Gaulle and certain top military advisors wanted to negotiate a "secret military agreement" with the United States and Britain. In fact, even in 1944 de Gaulle had been worried about the implications of an Anglo-Saxon troop withdrawal from Europe. See Mai, *Alliierte Kontrollrat*, p. 84n. On de Gaulle and the question of a security relationship with the United States, see Irwin Wall, *The United States and the Making of Postwar France, 1945–1954* (Cambridge: Cambridge University Press, 1991), pp. 33, 41–42. For French policy in the period after de Gaulle's resignation, see Georges-Henri Soutou, "La sécurité de la France dans l'après-guerre," in *La France et l'OTAN, 1949–1996*, ed. Maurice Vaïsse et al. (Paris: Editions Complexe, 1996), p. 27, and Soutou, "La politique française à l'égard de la Rhénanie," pp. 52, 56, 61, 65 (especially for Bidault's views).

[19] Murphy to Byrnes, October 2, 1945, FRUS 1945, 3:844.

policy quite seriously, but for Bidault it was essentially a lever. From the start, he and certain other French policymakers made it clear that the real reason they opposed setting up the central administrations was that such a system would "inevitably lead to the eventual setting up of a Soviet dominated central government in Germany."[20]

The two other western governments shared these basic concerns. The British, as noted above, opposed "effective" central administrations and shared the view that centralization might lead to a Communist takeover of all of Germany. The advantage of the zonal approach, Bevin pointed out, was that Soviet influence could be kept out of the vital western part of the country.[21] The British were not upset by the French vetoes, and disliked Clay's idea of organizing the great bulk of Germany on a tripartite basis—that is, with America and Russia, but without France.[22]

The American government also did not really disagree with key French policymakers on these fundamental issues. Byrnes, practically from the start, was thinking in terms of a rump Germany limited to the western part of the country. This is clear not just from his Potsdam policy, but also from his reference at an August 1945 meeting with Bidault to a Germany of forty-five million inhabitants, that figure being almost exactly the population of the three western zones at the time.[23] But the French, as early as July 1945, had also begun to think in terms of a western Germany run by the three western powers.[24] Bidault's goal was to keep Soviet influence out of western Germany, but this was a basic aim for Byrnes and Truman as well.[25] As a result, Byrnes was not upset by the French vetoes in the Control Council and did not press energetically for a more accommodating French pol-

---

[20] See, for example, Caffery to acting secretary, August 6, 1945, FRUS Potsdam, 2:1548–49; Caffery to Byrnes, August 13, 1945, 851.001/8–1345, RG 59, USNA (cited in an unpublished manuscript by James McAllister); Byrnes-Bidault meeting, August 23, 1945, FRUS 1945, 4:718–719; Caffery to Byrnes, September 27, November 3, and December 8, 1945, FRUS 1945, 3:878, 890–891, 916n. Bidault, in fact, later took credit for having blocked the central administrations. If France had gone along with the idea, he said in December 1947, "the Communists would now be in power in Cologne." This assessment was shared by such high American officials as Bohlen and Bedell Smith. "Conversations anglo-françaises," December 17, 1947, p. 13, Y/297/FFMA, quoted also in Buffet, *Mourir pour Berlin,* p. 73. For Bohlen and Bedell Smith, see Clay, *Decision in Germany,* p. 131. There is a sizeable literature dealing with France's German policy during this period. Soutou's "La politique française à l'égard de la Rhénanie" is the best summary account, but see also the four major studies cited in the first footnote of that article and a more recent work by Dietmar Hüser: *Frankreichs "doppelte Deutschlandpolitik"* (Berlin: Duncker and Humblot, 1996). For a brief and pithy statement of Hüser's interpretation, see his article "Charles de Gaulle, Georges Bidault, Robert Schuman et l'Allemagne," *Francia* 23 (1996), esp. pp. 57–64.

[21] Deighton, *The Impossible Peace,* pp. 70–71. See also Bevin's basic policy paper on Germany of May 3, 1946, CP(46)186, Cab 129/9, PRO.

[22] Mai, *Alliierte Kontrollrat,* pp. 97–98.

[23] Byrnes-Bidault meeting, August 23, 1945, FRUS 1945, 4:720. Bidault had argued that the shift in Germany's "center of gravity" to the west, resulting from the loss of the eastern territories, was a threat to France. Byrnes responded that the shrinking of Germany from a country of sixty-five million inhabitants to one whose population was only forty-five million should be a source of reassurance to France. Byrnes, however, went on to muddy the waters a bit, and referred in the same breath to the American policy of setting up central administrations—although he did take care to minimize their political significance.

[24] Mai, *Alliierte Kontrollrat,* p. 84; Young, *France, the Cold War and the Western Alliance,* p. 59.

[25] Franco-American meetings, August 22–23, 1945, FRUS 1945, 4:711, 721.

icy. The vetoes demonstrated the unworkability of the Control Council system, and that system had to be seen as a failure before anything else could be tried.

The Americans, in fact, secretly encouraged the French in their obstructionism. It was Robert Murphy, the U.S. political advisor in Germany and thus the top State Department official in that country, who delivered the message. He met with his French counterpart, Saint-Hardouin, in October 1945. The American military authorities in Germany were of course angry about the recent vetoes in the Control Council, but the French, Murphy said, should not get too upset about that. These military officers, he pointed out, had their orders and were not in the habit of wondering whether there was any valid basis for the obstacles they found in their way. Murphy then discussed America's German policy in more general terms. The United States, he said, was stuck for the time being with the policy of trying to work with Russia. Murphy did not like that policy, and, like the French, he was worried that a unified Germany might fall under Soviet control. But until public opinion changed, his government could not repudiate the Berlin-based Control Council regime. France, however, did not have to go along with it. He therefore urged the French to avoid the drawbacks of the Control Council system and to "orient your zone toward the west, rather than toward Berlin."[26]

But if, at the most fundamental level, the three western governments shared some very basic goals, there were certain things which kept the French from cooperating too closely, and above all, too openly with their Anglo-Saxon friends in the immediate postwar period. First of all, there was a whole series of problems having to do with political conditions at home. Both Bidault and Jean Chauvel, the top permanent official at the Quai d'Orsay, repeatedly made it clear in mid- and late 1946 that they sided with the United States in the developing dispute with the Soviets over Germany, and that it was only for "internal political reasons" that France could not overtly stand with America.[27] The power of the large French Communist party, though not the only factor, was certainly the key one, since the Communists were an important part of the governing coalition in France at the time. This problem of Communist strength within France continued to be a great concern in early 1947. When Bidault met with Marshall in April, he made this explicit: "To the American question 'Can we rely on France?', he said, the answer was 'Yes.' But France needed time and must avoid a civil war."[28] The internal crisis soon came to a head. In May, the Communists were forced out of the government, and later that year there was a wave of Communist-led political strikes. By November, however, Bidault was sure that the situation could be controlled and that

[26] Saint-Hardouin to Bidault, October 9, 1945, Y/283/FFMA.

[27] See Caffery to Byrnes, June 11, June 22, and August 30, 1946, FRUS 1946, 5:566–567, 567n, 596. For an open admission of the importance of domestic political considerations in France's German policy, see Byrnes-Bidault meeting, September 24, 1946, ibid., pp. 607–608. It was not as though Bidault, in taking a strong anti-Soviet line, was just telling the Americans what he thought they wanted to hear, in order, for example, to get economic or other concessions from them. His view, even in late 1946, was that the Americans were not tough enough with the Russians. See his comment to the British ambassador, Duff Cooper, of October 11, 1946, quoted in Soutou, "La sécurité de la France," p. 28.

[28] Bidault-Marshall meeting, April 20, 1947, FRUS 1947, 2:369–370. See also Bidault-Marshall meeting, March 11, 1947; Marshall to Acheson, March 24, 1947; Caffery to Marshall, March 25 and November 6, 1947; ibid., pp. 241, 396, 401, 702.

the Communists' "great bid for power" would fail.[29] He now felt freer to come out openly on the side of the other western powers, although even at this point there were limits to how forthright he could be. Indeed, Bidault's lack of candor was beginning to undermine his political position at home and would lead to his fall and replacement as foreign minister by Robert Schuman in July 1948.[30]

But domestic politics was not the whole story. There were also some real differences on foreign policy. The western strategy implied that Germany, or at least western Germany, was going to be built up—not just economically and politically, but ultimately in a military sense as well. It was obvious to military men in all three major western countries that German troops would eventually be necessary if western Europe was ever to be defended effectively. The British Chiefs of Staff had been thinking along these lines even during the war; American military authorities were arguing for German troops in 1947 and their French counterparts by 1948 at the latest.[31] The political leadership—or at least certain key policymakers—in America and Britain had come to the same conclusion by late 1947. The emerging American view in August of that year was that the non-Soviet world had to organize itself politically, economically, "and, in the final analysis, militarily" to deal with the Soviet threat, and that western Germany had to be brought into this bloc.[32] Bevin was beginning to think along similar lines; in January 1948, he believed the western countries had to come together to deal with the Soviet threat, and that Germany had to be brought into the western system "as soon as circumstances permit."[33] But to build up German power too quickly was seen as risky, and the French, given their geographic position, were particularly sensitive to those risks. Who could predict how the Soviets would react? Who could tell how a strong and independent Germany would behave? If the Americans came in on a more or less permanent basis—if they committed their power in a major way to the defense of western Europe, and in particular if they maintained a large military force in western Germany—the risks might be minimal. The Soviets would be held at bay, and German freedom of action could be curtailed. But who could

[29] Bidault-Marshall meeting, November 28, 1947, ibid., p. 739.

[30] Buffet, *Mourir pour Berlin*, pp. 66, 71, 78–80, 194. See also Elgey, *République des illusions*, pp. 386, 387; and unsigned note of May 24, 1948, MP/67/FFMA, reporting Chauvel explaining Bidault's backpedaling on the German question by referring to French domestic politics. On Bidault's great concern with the political situation in France, see also Caffery to Marshall, May 24, May 25, and May 28, 1948, FRUS 1948, 2:273–274, 281, 281n. On the backpedaling itself, see Bidault's memoranda of May 20, 1948, Z/Généralités/23/FFMA, and various documents in FRUS 1948, 2:266–281. For a wonderful example of the gap between the official rhetoric and Bidault's real beliefs, see Hüser, "De Gaulle, Bidault, Schuman et l'Allemagne," n. 55; note especially Bidault's private reference in September 1945 to the German threat as a "convenient myth."

[31] Rothwell, *Britain and the Cold War*, pp. 119–123; Joint Strategic Survey Committee report, April 29, 1947, FRUS 1947, 1:740; Pierre Guillen, "Les chefs militaires français, le réarmement de l'Allemagne et la CED (1950–1954)," *Revue d'histoire de la deuxième guerre mondiale*, no. 129 (January 1983): 3–33.

[32] Interdepartmental meeting and Bohlen memorandum, August 30, 1947, FRUS 1947, 1:762–764. The views Bohlen expressed were fully shared by the other top officials at the meeting.

[33] Summary of Bevin memorandum in Inverchapel to Marshall, January 13, 1948, FRUS 1948, 3:4–6, to be interpreted in the context of the general philosophy Bevin laid out in his December 17, 1947, meeting with Bidault, Y/297/FFMA and FO 371/67674.

be sure that the Americans would really be willing to play this kind of role, not just for the next year or two, but more or less permanently? If the French could not be certain, perhaps it made sense for them to hedge their bets and avoid too sharp a break with Russia.

The debate within France on the "western strategy"—on moving ahead in Germany without Russia, and siding with America and Britain in the Cold War—would turn largely on how this set of problems was resolved. In the internal debates in 1947 and 1948, the supporters of the western strategy used a whole series of arguments. If France cooperated with the other western powers, it was said, her interests—in Ruhr coal, for example, and in Marshall Plan aid—would be viewed more sympathetically than if she held herself aloof. Her Anglo-Saxon friends in that case would also be more willing to let her have her say on German questions, and especially on matters relating to the Ruhr. To stand aside would not prevent France from being overrun if war broke out—France's "fate would be the same, whether she wanted to stay neutral or not"—and it would not prevent the Anglo-Saxons from moving ahead in Germany without her. The French would then have little choice but to accept a situation that had come into being without her input. But if she acted now she might be able to head off unfavorable developments and put her imprint on the system while it was still taking shape.[34]

Such arguments had a certain force, but they were not enough in themselves to bring about wholehearted acceptance of the western strategy. What did bring this about was a fundamental shift in the way the German question was understood. Initially, the Cold War was seen as aggravating the problem: the conflict with Russia was pushing France to accept the distasteful and dangerous policy of building up Germany. But it gradually dawned on key French policymakers that the western strategy was a way of solving the German problem—that the system taking shape, a system based on the division of Germany and on a certain level of tension between east and west, was quite satisfactory from their point of view. With Soviet armies on the Elbe and with Germany weak and divided, western Germany would be dependent on the western powers for protection; even if most of the controls were ended, that west German state would be in no position to challenge the status quo; so the controls could be largely phased out, and western Germany could be brought into the western world as a kind of partner. The Soviet threat on the Elbe meant that American troops would remain in Germany, perhaps indefinitely, and American power would keep the Russians at bay. It was not a question,

---

[34] Buffet, *Mourir pour Berlin*, pp. 64–66, 141–142; Raymond Poidevin, *Robert Schuman, homme d'état, 1886–1963* (Paris: Imprimerie Nationale, 1986), p. 212; Raymond Poidevin, "Le Facteur Europe dans la politique allemande de Robert Schuman," in Poidevin, *Histoire des débuts*, p. 314; Humbert to prime minister, July 29, 1947 (for the quotation), box 4Q2, SHAT, Vincennes. For various archival documents with similar themes, see Massigli note, November 22, 1947, MP/65; Massigli to Foreign Ministry, June 3, 1948, MP/67; Massigli to Chauvel, February 14, 1949, MP/68; all FFMA. On Anglo-American pressure on France—and in particular the threat to move ahead on the German question without France if the French did not come along—see, for example, Lovett-Douglas phone conversation, March 2, 1948; Douglas to Marshall, May 21 and May 24, 1948; Douglas-Saltzman phone conversation, May 31, 1948; Douglas to Lovett, June 4, 1948; Douglas to Marshall, June 16, 1948; and Marshall to Douglas, June 14, 1948; in FRUS 1948, 2:112, 269, 273, 301, 319, 335, 378. Note also the discussion of the issue in the British cabinet, May 3, 1948, CM 34(48), Cab 128/12, PRO.

in other words, of one problem being piled on top of another; both problems—the German problem and the Russian problem—would be solved if such a system came into being. This sort of thinking became very sharp and explicit in the French foreign ministry around 1952.[35] But the basic idea had begun to take hold much earlier. Already in 1947 and 1948, the more clairvoyant French officials were coming to the conclusion that a system based on the division of Germany was the best arrangement that France could hope for.[36]

And an active French policy could perhaps make such a system even more satisfactory. France should now, some leading officials were beginning to argue, take the lead in "building Europe"—that is, in supporting the creation of west European transnational economic and political structures. Some officials had been thinking along these lines even in early 1945, but it was only in 1947 that the basic idea that Germany had to be dealt with in a European framework—or, more precisely, that *western* Germany had to be integrated into *western* Europe—really began to get off the ground. The focus was on economic integration, but what was ultimately driving this policy was the great political goal of tying western Germany to the West. A purely repressive policy could not keep Germany in the western camp. Controls on German power, a special status for the Rhenish area, and so on—all that might be very well and good, one high official at the Quai d'Orsay noted in October 1947, "but it is not with such measures that we will discourage the Germans from flirting with the Russians." A more creative policy was essential. A "plan for economic cooperation between France and Germany," a customs union or something similar, needed to be developed.[37]

The view was thus taking hold that West Germany would have to be treated as more of an equal, and that a framework had to be established within which this new relationship would be possible.[38] Only European institutions could effec-

[35] Note especially a series of memoranda written in 1952 and 1953 by Jean Sauvagnargues, especially his memoranda of June 25, 1952, and April 22 and June 10, 1953, Europe 1949–55/Allemagne/822 and 823/FFMA, and Europe 1949–55/Généralités/100/FFMA. The foreign ministers of the period— Bidault and, to my mind at least, Schuman as well—saw things in much the same way. See Marc Trachtenberg, *History and Strategy* (Princeton, N.J.: Princeton University Press, 1991), p. 179, and Georges-Henri Soutou, "La France et les notes soviétiques de 1952 sur l'Allemagne," *Revue d'Allemagne* 20 (1988): 270–272.

[36] See, for example, Massigli to Bidault, July 8, 1947, MP/92/FFMA: "je crois en définitive que la coupure vaut mieux pour nous." J.-C. Paris, the head of the direction d'Europe at the Quai d'Orsay, took the same kind of line in a note of July 18, 1948. "The cutting of Germany in two," he wrote, "has major advantages for us." Quoted in Buffet, *Mourir pour Berlin*, p. 189.

[37] Coulet to Massigli, October 31, 1947, MP/96/FFMA. See also a basic policy document drafted during the brief period in late 1946 and early 1947 when the veteran Socialist Léon Blum was prime minister: "In the economic area, but also in the political area, the integration of Germany into Europe has to be taken as the goal for both the allies and the Germans themselves. This of course means only western Germany and western Europe. But Europe is the only hope, aside from the Reich itself, which is open to the Germans, and for the victors of yesterday, it is the only way of giving life and substance to a Germany politically decentralized but economically prosperous, that they must take as their objective." Foreign Ministry to Koenig (draft), January 2, 1947, Y/298/FFMA. On the Blum interregnum in France's German policy, see Soutou, "La politique française à l'égard de la Rhénanie," p. 61.

[38] John Gillingham, *Coal, Steel and the Rebirth of Europe, 1945–1955* (New York: Cambridge University Press, 1991), p. 159; Buffet, *Mourir pour Berlin*, pp. 79, 138–139, 230, 243; Pierre Gerbet, "Les origines du Plan Schuman: Le choix de la méthode communautaire par le gouvernement français," in

tively limit Germany's freedom of action in that new environment. If controls were to be maintained, they would have to be Europeanized and apply equally to everyone: a west European structure, and not a fully independent Germany, would emerge as the occupation regime was dismantled.[39] The "European" policy, moreover, might head off a resurgence of German nationalist feeling. The "building of Europe" might capture the German political imagination: it was this great project, and not reunification, that might serve as the focus of German political energies and thus help the Germans live with the division of their own country.[40]

This emphasis on "building Europe" was thus another element tying French and American policy together. Bidault himself was personally a strong supporter of the policy of integrating western Germany into the western world, and in his April 1947 meeting with Marshall he did not mince words on this point: "Germany is part of the West, Germany is in Europe."[41] The Americans were of course delighted; the U.S. government by 1947 had also come to believe in the great importance of "building Europe." By 1948, the point about the need for an integrated western Europe of which western Germany would be an essential part had become one of the central dogmas of American policy.[42] Unless western Germany were tied to western Europe, "first through economic arrangements, and ultimately perhaps in some political way," Marshall wrote in February 1948, Germany as a whole might well be lost, "with obvious dire consequences for all of us."[43] As Lewis Douglas, the U.S. ambassador in London and a key policymaker in his own right, pointed out in a meeting with top French and British officials in February 1948, it was essential that the new arrangements being worked out for west Germany make the "German people feel part of Western Europe." Whatever controls were placed on the Ruhr should "be of such nature that Western Germany and Western Europe would be effectively integrated"; a more punitive approach might simply alienate the Germans and play into Soviet hands. The Americans, moreover, "attached very great importance" to the economic integration of western Europe as a whole. So "very tentatively and very informally" he suggested that the regime to be set up apply not only to the Ruhr but also to "similar industrial regions of Western Europe." This, of course, was the basic idea behind what two years later would be presented to the world as the Schuman Plan.[44]

Poidevin, *Histoire des débuts*, p. 209, and Poidevin, "Facteur Europe," pp. 314–315. See also Massigli to Chauvel, February 14, 1949, MP/68/FFMA.

[39] See Buffet, *Mourir pour Berlin*, pp. 230–231; Seydoux note, April 7, 1950, Europe 1949–1955/Généralités/87/FFMA.

[40] See Poidevin, "Facteur Europe," pp. 314–317; Poidevin, *Schuman*, p. 220; and Buffet, *Mourir pour Berlin*, p. 138. Note also Saint-Hardouin to Schuman, September 5, 1948, Y/312/FFMA.

[41] See Soutou, "La politique française à l'égard de la Rhénanie," pp. 64–65.

[42] See, for example, Marshall to Douglas, February 20, 1948, and Douglas to Marshall, March 2, 1948, FRUS 1948, 2:72, 114.

[43] Marshall to Caffery, February 19, 1948, ibid., p. 71.

[44] Douglas to Marshall, February 28, 1948, FRUS 1948, 2:99. The argument about the "American origins of the Schuman Plan," and in particular about Douglas's role, is developed at some length in René Massigli, *Une comédie des erreurs: Souvenirs et réflexions sur une étape de la construction européenne* (Paris: Plon, 1978), pp. 192–195. See also Poidevin, *Schuman*, p. 271; Pierre Mélandri, *Les Etats-Unis face à l'unification de l'Europe* (Paris: A. Pedone, 1980), pp. 155, 245, 272ff.; and Gillingham, *Coal, Steel and the Rebirth of Europe*, pp. 169–170.

But this emphasis on Europe did not mean that the French were thinking in terms of a purely European system. The European arrangements they had in mind were not meant as a substitute for a structure based on American military power. Indeed, the whole system based on the division of Germany presupposed a strong American presence in western Germany. The American troop presence there would not just protect western Europe from Soviet aggression, it would also automatically set limits to how far the Germans could go. It was the American presence, in fact, that made it possible to remove the controls, to treat Germany as a real partner, and thus to pursue the policy of "building Europe." In the French view, it was therefore vital that American power remain committed to the continent.[45] But would the Americans agree to take part in such a system?

The answer to that, it was becoming clear, would depend to a certain degree on the choices the French themselves made. The Americans might be tempted to push ahead in western Germany without limit, to re-create a strong and fully sovereign west German state, and then withdraw militarily from the continent. Or the Americans might limit their assistance to air and naval support: Europe would not be defended on the ground; in the event of aggression, the Soviets would be attacked from forces deployed on the periphery. For obvious reasons, neither of these possibilities was particularly attractive to the French. But suppose the French made it clear that they would be willing to cooperate on German questions if the U.S. government, for its part, was willing to pursue the other kind of policy—the policy of keeping U.S. troops in Germany, of maintaining limits on German power, and of providing an effective ground defense in western Europe. That might help tip the balance in Washington and lead to the kind of system the French really wanted.

And there was a good chance that French policy could make a major difference. From the U.S. point of view, French participation was important for a whole series of political and military reasons. It was not simply a question of adding another country to the anti-Soviet bloc. French participation would mean that western Germany would not just be the protectorate of the two great English-speaking powers, both based overseas. If France took part, the western system would have a broader basis, more of a continental flavor, greater legitimacy, greater viability, greater permanence. In military terms, it would provide more room for maneuver in the event of war, more secure lines of communication, and a major land force, all of which would help make it possible to defend Europe effectively on the ground—and an effective ground defense might be of fundamental importance in the long run if the western defense system was to be viable. In American eyes, it was therefore important that France be brought into the system. This meant that there was a good chance that the U.S. government would respond positively to a more forthcoming French policy and that quite satisfactory arrangements for Germany and for the defense of western Europe could be worked out.

So the idea was taking shape, especially in 1947, that France could support the western strategy for Germany, but that that support should not be unconditional. It would have to depend on America's willingness to help set up a security system

---

[45] On the key role that an American commitment to the defense of Europe played in French thinking at the time, see Soutou, "La sécurité de la France dans l'après-guerre," pp. 26, 29, 32.

for western Europe. This new French policy would have a major impact on the course of events in 1948.

In early 1948, British, French and American representatives met at London to work out terms for the creation of a west German state. On June 1, after three months of talks, they reached agreement on what were called the "London Recommendations." A constituent assembly was to draft a democratic constitution "of federal type," but the new state was not to be fully sovereign. The occupation would continue, and the occupation authorities would continue to exercise certain controls—over the Ruhr, for example, and over West Germany's military status and foreign relations—and indeed would have the right to "resume the exercise of their full powers" in an emergency, or if the democratic system within the new republic were threatened. The London agreement also laid out a procedure for the establishment of the new system: a constituent assembly was to meet no later than September 1, 1948.[46]

The London Recommendations were of fundamental political importance. The western powers were going to set up a new state in their part of Germany, and there was no telling how the Soviets would react. Many western leaders felt they might be heading into a full-fledged confrontation with the USSR. It had been clear even in late 1947 that a real test of strength was in the making. In August, for example, Bohlen had predicted a "major political showdown crisis" with Russia. The indications, he said, were that the conflict would come to a head in a matter of months.[47] High-ranking European officials also felt that the conflict over Germany

---

[46] For the main report of the London conference, see FRUS 1948, 2:309–312. For the principal annexes, see ibid., pp. 240–241, 260–262, 290–294, 305–307. The fact that America and Britain were serious about moving ahead quickly in Germany is reflected also in what was actually going on in the bizone. In January 1948, something that looked very much like a German government was brought into being there. The bizonal Economic Council was a kind of parliament, and the council's Executive Committee was made into a "proper executive body" ("really a cabinet but we are not calling it that"). Murphy to Marshall, January 7, 1948, ibid., p. 5. The structural changes in Germany were made without consultation with the French, even though the French had been assured at London in December that the Anglo-Saxons would bring them into the basic political process in Germany. The French government was livid and protested vigorously; the American and British governments were embarrassed. This was one of a series of incidents that confirmed the French in their view that when it came to foreign policy, the Americans did not quite have their act together. On this whole affair, see Caffery to Marshall, January 10, 1948, and Wallner to Bonbright, January 16, 1948, ibid., pp. 20–21, 27–28; and, for the French reaction, Massigli to Foreign Ministry, January 9, 1948, MP/65/FFMA, and two Chauvel notes and Chauvel to Bonnet, all dated January 12, 1948, Bonnet Papers [BP], vol. 1, FFMA. On the establishment of the Federal Republic, see two works by Wolfgang Benz: *Die Gründung der Bundesrepublik: Von der Bizone zum souveränen Staat* (Munich: Deutscher Taschenbuch, 1984), and *Von der Besatzungsherrschaft zur Bundesrepublik, 1946–1949* (Frankfurt: Fischer, 1984), esp. pp. 88–116, for the events described in the text. Note also two older but still useful English-language accounts: Peter Merkl, *The Origin of the West German Republic* (New York: Oxford, 1963); and John Golay, *The Founding of the Federal Republic of Germany* (Chicago: University of Chicago Press, 1958).

[47] Bohlen memorandum, August 30, 1947, FRUS 1947, 1:765.

was moving toward a climax. Bevin, Chauvel, and René Massigli, the French ambassador in London and another key policymaker, had no doubt that the western powers were rapidly moving into dangerous waters. The "organization" of western Germany, they all recognized, would lead to an increased risk of war with Russia.[48] There was a certain fear that the Soviets might lash out and launch a preventive war, pushing the western powers out of Germany and perhaps overrunning the continent as a whole. They might feel that they had to take action before events in western Germany had moved too far and before America and her friends had a chance to build up their defenses.[49]

In fact, in early 1948 the Russians did become more confrontational, more aggressive, as though they were getting ready for a major showdown with the West over Germany. In February the democratic order was brought down in Czechoslovakia, and a communist police state was imposed on that country. No Soviet troops were present as these events unfolded in Prague, but the shadow of Soviet power and the possibility of Soviet military intervention played a key role in the calculations of both sides in the Czech capital. Soviet Deputy Foreign Minister Zorin flew to Prague on February 19 and told the local Communists that Stalin wanted the matter to be brought to a head and that they should ask for Russian military help. Soviet troops, he said, were just across the border in Hungary, ready to move in. But the local Communists calculated that overt military intervention would be unnecessary. The simple fact that the Soviets were ready to send in troops while a western intervention was out of the question made resistance pointless.[50]

In late 1947, western statesmen had expected the Communists to take full control of Czechoslovakia in the near future.[51] The West was organizing itself into a bloc; the Soviets could therefore be expected to consolidate their own sphere as well; and Czechoslovakia lay on the Russian side of the line of demarcation. The events in Prague were nonetheless deeply disturbing. For many in the West, they underscored the brutality of Soviet policy. A servile ally was not good enough for the USSR. Whatever tactical flexibility the Russians might demonstrate in the short run, over the long run they would settle for nothing less than absolute control. It no longer mattered to the Soviets, one French diplomat argued, how world opinion reacted. Strategic considerations seemed to be the only thing they cared about,

[48] Oliver Harvey minute, October 20, 1947, MP/65/FFMA.
[49] Caffery to State Department and Douglas to Marshall, both May 21, 1948; Douglas to State Department, May 30, 1948; and Caffery to Marshall, May 25 and June 2, 1948; in FRUS 1948, 2:266n, 267, 281, 301n, 317. For the general French sense of the seriousness of the situation at this time, see, for example, Dejean to Foreign Ministry, March 12, 1948, and Chauvel to Bonnet, March 18 and May 19, 1948, BP/1/FFMA; for a discussion, see Buffet, *Mourir pour Berlin,* p. 89. See also Massigli to Foreign Ministry, May 3, 1948, MP/67/FFMA. Top American officials also felt that the West was skating on thin ice. See, for example, General Bradley's views, reported in Bonnet to Bidault, May 3, 1948, BP/1/FFMA; note also the cautious position taken by the JCS in April 1948, cited in JCS Historical Office, *History of the Joint Chiefs of Staff,* vol. 2: *1947–1949* (Wilmington, Del.: Glazier, 1979), p. 360. Truman himself later alluded to the possibility of a Soviet preventive war in his remarks to the NATO foreign ministers, April 3, 1949, published in the *Vierteljahrshefte für Zeitgeschichte* 40 (1992): 416.
[50] Kaplan, *The Short March,* p. 175.
[51] Policy Planning Staff, Résumé of the World Situation, November 6, 1947, FRUS 1947, 1:773. Note also Bidault's remarks in "Conversations anglo-françaises," December 17, 1947, Y/297/FFMA.

and Russia's "main preoccupation" now was to prepare for a conflict that might well be imminent.[52]

The situation in Berlin was an even greater source of concern. Czechoslovakia had long been recognized as part of the Soviet sphere, but western troops were in West Berlin. They were there by right of conquest, a right recognized by the Soviet government itself. Legal rights could not, however, alter geographical realities. The Soviets knew that the Berlin situation gave them an effective means of exerting pressure on the western powers, and indeed western leaders understood that the Soviets would be tempted to exploit the city's isolation and relative vulnerability. It was the obvious card for them to play.[53]

So it came as no great surprise when the Soviet authorities began in the early spring to interfere in a relatively minor way with western access to Berlin.[54] This pressure soon subsided, but the signal was clear enough. When the London Recommendations were adopted in June, the Soviets responded by stopping ground traffic between Berlin and western Germany. In imposing the blockade, they made it abundantly clear that their real goal was to challenge the West's policy of establishing a west German state: the London Recommendations had to be suspended, the western allies had to come back to the conference table. Stalin himself told the western ambassadors in his usual blunt way that Berlin was just a lever, that even trizonal economic fusion was not a problem, and that "the only real issue" was the establishment of a west German government.[55]

This comment of Stalin's was both important and revealing. He was accepting trizonal fusion—that is, the inclusion of France in the bloc of powers that was to run western Germany—and this implied that he had more or less accepted the more general idea of a western bloc. He was also making it clear that he was not opposed to economic recovery in western Germany. What he disliked was the idea of a German state—of the Germans getting too much independence and too much power. He wanted the western governments, and not the Germans, to be the real power in western Germany. This was in keeping with the Potsdam policy of accepting the division of Germany between the USSR and the West. The implication was that the USSR was not fundamentally opposed to a western system that limited German power and prevented a west German state from ever threatening the

---

[52] Dejean to Foreign Ministry, March 12, 1948, BP/1/FFMA. Dejean's analysis was endorsed in Chauvel to Bonnet, March 18, 1948, ibid. See also the discussion in Buffet, *Mourir pour Berlin,* pp. 87–91.

[53] See especially Murphy to Marshall, FRUS 1948, 2:1268–1270; and Seydoux to Foreign Ministry, November 14, 1947, Y/296/FFMA. See also Douglas to Marshall, March 3, 1948, FRUS 1948, 2:120, and Ann and John Tusa, *The Berlin Blockade* (London: Hodder and Stoughton, 1988), pp. 87–88.

[54] For the initial Soviet measures—what Murphy called the "series of strictures and annoyances" that the USSR had "inaugurated affecting our continued presence in Berlin"—and the U.S. reaction, see Murphy to Marshall, April 1, 2, and 13, 1948, FRUS 1948, 2:887–889, 892; and especially Clay teleconferences with Bradley and Royall, March 31 and April 10, 1948, and Clay to Bradley, April 1, 1948, in *Clay Papers,* 2:599–608, 621–623. Note especially Clay's comment (p. 623) that the "real crisis" would develop from the measures the western powers were about to take in western Germany, the currency reform followed by the establishment of a "partial German government."

[55] Smith to Marshall, August 3, 1948, FRUS 1948, 2:1003–1004.

status quo—that if the western powers could construct something of the sort, this was something the USSR would be willing to live with.

In 1948, Soviet and western leaders were not really able to discuss fundamental issues of this sort. For the Americans at the time, the real question had to do with the confrontation over Berlin and the policy they had adopted of establishing a west German state. They decided not to abandon their German policy, which meant that the conflict over Berlin would continue. But would they in the final analysis fight in order to defend their position in that city? The United States enjoyed a nuclear monopoly, but that was the only thing that balanced Soviet ground forces in Europe. The American military authorities thought that the United States was too weak to take a tough line and contemplated withdrawal from the city. In July 1948 the Joint Chiefs of Staff urged the political leadership to consider "the possibility that some justification might be found for withdrawal of our occupation forces from Berlin without undue loss of prestige."[56] In October, the Chiefs insisted that "in our present state of readiness," to go to war over Berlin "would be neither militarily prudent nor strategically sound."[57]

The view that the western position in Berlin was ultimately untenable, and that the western powers, in the final analysis, should be prepared to withdraw from the city, was in fact quite common at the time. One key State Department official argued in November 1947 that the Soviets had it within their power to make life in Berlin impossible for the western powers, that the West should hold on as long as it could, but should in the final analysis withdraw from the city rather than face war.[58] The British at times argued along similar lines.[59] There was a certain sense, in Europe especially, that Berlin was a strategic liability that needed to be liquidated: as long as the western powers hung on there, the Soviets would find it easy to exert pressure and limit what the West could do in western Germany. A withdrawal from Berlin was, from this point of view, a natural concomitant of the western strategy, both consequence and precondition of the policy of creating a west

---

[56] JCS to Forrestal, July 22, 1948, *JCS History,* 2:144. See also "Notes on the Berlin Situation (Army View)," enclosed in Maddocks to Army Chief of Staff, June 28, 1948, Army—Operations, Hot File, box 11, RG 319, USNA.

[57] JCS to Forrestal, October 13, 1948, in *JCS History,* 2:154. See also Avi Shlaim, *The United States and the Berlin Blockade, 1948–1949: A Study in Crisis Decision-Making* (Berkeley: University of California Press, 1983), pp. 218, 223–224, 259, 267.

[58] Seydoux to Foreign Ministry, November 14, 1947, Y/296/FFMA. One well-informed observer noted the widespread feeling among American officials even after the crisis had begun that the West would sooner or later have to withdraw. Reston memorandum, December 28, 1948, KP/1/212–216/ML.

[59] Bevin, in his important May 1946 paper on Germany, took it for granted that if a western strategy was adopted, the British would soon find themselves "forced out of Berlin." CP(46)186, May 3, 1946, Cab 129/9, PRO. And in late 1947, British representatives in Germany seemed to think that if the London foreign ministers' conference failed, a pullout from Berlin was inevitable. Seydoux to Foreign Ministry, November 14, 1947, Y/296/FFMA. During the crisis, Bevin sometimes took a firm line, but sometimes the British position struck the Americans as too soft. See Shlaim, *United States and the Berlin Blockade,* pp. 198, 212 (for the picture of Britain as very firm), and (for evidence pointing in the other direction) the report of a U.S. cabinet lunch, September 13, 1948, FD/12/FP/ML, and the evidence cited below, note 62. See also Murphy, *Diplomat Among Warriors,* pp. 313, 315.

German state tied to the western world. As a French official laid out the argument in July 1948, the whole thrust of recent events—"the organization of western Europe," "the cutting of Germany in two"—had "major advantages for us." But by agreeing to take part in the occupation of Berlin, the western powers had sacrificed their "freedom of action"; so, as painful as this might be, the West had to find some way to pull out.[60] Bedell Smith's views were not that different. He thought the western powers could hold out in Berlin if they wanted to, but that it made no military sense to maintain a presence in this "exposed salient." He thought, in fact, that it would suit the Russians' purposes "to let us stay on indefinitely." The ambassador in Moscow, a strong supporter of the western strategy, now called explicitly for a withdrawal from the city.[61]

But Marshall and Truman saw things differently. In their view, America was in Berlin by right, and to withdraw ignominiously would have a profound effect on the whole political situation in Europe. They therefore very much wanted to stay on in Berlin. The question was whether this would be possible without a war—or more precisely, whether they should in the final analysis be willing to risk war in order to remain in the city. There were those, not just in the State Department but military officers like General Clay, who had embraced the deterrence philosophy and who felt that the best way to stay without war was to make it abundantly clear that the United States would under no circumstances abandon Berlin, and would in the final analysis go to war rather than capitulate on the issue. The counterargument, which the British and French tended to make, was that the best way to get through the crisis was to avoid confrontation and "leave the issues blurred."[62]

These were difficult issues, and Truman and Marshall were pulled in both directions. When the blockade was imposed, Truman's first reaction was simple and straightforward: "we are going to stay period." He was careful to note, however, that this was "not a final decision." The political leadership soon did decide in principle to take a firm line and to stay on in Berlin no matter what the Soviets did.[63]

[60] Camille Paris, July 18, 1948, quoted in Buffet, *Mourir pour Berlin*, pp. 189–190. Similarly, see Massigli to Chauvel, July 17, 1948, MP/45/FFMA, discussed ibid., pp. 191–192.

[61] PPS meeting, September 28, 1948, FRUS 1948, 2:1194–1196.

[62] Marshall to Clay and Murphy, September 11, 1948, ibid., p. 1148. At a meeting with the Brussels Treaty countries at The Hague on July 19–20, Bevin had urged that the western powers take a relatively soft line on Berlin. He did not want to give in on essentials, but he did not want a confrontation either. He had no doubt, he said, that the Americans would object and accuse him of weakness. If they did, he would respond by asking them how many divisions they would deploy in Europe and what exactly they would bring to the defense of the West. And in fact the Americans did complain about a "definite weakening" in Bevin following his return from the Hague. Marshall characterized a British draft of a note to the Soviets as "redolent with appeasement." "Conférence de la Haye, 19–20 juillet 1948," p. 8, MP/67/FFMA; Marshall to Douglas, July 21, 1948, and Lovett-Douglas-Murphy teletype conference, July 22, 1948, FRUS 1948, 2:975, 978.

[63] *JCS History,* 2:135, 141, 151–152, 154–155; Royall to JCS, June 28, 1948, and Forrestal Diary entry for same date, FD/12/FP/ML. Truman's comment about this not being a "final decision" was deleted from the published *Forrestal Diaries,* p. 454. Note also that a series of "high level conferences" had resulted in a decision to stay in Berlin, and a top secret cable was sent out to Douglas informing him that in pursuit of that policy, the U.S. government was "prepared to use any means that may be necessary"—but the phrase "whatever the consequences" had been deleted before the document was sent out. See Marshall to Douglas, July 20, 1948, FRUS 1948, 2:971, 971n; see also the report of a July 22 NSC decision, ibid., p. 977n.

But in reality the American position on the Berlin question was not quite as firm as it appeared. When Ambassador Douglas, for example, said in April that if Berlin were cut off, America would fight rather than abandon the city, Marshall was quick to correct him. The United States would not "initiate the application of force" over Berlin.[64] As for Truman, he was unwilling even to shoot down a barrage balloon, since he was afraid of starting a war for which the "United States did not have enough soldiers."[65]

The basic American policy, the product of these conflicting feelings, was to put off the really vital decisions about the use of force until they absolutely had to be faced—that is, until the choice really was between war and capitulation. The best answer to the blockade was therefore an airlift, and West Berlin was supplied by air until the blockade was lifted in May 1949. But during that period the possibility of war had to be taken seriously. The Europeans were particularly alarmed. Marshall, returning to Washington in October 1948 after a brief trip to Paris, told President Truman that the Europeans were "completely out of their skin, and sitting on their nerves."[66]

It had in fact been clear from December 1947 on that the two sides were probably headed for a serious confrontation over Germany. This in turn, it was understood, implied that the defense of the West had to be organized, and the sooner the better. This was the theme of the very important talks that Bevin, Bidault, and Marshall had in London on December 17 and 18. Bevin began to call for a west European security organization. The British and French, he told Bidault on December 17, should begin military talks at once. As Bevin laid out his concept a few weeks later for the Americans, Belgium, Holland, and Luxemburg could then be brought in, followed by other western European countries, including Germany "as soon as circumstances permit." It was clear that the system ultimately had to be backed by American power.[67] Bidault agreed that a western defense system needed to be constructed. General Revers, the French Army chief of staff, was sent over to London for talks with his British counterparts. General Billotte, another top French military officer and from 1945 on an advocate of a military alliance with the United States, was sent over to Washington to negotiate a "secret Franco-American military agreement"; Bidault himself had long sought to bring about an arrangement of this sort.[68] In December 1947, moreover, Marshall and Bevin authorized the

[64] Douglas to Marshall, April 28, 1948, and Marshall and Lovett to Douglas, April 30, 1948, FRUS 1948, 2:899–900, 900n. A mere three weeks later, Douglas was telling Massigli that the United States would if necessary be the first to cross this threshold. Massigli to Foreign Ministry, May 20, 1948, MP/67/FFMA. It is not clear whether Douglas had been authorized to make this very important declaration.

[65] Samuel Williamson and Steven Rearden, *The Origins of U.S. Nuclear Strategy, 1945–1953* (New York: St. Martin's, 1993), p. 87.

[66] Quoted in Steven L. Rearden, *History of the Office of the Secretary of Defense,* vol. 1, *The Formative Years, 1947–1950* (Washington, D.C.: OSD Historical Office, 1984), p. 347.

[67] For the Bevin-Bidault and Bidault-Marshall talks, see Y/297/FFMA. For the Bevin-Marshall meeting, see FRUS 1947, 2:815–822; for Bevin's comment, see enclosure to Inverchapel to Marshall, January 13, 1948, FRUS 1948, 3:5. Cyril Buffet was the first scholar to bring out the full importance of these talks; see *Mourir pour Berlin,* p. 72.

[68] "Conversations anglo-françaises," December 17, 1947, p. 10, Y/297/FFMA; Revers report, January 25, 1948, 4Q37/2/SHAT. On Billotte, see Soutou, "La sécurité de la France," and Pierre Guillen,

American and British commanders in Germany to work out a very secret plan for joint military operations in the event of a Soviet attack. No one else was told about it, not even Truman or Attlee. A retreat was of course seen as inevitable. The purpose of the planning was to make sure it did not turn into a rout.[69]

In early 1948, the Europeans pressed hard for a formal American security commitment. They were fortunate that it had been Marshall who had lost patience and had decided on his own at the London conference to end to the talks with Molotov, since now they could say that the Americans had created the problem and could not leave them in the lurch.[70] In the months that followed, both governments, but the French in particular, insisted that the United States was primarily responsible for this very dangerous situation, that they were going along with America, but that they were entitled to something in exchange. Massigli, for example, said during the London talks that the American government was asking France to back an "extremely bold" German policy, one which might well lead the Soviets to take preventive action. If a new war broke out, France was in great danger of being overrun, and French diplomats argued repeatedly that the Americans had to do something about this problem. A formal guarantee of French security was not enough. The Americans had contracted a moral obligation and would not be let off cheaply with mere words. The simple fact that American troops were in Germany meant that if war broke out, America would be in it from the start. The real need now was for something more than a tripwire. Western Europe had to be defended on the ground. The European armies had to be built up with American aid; the U.S. military presence in Europe needed to be strengthened; the western armies should perhaps be welded into an integrated force, commanded by an American general.[71] Thus practically from the start the French were strong supporters of a western defense system under American command. They wanted the American commitment to Europe to be as strong and as "organic" as possible.[72]

The other great argument for a western security system had to do with Germany.

"Les militaires français et la création de l'OTAN," both in Vaïsse, *La France et l'OTAN*, pp. 25, 34, 77; note also General Humbert's analysis which Soutou cites on p. 32. See also Georges-Henri Soutou, "Georges Bidault et la construction europeénne, 1944–1954," in *Le MRP et la construction européenne*, ed. Serge Berstein et al. (Brussels: Complexe, 1993), p. 209, for more information on Billotte and his December 1947 mission to Washington. Soutou notes here that in the spring of 1946 Bidault and Armies Minister Michelet had already wanted to send Billotte to America to negotiate a security arrangement, but that this was blocked at the time by the Socialist prime minister, Félix Gouin.

[69] "Conversation Schuman-Marshall," October 4, 1948, p. 2, Z/Généralités/23/FFMA.

[70] See Bevin's remarks in his talk with Bidault on December 17, "Conversations anglo-françaises," pp. 3–4.

[71] Massigli to Foreign Ministry, May 3, 1948, MP/67/FFMA. See also Chauvel to Bonnet, March 18, 1948, Bidault to Marshall, April 14, 1948, and Chauvel to Bonnet, April 15 and May 19, 1948, all in BP/1/FFMA. In the last of these documents, Chauvel brought up the idea of an organized allied force with an American commander. For the idea that the Americans should not be let off cheaply, see Bidault's comments in "Conférence de la Haye, 19–20 juillet 1948, 2ème partie, les entretiens de Washington," MP/79/FFMA.

[72] See Guillen, "Les militaires français," pp. 78, 87; Pierre Guillen, "La France et la question de la défense de l'Europe occidentale, du pacte de Bruxelles (mars 1948) au plan Pleven (octobre 1950)," *Revue d'histoire de la deuxième guerre mondiale et des conflits contemporains*, no. 144 (1986): 78; and *JCS History*, 2:371.

For Bidault and the French generally, the long-term problem of German power, although now clearly overshadowed by the Russian problem, was still important both intrinsically and for domestic political reasons.[73] The American presence in Germany would keep that country from becoming a problem. In this way the two security problems were in effect merged. It had long been understood that the German threat could serve as cover for arrangements that were really designed to deal with the Russian problem.[74] Now it was becoming clear that measures officially directed against Russia would also serve to keep the Germans in line.

The key to the security problem was an American military commitment, and the U.S. government soon gave the Europeans the assurances they needed. "As long as European Communism threatens US vital interests and national security," Marshall wrote on February 28, "we could ill afford to abandon our military position in Germany." "The logical conclusion," he added, "is that three-power occupation may be of unforeseeable and indefinite duration, thus offering protracted security guarantees and establishing a firm community of interests." The maintenance of the occupation, he pointed out, meant in particular that the French would be secure against Germany.[75] They could thus take a more relaxed view and cooperate more readily with a policy rooted in the idea that western Germany would eventually be treated as a partner.[76]

It seemed that French persistence was now paying off. The U.S. government was making a very important commitment, and the Europeans reacted positively to the new American line. On March 17, Truman declared officially that American forces would remain in Germany until the peace was secure in Europe; this commitment was incorporated into the June 1 three-power agreement on Germany, thus giving it a certain contractual force. The French also received satisfaction on another point. The June 1 agreement called for a coordinated policy for dealing with the Soviet reaction to what the western powers now intended to do in Germany. The security arrangements were thus an integral part of the agreement reached on Germany, in a political as well as in a legal sense. This was particularly true in the French case: it was because France was receiving satisfaction in the security area that Bidault, as French officials pointed out at the time, was able to move openly toward a policy of "complete collaboration with the Anglo-Saxons" on the German question. The various commitments made during the negotiating process were adding up to a system; the central pillar of that system was a more or less permanent American military presence in Germany.[77]

---

[73] A passage from a Chauvel letter catches the prevailing mood nicely: "Il est une autre sorte de garantie, bien que moins actuelle et même un peu perdue de vue depuis quelque temps, qui nous intéresse néanmoins: il s'agit de la garantie contre l'Allemagne." Chauvel to Bonnet, April 21, 1948, BP/1/FFMA.

[74] See appendix 2, "The German Threat as a Pretext for Defense against Russia" (IS).

[75] Marshall to Douglas, February 28, 1948, 2:101.

[76] Douglas to Marshall, March 2, 1948, ibid., pp. 110–111.

[77] For the European reaction to the new U.S. commitment, see Douglas to Marshall, March 2, 1948, and Douglas to Lovett, March 6, 1948, ibid., pp. 111, 138–139. For Truman's declaration, see DOSB, March 28, 1948, p. 420. For the formal security commitment and the agreement to coordinate policy, see the London conference report, June 1, 1948, agreed paper on security (Annex L of the report), and London communiqué, June 7, 1948, ibid., pp. 292, 312, 316. For the point about France being able

Events now moved quickly. On March 17 the Brussels Treaty was signed by Britain, France, and the Benelux countries.[78] A common organization for the defense of western Europe was to be created. The U.S. government had originally insisted that the Europeans take the lead in this area, and the main purpose of Anglo-French cooperation was to pave the way for American involvement.[79] But the Americans now wanted to move ahead rapidly, and even before the Brussels Treaty was signed, Marshall informed the British and French that the United States was ready to discuss "the establishment of an Atlantic security system."[80] By May 11, the American government had agreed to take part in military talks with the Europeans.[81]

A basic security pact, the North Atlantic Treaty, was finally signed in April 1949. This very important agreement was to be the heart of the western security system for the entire Cold War period and beyond.[82] The next month the Berlin blockade was lifted, and the Basic Law of the Federal Republic of Germany was approved; elections were held that summer, and a West German government took office in September. Soon the Soviets created their own German state in the east, which for years would often be referred to in the West as the "so-called German Democratic Republic." Europe was now formally divided into blocs.

This did not mean that a stable political system had finally taken shape. The ending of the blockade did not mean that the Soviets had accepted the new status quo, or that they were ready to give the western powers a free hand on their side of the line of demarcation. Western Germany remained a very fundamental Soviet concern. But the military situation was such that the USSR for the time being could not push things any further.

A PRECARIOUS BALANCE

In 1948–49, neither side was willing to press the issue too close to the point of an armed confrontation. In the case of the Berlin blockade, the most serious episode

to cooperate on Germany because of what her partners had agreed to in the security area, see Chauvel to Bonnet, August 3, 1948, BP/1/FFMA. To understand how all these agreements added up to a system, see the London conference report (with twelve annexes cited in the footnotes), FRUS 1948, 2:309–312.

[78] See Maurice Vaïsse, "L'échec d'une Europe franco-britannique, ou comment le pacte de Bruxelles fut créé et délaissé," in Poidevin, *Histoire des débuts*, pp. 369–389.

[79] Lovett-Inverchapel meeting, February 7, 1948, and Marshall to Embassy in France, February 27, 1948, FRUS 1948, 3:23, 34.

[80] Marshall to Inverchapel and Marshall to Bidault, both March 12, 1948, ibid., pp. 48, 50.

[81] Lovett to Douglas, May 11, 1948, ibid., 2:233n. Bevin and Bidault had asked for the talks in a top secret letter to Marshall on April 17; see ibid., 3:91.

[82] For an account of the making of the North Atlantic Treaty which emphasizes the German question, see Ireland, *Creating the Entangling Alliance*. See also Kaplan, *The United States and NATO*; Baylis, *The Diplomacy of Pragmatism*; Don Cook, *Forging the Alliance: NATO, 1945–1950* (London: Arbor House, 1989); Nikolaj Petersen, "Who Pulled Whom and How Much? Britain, the United States and the Making of the North Atlantic Treaty," *Millenium: Journal of International Studies* 11, no. 2 (1982), 93–114; and the various articles in Joseph Smith, ed., *The Origins of NATO* (Exeter: University of Exeter Press, 1990), esp. Norbert Wiggershaus, "The German Question and the Foundation of the Atlantic Pact."

of the Cold War up to that point, Soviet policy was not nearly as confrontational as many western officials had feared. The airlift, for example, was successful because the Soviets chose not to interfere with it. Even nonviolent measures, especially the jamming of radars, would have gone a long way toward compromising its effectiveness. But the Soviets continued to work with western officials at the Berlin Air Safety Center, managing the air routes into the city, and thus bizarrely "doing something to help the airlift which was undermining their blockade."[83] And one is struck by the relatively friendly tone of U.S.–Soviet diplomatic interaction during the crisis: on July 31, for example, Molotov still referred to the four powers as "partners in Germany."[84]

The Americans, for their part, also ruled out extreme measures and sought to settle the crisis peacefully. In regional disputes more generally, the U.S. government felt at this point that it had to pursue a very cautious policy. The basic problem was that the American demobilization after World War II had been extremely rapid, and that by 1947 not much was left of the very impressive military machine that had been built up by 1945. It was not just that military manpower had dwindled from about twelve million at the end of the war to a mere one and a half million in mid-1947. "In terms of effective combat power," as the official JCS history points out, "the decline was even more striking." The United States had ninety-seven ground divisions at the end of the war, "all at a high pitch of combat effectiveness." Two years later, there were only twelve divisions, all under strength and most of them committed to occupation duties, with only two weakened Army divisions remaining in the general reserve based in the United States. In terms of air power, the story was the same. Very few operationally effective units remained, and none of units that were supposed to carry out the nuclear attack "was fully manned or operational." Thus by 1947 the extraordinarily powerful force that had been built up during the war "had almost ceased to exist."[85]

The result was that American leaders felt they could not really pursue a firm policy of containment in this period. It might have been "the policy of the United States to support free peoples who are resisting attempted subjugation by armed minorities or by outside pressures," as the president proclaimed in the Truman Doctrine speech in March 1947, but this policy was more honored in the breach than in the observance. The United States, for example, did not lift a finger to help the non-Communist side in Czechoslovakia when the political crisis in that country came to a head a few months later. On Korea, to take another example, the Chiefs argued strongly for a policy of disengagement, and their views ultimately prevailed. The key decision to withdraw "as soon as possible with the minimum of bad effect" was made in September 1947.[86] In late 1947 and at the beginning

---

[83] Tusa, *Berlin Blockade*, p. 274. On the non-jamming of the radars, see Richard Kohn and Joseph Harahan, eds., *Strategic Air Warfare: An Interview with Generals Curtis E. LeMay, Leon W. Johnson, David A. Burchinal and Jack J. Catton* (Washington, D.C.: Office of Air Force History, 1988), pp. 85–86.

[84] Smith to Marshall, July 31, 1948, FRUS 1948, 2:998. Note also Clay's comments in the NSC on July 22 about how the Soviets, whose attitude had been marked by "truculence and arrogance" just a few months ago, had now become "highly correct and considerate." FD/12/FP/ML.

[85] *JCS History*, 2:18–19.

[86] Butterworth to Lovett, October 1, 1947, FRUS 1947, 6:820–821. For the best analysis, see

of 1948, major decisions also had to be made about the use of American troops to prevent possible Communist takeovers in Italy and Greece. Certain State Department officials, especially Loy Henderson, the director of the Office of Near Eastern and African Affairs, wanted America to opt for a deterrent strategy, and felt that if America sent a small force into Greece as a demonstration of resolve, the Soviets would back off. No matter what the local military balance, these officials argued, the USSR would not take action that might lead to general war.[87] But the military authorities, who just a few years later were to embrace the deterrence philosophy with great zeal, now simply refused to see matters in those terms. They resented the idea that U.S. forces would be mere pawns in an essentially political game, and insisted on tests of "military soundness" that ruled out the deployment of troops. One top Army general, for example, told a Senate committee that he was "much opposed" to sending combat forces to Greece, that such a deployment would be a "'mousetrap' operation from the strategic viewpoint," and that this reasoning "applied to the entire Mediterranean" as a "possible theater of operations." These views were "characteristic of the general line of thinking" within military circles in Washington on the Greek question.[88]

In these disputes, the political leadership generally took the middle road. Truman and Marshall did not want to abandon key areas to the Communists, but neither of them was willing to commit American power to a full-fledged policy of containment. In early 1948, for example, when there was a real fear that both Greece and Italy would be lost to the Communists, the U.S. government did not adopt a policy of doing whatever was necessary to prevent them from falling into Communist hands—and this was true even though both countries lay within what had long been regarded as a western sphere of influence. On Italy, it was decided that American forces would in no event be sent to the Italian mainland, even if the Communists seized power there illegally; at most, forces might be sent to Sicily and Sardinia in the event of an illegal seizure of power by the Communists on the peninsula, but only if they were invited in by the legal government.[89] On Greece, the Henderson idea of being ready to send in troops as a demonstration of resolve was rejected. Marshall, of course, worried that if America took a weak line, she would "lose the game" and "our whole national position" would be compromised, but he was also deeply concerned about where a commitment of U.S. forces would lead. The problem was that if forces were deployed and then came under "heavy Soviet pressure," they would have to be either "backed up" or withdrawn "ignominiously." He felt that American military power had to be employed selectively:

William Stueck, *The Road to Confrontation: American Policy toward China and Korea, 1947–1950* (Chapel Hill: University of North Carolina Press, 1981), esp. pp. 75, 86–88.

[87] See especially Henderson to Marshall, January 9, 1948, and Hickerson to Lovett, June 1, 1948, FRUS 1948, 4:9–14, 98–99. Henderson's views had been reflected in the draft policy paper on Greece, NSC 5 of January 6, 1948, ibid., pp. 2–8. See also Henderson to McWilliams, February 10, 1948, ibid., p. 39.

[88] Henderson to Rankin, March 25, 1948, ibid., pp. 64–65. For JCS views, see JCS to Forrestal, January 8, 1948, and NSC 5/3, May 25, 1948, ibid., pp. 8, 94–95; see also *JCS History*, 2:28, 43–48.

[89] See NSC 1/2, February 10, 1948, FRUS 1948, 3:767–769.

"it was necessary to conserve our limited strength and apply it only where it was likely to be most effective."[90]

Was this, however, just foolishness on Marshall's part? Shouldn't he have understood that the American nuclear monopoly was such a powerful trump card that the United States could take a much tougher line in any disputes that developed, and that the Soviets would be sure to back down rather than face a general war with America that they would certainly end up losing? The answer is that the policies the U.S. government pursued made sense, given the strategic realities of the day.

What in fact was the situation as it appeared to policymakers at the time? First of all, it was universally understood that if war broke out, Europe would be overrun; but then the United States would gear up and begin a sustained campaign of atomic bombardment. To be sure, the initial American atomic strike on Russia would have only a limited effect on Soviet war-making capabilities. The fission bombs then in the American arsenal were of relatively limited destructive power, with a yield of only twenty-two kilotons; there were not many of them during this period—only thirteen in mid-1947 and only fifty a year later. Intelligence was poor and target selection was a problem; and it was not clear whether the bombs could be delivered on target in any case. But as long as it was a question of a purely one-sided air-atomic war, these problems, no matter how serious, would not affect the outcome of the conflict. Russian industry and war-making power would gradually be destroyed with bombs and bombers produced after the war had started. The United States was sure to win in the end. The Soviets would not start a war because they knew that an American victory would be simply a matter of time.[91]

American leaders were aware of these fundamental military realities. Indeed, it was because they understood the enormous significance of the American nuclear monopoly that they felt able to adopt the sort of military policy they did. The nuclear monopoly—the fact that the United States was bound to prevail in the end, no matter what happened during the initial phase of the war—meant that the United States did not have to maintain a massive military establishment, or deploy forces in western Europe capable of defending that area on the ground. The West could settle for a tripwire strategy. Very powerful, and very expensive, forces in

[90] Henderson's paraphrase of Marshall's informal testimony, in Henderson to Rankin, March 25, 1948, ibid., 4:64–65. For U.S. policy on Greece, see especially the minutes of NSC discussions of December 17, 1947, January 13 and February 12, 1948, President's Secretary's Files [PSF], HSTL. For other key documents bearing on the question, see FRUS 1948, 4:46–51, 93–95, 101, 205–208.

[91] On these matters in general, see Williamson and Rearden, *Origins of U.S. Nuclear Strategy,* and Trachtenberg, *History and Strategy,* pp. 119–121, 153–158. By far the most important work on American nuclear strategy was done by David Rosenberg. See especially the parts of two of his articles dealing with these issues: "American Atomic Strategy and the Hydrogen Bomb Decision," *Journal of American History* 66 (June 1979): 62–87, and "The Origins of Overkill: Nuclear Weapons and American Strategy, 1945–1960," *International Security* 7 (Spring 1983): 9–16. The two most important documents bearing on the problems America would face at the very beginning of a war are the Harmon and Hull reports of May 1949 and February 1950, analyzed in Rosenberg, "American Atomic Strategy and the Hydrogen Bomb Decision," p. 16, and in Richard Rowe, "American Nuclear Strategy and the Korean War" (M.A. thesis, University of Pennsylvania, 1984), pp. 26ff. For figures on yield and stockpile size, see Rearden, *The Formative Years,* p. 439.

being—in particular, ground forces in Europe—were not absolutely essential. The economic recovery of western Europe was a more pressing need. If the continent was not to be lost, this, and not the military area proper, was where limited resources had to be invested.[92]

But U.S. leaders also understood that the acceptance of a tripwire strategy inevitably limited their freedom of action. If war did break out, once the Soviets had overrun western Europe they would try to integrate the European economy into their war-making machine. America in turn would then have to bomb her own allies. This bombing, along with the ground war and the Soviet occupation, would devastate Europe. As Truman himself pointed out to the NATO foreign ministers in April 1949, "a Soviet attack today, while we could eventually defeat it, would involve an operation of incalculable magnitude in which, even if eventual victory is sure, the consequences to the US, and particularly to Western Europe itself, might well be disastrous." The American victory, in other words, would be Pyrrhic. The U.S. government, and even more the European governments, could scarcely relish the prospect of such a war, even if ultimate victory for the West was certain, and America herself could not take too tough a line for fear of alienating her main allies. And of course the Soviets understood that the western powers would be reluctant to take too unyielding or too belligerent a line in political disputes, and that this meant that they had a good deal of room for political maneuver.[93]

American leaders, in 1948 especially, were sensitive to all these problems. The Joint Chiefs of Staff in particular constantly hammered away at the point that American military resources were overextended. American commitments were not in line with the country's military capabilities: this was the central theme of the constant drumbeat of criticism coming from the military authorities.[94] And the political leadership was also very uncomfortable with the situation. As Marshall put it at a key NSC meeting on February 12: "The trouble was that we are playing with fire while we have nothing with which to put it out."[95] Marshall felt that "without even a token military establishment in being" he was skating on thin ice and had to proceed very cautiously. But he also felt that nothing could be done about the problem. "The country," he said, "could not, and would not, support a budget based on preparation for war."[96] In 1948, neither he nor Truman was willing to back a significant increase in the military budget.[97]

[92] See, for example, James Forrestal to Chan Gurney, December 8, 1947, *Forrestal Diaries,* pp. 350–351.

[93] Truman talk to Atlantic Pact foreign ministers, April 3, 1949, *Vierteljahrshefte für Zeitgeschichte* 40 (1992): 416. Note especially the reference here to the problem of using the bomb "against our occupied Western European allies." Note also the reference in a later American document to the "current JCS strategy" of attacking targets in western Europe, such as the Ruhr, in the "event of their take-over by the Soviets so as to deny additional military capabilities to the enemy." Fuller paper on U.S. policy toward Europe, September 10, 1954, FRUS 1952–54, 5:1171.

[94] *JCS History,* 2:360 and 3(1):12–28. *Forrestal Diaries,* pp. 374–377. Bradley to Joint Chiefs, March 11, 1948; Marshall to Forrestal, March 23, 1948; Forrestal to NSC, April 17 and 19, 1948; in FRUS 1948, 1:539–540, 541–542, 563–564, 566.

[95] NSC minutes, February 12, 1948, PSF/HSTL. See also *Forrestal Diaries,* p. 373.

[96] Marshall to Lovett, November 8, 1948, FRUS 1948, 1:655.

[97] *JCS History,* 2:164 and chap. 7; Marshall to Forrestal, November 8, 1948, FRUS 1948, 1:655; Rearden, *The Formative Years,* p. 319.

What this situation meant was that the defense of the West rested on a very narrow base. Even with the nuclear monopoly, American power only barely balanced Soviet power in central Europe. It followed that as soon as that monopoly was broken, the situation would be transformed radically, and practically overnight. The USSR would be much freer to press ahead on the German question. And this was exactly what happened: the Soviets exploded their first nuclear device in August 1949, and the world moved rapidly into a period of great crisis.

• PART II •

The NATO System

The Making of the NATO System

BY 1949 Europe was divided between east and west. Each side had "organized" its part of Germany and had incorporated it into its bloc. But the division of Europe did not lead directly to a stable peace. It was not as though the two sides now had little choice but to accept things as they were—that American and Soviet power now balanced each other so completely that both sides were locked into the status quo, and that both sides now knew that coexistence was the only viable option. The Soviets still felt that the question of German power, meaning now West German power, was a matter of utmost importance. Given how much they had suffered at Germany's hands during the war, they believed that they had the right to do whatever was necessary to prevent Germany from again being able to threaten their most basic interests, and that how far they would go in giving point to these concerns was solely a question of expediency. If the military balance was unfavorable, then a tough policy, leading perhaps to an outright military confrontation, would obviously have to be avoided. But if that situation changed, they might well be able to take a much harder line.

In late 1949 the balance did shift, suddenly and dramatically. The American nuclear monopoly was the one thing that had balanced Soviet superiority in ground forces in Europe; now, with the breaking of that monopoly, the Soviets were in a much better position to accept a showdown with the West. Indeed, by 1950, the USSR seemed to be getting ready for a real confrontation. Stalin told the Chinese in October of that year that the United States "was not prepared at the present time for a big war" and countries like Germany and Japan were currently unable to provide America with any real military support. The communist side, on the other hand, was in a strong position and need not fear an all-out war with the West. "If war is inevitable," he said, "let it happen now."[1]

The western powers were thus now faced with very serious problems. As western leaders saw the situation, their current difficulties were rooted in their military weakness, and the conclusion they drew was that they had to build up their military power, and build it up quickly. Western Europe had to be defended on the ground, and it was obvious that sooner or later German troops would be needed for that purpose. But German rearmament implied a transformation of the Federal Republic's political status: the occupation regime would have to be ended, and the German state would become stronger and more independent.

The problem was that movement in this direction might itself lead directly to

---

[1] Stalin to Mao, October 1, 1950, quoted in Stalin to Shtykov, October 7, 1950, cited in Zubok and Pleshakov, *Inside the Kremlin's Cold War*, pp. 66–67, and published in CWIHP *Bulletin*, nos. 6–7 (Winter 1995–96): 116. Note also Stalin's advice to the Chinese in early December 1950 to continue their advance in Korea—to "beat the iron while it is hot"—quoted in Mastny, *The Cold War and Soviet Insecurity,* p. 111.

war. The buildup of western power meant that the Soviets might feel that it was a question of now or never, and that they needed to act before the balance turned against them. A buildup of German power, involving as it did the restoration of German political rights, touched on a particularly sensitive Soviet nerve. The system of constraints on German power, the Russians were bound to feel, was disintegrating rapidly, and there was no telling how far this process would go. It might therefore make sense for them to act quickly, and deal with the threat before things got completely out of hand.

By the end of 1950, it seemed that the two sides were on a collision course and that a third world war might well be imminent. But in this atmosphere of crisis a system began to take shape which might have served as the basis of a stable peace in Europe. By October 1954, a whole series of interlocking agreements had been worked out. West Germany would be rearmed and would join NATO; Germany's political rights would in large measure be restored; but German sovereignty, German freedom of action, and German military power would be limited in major ways. The Germans, however, could accept the system, because it offered real protection against the threat from the east. And although the western system was directed against the USSR, it was in the final analysis something the Russians could also live with, since it solved their number one security problem, the threat of a resurgent and revisionist Germany. But a viable system depended also on strong American involvement, and this turned out to be the most problematic element in the equation. What role would the United States play in Europe? Would America remain the dominant force in the western alliance, or would the Europeans eventually have to provide for their own defense?

FROM TRIPWIRE STRATEGY TO FORWARD DEFENSE

In the late 1940s, Soviet pressure on western Europe was balanced by the American nuclear monopoly. Even the great industrial strength of the United States, it was understood, might not be enough in itself to keep the USSR at bay. If the Soviets overran western Europe and harnessed the vast resources of that region to their own war machine, they could confront America as an equal in terms of military-industrial potential. If it were not for nuclear weapons, this great Soviet-dominated bloc might well be unconquerable, and indeed might in the long run be more than a match for the United States. The American nuclear monopoly, on the other hand, meant that a U.S. victory in a third world war would be just a matter of time. Since the ultimate outcome was so clear, one could in the final analysis rely on a tripwire strategy for the defense of western Europe. It had to be made clear, of course, that an attack on Europe would lead to a nuclear war of this sort.[2] But if this were done, defense spending could be kept to a minimum and limited resources could be used elsewhere. The United State could concentrate on helping western Europe recover economically. Taxes at home could remain low, and

---

[2] The point was stressed by Marshall in meetings with Schuman and Bevin in October 1948. See Schuman–Marshall meeting, October 4, 1948, p. 4, Z/Généralités/23/FFMA, and Schuman-Marshall-Bevin meeting, October 5, 1948, pp. 7–8, BP/1/FFMA.

a generation of Americans that had struggled through long years of depression and war could perhaps now begin to enjoy a somewhat more comfortable life.

The tripwire strategy was by no means ideal. If general war broke out, Europe would be overrun and would have to be reconquered. The Europeans especially would scarcely relish the prospect of such a war, no matter who was sure to win in the end. In the late 1940s, the western powers had therefore been reluctant to take a tough line in their conflict with the USSR. In the various disputes that developed, western leaders felt themselves to be skating on thin ice. This was not a very comfortable situation, but on balance American and allied statesmen were willing to live with it—at least for the time being, until Europe had recovered economically and defense could be given a higher priority. It was, however, clear even then that sooner or later western Europe would have to be defended on the ground. The American nuclear monopoly would certainly not last forever, and when it was broken the whole basis of western defense strategy would have to be reconsidered. But in the late 1940s, as unsatisfactory as the situation was in some ultimate sense, the development of an effective defense in western Europe was not viewed as a matter of high urgency.

With the breaking of the American nuclear monopoly in August 1949, everything changed practically overnight. A final American victory in a general war could no longer be taken for granted. Nuclear weapons would certainly be used by both sides in such a war; each side could absorb very large numbers of those early atomic bombs and still survive as a functioning society. And those air-atomic offensives would dominate the war.

America and Russia, in such a war, would be racing against each other. In the period when only the United States could produce what was bound to be the decisive weapon, the Americans could go about destroying their enemy in a more or less leisurely fashion. Now suddenly time was of the essence. Each side's goal in a two-sided air-atomic war would be to gain a heavy advantage for itself in mobilizable war potential, which could then be used to develop a general military superiority in the sort of long war that was then anticipated. The aim of the bombing would therefore be to destroy as much as one could of the enemy's military-industrial power as quickly as one could, while protecting and indeed if possible building up one's own power base. To achieve this kind of superiority, it would be necessary to move with great speed. The top priority for each side would be to destroy and keep on destroying the enemy's air-atomic capability—his bombs and bombers and air bases, his nuclear and aircraft production facilities— as quickly and as thoroughly as possible. The faster and more effective the attack, the less able the enemy would be to mount a counterattack directed against similar targets in one's own homeland: thus the enormous premium placed on a rapid, massive, intensive bombing campaign—on forces in being as opposed to mobilizable war potential, on military readiness and effective command arrangements, and on adequate intelligence and secure overseas bases. Once success in this vital area had been achieved, the final outcome of the conflict would not be in doubt.

But it was by no means clear which side would win this race. From the American point of view, all of the problems relating to the small size of the stockpile, the inadequacy of military intelligence, the unreliability of the basing system, and so on, which had not mattered all that much during the period of the nuclear monopoly, were now suddenly seen as far more serious. And America herself was from the outset vulnerable to Soviet attack with TU-4 bombers on one-way missions. The Soviets knew where the American air bases and bomb stockpiles were, and a Soviet surprise attack might have a devastating impact on America's ability to recover and mount the kind of bombing campaign that would enable her to go on and win the war. The Soviets themselves, perhaps drawing on the great industrial and technological resources of western Europe, might ultimately be able to outproduce the United States in bombs and bombers, destroying American nuclear and aircraft facilities more quickly than the Americans were able to destroy theirs, thus permitting them to develop a general nuclear superiority which would guarantee ultimate victory in the war. Certainly an American victory in such a conflict could no longer be taken for granted. As General Omar Bradley, chairman of the U.S. Joint Chiefs of Staff, told the NSC in November 1950, if a global war were to break out, "we might be in danger of losing."[3]

American leaders expected the Soviets to be emboldened by this situation and looked for signs of an upsurge in Soviet aggressiveness. The evidence was not long in coming. The Soviets, for example, were telling the east European Communist leaders that their side currently enjoyed a strategic edge, that their superiority in Europe was, however, merely transitory and would not last for more than a few years, and that the time for action had now come.[4] The western governments got wind of this through intelligence channels, the east European regimes being far more effectively penetrated than the USSR itself.[5] The Soviets themselves were making extensive material preparations for a global conflict. Their economy was being placed on a war footing. In August 1950 the CIA outlined some of the most revealing material indicators:

> A program of extensive industrial mobilization for production of war materiel began throughout the Soviet Orbit about January 1949. Conversion of most plants in the entire Soviet Orbit scheduled to be converted under this program was completed by Jan-

[3] See, for example, Trachtenberg, *History and Strategy*, pp. 19, 107–108, 119 (for the Bradley quotation), 135. For the Soviet strike capability even in 1950, see CIA Intelligence Memorandum No. 323-SRC, "Soviet Preparations for Major Hostilities in 1950," August 25, 1950, Declassified Documents Reference System [DDRS] 1987/3151; and NIE 3, "Soviet Capabilities and Intentions," November 15, 1950, in *Selected Estimates on the Soviet Union, 1950–1959*, ed. Scott Koch (Washington, D.C.: CIA Center for the Study of Intelligence, 1993), pp. 172, 174.

[4] See especially Karel Kaplan, *Dans les archives du Comité Central* (Paris: Albin Michel, 1978), pp. 94, 162–166, and Kaplan's "Il piano di Stalin," *Panorama*, April 26, 1977. Kaplan is a Czech historian who had access to Czech documents during the 1960s. Note also the evidence that the Soviets were getting ready to attack Yugoslavia. See Béla Király, "The Aborted Soviet Military Plans against Tito's Yugoslavia," in *At the Brink of War and Peace: The Tito-Stalin Split in a Historic Perspective*, ed. Wayne Vucinich (New York: Brooklyn College Press, 1982), pp. 273–288; Beatrice Heuser, *Western "Containment" Policies in the Cold War: The Yugoslav Case, 1948–53* (London: Routledge, 1989), pp. 127–129; Mastny, *The Cold War and Soviet Insecurity*, pp. 71–72, 102.

[5] See, for example, Kennan's and Acheson's comments in the "Princeton Seminar," the transcript of a series of discussions held in Princeton in late 1953 and early 1954, pp. 1189–1190, Acheson Papers [AP], box 76, HSTL, and the intelligence briefing on "Soviet Activity in Europe during the past year which points toward offensive military operations," October 26, 1950, CD 350.09, RG 330 (July–December 1950 series), USNA.

uary 1950. Conversion of installations requiring major industrial readjustments will be completed in September or October 1950. Current industrial production plus the large stocks of military and civilian supplies which have been built up, are sufficient to support major operations. The current reserves stockpiling program has virtually been completed, with a flooding of reserves depots; the production of high octane aviation, jet, and diesel fuel has been stepped up beyond current consumption requirements and is straining storage capacity. (This is significant because part of the increase in aviation fuel stocks has been achieved by the use of stocks of components which are much more stable in storage than when blended in finished fuel.) In certain peripheral areas, military air fields are being rushed to completion; and supplies needed to support military operations have been moving into forward areas.[6]

As a result, as another intelligence report pointed out in early 1951, the USSR had been in "an advanced stage of readiness for war" since mid-1950 at least.[7]

In early 1950, American officials were coming to think that some Soviet action was imminent—perhaps against Yugoslavia, or around Berlin, or in Korea. As it turned out, of course, the North Koreans launched their attack on South Korea in June 1950. It was taken for granted—correctly, as we now know—that Stalin had approved the attack in advance. This act of military aggression was so overt that the American government, reversing its prior policy of disengagement from Korea, decided to intervene. But the fact of blatant armed aggression showed how dangerous the general situation had become. And then, of course, there was the obvious parallel between the two divided countries, Korea and Germany. The Soviets had set up a communist regime in East Germany, which they were now arming. Would East German forces be used as the spearhead of an attack on West Germany? East German leaders were suggesting that what had happened in Korea might well be repeated in central Europe, and defecting East German troops revealed that they had been training for action against the Federal Republic.[8]

In the fall of 1950 the situation worsened. Stalin might not have expected the United States to intervene in Korea when he gave the North Koreans the green light. The Americans, after all, had given many indications that they had written off South Korea. But now in November Communist China was coming into the war, inflicting serious defeats on U.S. forces and threatening to push America not

[6] Central Intelligence Agency, "Soviet Preparations for Major Hostilities in 1950," August 25, 1950, DDRS 1987/3151.

[7] Extract from the Intelligence Advisory Committee's "Weekly Report of Indications of Soviet Communist Intentions," May 23, 1951, FRUS 1951, 1:85–86. See also NIE 3, November 15, 1950, in Koch, *Selected Estimates,* pp. 169–178; NIE-15, December 11, 1950; NIE-25, August 2, 1951; and Watch Committee Circular Airgram, August 24, 1951, quoted in FRUS 1951, 1:7, 126, 169n. On the NIEs, see the editorial note in FRUS 1951, 1:4n.

[8] See Trachtenberg, *History and Strategy,* pp. 113–114. For the East Germans' threats, and in particular for their references to Korea, see Norbert Wiggershaus, "Bedrohungsvorstellungen Bundeskanzler Adenauers nach Ausbruch des Korea-Krieges," *Militärgeschichtliche Mitteilungen,* no. 1 (1979): pp. 101–103; Konrad Adenauer, *Memoirs 1945–1953* (Chicago: Regnery, 1966), pp. 274–275; Thomas Schwartz, *America's Germany: John J. McCloy and the Federal Republic of Germany* (Cambridge, Mass.: Harvard University Press, 1991), p. 126. Some typical threats cited by Schwartz are quoted in Trachtenberg, *History and Strategy,* p. 151n. On the East German defectors, see Gerhard Wettig, *Entmilitarisierung und Wiederbewaffnung in Deutschland, 1943–1955* (Munich: Oldenbourg, 1967), p. 225.

just out of North Korea but entirely off the Korean peninsula. This was a much more serious act than the initial North Korean invasion in June. It meant that the Communists had consciously decided to take on the United States in a major way. Why were they being so aggressive? Was it because they viewed the military situation as so favorable? Was it because they were tempted to precipitate a third world war at a time when victory might actually be within their reach?[9]

These were dark days for America, this period in late 1950 and early 1951, and it was a frightening time for Europe as well. The one thing that was clear was that the military balance would have to be rectified quickly, and that indeed a massive effort would be required. This, it was understood, entailed the risk that Stalin would be provoked into action—that he might feel that he would have to move before the western buildup wiped out the military edge he now enjoyed and made it impossible for him to accept a confrontation with the West. A real military showdown would of course be very risky, but if it was a question of now or never, perhaps he would be well advised to bring matters to a head while he still had a good chance of winning a war. U.S. leaders assumed that Stalin was poised on the brink and therefore held back from certain measures, relating especially to an expansion of the Korean conflict, which they were afraid might tip the balance and lead the Soviets to opt for general war. But on the central issue of building up U.S. military power they were undeterred. The risks of a buildup were clear, but Truman and Acheson—now secretary of state—would not be intimidated into accepting a situation where the USSR had the upper hand. The low military spending policy of the late 1940s was now seen as a terrible mistake. But the fact that a great error had been made then was no reason for holding back from a massive buildup now. And extraordinary steps were taken, especially in December 1950. Military spending more than tripled, and only a small fraction of the increase was directly related to the Korean War. The European allies also began to build up their military forces, both with American assistance and through greatly expanded defense budgets of their own.[10]

This enormous buildup had two main military objectives. The United States wanted to be able to launch a decisive attack on the Soviet homeland, and above all on the Soviet nuclear force, at the very start of a war; the Americans also wanted to be able to keep western Europe from being overrun. For Europe, it was now clear, had to be defended on the ground, and as far to the east as possible. Even in early 1949 it had been obvious that this strategy—what was called "forward defense"—was the only one that could hold the western alliance together over the long run. General Bradley, then U.S. Army chief of staff, made the point quite eloquently at the time. "It must be perfectly apparent to the people of the United

[9] Note Acheson's remarks, quoted in Trachtenberg, *History and Strategy,* p. 114, n. 46. See also *JCS History,* 4:67, 79.

[10] See Trachtenberg, *History and Strategy,* pp. 112–114, 123, 126–128. For the point that the extreme postwar demobilization had been a mistake, note, for example, Truman's remarks in the NSC in March 1952. The U.S. government, he said, had torn "up our military machine" after the war. "Everyone was involved in that development, and it is impossible to put the blame any one place." NSC minutes, March 24, 1952, PSF/220/HSTL. For data on the increase in allied defense spending, see extracts from briefing book for Eisenhower, and Cabot memorandum, March 27, 1951, FRUS 1951, 3:6, 104.

States," he said, "that we cannot count on friends in Western Europe if our strategy in the event of war dictates that we shall first abandon them to the enemy with a promise of later liberation." And yet that was what would happen under the then current strategy of relying on air power and wartime mobilization. That strategy, Bradley argued, would produce "nothing better than impotent and disillusioned Allies in the event of a war." If the people of western Europe were to be asked "to stake their lives on the common cause," the West would need a strategy that could offer them real security, and America, he said, would have to move toward a strategy of "sharing our strength" with the Europeans "on a common defensive front."[11]

With the U.S. nuclear monopoly broken, these arguments carried much greater force. The Soviets, it was assumed, would be more aggressive in this new strategic environment. They might well calculate that the prospect of a two-sided atomic war would lead the United States to back down. The weakening of the U.S. nuclear guarantee would thus mean that the USSR would feel freer to push ahead aggressively in political disputes. It also meant that it was more important than ever that a strong ground defense be built up in western Europe. This basic political argument was supported by a whole series of military arguments, which were particularly compelling in the context of a two-sided air-atomic war: arguments about the importance of avoiding the loss to the Soviet Union of western Europe with its great human and economic resources, which might be decisive in a long military conflict; arguments about the need to provide defense in some minimal depth for the U.S. medium bombers based in England; arguments about how essential it was to maintain a foothold on the continent, since a repeat of the Normandy invasion would obviously be impossible if the USSR possessed any nuclear weapons at all.

The basic point about the importance of an effective forward defense applied with particular force to western Germany. If the Germans were to stand with the West, they obviously had to be defended. As Acheson, for example, pointed out, one had to "offer security to Germany" if she were to be "irrevocably aligned" with the western powers.[12] Moreover, if the rest of western Europe was to be defended, the NATO allies would have to fight on German soil. Including German territory in the area of military operations was necessary if the western armies were to have any room for maneuver at all—and they needed to be able to maneuver, since fixed positions would be quickly overwhelmed.[13] If the war was to be fought in Germany, the cooperation of the German civil authorities would be of considerable value; but Germany would cooperate as an ally only if she were defended as an ally. If, on the other hand, the allies simply viewed German territory as the scene of military operations and not as an area to be defended, the effect on German opinion could be catastrophic. The French military authorities did in fact regard Germany as a buffer area. This was a natural attitude for people who thought in military terms to take: British military leaders, for example, were reluctant to commit themselves fully to the defense of continental Europe, and some of their Amer-

---

[11] Bradley remarks of April 5, 1949, quoted in draft aide-mémoire attached to Ives memo, June 24, 1949, CD 6-4-18, RG 330, 1947–50 series, USNA.

[12] Acheson to acting secretary, May 9, 1950, FRUS 1950, 3:1015.

[13] For a typical argument along these lines, see Secretariat Général de la Défense Nationale, "Note sur un système de sécurité en Europe," August 29, 1955, Europe 1949–55/Généralités/100/FFMA.

ican counterparts tended to feel the same way about Europe as a whole. But in each case that attitude was bound to be a source of resentment in the forward area. West Germany, as the most exposed area, and the country whose status as an ally was the most problematic, was particularly sensitive to this sort of problem. Kurt Schumacher, the leader of the German Social Democratic Party, the main opposition group in the Federal Republic, used this argument to discredit the pro-western policy of the West German government, headed from the start by Konrad Adenauer. The allies simply could not afford to alienate the Germans or to weaken the Adenauer government by adopting a strategy that treated West Germany as essentially a buffer zone. The obvious solution to all these problems was to make an effective defense of West Germany a fundamental objective of the western alliance.[14]

But if the Federal Republic was to be defended, it was clear that the other western countries should not have to do the whole job. It was only fair that West Germany contribute to her own defense. Without German troops it was hard to see how even Europe west of the Rhine could be defended, but if West German territory were included in the area to be defended, even more troops would be required, and no one but Germany could supply them. Officially in late 1949 the western powers still opposed German rearmament in any form, but in military circles in all three of the major western countries, it was taken for granted that German troops would be needed. And in November 1949, just a couple of months after the Soviet nuclear explosion had been announced, the whole issue of a German military contribution suddenly, and by no means coincidentally, moved to the top of the political agenda.[15]

A military contribution, however, implied a major change in West Germany's political status. For how could the Federal Republic really throw in her lot with

[14] For the French view of Germany as a buffer area, see especially the Revers report of January 25, 1948, 4Q37/2/SHAT and the "Avis du Comité des Chefs d'Etat-Major au sujet des problémes soulevés par le Plan des Possibilités du Commandant Suprême Allié en Europe," September 6, 1954, p. 9, in Series 1K145 (Papers of General Blanc, Army Chief of Staff), box 2, SHAT. For Schumacher's views, see in general Ulrich Buczylowski, *Kurt Schumacher und die deutsche Frage: Sicherheitspolitik und strategische Offensivkonzeption von August 1950 bis September 1951* (Stuttgart: Seewald, 1973); see also Schwartz, *America's Germany,* pp. 145–146. Schumacher wanted the West (including Germany) to build a "powerful offensive army" capable of making sure that any war that broke out was fought in eastern Europe, and not on German (including East German) territory; only if such a force were built up should the German government, in his view, take part in the western defense effort. For British reluctance to commit themselves fully to the defense of western Europe, see, for example, John Baylis, *Ambiguity and Deterrence: British Nuclear Strategy, 1945–1964* (Oxford: Clarendon, 1995), pp. 76–77.

[15] For the point that the Germans should contribute to their own defense, see, for example, McCloy to Acheson, September 23, 1951, FRUS 1951, 3:1523; Massigli, *Une comédie des erreurs,* p. 239; and the Ely-Stehlin note quoted in Jean Doise and Maurice Vaïsse, *Diplomatie et outil militaire, 1871–1969* (Paris: Imprimerie Nationale, 1987), p. 421. For the consensus view that a defense east of the Rhine would require more troops than a defense based on the Rhine, see, for example, Air Marshal Elliot memorandum, October 19, 1950, DBPO II, 3:177. For the point that the cooperation and support of the German people as a whole were necessary for an effective defense, see Acheson's remarks in western foreign ministers' meetings, September 14 and 15, 1950, FRUS 1950, 3:294, 316. On the sudden interest in German rearmament in late 1949, see, for example, Konrad Adenauer, *Erinnerungen,* vol. 1 (1945–1953) (Stuttgart: Deutsche Verlags-Anstalt, 1965), p. 341; Bonnet to Schuman, November 30, 1949, Europe 1949–55/Allemagne/182/FFMA.

the West and devote herself to the common defense if she were distrusted and subjected to all kinds of restrictions and discriminations—in short, if it were clear that she could never be more than a second-class member of the western community? If West Germany was to be a real partner in military terms, she could no longer be treated as an occupied country. Political relations would have to be recast and put much more on a basis of equality and mutual respect.[16] Allied troops would remain on German soil, but their role would change. They would no longer be a "symbol of coercion," but rather would be there to protect the West as a whole.[17] The Federal Republic and the North Atlantic powers would together be defending western civilization; their soldiers would be standing "shoulder to shoulder."[18] In such circumstances, they would have to relate to each other as partners, and that meant that the Germans' basic political rights would have to be restored, and restored rather quickly. If the energies of the Germans were to be mobilized effectively on behalf of the West as a whole, the Federal Republic could not be discredited in the eyes of its own people as a puppet state. But if West Germany was to be accepted into the western bloc as a partner, then it stood to reason that she should bear her fair share of the defense burden. Germany's willingness to provide troops and join in the common defense would be the test of her commitment to the West, of her sense of herself as part of the western world—just as the western countries, by standing "shoulder to shoulder" with Germany, would be demonstrating their willingness to accept the Federal Republic as one of their own.[19]

So everything was beginning to point in the same direction: toward the rearmament of the West, and the rearmament of the Federal Republic as part of the West; and, both as consequence and as cause, the restoration of Germany's political rights and her integration into the western community as a full, or nearly full, partner.

THE SETTLEMENT WITH WEST GERMANY

In late 1949 and early 1950, this whole way of thinking was beginning to have a major impact on the West's German policy. The western powers were certainly willing to live with the status quo in central Europe. In February 1949 Bevin had noted that the division of Germany was "essential to our plans," at least for the time being.[20] The French felt essentially the same way. Both they and the British had by this point rallied so completely to the western strategy that their main worry was that America might break with that strategy and make a deal with Russia providing for a unified Germany.[21] Indeed, throughout the whole period down to 1963 and beyond, both Britain and France felt quite comfortable with the status quo and had little real interest in German reunification.[22]

[16] See, for example, McCloy to Acheson, August 3, 1950, FRUS 1950, 3:182.
[17] Acheson to Acting Secretary, May 9, 1950, ibid., p. 1016.
[18] McCloy to Acheson, July 14, 1950, ibid., 4:698.
[19] McCloy to Acheson, September 23, 1951, FRUS 1951, 3:1523.
[20] Bevin memorandum, "Germany and Berlin," February 4, 1949, Prem 8/791, PRO.
[21] See Yost to Jessup, May 21, 1949, FRUS 1949, 3:874, 890–892, and also Buffet, *Mourir pour Berlin*, pp. 253, 261.
[22] For a revealing glimpse into both French and British feelings about keeping the status quo, see

The Americans did not approach the issue in quite the same way, and did not view the division of Germany as a fundamental element of the political system they wanted to create. Acheson, for example, would have been happy to add the eastern zone to the Federal Republic if the Soviets were willing to turn it over with no strings attached.[23] But if the USSR insisted that Germany could be reunified only if the whole country were removed from the western system, he would prefer to keep things as they were. Acheson had no intention of abandoning the basic strategy of linking western Germany to the western world and tying her to a bloc capable of standing firm against Soviet pressure. If that meant that reunification was a political impossibility, then a divided Germany would have to be accepted.

That basic strategy had not been universally accepted within the American government. George Kennan, then head of the State Department's Policy Planning Staff, was the main critic within the government of the official American line, and in 1948 and 1949 he argued forcefully for a radical shift in U.S. policy. The Germans, Kennan said, would never accept the regime that was being set up—the division of their country and the various constraints on their national power. A West German government, he thought, was bound to become "the spokesman of a resentful and defiant nationalism," and the "edge of this resentment" would "inevitably be turned against the Western governments themselves."[24] Under the emerging system, the three western powers would have to keep the West Germans "properly in their place and at the same time contain the Russians," but in Kennan's view they simply were not "strong enough to do it." The West should instead, he argued, allow a balance of power to come into being in Europe, with Germany, or a continental Europe dominated by Germany, as the prime counterweight to Russia. The Germans, after all, knew "more about how to handle" countries like Czechoslovakia, Yugoslavia, and Poland than the Americans did. He was aware of "the horrifying significance of this," which was that the Germans would again be playing a "very important" role. But it often seemed to him, "during the war, living over there, that what was wrong with Hitler's new order was that it was

---

Crouy-Chanel to Massigli, May 8, 1955 (handwritten), enclosing an account of a May 6 meeting with a high British official, MP/96/FFMA. For British views, see also Rolf Steininger, *The German Question: The Stalin Note of 1952 and the Problem of Reunification* (New York: Columbia University Press, 1990), pp. 34–35, and esp. p. 108. As for the French, the argument that a divided Germany was the optimal solution was developed most sharply in the early 1950s by the young Jean Sauvagnargues, head of the German desk at the Quai d'Orsay. See, for example, his memoranda of June 25, 1952, and April 22, 1953, Europe 1949–55/Allemagne/822–823/FFMA, and June 10, 1953, Europe 1949–55/Généralités/100/FFMA. For Schuman's views, see especially Schuman to Bonnet, June 16, 1952, Europe 1949–55/Allemagne/822/FFMA. The basic French attitude is reflected in many other documents. See, for example, Achilles to State Department, November 17, 1953, FRUS 1952–54, 5:1719; François-Poncet to Bidault, February 26, 1954, Europe 1949–55/Allemagne/11/FFMA; and Note de la Direction Politique, April 15, 1955, *Documents Diplomatiques Français* [DDF] 1955, 1:456–458. France's allies understood what her basic attitude was. "While they would not say so out loud, of course," Dulles noted, "the French would not be at all disturbed by the prospect of the continued division of Germany." NSC meeting, November 21, 1955, FRUS 1955–57, 5:806. On these matters in general, see the analysis in Soutou, "La France et les notes soviétiques de 1952 sur l'Allemagne," pp. 270–273, and also Trachtenberg, *History and Strategy*, pp. 178–179.

[23] See, for example, Acheson to Douglas, May 11, 1949, FRUS 1949, 3:872–873.

[24] Kennan paper, March 8, 1949, FRUS 1949:3, p. 98.

Hitler's." Something more like pre-1914 Germany, not a "westernized force," but "something between ourselves and the Russians," would be able to organize continental Europe, and would be "vigorous enough to back against the Russians."[25] But Kennan's views were not broadly shared. American policymakers, by and large, did not trust Germany enough to cast her "loose in the hope that things will work out for the best." The prevailing view was that Kennan's thinking was a little bizarre, and that the best course was still "to develop Western Germany politically and economically as part of a Western European system under the supervision and protection of the Western Allies."[26]

So by the time the Federal Republic was established in 1949, the three western powers knew in general terms how they wanted to deal with the German problem. Their long-term goal was to make the West German state part of the western bloc—to integrate it into western Europe and into the western community as a whole. Their aim in this period was not simply to prevent the USSR from taking over all of Germany. A strong and fully independent German state capable of standing up to the Soviet Union on its own was also unacceptable. Germany could not be allowed to become too powerful or too independent. She could not be permitted, as Acheson put it in July 1950, to "act as the balance of power in Europe." Instead Germany was to be "irrevocably aligned" with the West, integrated into the western system, incapable of making trouble on her own.[27]

But would the western powers be able to get the Germans to accept these arrangements? U.S. leaders did not think that success was certain. As the American high commissioner in Germany, John McCloy, put it, the allies were engaged in a "struggle for the soul of Faust." This was a struggle which they might conceivably lose, but if they played their cards skillfully, there was an excellent chance

---

[25] PPS meeting with Acheson, October 18, 1949, PPS 1947–53, box 32, RG 59, USNA. See also George Kennan, *Memoirs, 1925–1950* (Boston: Little Brown, 1967), p. 417 and chap. 19; John Lewis Gaddis, *Strategies of Containment: A Critical Appraisal of Postwar American National Security Policy* (New York: Oxford University Press, 1982), p. 33n.; and Yergin, *Shattered Peace,* p. 40.

[26] Reinstein to Thorp, September 6, 1948, FRUS 1948, 2:1288n. See also Wilson Miscamble, *George F. Kennan and the Making of American Foreign Policy* (Princeton, N.J.: Princeton University Press, 1992), pp. 166–173. At a meeting with Kennan, Murphy, and other top officials on March 9, 1949, Acheson did express a degree of sympathy for Kennan's position, but he also said that he did not "quite follow" Kennan's thinking or "understand how the proposed solution would work." He went on to say that he did not understand how the decision to create a West German state had been made, and wondered whether it had been "the brainchild of General Clay and not a governmental decision." Acheson certainly knew better than to think that a decision of this order of importance could possibly have been made in the field and not in Washington; he was probably in effect inviting Murphy to review the story of American policy in Germany, which in any event was what Murphy then went on to do. It seems, therefore, that the secretary of state was taking his distance from Kennan, but that he wanted to do this in the nicest possible way. He did not want to slam the door in Kennan's face or put an end to discussion of this fundamental issue. Acheson's own views—the official State Department line—were reflected in a memorandum he sent Truman three weeks later which stressed the importance of integrating at least western Germany in a west European system and also in an important analysis of the problem he personally made in May. See Acheson-Kennan-Murphy meeting, March 9, 1949; Acheson to Truman, with State Department paper, March 31, 1949; and Acheson to London Embassy, May 11, 1949; all in FRUS 1949, 3:102–103, 142–155, 872–874.

[27] Acheson-Truman meeting, July 31, 1950, Nitze in Lewis and Achilles to Byroade, May 2, 1950, and Acheson to acting secretary, May 9, 1950, in FRUS 1950, 3:167–168, 914, 1015.

that they would win in the end.[28] The western governments had to move ahead toward transforming their relationship with the Germans, but the assumption in 1949 was that they should not move ahead too quickly. They had to make sure that German nationalism remained under control. "We have the power," McCloy said, "and we should have the determination to crack down immediately on the Germans if they get out of line."[29] McCloy was worried about the possibility of "dangerous back-slidings" on the part of the Germans. The democratic elements the western powers were counting on, he wrote in early 1950, still needed "an umbrella under which to develop," and the allies therefore needed to hold on to their basic powers within Germany, at least for the time being.[30] On the other hand, the U.S. government understood from the very beginning that the West would not succeed if it opted for a simple policy of coercion. The Germans could not simply be forced to do what the western allies wanted them to do. Instead, Germany had to be brought in as a "willing participant" and eventually as a "full partner" in the "concert of democratic powers."[31] There was a risk that if the West was too hesitant and made concessions only grudgingly, the Germans would be alienated, and the pro-western Adenauer government discredited in the eyes of its own people.

British and French views were not fundamentally different. It was clear to all three governments, even in 1949, that the occupation regime was not consistent with the policy of integrating Germany into the western community. In the long run that regime would clearly have to go, but it would be dangerous to dismantle it too quickly. It was all a question of timing and of striking the right balance. The allies would have to move carefully and deliberately, gradually relaxing the controls as they became increasingly confident that things were going their way in Germany—that the pro-western elements in the Federal Republic would win out and that the Germans would take their place in the framework the western powers were constructing.[32]

That, at least, was the prevailing assumption in 1949 and early 1950. But by mid-1950 this basic strategy was being rethought. A quicker pace might be necessary; greater risks might have to be taken; a more radical transformation of West Germany's status might be essential. The defense of Europe had become a matter of considerable urgency. Perhaps there was no immediate threat of Soviet invasion, but there might well be a great crisis two or three years down the road.[33] And

[28] U.S. ambassadors' meeting, October 21, 1949, FRUS 1949, 3:287, 289–290. See also PPS, "The Current Position in the Cold War," April 14, 1950, and Nitze's remarks, reported in Lewis and Achilles to Byroade, May 2, 1950, FRUS 1950, 3:859, 914; and Byroade memorandum on "Germany in the European Context," February 11, 1950, ibid., 4:599.

[29] U.S. ambassadors' meeting, October 21, 1949, FRUS 1949, 3:290.

[30] McCloy to Byroade, April 25, 1950, FRUS 1950, 4:683.

[31] McCloy to Byroade, April 25, 1950, ibid., p. 633.

[32] Key French officials frequently argued along these lines. François-Poncet and Massigli both felt that the West had to move toward a system based on collaboration with Germany. In early 1949, they thought that the occupation statute had to be a lot more liberal than the one the allies were then drafting, and Schuman agreed. Massigli to Chauvel, February 14, 1949, MP/68/FFMA; Kennan–François-Poncet meeting, March 21, 1949, and Schuman-Acheson meeting, April 1, 1949, FRUS 1949, 3:114, 159.

[33] Wiggershaus, "Bedrohungsvorstellungen Bundeskanzler Adenauers," pp. 96, 98–99. For Bevin's

it was obvious that existing arrangements were far from adequate. The North Atlantic Treaty Organization, the military structure the allies had set up in 1949, was in Acheson's view "absolutely hopeless and was not getting anywhere," and this situation had to be rectified.[34] Military leaders in all three western countries had understood very early on that western Europe could not be defended without German troops, but the top political leadership had been reluctant to push ahead in this area. When the U.S. Joint Chiefs of Staff, for example, called for changing the existing demilitarization policy so that the West Germans could take part in NATO defensive arrangements and "contribute effectively to the security of western Europe," President Truman on June 16 sharply criticized their report as "decidedly militaristic." "We certainly don't want to make the same mistake," he wrote Acheson, "that was made after World War I when Germany was authorized to train one hundred thousand soldiers, principally for maintaining order locally in Germany. As you know, that hundred thousand was used for the basis of training the greatest war machine that ever came forth in European history."[35]

But Truman's resistance was soon overcome. Even in 1949, Acheson had felt that one could not "have any sort of security in western Europe without using German power," and now, in July 1950, he told the president that the real question was not whether Germany should be rearmed, but rather how it should be done.[36] It was quickly agreed that there could be no German national army under German command. The Germans, McCloy argued in August, could not be allowed to develop a degree of power that would enable them to play off east against west, and a national army would undermine "much that we have so far achieved in democratizing German society." To recreate such an army would in his view be a "tragic mistake," and Acheson called it "the worst possible move."[37] If the Germans were to make a military contribution without having a national army, there would have to be some kind of integrated force—a European army or a North Atlantic army—that would include German contingents but which would guarantee that the Germans could not operate independently. As one leading U.S. diplomat put it, reflecting what was by now the consensus view, a truly common effort was "the only way out."[38] The British felt the same way. An integrated force, in Bevin's view, was the only way the West could be certain that "Germany's defense effort" remained "under allied control."[39] But a German contribution, even at this level, implied a transformation of the Federal Republic's relationship with the western allies. She

---

view that the crisis was still a few years away, see, for example, U.S.-U.K. meeting, May 9, 1950, FRUS 1950, 3:1020.

[34] Evans memorandum, August 4, 1950, ibid., pp. 182–183.

[35] NSC 71, June 8, 1950, and Truman to Acheson, June 16, 1950 (two documents), ibid., 4:686–688.

[36] PPS meeting, October 18, 1949, p. 7, PPS 1947–53, box 32, RG 59, USNA; Acheson-Truman meeting, July 31, 1950, FRUS 1950, 3:167–168.

[37] McCloy to Acheson, August 3, 1950, and Acheson-Truman meeting, July 31, 1950, ibid., pp. 167–168, 181.

[38] Bruce to Acheson, July 28, 1950, ibid., p. 157. All the main American policymakers were arguing along similar lines. See, for example, Acheson-Truman meeting, July 31, 1950; McCloy to Acheson, August 3, 1950; and Kirk to Acheson, August 9, 1950; all ibid., pp. 167–168, 181, 193.

[39] Bevin to Harvey, October 9, 1950, DBPO II, 3:141.

would have to become much more of a partner, and more of an equal. The old gradualist strategy was no longer viable. The occupation regime would have to be transformed relatively quickly. But it was by no means clear how fast or how far the western powers would have to go.

According to the new thinking, there would have to be a strong American military presence in Europe, at least for the time being. The unified NATO army needed a supreme commander, and that commander would have to be an American.[40] Only an American general would have the authority and prestige needed to make the integrated system work. And the NATO commander would have to be backed up by a respectable U.S. combat force. The goal was to shore up the morale of the Europeans and to lay the basis for an effective defense of the continent; the U.S. force would be the backbone of the integrated structure into which the Germans could be brought.

The Americans now moved ahead rapidly in this direction. In September, at the New York foreign ministers' conference, the Europeans were presented with a package. If they wanted an American general as NATO commander and a respectable American military presence on the continent, they would have to accept German rearmament along the lines worked out in Washington—that is, as part of an integrated NATO force, with the Germans having no "capacity for independent action."[41] They were thus under enormous pressure to accept the American plan. The British suppressed their misgivings and went along with Acheson's proposal.[42] With the French, however, the problems ran deeper.

The French foreign minister, Robert Schuman, and other key officials personally agreed with the Americans on a whole range of basic issues: on the importance of drawing Germany into the West and transforming her into a partner; on the need for an effective ground defense in Europe and the impossibility of achieving this without a German contribution; and on the desirability of integrated structures that could provide a stable long-term basis for limiting German freedom of action. They understood that Germany could not be treated "as an economic and military ally" and at the same time as a political inferior.[43]

But French leaders who thought along these lines had to deal with a whole series of problems. The first was bureaucratic in nature. The policy of integrating Germany into the western system as a real partner had to a certain extent been sabotaged by the French military administration in Germany. In 1949, Schuman and his associates had therefore taken the lead in bringing about a major liberalization of the occupation regime: the military governors were replaced by a civilian High Commission and the occupation controls were relaxed.[44]

[40] Douglas to Acheson, August 8, 1950; "Establishment of a European Defense Force," enclosed in Matthews to Burns, August 16, 1950; Acheson to Bruce, September 2, 1950; all in FRUS 1950, 3:190–192, 215, 261.

[41] Acheson to acting secretary, September 17, 1950, ibid., pp. 316–319.

[42] See especially Bevin memorandum, October 6, 1950, and Bevin to Harvey, October 9, 1950, DBPO II, 3:133–135, 140–142. Note also Acheson to Truman, September 15, 1950, FRUS 1950, 3:1229.

[43] François-Poncet to Foreign Ministry, November 17, 1950, Europe 1949–55/Allemagne/ 913/FFMA.

[44] Kennan notes of meeting with François-Poncet, March 21, 1949, and Acheson-Schuman meet-

Political problems at home, however, could not be dealt with so easily. At the New York conference, Schuman made it clear that he personally understood the need for German troops, and he fully agreed that it was illogical to think that Germany should be defended without a German contribution. He was ready to accept the principle of a German defense contribution if this could be done secretly, but the Americans were insisting on public acceptance now. The problem, he said, was that in France only a minority understood "the importance of Germany in western defense." It was politically impossible for him to do what the Americans wanted right now. The French public was simply not ready to go along with German rearmament at this point. It would be better first to let the NATO regime take shape, for a U.S. general to come over as NATO commander, for a U.S. combat force to take up positions in Germany. After those things were done, it would be much easier to get the French parliament to accept some form of German rearmament.[45]

Domestic politics aside, there were major substantive reasons for moving ahead cautiously. To press the Germans on rearmament would transform the relationship between the allies and the Federal Republic. It would put the Germans in the driver's seat and encourage them to pose political conditions, and the allies might end up having to give them too much political freedom too soon. Even more important than that, it would provoke the Russians, possibly into a preventive war, before the allies had built up their power and were able to defend themselves.

But the American government was now determined to move ahead rapidly. The argument that the West was skating on very thin ice, and that a decision to rearm Germany might tip the balance in Moscow and provoke a Soviet attack, Acheson now simply dismissed out of hand. The only thing the Russians were interested in, he told the allies, was the overall balance of power between east and west. The rearmament of Germany had "little bearing on the matter," since it did not "really matter to the Russians whether we are building up strength by the creation of a German force or by other means." Acheson was proud of his performance. His arguments, he boasted to Truman, had "destroyed any logical basis" for the European fear that German rearmament as such, as distinct from "the mere creation of allied strength," might provoke a Soviet attack. The French in particular, he said, had been in favor of putting off the rearmament of Germany until after the general power of the West had been built up, but he had simply blown their arguments "out of the water."[46]

---

ing, April 1, 1949, FRUS 1949, 3:114, 159. On the undermining of the Schuman policy by the French occupation authorities in Germany, see Massigli to Chauvel, February 14, 1949, MP/68/FFMA.

[45] See Bevin to Foreign Office, September 13, 1950; Harvey to Bevin, October 7, 1950; and Schuman-Bevin meeting, December 2, 1950; all in DBPO II, 3:35–36, 136, 312–317. Schuman-Acheson meeting, September 12, 1950; meeting of western foreign ministers and high commissioners, September 14, 1950; Acheson to Truman, September 14, and September 16, 1950; and Schuman-Bevin-Acheson meeting, September 12, 1950; in FRUS 1950, 3:288, 296–302, 311–312, 1200. American officials had long felt that Schuman's domestic political problems were quite real and that he had taken France as far as he could. See Ambassador Bruce's remarks in U.S. ambassadors' meeting, March 22–24, 1950, ibid., p. 819.

[46] Meeting of western foreign ministers and high commissioners, September 14, 1950, and Acheson to Truman, September 15, 1950, ibid., p. 298, 1230.

The Europeans were not convinced by Acheson's reasoning, but an integrated military system, an American NATO commander, and a greatly increased U.S. troop presence on the continent were things that the British and French very much wanted. Acheson had made it clear, however, that the Europeans would first have to accept the principle of a German defense contribution. This heavy-handed tactic was generally disliked in Europe, but all the allies except France were willing to accept America's terms. The French were therefore under great pressure to come up with a proposal of their own.

On October 24, Prime Minister René Pleven therefore announced a plan for a European army and a European defense ministry. The Pleven Plan was similar in structure to the Schuman Plan for a European Coal and Steel Community proposed earlier in the year, and like the Schuman Plan, had been worked out principally by Jean Monnet, the great French champion of a unified Europe. Under the Pleven proposals, German troops were to be recruited and armed not by the Bonn government but by a supranational European authority. They would be welded into a highly integrated European army that would take its place alongside regular NATO national armies under the direct control of the NATO commander.[47]

The Pleven proposal had been worked out quickly. Neither the French military authorities nor the French foreign ministry had been consulted.[48] The plan soon developed into a proposal for a European Defense Community, and the EDC project played a central role in alliance politics until its final collapse in August 1954.[49] But the plan was never very popular. Military officers, especially in France, generally disliked the whole idea.[50] Their misgivings were shared by many key political figures. To Marshall, now back in office as secretary of defense, it was a "miasmic cloud"; to Churchill, who returned as prime minister in late 1951, the EDC was a "sludgy amalgam."[51] The prevailing view in late 1950 and early 1951 was that the Pleven Plan was unrealistic. The French had not come up with a practical solution to the problem of German rearmament; it seemed that the whole point of the proposal was to evade that basic problem. The American and British ambassadors in Paris both saw it as the "concoction of politicians designed to meet political difficulties," a view shared by a number of French officials.[52] The French

---

[47] For the statement outlining the Pleven Plan, see Royal Institute of International Affairs, *Documents on International Affairs, 1949–1950* (London: Oxford University Press, 1953), pp. 339–344. For a brief outline, see Acheson to Bruce, October 27, 1950, FRUS 1950, 3:410–412. On the Schuman Plan, see Gerbet, "Les origines du plan Schuman," pp. 199–222; Klaus Schwabe, ed., *Die Anfänge des Schuman-Plans, 1950/51* (Baden-Baden: Nomos, 1988); and William Hitchcock, "France, the Western Alliance, and the Origins of the Schuman Plan, 1948–1950," *Diplomatic History* 21 (1997): 603–630.

[48] British military attaché report, October 30, 1950, and Harvey to Dixon, November 3, 1950, DBPO II, 3:240n, 244.

[49] On the EDC, see Edward Fursdon, *The European Defence Community: A History* (London: Macmillan, 1980), and Hans-Erich Volkmann and Walter Schwengler, eds., *Die Europäische Verteidigungsgemeinschaft: Stand und Probleme der Forschung* (Boppard: Boldt, 1985).

[50] Acheson to Bruce, November 3, 1950, Spofford to Acheson, December 14, 1950, FRUS 1950, 3:428–429, 574; Guillen, "Les Chefs militaires français," esp. pp. 8–11; Hermann-Josef Rupieper, *Der besetzte Verbündete: Die amerikanische Deutschlandpolitik 1949–1955* (Opladen: Westdeutscher Verlag, 1991), p. 113.

[51] Defence minister to Bevin and Attlee, October 28, 1950, DBPO II, 3:228.

[52] Harvey to Dixon, October 31, 1950, ibid., p. 240. Note also the views of French diplomats in London quoted ibid., p. 220. See also Massigli, *Une Comédie des erreurs,* p. 257.

wanted to take what the Americans were offering in terms of U.S. combat divisions, an American NATO commander, and an integrated military system, while dragging their feet on German rearmament. It seemed that the Pleven plan had apparently been worked out with that goal in mind, and that the real French aim was to "play for time" on the German rearmament question.[53]

This, however, was not a purely French concern. For the Europeans in general at this point, the basic goal was to avoid provoking Russia by a decision to rearm Germany, without at the same time rejecting the American offer to begin building an effective system for the defense of Europe. In their view, the risk of war was now very real. Bevin, for example, had concluded by the end of 1950 that the great crisis was no longer two or three years off but that things might come to a head very quickly. It made sense, he now felt, for the western powers to build up their strength first before they took the plunge and decided to rearm Germany, something which might well "tip the balance" and provoke a Soviet attack.[54]

These fears were by no means a figment of the Europeans' fevered imaginations. As noted above, there was a whole series of indicators suggesting that the Soviets were getting ready for military action. That evidence had confirmed what many policymakers were inclined to believe on more theoretical grounds: that the nuclear monopoly was the one thing that had counterbalanced the USSR's enormous superiority in ground forces in Europe, so that the breaking of that monopoly would open up a window of opportunity for Russia, and would in all probability lead to a far more aggressive policy. Events—above all, the Chinese intervention in the Korean War—had now vindicated this whole way of looking at things. At the end of 1950, the level of risk was thus seen as very great. A general war, it was feared, might well break out in the very near future. The American military authorities were particularly sensitive to these problems. The JCS had taken a very cautious line in political disputes even in the late 1940s, and since then the strategic balance had worsened dramatically. In their view, the situation in late 1950 and early 1951 was quite dangerous: this was not the time to run major risks.[55]

The Soviets, it seemed, were poised on the brink. A decision to rearm Germany might well lead them to opt for war, especially since the West had embarked on a massive military buildup and action might no longer be possible in a year or two. McCloy, for example, thought in June that "the rearmament of Germany would undoubtedly speed up any Soviet schedule for any possible future action in Germany and would, no doubt, be regarded by them as sufficiently provocative to warrant extreme countermeasures." By December these fears had intensified. The CIA calculated in January 1951 that there was a better than fifty-fifty chance that German rearmament would lead to war with the Soviets, and Army intelligence was even more pessimistic. Soviet officials, from Stalin on down, made it clear, both publicly and in private talks with western diplomats, that the rearmament of

---

[53] Defence minister to Bevin and Attlee, October 28, 1950, DBPO II, 3:227.

[54] For the reference to "tipping the balance," see COS(50) 194th meeting, confidential annex, Defe 4/38, PRO, quoted ibid., p. 328n. For various documents reflecting similar concerns, see ibid., pp. 314, 327–328, 331, 331n, 337–338, 344n, 352 (calendar 133i), 358. Note also Attlee's views in the February 8, 1951, Cabinet meeting, Cab 128/19, PRO.

[55] See Trachtenberg, *History and Strategy*, pp. 113–114, 118–122.

Germany might well lead to preventive military action.[56] But Acheson—an "uncompromising hawk," as General Bradley called him—insisted on pushing ahead.[57] If the Europeans wanted a major American military presence, they would have to accept the principle of German rearmament, and accept it openly.

The Europeans were thus under enormous pressure, and finally, in December, an arrangement known as the "Spofford compromise" was worked out. The Western allies would begin at once to develop plans for a European Army, but while these arrangements were being negotiated, German units would be formed and placed, for the time being, under direct NATO command.[58]

The French accepted this arrangement, and it was the German government that now played the key role in slowing things down; indeed, it was probably because they had learned that the Germans would not go along with the plan that the French in the final analysis had been willing to accept it.[59] The German position had shifted dramatically since August. At that point, although Adenauer wanted a change in the Federal Republic's political status, he had felt that the long-term threat to German security was so great that the West Germans needed to do whatever the allies would let them do to help remedy the situation. But now the Adenauer government was laying down conditions: unless Germany's political status underwent a radical transformation, there would be no German defense contribution. Adenauer was concerned with the political situation within Germany, but, like the other Europeans, he also felt it was important not to provoke the Soviets at a time when the West was so weak. He therefore agreed with the French and the British that the main emphasis for the time being needed to be placed on building up NATO's strength, and that the specific issue of German rearmament should be placed on the back burner. And the way to slow things down was to stress his

[56] See McCloy to Acheson, June 13, 1950, PSF/178/Germany, folder 2/HSTL; "Soviet Courses of Action with Respect to Germany," NIE 4, January 29, 1951, and "Probable Soviet Reactions to a Remilitarization of Western Germany," NIE 17, December 27, 1950, both in PSF/253/HSTL. For the CIA's estimate at the beginning of 1951 that there was a better than fifty-fifty chance that German rearmament would lead to war with the Soviets, see the summary of the January 24, 1951, NSC meeting, p. 4, *National Security Council: Minutes of Meetings* (mic.), reel 1. As for the Russian threats, the most important declaration was a Soviet warning of October 19, 1950, which was frequently cited in the documents; for the text, see Beate Ruhm von Oppen, *Documents on Germany under Occupation* (London: Oxford University Press, 1955), pp. 520–521, and for remarks that show how seriously it was taken, see Clubb to Rusk, December 18, 1950, FRUS 1950, 1:479n; Strang in a meeting with Bevin and other top officials, December 5, 1950, and Bevin memorandum, December 12, 1950, in DBPO II, 3:331, 358. There were also warnings conveyed through more private channels. A Soviet diplomat in London, for example, told a Swiss diplomat toward the end of 1950 that the rearmament of Germany "would be an error similar to the crossing of the Thirty-eighth Parallel by U.N. forces"—an event which, of course, led to Chinese involvement and a transformation of the conflict into a great power war. And a TASS correspondent in Washington told a French diplomat about the same time that if Germany began to rearm, "Russia would strike." Massigli to Foreign Ministry, December 18, 1950, and Bonnet to Foreign Ministry, December 29, 1950, Europe 1949–50/Allemagne/300/FFMA.

[57] Omar Bradley, *A General's Life* (New York: Simon and Schuster, 1983), p. 519.

[58] On this arrangement, see FRUS 1950, 3:457–595 passim, esp. pp. 457–458, 531–547, 583–595.

[59] This point is made in a draft of a University of Pennsylvania dissertation by Norrin Ripsman. To support the point, Ripsman cites a note from the Direction d'Europe of December 5, 1950, in Europe 1944–60/Allemagne/189/FFMA.

very real domestic political problems, and to insist that a defense contribution would be politically possible only if the Federal Republic were treated as more of an equal. So Adenauer now declared that unless the occupation regime were replaced by a system of contractual relations, there would be no German troops. The allies, on the other hand, were bound to insist that Germany's political rights would not be restored until they got what they wanted from Germany by way of a military contribution, with adequate safeguards. What all this meant was that parallel negotiations would be necessary: both the political and the military issues would have to be settled as part of one great package. These issues were both complex and politically sensitive. The negotiations would obviously last for months, if not longer.[60]

Acheson was frustrated, but he understood that the German rearmament issue needed to be put "on ice for a little while." He now realized that the U.S. could not implement its threat not to send over a sizeable combat force or an American general as NATO commander unless the Europeans, including the Germans, made the kind of defense contribution the Americans expected of them. If America "tried to bargain," he said, and demanded more European army divisions, "everything would go to pieces."[61] So the U.S. troops were sent, Eisenhower went over as the first NATO commander—the Supreme Allied Commander, Europe, or SACEUR— and the NATO integrated command system was gradually set up.

In the meantime, western and German officials began to tackle the massive problem of regulating the Federal Republic's relations with the western powers— the whole cluster of issues relating to German sovereignty, a German defense contribution, the EDC, the structure of NATO, and so on. These problems were not easy to resolve and progress was slow, but gradually a package of interlocking arrangements took shape. The western powers, after all, saw eye to eye on essentials. None of them wanted Germany to be too independent or too powerful. That

[60] On the "hardening of the German line," see, for example, the report of the High Commission's December 1, 1950, meeting with Adenauer, calendar 120i, DBPO II, 3:309. See also the Adenauer paper quoted in McCloy to Acheson, November 17, 1950, FRUS 1950, 4:780–781, and McCloy to Acheson, January 16, 1951, reporting a conversation with Blankenhorn and Adenauer's Bielefeld speech of January 14, 1951, FRUS 1951, 3:1452, 1452n. Adenauer's earlier views were laid out in his memorandum on the security question of August 29, 1950, published in Klaus von Schubert, ed., *Sicherheitspolitik der Bundesrepublik Deutschland: Dokumentation 1945–1977,* part 1 (Cologne: Verlag Wissenschaft und Gesellschaft, 1978), pp. 79–83, and also in his presentations to the allied High Commission; see especially his remarks in the August 17, 1950, meeting, *Akten zur auswärtigen Politik der Bundesrepublik Deutschland* [AAPBD], 1:222–226. For his acceptance of the general European idea in late 1950 that the real need was to work out some kind of formula that would allow the Americans to begin building up "a strong Atlantic Army in Europe," and that the German defense contribution was not the "important question," see DBPO II, 3:210n. Even in October, Armand Bérard, François-Poncet's deputy, was struck by a certain parallelism between French and German policy: both countries were "preoccupied" by the need to avoid provoking the Soviets before the general power of the West had been built up. Bérard to Foreign Ministry, October 17, 1950, Europe 1949–55/Allemagne/70/FFMA. For U.S. acceptance of the idea that everything—the question of a German military contribution and the issue of Germany's political relationship to the western powers—had to be worked out in one all-encompassing plan, see Acheson to London Embassy, December 14, 1950, FRUS 1950, 4:801–802.

[61] Acheson-Lovett telephone conversation, December 15, 1950, and Acheson to McCloy, December 16, 1950, FRUS 1950, 3:579.

meant above all that the Federal Republic could not have an army capable of independent action. On the other hand, they agreed that the Germans had to be won over to the West, and that meant that the Federal Republic would have to be treated "substantially" as an equal. "A large degree of sovereignty" would have to be restored to Germany. This very phrasing, however, reflected the allies' unwillingness to go all the way and grant full sovereignty to the Federal Republic.[62] How far they would go would depend largely on whether structural arrangements could be worked out that would automatically limit German freedom of action, and perhaps everyone else's as well.

It was not obvious, however, what kind of structure was to be built. The great question was whether it should have a distinctly "European" or a broader "Atlantic" focus. Would the Europeans ever be able to pull together and defend themselves without direct American involvement? Could the problem of German power ever be resolved in a purely European context? Or was continuing American involvement needed to solve the two great interlocking problems that lay at the heart of international politics, the German question and the problem of defense against Soviet Russia?

The American government had long favored the "European" solution. To be sure, Byrnes at Stuttgart in 1946, and then Marshall and Truman in 1948, had given certain assurances about a long-term American commitment to the defense of Europe. But many American policymakers had come to think of the U.S. presence as a kind of crutch. It might be necessary for the time being, but eventually the Europeans needed to come together and take over primary responsibility for their own defense. America could then withdraw all or most of her forces. The goal was to get the Europeans ultimately to balance Soviet power on their own; at the same time there was to be no strong German force under national control, capable of independent action. The only way this could be accomplished was for the Europeans to delegate the war-making power to a central authority; this implied that foreign and military policy would be conducted on a unified basis, and thus that some sort of European federal state would have to be constructed. The Americans therefore attached enormous importance to the political unification of Europe, and generally supported whatever pointed in that general direction.

By the beginning of 1948, American policymakers were already talking about western Europe as an independent center of power, a "third force" strong enough "to say 'no' both to the Soviet Union and to the United States."[63] The feeling was that the Europeans had the resources to defend themselves. Faced with the great threat from the east, they should put their petty differences aside, pool their forces and ultimately unite politically. Unification would also solve the German problem,

---

[62] In December 1950, Acheson briefly considered relinquishing the supreme authority the allies had assumed in 1945, but he quickly drew back from that idea. From that point on, the references were always to "substantial" political equality or to a "large degree of sovereignty." Acheson to McCloy, December 12 and December 28, 1950; Spofford to Acheson, December 13, 1950; Acheson to London Embassy, December 14, 1950; Acheson in western foreign ministers' meeting, December 19, 1950; all ibid., 4:797, 799, 801–802, 809, 818. For various other references to the idea of "substantial" sovereignty and similar concepts, see FRUS 1951, 3:814, 840, 849, 850, 1166.

[63] Hickerson-Inverchapel meeting, January 21, 1948, FRUS 1948, 3:11.

and was probably the only solution if the United States was not to remain in Europe forever. So the American attitude toward European integration was unambiguous. "We favor it," Acheson told Schuman, "I favor it." This was the way to build a Europe strong enough to defend itself "against the attacks of Communist nihilism and Soviet imperialism," and it was "the soundest basis on which this generation could reinsure the next against another dangerous German aberration."[64]

But was a "European" solution viable? A simple supranational administrative structure would not be enough; for the system to work, there would have to be a genuine pooling of sovereignty, a centralized European political authority to control whatever common force was built up. But were the European countries ready to turn over the war-making power, the very heart of sovereignty, to a federal European authority? "Building Europe" might be a very nice way in theory to keep Germany from being able to act independently. But the European system had to be constructed on a basis of equality. Whatever constraints applied to Germany would therefore also have to apply to France and the other countries. But would the French, for example, agree that they could no longer act on a national basis, and that they could no longer have armed forces of their own?

Then there were problems having to do with the British role. A purely continental grouping might not work. France perhaps would not feel strong enough to deal with Germany by herself, even if she had Italy and the Benelux countries at her side. It might be a different story if Britain came in. Perhaps Britain and France together, especially if they could disengage from their burdensome overseas commitments and concentrate their energies on Europe, would be an adequate counterweight to West Germany within the European structure, and a grouping that included Britain might be strong enough to stand up to the USSR on its own. From the U.S. standpoint, what this meant was that Britain should be brought to think of herself as a primarily European power.[65]

But British leaders had little interest or faith in a solution of this sort. Indeed, they rejected the whole idea of Britain as primarily a regional European power, and even more as a key building block in a federal European system. Britain hoped to be treated as "the partner in world affairs of the United States." She refused to think of herself as just another European country, and British leaders resented American attempts to push their country "back into the European Queue." Britain was a world power with important overseas interests. This did not mean that the United Kingdom had any intention of disengaging from Europe. A "profound change" had in fact taken place in British defense policy in May 1950. The defense of continental western Europe was now considered "the first 'pillar' of British strategy," more important now than the defense of the Middle East. But the link with western Europe was, in Bevin's view, just one of "three pillars" on which British policy now rested. The ties with America and the Commonwealth were also of great importance. The Conservatives saw things in much the same way. Churchill

---

[64] Acheson to Schuman, November 29, 1950, FRUS 1950, 3:497. See also Eisenhower's remarks at White House meeting, January 31, 1951, and at North Atlantic Council, November 27, 1951, FRUS 1951, 3:450–451, 734.

[65] Note especially the U.S. views laid out in an Anglo-American meeting, April 25, 1950, DBPO II, 2:124, and also the PPS discussions, January 18 and 24, 1950, PPS 1947–53, box 32, RG 59, USNA.

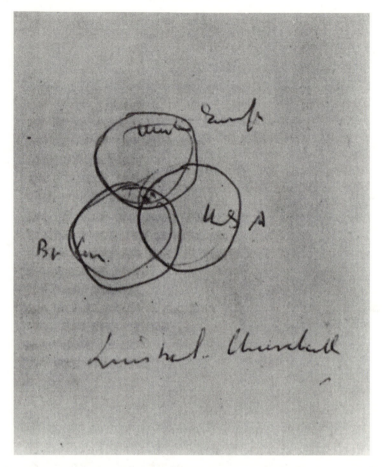

Figure 4 Churchill's Concept of Britain's Place in the World. From a sketch he made during a meeting with Adenauer in December 1951, reproduced from the copy in Adenauer, *Errinnnerungen,* 1:512.

especially had a clear vision of Britain's role in the world: Britain, as he saw it, lay at the center of three overlapping circles, western Europe, the British Commonwealth, and the United States of America.[66]

By 1950 Britain had thus become by far the most Atlanticist of the three major western powers. This was a fairly recent development. It was only in 1949 that

[66] On the "three circles" concept, see Winston Churchill, "United Europe," November 29, 1951, C(51)32, Cab 129/44, PRO, and also David Reynolds, *Britannia Overruled: British Policy and World Power in the Twentieth Century* (London: Longman, 1991), pp. 195, 202. Note also Bevin's reference to the Commonwealth, western Europe, and the United States as "the three main pillars of our policy," in his May 7, 1950, brief for Cabinet meeting, DBPO II, 2:261, calendar 74i. For the reference to Britain losing her status and being pushed "back again in the European Queue," see Oliver Franks memorandum, September 27, 1950, and Brook minute of December 16, 1950, DBPO II, 3:114, 383n. On the shift in British defense strategy, see Elliot memorandum, October 19, 1950, ibid., p. 178; see also ibid., 2:164, 164n.

Bevin had given up on the idea of a British-led "third force." Western Europe as a whole, he and most British officials were finally convinced, would never be strong enough to defend itself, whether Britain was included in a European system or not.[67] America had to be kept in Europe, and one therefore had to emphasize the "Atlantic" concept and reject the narrow "European" idea. "We cannot afford," Bevin wrote, "to allow the European federal concept to gain a foothold within N.A.T.O. and thus weaken instead of strengthening the ties between the countries on the two sides of the Atlantic. We must nip it in the bud."[68] The NATO structure— that is, a broadly based integrated force with an American general as supreme commander—was to be emphasized; the NATO system was a way of keeping the United States involved.

So the British disliked the Pleven Plan and the whole EDC idea. The French concept of a European army, Bevin wrote, was "out of harmony with our general policy of building up the Atlantic Community as the major grouping for the future." It would be "a sort of cancer in the Atlantic body," and might give the Americans an excuse to disengage from Europe.[69] Europe alone would never be able to defend itself, and the French plan would not provide an adequate framework for integrating Germany into the West. Indeed, a major goal of the French plan was to keep Germany from being directly admitted to NATO. Bevin, on the other hand, was "thinking in terms of a comprehensive Atlantic Confederation which would include *all* Atlantic countries and also Germany." "In this framework," he noted, "the Germans could do no harm."[70]

The British, however, were reluctant to oppose the Pleven proposal head on. They felt they had to go along with the idea, since this was now the only way to get the Americans to send over the combat divisions and a NATO commander. But they themselves would not join the force, and they resented American efforts to push them into a European grouping. The United States had to understand, Bevin told a high American official, that Britain "was not part of Europe; she was not simply a Luxembourg."[71] If the continental countries, however, sought to build a European federal force, the United Kingdom would not try to prevent them from doing so.[72]

In France, the attitude was somewhat different. Many officials felt that some kind of a continental grouping might serve as a counterweight to what would otherwise be overwhelming American power within the alliance. It was in part for this reason that the idea of "building Europe" was popular in France, especially among the parties in the governing coalition. But at the same time there was a strong sense that it might be unwise to push the "European idea" too far. France did not want to be left alone on the continent with Russia and Germany. She wanted her Anglo-Saxon partners, and especially the United States, to remain by her side. From the

[67] See above, pp. 67–68.
[68] Bevin memorandum, November 24, 1950, DBPO II, 3:294.
[69] Bevin memorandum, November 24, 1950, and Bevin to Franks, November 29, 1950, ibid., pp. 293, 306.
[70] Bevin to Nichols, November 23, 1950, ibid., p. 290.
[71] Bevin-Spofford meeting, August 23, 1950, ibid., p. 4.
[72] Cabinet Defence Committee meeting, November 27, 1950, ibid., p. 302.

start the French had pressed for a strong American military presence in Europe. They had pushed hard for an integrated defense system and for the appointment of an American as NATO commander, and in 1950 continued to champion the cause of a unified western defense authority under American leadership. "A common authority," Pleven said, would enable the United States to exercise the "preponderant role which it must play in the Atlantic defense effort."[73]

The U.S. presence, moreover, was also needed to deal with the German problem. The EDC concept, Schuman wrote Acheson in January 1952, could not solve that problem by itself. There was a danger that Germany might some day want to secede from the EDC, and by early 1952 the French were in effect asking their Anglo-Saxon allies to guarantee that they would intervene militarily if Germany ever tried to pull out.[74]

The U.S. government, however, was reluctant to play this kind of role. The Americans were not in Europe, Acheson said, "to police the obligations of friends but to prevent aggression from without."[75] The Europeans were constantly trying to pull the United States in—to deepen the American military presence in Europe, to make sure the United States continued to play a fundamental role there, to build a strong NATO structure in which America was the dominant power. The U.S. presence was the central pillar around which their political system was to be built. But the Americans were wary. The JCS especially did not want to tie U.S. power too tightly to Europe. The Chiefs were interested in safeguarding U.S. autonomy and from the outset resisted European, and especially French, pressure for a highly integrated system, even one under American control.[76]

[73] Bruce to Acheson, August 1, 1950, FRUS 1950, 3:171.

[74] On the issue of an eventual German secession, see Schuman to Acheson, January 29, 1952; Bruce to Acheson, February 1, 1952; Churchill-Acheson meeting, February 14, 1952; western foreign ministers' meeting, February 14, 1952; Anglo-American meeting, February 16, 1952; Acheson to Truman, February 16 and May 26, 1952; and Tripartite Declaration, May 27, 1952; all in FRUS 1952–54, 5:10, 12–13, 39, 41–43, 46–47, 78–79, 682, 687.

[75] Acheson to Truman, ibid., p. 79.

[76] For the reluctance of the U.S. military leadership to make a full commitment, see JCS History, 2:385, 392–393; see also Militärgeschichtliches Forschungsamt, Anfänge westdeutscher Sicherheitspolitik, 1945–1956, vol. 1 (Munich: Oldenbourg, 1982), pp. 244–245. The American military authorities made it clear that they wanted U.S. forces to be able to act, if necessary, on a national basis, and indeed it was for this reason that the U.S. European Command was eventually created. Eisenhower in 1951 had resisted that kind of policy, not because the establishment of an American command made any practical difference, but rather because of the symbolism involved: it suggested that the Americans were trying to keep their distance from the integrated NATO system. General Ridgway, who succeeded him as SACEUR, was of a more nationalistic bent, and the JCS view on this narrow issue eventually prevailed. But Eisenhower had been able to make sure that SACEUR would report directly to the president, and that he, and not the JCS, would have direct control over American forces in Europe. See H. H. Lumpkin, "The SACEUR/USCINCEUR Concept" (U.S. European Command, August 1957; Defense Department FOIA release), with the following attached documents: Eisenhower to JCS, October 3, 1951; JCS to Eisenhower, October 5, 1951; Ridgway to Handy, May 31, 1952; Ridgway to JCS, June 11, 1952. The first of these documents was also published in the Eisenhower Papers, 12:592–593; an editorial note (p. 594, n. 5) explained Eisenhower's conflict with the JCS and cited some additional documentation. The JCS was quoted there as contending that the U.S. war plan had to be "based upon national considerations alone." The immediate issue had to do with whether the United States would

The United States, in fact, was pulled into the NATO system reluctantly. America had not set out to build an empire for herself in Europe; U.S. hegemony was never sought as a kind of end in itself. The American government would have liked nothing better than for the Europeans to come together in some kind of federal union and take over the burden of their own defense. But if that was not to happen, there was no alternative to a system based on a strong American presence: there was no other way to construct an effective counterweight to Soviet power in Europe without at the same time allowing Germany to become too strong and too independent. It was to take years, however, before the U.S. government fully reconciled itself to this conclusion.

It was not that no American government in the 1950s ever accepted the idea of a more or less permanent American military presence in Europe. Acheson was won over to this notion in mid-July 1951. In late June and early July, he was still thinking in terms ultimately of a purely European solution. America would eventually withdraw from Europe, he argued, but when she did, some sort of integrated military system had to be left behind. A situation where nothing would remain on the continent "except national forces solely under national control"—meaning especially a German army under German control—had to be avoided. A "workable European army" was thus the aim; "practical steps" toward this goal should be taken even in the short run; and eventually a European system might evolve out of the present U.S.–dominated NATO structure.[77]

But other high officials were quick to criticize Acheson's basic assumptions. They were not convinced that an essentially European framework was viable or that American policy should be built on the assumption that the United States would pull out of Europe at some point in the future. They doubted whether western Europe was strong enough, even in the long run, to stand up to Soviet pressure by itself. America, therefore, could not afford to think of herself as involved in Europe on an essentially temporary basis. The European army thus had to be thought of as being embedded "permanently rather than temporarily" within the broader NATO framework. And even if the Europeans, in theory, had the resources with which to balance Soviet power on their own, there was a basic political problem which had to be overcome if a purely European system were to be viable. A purely European solution would be feasible only if arrangements were worked out providing for "supra-national political direction" of the European force. Without a "permanent European political structure," the U.S. ambassador in France pointed out, the European forces would "revert to separate national armies" after the American troops and the U.S. commander were withdrawn; this, of course, was something that American policymakers very much wanted to avoid. The problem was that the issue of "European supra-national civilian control" was

---

be able to plan, on a national basis, for a retreat from western Europe. This issue was resolved by having both a SHAPE plan (which did not provide for troop withdrawals in the event of a war) and a U.S. plan (which did, and to which the European officers at SHAPE were not privy). See ibid., p. 805, n. 2; and *JCS History*, 4:308.

[77] Acheson to Bruce, June 28, 1951, and Acheson memorandum, July 6, 1951, FRUS 1951, 3:802, 804, 816.

very hard to resolve. As Acheson himself recognized, it went "so deeply into the foundations of sovereignty" that no quick or easy solution was at hand. Indeed, it was by no means obvious that a viable solution could ever be worked out.[78]

So in mid-July Acheson's line shifted radically. The new line emphasized NATO and the long-term American commitment to Europe, rather than European institutions like the EDC. Acheson now complained about the growing tendency to "treat European integration and a European Army as final solutions for all problems including that of security against Germany," and to disregard the long-range importance of developing the Atlantic community as a whole. Two weeks earlier, he had accepted the idea that the American presence was temporary, but he now rejected the notion that U.S. participation in NATO would "terminate at some indefinite time in the future." America's "long-term interests" would be "best served" not just by the development of the European Army plan, but by a "policy of permanent association" with the NATO allies for the defense of the Atlantic area as a whole. The reason had more to do with Germany than with Russia: the west Europeans, he now thought, might not be strong enough "by themselves to outweigh German influence" in the future European Army.[79]

Thus NATO was to be stressed. With regard to what the Europeans were doing, their military effort was what now mattered, and their forces were to be integrated into the NATO framework. The idea of a European Army as a politically independent entity was to be played down.[80] This was in line with basic political realities in Europe. The Pleven Plan, as Schuman himself pointed out at the time, had not called for a European "super-state" vested with the power to make war, but simply for the establishment of European administrations to recruit, train, and arm the European force.[81] The EDC, in other words, was to be supranational only in an administrative sense. There was to be no true pooling of sovereignty on the part of the member states. When the EDC treaty was finally worked out in mid-1952, one of its provisions called for a study of this issue, and in fact a plan for political union was eventually proposed. But as it turned out, that idea had even less appeal than the EDC itself.[82]

The inability of the Europeans to create a supranational political structure of their own meant that effective power would remain in American hands. Who but the Americans, who but SACEUR, could fill the vacuum created by the absence of a European political authority?[83] In fact, the Americans and the Europeans now

---

[78] Acheson to Bruce, June 28, 1951; Bruce to Acheson, July 3, 1951; Acheson memorandum, July 6, 1951; Spofford to Acheson, July 8, 1951; all ibid., pp. 803–804, 806, 814, 818, 822.

[79] Acheson to Bruce, July 16, 1951, ibid., p. 835.

[80] The Americans now decided to use the term "European defense forces," and not "Army," to underscore the idea that they were now talking about a "military field organization only," rather than a force with a strong political personality. See MacArthur to Perkins and Byroade, July 7, 1951, and Bruce to Acheson, July 15, 1951, ibid., pp. 820, 837n.

[81] Schuman himself stressed this point in his Strasbourg speech of November 24, 1950; for the text, see *L'Année Politique* (1950): 381.

[82] See Georges-Henri Soutou, *L'alliance incertaine: Les rapports politico-stratégiques franco-allemands, 1954–1996* (Paris: Fayard, 1996), p. 21.

[83] It is interesting to note that the military authorities took the lead in arguing that this problem, the absence of a true supranational political authority to control the European force, was the central

agreed that the European force would have to be controlled by SACEUR and embedded in the NATO system.[84]

By May 1952, a fundamental series of agreements had been worked out, and the United States was to play a key role in the political system those agreements were designed to establish. The Federal Republic was to be given a good deal of authority over her own affairs, but full sovereignty was not to be restored. The western allies, for example, would retain the right to station troops in Germany and to intervene in extreme cases in internal German affairs. The EDC would be set up, but this would not be a purely continental structure. SACEUR, an American general, would command that European force, and Anglo-American involvement was underscored by the Tripartite Declaration of May 27, 1952, which Britain, France, and the United States issued when the EDC treaty was signed. In this declaration, Britain and America promised to regard a defection from the EDC as a "threat to their own security" and to take action in accordance with the North Atlantic Treaty. Their troop presence on the continent, and especially in Germany, was explicitly linked to their "interest in the integrity" of the EDC: the troops were a "guarantee against German secession."[85] The Anglo-Saxons had thus agreed to underwrite the whole EDC system.

These arrangements never took effect. Successive French governments knew that the EDC treaty would be voted down if it were submitted to parliament, so they kept dragging their feet on ratification. But this was something that the American government—and especially the new Eisenhower government, which took office in January 1953—could scarcely bring itself to accept.

The Eisenhower administration had its heart set on the EDC. This was not because it saw the scheme as the only way the Germans could make a military contribution. The U.S. government was very reluctant to accept alternative ways of providing for a German defense contribution even when they became politically feasible. Indeed, Eisenhower thought that "to resort to a national army was a second choice so far behind EDC that there could be no comparison." From a purely military point of view, a German army deployed within the NATO framework might be the best solution, but for Eisenhower, the decisive consideration was political in nature. The real point of the EDC, he and Secretary of State Dulles both felt, was to weld France and Germany together as the core of a strong European

flaw in the whole EDC concept. The French military leaders, for example, thought that a European army made sense only in the context of a politically unified Europe, and that if one was to do this at all, one had to begin by creating common political structures. See Guillen, "Les Chefs militaires français, le réarmament de l'Allemagne et la CED," pp. 10, 25, and especially the extract from the notes of the French Chiefs of Staff meetings, February 6 and November 15, 1951, quoted in Doise and Vaïsse, *Diplomatie et outil militaire, 1871–1969*, p. 422. This was also the view of the American military leaders. Eisenhower thought in March 1951 that to set up a European army before there was a real pooling of sovereignty amounted to "putting the cart before the horse," and the JCS was arguing along these lines even in 1950. See Cyrus Sulzberger, *A Long Row of Candles* (New York: Macmillan, 1969), p. 615, and (for the JCS) *Anfänge westdeutscher Sicherheitspolitik*, 1:355 n. 23.

[84] Interim report of EDC conference, July 24, 1951, and Acheson and Lovett to Truman, July 30, 1951, FRUS 1951, 3:845, 851. For a similar British view, see Spofford to acting secretary, November 7, 1951, ibid., p. 913.

[85] Tripartite Declaration, May 27, 1952, FRUS 1952–54, 5:687; Acheson-Eden meeting, February 16, 1952, ibid., p. 46.

federation that could stand up to Russia on its own, and thus make it possible for American forces to withdraw from Europe in the near future.[86]

So the coming to power of the Eisenhower administration brought about a major reversal of American policy in this key area. Once again, the idea was that the Europeans should come together in some kind of federal union, that they should carry the burden of their own defense, and that the United States should sooner or later withdraw from Europe. The idea of a system based essentially on American power was rejected. The EDC, whatever its shortcomings, pointed in what was for Eisenhower the right direction. If there was a European army, there would eventually have to be European political institutions to control that army; the war-making power would have to be centralized; there would be no way to avoid a certain pooling of sovereignty. The EDC would pave the way toward a political unification of Europe, and since a unified Europe was by far the best solution to the basic strategic problem, the EDC could not be allowed to fail. Thus the EDC was now considered to be of vital importance—for fundamental political reasons, and not because it was the only structure that would permit German forces to be raised.

The new administration was therefore determined to do everything it could to get the French to go along with the plan. The French government said that without new American assurances, the EDC treaty would be voted down in parliament. So grudgingly, and with considerable irritation, the Eisenhower government reiterated the old U.S. assurances about maintaining an American military presence in Europe.[87] But the other side of this coin was a blunt warning to France that a collapse of EDC could lead to an American withdrawal from the continent. The French were also told that if the EDC failed, the United States, together with Britain, would simply rearm Germany by themselves.[88] Dulles was particularly heavy-handed. In December 1953, he publicly threatened that the defeat of EDC would lead to an "agonizing reappraisal" of America's policy toward Europe, and in July 1954 he told Pierre Mendès France, the French prime minister, that "public sentiment in the United States was reaching a point where we could no longer tolerate indefinite delay on French action. A hornets' nest of trouble would be stirred up if German rearmament had to be arranged without an EDC. Indeed, if this actually happened, all further U.S. aid to NATO would be cut off."[89]

---

[86] For Eisenhower's comment, see Bermuda conference, December 5, 1953, ibid., p. 1783. See the "Annotated Order of Business at Bermuda," c. December 1953, Dulles State Papers [DSP], reel 12, frame 16320, ML, and also Dulles–Mendès meeting, September 27, 1954, p. 4, State Department Conference Files, CF 370, RG 59, USNA, for the U.S. view that the EDC was important for political far more than for military reasons. On the issue of a withdrawal of American troops, see Trachtenberg, *History and Strategy*, pp. 163–164, 167–168, 185. This issue will be treated in greater detail in the next chapter.

[87] NSC meetings, February 26 and March 4, 1954, FRUS 1952–54, 7:1230 and 5:886–890. The assurances were transmitted to the EDC countries on April 15; see DOSB, April 26, 1954, pp. 619–620.

[88] See appendix 3, "The United States, France and the German Question, 1953–1954" (IS).

[89] As early as January 1953, Dulles was talking about the importance of frightening the French by raising the specter of a retreat to the peripheral strategy. See State–JCS meeting, January 28, 1953, FRUS 1952–54, 5:712–713. For the threat of an "agonizing reappraisal," see his speech to the NATO Council of December 14, 1953; it was reiterated at a press conference later that day. Ibid., pp. 463, 468. See also Dulles-Mendès meeting, July 13, 1954, ibid., p. 1020; NSC minutes, July 16, 1954 (for

But Mendès was not intimidated. In his view, French policy was bankrupt, both in Europe and in the Far East, and his job was to clean up the mess he had inherited. One of his main goals was to find a way out of the "permanent crisis" the EDC business had caused.[90] He allowed the EDC to be killed by the French parliament in August 1954, infuriating Dulles, who viewed him practically as a tool of the USSR.[91] But the French leader, as he himself complained, had been completely misunderstood.[92] Indeed, Mendès at this point did more than any other single individual to save the NATO system.

Mendès understood that the strategic environment in 1954 was very different from what it had been in 1950. The great rearmament decisions of late 1950 had begun to pay off in 1952. By 1954, American power had been built up to absolutely unprecedented levels. In strategic terms, it was quite clear that the West, and especially the United States, now had very much the upper hand. In this new strategic environment, it was much harder to think of West Germany as posing a threat. Any German force would be totally dwarfed by the great nuclear-armed forces that had grown up elsewhere. Even France herself was going to build up a nuclear force. The key decisions in this area were in fact made by the Mendès France government in late 1954. German military power was no longer the problem. Indeed, in this new strategic environment, German conventional forces were "more necessary than ever" from the French point of view. German rearmament would provide western Europe with some defense in depth, and thus would make France herself more secure.[93]

It was therefore clear to Mendès that the shibboleths of the past were obsolete and would have to be abandoned—although this had to be done with some care, and with an eye to political realities within France. For earlier French governments, one of the main functions of the EDC had been to keep Germany out of NATO; in 1953, a French prime minister had threatened that if, over France's objections, Germany were allowed to come into NATO with her own army—that is, on the same basis as everyone else—the French "would destroy the effectiveness of any German national army by being so strongly in opposition that in practical effect the lines of communication between Germany and the Atlantic would be

---

the quotation in the text), DDRS 1986/1561; and Bonnet to Mendès, August 24, August 27, and September 16, 1954, DDF 1954, pp. 228, 228n., 378.

[90] Mendès to Massigli, August 14, 1954, Mendès France Papers, Accords de Paris (first box), folder "Correspondance avec nos ambassadeurs," Institut Mendès France, Paris. See also a remark of Mendès to this effect, quoted by René Girault, in François Bédarida and Jean-Pierre Rioux, eds., *Pierre Mendès France et le mendésisme* (Paris: Fayard, 1985), p. 527.

[91] NSC meeting, September 24, 1954, FRUS 1952–54, 5:1266.

[92] See Mendès to Bourgès-Maunoury, August 26, 1954, in Pierre Mendès France, *Oeuvres complètes*, vol. 3: *Gouverner, c'est choisir* (Paris: Gallimard, 1986), p. 249. For Dulles's misunderstanding of Mendès's policy, see Dulles to Dillon, August 12, 1954, and Dillon to Dulles, August 13, 1954, FRUS 1952–54, 5:1030, 1032; Mendès to Bonnet, August 13, 1954, and Lagarde to Mendès, November 26, 1954, DDF 1954, pp. 142, 799–800; and Pierre Guillen, "La France et l'intégration de la R.F.A. dans l'OTAN," *Guerres mondiales et conflits contemporains*, no. 159 (July 1990): 78–79.

[93] Aline Coutrot, "La politique atomique sous le gouvernement de Mendès France," in Bédarida and Rioux, *Mendès France*, pp. 309–316; Georges-Henri Soutou, "La politique nucléaire de Pierre Mendès France," *Relations internationales*, no. 59 (Fall 1989): 451–470, and "La France, l'Allemagne et les accords de Paris," *Relations internationales*, no. 52 (Winter 1987): 468.

broken."[94] To Mendès this sort of attitude made no sense at all. It was out of keeping with the whole thrust of the West's German policy. To some of its supporters, the EDC, moreover, had become a kind of end in itself, more a matter of theology than of practical politics.[95] But to Mendès political realities were fundamental, and it quickly became obvious that the EDC could not be brought into being: the allies would not accept major changes in the treaty, and in its present form no French parliament would ever vote to ratify it. What all this meant was that some other arrangement had to be worked out—and worked out quickly—that would enable Germany to take part in the defense of the West.[96]

In talks with British leaders on August 23, Mendès had already suggested an alternative to EDC. There would be a broader but looser European grouping that included Britain. This arrangement, embedded in the larger NATO framework, would in his view probably be acceptable to the French parliament. French political leaders, after all, felt a certain responsibility to be constructive: the EDC had originally been proposed by their own government, and it was embarrassing that France was now unwilling to take yes for an answer. The arrangement Mendès had in mind, moreover, was in line with basic British thinking on these issues. British leaders had supported the EDC out of loyalty to America, but their hearts were never in it. A united Europe, in their view, could only develop through a kind of organic process; the rapid creation of supra-national European institutions like the EDC was not the way to proceed. "European federation may grow but it cannot be built," Churchill wrote Eisenhower in September. "It must be a volunteer and not a conscript."[97] So although the British were at first reluctant to part company with the Americans and take the path Mendès was now proposing, after the collapse of the EDC they came around quickly. Indeed, they presented the idea as though it were entirely their own, which Mendès was happy to let them do, since this would make it more palatable to the Americans.[98]

The U.S. government, however, was not at all happy with a solution of this sort, and accepted it in the end with remarkably poor grace. At the time the EDC plan collapsed, Dulles told his top advisers that the very idea of "another route toward German rearmament" was "too perfunctory," that it might be "necessary to disen-

[94] Top Secret Staff Summary, February 5, 1953, DSP/82–83/73328/ML.

[95] See his remarks in the National Assembly, December 23, 1954, in his *Oeuvres complètes,* 3:614.

[96] For Mendès's basic thinking, see Massigli to Mendès, August 12, 1954, and Mendès to Massigli, August 14, 1954, Accords de Paris (first box), folder "Correspondance avec nos ambassadeurs," Mendès France Papers. See also Mendès to Massigli, April 1, 1969 (particularly important for its account of the Chartwell meeting with British leaders on August 25), in Accords de Paris (second box), folder "Polémique Spaak/PMF," Mendès France Papers, and Massigli, *Une comédie des erreurs,* chaps. 11 and 12.

[97] Churchill to Eisenhower, September 18, 1954, *Eisenhower Papers,* 15:1299n.

[98] Mendès-Eden-Churchill meeting, August 23, 1954, and Mendès to main French ambassadors, September 18, 1954, Mendès France, *Oeuvres complètes,* 3:246–247, 317–321; Massigli to Mendès, September 9, 1954, and Parodi to Massigli, September 9, 1954, with Mendès draft proposal, DDF 1954, pp. 308–310, 312–315. For the British view of the EDC, see especially Dulles to Eisenhower, September 18, 1954, FRUS 1952–54, 5:1227. Churchill, Dulles reported, had said he was glad the "EDC tomfoolery" was over, that "he had only supported it because" Eisenhower had wanted it, but that he "had never had faith in it." And indeed all along he sought to keep the door open for the simpler solution of admitting Germany directly to NATO.

gage ourselves," that "there was no use building up Germany until a reasonable political foundation in Europe was created." There was no point, he said, constructing a "beautiful" NATO superstructure, with armies, standing groups, and so on, without the strong political base that something like the EDC would give it. A "boggy political foundation, lacking the firmness of unity or integration, would create shambles in this beautiful superstructure at the first real strain." The British and French probed to see if the U.S. government would go along with the NATO solution, but Dulles reacted coldly, again threatening a major reappraisal of American strategy, warning that the United States might not remain committed to the defense of Europe, and expressing "grave misgivings" about any solution other than the EDC.[99]

Dulles was sullen and resentful, but that did not prevent a fundamental settlement from being worked out very quickly in two major conferences held at London and then at Paris in the early fall of 1954. That settlement was embodied in a large number of interrelated agreements and declarations, commonly referred to as the Paris accords.[100] After years of effort, it seemed that the western countries had finally constructed a political system.

THE NATO SYSTEM

The Paris accords ended the occupation regime. The Federal Republic was to have, in a term of art, "the full authority of a sovereign state" over her own internal and external affairs. The settlement, moreover, provided for West Germany's admission to NATO and created the framework for the reestablishment of a German national army. But the allies insisted on retaining important legal rights that limited German sovereignty in major ways.

First of all, the western powers retained the right to intervene in extreme cases if the democratic system in Germany was threatened. In those early days of the Federal Republic, the western governments were not yet convinced that the "basic democratic order" had taken root in that country.[101] McCloy and Acheson had

---

[99] Dulles meeting with State Department officials, August 25, 1954, Dulles-Bonnet meeting, September 14, 1954, Dulles-Adenauer meeting, September 16, 1954, p. 6, DSP/64, frames 62974, 63055 and 63071, ML. Note also the grudging tone of Dulles's remarks at the conference at which the NATO solution was worked out, and also in the NSC meeting of October 6, 1954, FRUS 1952–54, 5:1357–1361, 1379–1382.

[100] For the key documents, see FRUS 1952–54, 5:1345–1366, 1435–1457. One very important document, the Convention on Relations between the Three Powers and the Federal Republic of Germany, is not printed here in its final form, although the original May 1952 version appears ibid., 7:112–118, and the October 1954 amendments are given ibid., 5:1341–1342. For the final text, see Paul Stares, *Allied Rights and Legal Constraints on German Military Power* (Washington, D.C.: Brookings Institution, 1990), pp. 91–96.

[101] Rupieper, *Der besetzte Verbündete,* pp. 60–63. There was a good deal of attention paid at the time to polling data, much of it disquieting, tracking the Germans' feelings about the Nazi period. See, for example, "Germans Continue to Like Nazism," Top Secret Staff Summary, January 16, 1953, DSP/82–83/73244–73245/ML. For official U.S. polling data from the period of the military government, see Anna J. Merritt and Richard L. Merritt, *Public Opinion in Occupied Germany: The OMGUS Surveys, 1945–1949* (Urbana: University of Illinois Press, 1970).

therefore felt in 1951 that the allies should be able to intervene if democracy in Germany was seriously menaced.[102] The unratified May 1952 agreement had explicitly authorized the allied authorities to declare a state of emergency if the democratic order was in danger and to take appropriate action. That provision was dropped when the basic convention was renegotiated in 1954, but this did not mean that this allied right had disappeared. Another section of the 1952 treaty gave each of the three western military commanders the right "independently of a state of emergency" to take whatever action was necessary "to remove the danger" if the forces under his command were menaced. This provision in itself, it was argued, would allow the allies to take action if the democratic regime in Germany were threatened, since the overthrow of the democratic order would automatically endanger the security of the western troops. Since this provision was embarrassing to Adenauer, the allies were willing to delete it from the final 1954 agreement provided that it was kept as a "practical arrangement," and the German chancellor went along with this solution. He gave the allies a written assurance that the deletion of the clause would change nothing because it was an "inherent right of any military commander" to take whatever action was necessary to protect the forces under his command. The allies thus had a rather broad and rather loosely defined right to intervene in extreme cases in internal German affairs.[103]

Germany's international behavior was a more fundamental concern. The western powers were worried that the Germans might some day try to reunify their country through military action. Adenauer was therefore asked to promise that the Federal Republic would not use force to achieve reunification or to alter her present boundaries, and the commitment he gave was underwritten by the three western powers.[104] There was an even greater fear that the Federal Republic might be tempted to make a deal with Russia providing for reunification on the condition that Germany cut her ties with the West. The three western allies therefore insisted on retaining their rights on all-German matters. The Federal Republic was recognized in the Paris accords as the only legitimate representative of the German people in international affairs, but had no authority to negotiate a German settlement on her own. The three powers retained the legal right to block any German settlement of which they did not approve, and this applied in particular to a settlement that provided for the neutralization of Germany.

These constraints on German sovereignty were anchored in the most important of the reserved rights, the right to station military forces on German territory. Under the Paris accords, the Federal Republic did not have the legal authority to make the western countries withdraw their forces. This important right was taken quite seriously by western leaders. As late as 1958, when the issue came up of

---

[102] McCloy to Acheson, August 18, 1951; Acheson-Schuman meetings, September 11 and September 13, 1951; FRUS 1951, 3:1175–1176, 1251, 1273.

[103] Convention on relations, May 26, 1952, FRUS 1952–54, 7:115; McCloy's view cited in High Commission report, August 9, 1951, and Schuman in foreign ministers' meeting, September 13, 1951, FRUS 1951, 3:1273, 1505. Kidd memorandum, September 10, 1954, and working party report, October 2, 1954, FRUS 1952–54, 5:1169, 1341; Ruhm von Oppen, *Documents on Germany under Occupation*, p. 628.

[104] Declarations by the Federal Republic and the three western powers, October 3, 1954, FRUS 1952–54, 5:1352–1354.

whether a Socialist government in Germany might some day try to work out a reunification-cum-neutralization agreement with Russia, Eisenhower, for example, made it very clear that America would not permit her forces to be "kicked out." "If the Socialists did come to power in Germany," he pointed out, "we might have to put even more U.S. forces in that country." Whatever the Germans themselves thought, the western allies had both the right and ultimately the power to block a neutralist solution.[105]

But juridical constraints were only part of the system designed to limit German freedom of action. The military arrangements worked out in late 1954 played an even more important role. West Germany was to be admitted to NATO, but the size and character of the German military establishment would be restricted in various ways. These limits were to be enforced by the Western European Union, a purely European body including both Britain and the Federal Republic, whose main function was to oversee the controls on German military power. The most important constraint related to nuclear weapons. The German government promised not to build nuclear weapons on its own territory, and the WEU was to enforce this restriction.[106]

The new West German army, moreover, was to be integrated into the NATO structure, and SACEUR's powers were to be considerably strengthened. The new NATO framework would provide an effective means of dealing with the German problem. In an integrated military system, dominated by American power, the Germans would find it impossible to operate independently. The constraints on German freedom of action in such a system would be natural and organic, and hence much more palatable than a control regime that too obviously reflected a deep-seated distrust. The idea of a strengthening of the NATO system as an alternative to EDC had emerged very quickly following the collapse of that project. The NATO commander, General Alfred Gruenther, played a key role in developing the idea and in convincing Mendès France, Eden, and indeed his own government to look toward a strengthening of SACEUR's authority for a solution to the problem of German power.[107] But the Europeans needed little convincing. Eden, for example, now said that the "only real control over German forces" would come from putting Germany in a military organization together with the United States.[108] For Mendès also, it was obvious that for these reasons a high degree of military integration was of fundamental importance.[109]

All this—the strengthened NATO structure, the western military presence on

---

[105] NSC meeting, February 6, 1958, Ann Whitman File [AWF], NSC series, box 9, Eisenhower Library [DDEL].

[106] Protocols to Brussels Treaty (including Adenauer declaration), October 22, 1954, FRUS 1952–54, 5:1446–56.

[107] On the general issue of alternatives to EDC, see ibid., pp. 693–694, 713, 799, 859–860, and ibid., 7:502. On the emergence of the NATO solution—that is, the strengthening of the NATO institutional structure—see Martin to Moore, January 18, 1954, 740.5/1-1854, RG 59, USNA. For the role that this concept played following the collapse of the EDC, see FRUS 1952–54, 5:1199–1201, 1219, 1228, 1282, 1293.

[108] Gruenther to Dulles and Conant, September 16, 1954, FRUS 1952–54, 5:1201.

[109] See his remarks in the National Assembly, December 23, 1954, in his *Oeuvres complètes,* 3:613; see also p. 608.

German soil, the reserved rights, the limits on German military power—added up to a system. Germany was to be tied to the West, and in important ways made part of the West, but her freedom of action was to be curtailed and she was not to have the same sovereign rights as the other western powers. Would it be possible to to discriminate against Germany in this way and still expect the Federal Republic to remain a loyal ally?

The problem would be serious in any event, but exactly how difficult it would be would depend on Soviet policy. The Soviets had it within their power to drive a wedge between Germany and the western countries. They could offer to accept reunification on the basis of genuinely free elections, demanding only that the re-unified state not be part of the western bloc. It was commonly assumed that the Germans, if it were just up to them, would be strongly tempted to go along with such a plan.[110]

The western powers, however, were not prepared in the early 1950s to accept reunification on that basis. There were two basic variants of the neutralization idea: the reunified state might be weak, its military power limited by outside controls, or it might again become a strong and truly independent great power. But neither alternative was particularly attractive. A weak all-German state, unprotected by the West, would be vulnerable to pressure from the east, but a strong, reunified Germany maneuvering between east and west was bound (as Dulles put it) to be "the cause of future trouble." If, however, the western countries opposed the idea too directly and too openly, and especially if they said things that made it clear that the reason they opposed it was that they distrusted the Germans and did not want them to become too strong and independent, the Federal Republic might end up turning away from the western alliance and the NATO system would quickly un-ravel. The result was that any real flexibility on the Soviet side would put the western powers on the spot: from the western point of view, the more generous the Soviet offer, the more dangerous it would be.[111]

[110] See, for example, McCloy to Acheson, September 23, 1951, FRUS 1951, 3:1785–1786, and also NSC 5524 of June 10, 1955, the draft of a basic policy document on the question of a deal with the USSR involving Germany. Adenauer, according to this latter document (p. 12), was strongly opposed to neutralization as the price for reunification, but the German people, the drafters felt, might well support a proposal along these lines. In the event of what appeared to be "a genuine Soviet offer of reuni-fication after free elections," the chancellor might "lose control of the situation," and German opinion might "force him to accept neutralization as the price." In file for NSC 5524, NSC records, RG 273, USNA.

[111] For the Truman administration's policy, see, for example, Acheson to Douglas, May 11, 1949, and Acheson to Jessup, May 18, 1949, FRUS 1949, 3:872–873, 884. For the Eisenhower policy, see below, pp. 134–135. For the quotation and the point about how these things could not be said openly, see Dulles's remarks in a meeting with Pinay and Macmillan, October 31, 1955, FRUS 1955–57, 5:652. The assumption that a flexible Soviet line would put the western powers on the spot is reflected in a large number of documents. Note, for example, the French view in early 1951 that Soviet acceptance of the western proposal on free elections would be "the most embarrassing thing that could happen to us," or the British view in 1953 that "there was a great danger" in pursuing a policy that looked toward reunification based on free elections. For the sources and a sampling of additional documents showing British and French officials arguing along these lines, see Bruce to Acheson, February 27 and also October 11, 1951, FRUS 1951, 3:1763–1764, 1796–1797; Dulles-Bidault-Salisbury meeting, July 11, 1953, FRUS 1952–54, 5:1625, 1627; Gifford to State Department, May 6, 1952, ibid., 7:227. For the French attitude, see especially Schuman to Bonnet, June 16, 1952, and Bonnet to Schuman, June 16,

In the early 1950s, these problems were by no means purely hypothetical. It seemed, beginning in late 1951, that the USSR might actually be willing to accept reunification on the basis of genuinely free elections.[112] In March 1952 Stalin publicly proposed an arrangement designed to appeal to the Germans. Germany would be reunified on a democratic basis; foreign troops would be withdrawn and the new state would not be part of either bloc; the Germans themselves would be allowed to raise military forces "essential for the defense" of their country. This, along with other provisions in his proposal, suggested that what the USSR had in mind was the resurrection of Germany as a great power, able to stand on her own and play a truly independent role in international affairs.[113]

In public, the allies dismissed this offer as a mere ploy designed to sabotage the process leading to Germany's rearmament as part of the western bloc. It turns out that this claim was correct: the Soviet move really was essentially a maneuver.[114] But western officials had no way of knowing that at the time, and were in fact alarmed: the proposal was viewed as dangerous precisely because it was felt that the Soviets might well be in earnest this time. The Europeans, and increasingly the Americans as well, thought they could not just reject the Soviet offer point blank, because of the effect this might have on Germany. The problem therefore had to be finessed. The goal was to be firm enough to prevent agreement with the Russians, but not so intransigent as to upset German opinion—or, in the case of Britain and France, domestic opinion either, since there were important political forces in both of those countries favoring détente and thus also the idea of a general settlement with the USSR, which meant above all the settlement of the German question through some sort of reunification deal.[115]

1952, Europe 1949–55/Allemagne/822. Note also Bidault's remarks in Dillon to State Department, April 26, 1953, FRUS 1952–54, 5:390, and a Note de la Direction Politique, April 15, 1955, DDF 1955, 1:456–458. The Americans also felt that a "really attractive" Soviet offer would embarrass the western countries, and were relieved when the Soviets turned out to be intransigent. See Eisenhower's remarks in the October 1, 1953, NSC meeting, FRUS 1952–54, 7:542. Dulles was also worried, before the Berlin foreign ministers' meeting at the beginning of 1954, that the Soviets might offer a "genuine settlement" providing for the "neutralization of a united Germany"; had they done so, he pointed out after the conference, the western powers would have had to make "certain very difficult decisions," but fortunately Soviet rigidity meant that the West had not been "obliged to face such tough problems." NSC meeting, February 26, 1954, ibid., p. 1222.

[112] See the report of an important Communist overture in François-Poncet to Foreign Ministry, October 16, 1951, Europe 1949–55/Allemagne/301/FFMA.

[113] This episode has received a great deal of attention in the German historical literature. The more significant works are cited in Rupieper, Der besetzte Verbündete, p. 241n. One of the most important studies, Rolf Steininger's Eine vertane Chance: Die Stalin-Note vom 10. März 1952 und die Wiedervereinigung (Bonn: Dietz, 1985), was translated into English and published under the title The German Question: The Stalin Note of 1952 and the Problem of Reunification (New York: Columbia University Press, 1990). Rupieper's own discussion of the issue (pp. 240–300) is also quite useful, especially for the U.S. side of the story. For the French side, see Soutou, "La France et les notes soviétiques de 1952 sur l'Allemagne."

[114] See Gaddis, We Now Know, p. 127, especially the passage citing Alexei Filitov, "The Soviet Policy and Early Years of Two German States, 1949–1961," CWIHP conference paper (1994), p. 6. See also Gerhard Wettig, "Stalin and German Reunification: Archival Evidence on Soviet Foreign Policy in Spring 1952," Historical Journal 37 (1994): 411–419.

[115] For the seriousness with which the Soviet overtures were taken, see Noblet to Foreign Ministry,

Acheson, however, wanted to take a somewhat harder line. He took it for granted that the United States had to use "every means" in its power to head off talks with the USSR on the German question. But the very blunt tone he wanted to adopt would have hurt all three of the major European governments politically. In 1952 the allies therefore had to press hard to get him to take a less uncompromising line and not to close the door on talks with the USSR. The allied attitude upset him: he was "baffled" and "astonished" by the Europeans' willingness to meet with the Soviets. But these differences were more apparent than real: the allies might need to appear relatively flexible, but they, like the Americans, had no real interest in settling the German question along the lines the Soviets had proposed.[116]

How, then, could the western governments evade the pressure for a negotiated settlement without alienating the German people in the process, and without paying a major political price at home? The basic tactic was to pose conditions that would look good to German and domestic opinion, but which the Soviets were bound to reject. The tactic could be used to prevent a conference from convening, or to sabotage negotiations after they had begun.[117] The key thing here was to avoid focusing too narrowly on free elections. The French in particular were afraid

---

March 14, 1952, Europe 1949–55/Allemagne/819/FFMA, and Massigli to Foreign Ministry, March 18, 1952, MP/69/FFMA, giving both his and Eden's reaction to Noblet's dispatch. Both Massigli and Eden took these Soviet moves quite seriously. For the more skeptical reaction of the top permanent official at the Quai d'Orsay, see Parodi to Noblet, March 18, 1952, Europe 1949–55/Allemagne/820/FFMA. For more evidence of the seriousness with which top British officials took the Soviet initiative, see Roberts to Strang, March 14 and March 15, 1952, with appended comments, FO 371/97878 and 97879/PRO. For the U.S. reaction, see for example Rupieper, *Der besetzte Verbündete,* pp. 243–245. For the assumption that the proposal could not simply be rejected, that there were important political forces in Britain, France and Germany that had to be accommodated, and that the issue therefore had to be finessed, see, for example, Gifford to State Department, May 11, 1952, FRUS 1952–54, 7:239. Note also the British document quoted in Steininger, *German Question,* p. 168, n. 27. This concern with domestic opinion came to play an even greater role for Britain and France in 1955. See FRUS 1955–57, 5:137, 161, 171, 304.

[116] See Acheson to Gifford, April 18, May 9, May 12, June 10, and June 12, 1952, and Gifford to Acheson, May 6 and May 11, 1952; in FRUS 1952–54, 7:211, 229, 234–237, 239–242, 263, 268. Note also Bidault's remarks in western foreign ministers' meeting, July 11, 1953, ibid., pp. 1614–1615. The French foreign minister made it clear that although he disliked the pressure for talks with Russia, for domestic political reasons he had to accept the idea of negotiations.

[117] On the tactic of making offers that one hoped would be or knew to be unacceptable, see, for example, the French views cited in Bruce to Acheson, October 11, 1951, FRUS 1951, 3:1797; Acheson to State Department, June 28, 1952, and Donnelly to State Department, October 14, 1952, FRUS 1952–54, 7:277, 385. One typical point was that the western powers could make certain offers because the Soviets were not "likely to take them up." Dulles to Gifford, October 13, 1953, ibid., p. 655. Note also Bidault's comment that because the chances for a negotiation were so slight, the West would do well to offer the Soviets those guarantees "which they were not interested in anyway." Western foreign ministers' meeting, October 16, 1953, ibid., p. 695. British Foreign Office views were cut from the same cloth. See especially Eden marginal comments on Roberts to Strang, March 15, 1952, and Eden to Foreign Office, March 21, 1952, FO 371/97879, PRO. In a minute appended to the first of these documents, Strang had argued that if the Soviets were really willing to accept reunification on the basis of free elections, the West would have no choice but to go along, even though the elections would result in a Schumacher government that would probably reverse Adenauer's policy of integrating Germany into the West. But Eden was not so sure. "Is this really so?" he wrote on the margin. "Are there not other conditions we could add?"

that if this were left as the central issue, the Soviets might "well be ready to concede much or most of what we would demand." The allies had to retain some room for maneuver, and Schuman now said the West should call in addition for getting rid of four-power control. The slogan should be "not merely free elections, but free elections for a free Germany."[118] This sort of slogan would appeal to the Germans, but it also represented a position that the Soviets would not accept: they would not agree to reunification on terms that would give the new state the freedom to remain in the western bloc. The allies would thus be able to finesse the problem. But the very fact that maneuvering of this sort was necessary pointed to a basic weakness in the western system: it depended on German cooperation and loyalty, but at the same time one of its fundamental goals was to limit German power and independence. Could this sort of system be maintained indefinitely?

For the time being, however, the system worked, in large part due to the policy of the German government itself. That policy in turn was determined to a quite extraordinary extent by a single quite extraordinary individual, Konrad Adenauer, chancellor of the Federal Republic from its founding in 1949 until his fall from power in 1963.

Adenauer was by his own account far more pro-western in those early years of the Federal Republic than the German people as a whole. His great goal was to make Germany a western country. By tying her to the West politically, economically, and eventually militarily, she would be absorbed into the western world, and would in turn absorb western values. This pro-western policy went hand in hand with a certain coolness toward reunification. Since the Soviets would not permit a reunified Germany to be integrated into the western system, reunification would have to be put on the back burner. But Adenauer was not too eager for reunification in any case. The Germans in the east, he said, were not like the Germans in the western part of the country. They were Prussians, nationalistic and militaristic. The West Germans, on the other hand, especially Rhinelanders like himself, were more closely tied to western Europe. It did not make sense, therefore, to bring the east Germans, or even the West Berliners, into the Federal Republic too soon, before the system really had a chance to take root—that is, before Germany had really consolidated her position as part of the West.[119]

Adenauer was thus the western powers' great ally in dealing with the problems

---

[118] Gifford to State Department, May 6, 1952, FRUS 1952–54, 7:227; see also Schuman to Bonnet, June 16, 1952, Europe 1949–55/Allemagne/822/FFMA.

[119] For Adenauer's thinking and the gap between his views and the feelings of the German people as a whole, see, for example, Adenauer-Acheson meeting, November 13, 1949, FRUS 1949, 3:309–310; Adenauer-Murphy meeting, July 8, 1954, FRUS 1952–54, 7:581–582; Beam to State Department, April 28, 1955, ibid., 5:153; Schwartz, *America's Germany*, pp 52, 78; Steininger, *German Question*, pp. 22, 118–119; and Hans-Peter Schwarz, *Adenauer*, vol. 2; *Der Staatsmann, 1952–1967* (Stuttgart: Deutsche Verlags-Anstalt, 1991) pp. 145–147. For Adenauer's coolness even on bringing West Berlin into the Federal Republic—in part, in 1949 especially, because his plurality was so thin that he could not afford greater Socialist strength in the Bundestag—see Rupieper, *Der besetzte Verbündete*, pp. 161–162; François-Poncet to Schuman, October 19, 1949, Europe 1949–55/Allemagne/8/FFMA; U.S. ambassadors' meeting, October 22, 1949, FRUS 1949, 3:288; and above all Cyril Buffet, "Le Blocus de Berlin: Les Alliés, l'Allemagne et Berlin, 1945–1949" (doctoral thesis, University of Paris IV, 1987), p. 1004.

posed by the USSR's German policy in the early 1950s. His aim was to head off the possibility that four-power talks on Germany might develop a certain momentum and lead to reunification along neutralist lines. He pursued that goal with considerable tactical skill. He would not openly reject the idea of negotiations with the east, but rather, in the words of one of his closest advisers, sought "to feign flexibility in order to be free to go with the West."[120] One of his basic tactics was to outflank his nationalist opponents from the right—for example, by raising claims about the territories east of the Oder-Neisse line that he knew the Soviets would find unacceptable, or by talking about how Germany could be reunified not through concessions but through a "policy of strength," a strategy which he probably never took all that seriously himself.[121]

The western governments could scarcely believe how lucky they were that someone like Adenauer was in charge of German policy. Even the British, whose relations with Adenauer were always relatively cool, thought in late 1950 that he was "probably the best chancellor" they could get.[122] The French, whatever their difficulties with Adenauer on day-to-day issues, were from the outset delighted that he was at the helm in Bonn.[123] The U.S. government quickly came to see him as indispensable. As Eisenhower put it in October 1953, "our whole political program in Europe" was based on "Adenauer's continuance in power."[124] In 1955, the president referred to him as the West's "ace in the hole."[125] The western countries had to do everything they could to keep him in office, especially since the alternative in the early 1950s, a Socialist government led by the highly nationalistic Kurt Schumacher, was seen as appalling.[126] If left to themselves, the Germans

[120] Blank-Alphand meeting, October 11, 1951, cited in David Large, *Germans to the Front: West German Rearmament in the Adenauer Era* (Chapel Hill: University of North Carolina Press, 1996), p. 133.

[121] For Adenauer's calculations, and for the point that a certain degree of tension served his interests, see especially François-Poncet to Schuman, June 30, 1952, Europe 1949–55/Allemagne/10/FFMA, and François-Poncet to Foreign Ministry, June 14, 1952, Europe 1949–55/Allemagne/821/FFMA. On the use of the Oder-Neisse issue for the purpose of preventing a successful negotiation, see François-Poncet to Foreign Ministry, March 17, 1952, Europe 1949–55/Allemagne/820/FFMA. See also Steininger, *German Question*, pp. 48, 168. For a French official's appreciation of this strategy, see Bruce to Acheson, October 11, 1951, FRUS 1951, 3:1797. On the "policy of strength," see, for example, Klaus Erdmenger, "Adenauer, die Deutsche Frage und die sozial-demokratische Opposition" and Wilfried Loth, "Adenauers Ort in der deutschen Geschichte," in *Adenauer und die Deutsche Frage,* ed. Josef Foschepoth 2nd ed. (Göttingen: Vandenhoeck and Ruprecht, 1990), pp. 173–174, 282. Adenauer himself, in a talk with the Soviet ambassador, later dismissed the term "policy of strength" as a mere cliché. Adenauer, *Erinnerungen,* 3:453.

[122] Steininger, *The German Question,* p. 45.

[123] See especially François-Poncet to Schuman, November 6, 1949, Europe 1949–55/Allemagne/254/FFMA: "Le Cabinet ADENAUER est certainement, de tous ceux que nous avons connus et connaîtrons, le plus disposé à rechercher non seulement une amélioration des relations, mais une entente durable avec la France. Nous n'en aurons pas, de sitôt, de meilleur."

[124] Eisenhower diary notes, October 8, 1953, p. 9, DDE Diary/4/DDEL. See also Dulles's remarks in western foreign ministers' meeting, July 11, 1953, FRUS 1952–54, 5:1617.

[125] Meeting of western leaders, July 17, 1955, FRUS 1955–57, 5:345. This had been the U.S. attitude virtually from the outset. See, for example, McCloy to Acheson, November 17, 1950, FRUS 1950, 4:780. "Adenauer's outright championship" of the West had to be supported, the high commissioner argued. He could see "no one else" who had taken a "similar stand."

[126] For the western powers' view of Schumacher and for Adenauer's use of the specter of a Schumacher government as a way of exerting pressure on the allies, see Schwartz, *America's Germany,* pp.

might well opt for some kind of reunification-cum-neutralization deal, but Adenauer as chancellor could tip the balance in the other direction. Therefore Adenauer had to be supported.

Adenauer, of course, wanted the western powers to see him as an indispensable partner. He knew that their confidence in him was his single greatest domestic political asset and he did everything he could to cultivate it.[127] So he told the western governments what he knew they wanted to hear. When dealing with the Americans, he emphasized the importance of U.S. leadership, of America as a "preceptor" who would exercise a "guiding hand" in Europe.[128] When dealing with the French, he gave "Rhenish," anti-Prussian, and even anti-Berlin themes freer play—real views of his, but probably expressed in rather exaggerated terms, especially in the immediate postwar period.[129] When dealing with the allies in general, he and his assistants often stressed how important it was that he stay in power. In July 1954, for example, Adenauer "dwelt upon the fact" that the "whole responsibility" for the pro-western policy rested "on his old shoulders." He "foresaw nothing but trouble if he should die." In his view, "it would be a long time before the Western powers found another German political figure" who would pursue such a pro-western policy. He had gone much further in this direction "than the German people were prepared to go of their own inclination." If his policies were discredited, there would be "an inevitable drift towards a more independent policy and Germany's traditional interest in the East."[130]

In the 1950s, the western governments agreed that Adenauer had to be kept in power, and the Americans in particular were determined to give him what he needed to remain at the helm in Germany. Dulles, for instance, actually intervened

53–56, 80, 243, and François-Poncet to Schuman, September 1, 1952, ff. 182–189, Europe 1949–55/Allemagne/10/FFMA.

[127] This applied in particular to Germany's relations with America. Even in 1960, long after the honeymoon with the United States had ended, Adenauer still recognized this basic principle: "je enger die europäischen Staaten mit Amerika verbunden seien, desto stärker sei ihre innenpolitische Position." From account of Adenauer-Debré meeting, October 7, 1960, Adenauer, *Erinnerungen*, 4:75.

[128] Conant to Dulles, November 30, 1953, FRUS 1952–54, 7:683. On Adenauer's ability to lay it on with a trowel, see the wonderful anecdote in Schwartz, *Adenauer*, 2:62–64.

[129] For reports of three meetings with Adenauer during this period, see Stenger memorandum of conversation, September 18, 1945, Y/282/FFMA; French consul general in Düsseldorf to Saint-Hardouin, June 13, 1946, Y/286/FFMA; Arnal to Saint-Hardouin, March 25, 1947, Y/293/FFMA. In the first of these meetings, Adenauer said he favored the creation of three independent states in western Germany—the Rhineland, Bavaria, and northwest Germany—linked to each other in more or less the same way the British dominions were. These would become part of a French-led "United States of Western Europe." The French were also easily the best of the occupying powers. His comments in the two later meetings were a good deal less extreme. But in milder form Adenauer continued to emphasize his dislike for the East—including eastern Germany and even Berlin—in meetings with French officials (who, as a rule, shared those sentiments). See, especially, Buffet, "Blocus de Berlin," p. 1004; note also the sources cited in Schwartz, *America's Germany*, p. 332, n. 42. On Adenauer's flirtation in 1945 with the French occupation authorities, see also Schwarz, *Adenauer*, 1:449–462.

[130] See Kidd memorandum, July 8, 1954, FRUS 1952–54, 7:581–582. See also Adenauer to Dulles, August 9, 1955, p. 4, 762.00/8-955, RG 59, USNA; Loth, "Adenauers Ort," p. 271; Hallstein's and Adenauer's own comments in François-Poncet to Mendès France, August 16 and September 17, 1954, DDF 1954, pp. 155, 384–385; and Blankenhorn's remarks in a meeting with the French diplomat Jean-Marie Soutou, June 16, 1955, DDF 1955, 1:788.

in the German national elections in 1953, warning of disastrous consequences if Adenauer was not returned to power; one German politician claimed that this intervention brought Adenauer a million votes.[131] In mid-1954, the State Department was worried that with the impending collapse of the EDC, "Adenauer would be discredited and the Germans might adopt a more 'Germanic' attitude favoring independent action and playing off East against West." So when the German government at this point asked for a public statement that the return of Germany's political rights would not be further delayed—something, it pointed out, which Adenauer needed in connection with forthcoming elections in North Rhine–Westphalia—that statement was issued the very same day.[132] But it was not just that the western countries felt they had to make concessions in order to keep Adenauer in power. What was going on also had a more positive side: with Adenauer in charge of German policy, the western powers felt more comfortable about treating the Federal Republic as a full, or nearly full, partner.

And indeed the period from 1953 to 1955 saw a certain easing of the West's German policy. The Americans were coming to feel that the fundamental problem could not be finessed forever. As an important State Department paper pointed out in September 1953, the "demand for unification" was "the primary issue in Germany, which neither Adenauer nor the Western Powers could openly oppose without grave risk of alienating German public sentiment. In these circumstances, the tactics adopted by the West in the past may be no longer adequate."[133] By early 1955, there was an even stronger sense that the western countries needed to take the reunification issue seriously. Western policy on this question had so far been "like a promissory note on which, thanks to the Russians, we have never yet had to make payment." But one could not be sure that this situation would last forever, and in order to avoid losing the Germans, one had start thinking about what western policy should be if reunification became "a real possibility."[134]

To Dulles, it was obvious that the USSR was not simply going to hand over East Germany without getting anything in return. If the western countries were serious about reunification, they had to be prepared to offer the Russians something real. There would need to be some kind of "security agreement," the heart of which would be an arrangement to control the level and nature of German armament. The Soviets would have to be allowed to play a key role in such a system. As Dulles

---

[131] Editorial note, FRUS 1952–54, 7:532–533; U. W. Kitzinger, *German Electoral Politics: A Study of the 1957 Campaign* (Oxford: Clarendon, 1960), p. 251. For Dulles's continuing concern with Adenauer's domestic political position and his realization that western policy had to be framed with an eye to this problem, see Dulles to Eisenhower, July 21, 1955, FRUS 1955–57, 5:439.

[132] Dulles-Krekeler meeting, June 23, 1954 (with attachments), and Merchant meeting with senators, June 24, 1954, FRUS 1952–54, 7:574–578. Adenauer himself was quite open in talking with western leaders about his domestic political problems. See, for example, the Dulles-Adenauer meeting, September 16, 1954, pp. 4–5, DSP/64/63069–63070/ML, or Adenauer's remarks in a meeting with the allied High Commission, November 16, 1950, AAPBD 1:267–268.

[133] "Basic Position Paper on Germany for Four-Power Talks" (PTS D-1), September 8, 1953, enclosed in JCS 2124/94, September 12, 1953, CCS 092 Germany (5–4–49) sec. 17, SO File, JCS Chairman's Files, RG 218, USNA. The PTS papers—the series of papers on "Proposed Talks with the Soviets"—are not included in FRUS 1952–54, vol. 7.

[134] Cecil Lyon (German desk officer in the State Department) to Merchant, January 4, 1955, appendix on "German Unification," 762.00/1-455, RG 59, USNA.

pointed out in 1955, reunification "would be impossible unless it was achieved under some sort of international control in which the Soviet Union would have a voice. The Soviets would never simply throw East Germany into the pot to be added to West Germany and the united Germany to be further rearmed against the Soviet Union itself." If the level of German armament was to be controlled by the western powers alone, he said, if the West was simply to reject as a matter of principle the very idea of European security arrangements, "we might just as well give up all hope of unifying Germany."[135]

British and French attitudes were moving in the same direction. The professional diplomats at the Quai d'Orsay and in the Foreign Office might have been perfectly happy with the status quo, but the top political leadership in Britain and France viewed the question somewhat differently, in part because public pressure to pursue détente was a major factor in both of those countries.[136] For Bidault, back in office in 1953 as foreign minister, what this meant was that the western governments had to go through a kind of charade.[137] But in 1954 Mendès France was ready to take a fresh look at the whole complex of problems relating to Germany, Russia, and European security. Perhaps the controls outlined in the WEU Treaty could somehow be extended into some kind of all-European security system; maybe a general settlement could be worked out on that basis.[138] Churchill also thought the problem of a negotiated settlement had to be taken seriously, and in 1953 began to push actively for talks with the Russians.[139] Churchill's interest in détente was rooted in what was going on in the nuclear area, especially the coming of thermonuclear weapons. Dulles was also worried about the implications of the thermonuclear revolution, and in late 1953 began talking about the need for a "spectacular effort to relax world tensions on a global basis."[140]

Adenauer's views on reunification were also beginning to soften. In 1953 and again in 1955 he urged the western powers to seize the initiative in pressing for negotiations. The plan was for the West to propose reunification in the framework of a European security system, with a special military status for eastern Germany

[135] Dulles in State Department meeting, September 26, 1953, and Dulles-Molotov meeting, February 6, 1954, FRUS 1952–54, 7:636, 987; Dulles meeting with British, French, and German leaders, June 17, 1955, and (for the quotation) Dulles in NSC meeting, July 7, 1955, FRUS 1955–57, 5:238, 276–277.

[136] Gifford to State Department, May 11, 1952, FRUS 1952–54, 7:239; and Beam to Dulles, April 26, 1955, 396.1/4-155, RG 59, USNA. See also Watson-Elbrick-Beam-Tyler meeting, April 1, 1955; Beam to State Department, April 30, 1955; Dulles to acting secretary, May 8, 1955; Jackson log, July 11, 1955; all in FRUS 1955–57, 5:137, 161, 171, 304.

[137] Western foreign ministers' meeting, July 10, 1953, FRUS 1952–54, 5:1614–1615; western foreign ministers' meeting, October 16, 1953, ibid., 7:695. For Bidault's real views—his feeling that the status quo was by far the best solution—see especially Soutou, "La France et les notes soviétiques," p. 272.

[138] Note especially the Mendès France U.N. speech of November 22, 1954, in his *Oeuvres complètes,* 3:494–495.

[139] Steininger, *German Question,* pp. 103–109. See also Josef Foschepoth, "Churchill, Adenauer und die Neutralisierung Deutschlands," *Deutschland Archiv* 17 (1984): 1286–1301, and Rolf Steininger, "Ein vereintes, unabhängiges Deutschland? Winston Churchill, der Kalte Krieg und die deutsche Frage im Jahre 1953," *Militärgeschichtliche Mitteilungen* 36 (1984): 105–144.

[140] Dulles memorandum, September 6, 1953, FRUS 1952–54, 2:457–460.

and adjacent areas as well.[141] Adenauer's closest adviser, Herbert Blankenhorn, explained to Americans that the plan was essentially a tactical move designed to improve Adenauer's position in the forthcoming elections.[142] Domestic political considerations continued to play an important role in Adenauer's thinking when the issue came up again in 1955.[143] Yet it seems that Adenauer, especially in 1955, was not just going through the motions for internal political purposes. The chancellor's domestic political situation had improved dramatically as a result of the 1953 elections and he was no longer so worried about nationalist opposition at home.[144] But his position had become more flexible by 1955, and German tactics that year were very different from what they had been in the past. In 1951 and 1952, Adenauer had raised issues like the Oder-Neisse line with the goal of sabotaging negotiations. But now he and his government secretly made it clear to the Americans that they were prepared to make major concessions—to accept the Oder-Neisse line and the demilitarization of eastern Germany, and to include the WEU limits on German military strength in the settlement with the USSR—if negotiations were productive and a real agreement on reunification seemed within reach.[145]

The Americans now also hoped for an agreement and Dulles thought some arrangement might actually be negotiable.[146] There would be a European security

[141] For the best account, see Schwarz, *Adenauer,* 2:85–87 (for 1953), 186–187 (for 1955). See also Blankenhorn-Riddleberger meeting, July 10, 1953, FRUS 1952–54, 5:1606. There is also some information in the Thurston paper, "Proposed Talks with the Soviets (PTS)," September 24, 1953, 092 Germany (5-4-49) sec. 19, S.O. File, RG 218, USNA. For the German role in 1955, see Beam to State Department, April 28, April 29, and July 9, 1955; Merchant to Dulles, June 15, 1955; Dulles-Adenauer-Macmillan-Pinay meeting, June 17, 1955; all in FRUS 1955–57, 5:155–158, 229, 235, 309–310. See also *Anfänge westdeutscher Sicherheitspolitik,* 3:151. Note finally the list of documents relating to the "Adenauer plan—1955," DDRS 1989/3311.

[142] See, for example, Bruce diary, July 9, 1953, FRUS 1952–54, 7:484; and Blankenhorn-Riddleberger meeting, July 10, 1955, ibid., p. 1607.

[143] Note Blankenhorn's reference to putting forward proposals "for tactical and propaganda reasons" in U.S. Delegation to State Department, April 29, 1955, FRUS 1955–57, 5:157. See also U.S. to State Department, July 9 and July 15, 1955, ibid., pp. 309, 322, and Soutou-Blankenhorn meeting, June 16, 1955, DDF 1955, 1:789.

[144] Conant to Merchant, April 25, 1955, FRUS 1955–57, 5:147–148.

[145] Conant to Merchant, April 25, 1955; Adenauer-Dulles-Macmillan-Pinay meeting, June 17, 1955; Brentano in meetings with western foreign ministers, September 28 and October 24, 1955; all in FRUS 1955–57, 5:148, 238, 600, 625. Brentano's declaration in September and October about NATO, as part of an agreement with the Soviets, offering not to move troops into eastern Germany, represented a softening of the German position, and is thus further evidence of increased flexibility. For the earlier German view, shared by the Americans and the French but not by the British, see U.S. Delegation to State Department, July 9 and July 15, 1955, ibid., pp. 310, 323. See also Adenauer's comments in the CDU executive committee, May 2, 1955, in Günter Buchstab, ed., *Adenauer: "Wir haben wirklich etwas geschaffen": Die Protokolle des CDU-Bundesvorstands, 1953–1957* [CDU-BV] (Düsseldorf: Droste, 1990), pp. 432–433.

[146] For Dulles's optimism, see NSC meeting, May 19, 1955, and Dulles-Eisenhower meeting, August 11, 1955, FRUS 1955–57, 5:184, 546. For the argument supporting the optimistic view, see "Basic U.S. Policy on Four-Power Negotiations," June 10, 1955, in NSC 5524 file, RG 273, USNA; the line of argument developed here was watered down somewhat in the final version, NSC 5524/1, in FRUS 1955–57, 5:287–288. Note also Soviet Ambassador to France Vinogradov's statement that the Soviets were "now prepared to accept free all German elections subject to strict international control, provided

system—that is, German military power would be subject to outside control. The Americans were also beginning to be attracted to the idea of a disengagement agreement and the reunification of Germany outside of NATO. In Dulles's new view, a strong NATO was not "essential as a deterrent to war," and he was open to the idea of a "reunified Germany, friendly to the West," but not formally part of the western alliance. The best solution was still to keep a united Germany in western institutions like NATO and WEU, but if a reunified Germany remained outside as a pro-western "neutral," NATO strategy could be readjusted to deal with that situation.[147] The Soviets would also be offered certain far-reaching juridical guarantees. The western powers would promise to come to the aid of the USSR if she were attacked by Germany. This "undertaking by the United States to engage itself on the side of the Soviet Union in the event of a war in Europe" was, to Dulles's mind, a very important concession, and he wanted to hold it in reserve until it was really needed. "We did not wish to cheapen such a momentous decision," he said, "by pressing it upon the Soviets even before they had asked for it."[148] The United States was by this point taking the idea of a negotiated settlement very seriously indeed. In 1951 and 1952, the western governments had adopted an obstructionist strategy, but by 1955 U.S. tactics were designed to maximize the chance of a successful outcome.

All of this reflected a major shift in official American thinking. Dulles's inclination at this point to accept a formally neutralized, reunified Germany was the most remarkable aspect of the new policy. The Americans were now evidently willing to go a good deal further than they had been in 1953—and in 1953 policy had already become more flexible than it had been around 1951. By 1953 western policymakers had concluded that a reunified Germany should have the right to choose whether to ally with the West or with the East, or to remain neutral; the western powers were no longer insisting that the reunified state would have to remain in NATO, although they calculated that the Germans would probably maintain their alliance with the West if they were free to make that choice. But now in 1955 Dulles

---

only that foreign troops were withdrawn from German soil prior to the vote." Dillon to Dulles, June 23, 1955, 611.61/6-2355, RG 59, USNA. The CIA, however, was not impressed by such indicators and took a more pessimistic view. See the Intelligence Comments on NSC 5524, July 1, 1955, FRUS 1955–57, 5:251–252. Other governments, however, thought—or, in the case especially of some French officials, feared—that the Soviets were now really prepared to take a flexible line. See, for example, the Note de la Direction Politique, April 15, 1955, DDF 1955, 1:456–458.

[147] Dulles's meeting with his top advisers, May 3, 1955, DSP/64107-109/ML; NSC meeting, October 20, 1955, FRUS 1955–57, 5:616–617. See also the record of another meeting between Dulles and leading State Department officials, April 8, 1955, p. 5, DSP/66/64026/ML. For a further indication of the seriousness with which the issue was taken in May, see Wilson to Gruenther, May 6, 1955, and Gruenther to Wilson, May 25, 1955, CCS 092 Germany (5-4-49) sec. 30, RG 218, USNA. SACEUR was asked to give his views on the question, and the preparation of an answer caused him "considerable agony." His acceptance of the idea of the reunification of Germany outside of NATO and the withdrawal of western forces from German territory was subject to one basic condition: that "German potential can be related to the NATO system under all circumstances," and that a relationship with the Germans could be worked out "which would permit a satisfactory degree of joint defense planning." Dulles, in fact, had been toying with the troop disengagement idea even in 1953. See Dulles memorandum, September 6, 1953, FRUS 1952–54, 2:459–460.

[148] Dulles-Macmillan-Brentano-Pinay meeting, September 28, 1955, FRUS 1955–57, 5:598.

was inclined to go much further, and felt that the West could in the final analysis accept the Soviet condition that the reunified Germany would have to stay out of NATO, whether she wanted to be part of that alliance or not.

This, of course, marked a sharp break with prior American policy. Under Acheson, and in the early Eisenhower period as well, the very idea of a neutralization of Germany had been considered entirely out of the question. America could "hardly tolerate a neutralized Germany," Eisenhower's national security adviser said in 1953. In 1954, Bedell Smith, then under secretary of state, argued along similar lines. And in late 1954, Dulles had been livid when he had mistakenly thought that Mendès France favored the idea of a neutralized Germany, reunified on the basis of free elections. But now, just a few months later, he himself embraced this kind of approach, and public statements were beginning to reflect the new American thinking.[149]

Dulles's goal was to accommodate German national feeling, but his flirtation with the neutralization idea upset Adenauer and strained U.S.–German relations. After all Adenauer had done to bring Germany into the West, the Americans were now getting ready to cast Germany out of NATO, to put German security at risk, to side with his political opponents at home—and all this without any real consultation with his government. For years the Americans had taken the line that neutralization would be a disaster, and now, all of a sudden, they seemed to be taking the opposite position. How could one trust people like that? And yet in the current system Germany was supposed to remain absolutely dependent on the United States for her security.[150]

The new policy thus led to serious problems with one of America's most important allies, but it did not bring a real settlement with the Soviet Union any closer. Dulles had calculated that going the extra mile might well make a basic settlement possible, but he had been too optimistic. The USSR was simply not interested in the sort of arrangement Dulles had in mind. Even in 1952, the Soviets had not really favored a reunification-cum-neutralization deal. The huge American military buildup decided on at the end of 1950 had had a major impact on the

---

[149] NSC meeting, August 13, 1953, September 26, 1953, FRUS 1952–54, 7:505; Bonnet to Mendès France, August 16, 1954, DDF 1954, p. 158. Even as American policy was changing in 1955, the president and Dulles continued to tell the allies that a neutralization of Germany was practically "unthinkable." As Eisenhower himself put it: "there was no possibility of having 80 million hard-working people in the center of Europe as neutrals. It simply could not be done." See Eisenhower-Eden-Faure meeting, July 17, 1955, and Dulles-Pinay-Macmillan meeting, October 31, 1955, FRUS 1955–57, 5:348, 652. Of the public statements, Eisenhower's remarks in his press conference of May 18, 1955, were the most important. See *Anfänge westdeutscher Sicherheitspolitik 1945–1954,* 3:148–149; Rupieper, *Der besetzte Verbündete,* pp. 419–420; Schwarz, *Adenauer,* 2:184. Adenauer, incidentally, mistakenly thought that it was Eisenhower and not Dulles who was behind this sort of thing; Eisenhower, in his view, was "soft," and only Dulles was "tough." See ibid., p. 388, and Adenauer, *Erinnerungen,* 3:306, 328.

[150] For Adenauer's distrust of America, see Schwarz, *Adenauer,* 2:184, 205–206, 385. Note also the record of Adenauer's long meeting with Dulles on June 13, 1955, which was mainly devoted to a discussion of the issue. Adenauer described a whole series of German intelligence reports indicating the seriousness of what was going on; Dulles did not talk much about the substantive issue, but rather focused on the question of whether the president was pursuing this policy behind his back. DSP/66/64250–55/ML.

strategic balance, and the Soviets in 1952 had been deeply concerned by what the Americans were now saying and doing—especially by all the talk about rollback and having it out with the Russians before it was too late.[151] In such circumstances, the old Soviet policy of exploiting the divisions between Germany and the western powers—of developing the "contradictions" within the capitalist camp—still had a certain appeal. The Soviets felt they should try to get whatever mileage they could out of an appeal to German nationalism—as long as they were confident that they would never have to make good on that policy.

As it became clear, however, that the belligerent rhetoric about rollback and liberation was not really being translated into effective policy, Soviet concerns subsided, and the Russians lost whatever interest they had in playing the German card. Indeed, one is struck by how quickly, even in 1952, proposals designed to appeal to German nationalist feeling were superseded by references to the Potsdam agreement and to the principle of four-power control.[152] By 1954, Soviet appeals to German national feeling had become a mere propaganda exercise, and not a particularly effective one at that. Publicly, at the Berlin foreign ministers' conference in February of that year, Molotov, for example, condemned the Versailles system of 1919 as an "instrument of oppression," and said it had led to war. But when he met with Dulles privately, he laid out the real Soviet view. The problem with Versailles, he said, was that it had not been enforced, and he called for reunification under quadripartite control. His assumption was that the four victor powers had a common interest in keeping Germany down.[153] By 1955, it was obvious that the Soviets were simply not interested in the reestablishment of a strong, reunified, and fully sovereign German state, free of foreign troops and able to chart its own course in international affairs. A divided Germany, with the Federal Republic locked into the western system, dependent on powers who were comfortable with the status quo and whose fundamental interest was the maintenance of peace—this was clearly a much better solution from the Soviet point of view than a reunified Germany free of great power control.

In their talks with the Russians, western statesmen frequently argued that the NATO system worked to the USSR's advantage: a Germany tied into that system could not pose a threat to the USSR. The western, or at least the American goal was to persuade the Soviets to accept reunification without insisting that the new state leave NATO. But the more effective those arguments were, the less of an incentive the Soviets had to agree to reunification. The one thing that might get them to accept a formal settlement was a belief that the status quo was unstable. As Dulles pointed out, for the Soviets to agree to reunification, they would have to "receive the impression that by sitting on top of the German situation, there might

---

[151] See Trachtenberg, *History and Strategy*, chap. 3, esp. pp. 149–151. Note also the views of the Soviet diplomat Vladykin paraphrased in Daridan to Foreign Ministry, June 28, 1952, Europe 1949–55/Allemagne/302/FFMA.

[152] Soviet note, May 24, 1952, and Kennan to State Department, May 25, 1952; and Smith to Conant, August 17, 1953; all in FRUS 1952–54, 7:252–253, 625.

[153] U.S. Delegation to State Department, February 2, 1954, and Dulles-Molotov meeting, February 6, 1954, ibid., pp. 915, 985–987. Note also Dulles-Adenauer meting, February 18, 1954, PPS 1954, box 79, Germany, RG 59, USNA.

be an explosion."[154] But if the NATO system in its present form kept the Germans in line and thus removed that risk, what incentive did the Soviets have to negotiate a settlement that might lead to a general troop withdrawal from Germany? The current system—the limits on German sovereignty, the presence by right of western troops on German soil, and West Germany's political and military dependence on the western powers—was linked to the division of Germany and especially to the presence of Soviet troops on the Elbe. Why should the USSR agree to a peace settlement that would change all that? Reunification would probably mean full sovereignty for Germany, the withdrawal of Soviet troops, and the transformation of Germany's political relationship with the western powers. Germany would be less dependent on the West, more able to relate to her allies as a full equal. If the goal was to keep German power limited, wasn't the present system much better, even from the Soviet point of view? If the NATO system kept Germany from posing a threat, what was the point of putting that system at risk? Why not just keep things as they were?

So at the 1955 Geneva summit conference, Soviet leaders made it abundantly clear that they had little interest in a settlement that would provide for the reunification of Germany. The security guarantee that the western powers were willing to make in order to entice the Soviets into an agreement was dismissed out of hand: the USSR was a great power and did not need to rely on guarantees from the West. There was also a domestic factor that had a certain bearing on Soviet policy at this point. Stalin had died in 1953 and by now the post-Stalin struggle for power had run its course. Nikita Khrushchev, the head of the Communist party, was now the dominant figure in Moscow. His defeated rivals, especially Beria and Malenkov, had been associated with the flexible line on Germany, and this issue had played a certain role in the leadership struggle. Khrushchev had no great interest in vindicating his opponents after the fact by taking an accommodating position. Instead, the Soviets insisted that the division of Germany was a reality which both sides would have to accept, and they now recognized the Federal Republic of Germany and exchanged ambassadors with that state.[155]

A CHANCE FOR PEACE?

The fact that no formal east-west settlement was worked out in 1955 meant that the 1954 arrangements would remain intact. Could a stable peace have been based

---

[154] State Department meeting, August 28, 1955, FRUS 1955–57, 5:557.

[155] See especially Heads of Government meeting, July 20, 1955, and NSC meeting, July 28, 1955, ibid., pp. 391, 531. On the struggle for power within the Soviet Union and its impact on the USSR's German policy, see James Richter, "Reexamining Soviet Policy towards Germany during the Beria Interregnum," CWIHP Working Paper no. 3 (Woodrow Wilson Center, Washington, D.C., 1992). For the discussion within the Soviet leadership, see also Hope Harrison, "The Bargaining Power of Weaker Allies in Bipolarity and Crisis: The Dynamics of Soviet–East German Relations, 1953–1961" (Ph.D. diss., Columbia University, 1993), pp. 50–51, 109. Khrushchev (and the East German leaders as well) took what Beria and Malenkov were doing quite seriously. They had been willing, Khrushchev later told Ulbricht, to "liquidate the GDR." Khrushchev-Ulbricht meeting, November 30, 1960, in Hope Harrison, "Ulbricht and the Concrete 'Rose': New Archival Evidence on the Dynamics of Soviet–East German Relations and the Berlin Crisis, 1958–1961," CWIHP Working Paper no. 5 (Woodrow Wilson Center, Washington, D.C., 1993), appendix A.

on the system set up by the Paris accords? The answer turns on an analysis of Soviet, German, and American policy. Was this a system which all three major players were in the final analysis willing to accept?

The Soviets, first of all, would almost certainly have gone along with it. The NATO system, although officially directed against them, in practice solved their number one security problem. Assuming it worked the way the allies said it would, and assuming above all that the United States remained in Europe and continued to dominate the NATO structure, German power would be contained, and Germany could pose no threat. Western statesmen from the start argued that Germany's integration into the western system was the only viable solution to the German problem. This was the gist of Dulles's argument to Molotov at the Berlin conference in early 1954, and at Geneva in 1955 Eden told the Russians that it was much better, even from their point of view, to "see German military power contained in NATO than loose about the world." It was in part for this reason that the Americans had supported the EDC so strongly. The Germans, Eisenhower said in 1953, "must never be in a position where they could blackmail the other powers and say 'meet my terms or else,'" and the EDC would prevent them from ever being able to do so. The goal, he said, was to "integrate them in a federation from which they could not break loose." And in 1955 he told the Russians that the NATO system would serve the same function. It would make it impossible for German forces to engage in independent military operations, and the physical presence of western forces on German soil, he pointed out, would "constitute great security for all."[156]

The Soviets understood that there was something to this argument, and never simply dismissed out of hand the general idea that the western system could keep Germany in line. They certainly were aware of the fact that the western powers agreed that there was a German problem, and they recognized that the West's goal was never to build up as strong a German state as possible to serve as a kind of anti-Soviet battering ram. Stalin, for example, knew that the EDC was not directed against the Soviet Union, but was rather about "power in Europe"—that is, how much power Germany would have.[157] The USSR's great fear was that the system might not work as advertised. The Soviets were worried that America and the other western powers would "soon begin losing control over the Germans," and that West Germany might "become a loose cannon on the European boat." The western goal of a Germany "firmly anchored in NATO" and locked into a purely defensive policy they thought might well be beyond reach. Soviet reservations, in other words, were rooted in doubts about the viability of the NATO system. If it turned out, however, that the western powers were able to work out arrangements that would keep German power limited, the most basic Soviet interests would be

[156] Eisenhower-Churchill-Bidault meeting, December 5, 1953, FRUS 1952–54, 5:1783. U.S. Delegation to State Department, February 3, 1954 (two documents) and February 11, 1954; Dulles-Molotov meeting, February 6, 1954; ibid., 7:927, 934, 984–986, 1020. U.S. Delegation to State Department, July 20, 1955 (two documents), and Dulles-Ollenhauer meeting, November 7, 1955, FRUS 1955–57, 5:393, 395, 406, 696.

[157] Stalin meeting with East German leadership, April 7, 1952, in *Pieck: Aufzeichnungen,* pp. 396–397.

protected, and the USSR was evidently prepared to live with a system of that sort.[158]

Indeed, the Soviets in the late 1950s sought to work out an understanding with the Americans that would stabilize and formalize the status quo in Europe. The old Soviet idea about the importance of broadening "every fissure, every dissent and contradiction in the imperialist camp," which Molotov still championed in 1957, Khrushchev and his supporters now dismissed as dogmatic and old-fashioned. The new leadership was not interested in building up Germany as a counterweight to American power, but preferred to think in terms of a system dominated by America and Russia—a system, that is, in which American power dominated western Europe and in which Germany remained dependent on the United States for protection.[159]

And this, in the final analysis, was a system which the Germans themselves could also accept, even though German power and German freedom of action were limited in important ways. There was a whole series of reasons why this was so. The constraints on German sovereignty were not too discriminatory, and were not too overtly directed toward keeping the Germans in line. Some of them—the provisions extending SACEUR's authority, for example—had a perfectly straightforward military rationale. The goal of reunification had, of course, been put on the back burner, but reunification through force was practically out of the question anyway, and a peaceful solution was also highly unlikely, since the Soviets would insist on terms that would compromise German security and which the Federal Republic could therefore scarcely accept. In such circumstances, most of the constraints on German sovereignty, one could reasonably calculate, were of little practical importance and might well in time rust away through disuse. Instead of making a fuss over these provisions, it made more sense to be patient and ride the great political tides which would in time bring about a full transformation of Germany's political status.

Beyond that, there were certain juridical arguments for accepting the regime established by the Paris accords. Full sovereignty for the Federal Republic would imply that the division of Germany was definitive: the reserved powers, on the other hand, underscored both the provisional status of the West German regime and the allies' continuing responsibility for creating a unified German state.[160]

---

[158] Zubok, "Soviet Intelligence and the Cold War," p. 10; Vladislav Zubok, "Khrushchev and the Berlin Crisis (1958–1962)," CWIHP Working Paper no. 6 (Woodrow Wilson Center, Washington, D.C., 1993), p. 3. See also Zarubin's comment in a meeting with Bohlen, July 19, 1955, FRUS 1955–57, 5:387. For another indication (from 1962) that the Soviets wanted West German power to be contained within a system dominated by the United States—that they preferred this to a purely continental system—see Soutou, *L'alliance incertaine*, p. 264. The idea that the Soviets had a certain interest in the maintenance of an American military presence in Europe, and especially in Germany, is a central theme of Caroline Kennedy-Pipe, *Stalin's Cold War: Soviet Strategies in Europe, 1943 to 1956* (Manchester: Manchester University Press, 1995). For a related argument bearing on the later Cold War period, see John Keliher, *The Negotiations on Mutual and Balanced Force Reductions: The Search for Arms Control in Central Europe* (New York: Pergamon Press, 1980), pp. 144–145.

[159] Yuri Smirnov and Vladislav Zubok, "Nuclear Weapons after Stalin's Death: Moscow Enters the H-Bomb Age," CWIHP *Bulletin* (Fall 1994): 17.

[160] It was for the same sort of reason that the Federal Republic did not have a proper constitution,

There was also the special problem of Berlin to consider. The allies' right to be there was rooted in the occupation regime, but that regime had to be understood as a bloc. To liquidate it entirely in West Germany would to a certain degree undermine the allies' right to remain in Berlin, and to the extent (minor, but not negligible) that such juridical considerations affected both Soviet and western policy, a restoration of German sovereignty might not be a good thing for the Berliners.[161]

And then there was the Adenauer factor. In those early years, the chancellor did not want Germany to have complete freedom of action in any case. The German people, he thought, might not be able to resist Soviet blandishments after he left the scene, and might, if it were just up to them, opt for some sort of reunification-cum-neutralization deal with Russia. But a Germany not tied to the West, in his view, would not be strong enough either morally or materially to maintain "a free and independent central position in Europe." Germany had to be anchored in the West; he could therefore accept the idea that the Federal Republic's freedom of action needed to be curtailed.[162]

While all these factors were important, the fundamental taproot of German policy was geopolitical in nature. The geopolitical situation was very different now from what it had been after the First World War, and this meant that German foreign policy would now be cut from an entirely different cloth. In the 1920s, Germany's aim was to throw off the "shackles of Versailles" and resume her position as an independent great power. But Germany had been shielded from Soviet pressure at that time by a wall of independent east European states, tied to the West; and the Soviet Union had been much weaker in the 1920s than she was after World War II. Of the western powers, only France had tried to enforce the Versailles system; by the beginning of 1920, America had defected and Britain had half-defected; so not much had stood between Germany and her ambitions, and in fact the democratic governments of the Weimar Republic resisted Versailles practically from the start. Germany in the 1920s maneuvered between Russia and the west-

but only a "Basic Law," and that it had been drafted not by a true constituent assembly, but by a "Parliamentary Council." The Germans at that point were anxious to avoid anything that would suggest that a new sovereign state was being set up. See Murphy to Marshall, July 8 and July 9, 1948, and ministers president to Clay, July 10, 1948, FRUS 1948, 2:382–386.

[161] See Rupieper, Der besetzte Verbündete, pp. 151–180, esp. pp. 169, 178, and Schwartz, America's Germany, p. 238. The argument about Berlin was in fact a major theme in discussions of Germany's legal status. Bevin, for example, warned Acheson in December 1950 that "it might be dangerous for us to abandon the quadripartite concept in Western Germany and at the same time insist on maintaining it in Berlin." Calendar 139i, DBPO II, 3:374. See also McCloy to Acheson, December 1, 1950, and U.S. Delegation to Acheson, December 13, 1950, FRUS 1950, 4:791, 799; Foreign Ministry to Massigli and Bonnet, January 6, 1951, and Sauvagnargues memorandum on question of supreme authority, January 17, 1951, Europe 1949–55/Allemagne/914/FFMA.

[162] See McCloy to Acheson, July 6, 1951, FRUS 1951, 3:1489; Conant to Dulles, July 2, 1953, FRUS 1952–54, 5:1588; Schwartz, America's Germany, p. 247; and Steininger, German Question, pp. 22, 118–119. It is also worth noting in this context that Adenauer was prepared to go along with the French idea that America should underwrite the EDC system and take action in the event Germany tried to secede, but only if it were part of a more general system in which the U.S. would block such developments as a Communist takeover in Italy or a Gaullist regime in France. This was a call for a kind of Brezhnev Doctrine in reverse, and the Americans, of course, rejected the idea. But it is yet another illustration of the way pressure for a deepening of the American involvement came from Europe. See Acheson-Eden meeting and Acheson to Truman, both February 16, 1952, FRUS 1952–54, 5:46, 79.

ern powers, increasing her leverage in international affairs and gradually recovering her power; the "shackles of Versailles" had effectively been thrown off even before Hitler came to power. In the 1950s, however, a powerful Red Army was in the middle of Germany, not behind a hostile Poland tied to the West. And it was not just France, supported to a certain extent by Britain, that was now propping up the western system. The United States, a much stronger country, had become the principal western power. Germany was threatened, and a strong western alliance offered security; and Germany was being accepted into the western world as an almost equal partner. The Germans this time had a much stronger incentive to cooperate with the western allies and take their place in the system those powers were constructing.

All this was reinforced by another set of factors that was moral and historical in nature. In the Cold War environment, Germany had a strong incentive to embrace democratic values. The western countries could only be counted on to defend a democratic Germany, a Germany that rejected her Nazi past and had turned away from the nationalistic excesses that had poisoned her political life for so many years. This was a Germany that recognized the concerns of the rest of the world as having a certain legitimacy, and that was willing to accept certain limits on her power as the price she had to pay for what she had done in the past. World War II was very different from World War I, both in its origins and in terms of what happened while it ran its course. Since Germany really was guilty this time, the constraints on German sovereignty laid down in the 1950s could be accepted in a way that the milder constraints laid down at Versailles never could have been. And Germany's integration into the western system was a form of moral rehabilitation: Germany was being accepted into the western world as a real partner, with all that that implied, in moral as well as in material terms.

All these factors pointed in the same direction. What they meant was that the Germans could accept the 1954 system. They could live with the arrangements they and their allies had worked out, even though those arrangements limited their military power and political independence in important ways—but only if the United States remained on the continent and continued to play a fundamental political role in Europe.

The viability of the system, then, depended ultimately on American policy. The Russians would go along with it, and so, in the final analysis, would the Germans. It was the American attitude that was problematic. The U.S. presence was what made the whole system work. Who would protect Germany if the United States was not involved? Britain and France could obviously not provide the necessary degree of assurance. If America pulled out, the Germans would therefore have to build up their own forces. The regime of constrained German sovereignty, of a non-nuclear Federal Republic, of a highly integrated western military system, could scarcely survive an American withdrawal. But with America in, the system could work. Western Europe could be defended, but at the same time, the USSR would not feel threatened by a resurgent Germany.

American power was thus the heart of the NATO system, and the American presence in Europe was what held this whole political structure together. The 1954 arrangements could serve as the basis of a stable peace if, and only if, the United

States remained on the continent and continued to play a central political and military role. The problem was that Eisenhower and Dulles were determined "to get out of Europe" and make the Europeans carry the burden of their own defense.[163] Russia and Germany might be willing to go along with a system in which German power was limited and the United States was the dominant force in the West, but the American government had no interest in playing that kind of role on a permanent basis.

This basic policy choice—the determination to withdraw from Europe in the not too distant future—was to have enormous and far-reaching repercussions. It meant that the world would have to go through another great period of crisis before a relatively stable system would finally come into being.

[163] NSC meeting, July 7, 1955, FRUS 1955–57, 5:274.

Eisenhower and Nuclear Sharing

IN THE EARLY 1950s, the western powers had sought to construct a system that would provide for the defense of Europe without at the same time allowing Germany to become strong enough to act independently. With the signing of the Paris accords in late 1954, it seemed that they had finally achieved their goal. Soviet power would be balanced by an impressive NATO force that would include a German national army, but Germany's freedom of action would be limited in a whole series of ways. The most important constraint related to nuclear weapons. Technically, the Federal Republic had only promised not to build nuclear weapons on her own territory, but the spirit of the 1954 system was that Germany would not have a nuclear force under her own control. A non-nuclear Germany could not stand up to the USSR on her own. As long as the Federal Republic was dependent on her allies for protection, and as long as those allies were committed to an essentially defensive policy, there was no way West Germany, or the western bloc as a whole, would pose a threat to Soviet control of the east.

The Soviets could therefore live with the arrangements the western powers had worked out among themselves in 1954, and the Germans could also accept a system that provided security for the Federal Republic. But the viability of the system depended on a continuing U.S. military presence in Europe. If the Americans pulled out, a non-nuclear Germany would be vulnerable to Soviet pressure; the Federal Republic would then be secure only if she developed a strong nuclear capability of her own. But a powerful and independent Germany would no longer be locked into a purely defensive policy, and this was why, from the Soviet standpoint, anything that pointed in the direction of a resurgence of German power—above all, the building of a German nuclear force—was bound to be a source of great concern.

The problem was that Eisenhower very much wanted to withdraw American forces from Europe in the not too distant future. He thought the Europeans should be able to defend themselves as soon as they could. Europe should become a third great "power mass," capable of standing up to the USSR on its own. This implied that the Europeans, including the Germans, needed a nuclear capability under their own control. In fact, by the end of the Eisenhower period, the NATO allies had been given effective control of American nuclear weapons. This was not something that "just happened," because the military was out of control or because central authority was lax. It was the result of a basic policy choice that had been made at the highest political level: the U.S. government had in effect opted for what was called a policy of nuclear sharing.

The nuclear sharing policy was of enormous historical importance, and for that policy to be understood, its roots need to be examined in some detail. The meaning of what was going on in the field with regard to control of the weapons only becomes clear when one understands the depth and seriousness of the thinking in Washington. And, conversely, the thinking has to be taken seriously because of what was going on in the field. The next three sections therefore examine the three great taproots of the sharing policy: Eisenhower's basic views about the future of Europe and America's role in the world; the military strategy adopted in December 1954 for the defense of western Europe; and thinking about long-term changes in the overall strategic balance, especially about the implications of an eventual, and inevitable, loss of American strategic superiority. A final section will then deal with the sharing policy itself and with how it was actually implemented at the time.

THE EISENHOWER CONCEPT

Eisenhower's long-term goal was simple. He wanted to make western Europe into what he called "a third great power bloc." When that happened, he told the NSC in 1955, the United States would no longer have to bear the enormous burden of providing for the defense of Europe. America, he said, could then "sit back and relax somewhat."[1]

Eisenhower had been thinking along these lines well before he became president. The "great industrial complex of Western Europe," he had pointed out in February 1951, could obviously not be lost to the Communists, and America had to take the lead in organizing a defense system, since the European allies were still too weak to stand on their own. For the time being, a sizeable American army had to be physically present to make it clear that the United States "meant business." But sooner or later the Europeans would have to defend themselves. In the long run, the new NATO commander wrote from Europe, "there is no defense for Western Europe that depends exclusively or even materially upon the existence, in Europe, of strong American units. The spirit must be here and the strength must be produced here. We cannot be a modern Rome guarding the far frontiers with our legions if for no other reason than that these are *not,* politically, *our* frontiers. What we must do is to assist these people [to] regain their confidence and get on their own military feet."[2]

This was now his standard theme. Western Europe, with "about 350 million people, tremendous industrial capacity, and a highly skilled and educated population," he told a White House meeting in January 1951, could certainly generate the power to keep the Soviets at bay. Why was western Europe, with all its resources, so afraid of "190 million backward" Russians? The answer was that the USSR was a powerful, unified state, while Europe was weak and divided. The Europeans had to get moving, they had to take responsibility for their own military fate, they had to put their antiquated national differences aside and organize themselves into a strong and unified bloc. The western countries "could tell Russia to

---

[1] NSC meeting, November 21, 1955, FRUS 1955–57, 19:150–151. Note also the president's reference to the importance of western Europe becoming "a third great power complex in the world," in Eisenhower to Gruenther, December 2, 1955, *Eisenhower Papers,* 16:1919–1920.

[2] Eisenhower to Bermingham, February 28, 1951, *Eisenhower Papers,* 12:76–77. Emphasis in original.

go to hell if they only would get together, raise enough men, and produce enough equipment."[3]

While the Europeans were coming together and developing their military power, American forces obviously needed to be present. But the U.S. umbrella was not meant to be permanent. If Eisenhower said it once, he must have said it a thousand times: a large-scale American military presence in Europe was originally supposed to be temporary. "The stationing of U.S. divisions in Europe," he pointed out in a 1953 NSC meeting, "had been at the outset an emergency measure not intended to last indefinitely."[4] When it was decided to deploy those divisions, he noted later that month, no one had "for an instant" thought that they would remain there for "several decades"—that the United States could "build a sort of Roman Wall with its own troops and so protect the world."[5] U.S. forces had been sent to Europe, he pointed out in 1956, just "to bridge the crisis period during which European forces were building up."[6] And again in 1959: "the six U.S. divisions which we had deployed to the NATO area were originally intended to be our response to an emergency situation. These divisions were sent in order to encourage the European nations to become the first line of their own defense against the Soviet Union."[7] America's ultimate goal was to pull out and turn over to the Europeans responsibility for their own defense. Eisenhower himself felt, toward the beginning of his tour of duty as SACEUR, that "if in ten years, all American troops stationed in Europe for national defense purposes have not been returned to the United States, then this whole project"—meaning the whole NATO effort—"will have failed."[8] And he never really changed his mind on this basic point: his greatest frustration as president was his inability to withdraw the American forces from Europe.[9]

But if America was ever to pull out of Europe, the Europeans would first have to come together in a real political union. The power of western Europe could not "be fully developed" as long as that area was "just a hodge-podge of sovereign political territories," he wrote in December 1951. The Europeans should put their trivial national differences aside and create a kind of United States of Europe. With a united Europe, America would have nothing to worry about. "The whole 'German' problem would be solved," Europe would quickly be able to defend herself, and America would soon be able to withdraw her troops. In fact, there was "no real answer for the European problem until there is definitely established a United States of Europe." He was fed up with talk about the need for a cautious step-by-step approach. Unification should be brought about "in a single plunge" and "the sooner the better." In December 1951, he urged French Prime Minister Pleven to invite the continental NATO powers to a "constitutional convention" to create a

---

[3] White House meeting, January 31, 1951, FRUS 1951, 3:449–458.

[4] NSC meeting, October 7, 1953, FRUS 1952–54, 2:527.

[5] Eisenhower to Gruenther, October 27, 1953, *Eisenhower Papers,* 14:611.

[6] Eisenhower-Dulles meeting, October 2, 1956, FRUS 1955–57, 19:360.

[7] NSC meeting, March 26, 1959, FRUS 1958–60, 7(1):444.

[8] Eisenhower to Bermingham, February 28, 1951, *Eisenhower Papers,* 12:77.

[9] There are many documents that record Eisenhower expressing views of this sort. For a representative sample, see FRUS 1952–54, 2:456; FRUS 1955–57, 5:274; FRUS 1958–60, 7(1):479, 508, 516, 519; and the references cited in Trachtenberg, *History and Strategy,* p. 185, n. 56.

European union. American efforts, he wrote in June 1952, should be directed to "one great and ultimate purpose," the "political and economic unification of Europe."[10]

It soon became clear, however, that the great goal could not be achieved overnight. If it were to be achieved at all, a more gradual approach would have to be adopted. If Europe was not going to develop quickly into a "third great power bloc," American power would have to remain committed to the defense of Europe for a certain period of time. Eisenhower was thus coming to think in terms of a three-stage process. There was the initial emergency period when a sizeable American army would be stationed in Europe, lasting for perhaps five to ten years. There would be a second period when Europe would take over the burden of providing for her own ground defense. America, at this time, would continue to underwrite the defense of western Europe with her strategic nuclear force, but would station only token ground forces—perhaps only a single division—on the continent. And finally there would be a third period when Europe, while remaining friendly with America, would stand on her own militarily and would emerge as a truly independent "power mass" in world affairs.

Eisenhower wanted to move as fast as he could along this road, and all the major elements in America's European policy in the mid- and late 1950s were rooted in this kind of thinking. On the political level, the U.S. government pressed hard for European unification. On the military level, its basic goal was to turn over to the Europeans primary responsiblity for their own defense. And implicit in this policy was the assumption that the Europeans would have a nuclear capability of their own—that western Europe would not simply remain a strategic protectorate of the United States.

The support for European unification, to take the first of these general policies, was not rooted in a particularly sophisticated analysis of the issue. European unification was an important goal, and therefore anything that seemed to promote the "European idea" was worth supporting. A European union, a true merging of sovereignties, a common parliament, common elections, a real federal government—all that would be ideal. But if something this radical was beyond reach for the time being, and all one could get were integrated European administrative structures à la Jean Monnet, that was fine too, since it was taken for granted that this sort of thing might well in time develop into a true federal system.[11] The EDC was the great symbol of the "European idea," so the EDC had to be supported. This was why Eisenhower in mid-1951 shifted his position and decided to back the EDC concept, in spite of the fact that the plan, as he said at the time, "seemed, almost inherently, to include every kind of obstacle, difficulty, and fantastic notion that misguided humans could put together in one package."[12]

[10] U.S. Delegation to acting secretary, November 27, 1951, FRUS 1951, 3:734. Eisenhower diary, June 11, 1951; Eisenhower to Harriman, June 30 and July 9, 1951; Eisenhower to Lovett, December 13, 1951; and Eisenhower to Pleven, December 24, 1951; all in *Eisenhower Papers,* 12:340–341, 398, 408, 781, 812. Eisenhower to Gruenther, June 19, 1952, ibid., 13:1248.

[11] Note, for example, the tone of Dulles's comments in his meeting with German Atomic Affairs Minister Strauss, May 14, 1956, FRUS 1955–57, 4:439–440.

[12] Eisenhower to Marshall, August 3, 1951, *Eisenhower Papers,* 12:458.

After the EDC failed, the U.S. government threw its weight behind the two new projects on which the supporters of European unification placed their hopes, the European Common Market and the European Atomic Energy Community. The Common Market, and the already existing European Coal and Steel Community as well, were tied to the idea of Europe becoming a "third world force along with the US and the Soviet Union," and the Eisenhower administration strongly backed these efforts. Dulles, for example, made his standard veiled threat in May 1957 when he urged the Germans to ratify the Common Market treaty. A united Europe could stand on its own, he said, but if Europe remained weak and divided, the burden of defense would continue to fall disproportionately on the United States. The American people, however, would simply not go on carrying this burden indefinitely: "complete sovereignty for the many nations of Europe," he said, was "a luxury which European countries can no longer afford at US expense. If the Common Market treaty should fail, after the failure of the EDC, the Secretary thought that further support for Europe could hardly be expected from American public opinion."[13]

Eisenhower and Dulles were also strong supporters of the plan for a European Atomic Energy Community. Euratom, as it was called, was linked in their minds to the notion of western Europe as an independent "focus of power," of a "united Europe as a third great force in the World." "Were Western European integration to take place," Dulles remarked in this context, "this could remove the burden of Europe from the back of the United States, draw France and Germany together, and constitute a unified pool of power to balance the USSR."[14]

The Euratom project was in fact directly linked to the idea of an independent, integrated European nuclear capability. The idea of western Europe balancing the great nuclear power of Russia on its own obviously implied an eventual European nuclear force, and Eisenhower and Dulles wanted to move in that direction. To be sure, "a multiplicity of uncontrolled national atomic developments leading to multiplying atomic weapons programs" was to be avoided.[15] But an integrated European program was another matter entirely, and Dulles favored the idea. Some key State Department officials strongly opposed the very notion of an independent European nuclear infrastructure, and were very much against taking the one crucial step the U.S. government could take to help the Europeans "achieve atomic independence"—the sale to them of a gaseous diffusion plant for isotope separation—but Dulles disagreed. When the issue came up at a meeting between State Department and Atomic Energy Commission officials, and the AEC chairman declared his willingness to cooperate with the pro-Euratom policy "up to the legal

---

[13] See Eisenhower-Mayer meeting (for the Coal and Steel Community), February 8, 1956, Dulles-Strauss meeting (for the Common Market), May 14, 1956, FRUS 1955–57, 4:409, 441. For Dulles's threat about the Common Market treaty, see Dulles-Adenauer meeting, May 4, 1957, FRUS 1955–57, 26:240. Dulles took the same line in internal discussions with American officials. See meeting with U.S. ambassadors, May 6, 1957, ibid., 4:587.

[14] State Department memorandum on "Peaceful Uses of Atomic Energy and European Integration," December 6, 1955; State Department meeting, January 25, 1956; Eisenhower-Etzel meeting, February 6, 1957; all in FRUS 1955–57, 4:355, 391, 517. See also Stephen Ambrose, *Eisenhower*, vol. 2 (New York: Simon and Schuster, 1984), pp. 404–405.

[15] Dulles-Strauss meeting, May 14, 1956, FRUS 1955–57, 4:441.

limit," Dulles "said that he hoped the Commission might exceed those limits and consider all possibilities," based on what was the best policy for the United States. There had been some question about the legality of the sale of a gaseous diffusion plant; Dulles was in this context signaling his willingness to go ahead with such a sale and thus help the Europeans "achieve atomic independence." The real significance of this policy lay in the fact that although Euratom was supposed to be devoted to peaceful uses of atomic energy, everyone was aware of the military implications of the project: an independent nuclear infrastructure might ultimately mean an independent nuclear weapons capability.[16]

The basic Eisenhower defense policy ultimately pointed in the same direction. One of the president's central goals was to get the Europeans to take on more responsibility for their own defense. For the time being, this implied a policy of pressing the Europeans to build up their ground forces. In the early 1950s, Eisenhower certainly took the direct defense of western Europe seriously. He was unwilling as SACEUR in 1951 or in his first years as president to settle for a simple policy of relying almost exclusively on nuclear deterrence. A meaningful ground defense of the continent was from the start a central part of the Eisenhower strategy. The president wanted a NATO ground force capable of making a respectable military effort. He had no intention of "allowing Europe to be overrun," he said in late 1954, and was irritated whenever anyone suggested that it was American policy to "strip ourselves naked of all military capabilities except the nuclear." "It was ridiculous," he said, "to imagine anything of this sort."[17] But the Europeans were to provide the great bulk of the ground forces needed to implement the strategy. The United States would be the "central keep behind the forward forces." U.S. military power was not to be dispersed all along the periphery of Soviet power, but would be concentrated within the United States as a kind of mobile reserve.[18]

This was the main idea behind the "New Look," the military strategy the Eisenhower administration adopted not long after it took office in 1953, and it remained a key element in official U.S. thinking throughout the 1950s. The basic New Look

[16] State-AEC meeting, January 25, 1956, ibid., p. 395. Gerard Smith, the special assistant to the secretary for atomic energy affairs, was perhaps the leading State Department opponent of the administration's relatively liberal policy. Note especially the tone of his memorandum opposing the sale of the uranium enrichment plant: "we would be making the Europeans independent of us and giving up our monopoly on marketable enriched uranium." Smith to Merchant, December 8, 1955, ibid., p. 361. Note also his opposition a year and a half later to the NATO nuclear stockpile plan. He objected to a passage in a document on this question to the effect that the American government should try to make the allies less "dependent on the U.S. in the atomic field": "I think that such dependence is to our advantage." Smith to Timmons, May 21, 1957, 740.56/5–2157, RG 59, USNA. For the point about a nuclear infrastructure, in principle devoted to peaceful uses, inevitably laying the basis for a nuclear weapons capability, see for example an important State Department memorandum of December 6, 1955, FRUS 1955–57, 4:356–357. As this memorandum pointed out, it was understood, at least by the main Euratom participants, "that peaceful uses of atomic energy cannot, for technical reasons, be dissociated from potential possession of atomic power for military purposes."

[17] NSC meeting, June 24, 1954, FRUS 1952–54, 2:690–691.

[18] Eisenhower-JCS meeting, February 10, 1956, MR 80–224 No. 2, DDEL, also at the National Security Archive [NSA], Washington; NSC meeting, March 26, 1959, FRUS 1958–60, 7(1):444–445. The president frequently argued along these lines. See, for example, Cutler memorandum, September 3, 1953, FRUS 1952–54, 2:456; and NSC meeting, December 22, 1960, p. 16, AWF/NSC/13/DDEL.

document, the JCS report of August 8, 1953, explicitly argued for a "redeployment" of American forces back to the continental United States. America, it argued, had become "over-extended" under the existing policy of placing "major emphasis" on "peripheral deployments overseas." U.S. freedom of action was "seriously curtailed, the exercise of initiative severely limited." Military priorities had to be reversed. Primary emphasis had to be placed on the ability to wage a general nuclear war—on the "capability for delivering swift and powerful retaliatory blows" and for protecting "our Continental U.S. vitals" through an air defense that could "hold damage to nationally manageable proportions."[19] The assumption was that the bulk of whatever local defense forces were still necessary would be supplied by the allies in the region. America could not do everything: there had to be a division of labor. As Dulles pointed out in 1957, the theory was that "we would do the 'big stuff' (large-scale retaliatory attack). Our allies were expected to handle local hostilities." The president agreed: "our policy should be that our friends and allies supply the means for local defense on the ground and that the United States should come into the act with air and naval forces alone."[20]

The U.S. government therefore pressed the Europeans to build up their ground forces, and during the late Eisenhower period especially, American officials complained repeatedly about the Europeans' failure to bear their "fair share" of the common defense burden. Eisenhower wanted the Europeans to take over primary responsibility for ground defense, so that the great bulk of the American force on the continent could come home.[21] The question was how the European governments could be made to do this, and for one reason or another, the American government was never ready to bring this issue to a head with the allies. The administration itself was somewhat divided on this basic question. Dulles in particular did not see eye to eye with Eisenhower on the issue. From the start, the secretary of state thought that America had to be very cautious about broaching the subject of "redeployment." A U.S. withdrawal might well be interpreted as implying a return to isolationism and a "Fortress America" mentality. It might bring about a collapse of European morale, it would undercut Adenauer politically, it could lead to a drift toward neutralism, to a breakdown of the western alliance, and eventually to the loss of all of Europe.[22] The NATO allies, as Eisenhower himself pointed out,

[19] Joint Chiefs of Staff memorandum to the secretary of defense, August 8, 1953. This key document was the basis of an important NSC discussion of military policy on August 27, 1953. See FRUS 1952–54, 2:444–455. In compiling that volume, the editors of FRUS were unable to find a copy of the document (p. 444 n), but David Rosenberg located it in the archives and gave me a copy. Admiral Radford, the incoming JCS chairman at the time, considered it so important that he personally managed to get it declassified. See Stephen Jurika, Jr., ed., *From Pearl Harbor to Vietnam: The Memoirs of Admiral Arthur W. Radford* (Stanford, Calif.: Hoover Institution Press, 1980), p. 322.

[20] NSC meeting, February 28, 1957, FRUS 1955–57, 19:429.

[21] Eisenhower-Dulles meeting, October 2, 1956, ibid., 4:100; NSC meetings, December 11, 1958, and November 12, 1959, and Eisenhower-Norstad meeting, August 24, 1959, FRUS 1958–60, 7(1): 367, 479, 509. Note also Eisenhower's comments at a meeting with his top advisers, December 12, 1958 (document dated December 15, 1958), SS/S/DoS/3/State Department/DDEL.

[22] See, for example, NSC meeting, August 27, 1953, FRUS 1952–54, 2:445–453, and Dulles to Eisenhower, October 21, 1953, DP/WHM/8/General Foreign Policy Matters (4)/DDEL. For Dulles's differences with Eisenhower, see Eisenhower-Norstad meeting, November 4, 1959, and Eisenhower-McElroy meeting, November 16, 1959, FRUS 1958–60, 7(1):499, 517; Eisenhower-Gray meeting, July

became "almost psychopathic" whenever anyone talked about a U.S. with-drawal.[23] To assuage their anxieties, the State Department had over the years given the allies misleading assurances about America's intention to stay in Europe—as-surances contradicted from time to time by disconcerting noises about "redeploy-ment" coming from the Pentagon.[24]

But by the end of the decade Eisenhower had come to feel that American goals had to be made clear to the Europeans. The United States in the past had evaded the issue, he thought, and as a result the Europeans had come to take the Ameri-can presence for granted—America was being trapped in Europe, the "temporary" U.S. presence was in danger of becoming permanent, and a real shift in policy was becoming harder to engineer. Even in 1956, Eisenhower was complaining about the U.S. government's "unwillingness to put the matter squarely to the Europeans"; as a result, he said, the problem had now "become extremely difficult."[25]

By 1959, with Eisenhower's term of office due to end fairly soon, it was rapidly becoming a question of now or never. America by this time had begun to develop a serious balance of payments problem, and this gave additional weight to the ar-gument for cutting back on the very expensive military presence in Europe. The time for action was perhaps at hand. For five years, Eisenhower said, he had been trying to get the State Department "to put the facts of life before the Europeans concerning reduction of our forces." Given how prosperous the Europeans now were, there was "no reason" why they could not "take on" a greater share of the defense burden. America should not have to do everything. "We are carrying prac-tically the whole weight of the strategic deterrent force, also conducting space ac-tivities, and atomic programs. We paid for most of the infrastructure, and main-tain large air and naval forces as well as six divisions. He thinks the Europeans are close to 'making a sucker out of Uncle Sam.'" When it was a question of emergency help, that was one thing, but that time had passed.[26]

The U.S. government, however, could not use shock therapy. The Europeans had to be made to see that America would not be turning her back on her allies, but was only asking for a fair division of responsibilities. Eisenhower was "tired of having the whole defense burden placed on U.S. shoulders." "It was high time," he said, "that the thinking of Europe was reoriented and made more realistic be-fore the NATO situation is further crystallized; it was high time that the popula-tion of Europe did its part with respect to ground forces." If the Europeans refused, and if "responsibility for defending the world is to be imposed upon us, then per-

---

27, 1959 (document dated July 29), OSANSA/SA/P/4/Meetings with the President/DDEL, and Allen Dulles-Eisenhower meeting, August 22, 1961, National Security Files [NSF], box 82, Kennedy Library [JFKL], Boston.

[23] Eisenhower-McElroy meeting, November 16, 1959, FRUS 1958–60, 7(1):516.

[24] See especially Dulles and Eisenhower remarks in NSC meeting, December 10, 1953, FRUS 1952–54, 5:450–451. Note also Dulles's comments in a July 7, 1955, NSC meeting, FRUS 1955–57, 5:274.

[25] Eisenhower meeting with top advisers, October 2, 1956, FRUS 1955–57, 4:100. See also the president's remarks in the NSC, November 12, 1959, FRUS 1958–60, 7(1):508.

[26] Eisenhower-Norstad meeting, November 5, 1959, FRUS 1958–60, 7(1):498. For various docu-ments showing the impact of the balance of payments problem at this point, see ibid., pp. 488 n, 491, 494, 499.

haps," he said facetiously, "we had better rule the world." But if the Europeans wanted to play a real role, then they would have to make the kind of effort the United States was making. These shifts in policy, however, could not be imposed unilaterally. The Europeans would first have to be brought to understand these "facts of life" and agree to these structural changes voluntarily. America had made commitments and perhaps nothing could be done right now. There was also the ongoing crisis over Berlin to consider. An American pullout in the midst of this crisis would give the wrong signal. But after the crisis had passed, the whole issue could be pushed to the front burner, and in the meantime, America "must not drift." The problem, the president insisted, should be brought to the "attention of Europe bluntly and clearly."[27]

The U.S. government complained about the Europeans not doing their share, but it also understood why their effort was limited. The basic problem was that America and not Europe controlled what was unquestionably the dominant form of military power. Why should the Europeans embark on a major buildup of local defense forces if that effort, no matter how massive, would not give them any greater control over their own destiny—indeed, if it would make it easier for the Americans to withdraw the bulk of their ground forces and thus weaken the U.S. nuclear guarantee? The United States, in the final analysis, would be making the crucial decisions while the Europeans, with their conventional forces, would be merely "playing with marbles."[28]

If the Europeans were not doing their share, this was because all the power was concentrated in American hands, and that situation would have to be changed. The top U.S. leadership did not want western Europe to remain an American protectorate. Eisenhower wanted the Europeans to be real allies, the sort who felt responsible for their own defense. He complained increasingly that the Europeans had lost this sense of responsibility. They should be "ashamed" of that fact, and America had to do more to "wean our allies from overdependence upon us and to encourage them to make better efforts of their own."[29] The Europeans had to be made to see that their "security cannot always and completely depend on the U.S."[30] This implied that the Europeans needed nuclear forces under their own control, for how else would they be able to reduce their dependence on America and take on real responsibility for their own defense? And indeed, referring specifically to the idea of a NATO nuclear stockpile, Dulles said: "we do not ourselves want to be in a position where our allies are wholly dependent upon us. We don't think that is a healthy relationship."[31]

So if Europe's "overdependence" on the United States was a fundamental problem, if the real goal was to get the Europeans to take responsibility for their own fate, there was only one answer. The Europeans had to be armed with nuclear

[27] NSC meeting, November 12, 1959, ibid., pp. 508–509, 514.
[28] See Allen Dulles to John Foster Dulles, August 28, 1956, FRUS 1955–57, 26:148.
[29] Eisenhower-Dulles meeting, December 12, 1958, and Eisenhower-Spaak meeting, November 24, 1959, FRUS 1958–60, 7(1):370–371, 521, 524. See also NSC meeting, March 26, 1959, ibid., p. 445, and NSC meeting, June 15, 1956, FRUS 1955–57, 26:128.
[30] NSC meeting, December 11, 1958, FRUS 1958–60, 7(1):367.
[31] Dulles press conference, July 16, 1957, DOSB, August 5, 1957, p. 233.

weapons—and that meant nuclear weapons under their own control. As early as 1954, Eisenhower was already thinking along these lines. In a meeting with Dulles, he suggested telling the British and the French that "we were holding a certain number of atomic weapons of varied types for their possible use so as to place upon them a greater degree of responsibility in deciding whether or not in fact such weapons should or should not be used."[32]

So while the immediate aim was to work out a division of responsibilities with the Europeans whereby America would maintain the strategic nuclear force while the allies would concentrate on area defense, the administration never thought that what was obviously the dominant form of military power would remain exclusively under American control. Indeed, the very notion of a division of labor in this area implied that the U.S. government had to be open to the idea of nuclear sharing. The immediate goal might be to get the Europeans to concentrate on ground forces and leave the strategic air offensive to the United States. But this meant that the Europeans were dependent for their security on America's willingness, in the final analysis, to launch an all-out nuclear attack. Europe, that is, was being asked to trust America, to believe that the U.S. government would deliver on its promises. But how could Europe be expected to trust the United States, if the Americans were unwilling to trust their own allies by sharing their most important weapons with them? If the Europeans were treated as "second-class" members of the alliance, how could the alliance survive? The effect would be profoundly corrosive. "Trust," as Dulles pointed out, had to "operate both ways. It is not enough that others trust us. We must also allocate tasks to them. We must give them things to do. They all want to be in the missile business and do not wish to be mere cannon fodder."[33]

Eisenhower also took it for granted that the Europeans themselves would insist on a greater degree of independence; given that they had to face a massive Soviet military force armed with nuclear weapons, it was the most natural thing in the world for the European governments to want nuclear forces of their own. He thought that it was as "sure as day follows night that a number of countries would develop nuclear capabilities."[34] And it made no sense for them to build those forces entirely by themselves. A whole series of independent and uncoordinated national programs would be unconscionably wasteful. America had at great expense built up an enormous nuclear infrastructure. The best thing would be for the United States to treat the NATO countries as real allies and supply them with the weapons and the technology they needed.

All this was obvious to Eisenhower, as obvious as could be. "For God's sake," he exclaimed in 1955 (at the same NSC meeting where he talked about western

[32] Dulles-Eisenhower meeting, April 19, 1954, *Secretary of State's Memoranda of Conversation, November 1952 -December 1954* [SSMC], microfiche supplement to FRUS, no. 424.

[33] Notes of meeting between State Department officials and outside consultants, November 6, 1957, DP/GCM/3/Strictly Confidential—N-P (1)/DDEL. This view was widely shared at the time, even by veterans of the Truman administration. Note, for example, Spofford's comments at this meeting: "Sharing nuclear weapons with our allies would indicate that we share confidence in them. It would tend to interest them again in self-defense. Without facing up to that problem it will be very difficult to restore their confidence."

[34] NSC meeting, October 29, 1959, FRUS 1958–60, 7(2):290.

Europe as a "third great power bloc"), "let us not be stingy with an ally." It was absurd to "treat many of our NATO allies like stepchildren, and then expect them to turn around and commit themselves to fight with us. By such actions we cut our own throats."[35] The allies should be helped to acquire modern weapons. Indeed, he said in 1959, they had to be helped "if they were to remain allies."[36]

MC 48 AND ITS MEANING

In late 1950, the United States embarked on a great rearmament effort. Defense production expanded dramatically. Military deliveries increased from $1.2 billion in the first quarter after the outbreak of the Korean War to over $10 billion a quarter in mid-1953. U.S. defense spending increased from 4.7 percent of GNP in the last year before the Korean War to an extraordinary 17.8 percent in 1952–53, and only a small part of the expansion was due to the Korean War as such. It was America's general war-fighting power that was being built up, especially her ability to wage an air-atomic war against the Soviet Union. The NATO allies joined in the buildup. British defense spending, it was estimated at the time, rose from 5.7 percent of GNP in 1949–50 to 9.9 percent in 1952–53; for France, the increase in the same period was from 6.5 percent to 10.1 percent.[37]

But the raw numbers give only a faint indication of the impact of the buildup. This was a period of revolutionary change in military technology. In the nuclear area developments were especially dramatic. Advances in bomb design meant that weapons could be made small enough and light enough to be carried in fighter aircraft, including Navy carrier planes, and there was an enormous increase in the production of fissionable material and in the efficiency with which it was used. At the same time, weapons of ever higher yields were being tested, and a true thermonuclear device, a thousand times more powerful than the bombs dropped on Japan, was first detonated in 1952. This event was to have very far-reaching implications; the nuclear revolution of 1945 represented a radical break with the past, but the coming of thermonuclear weapons was an event of even greater importance.[38] And although these nuclear developments were fundamental, in many other areas—aircraft propulsion, military electronics (including the beginnings of military computerization), intelligence technology, and so on—impressive advances were constantly being made.

The fact that military technology was developing so rapidly meant that the strategic impact of the western rearmament effort was a good deal greater than the simple statistics might suggest. The American forces especially, armed with the

[35] NSC meeting, November 21, 1955, FRUS 1955–57, 19:151.

[36] Eisenhower–de Gaulle–Macmillan meeting, December 20, 1959, p. 16, Prem 11/2991, PRO. See also Eisenhower's remarks in the NSC meeting of November 17, 1960, FRUS 1958–60, 7(1):657.

[37] See Trachtenberg, History and Strategy, pp. 126–129. For the figures, see Key Data Book, n.d., PSF/NSC-Reports-Misc/HSTL; Report to the President, "Defense Expenditures of Soviet and NATO States as a Percent of Their Respective Gross National Products," September 5, 1952, DDRS 1988/2259. See also briefing book for Eisenhower, n.d., and Cabot to Acheson, March 27, 1951, FRUS 1951, 3:6, 104; Draft Statement of U.S. Policy on Germany, December 13, 1957, FRUS 1955–57, 26:335.

[38] See Trachtenberg, History and Strategy, pp. 119–120, 133–134.

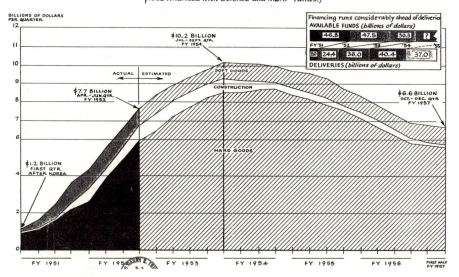

THE MOBILIZATION PROGRAM — PROCUREMENT AND CONSTRUCTION
(Military goods delivered and construction put in
place financed with Defense and MDAP funds.)

THE MOBILIZATION PROGRAM–
AIRPLANE PRODUCTION

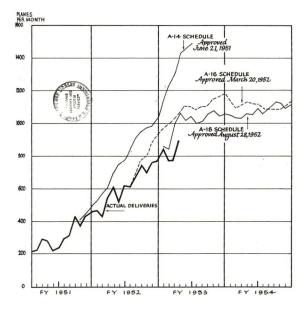

Figure 5. American Rearmament in the Late Truman Period. Charts from the "Key Data Book." From President's Secretary's Files, NSC—Reports—Misc, Harry S Truman Library.

most modern weapons, had by late 1952 developed a level of military power which the USSR, with its large stock of increasingly obsolescent weapons, simply could not match. The military balance had in fact been utterly transformed. In 1950–51, American leaders had been worried that if a third world war broke out, the United States might well lose. But by 1953–54, they had no doubt what the outcome of a general war would be. America would win, and the Soviet Union would be utterly destroyed.[39]

At the end of 1954 the western alliance adopted a strategy that took full advantage of America's enormous military superiority at that point. That strategy, embodied in the very important NATO document MC 48, and approved by the North Atlantic Council on December 17, 1954, was the second great taproot of the nuclear sharing policy.[40]

The MC 48 strategy placed an extraordinarily heavy emphasis on nuclear weapons for the defense of Europe, and NATO's acceptance of this strategy was an event of enormous historical significance. Its importance does not lie in the fact that this act marked NATO's formal acceptance of a strategy based on nuclear weapons. There was nothing particularly special about that. NATO strategy for the defense of Europe relied ultimately on nuclear forces for the entire Cold War period. What was special about the MC 48 strategy was that it was built on the assumption that there was one, and only one, way in which the Soviets could be prevented from overrunning Europe in the event of war, and that was through the very rapid and massive use of nuclear weapons, both tactically and strategically. A forward defense of western Europe had long been considered necessary for political reasons: a European commitment to the alliance could only be based on a sense that the alliance was doing everything it could to defend its European members against Soviet attack. The events of the early 1950s had made it abundantly clear that a non-nuclear defense was simply out of reach for reasons of domestic politics and finance. In the pre-1954 period, NATO strategy had been plagued by a

[39] On these matters in general, and on the impact of the shifting military balance on American policy in specific parts of the world, see Trachtenberg, *History and Strategy*, pp. 129–131, esp. n. 111. See also Sulzberger-Gruenther meeting, November 9, 1954, in Cyrus Sulzberger, *The Last of the Giants* (New York: Macmillan, 1970), p. 107; Dulles statement to NAC, December 14, 1953, and NSC meeting, December 23, 1953, FRUS 1952–54, 5:464, 480; and especially NSC meeting, October 20, 1955, FRUS 1955–57, 4:26. This basic issue—what strategic superiority meant, and why the U.S. had the upper hand in this period—will be discussed later in this chapter.

[40] My understanding of these matters is based in very large part on Robert Wampler's work, especially his Ph.D. dissertation, "Ambiguous Legacy: The United States, Great Britain, and the Foundations of NATO Strategy, 1948–1957" (Harvard University, 1991). I have also profited greatly from discussions with Wampler on these issues. There is also some information in the *JCS History*, 5:311–317. Aside from this official account and the documents published in FRUS 1952–54, 5:482–562, there is relatively little published material on this subject. A certain amount of very important archival material has, however, become available in recent years. The material in Defe 6/26 at the PRO proved particularly instructive, and some French material from the Blanc Papers at the SHAT in Vincennes was also extremely revealing. Some key extracts are given in my article, "La formation du système de défense occidentale: Les Etats-Unis, la France et MC 48," in Vaïsse et al., *La France et l'OTAN*. Note also the French Foreign Ministry memorandum on atomic war, December 13, 1954, DDF 1954, pp. 906–909. The text of MC 48 itself was declassified in 1996; I am grateful to the SHAPE historian, Gregory Pedlow, for providing me with a copy.

persistent and intractable gap between military "requirements" and the actual resources the NATO allies were willing to generate. But now it seemed possible actually to defend Europe on the ground. The goal was not simply deterrence, but a defense able to prevent the USSR from overrunning western Europe if a fighting war with the Russians were ever to break out.

A strategy of this sort was based on the notion that even forces of limited size, if geared to a nuclear battlefield, armed with nuclear weapons, and prepared to use them effectively against tactical targets (such as enemy stockpiles of war materiel, supply lines, and troop concentrations) could make sure that NATO Europe was not overrun during the relatively brief period when the basic sources of Soviet power were being destroyed through the strategic air offensive. Soviet offensive capabilities in Europe would soon wither, and until they did, a nuclear-armed covering force, trained to fight in a nuclear environment, would be able to hold the line on the continent. The MC 48 strategy was thus not, as is sometimes claimed, "a strategy based upon a tactical nuclear response to conventional aggression."[41] The essence of the new strategy was that the response would be *both* tactical *and* strategic; the attack on the Soviet Union would be massive, and, above all, very rapid. To quote from MC 48 itself: "it lies within NATO's power to provide an effective deterrent in Europe, and should war come despite the deterrent, to prevent a rapid overrunning of Europe," but only if "*the ability to make immediate use of atomic weapons is ensured. Our studies have indicated that without their immediate use we could not successfully defend Europe within the resources available. Any delay in their use—even measured in hours—could be fatal. Therefore, in the event of war involving NATO it is militarily essential that NATO forces should be able to use atomic and thermonuclear weapons in their defense from the outset.*"[42]

In adopting MC 48, NATO was embracing a strategy of extremely rapid escalation. No strategy up to that point, and indeed no NATO strategy since, placed such a heavy and unequivocal emphasis on rapid and massive nuclear escalation. This was not an aggressive strategy. It had to be clear, as President Eisenhower and other NATO leaders said repeatedly at the time, that the Soviets were responsible for the war. But as soon as it was clear that the Soviets were to blame, America and her allies had to open up with everything they had. "Our only chance of victory in a third world war against the Soviet Union," Eisenhower told the NSC in December 1954, "would be to paralyze the enemy at the outset of the war." "We are *not* going to provoke the war," he added; the blame had to rest with the other side. Only in

---

[41] Robert E. Osgood, *NATO: The Entangling Alliance* (Chicago: University of Chicago Press, 1962), p. 116.

[42] NATO Military Committee, "The Most Effective Pattern of NATO Military Strength for the Next Few Years," MC 48, November 18, 1954 (approved on November 22, 1954), SHAPE Historical Office. Emphasis in original text. The provision relating to immediate use was the first of three provisos relating to the viability of the new strategy; the other two had to do with a German defense contribution and the adoption of specific measures that would enable NATO forces to survive an attack and go into action rapidly. See also Comité de Défense Nationale, "Examen du 'Plan des Possibilités' établi par le commandement suprême des forces alliées en Europe," p. 4, September 7, 1954, folder "Comité de Défense Nationale du 10 Septembre 1954," Box 2, Papers of General Blanc (French Army Chief of Staff), fonds 1K145, SHAT, Vincennes.

such circumstances could America "use the nuclear weapon," and America had to be able to use it "if we are to preserve our institutions and win the victory in war."[43]

Did MC 48 presuppose a strategy of preemption? It was certainly taken for granted that the West would, if it could, be the first to launch a massive air-atomic offensive, even in response to a purely conventional Soviet attack. But was the new strategy preemptive in the stronger sense that it assumed that a full nuclear strike might be launched as soon as NATO judged that war was unavoidable, yet before the enemy had actually begun military operations? The indicators are mixed, but the bulk of the evidence does suggest that the MC 48 strategy was preemptive even in this sense. This important conclusion, however, rests largely on construction and inference—on the logic of the strategy as well as on the interpretation of certain key texts.

First of all, it is clear that the MC 48 strategy presupposed that a major war in Europe could not be limited, and that it would rapidly become an all-out conflict. Indeed, if anyone had any doubt on this score, the MC 48 strategy in itself would guarantee that escalation up to the level of all-out war would be extremely rapid. But if nuclear weapons were used against the USSR—and clearly the basic MC 48 decision was that in a European war they would be used against Soviet targets—then the Soviets would certainly want to retaliate in kind. For western Europe, a nuclear-based strategy would only be tolerable if it were not suicidal. It would be acceptable only if the Soviets could be prevented from retaliating on a major scale. But the only way this could be done was to destroy their nuclear capability while it was still vulnerable to attack, which is to say before the bomber force actually became airborne. It was common knowledge, as General Gruenther, the NATO commander and one of the principal architects of the MC 48 strategy, pointed out in a January 1954 press briefing, that "the best way to get control of the air is to destroy enemy planes while they are on the ground."[44] And it was clear enough that the only way to do this might well be to strike preemptively, as soon as it became clear that war was unavoidable—that is, while the Soviets were still getting ready for action, but before they had actually struck. With survival quite literally at stake, how could the West afford to allow the Soviets to set the timetable for action and concede to them the first nuclear blow?

This sort of thinking certainly lay at the heart of Eisenhower's basic defense philosophy—an important fact, since it was Eisenhower's personal thinking that was the most important source of the MC 48 strategy. Eisenhower throughout his presidency assumed that war in Europe could not be controlled. Local wars might be possible in the Third World, although even there America was not going to fight with her hands tied; nuclear weapons would in fact be used if U.S. troops were attacked by a sizeable enemy force. In the early part of his presidency, he took a very tough line and talked about the need, in such circumstances, to strike at the heart of enemy power; indeed, if such wars became too common, the United States, he said, might even attack the Soviet Union herself. Later on, his attitude became somewhat more moderate and reflected a certain reluctance to engage in nuclear

---

[43] NCS meeting, December 3, 1954, FRUS, 1952–54, 2:805–806.

[44] Transcript of Gruenther press briefing, January 11, 1954, Montgomery Papers, file "Philosophy of NATO military build-up," Imperial War Museum, London.

escalation. But even at that point he felt that the State Department, which thought that nuclear weapons "should be used only as a last resort," was being "overcautious" in its approach.[45]

With regard to Europe, the policy was a good deal less ambiguous. A war in Europe, Eisenhower insisted from beginning to end, would be a war with the USSR, and thus inevitably a general war. With so much at stake, both sides would use whatever forces they had. The whole argument about "mutual deterrence"—the idea that both sides would hold back from nuclear use for fear of retaliation, and would therefore fight with conventional weapons only—was in his view "completely erroneous." A war between America and Russia would, practically by definition, be a general war, and nuclear weapons would certainly be used. "It was fatuous," he said in 1956, "to think that the U.S. and USSR would be locked into a life and death struggle without using such weapons." And again in 1960 he stated flatly that no war in Europe could be kept from becoming a general war. That was why, he said, "we must be ready to throw the book at the Russians should they jump us. He did not see how there could be such a thing as a limited war in Europe, and thought we would be fooling ourselves and our European friends if we said we could fight such a war without recourse to nuclear weapons."[46]

In this sort of situation, in Eisenhower's view, there could be only one war aim, and that was national survival. There could be no winner in such a war, he said, but "we just don't want to lose any worse than we have to." He would hit the Soviet Union as hard as he could. The attack would be unrestrained. "In such a war," he said, "the United States would be applying a force so terrible that one simply could not be meticulous as to the methods by which the force was brought to bear." The president was certainly aware of how devastating a full-scale Soviet nuclear attack on America would be. If America were to survive, the USSR would have to be prevented from mounting such an attack. Given the limited effectiveness of air

[45] For evidence of Eisenhower's willingness to escalate even in local wars in the Third World, see NESC briefing, January 23, 1956 (where the president said he would "never commit our forces to battle where I cannot get at the heart of the enemy's power and support"); NSC meeting, February 27, 1956; Eisenhower-Radford-Taylor meeting, May 24, 1956; NSC meeting, January 3, 1957; and NSC meeting, May 27, 1957; all in FRUS 1955–57, 19:191, 211, 313–314, 397, 503. Note also the series of public statements quoted ibid., p. 61, and also Eisenhower's remark, during the first Taiwan Straits crisis in 1954, about the need "to go to the head of the snake" and attack Russia rather than fight a ground war with China; NSC meeting, September 12, 1954, FRUS 1952–54, 14:617. But the evidence on this question is not unambiguous: some documents indicate a certain reluctance to escalate. See, for example, NSC meeting, May 17, 1956, FRUS 1955–57, 19:307. For the comment about limited wars only being possible in "underdeveloped areas," see NSC meeting, May 27, 1957, ibid., p. 503. For the remark about having to fight a major war if local wars become too common, see NSC meeting, August 4, 1955, ibid., p. 97. For the treatment of this issue in the later period, see Eisenhower-Herter-McElroy-Radford meeting, July 2, 1959; NSC meetings, July 9, 1959, and October 6, 1960; and Furnas to Smith, July 15, 1959; in FRUS 1958–60, 3:228–235 (the quotations are on pp. 233 and 235), 238–248, 255–258, 483–484.

[46] See also Eisenhower-Taylor-Radford meeting, May 24, 1956, FRUS 1955–57, 19:311–315; Eisenhower-Bowie meeting, August 16, 1960, FRUS 1958–60, 7(1):612, 614. For other documents reflecting Eisenhower's belief in the uncontrollability of major war in general, and his dismissal of the idea that in a major conflict the fighting might be kept limited because both sides would be too frightened to use nuclear weapons, see NSC meeting, June 24, 1954, FRUS 1952–54, 2:689–690, and Eisenhower-JCS meeting, February 10, 1956, DDRS 1982/798.

defense, the only way to protect the United States was therefore to destroy the Soviet force before it got off the ground. This is what Eisenhower meant when he said in May 1956 that "massive retaliation" was "likely to be the key to survival." "Retaliation," for Eisenhower, although he sometimes said the opposite, did not mean simply striking back after absorbing an enemy attack: a simple counterattack of that sort would do nothing to assure the survival of American society. When Eisenhower said that "there is in reality no defense except to retaliate," what he really meant was that America would have to be the first to launch a "retaliatory" attack—that the United States, as he put it that same day, "must not allow the enemy to strike the first blow."[47]

And America, he thought, had to concentrate on developing a military force that would enable her to do just that. At the end of 1956, after being briefed about the effects of a nuclear war, Eisenhower wondered "why we should put a single nickel into anything but developing our capacity to diminish the enemy's capacity for nuclear attack."[48] A few months later, he noted that given the enormous destruction that would result from a Soviet nuclear attack, "the only sensible thing for us to do was to put all resources into our SAC capability and into hydrogen bombs."[49] He fully understood that the only way this additional capability could make a real difference was if the United States used it to destroy the Soviet force before it launched its initial attack—and given the limited effectiveness of air defense, that meant before it had actually left the ground.

Thus massive retaliation, as David Rosenberg says, really meant massive preemption—certainly in operational terms, and to a considerable extent in fundamental strategic terms as well.[50] In the words of a major historical study sponsored by the Defense Department, the whole U.S. operational posture, as it had developed during the Eisenhower period, "strained for rapid (indeed preemptive) and massive response to an imminent attack."[51] It was not as though the United States had decided not to launch an attack until after absorbing the enemy's first strike. Under Eisenhower, the top priority, as the president himself said, was "to blunt the enemy's *initial* threat—by massive retaliatory power and ability to deliver it; and by a continental defense system of major capability."[52] The "blunting" of the attack meant, in the idiom of the day, the neutralization to the extent possible of the enemy's strategic capability, and it is important to note that this was not to be

---

[47] NSC meeting, March 25, 1954, FRUS 1952–54, 2:640–642. See also NSC meeting, January 22, 1959, FRUS 1958–60, 3:178; Eisenhower-Radford-Taylor meeting, May 24, 1956, FRUS 1955–57, 19:313. For the point that the enemy could not be allowed to strike first, see the November 1957 document cited in Rosenberg, "Origins of Overkill," p. 47. Note also a comment he made in passing in an NSC discussion of general war strategy on March 5, 1959: "if you get into a fight you try to shoot your enemy before he shoots you." FRUS 1958–60, 3:197.

[48] NSC meeting, December 20, 1956, FRUS 1955–57, 19:381.

[49] NSC meeting, February 7, 1957, ibid., p. 416.

[50] David Rosenberg, "Toward Armageddon: The Foundations of U.S. Nuclear Strategy" (Ph.D. diss., University of Chicago, 1983), p. 221. See also pp. 197–201.

[51] Ernest May, John Steinbruner, and Thomas Wolfe, "History of the Strategic Arms Competition, 1945–1972," pt. 1 (Office of the Secretary of Defense, Historical Office, 1981), p. 588. Available from the Department of Defense Freedom of Information [DOD-FOIA] Office.

[52] Eisenhower-JCS meeting, December 22, 1954, AWF/ACW Diary/3/DDEL. Emphasis added.

done by air defense alone. The "retaliatory" force was to do the major part of the job, and it could do this only if it destroyed that enemy force—the force to be used for the *initial* attack, and not just whatever was being held in reserve for follow-on strikes—while it was still on the ground.

Eisenhower believed in the importance of "diminishing as much as possible the *first* blow of an enemy attack," and his policy reflected that basic principle.[53] In the president's view, America's "only chance of victory"—really her only chance of survival, since he did not believe it made sense to talk of winners and losers in a war of this sort—was "to paralyze the enemy at the outset of a war."[54] And the very top priority was to destroy the enemy's strategic force.[55]

But did this mean that the United States would strike before the Soviets had actually started the war by beginning hostile military operations? Or was it assumed, for example, that the war might begin with a Soviet conventional attack in Europe, so that the American first strike would take place only after the Soviets had already committed actual acts of military aggression? It is important to understand that American strategy was *not* built on the assumption that the war would begin in this way, and in fact the idea that the Soviets would deliberately start a war *without* launching a massive nuclear attack on America was explicitly ruled out by Eisenhower. The president had little doubt that the Soviets would be under "extremely great" pressure to use atomic weapons "in a sudden blow" if they decided to go to war; "he did not see any basis for thinking other than that they would use these weapons at once, and in full force."[56]

What this meant was that if America was to get in the first nuclear blow— viewed as vital to the survival of the western world, and thus a prime goal of the strategy—she would in all likelihood have to launch her attack *before* the enemy had actually struck. Hence the great emphasis placed on speed, something that would have made little sense if America and NATO as a whole had opted for a simple retaliatory strategy in the normal sense of the term. "Victory or defeat," Eisenhower wrote, "could hang upon minutes and seconds used decisively at top speed or tragically wasted in indecision."[57]

This view was widely shared by top American military authorities. General J. Lawton Collins, former Army chief of staff and now America's representative on the NATO Military Committee, stressed the point in his remarks to that body in December 1953. "Even short delays in granting Commanders the authority to initiate retaliatory operations," Collins declared, "might well lead to a serious disintegration of our military position."[58] And General Alfred Gruenther, the NATO commander, emphasized the point in his very important "Capabilities Study," one of the key documents on which MC 48 was based. To accomplish his main mission of defending Europe, Gruenther wrote, SACEUR's "authority to implement the planned use of atomic weapons must be such as to ensure that *no delay what-*

[53] NSC meeting, July 29, 1954, AWF/NSC/5/DDEL. Emphasis added.
[54] NSC meeting, December 3, 1954, FRUS 1952–54, 2:805.
[55] See Rosenberg, "Origins of Overkill," esp. p. 38.
[56] Eisenhower-Radford-Taylor meeting, May 24, 1956, FRUS 1955–57, 19:312.
[57] Eisenhower to Churchill, January 22, 1955, *Eisenhower Papers,* 16:1523.
[58] Quoted in Wampler, "Ambiguous Legacy," p. 602.

soever will occur in countering a surprise attack." The choice of the term "countering," as opposed to "responding to" or "reacting to," probably again reflected an assumption that the West might have to act preemptively in a crisis.[59]

The MC 48 strategy was rooted in this kind of thinking. NATO, it was assumed, would have to move fast. If the USSR's nuclear capability was to be effectively neutralized, the West's air-atomic offensive had to be launched "without any delay." It was vital, in SACEUR's view, that the attack be "directed initially against the adversary's atomic capability and his key positions: in this area, where the time factor is decisive, measures must be taken to reduce to a minimum the time needed for decision and execution." The aim here was to "free the West from the threat of a Soviet nuclear attack." But the only way NATO could do this was to destroy the Soviet nuclear force before it was able to strike at the NATO countries. And since no one could take it for granted that the USSR would be so obliging as to start a war with a purely conventional attack and then wait patiently for the West to deliver the first nuclear strike, this implied that NATO might have to strike before the Soviets committed an overt act of aggression.[60]

Western leaders, of course, thought of themselves as the kind of people who would never start a war, and in a number of documents a strategy of preemption was explicitly ruled out.[61] But it is hard to take such statements at face value, given both the logic of the strategy and the many documents that point in the opposite direction.[62] Thus Dulles, for example, commented in December 1953 on the "great importance" of developing a "mechanism which can go into effect instantly on an alert."[63] And Eisenhower himself, just days after MC 48 was adopted, emphasized "his firm intention to launch a strategic air force immediately in case of *alert* of actual attack."[64] Once again, the phrasing is significant, suggesting that the bomber force would be launched when it became clear that the Soviets were still preparing for war but had not yet actually begun their attack.[65]

---

[59] Quoted in "Standing Group Report to the Military Committee on SACEUR's Capability Study, 1957," annex to JP(54)76 (Final), September 2, 1954, Defe 6/26, PRO. Emphasis added.

[60] "Avis du Comité des Chefs d'Etat-Major au sujet des problèmes soulevés par le Plan des Possibilités du Commandant Suprême Allié en Europe," September 6, 1954, and "Examen du 'Plan des Possibilités' établi par le commandement suprême des forces alliées en Europe," Blanc Papers, fonds 1K145, box 2, SHAT.

[61] See, for example, Eisenhower's diary entry for January 23, 1956, *Eisenhower Papers,* 16:1974, and his comments in NSC and other meetings in 1954, 1957 and 1960, in FRUS 1952–54, 2:641, FRUS 1955–57, 19:675, FRUS 1958–60, 3:413.

[62] One should note that some of the arguments Eisenhower made when ruling out preemptive action were explicitly contradicted by comments made in other contexts. Thus in the January 1956 diary entry just cited he said that no attack could be ordered unless Congress first met and declared war, something he considered impossible. But when he met with congressional leaders during the Berlin crisis in 1959, and said that if the Soviets cut off access to the city, he would come before Congress, one senator interrupted to tell him "not to come to Congress, but to go ahead." Eisenhower "assured him that in the event of a *real* emergency he would do just that." Eisenhower meeting with congressional leaders, March 6, 1959, p. 7, DDRS 1996/3493.

[63] North Atlantic Council meeting, December 16, 1953, FRUS 1952–54, 5:479.

[64] Eisenhower-JCS meeting, December 22, 1954, AWF/ACW Diary/3/December 1954 (2)/DDEL. Emphasis added.

[65] The same kind of point applies to a sentence from one of the key French documents describing the new strategy: "Le Commandant Suprême des forces alliées en Europe (SACEUR) prend pour postulat de base de l'ensemble de ses conceptions, *l'emploi immédiat des armes nouvelles dès la première man-*

The general thinking at NATO headquarters during this period was that, for the time being at least, the Soviets would have to build up their forces in central Europe before they could launch an assault on NATO Europe and that such a buildup would in itself give warning of attack. Gruenther thought the "alert period" would last for five to seven days. When warning was received, a general alert would be called, carrying with it an automatic grant of authority to SACEUR to order nuclear operations. In other words, the decision to use nuclear weapons would be made "before either side opens fire."[66]

As Eisenhower put it in a letter to Churchill, one had to consider most carefully the circumstances in which the NATO should react "explosively."[67] The fact that this is treated as a difficult issue once again supports the idea that Eisenhower and the other makers of the strategy were thinking in terms of preemption. A decision to retaliate against a Soviet nuclear attack, or even to order a full nuclear strike in response to a massive Soviet conventional attack on western Europe, would not be hard to make, but defining the conditions for preemptive action was obviously a much more difficult problem.

And indeed, at an NSC meeting held on November 4, 1954, Eisenhower issued a directive ordering the establishment of a special subcommittee of the NSC Planning Board. This committee was to prepare a report on "possible Soviet actions which might constitute clear indication of hostile intent." Eisenhower personally drafted the subcommittee's terms of reference. This body was, first of all,

to try to anticipate, by a judgment on indications of Soviet hostile intent, the need for immediate U.S. military action to save the U.S. from attack. Our own countermeasures to such established indications would include orders for the evacuation of American cities, for the dispersal of SAC, for mobilization, etc., and for *possible U.S. preventive military action*. The President indicated that should the need so require, he might be prepared to give *advance authority to local commanders to act.*"[68]

---

ifestation d'hostilité." "Avis du Comité des Chefs d'Etat-Major" (see above, note 60). The precise language is significant. The reference is not to launching the NATO attack at the start of hostilities (*dès le début des hostilités*); the attack, the actual language suggested, would instead begin as soon as the enemy's warlike intent became clear. Similarly, consider the following passage from a British document on the new strategy. Under the proposed arrangements, the general alert would authorize commanders whose forces were "attacked or menaced" to "conduct operations in accordance with the emergency plans." The use of the word "menaced" again suggests that the door was being kept open for preemptive action. "Standing Group Report to the Military Committee on SACEUR's Capability Study, 1957," annex to JP(54)76 (Final), September 2, 1954, Defe 6/26, PRO.

[66] See Vice Admiral Royer Dick to Lord Ismay, February 11, 1954, Ismay Papers, III/12/22/1, Liddell Hart Centre for Military Archives [LHCMA], King's College, London, cited in Wampler, "Ambiguous Legacy," p. 615. See also Standing Group Report to the Military Committee on SACEUR's Capability Study, 1957, annex to JP(54)76 (Final), September 2, 1954, para. 11, Defe 6/26, PRO, and Gruenther's "Remarks to SHAPE Correspondents," January 11, 1954, Montgomery Papers, file "Philosophy of NATO Military Build-up," Imperial War Museum, London.

[67] Eisenhower to Churchill, January 22, 1955, *Eisenhower Papers,* 16:1523. For another example of Eisenhower's interest in this question, see his comment in an NSC discussion of a study of "constitutional authority for use of U.S. forces in reacting promptly to aggression." The "great problem," he said, was "what the President could and should do in the event he had knowledge that Russia was on the point of attacking the United States." This again suggests that the option of preemptive action was not being ruled out a priori. NSC meeting, April 13, 1954, DDRS 1992/2735.

[68] Beam memorandum, December 31, 1954, and n. 3 appended to this document, FRUS 1955–57,

The MC 48 strategy, in fact, explains one of the most extraordinary features of the NATO system that took shape in the 1950s: the effective delegation to SACEUR of authority to initiate nuclear operations in an emergency. At the time, it was argued repeatedly that with survival hanging in the balance, one simply could not afford to waste precious minutes going through a cumbersome process of political consultation, and the American government insisted from the very outset on its ultimate right to order its nuclear forces into action unilaterally. There could be no doubt, Eisenhower wrote Admiral Radford, the JCS chairman, about what the United States would do if one of the allies tried to "impose a veto on actions which the United States considers essential to its security or to the security of its armed forces exposed to enemy attack. We should not let the British and French have any illusions as to U.S. intentions." And Secretary Dulles often argued forcefully along similar lines.[69]

But it is important to note not just that the U.S. government was reserving to itself this supreme power. The more crucial point to emerge from the new evidence is that this authority was effectively delegated to the NATO commander—or more precisely, to SACEUR in his capacity as the U.S. commander in chief in Europe, or CINCEUR. The NATO military authorities for some time had been pressing for a predelegation of authority to launch a nuclear attack. General Ridgway, in one of his last acts as SACEUR in 1953, had requested a delegation of authority "to put into effect his atomic counter-offensive immediately on the outbreak of war."[70] The idea was also a basic feature of the Gruenther strategy in 1954.[71] The military authorities in Washington wanted to get a formal acceptance of this principle by the allies as part of the MC 48 strategy.[72]

19:1–2. Emphasis added. The subcommittee's report, dated March 21, 1955, was submitted to the NSC and discussed at its March 31, 1955, meeting. The report listed a whole series of Soviet actions which "should leave no doubt in the President's mind as to the need for taking immediate military action to save the United States from the consequences of enemy attack, or to postpone, lessen or prevent imminent enemy attack." Among other things, a Soviet attack on Yugoslavia and a Soviet occupation of Finland were considered in and of themselves "clear evidence that Soviet attack upon the continental U.S. is certain or imminent." The report did not call for preemptive action in the event of obvious Soviet preparations for a ground war in Europe, although the original version of the report did contain an annex which listed various indicators of this sort. NSC meeting, March 31, 1955, ibid., p. 69; "Study of Possible Hostile Soviet Actions," NSC 5515/1, April 1, 1955, ibid., pp. 71–75. The annex to the original draft can be found in DDRS 1986/2158. The annex was deleted because the JCS felt it was arbitrary and thus misleading, and in any case unnecessary. FRUS 1955–57, 19:70, n. 11.

[69] Eisenhower to Radford, December 8, 1954, CJCS Radford 092.2 NAT, RG 218, USNA. For Dulles, see his statement to the North Atlantic Council, April 23, 1954, FRUS 1952–54, 5:512; Dulles to Wilson, Feb. 8, 1955, 740.5/2–855, RG 59, USNA; Dulles-Brentano meeting, November 23, 1957, FRUS 1955–57, 4:191; Dulles to Adenauer, November 29, 1957, DDRS 1988/3308; and especially Dulles-Macmillan meeting, December 14, 1957, DDRS 1987/3307. Note also Wampler, "Ambiguous Legacy," pp. 650, 971.

[70] See SACEUR's "Estimate of the Situation and Force Requirements for 1956," October 2, 1953, para. 26, COS(53)490, Defe 5/49, PRO, cited in Wampler, "Ambiguous Legacy," p. 501.

[71] "Standing Group Report to the Military Committee on SACEUR's Capability Study, 1957," September 2, 1954, annex to JP(54)76 (Final), and Joint Planning Staff report on "The Most Effective Pattern of NATO Military Strength for the Next Few Years," October 21, 1954, JP(54)86 (Final), both in Defe 6/26, PRO.

[72] *JCS History*, 5:305.

It was clear from the start, however, that it would be hard to win explicit allied approval for such an arrangement. The Europeans were in fact sensitive to the great dilemma posed by the new strategy: the conflict between the military need for extremely rapid action, and the political requirement that the crucial decision be made by duly constituted civil authority. This sense of basic imperatives in conflict comes out over and over again in the newly released documents. Thus a British document discussed a NATO Standing Group report on Gruenther's "capabilities study" as follows:

> Politically the implications of initiating atomic warfare are so grave that there would be the greatest objection to delegating the decision to use atomic weapons to SACEUR. Militarily there is no question now as to the importance of instant atomic retaliation to any major attack whether with or without the use of atomic weapons; this will be of even greater importance by 1957 since SACEUR's forces will be committed to the atomic warfare strategy. . . . The proposal in the Standing Group Draft goes some way towards meeting SACEUR's requirement but still leaves open the question of what will happen in the event of there not being time for SACEUR to obtain the Council's consent to a General Alert. *Militarily it is desirable to give SACEUR discretion in this event, politically this is probably impossible.*[73]

The French saw things in much the same light: the question of who would be authorized to order a nuclear attack was "the most delicate problem."[74] Extremely rapid action might well be necessary, but could a decision of such enormous gravity be made by SACEUR alone? The French wanted the crucial decision to be made by the political authorities on a three-power basis, perhaps by a small committee with British, French, and American representation.[75] But the Americans were unwilling to see their hands tied. And the British agreed with the Americans that formal arrangements were not necessary—that in an emergency the matter would be "dealt with informally" by consultations at the "highest level."[76]

In the end, no formal decision was reached on the control question. The French plan for a three-power committee was not adopted, but the Americans decided not to press the Europeans too hard on the fundamental question of nuclear use. General Gruenther was against pushing for "express agreements in NATO on the right to use nuclear weapons." "Getting a plan" like MC 48 "approved in principle," he argued, would "permit implementation in fact to take place and lay the groundwork for any future action."[77] Dulles agreed, and the JCS went along with this approach. Instead of America pressing for categorical

[73] "Standing Group Report to the Military Committee on SACEUR's Capability Study, 1957," September 2, 1957, annex to JP(54)76 (Final), Defe 6/26, PRO. Emphasis added.

[74] "Examen du plan des possibilités," 1K145/2/SHAT.

[75] Foreign ministry note on atomic warfare, December 13, 1954, DDF 1954, pp. 906–909; Dulles-Mendès meeting, November 20, 1954, Dulles-Mendès-Eden meeting, December 16, 1954, SSMC, nos. 800 and 853.

[76] Dulles-Makins meetings, December 4 and December 8, 1954, and Dulles-Eisenhower meeting, December 14, 1954, SSMC, nos. 827, 849.

[77] Elbrick to Dulles, October 12, 1954, 740.5/10–1254, RG 59, USNA. These remarks were deleted from the version of the document published in FRUS, 1952–54, 5:527.

commitments, the view was that "the Europeans should be led into the atomic era gradually and tacitly."[78]

In formal terms, the NATO Council simply approved MC 48 "as a basis for defense planning and preparations by the NATO military authorities, noting that this approval does not involve the delegation of the responsibility of governments for putting plans into action in the event of hostilities."[79] But this sort of phrasing was somewhat disingenuous. In agreeing to MC 48, the NATO governments were not just approving it as a basis for planning. They were also accepting—and, in the case of the British and French at least, knowingly accepting—the whole concept of operations it embodied.[80] As for the Americans, the Eisenhower administration certainly did not take the proviso about the governments' responsibility for deciding on war and peace too literally. "For political purposes" the U.S. government was willing to go along with a text reserving "final decisions" to the governments. But when the time came, the United States was not going to hold back simply because an allied government was opposed to action.[81] In general, when pressed on the question of how NATO would actually go to war, the basic tactic was to finesse the issue. "Events would take care of the political decisions," Dulles said in this context, especially since the United States retained "its own freedom of action" and would do what was necessary "because it would be our troops that would have the atomic weapons which they would be able to use in their own defense and that would be decisive."[82] Indeed, throughout the 1950s, NATO did not have a real procedure for determining when and how force would be used: this crucial issue was deliberately evaded throughout the Eisenhower period.[83] So in December

[78] Top-level meeting, November 3, 1954, 740.5/11–354, RG 59, USNA. The passage quoted was deleted from the version of this document published in FRUS 1952–54, 5:532. Goodpaster to Eisenhower, November 16, 1954, SS/ITM/3/NATO file no. 1 (4)/DDEL.

[79] *JCS History*, 5:317.

[80] See, for example, Foreign Ministry note on atomic warfare, December 13, 1954, DDF 1954, p. 907.

[81] Memorandum for Radford, December 8, 1954, CJCS Radford 092.2 NAT, RG 218, USNA.

[82] Dulles-Eisenhower meeting, December 14, 1954, SSMC, no. 849.

[83] Thus, according to one U.S. document, by the end of the Eisenhower period a NATO system had taken shape full of ambiguities about "how war starts and who has the authority to start it." State Department memorandum on "The Problem of Berlin," p. 5, enclosed in McGhee to Bundy, March 24, 1961, NSF/81/JFKL. And in mid-1960 a British official characterized the system for the political control of nuclear use as "woolly and diffuse." Sir Solly Zuckerman, in a meeting with Macmillan and the defence minister, June 13, 1960, Prem 11/3713, PRO. That this kind of system had taken shape was no accident. The NATO commander, General Norstad, whose views carried a good deal of weight in this area, was very much against the idea of trying to work out a precise procedure to cover this fundamental issue. See, for example, Norstad-Adenauer meeting, December 16, 1957, DSP/231/107951/ML; Norstad-Adenauer-Spaak meeting, reported in Houghton to Herter, September 10, 1960, SS/ITM/5/NATO (4) [1959–1960]/DDEL; Norstad-Lloyd meeting, July 11, 1960, Prem 11/3713, PRO. Nor was it just the Americans who felt this sort of issue was best avoided. Adenauer, in his meetings with Norstad, basically saw eye to eye with SACEUR, and was irritated when Spaak brought up the issue in the September 1960 meeting. The British also, as a rule, were in favor of avoiding the issue. See, for example, Ismay meeting with U.S. State Department officials, March 13, 1953, FRUS 1952–54, 5:361. In late 1957, a top British defense official also argued that NATO had to "stay away from effort at advance planning on how decision to use will be made." Martin to Timmons, November 29, 1957, State Department Freedom of Information Act release [DOS-FOIA] 90-1102-25. And according to a

1954, Dulles did not press for a clear grant of authority. It was enough simply to rule out any NATO Council decision suggesting that action by SACEUR, in an emergency, had to await approval by all the NATO members.

The real American view was that for the MC 48 strategy to be effective, very rapid action—and probably even preemptive action—might be essential. But such swift action might only be possible if SACEUR was authorized to make the crucial decision in an emergency. Eisenhower, a former SACEUR himself, certainly felt the NATO commander had to be given some discretionary power in extreme circumstances.[84] And Admiral Radford, the JCS chairman, later remarked that the "decision would really have to be made by SACEUR."[85]

In fact, SACEUR actually did have a certain recognized authority to order his forces into action in extreme cases. The NATO Council in 1954, in approving the principle that SACEUR should seek political guidance "when appropriate," had recognized the NATO commander's authority to interpret the "when appropriate" proviso as he saw fit.[86] In 1956, a NATO Military Committee paper noted that SACEUR did not have to seek political guidance "in cases where the degree of urgency precludes following the full procedures."[87] And of course, given America's clear refusal to accept any allied veto on the use of American forces in an emergency—and this to a certain extent even included forces based on that ally's territory[88]—no specific NATO authorization was even necessary for SACEUR to have predelegated power. Given that the NATO nuclear forces at this time were essen-

1960 U.S. document, the members of NATO had as a whole informally agreed that it was "undesirable to set up formal procedures for a NATO Council approval of the institution of nuclear warfare." "NATO in the 1960's: U.S. Policy Considerations" (draft), September 9, 1960, p. 22, SS/ITM/5/NATO (5) [1959–1960]/DDEL.

[84] JCS History, 5:317, and Wampler, "Ambiguous Legacy," p. 1041.

[85] Radford-Strauss meeting, December 10, 1956, Conference Files, CF 814, RG59, USNA, cited in Wampler, "Ambiguous Legacy," p. 976.

[86] See Wampler, "Ambiguous Legacy," p. 629.

[87] Quoted ibid., p. 1005. It was a draft of the NATO document MC 57 that was being quoted here. Note also Dulles's reference in early 1955 to a NATO alerts paper, which provided for political consultation to be omitted "in case of sudden and extreme emergency." Dulles to Wilson, February 8, 1955, Records relating to Disarmament, 1953–62, box 83, NATO—Nuclear Weapons, 1954–56, RG 59, USNA.

[88] The Americans—especially the military authorities—were very reluctant throughout this period to see their hands tied by agreements with even the friendliest foreign powers. Even arrangements governing the use of the American bases in Britain were left rather loose and informal, and could be interpreted differently by the two governments. U.S. officials had indicated that the British "obviously" had the right to be consulted before attacks were mounted from the bases. But according to the formal agreement reached in January 1952, the use of the bases "would be a matter for joint decision" by the two governments "in light of the circumstances prevailing at the time." The British could argue that this gave them the right to be consulted; the Americans could, however, proceed on the basis of the assumption that the proviso about "circumstances prevailing at the time" implied that they had to right to launch strikes from the bases on their own, if time did not permit consultation—and Dulles, in fact, endorsed this interpretation in a phone conversation with Senator Knowland in December 1957. See Timothy Botti, The Long Wait: The Forging of the Anglo-American Nuclear Alliance, 1945–1958 (New York: Greenwood, 1987), pp. 80–86 (for U.S. reluctance to make any commitment at all), pp. 84 and 93 (for earlier assurances about the use of bases in Britain), p. 101 (for the key passage in the agreement and the "implied consent" theory), and p. 206 (for Dulles's interpretation).

tially American, the predelegation could be made to SACEUR in his capacity as the U.S. commander in Europe.

Eisenhower understood that authority to initiate military operations could legally be delegated to high military commanders, provided that they were Americans. The principle of predelegation was recognized in the Basic National Security Policy document for 1956, and had in fact been implicit in the interpretation given to an important paragraph on the use of nuclear weapons in NSC 162/2, the first BNSP paper in the Eisenhower period.[89] What if action absolutely had to be taken immediately? If a fleet of enemy bombers suddenly showed up on the radar screens, Eisenhower asked, wasn't a commander justified in using "every weapon at hand to defend himself and his forces?"[90] This sort of argument was the standard foot in the door, the device commonly used to establish the legitimacy of a certain degree of predelegated authority. But how far could the principle be carried? Should it in fact include the authority to launch a preemptive strike?

It seems that this issue was dealt with mostly on an informal basis: the president reached a certain understanding with his top military commanders, especially SACEUR and the commander of the Strategic Air Command (CINCSAC). Even as late as 1959, the assumption was that SACEUR, in his capacity as the U.S. commander in Europe, "would probably begin the fighting on the principle of the inherent right of a commander to defend his forces."[91] Eisenhower's personal relations with General Gruenther, the man he had effectively chosen as SACEUR in 1953, were so close—the two men were on such intimate terms and had such a high regard for each other personally—that formal arrangements were never really necessary during the period when Gruenther was NATO commander. With Gruenther's successor, Air Force General Lauris Norstad, the president's relations were not so intimate, but even here the issue of war-making power was apparently handled in a relatively informal way. When Norstad was asked by the British foreign secretary in 1960 whether the U.S. government had "delegated authority to him on its behalf," he replied simply "that the answer to that question depended upon the relationship between him and the President," and he implied "that his present relationship with President Eisenhower was such that no understanding was required."[92]

---

[89] NSC 5602/1, March 15, 1956, para. 11, FRUS 1955–57, 19:246. Paragraph 39b of NSC 162/2 of October 30, 1953, said that "in the event of hostilities, the United States will consider nuclear weapons to be as available for use as other munitions." The State and Defense departments differed on the interpretation of this provision; the JCS argued that it meant that in the event of armed conflict, authority to use nuclear weapons was automatic. At the end of 1953, the president decided that use would be "automatic" only in the case of an atomic attack on western Europe or the United States; in other circumstances, a political decision would have to be made. Cutler to secretary of state, secretary of defense, and AEC chairman, March 14, 1955, summing up a memo from Lay to those three officials of January 4, 1954, on the interpretation of paragraph 39b, in OSANSA/NSC/S/1/Atomic Weapons (1953–60)(1)/DDEL. The BNSPs for the Eisenhower period, including NSC 162/2, were published in Marc Trachtenberg, ed., *The Development of American Strategic Thought, 1945–1969*, vol. 1 (New York: Garland, 1988).

[90] NSC meeting, February 27, 1956, FRUS 1955–57, 19:204.

[91] Deputy Secretary of Defense Quarles and Captain Schneider of the Chief of Naval Operations office, in notes of Eisenhower meeting with Twining, Quarles, et al., March 12, 1959, FRUS 1958–60, 7(1):436. The president, it is worth noting, did not disagree with this view.

[92] Notes of Norstad-Lloyd meeting, July 11, 1960, Prem 11/3713, PRO.

Similarly, it seems that the SAC commander, General Curtis LeMay, had reached a certain informal understanding, with Eisenhower on these issues. In 1957, LeMay met with Robert Sprague, one of the members of the Gaither Committee, a body that had been set up to look into the problem of surprise attack. He told Sprague that he might strike preemptively in extreme circumstances, without direct presidential authorization, but simply on his authority as SAC commander. "If I see the Russians are amassing their planes for an attack," he said in substance, "I'm going to knock the shit out of them before they get off the ground." When Sprague objected that this was not national policy, LeMay replied that he did not care, that this was his policy, this was what he was going to do.[93] It is hard to imagine that LeMay would have been so open with Sprague—the comment might well have gotten back to the president—unless he had been given some indication that Eisenhower understood the need for such a policy.

In any event, it was about this time that formal rules governing predelegation were being worked out. The development by 1957 of a Soviet rocket with enough thrust to deliver a thermonuclear warhead halfway around the world meant that warning time was soon going to be cut very considerably, and that the national command authority in Washington might be wiped out before it had a chance to authorize nuclear operations. For the sake of deterrence if nothing else, something explicit in the way of predelegated authority was needed to cover this contingency.[94]

In May 1957, the president issued a basic "authorization for the expenditure of nuclear weapons," and this was followed by other documents spelling out the nature of this predelegated authority in greater detail. Under these arrangements, certain commanders—especially the SAC commander and the U.S. commander in Europe—were authorized to make the crucial decisions on their own, if they were unable to "contact higher authority at a time when survival depends upon immediate action."[95]

The whole issue of predelegation is considered quite sensitive, and the relevant documents have still not been fully declassified. But even if the delegation letters and related documents were available, they would probably tell us little about what was in the minds of people at the time—about what Eisenhower really intended, how he explained his thinking to top military officers, or how the commanders

[93] Quoted in Fred Kaplan, *The Wizards of Armageddon* (New York: Simon and Schuster, 1983), pp. 133–134. The accuracy of this account was confirmed in a letter Sprague sent me dated January 15, 1986. Note also LeMay's comments in Kohn and Harahan, *Strategic Air Warfare*, pp. 92–95.

[94] This was reflected in the attention given at this point to the problem of developing a "response doctrine." See, for example, Eisenhower-Gray meeting, July 19, 1960, OSANSA/SA/P/5/DDEL, and Rubel briefing on continental defense, September 15, 1960, p. 13, SS/S/A/16/National Security Council [vol. 2](6)/DDEL. See also the editorial note relating to this issue in FRUS 1958–60, 3:353.

[95] Rosenberg, "Origins of Overkill," pp. 48–49; "Note on Implementing Instructions for the Expenditure of Nuclear Weapons," JCS 2019/238, August 15, 1957, CCS 471.6 (8-15-45) sec. 99R8, RG 218, USNA and DDRS 1980/272B; interview with Carl Kaysen, August 1988. For the heavily sanitized predelegation letters, see DDRS 1997/1280–1282. Note also McGeorge Bundy's reference at the beginning of the Kennedy period to "a situation today in which a subordinate commander faced with a substantial Russian military action could start the thermonuclear holocaust on his own initiative if he could not reach [the president] (by failure of communication at either end of the line)." Bundy to Kennedy, January 30, 1961, NSF/313/NSC no. 475/JFKL. For a number of documents, mostly highly sanitized, bearing on the issue, see the National Security Archive website: http://www.seas.gwu.edu/nsarchive/news/predelegation/predel.htm.

understood the authority they were being given. One does get the sense, however, that Eisenhower was willing to give high military commanders a good deal of latitude in situations where hours, perhaps even minutes, were crucial. His basic thinking was fairly straightforward. In a U.S.–Soviet war in Europe, nuclear weapons would certainly be used. To limit damage to themselves, the western countries had to prevent the Soviets, to the extent possible, from launching a nuclear attack. That meant that the western forces had to strike as soon as they could, and as effectively as they could, focusing their initial attack on the USSR's nuclear force. The West was not going to "start" the war, but this meant simply that the United States and her allies would wait until Soviet responsibility was clear. They could not, however, wait too long: the greater the delay, the greater the risk of disaster.[96] One might therefore have to strike preemptively. As Eisenhower put it in a meeting with the congressional leadership during the Berlin crisis in 1959: "when we reach the acute crisis period" it might be "necessary to engage in general war to protect our rights."[97] The nuclear attack, in other words, might have to be launched before the enemy had begun to fire on NATO forces, or at least before large-scale conventional fighting had broken out. And a policy that placed such a great emphasis on extremely rapid, and indeed on preemptive action, implied that the high military authorities, especially SACEUR, would play a key role in deciding when the attack had to be ordered.

Eisenhower was not thinking in terms of SACEUR exercising his predelegated authority entirely on his own, and certainly not in terms of SACEUR ordering an attack semidefiantly, against the wishes of the president, in order to force his hand and oblige him to order SAC into action. What Eisenhower probably had in mind was a process of constant and intense consultation between the president and SACEUR, with some additional consultation with the three main allied governments. The decision to execute the war plans would develop from that process in a natural way, on the basis of political and especially military data. The presumption was, however, that the president would be strongly inclined to defer to the military judgment of SACEUR, the commander on the scene.

It was this presumption that lay at the heart of SACEUR's special authority. For SACEUR in the 1950s was no ordinary military commander. He occupied a "unique position" with the president; he did not take orders from the JCS; he had a considerable degree of personal autonomy, which enabled him to relate to the European governments as something more than a mere tool of U.S. policy. Eisenhower, the first SACEUR, had played a key role in developing the system based on this concept. Before he had agreed to accept that appointment, he had gotten Truman to grant SACEUR the degree of autonomy that he had felt was necessary.[98]

---

[96] Note, for example, Eisenhower's account of a meeting he had with Churchill and Eden on December 5, 1953: "I told them that quite naturally in the event of war, we would always hold up enough to establish the fact before the world that the other was clearly the aggressor, but I also gave my conviction that anyone who held up too long in the use of his assets in atomic weapons might suddenly find himself subjected to such wide-spread and devastating attack that retaliation would be next to impossible." *Eisenhower Papers,* 15:733.

[97] Eisenhower meeting with congressional leadership, March 6, 1959, FRUS 1958–60, 8:433.

[98] See General Coiner to SHAPE chief of staff, September 2, 1960, DDRS 1990/1880; Eisenhower

And after he became president, he continued to support the basic concept of a strong SACEUR—that is, a SACEUR with considerable war-making power. Even at the very end of his presidency, he was still thinking in these terms. SACEUR, he thought in late 1960, should have the authority to decide when and how nuclear weapons would be used.[99]

The MC 48 strategy, especially the premium it placed on preemptive action and the incentives it created for the transfer of war-making power to high military commanders, naturally made many people uneasy, particularly in the European governments. How then did this strategy come to be accepted? Was it essentially forced on the Europeans by the United States?

The U.S. government certainly took the lead in pressing for the new strategy, and indeed Eisenhower's personal role was fundamental. From the outset he knew that nuclear weapons could play a major role in the defense of Europe. In January 1951, shortly after his appointment as SACEUR, he laid out his basic strategic concept at a meeting in the White House. NATO could build up its air and naval power in England and the North Sea, and in the Mediterranean and North Africa. Then "if the Russians tried to move ahead in the center, I'd hit them awfully hard from both flanks. I think if we built up the kind of force I want, the center will hold and they'll have to pull back."[100] Nuclear strikes would be particularly effective in this context, and in fact from 1949 on, Army thinking on the defense of Europe had focused on the tactical use of nuclear forces.[101] Eisenhower himself was particularly interested in using atomic weapons in this way.[102] But the weapons only started to become available for this purpose in 1952, with the dramatic expansion of the nuclear stockpile and the advances in weapons design that made it possible for fighter aircraft to be armed with nuclear explosives.[103]

By this time, however, Eisenhower was no longer SACEUR. His successor, General Ridgway, was of a more conservative bent. Ridgway's whole approach to the problem of the defense of Europe, it was widely felt, just did not take adequate account of the effect nuclearization was bound to have on the nature of ground warfare. Ridgway sought simply "to superimpose nuclear planning on conventional force postures." Hence the requirement for very high force levels: whenever a NATO unit deployed in the standard way was wiped out by nuclear fire, it would have to be replaced. And Ridgway's requirements for the defense of Europe simply ignored the impact of the strategic air war: it was as though NATO and SAC would be fighting two entirely separate wars, with neither campaign having any

---

recollection in meeting with military leaders, March 12, 1959, FRUS 1958–60, 7(1):435; and Lumpkin, "SACEUR/CINCEUR Concept."

[99] Notes of Eisenhower-Spaak meeting, October 4, 1960, SS/ITM/5/NATO(6)[1959–1960]/DDEL. This version of the document was declassified in 1979; in the version published fourteen years later (FRUS 1958–60, 7(1):638–642), the relevant passage was deleted.

[100] White House meeting, January 31, 1951, FRUS 1951, 3:454.

[101] See Trachtenberg, *History and Strategy*, pp. 156–157. As Robert Wampler pointed out to me, some of the officers who had developed the Army point of view moved on to SHAPE, where they played a certain role in the process leading to MC 48, General Schuyler, for example, becoming Gruenther's chief of staff.

[102] See the long footnote in the *Eisenhower Papers*, 13:1225–27.

[103] See Trachtenberg, *History and Strategy*, p. 129.

impact on the other. The result, again, was to magnify estimates of force requirements, and thus to trap Europe in a situation where, given political realities, even great efforts were bound to be considered totally inadequate. The Ridgway approach meant that an effective forward defense would be forever beyond reach.[104]

Eisenhower and Gruenther from the start disliked this hidebound military philosophy, which, incidentally, was shared by many top Army officers.[105] The "Tank-for-Tank and Division-for-Division approach," they felt, was "exactly what we most wish to avoid."[106] The problem was not insoluble: "we can have security without paying the price of national bankruptcy," Eisenhower wrote, "if we will put brains in the balance." "Preconceived notions" had to be put aside; if a radical change in strategy was appropriate, then so be it; the implications of the nuclear revolution had to be thought through and accepted unflinchingly.[107]

When Eisenhower took office as president in January 1953, he knew exactly where he wanted to go, and the first thing he did was to take control of the strategy-making process. The terms of the principal members of the Joint Chiefs of Staff were about to expire, and the new chief executive decided to replace them all. He then pulled Ridgway back from Europe by making him Army chief of staff; the other new chiefs, especially the chairman, Admiral Radford, and the Air Force chief of staff, General Twining, placed much greater reliance on nuclear, and especially on strategic nuclear, weapons. This meant, first of all, that the JCS would be divided on the most fundamental issues of strategy, and Eisenhower would therefore play the crucial role of arbiter. But Eisenhower had also created an opening in Europe: he had gotten rid of Ridgway and could now make his close friend Al Gruenther the new SACEUR. If Eisenhower had had his way, Gruenther would have been his immediate successor as NATO commander, but Truman had given the job to Ridgway instead. Now, however, shortly after taking office as president himself, he was able to arrange things the way he wanted. And with Eisenhower's full support, Gruenther was able to stage-manage the process culminating in the adoption of MC 48 in December 1954.

But this is not to say that the new strategy was simply rammed down the throats of the Europeans, who accepted it only grudgingly and with serious misgivings. Indeed, one can almost say the opposite. The French military authorities, and certain key British officials as well, were as concerned as anyone else with the glaring defects of the Ridgway strategy. Under that strategy, there was a persistent gap between NATO capabilities and requirements, and thus an insatiable demand for increased military spending. Yet the NATO countries were clearly reaching the limits of what they could realistically be expected to devote to defense; military

---

[104] General Robert C. Richardson III, "NATO Nuclear Strategy: A Look Back," *Strategic Review,* 9, no. 2 (Spring 1981), esp. pp. 38–40; Robert Wampler, "The Die is Cast: The United States and NATO Nuclear Planning" (unpublished paper), pp. 13, 15, 19, 24, and esp. 27–28; and Wampler, "Ambiguous Legacy," pp. 500, 503–504. For the Ridgway strategy, see "SACEUR's Estimate of the Situation and Force Requirements for 1956," COS(53)490, October 2, 1953, Defe 5/49, PRO.

[105] Note, for example, JCS Chairman Bradley's views, in *JCS History,* 4:309–310.

[106] Gruenther to Army Department, October 5, 1951, quoted in *Eisenhower Papers,* 13:1226.

[107] Eisenhower diary, October 18, 1951, *Eisenhower Papers,* 12:651.

spending was in fact leveling off. Wasn't the obvious solution to take into account the implications of the "new weapons" then becoming available, and to radically adjust one's way of fighting a war in Europe so as to take full account of the nuclear revolution? Didn't it make sense to have a more integrated defense strategy, and especially to develop a strategy for the defense of western Europe more closely bound up with America's strategy for general war?[108]

If this was the problem, the solutions were obvious, especially from the point of view of the French military leaders. A highly integrated NATO defense strategy, a strategy in which nuclear weapons played the major role and in which the defense of Europe was tightly linked to the American air-atomic offensive—all this had been the goal of French military policy for quite some time.[109] This was why the French military authorities embraced MC 48 as unambiguously, as wholeheartedly, and indeed as enthusiastically as they did. This policy, the French chiefs stressed, would "for the first time" make an effective defense of Europe possible. If it were rejected, the Americans might well give up on forward defense and revert to the "peripheral strategy." But forward defense was vital for France, and the French chiefs had no problem accepting a German military contribution, which, they agreed with Gruenther, was essential to the success of the new strategy. The French had for years taken the lead in pressing for highly integrated NATO structures with three interlocking objectives in mind: keeping the Americans in Europe by linking them as closely and as inextricably as possible to the rest of NATO; providing a framework for German rearmament while still limiting German freedom of action, but in a way the Germans themselves would not find too offensive; and providing for a pooling of effort that would make for a more militarily efficient use of the NATO countries' limited military resources. The new strategy brought them closer to all these goals. If the price they paid was a certain sacrifice of French independence, well, wasn't that implicit in the very nature of the alliance, one in which the United States was bound to play by far the most important role? As for the political leadership, the Mendès France government certainly had qualms about the new strategy, but in the final analysis it was persuaded by the arguments

---

[108] French General Staff memorandum, November 25, 1953, Ismay Papers III/12/13a/LHCMA; Ismay's notes for December 6, 1953, meeting, Ismay Papers, III/12/17/LHCMA; summary of foreign ministers' meeting, December 6, 1953, FRUS 1952–54, 5:1789–1790.

[109] As the French military authorities were themselves aware: the Chiefs of Staff Committee appointed to report on the new strategy expressed "également son accord quant à l'intégration des moyens atomiques dans les dispositifs de défense occidentaux, et à l'étroite conjugaison des possibilités des forces stratégiques américaines avec ceux-ci, *dispositions qui jusqu'à ce jour n'avaient cessé de faire l'objet des demandes françaises.*" "Avis du Comité des Chefs d'Etat Major," September 6, 1954, 1K145/3/SHAT; emphasis added. And in other internal discussions, the French military authorities took a certain credit for the emergence of the new strategy. See, for example, the reference made at this time by General Blanc, the Army chief of staff, to "la réforme des systèmes militaires et des structures des forces, idée lancée par le Général ELY au standing group dès 1950, soutenue par le Général VALLUY avec une tenacité qui porte aujourd'hui ses fruits . . . " Notes of Blanc talk to Conseil Supérieur des Forces Armées, November 5, 1954, 1K145/4/SHAT. For the thinking of French military leaders during this period, very much in line with the MC 48 philosophy, see also Billotte, *Passé au futur*, pp. 41–42; Maréchal Juin, *Mémoires*, vol. 2 (Paris: Fayard, 1960), pp. 255–258; Bernard Pujo, *Juin, Maréchal de France* (Paris: Albin Michel, 1988), pp. 294–296.

the top French military leaders were making, and it swallowed whatever misgivings it had and fully accepted the new system.

Indeed, western Europe as a whole was quick to embrace the new strategy. The Americans had anticipated much greater opposition to MC 48 than they actually found, and were pleasantly surprised by the fact that the Europeans accepted the new strategy so readily at the NATO Council meeting in December 1954.[110] Even on the sensitive issue of predelegation, the Europeans quickly moved toward acceptance of American views on the subject—if indeed such views had not already been effectively accepted in 1954. At the NATO Council meeting in December 1956, NATO defense ministers generally backed the principle of delegating to NATO commanders authority to use nuclear weapons. The Dutch and West German defense ministers were particularly outspoken on this subject. The general attitude in NATO Europe was perhaps best summed up by a comment to Gruenther made by Portugal's NATO ambassador in an earlier discussion of nuclear use: "If the time comes, use them. Don't wait to ask us. We may hang you afterwards but for God's sake use them."[111]

The American government was pleased with the way the European attitude had evolved. The United States, Eisenhower said in 1956, had "made real progress in convincing our friends of the validity of our views on the use of atomic weapons. For example, the NATO powers were now clamoring that we share atomic weapons with them; whereas only a couple of years ago they had recoiled in horror from all thought of employing nuclear weapons."[112] But this was a fundamental point: the MC 48 strategy implied that the European armies needed to be equipped with nuclear weapons. And this in turn meant that the United States, if it was serious about the strategy and serious about the alliance, had to help the Europeans acquire a certain nuclear capability.

Thus nuclear sharing was implicit in MC 48. A war in Europe would be nuclear from the start; it followed that forces geared to the nuclear battlefield were practically the only forces worth building up. The allies, as long as they were not armed with nuclear weapons, would essentially be marginalized by the new strategy. "We are now in effect indicating to our allies that the next war, if it occurs, will be largely an atomic war," Dulles told the NSC in late 1956. "Since they do not have atomic weapons they naturally deduce, from our statements, that they will be expected to sit on the sidelines while we fight the war. This attitude is not desirable either from their point of view or from ours."[113] The allies, he said a year later, were being placed in an untenable situation. Nuclear forces were coming to play an "ever-increasing role" in the defense of the West. The result was that those allies without nuclear forces of their own, and who therefore felt that "they would have no voice" in the decision to use those forces, were left in a "state of considerable uncertainty and bewilderment."[114]

[110] See, for example, Secretary Humphreys' remarks in the December 21, 1954 NSC meeting, FRUS 1952–54, 5:562.

[111] Wampler, "Ambiguous Legacy," pp. 987–988, 1039.

[112] NSC meeting, May 10, 1956, FRUS 1955–57, 20:399.

[113] NSC meeting, October 4, 1956, p. 8, AWF/NSC/8/DDEL. See also Dulles's remarks in the May 11, 1956, NSC meeting, FRUS 1955–57, 4:81, and Trachtenberg, *History and Strategy,* pp. 182–183.

[114] Dulles meeting with Macmillan and Lloyd, October 22, 1957, DDRS 1987/3272.

A more generous American policy was thus essential if the alliance was to be saved. The United States, Dulles explained to a very receptive Eisenhower, could not tell her allies "in effect that these new weapons are becoming conventional weapons, and at the same time tell them that they cannot have such weapons. He felt that now [late 1957] is the time for a decision in this matter—the alternative is that the alliances will fall apart."[115] Even as early as December 1953, Dulles commented that the U.S. government wanted to make sure that the allied forces would not have to "fight with obsolete equipment."[116] How could America deny to her allies a form of weaponry the Soviets already had and indeed were deploying against them? What kind of alliance would it be if America so obviously did not trust her own allies?

With the MC 48 strategy, the United States was essentially asking the allies to put their fate in American hands—indeed, largely in the hands of an American general. Could one expect them to place such trust in America while the United States would not trust them with the very weapons most essential to their own defense? NATO had developed an integrated command structure. But if this simply meant that the Americans would be running the show and giving orders that the Europeans would have to carry out, would the alliance be viable? Didn't the basic idea of military integration imply that the NATO forces would be armed in a uniform way, without regard to national distinctions? It was absurd to think that a truly integrated force could be composed of national contingents, some of which had the most modern armament while others were denied on principle the very form of weaponry most vital in modern warfare.

For Eisenhower and Dulles, the need for nuclear sharing was obvious from the start. It was impossible, Dulles said in 1957, to "contemplate a situation in which there were first and second class powers in NATO"—and this, in fact, had been his and especially Eisenhower's view all along.[117] Already in 1953 Dulles had been talking about the idea of "atomic weapons 'being meshed into' NATO forces" so that the allies would not have to fight with "obsolete weapons."[118] In late 1954, at the time MC 48 was being prepared, the U.S. government decided that henceforth American military assistance would be "geared into" the development of European forces "prepared for integrated action" in line with the new strategy. The goal was to make sure that the NATO forces would have a nuclear capability of their own.[119] And in 1956, Dulles agreed with the British foreign secretary that "the

[115] Eisenhower-Dulles meeting, October 22, 1957 (document dated October 31), AWF/DDE Diaries/27/October 1957 Staff Notes (1)/DDEL. The passage quoted here, although it was declassified in 1982, was nevertheless deleted from the version that was published in 1992 (FRUS 1955–57, 27:800).

[116] Foreign ministers' meeting, December 6, 1953, FRUS 1952–54, 5:1790.

[117] Dulles-Brentano meeting, November 21, 1957, 740.5/11-2157, RG 59, USNA. This particular sentence was deleted from the version of the document that was published in FRUS 1955–57, 4:202. See also Eisenhower's comments in a November 17, 1960, NSC meeting, FRUS 1958–60, 7(1):657.

[118] Heads of government meeting, December 6, 1953, DDRS 1985/307.

[119] Goodpaster to Dulles, Wilson, and Radford, November 4, 1954; Goodpaster to Eisenhower, November 16, 1954; contingency paper on assurances which may be given on availability of aid programs,

strategic concept contemplated that everyone should have an atomic capability," and that this "was the implication of MC 48."[120] Indeed, the great premium MC 48 placed on rapid action, and thus on forces in being and on operational readiness, meant that the weapons placed in European hands would have to be under their effective control for the strategy to work. In this way also, MC 48 pulled the United States toward a full-fledged policy of nuclear sharing.[121]

The U.S. government was thus determined to reach out to the allies. The French, for example, were told about the nuclear sharing policy in January 1956. Nuclear weapons were becoming normal weapons, Dulles told the French ambassador, and the American government wanted to provide the European allies with an atomic capability. It would be foolish and wasteful for the various allies to duplicate each others' efforts and develop nuclear forces on an independent national basis. It made much more sense to capitalize on the enormous investment the United States had already made. The weapons could be produced relatively cheaply in the United States and, he thought, provided directly to the allies. But he and Eisenhower first had to overcome one great obstacle: the U.S. Congress. The Atomic Energy Act first had to be liberalized, and this would not be easy.[122]

This issue, in fact, turned out to be quite important. Eisenhower strongly believed that the law needed to be changed. The McMahon Act, as the Atomic Energy Act was sometimes called, was in his view foolish, antiquated, and destructive. At a time when the United States was trying to get the allies to put nationalist sentiment behind them—especially in the context of MC 48—here was the American Congress taking a more nationalistic line than anyone else. Here was this Joint Committee on Atomic Energy, given great powers under the McMahon Act, which seemed to think that it knew better than Eisenhower himself what the heart of American defense policy should be. All of this was just poison in the alliance, it was just intolerable, and yet the administration simply did not have the votes to change the law.[123] The American people, Eisenhower felt, therefore had to be "educated" about these new weapons. They had to be made to see that they were "becoming conventional and that we cannot deny them to our allies."[124]

December 10, 1954; and Wilson and Dulles to Eisenhower, December 10, 1954; in Conference Files, CF 420, RG 59, USNA. The first two documents also appear (the second in sanitized form) in FRUS 1952–54, 5:533–535.

[120] Anglo-American meeting, December 11, 1956, FRUS 1955–57, 4:125.

[121] For the premium placed on operational readiness and its relation to the sharing policy, see, for example, Office of the Assistant to the Secretary of Defense (Atomic Energy), "History of the Custody and Deployment of Nuclear Weapons, July 1945 through September 1977," February 1978, pp. 37, 43, DOD-FOIA; Gruenther to JCS, October 15, 1956, CCS 471.6 (8-15-45) sec. 86 RB, RG 218, USNA; and Eisenhower in NSC meeting, November 17, 1960, FRUS 1958–60, 7(1):655.

[122] Couve to Massigli, February 2, 1956, MP/96/FFMA.

[123] Eisenhower meeting with Gaither committee, November 4, 1957, FRUS 1955–57, 19:623; Eisenhower remarks in meeting with Macmillan and de Gaulle, December 20, 1959, pp. 15–16, Prem 11/2991, PRO. Eisenhower-Norstad meeting, August 3, 1960, Eisenhower-Bowie meeting, August 16, 1960, and Eisenhower-Spaak meeting, October 4, 1960, all in FRUS 1958–60, 7(1):610, 612, 640. For Dulles's views, see foreign ministers' meeting, December 6, 1953, FRUS 1952–54, 5:1790, and Dulles-Pineau meeting, September 7, 1957, FRUS 1955–57, 27:169.

[124] Eisenhower-Dulles meeting, October 22, 1957, AWF/DDE Diaries/27/October '57 Staff Notes (1)/DDEL. This passage was deleted from the version published in FRUS 1955–57, 27:800.

THE SHADOW OF PARITY

Nuclear sharing was thus implicit in the MC 48 strategy. But that strategy only made sense at a time when the United States enjoyed an enormous military advantage over the Soviet Union, and it was clear from the outset that that advantage would not last forever. No matter how much America spent or how many nuclear weapons were constructed, it was taken for granted, certainly from 1954 on, that her great strategic edge would eventually waste away. The United States might retain a large lead in numbers of weapons, and if the Americas struck first, the U.S. force might be able to wipe out the bulk of the Soviet nuclear arsenal. But if that arsenal was big enough, and if the Soviets were able to retaliate with even part of what they had left, America would still suffer enormous devastation. And with thermonuclear weapons, the surviving force did not have to be very large. A force that could place even forty or fifty bombs on target could effectively destroy the United States as a functioning society. And it was clear that sooner or later the Soviets were bound to develop such a force; sooner or later, they would build up their forces to a point where a full-scale American nuclear attack on Russia would for all intents and purposes be suicidal. No matter how massive that American attack, no matter how rapidly it was mounted, no matter how thoroughly Soviet society was destroyed, thermonuclear weapons were so enormously powerful that the USSR's surviving forces would by that point be able to utterly devastate the western countries in a retaliatory strike.

In the mid-1950s, it was assumed that this sort of world was not very far off. Within a few years, perhaps by the end of the decade, general war would mean total devastation. Would America at that time still be able to threaten to attack the Soviet Union with strategic nuclear weapons, or would she be held back by fear of retaliation? But the threat of nuclear bombardment was the heart of American military power. If this threat were effectively neutralized by the growth of Soviet nuclear capabilities, what then would protect western Europe? What then would counterbalance the massive land power of the USSR?

Even forces that were in theory capable of holding the line in Europe against a full-scale Soviet conventional attack would not be a complete answer: the NATO armies might be able to keep the Soviet ground forces from overrunning Europe, but they could not keep Soviet planes and missiles from conducting a nuclear offensive well behind the front lines. With American cities increasingly at risk, the American nuclear deterrent was bound to decline in value: the Americans might not retaliate against Russia even in the event of a nuclear war in Europe. In such circumstances, how could the Europeans put their fate so completely in American hands? Didn't they need nuclear forces under their own control? And wasn't it in the interest of the United States to make sure that the Europeans developed a nuclear capability of their own, so at least part of the burden of maintaining a credible deterrent could be removed from American shoulders? What all this implied was that the NATO allies needed a deterrent force free of American control. This concern with the implications of strategic parity was thus the third great taproot of the nuclear sharing policy.

For the time being, of course, the United States had very much the upper hand in strategic terms. When MC 48 was adopted, NATO leaders were no longer worried that the USSR might invade western Europe in the near future. In late 1954, General Gruenther said "flatly that we have such an enormous edge over the Soviet bloc that there is absolutely no danger of their attacking us now."[125] In 1955, he thought that "if the Soviets were to attack now, the NATO forces could lick them."[126] The Americans were capitalizing on their very heavy advantage in strategic nuclear weapons and delivery systems, and this advantage lasted throughout the Eisenhower period and into the Kennedy years. "There was a time in the 1950s," according to General LeMay, the SAC commander during this period, "when we could have won a war against Russia. It would have cost us essentially the accident rate of the flying time," because Soviet air defenses were so weak.[127] Eisenhower himself made a similar point in 1959. "If we were to release our nuclear stockpile on the Soviet Union," the president said, "the main danger would arise not from retaliation but from fallout in the earth's atmosphere."[128]

In keeping with standard bureaucratic practice, formal estimates were generally a good deal more cautious, but even at the start of the 1960s, some of the people most closely involved with these issues felt that the United States had something close to a first-strike capability. When Carl Kaysen, then a top White House official, analyzed the issue during the Berlin crisis in 1961, he reached the conclusion that with a limited attack the United States could have destroyed the USSR's ability to inflict really heavy damage on America.[129] And during the Cuban missile crisis in 1962, a high Air Force general said that "if it came to a U.S. strike," the military authorities "could give a 90 percent assurance that 99 percent of the Soviet nuclear force aimed at the United States would be destroyed before it could get off the ground, or a 99 percent assurance that 90 percent would be destroyed."[130] This calculation did not take into account either the damage that would be inflicted by the nuclear forces under NATO command, nor the damage that Europe would suffer through Soviet retaliation. But according to a major Defense Department historical study, the Soviet strategic situation might well have seemed "little short of desperate," and a "coordinated U.S.–NATO first strike" might have been able to destroy enough of the Soviet force targeted on the NATO area "to negate the deterrent effect of hostage Europe."[131]

This sort of superiority was important not because anyone thought that America's enormous nuclear strength was likely to be used. No one, for example, thought that if the Soviets did something minor, such as stopping a couple of jeeps

[125] Sulzberger, *Last of the Giants.* p. 107.
[126] NSC meeting, October 20, 1955, FRUS 1955–57, 4:26.
[127] Kohn and Harahan, *Strategic Air Warfare,* p. 95.
[128] Dwight Eisenhower, *Waging Peace, 1956–1961* (Garden City, N.Y.: Doubleday, 1965), pp. 347–348.
[129] Kaysen interview, August 1988.
[130] Raymond Garthoff recollection, from the record of a conference on "Europe and the Cuban Missile Crisis" held in Paris in October 1992. Garthoff's comment was made in the morning session on October 17. The tapes of the discussion are in my possession.
[131] May et al., "History of the Strategic Arms Competition," p. 475.

	United States			Soviet Union	
	Total Stockpile	Strategic Weapons	Total Yield (megatons)	Total Stockpile	Strategic Weapons
1945	2	2	0.04	—	—
1946	9	9	0.18	—	—
1947	13	13	0.26	—	—
1948	50	50	1.25	—	—
1949	170	170	4.19	1	—
1950	299	299	9.53	5	—
1951	438	438	35.25	25	—
1952	841	660	49.95	50	—
1953	1,169	878	72.80	120	—
1954	1,703	1,418	339.01	150	—
1955	2,422	1,755	2,879.99	200	—
1956	3,692	2,123	9,188.65	400	84
1957	5,543	2,460	17,545.86	650	102
1958	7,345	2,610	17,303.54	900	186
1959	12,298	2,496	19,054.62	1,050	283
1960	18,638	3,127	20,491.17	1,700	354
1961	22,229	3,153	10,947.71	2,450	423
1962	27,100	3,451	12,825.02	3,100	481
1963	29,800	4,050	15,977.17	4,000	589

Figure 6. Estimates of American and Soviet Nuclear Stockpiles. From "Estimated U.S. and Soviet/Russian Nuclear Stockpiles, 1945–94," *Bulletin of the Atomic Scientists,* November–December 1994, p. 59. For additional data, see the Natural Resources Defense Council Nuclear Program website, http://www.nrdc.org/hrdcpro/nudb/datainx.html.

on the autobahn to Berlin, the "go code" would be issued and a full-scale nuclear attack would be launched. That was never the strategy, although it was often caricatured that way. The basic idea was that the American authorities would be in a position to undertake more limited forms of military action, regardless of what the balance of forces was at that level, because they were in a position to escalate the conflict. America, in the final analysis, had the ability to launch a full-scale nuclear attack; the USSR had nothing comparable. The Soviets would therefore have to back down if the American government pushed things far enough. It was like a game of chess, Dulles said: "In a chess game you wouldn't normally ever go so far as to take your opponent's king; you checkmate that king and don't play out the rest." And America could accept Soviet challenges because she knew her "own military establishment was superior to Russia's and that the Russians knew it was superior. Thus, if necessary, we could call checkmate on the Soviet Union."[132]

The United States thus had a clear strategic advantage throughout the Eisenhower period; indeed, what was surprising was that it was taking the USSR so long

---

[132] NSC meeting, January 11, 1957, FRUS 1955–57, 19:407. Note also some remarks by General LeMay, who at the time was one of the more extreme proponents of the strategy of massive nuclear attack: "I think too many people thought of massive retaliation as automatically pushing all buttons,

to build an effective nuclear force. To analysts familiar with the situation, Soviet behavior in this crucial area was quite puzzling. The "irrationality" of Soviet basing, the Rand Corporation analyst Andrew Marshall pointed out in 1960, was "fantastic." It took six to eight hours just to get the planes loaded. "In those circumstances," he said, "they are just sitting ducks."[133] In late 1955, two other Rand analysts made the same kind of point: "we cannot help being impressed by evidence that the Russians have not taken certain elementary steps to protect themselves" against a U.S. surprise attack with high-yield nuclear weapons.[134] And in July 1963 Marshall and Joseph Loftus, formerly the civilian director of target intelligence for the Air Force and now Marshall's colleague at Rand, analyzed the issue in some detail. The defects in the Soviet strategic posture were extraordinary. The Soviets, they said, were "extremely reluctant to marry nuclear warheads to their delivery vehicles." Warheads were kept well away from missiles. For Soviet MRBMs, the weapons storage sites were on the average fifty miles away. The USSR had been surprisingly slow to build an intercontinental force, and this was not because they had been strapped for money. Resources were wasted, especially on ineffective air defense systems. The Soviets had evidently spent a good deal more on "antiaircraft artillery alone since the end of World War II than they have on the entire intercontinental mission, including BEAR and BISON bomber programs, ICBM's, and missile submarines." The Soviet strategic air force was quite vulnerable to attack: of the five main bomber bases, only three were defended by surface-to-air missile batteries, and even they were not deployed for quick reaction. The various efforts the United States had made to reduce aircraft vulnerability had no parallel in the Soviet system. "Such common USAF measures as bombs on board, airborne alerts, and aircraft on quick reaction ground alert with bombers parked at the end of the runway," they pointed out, "are not characteristic of Soviet bomber operations. Nor, apparently, does the situation change appreciably even in times of crisis with the West." The same general point applied to the Soviet ICBM force: "the missiles, the nature of the launch complex, and the mode of system operation, all suggest that the force is not designed for fast reaction." These were all "extremely puzzling phenomena," and "even more puzzling than the soft basing and slow reaction time of the Soviet intercontinental force are the questions of its late emergence and small size." And on it went: it was Soviet incompetence that had enabled the United States to hold on to its nuclear superiority as long as it had.[135]

It was only in late 1963 that the U.S. government finally came to the conclusion

---

shooting all guns, that sort of thing, in response to virtually anything the Russians did. Nobody that I knew in the military ever thought of it that way." And General Catton, one of LeMay's main subordinates at SAC in the 1950s, elaborated on the point: "Massive retaliation was a phrase that did not describe what we intended to do at all. The important thing, of course, was always to be able to prevail at the highest level of intensity, so that any kind of an escalation would be to the disadvantage of the enemy." Kohn and Harahan, *Strategic Air Warfare,* p. 108.

[133] See Trachtenberg, *History and Strategy,* p. 29.

[134] M. J. Ruggles and A. Kramish, "Soviet Atomic Policy," D(L)-3297, November 9, 1955, Rand Corporation archives.

[135] Joseph Loftus and Andrew Marshall, "Forecasting Soviet Force Structure: The Importance of Bureaucratic and Budgetary Constraints," RM-3612-PR, July 1963, pp. 23 ff., 69–72, Rand Corporation

that a preemptive strike was no longer a viable option. In September of that year, the NSC's Net Evaluation Subcommittee, the group responsible for assessing the damage that would result from a nuclear war, delivered a report to top administration officials. President Kennedy wondered whether Soviet retaliation would result in unacceptable losses, "even if we attack the USSR first." The NESC chairman, General Leon Johnson, said that this was indeed now the case: that "even if we preempt, surviving Soviet capability is sufficient to produce an unacceptable loss in the U.S. The President asked whether then in fact we are in a period of nuclear stalemate. General Johnson replied that we are." The president then summed up the basic conclusion he was drawing from the report: the new facts showed that "preemption was not possible for us."[136]

But it had taken many years for this conclusion to be reached, and the fact that American nuclear superiority was going to last as long as it did was by no means obvious in the early 1950s. Hence the problem of mutual deterrence, as a situation that was bound to arise sooner or later, was from the outset a great source of concern. High officials, and especially Dulles, were worried about what would happen when America's freedom to "initiate the use of strategic nuclear bombing" was "circumscribed" by the fear of retaliation.[137] How would Europe then be defended? How could the alliance be kept together if America remained wedded to a military strategy that might result in the destruction of European society, and perhaps of civilization itself? And if the present strategy would soon be bankrupt, what was the alternative?

These were the great questions that dominated not just American policy but the politics of the North Atlantic alliance in the period from 1954 on. The problem of "mutual deterrence" was an object of intense interest within the Eisenhower administration in the mid-1950s. Beginning in late 1954, various "time charts" were developed to enable the administration to get a handle on this problem.[138] What they all suggested was that the world was moving inexorably and probably quite rapidly toward a "condition of mutual deterrence, in which each side would be strongly inhibited from deliberately initiating general war or taking actions which it regarded as materially increasing the risk of general war."[139]

archives. The passages quoted were declassified in 1986. On Soviet strategic inaction during the Cuban missile crisis, see Trachtenberg, *History and Strategy*, pp. 253–257. For additional technical information on Soviet strategic vulnerability in this period, see May et al., "History of the Strategic Arms Competition," pp. 474–476.

[136] NSC meeting, September 12, 1963, FRUS 1961–63, 8:499–507.

[137] NSC Planning Board study, NSC 5422, June 14, 1954, and "Basic National Security Policy (Suggestions of the Secretary of State)," November 15, 1954; FRUS 1952–54, 2:655, 773.

[138] In addition to the time chart reproduced here, "timetables" of this sort were the focus of the analysis in two very important reports, the Killian report on the surprise attack problem in 1955, and the Gaither report of 1957. Both reports were published in Trachtenberg, *Development of American Strategic Thought*, vol. 1; the timetables are on pp. 342–345 and 540–542. For the seriousness with which these "timetables" were taken during the mid–Eisenhower period, see NSC meetings, August 4, 1955, November 15, 1955, and June 15, 1956, and annex to NSC 5602/1, March 15, 1956; all in FRUS 1955–57, 19:95–96, 147, 258, 319, 324–325, 327–328. But by early 1958, Eisenhower had become fed up with the timetable approach. "He was sick to death of timetables," he told the NSC; "they never proved anything useful." NSC meeting, January 6, 1958, FRUS 1958–60, 3:7.

[139] Annex to NSC 5602/1, March 15, 1956, FRUS 1955–57, 19:258. See also NSC 5501, January

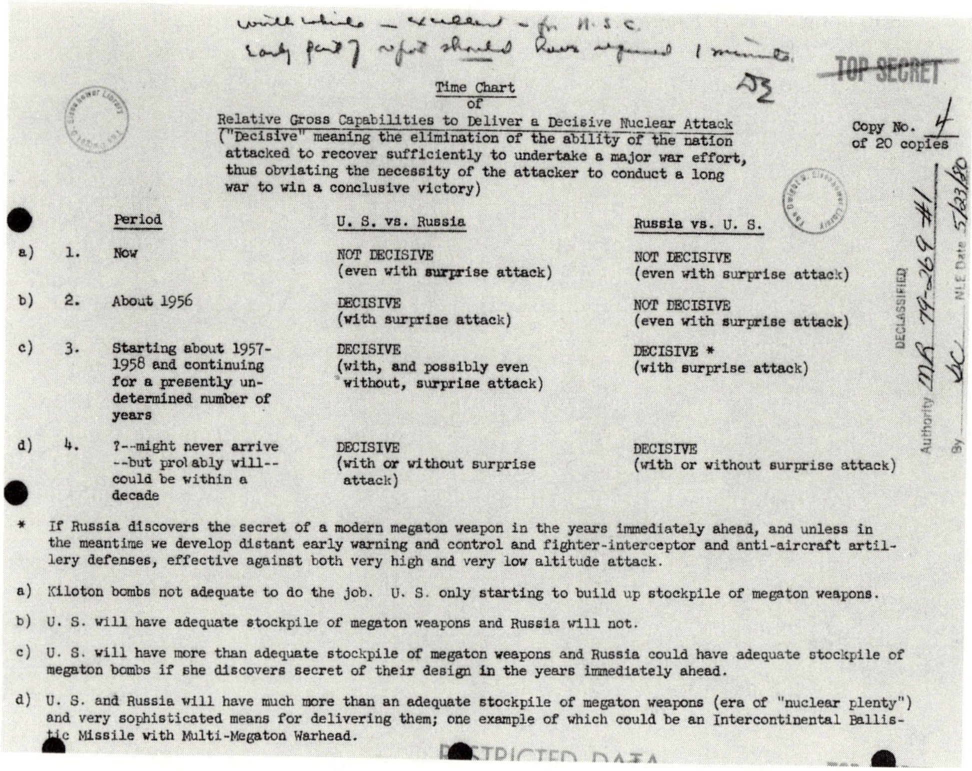

TOP SECRET

Copy No. 4 of 20 copies

Time Chart of Relative Gross Capabilities to Deliver a Decisive Nuclear Attack ("Decisive" meaning the elimination of the ability of the nation attacked to recover sufficiently to undertake a major war effort, thus obviating the necessity of the attacker to conduct a long war to win a conclusive victory)

		Period	U. S. vs. Russia	Russia vs. U. S.
a)	1.	Now	NOT DECISIVE (even with surprise attack)	NOT DECISIVE (even with surprise attack)
b)	2.	About 1956	DECISIVE (with surprise attack)	NOT DECISIVE (even with surprise attack)
c)	3.	Starting about 1957-1958 and continuing for a presently undetermined number of years	DECISIVE (with, and possibly even without, surprise attack)	DECISIVE * (with surprise attack)
d)	4.	?--might never arrive --but probably will-- could be within a decade	DECISIVE (with or without surprise attack)	DECISIVE (with or without surprise attack)

* If Russia discovers the secret of a modern megaton weapon in the years immediately ahead, and unless in the meantime we develop distant early warning and control and fighter-interceptor and anti-aircraft artillery defenses, effective against both very high and very low altitude attack.

a) Kiloton bombs not adequate to do the job. U. S. only starting to build up stockpile of megaton weapons.

b) U. S. will have adequate stockpile of megaton weapons and Russia will not.

c) U. S. will have more than adequate stockpile of megaton weapons and Russia could have adequate stockpile of megaton bombs if she discovers secret of their design in the years immediately ahead.

d) U. S. and Russia will have much more than an adequate stockpile of megaton weapons (era of "nuclear plenty") and very sophisticated means for delivering them; one example of which could be an Intercontinental Ballistic Missile with Multi-Megaton Warhead.

Figure 7. A Time Chart Developed by Robert Sprague and Presented to the National Security Council in November 1954. Note the president's handwritten comment at top: "worthwhile—excellent—for NSC." See Sprague's report to the NSC on continental defense, June 16, 1955, para. 10, Declassified Documents Reference System, 1997/1052. The copy of the document with Eisenhower's comment on it is in the Ann Whitman File, Ann Whitman Diary, box 3, November 1954 (1), Dwight D. Eisenhower Library.

Eisenhower, however, was very reluctant to accept this argument. It was "fatuous," he thought, "to think that the U.S. and USSR would be locked into a life and death struggle without using such weapons."[140] But in rejecting the argument out of hand, he soon felt himself to be on increasingly shaky ground. Things would soon reach the point, he said in 1955, where full-scale warfare would be absurd. With long- and medium-range missiles, general war would no longer make sense, and he himself "would never wage" such a war.[141] "War up to now," he said the following year, "has been a contest," but with "nuclear missiles, it is no longer a contest, it is complete destruction."[142] The whole Eisenhower strategy, so clear in 1953–54, was coming unglued.

7, 1955; NIE 100-7-55, November 1, 1955; Taylor in meeting with Eisenhower, May 24, 1956; Cutler in NSC meeting, February 28, 1957; all ibid., pp. 26, 135, 311, 428–429.

140 Eisenhower meeting with Radford and Taylor, May 24, 1956, ibid., p. 312.

141 NSC meeting, August 4, 1955, ibid., p. 102.

142 Eisenhower meeting with Congressional leadership, February 14, 1956, ibid., p. 198. See also Eisenhower-Quarles-Twining-Killian meeting, March 4, 1959, FRUS 1958–60, 3:185, 187.

The president understood the problem, but he had no real answer. Some world problems, he told the NSC in early 1957, seemed "insoluble." The problem posed by ballistic missiles was the main case in point. "The concept of deterrent power," he said, had "gone as far as it can. In view of this incredible situation we must have more fresh thinking on how to conduct ourselves."[143] In early 1956 he even seemed ready to concede the heart of the "mutual deterrence" argument: both sides would back away from situations that could lead to general war, and "the deterrent against the use of all-out thermonuclear warfare would grow in proportion to the magnitude of the capability." But practically in the same breath he said that America had to continue to rely primarily on her nuclear capability, and if U.S. forces ever were engaged in battle, it would be vital to strike "at the heart of the enemy's power."[144]

So Eisenhower could never quite bring himself to break with the fundamental tenets of his original strategic philosophy: that in a major U.S.–Soviet conflict, neither side would be willing to fight for long with one hand tied behind its back, that escalation was therefore inevitable, that strategic nuclear weapons were the dominant instrument of warfare, and that primary reliance had to be placed on America's ability to fight a general nuclear war. The very idea of restraint in general war he continued to dismiss out of hand. "Once we become involved in a nuclear exchange with the Soviet Union," he said in 1959, "we could not stop until we had finished off the enemy." There was no point to talking about "negotiating a settlement in the midst of the war," no alternative therefore to hitting "the Russians as hard as we could."[145]

Dulles, on the other hand, was not quite so fatalistic. He knew that there was a real problem here and pressed for an alternative policy. It is perhaps ironic, given Dulles's reputation as the great champion of the "massive retaliation" strategy, that he was the leader of those forces within the administration that wanted to do away with that strategy, at least in the near future, and put something very different in its place. "The massive nuclear deterrent," Dulles told the NSC in 1958, "was running its course as the principal element in our military arsenal"; he had been arguing along similar lines since at least 1953.[146] The secretary of state had accepted the argument about "mutual deterrence" very early on, and was probably largely responsible for making sure that language expressing this general idea was included in the basic policy documents.[147]

The idea that "nuclear parity" was unavoidable had certain very important implications. It meant that the United States would have to move toward what would later be called "flexible response": with the "coming of nuclear parity," the BNSP documents pointed out, "the ability to apply force selectively and flexibly" would become "increasingly important."[148] The West needed to make sure that it could

---

[143] NSC meeting, January 11, 1957, FRUS 1955–57, 19:409.

[144] NESC briefing, January 23, 1956, ibid., pp. 190–191.

[145] NSC meeting, January 22, 1959, FRUS 1958–60, 3:176–179.

[146] NSC meeting, May 1, 1958, ibid., p. 86. For a typical example of an earlier Dulles argument along these lines, see foreign ministers' meeting, December 6, 1953, FRUS 1952–54, 5:1790.

[147] "Basic National Security Policy (Suggestions of the Secretary of State)," November 15, 1954; and Dulles in NSC meeting, November 24, 1954; ibid., 2:773, 789.

[148] NSC 5501, January 7, 1955, and NSC 5602/1, March 15, 1956, FRUS 1955–57, 19:26, 32–33, 247.

deal with local aggression without automatically running a great risk of nuclear devastation—or, as people would later say, that "holocaust" and "surrender" were not the only options. Dulles argued repeatedly, especially in 1958, for shifting the emphasis away from strategic nuclear forces and toward area defense.[149] The United States, he told the NSC, "must be in a position to fight defensive wars which do not involve the total defeat of the enemy."[150] America should "cut down on the nuclear effort," he noted later that year, "on the theory that all we needed there was enough to deter; that we did not need to be superior at every point."[151] Greater emphasis had to be placed on conventional forces, which, as he pointed out, "we use everyday in our business."[152]

Dulles's views were to one extent or another shared by a number of key officials—by Robert Cutler, the president's national security adviser, by General Maxwell Taylor, the Army chief of staff (who, however, irritated Eisenhower by repeatedly speaking out publicly in this sense), by the chief of naval operations, Admiral Arleigh Burke, and by Air Force General Lauris Norstad, Gruenther's successor as SACEUR.[153] This general approach emphasized the importance of the NATO shield forces—that is, the forces designed for the direct defense of the NATO area. The shield forces, as Norstad put it, would provide an "'essential alternative' to the employment of ultimate capability."[154]

What was at stake in this debate was of fundamental importance, and in the course of the 1950s the lines began to be drawn more sharply. On both sides, there was movement away from the MC 48 strategy. On the "massive retaliation" side, people began to feel that direct defense in Europe was hopeless, that whatever happened on the front lines, no one could prevent the Soviets from devastating all of Europe, that all the West really had was the strategic nuclear deterrent, and (in the more extreme versions of this argument) that this was all the west really needed, since these great capabilities on both sides would make all war impossible—even limited aggression and conventional war, because of the irreducibly high risk of escalation this would involve.

This was, for example, the British view, or at least the view the British government put forward in pressing for a reassessment of NATO strategy: U.S. officials assumed (quite accurately in fact) that this British concept was mainly a way of ra-

---

[149] For some typical examples, see Dulles-Eisenhower meeting, April 1, 1958, DDRS 1989/3430; State-Defense meetings, April 7 and June 17, 1958, SS/S/A/21/Nuclear Exchange [September 1957–June 1958](3)/DDEL, and DDRS 1982/1578.

[150] NSC meeting, May 1, 1958, FRUS 1958–60, 3:86.

[151] Dulles-Anderson meeting, November 6, 1958, DP/GCM/1/DDEL.

[152] Anderson-Dulles phone call, December 3, 1958, DP/TC/9/DDEL.

[153] See Cutler's and Taylor's remarks in the May 1, 1958, NSC meeting, cited above. For Taylor's acceptance of the "mutual deterrence" argument, see also the notes of his meeting with Eisenhower, May 24, 1956, FRUS 1955–57, 19:311–312. On the Navy's attitude in general, and in particular its support, especially at the end of the 1950s, for a "finite deterrence" nuclear posture, see Rosenberg, "Origins of Overkill," pp. 56–57.

[154] Nolting to State Department, October 2, 1957, FRUS 1955–57, 4:170–171. For Norstad's views—increasingly at odds with Eisenhower's—see U.S. Delegation to State Department, December 18, 1958, and Herter-Anderson-McElroy meeting, October 24, 1959, FRUS 1958–60, 7(1):387, 489. Norstad "nearly had a fit" in August 1959 when he heard Eisenhower argue for massive troop reductions. Merchant-Eisenhower meeting, August 24, 1959, Merchant Papers, box 5, ML.

tionalizing cuts in their defense budget, and especially reductions in British force levels in Germany.[155] Norstad, in fact, told the British that it would be better to follow "a frank and open policy" and admit they had to reduce their forces in Europe for economic reasons, than to base those cuts on a strategic concept that he felt to be deeply flawed. But this was something the British government could not do. To explain the cuts in terms of Britain's "financial plight," would, as their defense minister pointed out, "further weaken the pound, endanger British financial stability, and prove generally damaging to Britain's economic situation."[156]

Economic factors also played a certain role on the U.S. side in the late Eisenhower period. Since cutting back on force levels was a way of dealing with America's growing balance of payments problem, Treasury officials generally favored the idea of moving toward a tripwire strategy.[157] But many people—Secretary of Defense McElroy, for example—were coming to support this kind of strategy for mainly military reasons.[158] Eisenhower himself, although by no means dogmatic on this issue and unwilling to force his personal views on the government as a whole, was increasingly coming to favor a purer "massive retaliation" strategy. As early as May 1956, he considered current NATO strategy, which of course did aim at a direct defense of Europe, as "completely outmoded" in the light of "recent weapons developments."[159] By 1959, he had become more assertive. A limited war in Europe, in his view, was impossible; the NATO shield should therefore be "symbolic"; and the U.S. troop presence in Europe could be cut back dramatically, perhaps to only a single division.[160]

But the other side—the people thinking more in terms of an effective shield, limited war, a high threshold for the use of nuclear weapons, and even a "no first use" policy and nuclear forces designed for simply deterring the enemy from initiating a nuclear exchange—was at the same time moving toward an even more radical break with the MC 48 strategy.[161] Even under MC 48, sizeable ground forces had a major role to play. Their function was to "raise the stakes" to the point where the enemy attack, to have any chance of success, would have to be on such a scale as to lead virtually automatically to general war; a strong shield was thus an integral part of a strategy of deterrence. This point remained intact, but by 1956

[155] See Wampler, "Ambiguous Legacy," chap. 12, esp. pp. 877, 884, 960.

[156] Norstad-Head meeting, December 12, 1956, DSP/52/57492/ML.

[157] For various documents that reflect the increasing importance of this problem and its growing bearing on strategic issues, see FRUS 1958–60, 7(1):488 n, 491, 494, 498–499, 512–513, 679.

[158] Smith to Herter, October 29, 1959, ibid., p. 495.

[159] NSC meeting, May 17, 1956, FRUS 1955–57, 19:306.

[160] Eisenhower meeting with Herter et al., October 16, 1959, and Herter-McElroy-Anderson meeting, October 24, 1959, FRUS 1958–60, 7(1):488 n, 489.

[161] The Army was the great champion of this approach. See especially Taylor in NSC meeting, May 1, 1958, ibid., 3:82. In February 1961, the Army called for a NATO strategy that would "emphasize a concept of limited war with the Soviets in the NATO area," develop a force structure designed to support that concept, and "use nuclear weapons only in response to Soviet use." This extraordinary position, put forth so early in the Kennedy presidency, obviously reflected the kind of thinking that had taken shape in Army circles under Eisenhower. Briefing sheet for JCS Chairman on JCS 2305/386, "NATO Strategy and Nuclear Weapons," March 1, 1961, CCS 9050 (11 Feb 61) sec 1, JCS Central Files, RG 218, USNA. The State Department position at the end of the Eisenhower period was not very different. See draft record of action for November 17, 1960, NSC meeting, pp. 2–3, DDRS 1992/2709.

it was being supplemented by a new argument. That same strong shield force, Gruenther now argued, would also make it possible to contain local aggression "on a scale less than that likely to lead to general war." The deterrent was being rounded out. No matter what the enemy did, aggression would be unprofitable. The same forces needed for the "strategic" function of forcing an enemy contemplating large-scale aggression to attack on such a scale that he would have to reckon with general war, would also serve the "tactical" function of enabling NATO to defend against limited aggression.[162]

This represented a certain movement away from an MC 48–style rapid escalation strategy. Escalation there might well be, but it would take place in a more controlled manner. The West, worried about retaliation, was not going to rush headlong into a full-scale nuclear war. The Soviets would first be made to see how serious NATO was, how ready the West was to risk escalation: by putting a sizeable ground force into action, NATO could force the enemy to confront the specter of escalation and thus to reassess his position. Ground forces were thus an integral part of a deterrent strategy based on something more than simple apocalyptic threats. They were the chips one needed to play the poker game of controlled escalation.[163]

This was not a full-fledged limited war strategy, but it certainly was a step in that direction: Gruenther's 1956 concept explicitly accepted the possibility of a local military conflict in Europe that might be contained without a general war. Norstad took the idea a bit further with his notion of shield forces strong enough to enforce a "pause" before general war broke out, and thus able to provide an "essential alternative" to strategic nuclear attack.[164]

NATO formally accepted this more flexible strategy in 1956 and 1957, with the adoption of a new NATO Political Directive and a new fundamental strategy document, MC 14/2, based on it. It is often said that the adoption of MC 14/2 represented the alliance's acceptance of a "massive retaliation" strategy. But in reality MC 14/2 needs to be seen as a major move *away* from "massive retaliation"—in fact, as a kind of halfway house between MC 48 and the "flexible response" strategies of the 1960s and beyond.[165] The Political Directive and MC 14/2 represented the climax of a process that had been set in motion, at least to a considerable extent, by British efforts to get the alliance to embrace a pure "massive retaliation"

---

[162] Wampler, "Ambiguous Legacy," pp. 940–941. The key document summarizing what Wampler aptly refers to as Gruenther's "testament" is "SACEUR's Force Requirements 1960/62," annex to JP(56)162 (Final), November 16, 1956, Defe 4/92, PRO.

[163] The poker metaphor was often used at the time. Note, for example, Eisenhower's reference to pushing "our chips into the pot" in his meeting with the congressional leadership on Berlin, March 6, 1959, FRUS 1958–60, 8:433. See also Eisenhower-Kennedy meeting, January 19, 1961, cited in Fred Greenstein and Richard Immerman, "What Did Eisenhower Tell Kennedy about Indochina? The Politics of Misperception," *Journal of American History* 179 (September 1992): 576, and Kennedy-Norstad meeting, October 3, 1961, p. 7, in FRUS 1961–63, vols. 13–15 (mic. supp.), no. 191.

[164] See, for example, Nolting to State Department, October 2, 1957, FRUS 1955–57, 4:170–171, and U.S. NAC delegation to State Department, December 18, 1958, FRUS 1958–60, 7(1):387.

[165] For the conventional interpretation of MC 14/2 as representing NATO's adoption of "massive retaliation," see the references cited in Wampler, "Ambiguous Legacy," p. 1058, n. 2. Wampler has shown that this interpretation is not well founded, and my discussion here relies heavily on his analysis.

strategy, one that (unlike MC 48) did not recognize the need for substantial ground forces in Europe. But in the process that led to the Political Directive and MC 14/2, the official British view was defeated. It was the American concept, the idea that substantial ground forces were necessary, that prevailed.[166]

The NATO Council adopted the Political Directive on December 13, 1956. The key passage called for forces able "to deal with incidents such as infiltrations, incursions or hostile local actions"; it declared that these forces should "have the capability to deal with" such situations "without necessarily having recourse to nuclear weapons." MC 14/2, adopted in April 1957, echoed this language at a number of points, and included also a "Statement on Limited War" that defined basic NATO thinking on this question in some detail:

> The Soviets might therefore conclude that the only way in which they could profitably further their aim would be to initiate operations with limited objectives, such as infiltration, incursions or hostile local actions in the NATO area, covertly or overtly supported by themselves, trusting that the Allies in their collective desire to prevent a general conflict would either limit their reactions accordingly or not react at all. Under these circumstances NATO must be prepared to deal immediately with such situations without necessarily having recourse to nuclear weapons. NATO must also be prepared to respond quickly with nuclear weapons should the situation require it. In this latter respect, the Military Committee considers that, if the Soviets were involved in a local hostile action and sought to broaden the scope of such an incident or to prolong it, the situation would call for the utilization of all weapons and forces at NATO's disposal, since in no case is there a NATO concept of limited war with the Soviets.[167]

NATO strategy was in transition. Increasingly, the official goal was to build more flexibility into the alliance's posture. By the end of the Eisenhower era, top American officials were using language indistinguishable from the "flexible response" rhetoric of the Kennedy period. "In case of an attack," Secretary of State Herter told the NATO Council in December 1960, "NATO forces should be able to meet the situation with a response appropriate to the nature of the attack." He then referred to Norstad's call for forces with a "substantial conventional capability" and his insistence that "the threshold at which nuclear weapons are introduced into the battle should be a high one." Without a substantial shield force, Herter said, NATO's military commanders would "not have that flexibility of response that will enable them to meet any situation with the appropriate response."[168] And Secretary of Defense Gates also stressed the importance of forces, both "nuclear and nonnuclear," that would provide NATO with "adequate flexibility of response." "We must be prepared," he said, "to meet any overt Soviet Bloc military action with sufficient strength and determination to force the Soviet either to withdraw or to accept the full risk of retaliation."[169]

[166] See ibid., chap. 12 and 13.

[167] Extracts from the Political Directive and MC 14/2 pieced together from a variety of British and American sources are given in Wampler, "Ambiguous Legacy," pp. 1074–1079. The full text of MC 14/2 was declassified after Wampler finished his dissertation, and is available from the SHAPE Historical Office.

[168] Herter statement at NATO ministerial meeting, December 16, 1960, FRUS 1958–60, 7(1):678.

[169] Gates statement to NATO ministerial meeting, December 1960, DDRS 1987/1141.

Eisenhower's personal views were of course very much at variance with this general approach, and the fact that such statements were nonetheless presented as official American policy shows how strong the "flexible response" philosophy now was within the Eisenhower administration. Its strength rested not just on the military case for a degree of flexibility. Political arguments also played a major role. People like Dulles were for obvious reasons reluctant to challenge Eisenhower's military judgments directly, but they were on much firmer ground in emphasizing the political effect of continuing to place such heavy reliance on nuclear weapons. A European war, Dulles and his followers freely admitted, might well run its course as Eisenhower said it would. There might be little chance of keeping such a conflict under control. But long before such a war broke out, a strategy placing such heavy emphasis on strategic nuclear forces would have very serious political consequences. The Europeans would turn away from an American policy that might well lead directly to their destruction, and the NATO alliance might well fall apart. Even in 1953, Dulles was concerned about the NATO concept "losing its grip" in Europe, about American military bases there coming to be seen more as "lightning rods" than as "umbrellas."[170] Too great a reliance on nuclear forces, and especially on strategic nuclear forces, would lead the Europeans to separate themselves from the United States. It would, he said, "strain the will to fight and spur neutralism."[171]

The Europeans, Dulles argued in 1954, therefore had to be given "some sense of choice as to the actual character of warfare." In 1958, he made the point even more bluntly. The NATO allies, he said, "must at least have the illusion that they have some kind of defensive capability against the Soviets other than the United States using a pushbutton to start a global nuclear war." If they did not get that capability, they would "disassociate" themselves from America—that is, from an alliance that might well lead directly to their nuclear destruction.[172]

Dulles was thus firmly against the idea of America putting "all of our eggs in the general nuclear-war basket."[173] NATO needed to develop a strong area defense, and in the mid-1950s he thought that a defense of Europe based on low-yield, low-fallout tactical nuclear weapons might well soon be feasible. The strategy of massive retaliation would sooner or later drive the Europeans away from the United States, but a new strategic concept based on "the tactical defensive capabilities inherent in small 'clean' nuclear weapons" might enable America to save the alliance.[174]

But Dulles was just about the only major figure in the administration who

---

[170] Dulles memorandum, September 6, 1953, FRUS 1952–54, 2:457–460.

[171] Dulles paper, November 15, 1954, ibid., p. 775.

[172] Dulles paper, November 15, 1954, ibid., p. 775; NSC meeting, May 1, 1958, FRUS 1958–60, 3:85, 88.

[173] Dulles to Eisenhower, May 7, 1958, DDRS 1991/823.

[174] NSC meeting, May 1, 1958, FRUS 1958–60, 3:85. For Dulles's interest in a defense based largely on tactical nuclear weapons, see Dulles-Adenauer meeting, May 4, 1957, FRUS 1955–57, 26:237; Dulles-Eisenhower meeting, April 1, 1958, DDRS 1989/3430; and the editorial note, FRUS 1955–57, 19:60–61. Dulles had long been thinking in terms of an area defense in which nuclear weapons would be "meshed in." Note, for example, his remarks at a meeting with Bidault and Eden on December 6, 1953, FRUS 1952–54, 5:1790.

thought that this was the way to go. A defense strategy based on tactical nuclear weapons might have made sense if the West was the only side to possess them. The problem, as a top Pentagon official pointed out to him, was that "the enemy can use the same kind of weapons against us."[175] NATO might have had its "constraints policy" limiting the yield of nuclear weapons that could be used in the east European satellites and especially in East Germany, but there was no guarantee that the USSR would observe similar restraints.[176] And in any event the sheer number of weapons that would be used, not their average size, might well be the controlling factor. Responsible military officers were at this time talking about fantastic numbers of such weapons. General Gavin, for example, referred to an Army requirement for 151,000 weapons, 106,000 of which were for tactical battlefield use and 20,000 for "support of our allies."[177] A war fought mainly with tactical nuclear weapons might well destroy all of Europe, while Russia and America were left intact. And such a shift in strategy was meant to save the alliance?

The basic problem, in fact, with any strategy that emphasized area defense, even one that relied essentially on conventional forces, was that the NATO side could exert only limited control over the nature of the war. The NATO powers might themselves not want to use nuclear forces, but the USSR might still be tempted to use nuclear weapons against European targets, calculating that the United States would be reluctant to escalate the war and risk the destruction of American cities. So no matter how strong the shield forces were, western Europe still needed something in the way of nuclear deterrence. A degree of flexibility was certainly a good idea, but NATO Europe needed something more.

How, then, could the Soviet nuclear threat to Europe be countered? One basic approach was to tie the American nuclear deterrent closely to Europe—to try to make sure that if Soviet nuclear weapons were used against Europe, the Americans would retaliate with a nuclear attack on the USSR. The idea, that is, was to guarantee that nuclear retaliation would be as automatic as possible. The United States should thus continue to maintain a large military force in Europe; the larger the force, the more inescapable the commitment, and the greater the likelihood of nuclear escalation in the event of a European war; and this meant that the Soviets would probably be deterred from starting a serious conflict, and especially a nuclear conflict, in the first place.

A strong U.S. presence also meant that SACEUR, with his control over nuclear forces, would continue to be an American. This was another major source of reassurance for the Europeans. It was like the old theory from the American colonial period of "virtual representation": European interests in the event of a crisis would be championed within the American government by a general whose whole

---

[175] Deputy Secretary of Defense Quarles, in State-Defense meeting, April 7, 1958, SS/S/A/21/Nuclear Exchange [September 1957–June 1958] (3)/DDEL.

[176] On the "constraints policy," see Roberts to Foreign Office, October 7, 1960, Defe 11/313; U.K. NATO Delegation to Foreign Office, October 17, 1962, Prem 11/3715; and Joint Planning Staff, "SACEUR's Revised Emergency Defence Plan," JP(62)18 (Final), March 19, 1962, para. 11, in COS(62)23rd meeting, Defe 4/143; all PRO.

[177] Office of the Assistant to the Secretary of Defense (Atomic Energy), "History of the Custody and Deployment of Nuclear Weapons," p. 50, DOD-FOIA.

way of looking at things had been shaped over the years by his fundamental responsibility, the defense of western Europe. Norstad, in fact, did come to play this kind of role. "The NATO nations," as one official noted in 1961, "have grown to trust Norstad because they feel he is one of them, not an advocate of some American policy."[178] But whatever confidence the Europeans might have in the NATO commander as an individual, the feeling was that SACEUR could play this role only if explicit arrangements defining his war-making authority were worked out with the allies: during the predelegation discussions in 1957, Dulles argued that it "would be more assuring to our allies" to give SACEUR in his capacity as the U.S. commander in Europe formal authority to use nuclear weapons in the NATO area.[179]

But even this approach might not solve the problem completely. No matter what was said and what sort of assurances were given, the fundamental questions would remain. SACEUR might in theory have broad war-making powers, but in the final analysis he remained an American general, and would any American president (except perhaps for Eisenhower himself) ever really be willing to surrender effective control over American forces? And if the ultimate decision was in the president's hands, what guarantee was there—no matter what was happening to the American army in Europe—that he would order a nuclear attack on the Soviet Union if such an attack would inevitably lead directly to the destruction of American society? Would the Europeans necessarily even want him to do so, if the attack would inescapably lead to their own destruction? Wouldn't the Europeans want to have some control over what was done, so that they might have some real influence on the decisions that would have to be made in the light of circumstances at the time? Indeed, how could the Europeans accept a situation where their fate rested, in the final analysis, so completely in American hands?

The fundamental issue, then, was the question of control—and of responsibility. From Dulles's and Eisenhower's point of view, a situation where America had all the power, and therefore all the responsibility, was unhealthy, and indeed lay at the root of a "certain malaise" in the alliance.[180] In the current situation, the Europeans could behave irresponsibly. The United States could be criticized from both sides. The charge could be made—and in fact increasingly was being made—that America would not launch a full-scale nuclear attack in defense of Europe once America's own cities were at risk. At the same time, the Europeans could complain that America would indeed go to general war rather than suffer a major defeat, and that Europe would be destroyed in the process. The fact that the criticism came from both ends shows that it was not American policy as such that was the root of the problem.[181] The difficulty was built into the situation, or at least

[178] Legere to Bundy, October 24, 1961, Taylor Papers [TP], box 35, NATO 1961–62 T-38–71, National Defense University [NDU], Washington.

[179] Telephone call to General Cutler, April 27, 1957, DP/TC/12/DDEL.

[180] See, for example, Dulles's remarks in a meeting with top British officials, October 24, 1957, FRUS 1955–57, 27:819. Dulles here included the U.K. in the nuclear club, but the basic thrust of his thinking is clear.

[181] See a high British official's account of Dulles's views in Chauvel to Pineau, October 31, 1957, DDF 1957, 2:617–618.

into the situation that would exist in a few years when general war would mean virtually total devastation. The Europeans had to be made to face up to the real problem, and that meant that they had to be given some real control over what would happen in a crisis.

It was not that European doubts about American resolve were fundamentally baseless. The timing was perhaps be a bit off. Many Europeans thought in the 1950s that the world of nuclear parity, of mutual deterrence and "strategic stalemate," had already arrived. Some European leaders questioned the resolve of even Eisenhower, a president who believed in the soldierly ethic of death before dishonor, and who, even more than Dulles, felt that America would have to follow through and launch a full-scale nuclear attack if she were pushed far enough, almost regardless of consequence. But would any other American president be willing to take the plunge? Dulles, for one, did not think so, and was therefore convinced that the "European doubt" was basically "rational."[182]

The problem was fundamental and inescapable, and as top officials in the late 1950s thought through the problem, one basic conclusion began to emerge. Solutions based on strengthening the NATO shield, on making NATO strategy more flexible, on keeping a sizeable American army in Europe, or on giving SACEUR greater formal authority, might all be useful, but they would not solve the problem. Over the long run, there was perhaps only one really viable solution, and that was for the Europeans to get a nuclear deterrent of their own.

NUCLEAR SHARING UNDER EISENHOWER

Around 1956 and 1957, the various elements in the nuclear sharing equation were falling into place. The Europeans, who only a few years earlier had "recoiled in horror" at the thought of using nuclear weapons, were now, as Eisenhower put it, "clamoring" for the United States to share these weapons with them.[183] And indeed official European attitudes had undergone an amazing transformation. In late 1953, Eisenhower and Dulles had been complaining to each other about how the NATO allies were refusing to accept the realities of the atomic age. The Europeans, the president thought, were "lagging far behind us and think of themselves only as the defenseless targets of atomic warfare." Dulles agreed: "while we regarded atomic weapons as one of the great new sources of defensive strength, many of our allies regarded the atomic capability as the gateway to annihilation."[184] But by 1956 the Europeans were if anything too "pro-nuclear" for Dulles's taste. At the December 1956 NATO Council meeting he had to resist strong allied pressure for what he viewed as an excessively heavy emphasis on nuclear forces and a consequent slighting of conventional capabilities.[185]

As for the Americans, the top officials in the Eisenhower administration were

---

[182] State-Defense meeting, June 17, 1958, DDRS 1982/1578; NSC meeting, May 1, 1958, FRUS 1958–60, 3:89.

[183] NSC meeting, May 10, 1956, FRUS 1955–57, 20:399.

[184] NSC meeting, December 11, 1953, FRUS 1952–54, 5:451–452.

[185] See Wampler, "Ambiguous Legacy," pp. 987–990.

willing by this point to go a long way toward meeting European concerns by providing them with the weapons they needed. The basic thrust of American policy
at this time was to set up a system that would indeed give the European allies confidence that the weapons would be available to them in the event of an emergency.
The NATO nuclear stockpile plan, formally proposed at the NATO heads of government meeting in December 1957—perhaps the most important policy initiative ever undertaken by the Eisenhower administration—was framed with this objective in mind. This plan was based on the idea that "a naked promise of nuclear
protection" by America was "no longer a sound basis for any major country's security." NATO Europe needed a system that would assure the availability of American nuclear weapons in an emergency, and the "best assurance" that nuclear
power would "in fact be available lies in our allies actually having a share in this
power close at hand and a capability to employ it effectively." America had been
"moving in this direction" for some time, but now the process had to be acceler-
ated. Under the stockpile plan—which, incidentally, had originally been proposed
by the French government—the allies could be reasonably certain that the warheads would, when the time came, "be available to the appropriate NATO commanders for allied purposes."[186] The Europeans could in this way be confident
that nuclear forces would be used "automatically in response to nuclear attack"
and "if necessary to meet other than nuclear attack."[187]

This plan did not call for a formal surrender of ultimate American authority, but
U.S. officials at the time thought that an "extremely important" policy decision had
been made.[188] The assumption was that the United States was taking a major step
in the direction of full nuclear sharing—that is, of putting the weapons under effective European control. The Americans were already arming the NATO allies
with nuclear-capable weapons (with nuclear components released to them in the
event of a defense emergency). If the stockpile plan was considered "extremely important," this could only be because it meant that the U.S. government had decided to go well beyond the existing policy and give the Europeans a good deal
more.

And indeed over the next few years the NATO allies were given effective control over American nuclear weapons. By the end of the Eisenhower period, about
five hundred American nuclear weapons were deployed to non–U.S. NATO forces
in Europe, and the basic picture regarding control of these weapons has been clear
for many years.[189] American control over these weapons was extraordinarily weak
and ineffectual. The Joint Committee on Atomic Energy (JCAE) conducted an im-

[186] "Nuclear Policy," background paper prepared by State Department Policy Planning Staff for
NATO Heads of Government Meeting, December 4, 1957, pp. 5–7, Wampler FOIA release. On the
French origins of the proposal, see the reference in Dulles to Paris embassy, November 30, 1957,
740.56/11-3057, RG 59, USNA, and Parodi to Foreign Ministry, May 6, 1957, note of general secretariat, May 7, 1957, and Dulles-Mollet-Pineau meeting, May 6, 1957, in DDF 1957(1): 734, 734 n,
738–739.

[187] From the "Nuclear Policy" briefing paper just cited.

[188] Norstad remarks to the NATO Council, April 30, 1959, Norstad Papers [NP], box 85, Atomic-
Nuclear Policy 1957–59 (1), DDEL. See also Loper briefing on nuclear sharing, April 26, 1960, p. 6,
NP/96/Atomic-Nuclear Policy (2)/DDEL.

[189] For the figures, see White House briefing for JCAE, May 1, 1962, 740.5611, RG 59, USNA.

portant investigation of these matters in late 1960; it concluded that the arrangements that had taken shape were a travesty of the very idea of American "custody." By 1960, allied fighter-bombers on quick reaction alert were sitting on runways, armed with American nuclear weapons, ready to take off on a moment's notice. A lone American sentry standing on the tarmac, armed only with a rifle, not even knowing what to aim at if the pilot tried to take off without authorization—often a mere eighteen-year-old "required to stand long watches in the open for periods extending as long as eight hours at a time"—this was what American custody of those weapons had come to mean.[190]

It was not just a question of effective control over nuclear-armed aircraft. People were also concerned with the problem of the control of the strategic missiles that NATO had decided to deploy in the late 1950s, the Thors based in Britain and the Jupiters eventually based in Italy and Turkey. These intermediate-range ballistic missiles were theoretically under joint control. There was a "dual key" system designed to make sure that armed missiles could be launched only if officers from both America and the host country used their keys. In reality, however, it was by no means clear that the American government had the physical ability to prevent the use of the weapons. A congressman visiting a Thor base in England in 1959, for example, was amazed to find a British officer in possession of both keys; no warheads were on the base, but when they were deployed there, the possession of both keys (or duplicates, which it was presumed the British would have made) would give British authorities effective control of an armed IRBM. In any event, the U.S. officer might be overpowered by the host country forces in a crisis and his key taken away.[191]

[190] For some standard descriptions, see John Steinbruner, *The Cybernetic Theory of Decision: New Dimensions of Political Analysis* (Princeton, N.J.: Princeton University Press, 1974), pp. 182–183; Peter Stein and Peter Feaver, *Assuring Control of Nuclear Weapons: The Evolution of Permissive Action Links,* CSIA Occasional Paper no. 2 (Boston: University Press of America, 1987), pp. 28–31; and Peter Feaver, *Guarding the Guardians: Civilian Control of Nuclear Weapons in the United States* (Ithaca, N.Y.: Cornell University Press, 1992), pp. 178–183. The picture these accounts give of American nuclear weapons under effective allied control is confirmed by various archival sources. See, for example, some comments made by General Truman Landon, the U.S. air commander in Europe in 1961, in an oral history interview. Not just French and British aircraft, he said, but German and Canadian planes as well, were armed with American nuclear weapons. "Theoretically, they were in our hands," he said, but the allied forces had been trained to use those weapons. "I am sure that we violated rules 1 through 13, maybe more. But to us, it seemed necessary that they be trained and they appreciated the fact that they got it." Oral History interview with General Truman H. Landon, p. 481, Office of Air Force History, Bolling Air Force Base, Washington, D.C. Note also Acheson's comments in a meeting with the British in April 1961: "The armed forces of many of the European Allies," he said, "—e.g., the Dutch, the Italians and the French—were in fact holding nuclear weapons." "The United States control of these weapons," he pointed out, "was in some cases theoretical; there was not always a duplicate key and sometimes the control amounted to nothing more than a United States sergeant who was supposed to see that the weapons were not released without authority." Anglo-American talks, April 5, 1961 (second meeting), p. 1, Cab 133/244, PRO. The most important archival source, and the source (on p. 31) for the quotation in the text, is the Holifield Report on U.S. nuclear weapons in NATO. Holifield had chaired an ad hoc subcommittee of Congress's Joint Committee on Atomic Energy which had recently gone to Europe to look into the question. The summary portion of the report is enclosed in Holifield to Kennedy, February 15, 1961, and is available at the National Security Archive [NSA] in Washington.

[191] See Joel Larus, *Nuclear Weapons Safety and the Common Defense* (Columbus: Ohio State Univer-

From the JCAE's point of view, the overall picture was disturbing. American control was essentially "fictional"; the arrangements that had taken shape were "of dubious legality"; the old norms of U.S. custody and control were "being stretched beyond recognition."[192] But how did this system come into being? Was it basically a question of the military working out these arrangements on its own, of a "gradual, step-by-step surrender to the pressure of our strong and entrenched military bloc," of Eisenhower losing his grip on policy, too tired, too soft to assert himself and do what was obviously necessary?[193]

This interpretation is simply incorrect. Eisenhower, in fact, was the driving force behind the nuclear sharing arrangements. The president pressed consistently for a very liberal policy in this area, even at a time when the military was still dragging its feet.[194] The transfer of physical control over American nuclear weapons to the NATO allies has to be seen as an act of high policy. It was not just some-

---

sity Press, 1967), pp. 80–86; also David Schwartz, *NATO's Nuclear Dilemmas* (Washington, D.C.: Brookings, 1983), p. 78. Note also Albert Wohlstetter's comment at the time that the deployment of the Thor and Jupiter IRBMs in Europe appeared to "give our allies a deterrent of their own, independent of our decision." Albert Wohlstetter, "The Delicate Balance of Terror," *Foreign Affairs* 37 (January 1959): 224; Wohlstetter was an exceptionally well-informed observer. And even in the government, top officials were by no means certain that control of the IRBMs was firmly in American hands. Norstad, for example, was unsure whether the Jupiters in Italy could be fired by the Italians without American authorization and at one point had to send an American general to check on this for him. Kohn and Harahan, *Strategic Air Warfare*, p. 94. And during the Cuban missile crisis in 1962, the authorities in Washington were worried about whether the Jupiters in Turkey could be launched without specific presidential authorization; CINCEUR was instructed to destroy the missiles or make them inoperable if any unauthorized attempt to fire them was made. White House meeting, October 22, 1962, in Ernest May and Philip Zelikow, *The Kennedy Tapes: Inside the White House during the Cuban Missile Crisis* (Cambridge, Mass.: Harvard University Press, 1997), pp. 222–223; JCS Joint Secretariat, Historical Division, "Chronology of JCS Decisions Concerning the Cuban Crisis," December 1962, p. 34, DOD-FOIA; Philip Nash, *The Other Missiles of October: Eisenhower, Kennedy and the Jupiters, 1957–1963* (Chapel Hill: University of North Carolina Press, 1997), p. 126. The process of installing permissive action links [PALs] on these weapons began in the summer of 1962, but had not been completed by the time the crisis began; see White House briefing for Joint Committee on Atomic Energy, May 1, 1962, 740.5611, RG 59, USNA, and Nash, *Other Missiles of October*, p. 125. Finally, it is worth noting that according to the understanding between the administration and Congress, "custody" meant that access would be controlled to the extent that "it would take an act of force" to gain control of the weapons. Loper presentation to NSC Planning Board, April 26, 1960, p. 8, NP/96/Atomic-Nuclear Policy (2)/DDEL. Thus, almost by definition, the custody arrangements were not proof against a host country effort to take over the weapons by force.

[192] Holifield Report, pp. 28, 48–49; Senator Clinton Anderson to President-Elect Kennedy, November 16, 1960, JCAE records, General Correspondence/323/International Negotiations: NATO, RG 128, USNA; Feaver, *Guarding the Guardians*, pp. 179–180.

[193] The quotation is from a speech given by Congressman Chester Holifield, a leading member of the JCAE, in February 1960, and quoted in Feaver, *Guarding the Guardians*, p. 178.

[194] For the relatively cautious approach of the military authorities, see, for example, Radford to assistant secretary of defense for international security affairs, September 21, 1956, JCS Chairman's Papers (Radford), CCS 471.6 (1 August 1956), RG 218, USNA; and Radford to Wilson, November 21, 1956, CCS 350.05 (3-16-48) sec. 8, RG 218, USNA. See also the discussion of the issue in the NSC on May 27, 1957, FRUS 1955–57, 19:496, 498. Note finally Radford's complaint to Dulles (in the context of an impending discussion on nuclear sharing with the French) that "NATO was going too far in terms of modern weapons." Dulles-Radford meeting, July 2, 1957, DP/GCM/Memoranda of Conversation— General—N through R (1)/DDEL.

thing that was allowed to happen because of laxness at the top, but was rather the result of a fundamental policy decision taken at the very highest level of the government.

Eisenhower and other high American officials in the 1950s strongly supported the basic idea of nuclear sharing. With increasing fervor, the president argued unambiguously for the sharing policy. The allies, he said in this context in 1955, could not be treated as "stepchildren," but rather had to be treated generously.[195] He disliked the "attitude that we will call the tune, and that they," the Europeans, had "inferior status in the alliance."[196] The mere idea that the U.S. government should try to keep these weapons away from its allies was in his view almost insane. It was as though "we had been fighting wars with bows and arrows and then acquired pistols. Then we refused to give pistols to the people who were our allies even though the common enemy already had them."[197]

He personally, as he said in February 1960, had therefore "always strongly favored the sharing of our weapons."[198] But under the law, the weapons had to remain in American custody. The real problem, in his eyes, was the attitude of the Congress, which seemed "to think that our situation was the same as in 1947 when we had a monopoly of the nuclear secret."[199] It refused to get rid of the Atomic Energy Act, a "terrible" piece of legislation which had done "great harm" to American relations with the NATO allies.[200] "The stupidity of Congress in this regard never ceased to amaze him."[201] Over and over again, he made the same point. The Atomic Energy Act, he said in October 1957, had been "a great mistake." The policy it mandated "seemed to run counter to common sense," he told de Gaulle in September 1959. The law, he told the French leader a few months later, was "somewhat absurd," but de Gaulle had to understand that "there was as much nationalism in the United States as elsewhere." The president took exactly the same line in meetings with U.S. officials. In May 1959, for example, he complained about being "handcuffed" by the "senseless limitations" Congress had placed on the administration.[202]

[195] NSC meeting, November 21, 1955, p. 11, AWF/NSC/7/DDEL. See also his comments in the NSC meeting, November 17, 1960, FRUS 1958–60, 7(1):657.

[196] Eisenhower-Norstad meeting, August 3, 1960, ibid., pp. 609–610.

[197] NSC meeting, August 18, 1959, ibid., 7(2):251.

[198] Eisenhower-Herter meeting, February 8, 1960 (document dated February 12), DDRS 1985/529.

[199] NSC meeting, October 29, 1959, FRUS 1958–60, 7(2):292. These remarks are not attributed specifically to Eisenhower in this sanitized document, but it is obvious from context and content that this was the president speaking.

[200] Eisenhower-Norstad meeting, August 3, 1960, FRUS 1958–60, 7(1):610.

[201] NSC meeting, October 29, 1959, ibid., 7(2):292.

[202] Anglo-American meeting, October 24, 1957, FRUS 1955–57, 27:820; Eisenhower-Herter meeting, May 2, 1959, and Eisenhower-de Gaulle meeting, September 2, 1959, FRUS 1958–60, 7(2):204, 262; Eisenhower-de Gaulle-Macmillan meeting, December 20, 1959, pp. 15–16, Prem 11/2991, PRO. See also Anglo-American meeting, June 9, 1958, DDRS 1987/2777; Couve to Massigli, February 2, 1956, reporting Dulles's liberal views on nuclear sharing, and saying that the Atomic Energy Act and the attitude of Congress was the only major obstacle, MP/96/FFMA; and John Baylis, *Anglo-American Defense Relations 1939–1984: The Special Relationship,* 2d ed. (New York: St. Martin's, 1984), p. 90 (for Eisenhower's description of the McMahon Act "as one of the most deplorable incidents in American history, of which he personally felt ashamed").

Eisenhower particularly disliked the way the act gave special powers to the Joint Committee on Atomic Energy that encroached on the authority of the executive branch. Consulting with the JCAE, he said, "only amounted to letting politicians tell us how to carry out our defense policy."[203] The JCAE was "unconstitutional in its functions."[204] It violated not just the basic constitutional principle of the separation of powers, but also the president's authority as commander in chief. But he was reluctant to challenge the system head-on, since he was a "minority president," and could not afford to alienate the Democratic majority in Congress.[205] He knew that the administration, in the final analysis, just did not have the votes to bring about the great liberalization of the law that he wanted.

There was only one way out of the box. The weapons would not be overtly turned over to the allies. They would remain technically in American hands and the administration could thus claim that it was not violating the law. But the custody arrangements would be so weak and ineffectual that the NATO allies would be given effective control over these American nuclear weapons. In this way, Eisenhower could do an end-run around the Atomic Energy Act.

American officials thus referred to the custody arrangements as purely "token" in character, something that had to be done in order to be in "technical" compliance with the law.[206] And they were not just talking about battlefield weapons. These arrangements applied also to strategic missiles with megaton-range warheads. In December 1956, for example, Secretary of Defense Wilson hinted to his British counterpart that the American government would provide Britain with IRBMs. "Some arrangement would have to be made for the custody of the warheads," the British record noted, but Wilson "gave the impression that it might be possible to devise means of putting the warheads into the hands of the United Kingdom."[207] Two days later, a top British defense official had a follow-up meeting with Gordon Gray, another high Pentagon official and later Eisenhower's national security adviser. Again, the custody provisions were not taken too seriously: "Custody of the warheads would have to remain technically with the United States owing to the terms of their Atomic Energy Act," the British official noted, "but I understood that this requirement could be complied with by stationing a few Army Ordnance personnel in this country."[208]

---

[203] NSC meeting, August 25, 1960, FRUS 1958–60, 7(1):619–620.

[204] Eisenhower-Bowie meeting, August 16, 1960, ibid., p. 612; see also Eisenhower-Spaak meeting, October 4, 1960, ibid., p. 640.

[205] Eisenhower meeting with Gaither committee, November 4, 1957, FRUS 1955–57, 19:623; and Eisenhower-Spaak meeting, October 4, 1960, FRUS 1958–60, 7(1):640.

[206] See, for example, Haskell to Nolting, November 3, 1959, enclosed in Haskell to Burgess, November 4, 1959, 740.5/11-459, RG 59, USNA.

[207] Meeting of British defense minister with Secretary of Defense Wilson, Admiral Radford, and Gordon Gray, December 12, 1956, Defe 7/1162, PRO.

[208] Powell notes of meeting with Gray, December 14, 1956, Defe 7/1162, PRO. The State Department earlier in the year had been upset by Gray's dealings with the British; one official in January had "expressed incredulity at report that the United States was proposing to 'turn the control of the IRBM over to the British.'" Ian Clark, *Nuclear Diplomacy and the Special Relationship: Britain's Deterrent and America, 1957–1962* (Oxford: Clarendon, 1994), p. 47. Note also the way the top British atomic energy official described the proposed custody arrangements to the French in December 1957. The custody question was "largely artificial," he said; the same kind of fiction that applied to the American

This was not a case of the British being singled out for preferential treatment. The administration intended to treat other NATO powers, in particular France, in much the same way. In November 1957, for example, top U.S. officials met with French leaders. The French wanted not just battlefield weapons, but "longer range missiles with which they could strike the vital centers of the Soviet Union." The Americans were sympathetic. Deputy Secretary of Defense Quarles said that "French thinking was consistent with ours and it is a matter of working out arrangements."[209] He thought the United States should be "more forthcoming with the French" in the nuclear area, and Dulles agreed.[210] The secretary in fact told his French counterpart that he hoped "that such missiles could be available for use by any NATO country concerned in the event of hostilities in accordance with NATO strategy." The warheads, he pointed out, "would have to remain *technically* under U.S. custody"—"*nominalement* sous garde américaine" in the French record of the meeting—but in reality things would be set up in such a way that France could be confident "that in the event of war" the warheads would be "immediately available."[211] The aim here was not just to give France the same special status as Britain. The ultimate goal was to put control of the IRBMs in the hands of the NATO allies more generally: by 1957, it was "considered to be to the mutual advantage of the United States and the host country to plan for the assumption of manning and control responsibilities of certain units by indigenous forces as rapidly as possible."[212]

There can be little doubt about what was going on. Given what was actually done in terms of the transfer of physical control over American nuclear weapons in Europe; given the importance Eisenhower and other top officials attached to nuclear sharing, and the depth and seriousness of the thinking in which that attitude was rooted; given Eisenhower's belief in the unconstitutionality of the Atomic Energy Act; and given the way high officials spoke of the custody arrangements as essentially nominal in nature—given all this, there is no way to avoid the conclu-

---

weapons—that they were under AEC and not military control—would also apply to the weapons in the NATO stockpile. Chauvel to Pineau, December 11, 1957, DDF 1957, 2:879–880. Macmillan, it should be noted, saw the IRBM deployment as giving Britain "a rocket deterrent long before we could hope to produce one ourselves." See Baylis, *Anglo-American Defense Relations,* pp. 89–90.

[209] Pineau meeting with U.S. Defense Department officials, November 20, 1957, FRUS 1955–57, 27:202.

[210] Quarles-Dulles meeting, December 27, 1957, DSP/69597/ML.

[211] Dulles-Pineau meeting, November 19, 1957, 740.5/11-1957, RG 59, USNA (for the U.S. record), and DDF 1957, 2:712 (for the French record). Emphasis added.

[212] Defense Department background paper on IRBMs for NATO Heads of Government meeting, circulated December 6, 1957, DSP/229/106963. A week earlier, the Joint Chiefs of Staff, deferring to the basic Eisenhower policy, had endorsed the "principle that it is to the mutual advantage of the United States and the host country to plan for the gradual and eventual assumption of manning and control responsibilities of certain units by indigenous forces." JCS to secretary of defense, November 27, 1957, CCS 092 Western Europe (3-12-48), RG 218. There was some question about how far this policy should be carried. Some State Department people, for example, were worried about "the Turks misusing IRBMs," but Norstad pointed out that the U.S. could "drag out indefinitely" arrangements under which the weapons would remain under U.S. control; he noted that the Turks "were obviously not ready" to take control of the weapons "immediately." Norstad-Dulles meeting, February 4, 1959, DSP/243/123621.

sion that the transfer of effective control was a deliberate act of policy, and that an extraordinarily important decision had been made at the highest level of the government. Eisenhower himself certainly understood what the real policy was. As he told General Norstad in June 1959: "we are willing to give, to all intents and purposes, control of the weapons. We retain titular possession only."[213]

[213] Eisenhower-Norstad meeting, June 9, 1959, FRUS 1958–60, 7(1):462.

An Alliance in Disarray

IN THE LATE Eisenhower period, the NATO allies were given effective control over many of the American nuclear weapons deployed in Europe. But this was by no means regarded as a final answer to the nuclear sharing question, and from Eisenhower's point of view a great deal remained to be done. A de facto arrangement that did not correspond to any clearly articulated strategy—indeed, one that skirted the edge of legality—was obviously not a permanent solution. A more stable system had to be put in place. Allied control over the weapons had to be overt, straightforward, and legitimate. And the way to do this was to set up some kind of NATO nuclear force. Eisenhower's idea was that the American presence in Europe would eventually wither away, perhaps down to the single division level, conceivably down to zero, and the NATO force would become a European nuclear force. The assumption was that this force would ultimately be truly independent: its use would not be subject to an American veto.[1]

How would this NATO or European force be organized? The issue of the war-making power—that is, the question of who would authorize the use of nuclear weapons—was fundamental. In a system dominated by the United States, the answer was relatively simple: the Americans would make the key decisions. In the 1950s, everyone knew that this was the case, but the NATO countries preferred not to deal with this question explicitly. The issue of control, the argument ran, was "academic." It would only be resolved "in the event." To focus on such questions would reflect distrust and would accomplish little of real value.[2] But with a force divided more evenly among a number of NATO powers, this sort of approach would no longer be viable. More explicit arrangements for the control of that force would have to be worked out.

There were two basic ways of dealing with the issue of control of a NATO, and eventually a European, nuclear force. In both cases the problems were enormous.

---

[1] The Bowie Report of August 1960, "The North Atlantic Nations: Tasks for the 1960's," called for a NATO force that would not be subject to an American veto. See the full text of the report, especially pp. 7–8, and 66, which was made available through the Nuclear History Program in 1991. (The passages referring to a "veto-free NATO strategic force" and so on were deleted from the sanitized version of the part of the report published two years later in FRUS 1958–60, 7(1):623.) For Eisenhower's general support for the Bowie approach, see Bowie-Eisenhower meeting, August 16, 1960, and Eisenhower-Merchant-Gates meeting, October 3, 1945, ibid., pp. 611–614, 634–635. For the idea of a withering away of the U.S. troop presence down to the single-division level, and the related notion of a European-controlled force, see Eisenhower-Herter meeting, October 16, 1959, ibid., 9:70. For Eisenhower's reference to taking all six American divisions out, see NSC meeting, August 18, 1959, ibid., 7(2):249.

[2] See in general the discussion in chapter 5, p. 168, and especially note 83. For Eisenhower's remark that the issue was academic, see Eisenhower-Spaak meeting, October 4, 1960, FRUS 1958–60, 7(1):641.

The first alternative was for this force to be organized in the same way as the rest of NATO—on a national basis, under ultimate national control, but with plans worked out within the NATO structure, and with a unified command becoming fully effective in the event of war. Planning, and especially targeting, could be done primarily on an alliance-wide basis, although there was no reason why arrangements for various fallback contingencies could not also be worked out on a national basis.

But there were two great problems with this relatively loose approach. There was first a problem of military efficiency. Nuclear decisions might have to be made quickly, and authority over nuclear operations therefore had to be centralized. The basic trend in NATO, in fact, was toward a greater degree of military integration. As the British ambassador to NATO pointed out, this trend was a "quite straightforward technical consequence of the increased speed of modern warfare and the increased violence of modern weapons." Air defense was the obvious case in point: "If you have central control both of the information that is coming in from the long-range early-warning system that guards the Alliance and of the fighter forces and surface-to-air missiles that are ready to fight off an attack, you have some hope of success. If each country relies on the information available to itself and on the forces it can itself put into the air, the attack will be over in most cases before anything can be done to repel it." The NATO Military Committee had studied the issue and had reported in November 1958 (in MC 54/1) that SACEUR needed operational control of NATO air defense forces "in peace and war." Anything short of that, General Norstad said, would be a "loose ineffective co-ordination of forces."[3] Norstad's basic assumption was that a strategy of preemption was Europe's only hope: "the real air defense of Western Europe would not so much be in the air battles over Western Europe but what we did to the Soviet Air Force on its bases"— a strategy that, of course, would be meaningful only if the enemy force was destroyed before it launched its attack.[4] The NATO command, Norstad thought, therefore had "to have the power to attack certain targets *immediately.*"[5] The Americans were thus serious about nuclear war-fighting, and this was a major reason why they were drawn to the idea of a tight, centralized NATO command structure, especially in the nuclear area.

The second and more basic problem with a NATO or European nuclear force organized on a national basis was that it meant a German finger on the nuclear trigger.[6] A German state with a nuclear capability of its own would no longer be

[3] Roberts to Lloyd, "General de Gaulle's Attitude to NATO," December 3, 1959, Prem 11/3002, PRO. See also Norstad's remarks in his meeting with Adenauer, December 16, 1957, p. 2, DDRS 1987/563.

[4] Vernon Walters, *Silent Missions* (Garden City, N.Y.: Doubleday, 1978), pp. 502–503. See also de Gaulle–Norstad meeting, January 21, 1960, FRUS 1958–60, 7(1):568. As noted in the previous chapter, this sort of thinking had already taken hold during the Gruenther period. Norstad's predecessor had called at the end of 1955 for an air defense system that would include arrangements for the "timely" implementation of NATO "atomic strike plans." Gruenther's proposal is described in two JCS documents from late 1955 and early 1956, cited in *JCS History,* 6:144.

[5] The quotation is from a British paraphrase of a study by the NATO command, "MRBMs in Allied Command Europe," annex to UKNMR/8/6(431), March 24, 1960, Defe 11/312, PRO. Emphasis in original text.

[6] The central importance of this issue is reflected in a great many documents, especially from the

locked into a purely defensive policy; and if it looked like Germany was developing a nuclear force under national control, the Soviets might be tempted to act before it was too late. It followed, or so it seemed to many western leaders, that the three western powers had a certain interest in preventing the situation from developing along these lines—that is, that they had an interest in keeping Germany dependent on her allies, and without nuclear forces under her own control.

This was certainly the British view in the late 1950s, and to a certain extent the French view as well. As for the Americans, while Eisenhower personally was quite relaxed about a buildup of German power, leading officials in the State Department and elsewhere were increasingly hostile to the idea of a German nuclear force.[7] From their point of view, if a German force was to be avoided, national nuclear forces (other than America's, of course) had to be opposed as a matter of general policy. The idea of a British or a French nuclear force was not particularly troubling in itself. The problem was the spillover effect on Germany. For how could one say yes to the French, but no to the Germans? And if one said no to the French, how could one go on cooperating with the British nuclear program? If the goal was to keep Germany non-nuclear, then national nuclear forces in general would have to be discouraged. The idea of a NATO or eventually a European force built up from national components which in the final analysis would be under national control thus cut against the grain of this whole way of thinking.

A tighter, more centralized system, in which it would be impossible for the Europeans to use their forces on a national basis, was thus the second major alternative. But here again the problems were enormous. How would such a force be controlled? Could the war-making power, the very heart of sovereignty, be turned over to some sort of international committee, or perhaps even to the commander of the force? In the first case, Germany would still be totally dependent on her allies—if not on America this time, then on Britain and France, which was scarcely an improvement from the German point of view. In the second case, the decision to go to war would be turned over to a high military officer. But that decision was political at its core: in a sovereign state, a state able to chart its own course in international affairs, this was a decision which the political leadership had to make. For Germany in particular, the basic problem, at least as Adenauer saw it, was her inability to control her own political fate. It was hard to see how in the long run this fundamental political problem could be solved by any arrangement that provided for tight, centralized control and made it impossible for the German government to act independently.

---

end of the Eisenhower period. See, for example, Norstad's remarks in a meeting with top U.S. officials, August 2, 1960, DDRS 1989/2751, and Kohler's comments in a meeting with Spaak, June 13, 1960, NP/Policy File/NATO General (4)/DDEL.

[7] Eisenhower-Macmillan meeting, March 28, 1960, FRUS 1958–60, 9:260–261. Even in 1951 and 1952, Eisenhower had felt that the overriding goal had to be to get Germany to come in "wholeheartedly on our side in the struggle against Communism," and had little patience for French concerns about Germany getting too much power. See, for example, his diary for July 2, 1951, and Eisenhower to Truman, February 9, 1952, *Eisenhower Papers*, 12:399 and 13:959–960; and also NSC meeting, November 12, 1959, FRUS 1958–60, 7(1):511.

THE TURNING OF THE TIDE

Eisenhower was drawn in both directions—toward the idea of a force built up from components under ultimate national control, but also toward the idea of a highly centralized NATO, and eventually European, nuclear force. On the one hand, he felt that a real alliance had to be based on voluntary cooperation and mutual trust. But as a military man, he also understood the importance of a strong, centralized command structure. And given his commitment to European unification and his belief in the importance of Europe becoming a "third great power bloc," a highly integrated system, which might well devolve into a purely European system, was also desirable on fundamental political grounds.

It was this commitment that gave the State Department its opening.[8] Many key officials there were deeply out of sympathy with the basic thrust of the Eisenhower nuclear sharing policy.[9] National nuclear capabilities, in their view, were not just wasteful and militarily inefficient. The real problem ran deeper. Nuclear forces under national control were viewed with great disfavor, quite apart from the costs involved. An independent German force was the central problem, both in itself and because of the presumed Soviet reaction. But "Europe" clearly needed "something" in the way of greater control over nuclear use. A single, integrated NATO force or European nuclear force was thus the only way out.

These State Department officials did not all view the problem in exactly the same way. For some, an integrated NATO force not subject to an American veto was barely acceptable—a device to absorb European pressures for "something" in the nuclear area, and to deflect and channel Eisenhower's insistence on the need for a generous policy toward the NATO allies. For others, it was an important goal in itself, a means of bringing about a truly unified and independent Europe, which they viewed as the only permanently viable solution to the whole cluster of problems the U.S. government faced in Europe.

But no matter how divided these people were among themselves, they shared a common hostility to national nuclear forces, and therefore backed the idea of a highly centralized system. In this they were supported by the strong NATO lobby, led by General Norstad himself, which saw centralized control, meaning essentially SACEUR control, as vital for military reasons. And this general view also had strong support in Congress and in the more nationalistic parts of the U.S. defense and atomic energy establishment. There was a certain unwillingness to turn over America's nuclear secrets too freely, and, in the Congress especially, a certain anxiety about the spread of nuclear capabilities and a reluctance to be a party to that process. On top of these general considerations, there was the growing problem

[8] See especially Owen to Courtney, February 26, 1960, Records relating to atomic energy, box 384, Regional Programs: NATO, RG 59, USNA.

[9] Note in this context an exchange between Eisenhower and his national security adviser, Gordon Gray. There had been something of a stir after the president had endorsed the idea of nuclear sharing at a press conference on February 3, 1960. Eisenhower, as he himself noted, had simply said "what he believed and what he had said before," and Gray agreed: "I observed to the President that I had heard him say the same thing at least four times in NSC meetings in forcible terms but that the State Department hadn't really agreed." Gray-Eisenhower meeting, February 9, 1960, OSANSA/SA/P/4/1960—Meetings with the President-vol. 1 (7)/DDEL.

with de Gaulle. The French leader, who had returned to power in mid-1958, was beginning to make trouble in NATO and was thus forfeiting whatever claim he had to American nuclear cooperation.[10] From the administration's point of view, it thus seemed that if anything were to be done, it would have to be on an alliance-wide rather than on a country-to-country basis.[11]

The American government was therefore coming increasingly to favor the second basic approach. The nuclear sharing arrangements, U.S. representatives began to insist in the late Eisenhower period, would have to have a "NATO flavor." More emphasis was now placed on centralized control. Official U.S. policy was turning away, to a degree that Eisenhower himself never felt entirely comfortable with, from support for, or even acceptance of, national nuclear weapons programs.

In 1956 and 1957, the American government had by no means been opposed to the principle of such programs. Eisenhower certainly never wanted the NATO allies to go off on their own and build forces that would be used in a totally independent way. But this did not mean that he was against the Europeans developing forces that would ultimately be under national control. In his view, it was inevitable that the Europeans would develop forces of this sort. His hope, however, was that the allies would cooperate with each other—on production, deployment, targeting, and so on—within the NATO structure. "Italy, Germany, France and Britain," the president thought, "would all want such weapons." But this was no problem as long as these forces were coordinated within the NATO framework: the weapons, he said, "should be handled as NATO weapons, to be utilized in 'over-all' or strategic purposes."[12] And the further that process reached, the more of a "NATO flavor" and the more of a European flavor those nuclear arrangements had, the better from his point of view.

Eisenhower always favored cooperative arrangements, even multi-national arrangements worked out just by the continental countries. This was clear during the Euratom affair in 1955 and 1956, but Euratom never got off the ground, mainly for economic reasons. In 1957 and 1958, however, France and Germany, later joined by Italy, embarked on the path of nuclear cooperation. A number of agreements, the so-called FIG (France-Italy-Germany) agreements, were signed at this time.[13] The goal was to create a "European strategic entity": the continentals would

[10] On the specific problems relating to nuclear cooperation with France, see Eisenhower-Macmillan meeting, June 9, 1958, DDRS 1987/2777 (for a reference to Congress being "pretty sore at the French," which made a change in the law "very doubtful"); NSC meeting, October 29, 1959, FRUS 1958–60, 7(2):292 (for evidence that opposition to nuclear assistance to France was rooted in a sense that the French were "out of step in NATO"); and Gates-McCone-Dillon meeting, August 24, 1960, NP/85/Atomic-Nuclear Policy 1960 (2)/DDEL (for the persuasive Norstad argument "that it would be bad policy to reward General de Gaulle" with nuclear sharing "after his continuous non-cooperation with NATO").

[11] See, for example, NSC meeting, August 18, 1959, p. 16, DDRS 1990/890.

[12] Eisenhower-Norstad meeting, August 3, 1960, FRUS 1958–60, 7(1):610.

[13] On the FIG agreements, see Colette Barbier, "Les négociations franco-germano-italiennes en vue de l'établissement d'une coopération militaire nucléaire au cours des années 1956–1958," Eckart Conze, "La coopération franco-germano-italienne dans le domaine nucléaire dans les années 1957–1958: Un point de vue allemand," and Leopoldo Nuti, "Le rôle de l'Italie dans les négociations trilatérales, 1957–1958," all in the *Revue d'histoire diplomatique* (1990), nos. 1–2; Peter Fischer: "Das Projekt einer trilateralen Nuklearkooperation," *Historisches Jahrbuch* 112 (1992): 143–156, and also

develop some sort of nuclear capability of their own.[14] After returning to power in May 1958, de Gaulle officially put an end to these efforts—they had in fact been effectively abandoned by his predecessors—but it is important to note how the Americans viewed the FIG project. Some State Department officials, Gerard Smith for example, were hostile to the idea.[15] But Dulles was more supportive.

The matter came up when Dulles met Adenauer at the NATO meeting in Paris in December 1957. Adenauer referred to the FIG proposal for nuclear weapons research and wanted to make sure the United States was adequately informed. Dulles said he would like to know more, but his tone was not the least bit hostile. He brought up the possibility of broadening the arrangement and creating "something like a nuclear weapons authority" which would include the three continental countries plus America and Britain. The State Department officials who worked on this idea in early 1958 tried to make sure that the plan would not result in the European countries getting nuclear forces under their own control. The whole point of the proposal, as they were developing it, was in fact to "deter the creation of additional national nuclear capabilities in Europe." But it is not at all clear that this corresponded to what Dulles had in mind.[16]

As for Eisenhower, his attitude was probably reflected in some remarks Secretary of Defense McElroy made at the NATO defense ministers' meeting in April 1958. The United States, McElroy said, had "no objection" to such arrangements as the "French-Italian-German collaboration, provided that the work is carried out under the aegis of NATO. In that event the U.S. would be able to furnish technical and certain financial assistance."[17] Given that this position was a good deal

---

pp. 125–129 in Fischer's article, "Die Reaktion der Bundesregierung auf die Nuklearisierung der westlichen Verteidigung," *Militärgeschichtliche Mitteilungen* 52 (1993); Schwarz, *Adenauer,* 2:332, 394–401; and above all Georges-Henri Soutou, "Les accords de 1957 et 1958: Vers une communauté stratégique et nucléaire entre la France, l'Allemagne et l'Italie?" in *La France et l'atome: Etudes d'histoire nucléaire,* ed. Maurice Vaïsse (Brussels: Bruylant, 1994). Another scholar has pointed out that high French military officers (Generals Stehlin and Valluy) had raised the issue of nuclear cooperation with the top German military officer, General Heusinger—in America, incidentally—as early as July 1956. Christian Greiner, "Zwischen Integration und Nation: Die militärische Eingliederung der Bundesrepublik Deutschland in die NATO, 1954 bis 1957," in *Westdeutschland 1945–1955: Unterwerfung, Kontrolle, Integration,* ed. L. Herbst (Munich: Oldenbourg, 1986), p. 275; also cited in Greiner's article in *Anfänge westdeutscher Sicherheitspolitik,* 3:737, 739. For the most complete account of the FIG affair, see Soutou, *L'Alliance incertaine,* chaps. 3 and 4.

[14] Georges-Henri Soutou, "Les problèmes de sécurité dans les rapports franco-allemands de 1956 à 1963," *Relations internationales,* no. 58 (Summer 1989):229.

[15] See, for example, Smith to Dulles, March 3, 1958, and Elbrick to Dulles, on "production of nuclear weapons in Europe" (with Smith concurrence), March 6, 1958, PPS records, 1957–61, box 151, Europe 1958.

[16] Dulles-Adenauer meeting, December 14, 1957, DDRS 1987/750. The idea may have been planted in the Americans' minds by the French. A few weeks earlier, France's NATO ambassador had proposed a NATO "mechanism involving a common effort in the field of modern weapons, including evaluation, production and common use." Thurston to Timmons, October 29, 1957, 740.5611/10–2957, RG 59, USNA. For the development of the NATO nuclear authority idea by Dulles's subordinates in the State Department, see "Franco-German Italian Collaboration in the Production of Nuclear Weapons," enclosed in Smith to Dulles, March 3, 1958, PPS 1957–61, box 151, Europe 1958, RG 59, USNA.

[17] Elbrick to Dulles, April 24, 1958, FRUS 1958–60, 7(1):318. Note also Quarles's remarks in meeting with Pineau and McElroy, November 20, 1957, FRUS 1955–57, 27:203.

more liberal than what McElroy personally favored, one assumes that he was taking this line out of loyalty to, or upon the instructions of, the president.[18]

The U.S. government took another major step at this time that reflected support for an independent European nuclear capability. The Americans were not only willing to help the Europeans get control of U.S.–built ballistic missiles, they were even prepared to help the Europeans build those weapons in Europe. In November 1957, Dulles told the French leaders that the Americans intended to turn over blueprints for IRBMs to their European allies, and Eisenhower made the formal offer at the NATO heads of government meeting the following month. The American government, he said, "believes that the follow-up development and production of IRBMs could advantageously be undertaken in Europe. To this end, we are prepared to make available under appropriate safeguards blueprints and other necessary data relating to the IRBM delivery system, if this Council decides that the further development and production of the IRBM should be undertaken on a cooperative basis by NATO countries in Europe."[19]

The United States was not at this time insisting that the missiles the Europeans would be building with American help would be subject to SACEUR control.[20] Eisenhower instead was taking a big step toward helping the European countries acquire a strategic nuclear capability of their own on what was essentially a national basis. He obviously hoped that resources would be pooled to avoid a senseless duplication of effort, and that in an emergency the allies would use their forces in a coordinated way—that is, within the NATO framework. But he was not insisting on a tight institutional structure that would make independent national use impossible.

This was reflected in American policy on sharing with the main allied governments. In early 1957, Eisenhower formally accepted the principle of providing the British with IRBMs. He did not insist or even suggest at the time that these missiles would be subject to NATO control.[21] The agreement with Britain simply called for missiles to be "made available by the United States for use by British forces" and said nothing at all about NATO.[22] It was clear that Eisenhower in-

[18] For McElroy's views, see, for example, NSC meeting, July 16, 1959, FRUS 1958–60, 3:261. The defense secretary "disassociated" himself personally here from the views of his own department. As McElroy's remark indicates, the bureaucratic politics of this issue is not easy to sort out. Each of the three major governments involved—France, Germany, and the United States—was divided within itself on these matters, and those factional differences interacted with each other in a fairly complex way. See appendix 4, "The Politics of the Nuclear Sharing Question" (IS).

[19] Pineau-Dulles meeting, November 19, 1957, DDF 1957, 2:713. For an extract from the president's speech, see DDRS 1987/558. A background paper outlined what the U.S. government wanted to accomplish: "A European production capacity for such missiles should be established in the near future. A European missile research and development capacity to design future missile types should also get underway now. U.S. transfer of missile technology will be essential to the success of any such venture. U.S. disclosure policy must be modified to enable this." Nuclear policy background paper, December 4, 1957, Wampler FOIA release.

[20] This point was noted in Haskell to Nolting, November 3, 1959, attached to Haskell to Burgess, November 4, 1959, 740.5/11–459, RG 59, USNA.

[21] Eisenhower-Macmillan meeting, March 22, 1957, FRUS 1955–57, 27:737–739.

[22] Bermuda communiqué, March 24, 1957, DOSB, April 8, 1957, p. 561. See also Wilson and Herter to Eisenhower, March 14, 1957 (with appended documents), DDRS 1997/1857.

tended to treat the British generously. In late 1957, he wanted to "take the British into the fold on the basis of mutual confidence," and called for a full exchange of information. Each side "should be able to expect to receive whatever the other has."[23] The president's attitude was so positive that the chairman of the Atomic Energy Commission was worried that Eisenhower had decided "to turn everything over to the British irrespective of whether or not this involved information of a very secret character." Dulles, however, thought that the president had not intended to go quite that far. Eisenhower did not want to risk compromising "highly secret information" that would not do the British much good, but had simply wanted a practical program to be worked out.[24]

In developing this relationship with the British, Eisenhower and Dulles were not trying to set up a special Anglo-American nuclear alliance. The British were always trying to stress their "special relationship" with the United States, Dulles pointed out, but the American government had to "demonstrate an interest in all of our allies." In dealing with Britain, the U.S. government needed to take "the kinds of action that we can broaden to the whole alliance." He felt, in particular, that the time had come "to close up the IRBM agreement with Britain and then to extend it to other countries."[25] The arrangements with Britain were thus seen as a kind of opening wedge. They would be more acceptable to Congress than a more general sharing policy, so this clearly was a good place to start. But the sharing system, in the administration's view, would eventually have to be extended to the main continental allies as well.

The great test of the Eisenhower administration's seriousness in this regard was its willingness to help France develop a nuclear capability. Of all the continental allies, France was the most interested in building a nuclear force and had in fact moved furthest in that direction. Eisenhower and Dulles did not strenuously object to that French policy. Indeed, from the start the president especially was sympathetic to French nuclear aspirations and understood why France should want nuclear forces under her own control. Dulles in early 1956 told the French ambassador, Couve de Murville, that he and Eisenhower wanted to help the Europeans arm themselves with nuclear weapons, that Congress was the problem, but that some way would be found to make sure that the allies would have access to those weapons in an emergency.[26] And when American leaders met with their French counterparts in November 1957, they made much the same point. The French wanted IRBMs and the Americans made it clear that they intended to help

[23] Meeting with the president, October 26, 1957, cited in Clark, *Nuclear Diplomacy*, p. 85.

[24] Peacock memo, October 29, 1957, DP/GCM/1/Memoranda of Conversation, General S(4)/DDEL. For more information on the internal politics of this issue within the U.S. government (somewhat at variance with what bureaucratic politics theory would lead one to expect), see Farley to Dulles, November 19, 1957, PPS 1957–61, box 130, Great Britain, RG 59, USNA.

[25] Eisenhower-Dulles meeting, October 22, 1957, FRUS 1955–57, 27:800–801. Dulles and Eisenhower were preparing for forthcoming talks with Macmillan. Shortly after those talks, Dulles reported that he had gotten the British to accept "the proposition that nothing would be agreed to between them and us which could not be extended to the free world as a whole. He had tried to avoid any exclusiveness in the United States–British relationship." State Department meeting, November 6, 1957, DP/GCM/3/Strictly Confidential, N-P (1)/DDEL.

[26] Couve to Massigli, February 2, 1956, MP/96/FFMA.

France get them, with the warheads only "nominally" in American hands.[27] It was clear that Eisenhower wanted to go as far as he could under the law, and perhaps a bit further still, in transferring these weapons to France.

After de Gaulle returned to power in the spring of 1958 and placed the nuclear issue at the heart of French policy, this aspect of U.S. policy remained intact. The American leaders wanted to explore with French officials "what could be done by a liberal interpretation of existing authority."[28] In July 1958 Dulles flew over to Paris to explain U.S. policy on nuclear matters to the new French leader. If France wanted to develop an independent nuclear capability, that was "a matter for France itself to decide," but it would be terribly wasteful if one NATO state after another went down that path. The best course of action was to develop the NATO system in such a way as to make sure that all the major allies had access, in the event of an emergency, to the alliance's nuclear weapons—that is, to work out an arrangement that would guarantee that the "use of the weapons" would not "depend on a political decision from far way." Dulles therefore suggested that the two governments get together to see what could be done to "ensure that in the event of a major attack on French or United States forces in Europe, nuclear weapons available to NATO would be used immediately without having to depend on a United States political decision, concerning which the French might have some doubts."[29] And with regard to the IRBMs, Eisenhower personally told de Gaulle in December 1959 that "France could at any time have the same arrangement as the United Kingdom under which missiles were given subject only to the 'key of the cupboard' [i.e., dual key] arrangement. In fact it would not be too difficult to obtain a key in a real emergency." The dual key arrangement, he pointed out, would not in reality enable the United States to prevent the weapons from being used: it was an "illusory precaution" because the host countries could "always arrange to seize control of the key."[30]

Even with Germany, the U.S. government—or at least the top American leadership—was willing to go along with the idea of nuclear forces under national control. The issue came up in two important NSC meetings in 1959. Dulles had been forced by illness to resign earlier in the year, and the basic post-Dulles State Department view was that the United States should try "to prevent any additional nations from achieving a nuclear capability." Eisenhower agreed that this was a good idea—that is, until the NATO allies "came into the picture." He supported the JCS view that the United States should help key allies develop a nuclear capability by exchanging scientific and technical information with them; better still, the U.S.

[27] Dulles-Pineau meeting, November 19, 1957, DDF 1957, 2:712, and (for the U.S. account) 740.5/11–1957, RG 59, USNA.

[28] Dulles–de Gaulle meeting, July 3, 1958, FRUS 1958–60, 7(2):52.

[29] Dulles–de Gaulle meeting, July 5, 1958, ibid., pp. 55–56. See also Elbrick-Alphand meeting, July 9, 1958, ibid., p. 74. It seems that Eisenhower was behind the policy Dulles presented to de Gaulle; see Eisenhower-Dulles-Quarles meeting, July 3, 1958, DDRS 1995/2903. Dulles's personal views in this area are somewhat unclear, and the evidence points in both directions. But my sense is that he was more conservative than Eisenhower on the sharing issue, but more liberal than many of his subordinates in the State Department.

[30] Eisenhower–de Gaulle–Macmillan meeting, December 20, 1959, Prem 11/2991, PRO, and DDF 1959, 2:770.

government should make American weapons available to those allies, so they would not have to build them themselves. And it was clear that he considered Germany one of the "selected allies" to be helped in this way. When the secretary of defense, for example, objected to the idea of a German nuclear force, Eisenhower dismissed his concerns out of hand. "Germany," the president said, "had been his enemy in the past, but on the principle of having only one main enemy at a time, only the USSR was now his enemy."[31]

Dulles, whether out of conviction or out of loyalty to Eisenhower, had taken much the same line. In a May 1957 meeting with Adenauer, for example, he had advised the chancellor on how to respond to a Soviet note complaining about German nuclear aspirations. The Federal Republic, he suggested, should once again declare that it would not allow its territory to be used as a base for aggression. But "as for the means of its own defense," he advised Adenauer to reply, "the Federal Republic will not accept the dictates of any country; least of all of a country which forcibly holds some 20 million Germans in bondage."[32] This was scarcely the line someone firmly opposed to the very idea of a German nuclear force would have taken.

When Dulles met with the German foreign minister in November 1957, he was even more explicit. He again emphasized the importance of guaranteeing that nuclear weapons would be available to the allies in an emergency. This would be necessary if the Europeans were not to get involved in the costly and wasteful process of building such weapons on their own. The weapons would be made available "on a basis of impartiality, in light of the military judgment of SACEUR." As far as America was concerned, it was not possible "to contemplate a situation in which there were first and second class powers in NATO." It was true, he said, that at the time of the Paris accords Germany had promised not to produce nuclear weapons on her own territory, but at that time those weapons "were regarded as something apart, both from a political and a moral point of view." Dulles, however, "did not think this would always be the situation." This again implied that Dulles was not ruling out for all time a nuclear force under full German control—or even a force built by the Germans themselves.[33]

American policy in this area was thus extraordinarily liberal in 1957 and 1958. The Eisenhower administration was in principle ready at this point to help the European allies acquire a nuclear capability. But soon the tide began to turn. By 1960, whatever the president's personal views, the American government had come to place much greater emphasis on strong centralized controls. It was clear, for example, that the U.S. government was backing away from the commitment Eisenhower made about European production of IRBMs, and indeed also from the policy of supplying these missiles to the allies—even to the British—on a national basis. In late 1959, State Department officials began talking explicitly about adding "political conditions" to the offer of U.S. technical assistance. Eisenhower's offer, which was still recognized as a "commitment," had said nothing about NATO con-

---

[31] NSC meetings, July 16 and 30, 1959, FRUS 1958–60, 3:260–261, 288–289.

[32] Adenauer-Dulles meeting, May 4, 1957, FRUS 1955–57, 26:238–239.

[33] Dulles-Brentano meeting, November 21, 1957, 740.5/11–2157, RG 59, USNA. These passages were deleted from the sanitized version published in FRUS 1955–57, 4:202.

trol, but now U.S. help would be given only for "NATO," and not "national," weapons. Some officials were worried that the Europeans would regard this as America defaulting on her December 1957 pledge. But in early 1960, that was the path the U.S. government chose to take.[34]

This shift in policy was tied in with what was going on in the military sphere. General Norstad, ostensibly for purely military reasons having to do with the increasing vulnerability of NATO aircraft on the ground and growing problems of penetrability in the light of Soviet advances in air defense, was calling for a sizeable number of intermediate-range (the more advanced models now coming to be called medium-range) ballistic missiles to be placed under his command.[35] In October 1959, Norstad had asked for 300 second-generation MRBMs, with a range of up to 1500 miles, to be deployed in western Europe in 1963–65; eventually about a thousand such missiles might be deployed. These would be targeted mostly at the "enemy's aircraft strike force"—that is, air bases, nuclear stockpiles, control centers, and air defense centers—but eventually a variety of targets well within the USSR would be covered: ports and naval bases, "army bases and forces," missile bases, and "military and governmental centers." These missiles, Norstad said, were needed to allow the NATO command "to force a halt on an enemy penetration."[36]

Given the location and nature of the targets, many people doubted whether this was a realistic objective. The MRBM was not a limited war-fighting weapon, and in a general war external forces—preeminently the U.S. Strategic Air Command, supplemented by the British Bomber Command and the U.S. Polaris missile submarine force, just beginning to be deployed at the end of the Eisenhower period—would provide coverage of those targets.[37] But Norstad, even in the case of general war, still wanted direct control over a missile force of this sort: the "value of external forces" was recognized, but the NATO command needed "the power to attack certain targets *immediately;* therefore external forces cannot be relied upon."[38] This was in line both with the preemptive strategy and the idea of a semiautonomous SACEUR.

[34] State-Defense meeting, September 25, 1959, FRUS 1958–60, 7(1):484–488. For the State Department attitude, see also Note de la Direction politique, September 4, 1959, DDF 1959, 2:302–303.

[35] I say "ostensibly," because although Norstad claimed the request reflected no change in strategy and that the missiles were simply theater weapons, missiles with this range, armed with high-yield warheads, would give NATO a true strategic capability of its own. Indeed, Norstad wanted to make NATO, as he put it, a "fourth nuclear power." One suspects that whatever his original motivation in pressing for the MRBMs, he was well aware of the fact that deployment of these weapons under the control of SACEUR would allow NATO to get a strategic nuclear capability of its own through the back door. On these matters in general, and in particular on Norstad's idea of NATO as a "fourth nuclear power," which he presented in his Pasadena speech of December 6, 1959, see Gregory Pedlow, "General Lauris Norstad and the Second Berlin Crisis" (unpublished paper), pp. 5–6, 24, 26.

[36] U.K. SHAPE representative to COS, March 24, 1960, annex, and annex to JP(60)72 (Final), June 29, 1960, both Defe 11/312, PRO.

[37] This was a standard British argument. See, for example, "Mid-range Ballistic Missiles in ACE," annex to JP(60)72 (Final), June 29, 1960, Defe 11/312, PRO.

[38] This paraphrase of the thinking at NATO headquarters is from the annex to UKNMR/8/6(431), attached to "MRBMs in Allied Command Europe," March 24, 1960, Defe 11/312, PRO. Emphasis in original. It was for the same sort of reason that Norstad disliked the idea of a sea-based MRBM force.

The Norstad request for a NATO MRBM force now gave the State Department the opportunity it needed. The missiles the United States had promised to help the Europeans acquire would have to be placed under NATO and not national control; this would be how the European allies would help Norstad meet his MRBM requirement. So on April 1, 1960, the same day that the French conducted their second atomic test in the Sahara, the U.S. government made a proposal. Secretary of Defense Gates offered the Europeans a choice: they could either buy MRBMs from America for deployment in Europe, which was the option the U.S. government preferred, or they could produce them in Europe, with American help, on a multilateral basis. In either case, these would be NATO, and not national, weapons.[39] In the past, there had been a good deal of talk, especially with the French, about working out some kind of a deal: the weapons might be built in Europe, some would go to NATO, some would be under full national control. But now "America was ready to sell Polaris"—a land-based version of the one second-generation MRBM that would be available in the period in question—"to NATO and that was all."[40] It was clear that American policy had shifted and that nuclear forces under national control were viewed with growing disfavor. The president had made a commitment, of course, but the State Department had been looking for a way to renege on it, and the Gates two-option offer meant that a way out had been found. On March 21, Secretary Herter bluntly explained the thinking to the British. The United States, he said, had "to make some offer which would at least appear to be honouring the pledge of December 1957, but he himself expected that the form of the offer would not be sufficiently attractive to be taken up." The idea was to tie the U.S. proposal "to conditions which, while reasonable in themselves, would be unlikely to prove acceptable to European NATO governments"— conditions, in other words, which would rule out national use.[41]

But what if the Europeans actually accepted one of the options Gates had offered? The view was beginning to take hold that even the April 1 proposal went too far. Robert Bowie, for example, who in early 1960 had been asked to conduct a major study of the whole NATO problem, "thought we should explicitly back away from that proposal," and he told Eisenhower so in September.[42] It was not enough that the missiles would be assigned to SACEUR, or that the countries involved would promise to use them only in accordance with NATO plans and only when authorized by appropriate NATO authority. Physical control of the weapons was crucial; the great fear was that placing the weapons in western Europe might come dangerously close to giving the host countries (meaning mainly Germany)

Polaris submarines would not meet his needs: "he himself would have no control over submarines earmarked for SACLANT [Supreme Allied Commander, Atlantic], more especially as naval forces were in any case much more loosely attached to NATO than land or air forces." U.K. NATO Delegation to Foreign Office, July 7, 1960, Defe 11/312, PRO.

[39] See FRUS 1958–60, 7(1):582 n.

[40] Herter-Couve meeting, April 15, 1960, ibid., 7(2):339.

[41] Caccia to Foreign Office, March 21, 1960, Defe 11/312, PRO.

[42] Eisenhower-Norstad-Bowie meeting, September 12, 1960, FRUS 1958–60, 7(1):631. The Bowie study had been proposed by Gerard Smith, one of the high State Department officials most opposed to national nuclear forces.

effective control over what were in reality strategic nuclear weapons: missiles with megaton-yield warheads able to strike at targets well within the USSR.[43]

It was clear that Europe, as Adenauer told Norstad, needed "something" in the nuclear area.[44] If national nuclear forces, even forces coordinated within the general NATO system, were to be ruled out, then the only answer, Bowie thought, was for Europe to build up some sort of multinational force under such tight centralized control that independent action on a national basis would be impossible, and so thoroughly multinational in character that no participating "ally could withdraw units and employ them as a national force."[45] To underscore its international character, the force would not be stationed on anyone's national territory: it would be deployed at sea, with the missiles either on submarines or on surface ships manned by international crews.

Eisenhower liked the idea, and a proposal along these lines was presented to the NATO Council in December 1960. The presidential election had been held the previous month; Eisenhower would soon be leaving office and the incoming president was from the other party. The December proposal was, however, taken very seriously. It was to be Eisenhower's "legacy": it would embody "the finest ideas and plans this administration could develop."[46]

In a sense the December 1960 proposals—more "a concept than a plan," as Secretary Gates pointed out—really did represent the culmination of the Eisenhower NATO policy.[47] The goal, at least in the president's mind, was by no means to perpetuate and institutionalize American domination of the western alliance. The NATO nuclear force would be centrally controlled, but for Eisenhower and other top officials, the system ultimately was not to be run by the United States. The aim was to pave the way for an independent *European* deterrent. The use of the force, Bowie stressed, would not be subject to an American veto.[48] The project, as top American officials pointed out in late 1960, would "give NATO its own deterrent strength." NATO would be getting a "striking force of its own."[49] Secretary Gates, for example, even suggested that the United States might be willing to do away with the "two-key system"—that is, with official American control over the warheads.[50]

The project was considered to be of fundamental importance, and the reason had to do with SACEUR: with SACEUR's powers and SACEUR's nationality. The heart of the plan was to delegate, this time formally, an extraordinary degree of war-making authority to the NATO commander, who would act on his own and would not simply be taking orders from the American president. The delegation

---

[43] On the fear of "seizure by national forces," see, for example, the Bowie Report, pp. 8, 64.

[44] Thurston to Herter, September 10, 1960, SS/ITM/5/NATO(4) [1959–1960]/DDEL.

[45] Bowie Report, pp. 9, 61.

[46] NSC meeting, November 17, 1960, FRUS 1958–60, 7(1):654.

[47] Gates-Watkinson meeting, December 12, 1960, Defe 13/211, PRO.

[48] Bowie Report, pp. 7, 8.

[49] Merchant in meeting with Eisenhower and top State and Defense Department officials, October 13, 1960, DDRS 1986/3551; Herter in NSC meeting, November 17, 1960, FRUS 1958–1960, 7(1):651.

[50] Gates-Watkinson meeting, December 12, 1960, p. 4, Defe 13/211, PRO.

had to be formal, since the weapons themselves would no longer be solely in American hands. One could no longer rely on arrangements that the Americans had worked out among themselves, with SACEUR in his capacity as CINCEUR beginning "the fighting on the principle of the inherent right of a commander to defend his forces."[51] So SACEUR was to be given official control over the force: when people referred to NATO getting a "striking force of its own," or to a force "responsive only to NATO authority," this was what they had in mind.[52] Eisenhower's own views on this point could scarcely be clearer. On October 4, the NATO secretary general, Paul-Henri Spaak, brought up this basic issue in a meeting with the president. "If the United States turned nuclear weapons over to NATO," Spaak asked, "who would have the authority to decide on their use?" Eisenhower's answer was unambiguous: "The President said that such authority should be vested in NATO and in particular in the Supreme Allied Commander in Europe."[53]

The British were soon given the same message. Under the new American plan, their ambassador reported on October 17, "the U.S. government could not block the use of those weapons in the event of an attack in Europe." The Americans made it clear "that their proposals to delegate authority to SACEUR to use the MRBM force at his own discretion will relieve him of any obligation to seek clearance from the President and the Prime Minister before declaring H-hour for that part of his forces." The U.S. government was thus willing to go very far in terms of surrendering "ultimate control" over the nuclear force they were willing to give NATO.[54]

In turning over formal authority, however, how much of a concession would the American government really be making, especially given the substantial degree of delegated authority SACEUR already had? As long as the NATO commander was an American general, one could fairly argue that not much was being given away. It is therefore important to note that Eisenhower sought to move to a system where SACEUR was a European officer. This was, of course, in line with his general philosophy of getting the Europeans to pull together and take over responsibility for their own defense.

From the very outset, Eisenhower had wanted to create a system where the defense of Europe was in European hands. When he assumed command of the NATO forces in 1951, he took it for granted that a European general would eventually become SACEUR. At that time, he had had no idea that "United States command of NATO forces" would last even through the late 1950s.[55] By 1959, he was think-

[51] Eisenhower meeting with Quarles and military officers, March 12, 1959, FRUS 1958–60, 7(1):436.

[52] Thurston to Irwin, October 15, 1960, p. 5, DDRS 1989/2732; Merchant in meeting with Eisenhower, October 13, 1960, DDRS 1986/3551.

[53] Eisenhower-Spaak meeting, October 4, 1960, SS/ITM/5/NATO(6)[1959–1960]/DDEL. Eisenhower's reply, released in full in the version of this document declassified in 1979, was deleted from the sanitized version published in 1993; see FRUS 1958–60, 7(1):641.

[54] Hood to Shuckburgh, October 17, 1960; Working Party on Policy on Nuclear Weapons for NATO, "United States Proposals for a NATO MRBM Force," PNWN/P(60)3, October 26, 1960; and memo for Macmillan, "NATO MRBM," October 27, 1960; all in Prem 11/3714, PRO.

[55] Eisenhower-Spaak meeting, November 24, 1959, FRUS 1958–60, 7(1):519.

ing increasingly in terms of "making the Europeans furnish the Commander for the European NATO command."[56] At Rambouillet in December 1959 he told de Gaulle flatly that he wanted a European—indeed a French—SACEUR. "When there was an American commander," he said, "other countries looked too much to the United States to help them and did not accept their own responsibilities."[57] And in September 1960, he was still thinking of "saying that we are ready to let a European take over the command of NATO in Europe."[58]

This was why the issue of giving SACEUR the authority to decide on the use of nuclear weapons raised such serious problems. The president had the right under American law to delegate this authority to American military commanders. But Eisenhower explicitly rejected the idea that the commander of the NATO force would have to be an American. "Such a condition," he said, "could not be justified and should not be contemplated."[59] This was why the U.S. plan, as Secretary of Defense Gates pointed out, would ultimately "require fundamental changes in U.S. law, if not in the Constitution."[60] It is a measure of Eisenhower's seriousness about creating a nuclear force independent of American control that he made so far-reaching a concept the centerpiece of his policy in his final months in office.

So by the end of the Eisenhower period a policy had taken shape. The American government favored the idea of an independent and ultimately purely European nuclear force, whose use would not be subject to an American veto. The NATO force, in the emerging view, would be effectively controlled by the NATO commander, who might not be an American officer. Indeed, the assumption was that a European general would eventually take command of the force. This was what was behind the December 1960 proposal for what was coming to be called the "multilateral force"—the famous "MLF." Eisenhower in particular was a strong supporter of a concept that was so clearly in line with his basic thinking about the defense of Europe and the future of U.S.–European relations. He "favored the theory of the proposal," he told his main advisers in October 1960. "He favored the establishment of a multilateral force. He felt it would help pull NATO together and raise the morale of the NATO members."[61]

THE WESTERN ALLIES AT CROSS-PURPOSES

The new policy did not pull the alliance together. It had exactly the opposite effect. The U.S. government had turned against the idea of national nuclear forces, while the three main European allies were all determined to hold on to, or even-

---

[56] Eisenhower-Herter meeting, October 16, 1959, ibid., 9:70.

[57] De Gaulle-Eisenhower-Macmillan meeting, December 20, 1959, p. 21, Prem 11/2991, PRO, and DDF 1959, 2:772; and Eisenhower–de Gaulle meeting, December 19, 1959, ibid., p. 761.

[58] Eisenhower-Macmillan meeting, September 27, 1960, FRUS 1958–60, 7(2):421.

[59] Eisenhower-Spaak meeting, October 4, 1960, ibid., 7(1):641.

[60] Gates-Watkinson meeting, December 12, 1960, Defe 13/211, PRO, and NSC meeting, November 17, 1960, FRUS 1958–60, 7(1):651.

[61] Eisenhower meeting with State and Defense department officials, October 3, 1960, ibid., p. 635.

tually to acquire, nuclear forces under ultimate national control. This conflict lay at the heart of a long crisis in the Atlantic alliance—a crisis that came to a head during the Kennedy period and which was to play a very important role in the larger story of great power politics during this climactic phase of the Cold War.

Even relations with Britain were strained by the new policy. America had long had a goal for that country. The British should give up thinking of themselves as a world power. Britain no longer had the strength to play that kind of role. She should instead view herself as primarily a European power and become, along with Germany and France, one of the three great building blocks of a united Europe.

The British had from the outset disliked that aspect of American policy. Britain was, of course, no longer strong enough to play a truly independent role in world affairs. This had been made quite clear at the time of the Suez affair in 1956. The new prime minister, Harold Macmillan, realized that the British action in Egypt had been "the last gasp of a declining power." And although he resented the way Britain had been treated by America—he remarked bitterly to Dulles that "perhaps in two hundred years the United States 'would know how we felt'"[62]—he made the cultivation of a close relationship with the United States the centerpiece of his policy. The Americans had to begin trusting Britain again, and so Macmillan's first step was to apologize for "the deception practiced upon" the U.S. government in connection with the Suez affair.[63] The implication was that this would not happen again, and that the two governments needed to be open with each other.

In Macmillan's view, Britain might not be strong enough to stand entirely on her own, but she could be a kind of smaller version of the United States, standing at America's side and helping her more powerful partner direct the affairs of the West as a whole. His great dream was for Britain to "play Greece to America's Rome." Britain would not be a mere regional power, but would continue to play a certain role on the world stage. This vision meant that Britain should not put her limited military resources primarily into building an army prepared to fight on the continent; the emphasis instead would be on the development of strategic nuclear forces. Britain needed an independent nuclear deterrent, a scaled-down version of the American Strategic Air Command. And this in turn implied the adoption of military strategies that would rationalize the development of forces of that sort, strategies that played down the importance of ground forces and strategic "flexibility," and that justified a heavy reliance on strategic nuclear deterrence.[64]

The Americans were never entirely happy with British attempts to play up their "special relationship" with the United States—to piggyback on American power and thus shore up their declining influence in the world.[65] In 1956–58, a very

[62] Macmillan-Dulles meeting, December 12, 1956, FRUS 1955–57, 27:677.

[63] Dulles to Eisenhower, December 12, 1956, DSP/141/58630/ML.

[64] There is a large literature on British defense policy, British nuclear weapons policy, and Anglo-American nuclear relations in this period. John Baylis's *Ambiguity and Deterrence*, an excellent overview, provides a critical assessment of much of this literature.

[65] The U.S. government felt that British pretentions were not in line with Britain's real strength, that British attempts to portray themselves as standing side by side with America as the West's two leading powers were to be discouraged, and that it would be best if Britain came to think of herself as a regional power, "join Europe," and concentrate on ground defense in the NATO area. See, for example, Dulles-Eisenhower meeting, October 22, 1957, FRUS 1955–57, 27:800, and Bowie-Eisenhower meeting of

important relationship did of course develop in the key nuclear area. But from the U.S. point of view, this was intended to be a prelude to a broader system. The original hope (as noted above) was that the sharing arrangements worked out with the British would ultimately be extended to the other main NATO allies. But then American policy shifted. The "specialness" of the nuclear relationship with the U.K. resulted from the new American coolness toward national nuclear capabilities in general, and not from any belief on the U.S. government's part that Britain should be an exception to the new rule. Indeed, the new policy implied a cooling of American support for an independent British nuclear capability. One could not discriminate so sharply between allies; one could not say yes to the British but no to the French and the Germans. To try to do so would poison America's relations with the allies getting the short end of the stick, and would also have the counterproductive effect of sustaining British illusions about their place in the world. Sooner or later, in the American view, British leaders would have to face reality and forget about playing a major role in global politics. Ideally, Britain should become part of a unified Europe, with military forces geared primarily to the defense of western Europe as a whole.

So the U.S. government gradually moved away from the earlier policy of helping the British develop a force under national control. The 1957 Anglo-American IRBM agreement, for example, had said nothing about NATO control. But by early 1960 NATO strings were being attached. The American government started to link the question of missiles for Britain—the Skybolt air-launched and the Polaris submarine-launched missiles—to the NATO MRBM question.[66] On March 29, 1960, Eisenhower and Macmillan reached an agreement. If Skybolt turned out to be worth producing, the British could buy those missiles. But Britain would in any event be able to "acquire in addition or substitution a mobile MRBM system"— meaning Polaris—"in the light of such decisions as may be reached in the discussions under way in NATO." Macmillan was satisfied with the arrangement he had reached with the president. As he told his defense minister, he was confident that "we shall get what we need."[67] The new U.S. secretary of state, Christian Herter, in fact had just told the British that after America had gone through with the charade of the Gates two-option plan for NATO MRBMs, "the way would be clear for bilateral arrangements" to provide the British with the missiles directly; Polaris was mentioned in this context as the preferred weapon. This implied that the British

---

August 16, 1960, ibid., 7(1):613. The Americans had felt this way even during the Truman period. Note, for example, a State Department comment from 1951 about the British always liking to "inflate their special relationship with the U.S.," quoted in *Eisenhower Papers,* 12:130.

[66] See Caccia to Foreign Office, March 18 and 20, 1960, Defe 11/312, PRO.

[67] The State Department position at this point was a good deal tougher than the line Eisenhower took with Macmillan. A memorandum from Under Secretary Dillon handed to Macmillan on March 29 ruled out a bilateral deal on Polaris until the NATO MRBM issue had been "satisfactorily disposed of in NATO." Eisenhower's own position, which was not nearly so stringent, is reflected in Macmillan to Eisenhower, March 29, 1960; Macmillan here was simply repeating back to Eisenhower what the president had told him in their meeting that day. See Macmillan to defense minister, March 29 and 30, 1960, Defe 13/195, PRO; Macmillan to Eisenhower and Dillon to Macmillan, both March 29, 1960, in "Prime Minister's Visit to Washington, March 26–30, 1960," Cab 133/243, PRO. The Dillon memorandum is attributed to Eisenhower in FRUS 1958–60, 7(2):863–864.

MRBMs—Skybolt or Polaris or the two together—would not be under tight NATO control.[68]

By June, however, the U.S. government was placing somewhat greater emphasis on giving the British MRBMs a "NATO flavor." The Americans were claiming, without much evidence, that the British had committed themselves to support "some kind of European MRBM scheme"; the U.K. contribution would be two Polaris submarines (with sixteen missiles each) which the Americans would sell them. This was still no problem for Macmillan: as long as the weapons would be "under the sole ultimate control of the United Kingdom Government," there was no reason why they should not be regarded as the British contribution to the NATO MRBM project.[69]

By the end of the year, the Americans—now meaning mainly the State Department—had gone a bit further. They were by this point placing even greater emphasis on NATO control over the MRBMs. The Skybolt program, it seemed in December, might not work out, and the British wondered whether they could get Polaris as a straight replacement—that is, as weapons under full national control. Secretary Gates told them that "he doubted whether supplying the U.K. with Polaris submarines for use outside a NATO force would be consistent with current State Department objectives as he understood them." But he still left the door open a bit: "If, however, discussion of the U.S. offer in Paris broke down"—meaning the December 1960 proposal for a multilateral force—"the U.S. might then be readier to contemplate bilateral arrangements, though such arrangements might not be confined to the United Kingdom."[70]

The British did not like the drift of U.S. policy on this issue, and especially the way the American were backing out of their commitments. But in a sense they had no real basis for complaint, since the new American policy was in line with fundamental British thinking. The British had from the start been against the idea of western Europe standing on its own, and thus against the idea of an independent European nuclear force. They had therefore disliked Eisenhower's December 1957 pledge to support European production of IRBMs, and when the issue of a joint Anglo-Franco-German program to develop and produce an IRBM (with American technical and financial help) came up in 1959 and 1960, they were determined to "kill this project"—but not openly, since they did not want to harm their relations with the French and the Germans.[71] And as for the more general idea of a NATO

[68] Caccia to Foreign Office, March 20, 1960, Defe 11/312, PRO. In an internal American document, however, Herter, or whoever in the State Department wrote the document for him, was a good deal more hostile to the idea of an independent British deterrent, and thus more insistent on the goal of centralized NATO control. Herter to Eisenhower, March 27, 1960, FRUS 1958–60, 7(2):860. This typified the incoherence of U.S. policy in this area in 1960.

[69] Defence Minister Watkinson to Macmillan, June 7, 1960 (see both such memoranda with this date); Gates-Watkinson meeting, June 6, 1960 (document dated June 9); de Zulueta to Macmillan, June 10, 1960; and (for Macmillan's views) Macmillan-Watkinson meeting on "Nuclear Deterrent Policy," June 15, 1960; all in Prem 11/3261, PRO.

[70] Gates-Watkinson meeting, December 12, 1960, Defe 13/211, PRO.

[71] See especially Bishop to Macmillan, "European Rocket Project," June 30, 1959, Prem 11/3713, PRO (for the quotation). Caccia to Foreign Office, March 18, 1960, and Chilver to minister of defence, "Discussions with the Americans on M.R.B.M.s and on deterrent weapons," March 21, 1960, in Defe

nuclear force, the British, as their defense minister, Harold Watkinson, noted in April 1962, "always believed this to be nonsense."[72]

But they were not going to push their opposition to the point where the Americans became really irritated with them. The British government very much wanted to remain America's closest ally. Another note to Macmillan from Watkinson captures this attitude quite nicely. "Whatever price we have to pay," he said, "to be regarded by the Americans as being closest to them in defence matters and to whom they will talk frankly and freely as I believe they talk to none of their other allies, is well worth paying." It was therefore important that the British participate, "even if in a very small way, in all their major projects," because this was the only way they could make sure that their views would continue to carry some weight with the U.S. government and that they would thus be able to exercise "a restraining influence" on American policy. The "peace of the world," he added, might well depend on Britain continuing to play this privileged role as America's closest ally.[73] So no matter how absurd they felt the NATO MRBM scheme to be, they were not about to oppose the United States directly on this issue. They would "play it long"—that is, drag their feet—hoping that the project would sooner or later just fade away.[74]

There was one overriding reason why the British were so deeply opposed to these projects: they, far more than any other major western power in the late 1950s, were worried about Germany getting her finger on the nuclear trigger. This was the great taproot of British thinking on the whole complex of issues relating to NATO and nuclear weapons. They understood that the Germans wanted sooner or later to throw off the constraints that had been worked out in 1954.[75] The Germans, they assumed, were interested in ultimately developing a nuclear force under their own effective control. The German defense minister, Franz-Josef Strauss, had begun in late 1958 to press for IRBMs to be deployed in Germany, and this, the British felt, would be a major step toward Germany acquiring an "independent deterrent."[76] The British were very much opposed to any movement in

---

11/312; all in PRO. The British even opposed an Anglo-French project when the French proposed it in early 1960. See Roberts to Foreign Office (for meeting of British and French defense ministers), March 31, 1960, Defe 11/312, PRO.

[72] Watkinson to Macmillan, April 12, 1962, Prem 11/3712, PRO.

[73] Watkinson to Macmillan, June 7, 1960, Prem 11/3261, PRO. Note also the following passage from an unsigned paper on "Mid-range Ballistic Missiles," undated, but written around September 1960, which began with a short section reviewing the history of the issue: "In July and August, 1959, the United Kingdom expressed to the Americans anxiety about the manufacture of such a weapon in Europe, particularly in the event of German participation, but stated that the British attitude to the project would be greatly influenced by that of the United States Government and that the United Kingdom did not wish to discourage the project if the U.S.A. were going to support it." Defe 11/312, PRO.

[74] Watkinson to Macmillan, May 12, 1960, Prem 11/3713, PRO. See also a memorandum to the prime minister on the "N.A.T.O. M.R.B.M." of October 27, 1960, in Prem 11/3714. The author asked whether Britain should continue "to do what we have done so far"—namely, "avoid any commitment" and "play the question along, in the hope that the project will die away."

[75] Bishop to Macmillan, "European Rocket Project," June 30, 1959, Prem 11/3713, PRO.

[76] Macmillan note of meeting with Norstad, November 26, 1958, and Richards to de Zulueta, December 1, 1958, Prem 11/3701, PRO; Roberts to Lloyd (reporting on meeting with Norstad), December 18, 1958, Prem 11/2929, PRO. On the German desire for IRBMs, see Nash, *Other Missiles of October,* pp. 57–60.

this direction. This was the main reason why they were so hostile in particular to the idea of European production of IRBMs. The 1954 constraints, they thought, could not survive German participation in such a project.[77]

The British government was therefore relieved when in late 1960 the Americans backed off from the idea of manufacturing the missiles in Europe. The allies would no longer be forced to choose between two distasteful alternatives: easing the 1954 constraints or discriminating overtly against the Federal Republic. Deploying the missiles at sea would further reduce the risk of their falling under national (that is, German) control, so that aspect of the new American thinking was also welcome. But the risk had not disappeared completely. Land-based weapons might still be deployed in the future, especially after a missile smaller and more mobile than the land-based variant of Polaris was developed. Norstad did not intend to deploy such missiles in Germany, but there was no telling what his successor might do. And even with a seaborne deterrent, there was the "danger that the Germans may contribute a German manned ship" to that force. Any scheme that seemed to give the Germans effective control over nuclear weapons "would arouse serious disquiet in the U.K. and, to a lesser extent, abroad." But the British had to tread carefully: "*Open* discrimination against the Federal Republic would, however, be contrary to our policies."[78]

More generally, the British sought to keep German power limited. They were quite comfortable with the status quo in central Europe—a divided Germany, with a West German state dependent on the western powers for protection, locked into the NATO system, and incapable of independent military action. "The division of Germany," Bevin had declared in early 1949, "at all events for the present, is essential to our plans." In July 1961, Lord Home, at that point British foreign secretary, took exactly the same line: "Nor, in fact, do we really want German reunification, at least for the time being, though we cannot abandon the principle of self-determination for the Germans." Macmillan felt the same way. In June 1958, de Gaulle asked him point blank how he felt about German reunification, whether he was in favor of it in reality or simply in theory. "In theory," he replied. "We must always support reunification in theory. There is no danger in that."[79]

A powerful Germany was seen as a threat to stability, and one of the reasons the British were so attached to the NATO system was that it kept the Germans in line.

[77] Chilver to minister of defence, March 21, 1960, Defe 11/312, PRO. British efforts to bring about a rethinking of NATO strategy, especially in 1961–62, were in large part driven by the goal of undercutting the military rationale for MRBMs, which they opposed mainly on political grounds: their primary concern was to keep control of strategic nuclear weapons out of German hands. See especially Defe 13/254, PRO, a very rich file on this whole question. For two published documents reflecting British concern with Germany acquiring strategic weapons, see Irwin in State-Defense meeting, September 25, 1959, FRUS 1958–60, 7(1):485, and Lloyd in foreign ministers' meeting, June 1, 1960, ibid., 7(2):374–376.

[78] Working Party on Nuclear Weapons for NATO, "United States Proposals for a NATO MRBM Force," PNWN/P(60)3, October 26, 1960, Prem 11/3714. Emphasis added. This document reflects what by this point had become the conventional wisdom in official British circles.

[79] Bevin memorandum on "Germany and Berlin," February 4, 1949, Prem 8/791, PRO. Lord Home, "Berlin," July 26, 1961, C(61)116, Cab 29/106, PRO. De Gaulle–Macmillan meeting, June 29, 1958, DDF 1958, 1:871.

As Macmillan explained to the French ambassador in early 1959: "France and England had suffered a great deal in the past from the Germans cutting loose, and his own feeling was that one of the great advantages of NATO and other European institutions was that they mixed the Germans up very thoroughly with the West and made it difficult for them to escape."[80]

At the same time, however, the British were pushing for policies that would reduce the western military presence on German soil—a reduction in British force levels there, a revision of NATO strategy that would rationalize those cutbacks, and negotiations with the USSR that would provide for at least a degree of military disengagement from central Europe. Britain was in fact by now the only major western power to support the general idea of "disengagement." A March 1958 British plan, for example, called for a "zone along the present demarcation line in Germany from which nuclear weapons would be barred and from which non-German troops would be withdrawn." That zone would evidently include both parts of Germany, and Poland, Czechoslovakia and Hungary as well, and the scheme would take effect even if Germany remained divided. But didn't these ideas cut against the basic thrust of British thinking about how NATO prevented Germany from "cutting loose"? As the State Department pointed out in its comments on the British proposal, disengagement would be destabilizing, in large part precisely because the presence of U.S. and British troops acted "as a restraint on the possibility of any independent German action."[81]

And how could the British expect Germany to remain non-nuclear when they themselves were so determined to hold on to their own independent deterrent? The Americans—or at least some State Department officials—were coming to the conclusion that to keep nuclear weapons out of German hands, they would now have to try to get the other allies, including Britain, "out of the nuclear business": the United Kingdom should merge her nuclear force into a broader NATO or European force over which no single country could exercise effective control. And in fact there were some influential people in England—in particular, a group around Sir Norman Brook, the Cabinet secretary—who saw the logic in this position and began to argue along precisely these lines.[82] But not Macmillan: he was determined to keep the British force under the "sole ultimate control of the United Kingdom government."

From the American point of view, these different elements in British thinking just did not add up to a consistent policy. What Macmillan was doing did not make sense in terms of Britain's most fundamental foreign policy goals. He instead was pandering to the domestic political pressure for "peace" through disengagement, and was clinging for prestige reasons to a role in the world which British power was no longer sufficient to sustain. And indeed it was a common (and not unwar-

[80] Macmillan-Chauvel meeting, February 5, 1959, FO 371/145858. Macmillan frequently expressed views of this sort. As late as October 1962, he still made a point of saying that "our great fear is Germany." Reston-Harriman meeting, October 30, 1962, Harriman Papers [HP], box 565, chronological files, Library of Congress, Washington.

[81] State Department comments on British paper on European security, attached to Hood-Reinstein meeting, April 18, 1958, 740.5/4–1858, RG 59, USNA.

[82] See chapter 8, note 81.

ranted) assumption in the West that British policy on every important issue was to be understood to a quite extraordinary degree in terms of domestic political concerns.[83] Dulles especially had soured on the British during his last few months in office in early 1959.[84] But these American views had little impact on British policy. The United Kingdom was not going to alter the heart of her defense policy: Britain was determined to hold on to a nuclear force under national control.

The French were far more outspoken in their opposition to the new American policy. Even before de Gaulle came to power, the French government had decided not to settle for half a loaf, and had come to the conclusion that France needed a nuclear force under national control. In early 1957 the French had been great champions of the stockpile idea. It was the French delegation that had taken the lead and proposed an arrangement of this sort at the Bonn NATO Council meeting in May of that year, and French officials were initially delighted that the Americans were so receptive to the proposal. But when a few months later the U.S. government came up with a plan that corresponded quite closely to what the French had initially suggested, they began to complain that the U.S. plan did not go far enough toward giving the Europeans full control over the weapons.[85]

Under de Gaulle this basic attitude became still more pronounced. For the new French leader, the nuclear issue was of absolutely fundamental importance, and

[83] See, for some typical examples, Dulles-Eisenhower telephone conversations, January 20 and 25, 1959, 5:15 P.M., DP/TC/13/DDEL; Steel to Foreign Office, February 3, 1959 (for an Adenauer view) FO 371/145773, PRO; Chauvel to Couve, July 11, 1959, Eisenhower–de Gaulle meeting, September 2, 1959, Adenauer–de Gaulle meeting, December 2, 1959, DDF 1959, 2:37, 284, 658; and Massigli note of meeting with Macmillan, January 28, 1959 (for an account by an astute and experienced French observer), MP/100/FFMA. British leaders themselves often stressed the importance of domestic political considerations. See, for example, Beam to State Department, April 30, 1955, and Jackson log, July 11, 1955, FRUS 1955–57, 5:161, 304; and Dulles's note of a meeting with Lloyd, October 19, 1958, DP/GCM/1/DDEL.

[84] For Dulles's concern about the drift of British policy, see, for example, Dulles–McElroy meeting, September 11, 1958, FRUS 1958–60, 7(2):821–822; Dulles's "Thinking Out Loud," January 26, 1959, DP/WHM/7/White House Correspondence—General 1959/DDEL, and MI, a short essay provoked by a similarly-entitled "think piece" by British Foreign Secretary Selwyn Lloyd; and especially Dulles-Herter meeting, April 24, 1959, with attached outline, "British and United States Views on Dealing with the Soviet Union," DP/SACS/14/DDEL.The British were also aware of a certain deterioration in their relations with the United States. See especially de Zulueta to Macmillan, March 8, 1960; for an analysis, see de Zulueta's "The Future of Anglo-American Relations"; both in Prem 11/2986, PRO.

[85] For the French proposal for integrating American nuclear weapons into the NATO forces in Europe, see Dulles-Mollet-Pineau meeting, May 6, 1957, DDF 1957, 1:738–740. The corresponding passages were deleted from the American account of the meeting published in FRUS 1955–57, 27:121, but were released subsequently; see DSP/225/103315/ML. See also Elbrick to Dulles, July 9, 1957, with attached July 6 memorandum for talks with Joxe on NATO atomic stockpile, 740.5611/7–957, RG 59, USNA. When Dulles endorsed the idea in his July 16 press conference, the French were delighted. Their defense minister was "tremendously pleased" and told the Americans a couple of days later that if American nuclear weapons could be made available immediately in the event of an emergency, "either directly or through NATO," and if French forces could be trained in their use, the whole problem of a French nuclear capability "would be solved." Houghton to Dulles, July 18, 1957, 740.5611/7–1857, RG 59, USNA. But when the Americans presented a formal proposal along these lines at the NATO heads of government meeting in December, the French were unhappy and felt it did not go far enough toward giving them outright control of the weapons. Burgess to Dulles, December 5, 1957, 740.5611/12–555, and State Department to embassy in Paris, December 6, 1957, 740.5611/12–557, RG 59, USNA.

the question of control was the nub of the problem. He did not insist from the start on developing a totally independent nuclear infrastructure. He was perfectly willing in 1958 to build a national nuclear capability with weapons provided by the United States. To serve French political purposes, that capability did not have to be particularly large; the balance of France's nuclear force could be under joint French and American control.[86] (This was the British model.) But the key point was that France had to acquire a certain nuclear capability under purely national control, and that control had to be overt and explicit. Anything less simply would not do.

So de Gaulle rejected the early American overtures, which were based on the idea that American control would be nominal and that in reality the weapons would be available in an emergency. For the French leader, any system in which the Americans retained even formal control was just not good enough. If the weapons could be used only if America or SACEUR gave the green light, he said, "this proposition had little interest" for France.[87] The Americans brought up the problem of the Atomic Energy Act, but for de Gaulle this was just a convenient excuse: he took it for granted that what was behind American policy was what he saw as a very natural desire to hold on to something close to a nuclear monopoly in the West.[88] And the French president was in the final analysis prepared to take this American policy philosophically. It was as though a law of nature was at work. This was the way a great power more or less had to behave,[89] indeed, he himself would behave the same way if he were the one who had an effective nuclear monopoly.[90]

But if U.S.–European tensions were rooted in hard, unalterable political realities, there was little point to trying to deal with them through negotiation and compromise. Fundamental problems could not be swept under the rug. The simple fact was that the European countries, and France above all, were no longer going to remain American protectorates, without a distinct political personality of their own. France was going to develop a nuclear force under her own control, and by her own efforts, since the United States did not trust her enough to turn American nuclear weapons over to her directly.[91] And since NATO was an instrument of American domination, France was no longer interested in cooperating within the NATO framework. In the NATO system, the "whole show was being run by the U.S."[92] This was intolerable; fundamental changes were absolutely necessary; and noncooperation on such matters as air defense and NATO nuclear stockpiles in

---

[86] De Gaulle–Macmillan meeting, June 29–30, 1958, DDF 1958, 1:883.

[87] De Gaulle–Dulles meeting, July 5, 1958, FRUS 1958–60, 7(2):59.

[88] De Gaulle–Dulles meeting, July 5, 1958, ibid., p. 58. This particular charge was not justified, but one should note that the Eisenhower administration was not above using arguments about Congress in this way. See, for example, Dulles-Eisenhower telephone conversation, September 24, 1954, SSMC, no. 669.

[89] For a striking example, see Alain Peyrefitte, C'était de Gaulle (Paris: Fayard, 1994), pp. 367–368.

[90] See Hervé Alphand, L'étonnement d'être (Paris: Fayard, 1977), pp. 331, 343, 397.

[91] As the French leader bluntly pointed out in a letter to the American president: De Gaulle to Eisenhower, November 24, 1959, in Charles de Gaulle, Lettres, notes et carnets (juin 1958—décembre 1960) [LNC 1958–60] (Paris: Plon, 1985), p. 283.

[92] Dulles to Eisenhower, December 15, 1958, FRUS 1958–60, 7(2):154.

France was a way of driving home the fact that France insisted on radical change in the structure of the alliance.[93]

From the American point of view, de Gaulle was becoming "increasingly troublesome."[94] He had a "Messiah complex," Eisenhower said. He saw himself as a "cross between Napoleon and Joan of Arc."[95] The French president thought in old-fashioned nationalistic terms, and his point of view, if carried to its logical conclusion, would wreck the alliance.[96] Modern military realities, if nothing else, made that kind of attitude obsolete. The premium they placed on rapid action meant that only a high degree of integration—above all, in the area of air defense—would be militarily efficient.[97]

An even more basic problem, in Eisenhower's view, was that de Gaulle had "no idea of what the U.S. is really trying to do."[98] The United States, he pointed out to the French leader, had never sought to "push itself into a place of prominence." It was the Europeans, he told his subordinates, who had "insisted there be an American command." It was their inability "to get together" that had led to an American SACEUR. De Gaulle seemed to resent America's "overpowering influence in

[93] See, for example, de Gaulle's views cited in Burgess to State Department, March 9 and 10, 1959, ibid., 7(1):424, 426. French officials, including de Gaulle himself, often minimized the practical importance of these moves, implying that they were essentially gestures. See Alphand-Herter meeting, March 3, 1959, and de Gaulle–Norstad meeting, January 21, 1960, ibid., pp. 417, 569. U.S. policy on Algeria, which was not nearly as supportive of France as de Gaulle would have liked, was also an important—probably the most important—factor. For various documents reflecting the importance of the Algerian issue, see ibid., pp. 416, 418, 421, 423, 437.

[94] Dulles in meeting with Eisenhower, December 12, 1958, ibid., 7(2):145.

[95] Eisenhower, in meeting with Herter, May 2, 1959, ibid., p. 206.

[96] Eisenhower, in meeting with Spaak, September 3, 1959, and in letter to Norstad, January 11, 1960, ibid., 7(1):482, 566.

[97] The Americans frequently argued along these lines. See, for example, Norstad in meeting with Adenauer, December 16, 1957, SS/ITM/4/NATO Heads of Government Meeting, Paris, Chronology, December 16, 1957 (1)/DDEL; Eisenhower-Debré meeting, December 21, 1959, FRUS 1958–60, 7(1):559; and Eisenhower to de Gaulle, August 30, 1960, ibid., 7(2):415. For a perceptive analysis of the question, see Roberts to Lloyd, "General de Gaulle's Attitude to NATO," December 3, 1959, pp. 4–7, Prem 11/3002, PRO.

[98] Eisenhower-Herter meeting, April 22, 1960, FRUS 1958–60, 7(2):342. Eisenhower's basic strategic concept was in some ways quite similar to de Gaulle's. The U.S. president's notion of America as the "central keep behind the forward forces" (cited above, p. 151, and chapter 5, note 18) was, for example, in line with de Gaulle's idea of America providing the reserve force for the West. The difference was that while for Eisenhower the European forces were ultimately to be highly integrated, with American power fading increasingly into the background, for de Gaulle each of the major European countries was to play a very distinctive role. Germany, in his view, should be the "advance guard," France should "provide the main armies," and Britain should defend the "coastal flank." For de Gaulle's concept, which he laid out many times, see, for example, de Gaulle–Macmillan meeting, March 12–13, 1960, p. 5, FO 371/154096, PRO, and also Macmillan diary entry, March 13 1960, in Harold Macmillan, *Pointing the Way, 1959–1961* (London: Macmillan, 1972), p. 182; de Gaulle–Adenauer meetings, July 29–30, 1960, cited in Georges-Henri Soutou, "De Gaulle, Adenauer und die gemeinsame Front gegen die amerikanische Nuklearstrategie," in, *Politischer Wandel, organisierte Gewalt und nationale Sicherheit: Beiträge zur neueren Geschichte Deutschlands und Frankreichs*, ed. Ernst Hansen et al., (Munich: Oldenbourg, 1995), pp. 496–497 (for the French record), and Schwarz, *Adenauer*, 2:569–570 (for the German record); de Gaulle–Macmillan meeting, January 28, 1961, p. 11, Prem 11/3714, PRO; de Gaulle–Kennedy meeting, June 1, 1961, FRUS 1961–63, 13:313; de Gaulle–Alphand meetings, May 25, 1961, and June 26, 1962, Alphand, *L'étonnement d'être*, pp. 351, 379.

NATO," but this situation, he noted, was "not a product of our own choice." Eisenhower certainly knew what he was talking about. The Europeans, and especially the French, had from the outset pressed for a major American military presence in Europe, for an American SACEUR, and for a highly integrated defense system. America had cooperated, but from the start had had no wish to play this kind of role on a permanent basis. Eisenhower wanted to tell de Gaulle quite bluntly that the United States did "not want command in Europe," and would be delighted to pull her troops out and see the Europeans take over responsibility for their own defense. What was grating was that after all these years of acting "in a spirit of allied helpfulness," America should now find herself dealing with Europeans who resented a system that had come into being in large part as a way of meeting their concerns, and refused now to act the way real allies were supposed to.[99]

It was clear what de Gaulle objected to, but not at all clear how he proposed to change things. The NATO system and the American presence had served the great political purpose of controlling German power. Had this fundamental objective, so central to French policy during the Fourth Republic, now been totally abandoned?[100] Did de Gaulle really want to demolish the limits on German power embodied in the NATO system? On the one hand he made it clear to American and British leaders that the prospect of a resurgence of German power was a fundamental French concern, that he was (like the British) in no rush to see Germany reunified, and that he was against Germany acquiring a nuclear capability.[101] On the other hand, the central thrust of his policy, and the rhetoric that surrounded it, was a standing goad to the Germans to reach for full independence and to go nuclear themselves. If France could not rely so heavily on America, why should Germany have to? If a France without nuclear weapons was nothing more than a satellite, why should Germany remain an American nuclear protectorate?

All this made it hard for Eisenhower to "understand exactly" what de Gaulle was "getting at" when the French leader complained about NATO. De Gaulle's theories were "so hazy," he said, that he had "never been able to respond ade-

[99] Eisenhower to de Gaulle, August 30, 1960, Eisenhower-Herter telephone conversation, August 10, 1960, and Eisenhower-Herter meeting, April 22, 1960, FRUS 1958–60, 7(2):414, 404, 342.

[100] See, for example, Herter-Couve-Home meeting, September 23, 1960, DDRS 1997/2558. On French policy in this area in the pre-Gaullist period, see Dulles-Mollet-Pineau meeting, May 6, 1957, DDF 1957, 1:738–740. Mollet and Pineau argued here that an integrated system—an "armement atomique européen integré"—was the only way to both provide for the defense of Europe and deal with the "special problem posed by Germany"—that is, to prevent Germany from acquiring an independent nuclear capability. This strand of thinking did not entirely disappear from French policy during the Gaullist period. As late as mid-1962, de Gaulle himself, for all his attacks on the principle of integration, his criticism of American predominance in NATO, and his calls for a Franco-German Europe with a strategic personality of its own, unambiguously favored the idea of a combined U.S.–British-German-French force in Germany, under American command, "afin d'éviter surtout que l'armée allemande forme des divisions indépendantes." De Gaulle–Alphand meeting, June 26, 1962, Alphand, *L'étonnement d'être*, p. 379.

[101] For de Gaulle and the question of German reunification, see Eisenhower–de Gaulle–Macmillan meeting, December 20, 1959, pp. 5, 8, Prem 11/2991, PRO, and especially U.S. State Department Historical Office, "Crisis over Berlin: American Policy Concerning the Soviet Threats to Berlin, November 1958–December 1962" (October 1966) [DOS Berlin History], pt. 1, p. 53. For de Gaulle and the German nuclear question, see below, pp. 332, 336–337, 371–373.

quately."[102] France took a nationalistic line and rejected the concept of a strong NATO defense system. But de Gaulle had also called for a tripartite directorate: France, Britain, and America would together work out policy for the West as a whole. Military plans would also be developed and implemented on a tripartite basis. This proposal, "with all the implications of the veto and of imposition of decisions on others which this suggestion holds," did not seem compatible with the basic nationalistic thrust of French policy.[103] If the fundamental concern was that with American cities increasingly at risk, nuclear deterrence was becoming hollow, then presumably the last thing the French would have wanted was an arrangement designed to hold the Americans back. A system where each power had a veto would enable not just the French but the British as well to keep the Americans from using their nuclear forces; and in such a system the United States and even Britain would also in theory be able to prevent France from using whatever nuclear weapons she was able to build. Could de Gaulle really have had such an arrangement in mind? At first even Couve de Murville, now the French foreign minister, and Hervé Alphand, the French ambassador in Washington, took it for granted that this was not what de Gaulle intended.[104] But it soon became clear that this was precisely what the French president was demanding.[105] And de Gaulle was in fact making demands. Either the alliance would change in accordance with his proposals, he said, or France would withdraw from NATO.[106]

What was de Gaulle trying to do? Was he deliberately picking a fight with America? On the nuclear question, Dulles was as forthcoming as any U.S. secretary of state could possibly have been. The American aim, he had told de Gaulle in July 1958, was to create a system where the use of nuclear weapons would not depend on an American decision. Things would be set up in such a way, he said, that the Europeans could have "complete confidence" that the weapons would be used in accordance with NATO plans.[107] But the French leader showed no interest in pursuing the idea—a reaction so bizarre that even his ambassador in Washington thought that de Gaulle had not understood what Dulles was proposing.[108] And the French leader later showed little interest in Eisenhower's idea of a European— and in fact a French—SACEUR in control of a strong NATO nuclear force. What exactly did de Gaulle want? On the one hand, he argued in September 1958 that it was vital that the three western powers cooperate in the formulation of military plans. But on the other hand, he was unwilling to proceed actively with joint plan-

[102] Eisenhower memorandum, August 10, 1960, FRUS 1958–60, 7(2):405–406. See also Eisenhower-Macmillan meeting, September 27, 1960, p. 3, DDRS 1997/1698.

[103] Eisenhower to de Gaulle, August 30, 1960, FRUS 1958–60, 7(2):417.

[104] Couve to Alphand, November 3, 1958, and Alphand to Couve, October 31, 1958, DDF 1958, 2:620, 620 n; see also Alphand to Couve, December 4, 1958, ibid., p. 805.

[105] Couve to Alphand, January 18, 1959, DDF 1959, 1:68; de Gaulle to Eisenhower, October 6, 1959, LNC 1958–60, p. 263.

[106] De Gaulle–Jebb meeting, October 22, 1958, DDF 1958, 2:565.

[107] Dulles–de Gaulle meeting, July 5, 1958, FRUS 1958–60, 7(2):55–56, and DDF 1958, 2:24.

[108] Alphand-Elbrick meeting, July 9, 1958, FRUS 1958–60, 7(2):74. Dulles and Norstad also felt that de Gaulle had not "appreciated the far-reaching character" of the U.S. proposal. Dulles-Norstad meeting, September 26, 1958, DSP/79/71882/ML.

ning for the use of force when the Soviets threatened in November 1958 to "liquidate" western rights in Berlin—the area where the right of the three powers to
act as a bloc was most firmly established.[109] If the fear was that the United States
would not react quickly enough if war broke out in Europe, why was de Gaulle
against the air defense measures that the rest of the alliance was ready to accept?
This was a system that reflected American seriousness about nuclear war-fighting
and American willingness to take action very quickly.[110] Why, then, was de Gaulle
out to undermine those arrangements? And more generally, if de Gaulle was worried that the United States would eventually abandon Europe, why was he attacking the whole NATO framework, which the Americans viewed as the basis for their
involvement on the continent? If he was so worried about a possible American
withdrawal, why was he pursuing a policy that alienated the United States—gra-
tuitously, in the American view—and thus made it more likely that America would
in fact pull out? De Gaulle, it seemed—even to former high-ranking French officials looking back at the period—was more interested in posturing than in dealing with real problems.[111] And in America the idea was beginning to take hold
that the French president was insatiable, that it was pointless trying to "appease"
him, that he was simply a problem that the other western countries would have to
find some way around.[112]

But in spite of all this, Eisenhower personally always felt a certain sympathy for
de Gaulle, and American policy toward France during his presidency was never
marked by the kind of antagonism that took hold, especially in the State Department, during the Kennedy period. For at the most basic level, Eisenhower and de
Gaulle wanted the same thing. They both wanted the Europeans to stand on their
own, to move away from a situation characterized by excessive dependence on the
United States. It was a source of intense frustration to the American president that

[109] This issue will be treated in detail in the next chapter, but French reluctance to engage in joint
planning was clear at the outset. See especially Couve to Alphand, January 11, 1959, DDF 1959, 1:37.
Alphand, the French ambassador in Washington, was embarrassed by the French response to the American proposal for joint planning, and indeed thought that the American position was correct. See Alphand, L'Etonnement d'être, pp. 297–298.

[110] On the air defense issue, and the meaning of American pressure for an effective air defense system, see above, p. 202.

[111] See, for example, Jean Chauvel, Commentaire, vol. 3, De Berne à Paris (1952–1962) (Paris: Fayard, 1973), p. 281. If de Gaulle had wanted joint planning (on African or Levantine questions, for example), Chauvel wrote, he should have made precise proposals, but he never did, because he was not
really concerned with what was strategically effective, but rather sought to do "spectacular" things for
domestic political purposes. Couve's view was not all that different, as one can tell from certain comments he made many years later. These remarks were phrased in general terms—"il ne faut pas con-
fondre indépendance et irresponsabilité," "la dramatisation serait la pire des politiques"—but it is not
hard to imagine what he had in mind. The basic problem from his point of view was not that de Gaulle's
instincts were wrong, but rather that he was not subtle, that he tended to oversimplify things. While
de Gaulle, for example, spoke of Russia coming to dominate all of Europe east of the Elbe "thanks to
the consent given by the Anglo-Saxons at Yalta," Couve referred to the partition of Europe "improperly
called that of Yalta." See Maurice Couve de Murville, Le monde en face: Entretiens avec Maurice Delarue
(Paris: Plon, 1989), pp. 17, 69, 249; de Gaulle, Mémoires d'espoir: Le renouveau, p. 239.

[112] See, for example, Norstad's remark that it was "impossible to satisfy de Gaulle's appetite," in
Norstad-Eisenhower meeting, June 9, 1959, FRUS 1958–60, 7(1):462.

de Gaulle was simply incapable of grasping this central fact—of seeing what Eisenhower really wanted, and understanding the various factors that kept him from moving quickly toward that goal.[113]

This applied especially to problems in the nuclear area. Control over nuclear weapons was the key to political independence. This was why de Gaulle put it at the heart of his policy. And Eisenhower sympathized with French nuclear aspirations. In June 1959, for example, the president remarked to General Norstad (who by this point was quite fed up with de Gaulle) that "we would react very much as de Gaulle does if the shoe were on the other foot."[114] A year later, he told Norstad that the United States should be "generous" with the allies on the nuclear sharing issue, that cooperation could not be a one-way street, and that "he had considerable sympathy for the point of view of de Gaulle in this question. He is trying to build up his country, and we persist in treating them as second-rate."[115] He told Herter that on the question of a French nuclear capability, "he really was sympathetic."[116] Indeed, he never fully blamed de Gaulle for the difficulties in relations between the two countries. The more basic problem, in his view, lay at home. In May 1959, for example, the president again "expressed sympathy with the French." The problem was that the administration was "handcuffed" by the "senseless limitations" Congress had placed on the executive branch.[117] France, he thought, should have the bomb. "I would like to be able to give it to you," he told

---

[113] In fact, French leaders did grasp the basic thrust of the Eisenhower policy and understood that his goal was to make the Europeans more responsible for their own defense and less dependent on America. Unlike Adenauer, who was alarmed when he heard that Eisenhower was thinking along these lines, the French thought that what the president had in mind was natural and indeed desirable. Adenauer-Couve-Debré meeting, December 1, 1959, DDF 1959, 2:651–653. What is surprising, however, is that the French did not press actively for arrangements that would make for a smooth transition to a new, European-based defense system—above all, by supporting Eisenhower's plans for a European SACEUR, a NATO force not subject to a U.S. veto, and so on—and instead took a line that made it much harder for the United States to cooperate with a policy of devolving authority to the Europeans, above all in the nuclear sphere.

[114] Norstad-Eisenhower meeting, June 9, 1959, FRUS 1958–60, 7(1):462.

[115] Norstad-Eisenhower meeting, August 3, 1960, ibid., p. 610.

[116] Eisenhower-Herter telephone conversation, August 10, 1960, ibid., 7(2):403.

[117] Eisenhower-Herter meeting, May 2, 1959, ibid., 204. See also Eisenhower's comments at NSC meetings, August 18 and October 29, 1959, ibid., pp. 251–252, 292. The president's attitude was reflected in the position his government took on the question of legal authority to help the French with their nuclear program. The Atomic Energy Act had been liberalized in 1958 to permit America to help allies who had "made substantial progress in the development of atomic weapons," but the JCAE Report accompanying that piece of legislation had been "loaded in favor of the U.K. and against France." The administration, however, wanted to take as liberal a line as it could with regard to the French nuclear program. From Congress's point of view, the setting off of a single bomb was not meant to be the test of "substantial progress," but Secretary Herter told top French officials in May 1959 that "once the French had effected their first atomic explosion," the legal situation would be different and the U.S. "could talk substance to them." Eisenhower took a similar line in a meeting with de Gaulle a few months later. The U.S. law, he said, was a "mistake": "It seemed to run counter to common sense, but France could receive assistance only after she had expended large sums of money and a great deal of time and had herself detonated nuclear weapons. He regretted this but there was no way he could get around it." Herter-Debré-Couve meeting, May 1, 1959, and Eisenhower–de Gaulle meeting, September 2, 1959, ibid., pp. 199, 262, and DDF 1959, 2:279; NSC meeting, August 25, 1960, FRUS 1958–60, 7(1):619–620.

de Gaulle when the two men discussed the issue in December 1959. It was "stupid" that France had to spend huge sums of money developing a weapon her allies already had.[118] And the president never shut the door entirely on bilateral nuclear cooperation with France.[119]

Nevertheless, it was clear that relations between the two countries had gone downhill, and that the nuclear question lay at the heart of the problem. Certain sections of the American government, largely in reaction to de Gaulle's own policies, had turned with particular force against the idea of nuclear cooperation with France. It was not just that Congress had been alienated by de Gaulle and was now less willing to liberalize the law. Even within the administration, the balance was shifting against the idea of helping the French with their nuclear program. It was because of de Gaulle's generally uncooperative attitude on NATO issues in general that Norstad came to oppose so sharply the idea of nuclear assistance to France, and his opposition played a key role in shaping opinion within the administration. There was no military need for any sharing arrangement that went beyond the stockpile scheme, Norstad told top officials in August 1960, and he threatened to testify to that effect before Congress. There was no point trying to appease de Gaulle; helping the French nuclear program, he said, would "not 'buy' any better French cooperation in NATO." The intensity of Norstad's feelings convinced Secretary of Defense Gates not to press the issue of nuclear assistance to France. Gates had earlier thought the issue had to be resolved, even if that meant a showdown with the State Department. But Norstad's strong opposition had "shaken" Gates and had led him to instruct "his people to prepare the paper [on nuclear sharing] in a way that would show no sharp splits with the Department of State position." The issue was in effect put on ice for the rest of the Eisenhower period.[120]

[118] Eisenhower–de Gaulle meeting, December 19, 1959, and Eisenhower–de Gaulle–Macmillan meeting, December 20, 1959, DDF 1959, 2:761, 770.

[119] See the policy guidance in NSC 5910/1, "Statement of U.S. Policy on France," November 4, 1959, para. 42(a), FRUS 1958–60, 7(2):308—this represented an overruling, after an NSC discussion on October 9, of the majority view, which sought to put off the issue of bilateral aid and focus efforts on a multilateral solution; see ibid., pp. 290 n, 290–295; editorial note, ibid., p. 412; NSC meeting, August 25, 1960, FRUS 1958–60, 7(1):616–617. This was all at the level of formal policy. What was going on in practice is again a clearer test of American policy—or at least of the policy that Eisenhower and a good part of the U.S. national security establishment wanted to pursue. Thus the comment of one exceptionally well-informed French student of these issues is of considerable interest: "Sur le plan nucléaire, on le sait bien maintenant, c'est avec Washington que nos rapports ont toujours été déterminants, sous la forme d'échanges scientifiques ou d'achats de certain matérials sensibles. L'orthodoxie 'gaulliste' a fait que l'on a occulté cette réalité: il existe depuis le début (et le Général regrettait surtout qu'elle ne fût pas plus développée!) une relation nucléaire franco-américaine." One should add that it was not just the Gaullists who had an interest in suppressing the truth; so did the U.S. government, albeit for different reasons. Georges-Henri Soutou, "Dissuasion élargie, dissuasion concertée ou dissuasion pour le roi de Prusse," Géopolitique, no. 52 (Winter 1995–96):40; emphasis added. For other evidence of the interest of at least certain sections of the U.S. government in taking a liberal line, see the notes of a discussion of this subject with a U.S. official, September 4, 1959, DDF 1959, 2:304–305.

[120] Norstad meeting with State and Defense Department officials, August 2, 1960, DDRS 1989/2751; Gates in meeting with Acting Secretary of State Dillon and McCone, August 24, 1960, DDRS 1997/1348. On de Gaulle being unappeasable, see Norstad-Eisenhower meeting, June 9, 1959, FRUS 1958–60, 7(1):462. Up to this point, Gates had felt that the U.S. government should push ahead with the policy of helping the Europeans build MRBMs in Europe. It was, in his view, inevitable that

The French, for their part, also hardened their line, and showed no interest in anything the Americans now suggested. If the remarkably liberal U.S. policy that Dulles had outlined to de Gaulle in 1958 had not been enough to win his cooperation, it was scarcely to be expected that the new proposals for a "NATO nuclear force" would lead to a more forthcoming French policy. To de Gaulle all this talk of "NATO control" or even "European control" was just smoke and mirrors. The whole "idea of a NATO nuclear force," he told Macmillan, "had no reality. The nuclear forces were American and the Americans would use them or not as they wished."[121] SACEUR in the final analysis was just an American general. Giving Norstad control over the Polaris missiles would "change nothing." "What do we care," he asked, "if the U.S. forces in Europe are under the control of an American in Europe or in Washington?" It was a question of same pants, different pockets: "In reality the United States would continue as before to control these nuclear weapons." So the idea of a powerful SACEUR, with a nuclear force under his own control, "had little interest" for France—although de Gaulle would complain loudly enough when, during the Kennedy period, SACEUR's wings really were clipped and he became little more than an ordinary American field commander.[122]

Even the idea of a "European force," as it was taking shape in American minds, had little appeal for de Gaulle. There was no sovereign European authority to control that force, only an ersatz Europe with no real political personality of its own. This "'integrated' Europe, as they call it," he said, would have no policy, and would thus follow the lead of "some outsider who did have a policy."[123] Such a Europe would be a passive instrument in America's hands, and indeed this was why, he claimed, the U.S. government had been such a strong supporter of an integrated Europe à la Jean Monnet. For the Americans, the proposal for a multilateral force was meant to be a major new departure. But de Gaulle had seen it all before. The MLF, like the EDC before it, was simply a gimmick: a new structure would be set up, but the basic political question, the question of control, was being evaded. The Americans could go ahead with this nonsense if they wanted, since it would make no difference one way or the other. But France would not take part in the charade and would continue to build a force under full national control.

So in their very different ways, neither Britain nor France was willing to go along with the new thrust of American policy. But it was Germany that was the crucial country in this context. Indeed, it is scarcely an exaggeration to say that no one

---

they would attain a missile capability; given that, it was in America's "interest that they attain such capability with U.S. help." There was "no question," one high State Department official unhappily noted, "that Defense is anxious to make an offer sufficiently attractive to invite acceptance." State took the opposite line, so the two departments were at odds with each other on this issue, especially in late 1959 and through the first half of 1960. The matter can be followed in 740.5611 for this period; for the quotations, see Gates to Merchant, November 25, 1959, and Merchant to Herter, March 4, 1960, both in that file in RG 59, USNA.

[121] De Gaulle–Macmillan meeting, January 28, 1961, Prem 11/3714, PRO.

[122] De Gaulle–Sulzberger interview, February 14, 1961, in Sulzberger, *Last of the Giants,* pp. 64–65; Dulles–de Gaulle meeting, July 5, 1958, FRUS 1958–60, 7(2):59; De Gaulle–Lemnitzer meeting, July 23, 1962, NSF/71a/France—General/JFKL.

[123] Quoted in John Newhouse, *De Gaulle and the Anglo-Saxons* (London: Andre Deutsch, 1970), p. 165. See also de Gaulle, *Mémoires d'espoir,* p. 212.

would have cared much about British or French nuclear weapons if it had not been for the implications with regard to Germany. And the most important point to note about German policy is that the German government, and Adenauer in particular, also very much wanted eventually to acquire an independent nuclear capability.

Beginning in 1955, German policy began to take on a more "nationalistic" cast. With the ratification of the Paris accords and the beginning of German rearmament, with Germany's admission into NATO and the establishment of diplomatic relations with the Soviet Union, the Federal Republic had come of age: Germany, Adenauer declared, had once again become a great power.[124] And a major country like Germany, he felt, could not forever remain a mere "atomic protectorate." A state incapable of defending itself, in his view, was no real state at all. It was "intolerable," he said, that only America and Russia had large nuclear forces—"intolerable" that those two countries had so much power, and that the fate of every nation on earth rested so exclusively in their hands.[125]

In 1955, German relations with the United States cooled dramatically. The great 1949–54 love affair between Adenauer and the Americans now came to an end. There was a real danger, the chancellor thought, that the Americans were getting ready to make a deal with Russia at the expense of their European allies—above all, at the expense of Germany.[126] He disliked the 1955 Geneva summit conference and everything it symbolized—in spite of the fact that he had pressed strongly for talks and that American policy at that meeting was very much in line with the plan he himself had put forward at the time.[127] It sometimes seemed at this point that it was the simple idea of détente that he objected to. Détente seemed to imply that both sides had come to accept the status quo and thus the division of Germany. The notion of détente thus merged in his mind with the idea of the United States and the Soviet Union dividing up the world between themselves, and of America selling out German interests in the process. But Adenauer did not believe that an intransigent policy would force the Soviets to disgorge East Germany or that détente would rule out reunification. He in fact took exactly the opposite line when discussing the issue with other CDU leaders in early 1955. Reunification, he argued, would have to follow détente—the implication being that if one were serious about reunification, one would first have to achieve a relaxation of tensions in Europe, and thus that his criticism of the détente policy was unwarranted.[128]

By 1956 it seemed as though Adenauer was looking for excuses to attack American policy. He now questioned America's willingness to go to war for the sake of

[124] Schwarz, *Adenauer*, 2:159, 218.

[125] Ibid., pp. 178, 299; Adenauer in Buchstab, CDU-BV, 1953–57, September 20, 1956, pp. 1029, 1073, 1079; Adenauer, *Erinnerungen*, 3:303, 325–328. He was still talking along these lines in 1963 and even 1967. See, for example, Adenauer–de Gaulle meeting, January 22, 1963, AAPBD 1963, 1:141, and Adenauer, *Erinnerungen*, 4:205, 240, 243–244.

[126] Schwarz, *Adenauer*, 2:205–206, 306, 385. See also Couve to Pineau, October 10, 1956, DDF 1956, 2:553–554; Adenauer-Mollet meeting, November 6, 1956, DDF 1956, 3:234–237.

[127] Adenauer to Dulles, August 9, 1955, 762.00/8-955, RG 59, USNA, and Schwarz, *Adenauer*, 2:205–206. For the U.S. reaction, see Dulles to Adenauer, August 15, 1955, DDRS 1989/3308, and Dulles to Eisenhower, August 10, 1955, DP/GCM/2/Strictly Confidential A-B(1)/DDEL.

[128] Adenauer in Buchstab, CDU-BV, 1953–57, June 3, 1955, p. 527.

Europe. In a world ruled by the United States and the Soviet Union, Europe would no longer count, and NATO would be superfluous. That, he said, was why America was thinking in terms of a withdrawal from the continent, and why the Pentagon was working out plans—the so-called "Radford Plan"—for cutting back on the American troop presence in the NATO area. The United States, he insisted, could not be trusted. Donald Quarles, the U.S. Air Force secretary, had met with him in September and had told him, Adenauer said, that even if the Soviets launched a nuclear attack on the United States, the Americans would allow a whole week to go by before retaliating. It was not hard to see what Adenauer was implying. If the Americans would be so slow to respond even if they themselves were struck, how could one expect them to react quickly in the event of an attack on Europe?[129]

And this was no isolated incident. Adenauer was now highly critical of American policy in general. The United States, he complained to Dulles, was placing excessive emphasis on nuclear weapons. As a result, any U.S.–Soviet war, "even if arising from a cause of no decisive importance in itself," would lead to the "complete annihilation" of most of the human race. Europe, including Germany, was therefore "losing confidence in the reliability of the United States."[130]

The Americans were puzzled, and wondered what they had done to provoke this kind of reaction. The point of view Adenauer had attributed to Quarles was absurd, as Robert Murphy, now deputy undersecretary of state, told the chancellor when the two men met in October. In fact, even the German record of the original meeting with Quarles shows that Adenauer had totally misunderstood, or had deliberately misrepresented, what the Air Force secretary had said.[131] As for Adenauer's criticism of America's general military policy, it soon became clear that his complaints could not be taken at face value. He was not interested in getting the United States to support a more balanced NATO strategy. He ignored the American response that ground forces were indeed necessary, that the United States could not do everything, and that countries like Germany had to "carry the part of the task most appropriate for them."[132] What he actually objected to was that America, by herself, should have this life-or-death power. To complain about the United States was to lay the basis for some sort of arrangement that would give the Europeans some real control over their own fate: if America was "unreliable," then the European countries, including Germany, needed nuclear forces of their own.

German defense policy now shifted course. The emphasis was placed not on conventional forces but on a relatively small but highly trained and well-equipped army prepared to operate on the nuclear battlefield. German units would not be

[129] See, for example, Schwarz, *Adenauer*, 2:291–292, 302, 306; Adenauer in Buchstab, CDU-BV, 1953–57, pp. 1028–1030; and especially Adenauer-Mollet meeting, DDF 1956, 3:235. For the claim about Quarles, see also Adenauer–Murphy meeting, October 4, 1956, 762a.5/10-456, RG 59, USNA.

[130] Adenauer to Dulles, July 22, 1956, DP/WHM/5/Meetings with the President, Aug.–Dec. 1956 (8)/DDEL; also quoted in Schwarz, *Adenauer*, 2:292–294.

[131] Adenauer-Murphy meeting, October 4, 1956, 762a.5/10-456, RG 59, USNA. The record of the September 10 meeting between Adenauer and Quarles made by the German interpreter Weber is in the Blankenhorn Papers (NL-351) at the Bundesarchiv in Koblenz; a translation of Weber's record is in DOS-FOIA release 901011.

[132] See Dulles to Adenauer, August 10, 1956, FRUS 1955–57, 26:139–143.

mere "cannon fodder." The Federal Republic had to be treated as an equal, and that meant that the Bundeswehr had to be armed with the same weapons as the other NATO forces—that is, nuclear-capable weapons, with the Americans turning over the warheads in an emergency.[133] But the question of whether an arrangement of this sort should be set up was never the real issue. It was obvious to both Dulles and Adenauer that the German army had to be prepared to fight with nuclear weapons. A purely conventional force would be no match for a powerful nuclear-armed adversary. Even in 1953 the Americans had understood that German forces would have to be equipped "with new weapons as they become available." The Americans had worried that France would take a different line, but by 1957 the French had reached the same conclusion. Their foreign minister, for example, now "stressed the importance of nuclear weapons for Germany." This had by now become the standard view within the western alliance.[134]

The key issue was not whether the Bundeswehr should be armed with nuclear-capable weapons, but rather whether the warheads would be under German national control—that is, whether the Americans would have to give the green light before the weapons could actually be used. And Adenauer's view was that the Federal Republic needed an independent nuclear capability. In October 1956, he thought Euratom might provide a way for Germany to "produce nuclear weapons herself."[135] A year later, when the French proposed joint production of nuclear weapons, Adenauer was delighted to go along. It was not enough that the weapons be available in an emergency. "Wir müssen sie produzieren," he declared—"we must produce them."[136] This remained his view even in the 1960s. Just weeks before his death in 1967, for example, he attacked the Nuclear Nonproliferation Treaty, which confirmed the non-nuclear status of the Federal Republic, as the "Morgenthau Plan squared."[137]

[133] Fischer, "Reaktion der Bundesregierung," pp. 116–117; Schwarz, *Adenauer*, 2:158, 329–333.

[134] Dulles-Adenauer meeting, May 26, 1957, DSP/226/103684–87/ML. See also Buchstab, CDU-BV 1957–61, pp. 128, 132, 387–388. For the assumption that the Bundeswehr would be armed with nuclear weapons, see the Annotated Order of Business at Bermuda, and the memorandum for Eisenhower on NATO problems (almost certainly by Dulles), both December 1953, DSP/12/16321 and 16354/ML, and the State Department position paper on "Development of NATO Nuclear Capability," December 7, 1956, DSP/51/56848/ML. For the French view: Dulles-Mollet-Pineau meeting, May 6, 1957, DSP/225/103315 (containing an important passage deleted from the version in FRUS 1955–57, 27:121, and not adequately reported in the French account in DDF 1957, 1:738–740).

[135] Adenauer's language in September and October 1956 was unambiguous: "Deutschland kann nicht Atomprotektorat bleiben . . . Er möchte über EURATOM auf schnellstem Weg die Möglichkeit erhalten, selbst nukleare Waffen herzustellen." A related document also spelled out his thinking in very explicit terms: "Abschluss von EURATOM gibt uns auf die Dauer die Möglichkeit, auf normale Weise zu nuklearen Waffen zu kommen." The documents are quoted in Schwarz, *Adenauer*, 2:299. For a French translation, see Hans-Peter Schwarz, "Adenauer, le nucléaire, et la France," *Revue d'histoire diplomatique* 106 (1992): 300. Note also Adenauer's reference to German production of nuclear weapons in a December 19, 1956, Cabinet meeting, quoted in Greiner, "Zwischen Integration und Nation," p. 276, and also cited in Greiner's contribution to *Anfänge westdeutscher Sicherheitspolitik*, 3:734–735.

[136] Schwarz, *Adenauer*, 2:332, 394–401; the quotation is on p. 396. See also Fischer, "Die Reaktion der Bundesregierung," p. 126 (citing another source for the same key document), and giving some further information in the same vein (esp. p. 127), and Franz-Josef Strauss, *Die Erinnerungen* (Berlin: Siedler, 1989), pp. 313–314.

[137] Schwarz, *Adenauer*, 2:974. For other evidence reflecting Adenauer's desire to possess nuclear

This goal of making Germany something more than an American "atomic protectorate" obviously did not mean that Adenauer was determined to end the alliance with America or to pursue a totally independent course in international affairs. The other major western powers all wanted nuclear forces under national
control, but this did not mean that any of them wanted to end the western alliance.
Why should it be different for Germany? What Adenauer was striving for was natural, especially in the context of 1950s attitudes about nuclear weapons and nuclear warfare. But he knew that his goals would not be easy to reach. Enormous
obstacles lay in his path. The mere thought of a nuclear-armed Germany aroused
great anxiety even in the other western countries, and there was a major domestic
problem as well. So he had to proceed cautiously and opportunistically, preparing the ground for later action and testing the waters as he went.

It was for this reason that he now stressed—indeed, exaggerated—America's
"unreliability." If the United States was not to be trusted, the Europeans had the
right to build up their own defenses. At the same time, he began to talk vaguely
about the need for changes in the 1954 treaties which had limited Germany's freedom to move ahead in the nuclear area.[138] As for the unilateral declaration he had
made in conjunction with those treaties, promising that the Federal Republic
would not build nuclear weapons on her own territory, he started to tell the story
that when he made that pledge, Dulles came over to him and stated that it would
apply in accordance with the legal principle *rebus sic stantibus*. This implied that
as the general situation changed, the pledge would no longer be binding; Germany
would thus eventually be able to build nuclear weapons of her own. But although
the story was not entirely without foundation and Dulles did sometimes express
this kind of thought, the American secretary of state had not made an explicit declaration to that effect at the time.[139] If Adenauer was exaggerating things, it was
because this helped clear the way for measures that would lead to a greater degree
of German strategic independence—that is, for an eventual German nuclear program. Similarly, in 1961, Strauss intimated that the 1954 pledge was binding only
as long as NATO was able to protect Germany. To argue that the NATO system

---

weapons, see the record of the Adenauer-Gaillard meeting of December 15, 1957, quoted ibid., p. 400,
and the discussion based on some new material from the Blankenhorn Papers in Soutou, "Les accords
de 1957 et 1958," pp. 141–142. For additional information bearing on the question, and especially on
the views of foreign minister Brentano and defense minister Strauss, see Daniel Kosthorst, *Brentano und
die deutsche Einheit: Die Deutschland- und Ostpolitik des Aussenministers im Kabinett Adenauer 1955–1961*
(Düsseldorf: Droste, 1993), pp. 137–143; Pertti Ahonen, "Franz-Josef Strauss and the German Nuclear
Question, 1956–1962," *Journal of Strategic Studies* 18:2 (June 1995), esp. pp. 32–34; and (also on
Strauss) Soutou, *L'Alliance incertaine*, p. 77.

[138] See, for example, Fischer, "Reaktion der Bundesregierung," p. 117. Note also Lloyd's comments
in meetings with French officials, November 12, 1959, DDF 1959, 2:558.

[139] Schwarz, *Adenauer*, 2:157–158, 299. For the best analysis of this issue, see Hanns Jürgen
Küsters, "Souveränität und ABC-Waffen-Verzicht: Deutsche Diplomatie auf der Londoner Neunmächte-Konferenz 1954," *Vierteljahrshefte für Zeitgeschichte* 42 (1994): 531–535. For a Dulles comment along these lines, see Dulles-Brentano meeting, November 21, 1957, p. 10, 740.5/11–2157, RG
59, USNA. The German foreign minister had raised the NATO nuclear issue, and Dulles told him that
"he knew that at the time of the London and Paris Agreements, and to some extent still, atomic weapons
were regarded as something apart, both from a political and a moral viewpoint. He did not think this
would always be the situation."

and American power did not give the Federal Republic the security she needed— and Adenauer's complaints about America implied that Germany did not feel fully protected by existing arrangements—was thus to suggest that the Germany was entitled to some real control over what was obviously the dominant form of military power.[140]

Collaboration with France seemed at times to offer an important avenue of advance. Adenauer understood that it was easier, especially given the American attitude and political conditions within Germany, to move ahead in a "European" framework than for Germany to proceed on a purely national basis.[141] In October 1956, in a meeting with the French ambassador, he attacked the Americans for trying to keep nuclear weapons away from their allies, and linked this to what he saw as the prospect of America making a direct deal with Russia, selling out Europe in the process. He returned to the theme a month later. The European countries, he told some rather astonished French leaders, had to "unite against America."[142] But Europe, he felt, could become a power factor only if it had some sort of nuclear capability of its own. The European countries should therefore cooperate with each other in developing nuclear forces: hence his interest first in Euratom in 1956 and then in the FIG arrangements in 1957 and early 1958.

After de Gaulle returned to power in 1958 and put a final end to the FIG project, the only road that remained open was the American stockpile plan. This brought Germany closer to a nuclear force of her own, and as a NATO arrangement it was more acceptable to other countries than a nuclear force under full national control. The stockpile plan, however, was simply a way station. In 1960 especially, there were many indications that the German government wanted to go a good deal further—although Adenauer understood that he could not be too open about his nuclear ambitions.[143]

[140] See Ahonen, "Strauss and the German Nuclear Question," p. 29, and the November 22, 1961, document cited there. See also n. 71 in the Ahonen article for a German document reporting Norstad's "concern and disappointment" regarding "Strauss's and Adenauer's lack of confidence in the U.S."

[141] See especially Adenauer to Erhard, April 13, 1956, quoted in Schwarz, *Adenauer*, 2:291.

[142] Couve to Pineau, October 10, 1956, DDF 1956, 2:553–554; Adenauer-Mollet meeting, November 6, 1956, ibid., 3:234–237. For the French reaction, see Schwarz, *Adenauer*, 2:306. Three weeks later the Americans were given a detailed account of the November 6 meeting by a French official in Washington, who read "substantial parts" of the minutes of the meeting. Meeting with Reinstein, November 27, 1956, 611.62A/11–2756, RG 59, USNA. One should note that Adenauer's initiative did not result from a sudden change in his thinking. His interest in giving continental Europe a strategic personality of its own—in making western Europe something more than a protectorate of the United States—was apparent very early on. In late 1950, for example, just before the Pleven Plan was proposed, he had urged the French government to take the lead in calling for a European army under a French commander: Germany "did not want to take her place in an American army." Bérard to Foreign Ministry, mid-October 1950, ff. 6–8, Europe 1949–55/Allemagne/70/FFMA. Note also Bérard's very interesting commentary on this, stressing the parallels between German and French policy, in Bérard to Foreign Ministry, October 17, 1950, same volume, ff. 15–19.

[143] See, for example, Herter's comments in a meeting with Lloyd and Couve, June 1, 1960, FRUS 1958–60, 7(2):375–376. The Germans were quite interested in eventually acquiring Polaris missiles, although they felt they could not be too open about this: the issue, one key German official said in October 1960, was still "too hot to discuss." See Morris to Herter, October 6, 1960, Bonn Embassy Files, 1959–61, box 21, RG 84, USNA. Note also Strauss's point at about the same time that the Germans would be able to place large defense orders in the United States (which the Americans very much

A NATO nuclear force, with missiles able to destroy targets well within the Soviet Union, was yet another step in the right direction, so the chancellor backed this idea and indeed was ready to tell the Americans what he thought they wanted to hear. The NATO force, he said, was necessary to head off an independent German program. The French argument that a country without its own nuclear force was a mere satellite had angered him, Adenauer told Norstad in September 1960. He was afraid that French nationalism would lead to German nationalism, and that after he was gone, no successor would be strong enough to oppose a German national force. The NATO MRBM plan was the only solution. If that plan failed, "nobody would be able to prevent Germany in the future from creating such a system for itself. And Germany could do that better and sooner than France!"[144]

Adenauer's strategy was to stress the points that the world could most easily accept: that a system based on total American control was unacceptable, that Germany could not be discriminated against, that the Bundeswehr had to be armed with the same weapons as the other NATO armies, that a special military status for the Federal Republic was a step toward neutralization and was therefore out of the question. The members of NATO, he told British leaders in early 1961, "could not accept that these weapons would only be used on the orders of the United States President, since in an emergency things might look very differently from Washington. Unless the situation was changed, one or another member would start to manufacture its own weapons, which were cheaper now. France was already doing so, and she would not be the last." The implication was clear enough. It was not hard to imagine which he thought the next country would be.[145]

To be sure, he now officially supported the idea of a NATO nuclear force, and said—in the meeting with the British, for example—that SACEUR had to have the authority to use the weapons, but "not in his capacity as a United States General." In reality, however, a system that put the most fundamental decisions about war and peace in the hands of a military officer, especially an American general, could never be fully satisfactory to a political creature like Adenauer, and at no point was he enthusiastic about the idea of a NATO multilateral force under the control of SACEUR.[146] He thus often spoke about "European," and not just German, needs in this area, implying that some kind of European force, not subject to an American veto, might be a possible solution. But he was probably not thinking in terms

wanted for balance of payments reasons) only if they could get advanced weapons "like Polaris." Burgess to Herter, December 17, 1960, 762a.5-MSP/12–1760, RG 59, USNA. Both of these documents were provided by Hubert Zimmermann.

[144] Stikker to Acheson, December 19, 1960, AP/85/State Department and White House Advisor [SDWHA], HSTL. For Norstad's account of this four-hour luncheon meeting, see Thurston to Herter, September 10, 1960, SS/ITM/5/NATO(4) [1959–1960]/DDEL. This document was released in full in 1978; a copy of the same document in the Norstad Papers, box 90, was reviewed for declassification in 1992, and most of the important parts were deleted. For Adenauer's handling of the issue, and especially for more information on the way he manipulated American perceptions, see appendix 4, "The Politics of the Nuclear Sharing Question" (IS).

[145] For the quotation: Adenauer-Macmillan meeting, February 23, 1961, p. 5, Prem 11/3345, PRO. See also the views he expressed in a meeting with Norstad and Stikker, September 10, 1962, NP/90/NATO General (1)/DDEL (p. 4 in the document). For Adenauer's basic thinking on these issues, see Schwarz, *Adenauer,* 2:157–158, 299, 330–332, 396, 431, 501, 554, 813.

[146] Ibid., pp. 811, 813.

of a true pooling of sovereignty and of a force controlled by a supranational European authority. He was a good European, he said, but not a "super-European." He understood that a true European political union was not in the cards, not for many years at any rate.[147] That meant that a European force would have to be built up from national components, coordinated within, even integrated into, the common structure, but ultimately under national control—that is, the same way NATO as a whole was organized.

By taking the line he did, Adenauer was thus killing a number of birds with one stone. By supporting the plan for a NATO nuclear force, he was ingratiating himself with the Americans, and confirming their view of him as a key ally in the struggle against the dark forces of German nationalism—someone who had to be supported and whose views, especially in the key nuclear area, needed to be accommodated.[148] At home, he would be coming across as an "Atlanticist": people could be confident that he was not the one who would put Germany's vital relations with America at risk.[149] But at the time he was taking another step toward achieving his nuclear objectives. The Americans might agree that the NATO force would be built up from national contingents, ultimately under national control. A German force would then emerge as the Federal Republic's contribution to the NATO force, and the NATO framework would legitimate the German nuclear effort. But if things did not work out this way—if the NATO effort failed or was deemed inadequate—Germany would be justified in moving ahead in this area, if possible, together with her European friends.[150] The NATO project, after all, was based on the premise that Europe needed "something" in the nuclear area, free of American control; and if an effective NATO force could not be set up, that principle meant that it was legitimate for the individual countries, including Germany, to proceed on a national basis. Indeed, the chancellor predicted in late 1960 that if there was no agreement on a NATO force in which France participated, Germany would begin to build a nuclear force of her own—and he took this position knowing full well that de Gaulle did not support the idea of a NATO force and would take no part in such an arrangement.[151] This was just a prediction, and his tone might even have been regretful: Adenauer certainly wanted to make his po-

[147] Ibid., p. 298.

[148] Note especially in this context the way Adenauer used Strauss, described in some detail in appendix 4 (IS).

[149] Note especially his comments in his October 7, 1960, meeting with Debré, quoted in Adenauer, *Erinnerungen,* 4:75.

[150] For example, Strauss called in November 1961 for a NATO nuclear force "composed of national contingents," and told the Americans that if no progress were made on this proposal, he might then seek to create such a force on a European basis. Earlier that year, he had again begun to press for Franco-German nuclear collaboration. McNamara to Strauss, December 5, 1961, DDRS 1997/1255; Georges-Henri Soutou, "Le Général de Gaulle et le Plan Fouchet d'union politique européenne: Un projet stratégique," *Revue d'Allemagne* 29 (1997): 216.

[151] At the Rambouillet meeting with de Gaulle on July 29–30, 1960, Adenauer made an argument that a French diplomat paraphrased as follows: "Il fait d'ailleurs savoir que, faute d'un accord sur une force nucléaire de l'OTAN avec la participation française, l'Allemagne se lancera dans une aventure nucléaire nationale.'" De Leusse note, October 26, 1960, quoted in Vaïsse, "Indépendance et solidarité," p. 236. For Adenauer's understanding of de Gaulle's position on a NATO force, see, for example, Schwarz, "Adenauer, le nucléaire, et la France," p. 307.

sition as palatable as possible to his allies, and to come across as the great opponent of German nationalistic tendencies. But he was doing important spadework:
he was preparing the ground for a policy he wanted Germany eventually to adopt.

Adenauer complained to the Americans about France, but the new thrust of
French policy fit in perfectly with what he was trying to do. The basic philosophy
that de Gaulle was articulating—the idea that Europe could not depend so heavily on America, that the European countries had to take charge of their own destiny, and that they therefore had to acquire nuclear forces under their own control—struck just the right chord as far as Adenauer was concerned. This was not
a philosophy which he himself could openly espouse. Germany was too dependent on America and too burdened by the past for him to take that kind of line in
public. But de Gaulle was doing his work for him. The French leader was establishing the legitimacy of principles which could sooner or later be taken over,
ready-made, and put at the heart of German policy. From Adenauer's point of
view, it did not matter all that much that on a whole series of issues France and
Germany were at odds. De Gaulle's proposal for an Anglo-Franco-American directorate obviously had little appeal for Germany; the French leader's acceptance
of the Oder-Neisse line as a reunified Germany's final border was not in line with
German policy, which wanted to keep the issue formally open as a bargaining chip;
his apparent opposition to German nuclear weapons, reflected in the cancellation
of the FIG agreements, also ran counter to Adenauer's policy. But none of this was
of fundamental importance. What really mattered was what de Gaulle stood for.
It was his basic political message that resonated with Adenauer, and that fact lay
at the heart of an increasingly close Franco-German relationship. Adenauer sympathized with the basic thrust of de Gaulle's policy. In particular, he strongly supported the French nuclear program—although here again, for tactical reasons, he
sought to give the Americans the opposite impression.[152]

So by 1960 serious problems were beginning to develop within the western alliance. America and Europe were increasingly at odds in the nuclear area. The three
main European allies had all come, in their different ways, to see nuclear forces
under their own control as of fundamental importance, while American policy, or
at least State Department policy, had evidently turned against the idea of nuclear
capabilities under national control.

This conflict between the United States and the European allies on the nuclear
issue was a basic source of tension, but it is important to see it in context: the western political system as a whole was in disarray, and the problems were growing. On
the most fundamental issues, the western countries did not quite know what they
wanted or how to go about achieving their goals. Britain and France, for example,
both very much wanted to keep Germany from becoming too powerful and inde-

---

[152] For Adenauer's support of the French program, see Adenauer-Debré-Couve meeting, December
1, 1959, and Adenauer–de Gaulle meeting, December 2, 1959, DDF 1959, 2:653; Adenauer-Debré
meeting, October 7, 1960, Adenauer, *Erinnerungen*, 4:71; Adenauer–de Gaulle meeting, January 22,
1963, AAPBD 1963, 1:141. For an example of Adenauer giving the Americans the opposite impression, see the account of his meeting with U.S. Under Secretary of State George Ball in January 1963, in
Richard Neustadt, "Skybolt and Nassau: American Policy-Making and Anglo-American Relations," November 1963, pp. 106–107, NSF/322/Staff Memoranda: Neustadt/JFKL. See also appendix 4 (IS).

pendent, but each had adopted a set of policies that pulled in the opposite direction. The presence of western troops, and especially American troops, on German soil was the heart of the NATO system, and this system had been designed in large part to keep Germany from posing a threat to the status quo. Yet the British were attracted to the general idea of disengagement, favored even unilateral cutbacks in allied troop strength in Germany, and to rationalize those reductions in force levels supported a change in NATO military strategy that would place much greater emphasis on nuclear deterrence—policies that not only tended to undermine the system for limiting German power and independence, but also directly alienated the Germans and weakened the bonds of confidence tying Germany to the West.

For France also, the control of German power was a fundamental goal, yet de Gaulle seemed determined to destroy the system that had been designed to keep Germany from becoming too strong and too independent. In de Gaulle's view, America was a hegemonic power and sought to keep the European nations down. If the Europeans were to assert their own political identities, the American grip had to be broken. NATO was the instrument of American hegemony; the NATO structure therefore had to be radically transformed. The message was that the American presence was no longer appreciated; the implication was that the Europeans countries would ultimately have to look to themselves for their security. All this was a matter of basic political philosophy and had little to do with anything the United States had actually done. But it was hard to see how this policy fit in with the other fundamental goal of making sure that Germany did not pose a threat to European stability. The American presence was the linchpin of the structure within which German power was contained, a structure which made it possible to keep the Soviets at bay without a massive buildup of German power. Why, then, did de Gaulle seem determined to wreck that very structure? And in particular, wouldn't a nationalistic French policy, especially a policy of nuclear independence, by its very nature encourage the Federal Republic to go down the same path?

As for the Germans themselves, a policy of reaching for political, and thus military, independence made eminent sense, except for one thing. It was natural that the German government would not want to be so absolutely dependent on the United States for protection, and thus would want a nuclear force of its own. The only problem was that the Soviets were dead set against the idea of a German nuclear capability. Did it make sense, in such circumstances, to provoke the USSR by trying to establish German nuclear independence? The Soviets might react violently; it would be very easy for them to put pressure on the west by again threatening Berlin. If Adenauer had been willing to go to war over the Berlin issue or, alternatively, had been prepared to write off the city and allow it to fall into Communist hands, then his policy would at least have been consistent. But as it turned out, he was neither willing to go all the way and accept a real military confrontation over Berlin, nor was he prepared to accept the very serious and possibly catastrophic long-term political consequences that a sacrifice of Berlin would entail. It was as though he had not thought the problem through—as though he were determined to move ahead without regard for the consequences.[153]

---

[153] These issues will be treated in some detail in the next two chapters.

The whole situation was a mess. Problem had been piled on top of problem. And the United States, by far the most important western power and thus the leader of the western alliance, did not really know how to proceed. By 1960 it seemed, in fact, that Eisenhower had lost his grip on policy.

EISENHOWER AT LOOSE ENDS

Secretary Herter was scheduled to give a major speech at the December 1960 NATO Council meeting in Paris. That speech was supposed to lay out the administration's basic thinking on the future of the alliance. Eisenhower wanted to take advantage of this opportunity to leave a kind of testament: as noted above, he wanted to leave "a legacy of the finest ideas and plans this administration could develop."[154] Yet the position Herter took at the Paris meeting did not come close to capturing the president's fundamental point of view. Herter's call for a "substantial conventional capability" in Europe so as to give NATO commanders the "flexibility of response" they needed clearly did not reflect Eisenhower's thinking. The "flexible response" line implied that the large U.S. troop presence in Europe would have to be maintained indefinitely, which again directly contradicted the president's basic point of view. Eisenhower had wanted to take a relatively tough line with the Europeans. He thought they needed to be told that the time had come for them to take on more of the burden of providing for their own defense—that a "redeployment" of U.S. forces was now necessary, if only for balance of payments reasons. The State Department, however, did not see things that way at all, and Herter's language on this point remained quite mild—far too mild, in fact, for Eisenhower's taste. It "was not as tough a statement," the president said, "as he would have made."[155]

The line Herter took on the NATO nuclear issue was also very much at variance with Eisenhower's thinking. It was not just that the Herter speech was considerably more hostile to "additional national nuclear weapons capabilities" than Eisenhower ever was. The more important point is that it failed to propose anything real as an alternative. The whole Eisenhower concept of an independent European nuclear force, not subject to an American veto, and under the command of a European SACEUR, was not held out to the Europeans even as an ultimate goal. These aspects of the president's thinking, although they surfaced from time to time in the press, were but dimly reflected in the Herter statement. The control of the force would be "truly multilateral," Herter said, without making it at all clear what this was supposed to mean, and in particular whether America would be giving up her veto on the use of the weapons. "A suitable formula to govern" use of the force would be worked out eventually, which was another way of saying that the United States had no answer to this question right now. A NATO *strategic* force was simply an "extremely interesting thought." The NATO MRBMs might form the basis of such a force. Or they might not, since, as Herter pointed out, they were "required as modernization of the *tactical* strike capability." But on the other hand,

---

[154] NSC meeting, November 17, 1960, FRUS 1958–60, 7(1):654.

[155] NSC meeting, December 22, 1960, p. 16, AWF/NSC/13/DDEL.

the "line between 'tactical' and 'strategic' capabilities" was becoming "ever more blurred." In any event, the NATO MRBMs would be targeted in "coordination" with external forces such as SAC, a point that suggested that the U.S. government was not thinking in terms of an *independent* NATO force. This was not a plan for giving "NATO," let alone NATO Europe, independent power in the area of nuclear war-fighting. At most, the door was being left open for the "exploration of the concept of increasing the authority of the Alliance" in the nuclear area. The basic Eisenhower concept had been watered down practically beyond recognition, and there was very little in the plan to capture the imagination of the Europeans. None of this is to be understood in domestic political terms. The administration was about to leave office and was thus free to speak its mind and say where it thought the alliance ought to be headed. But it was evident from the Herter speech that it was incapable of laying out a clear concept.[156]

If the December 17 statement did not reflect the president's own point of view, this was because Eisenhower was no longer the same man who had taken control of the policymaking process in 1953–54. The president had no great personal regard for Herter, and he knew that the State Department as a whole was fundamentally out of sympathy with his basic thinking.[157] He in fact complained sharply from time to time about the behavior of American officials. In 1960, for example, he told Norstad that he had become "very dissatisfied regarding our relationships with our allies in the matter of atomic weapons and missiles. The US Government seems to be taking the attitude that we will call the tune, and that they have inferior status in the alliance."[158] But he was no longer willing to put his foot down and make the State Department follow his lead. To be sure, in the formal policy documents, his views had to be taken into account, and the final texts did not take as firm a line as the State Department would have liked.[159] But the president, for his part, did not insist on language that really expressed his own thinking. The result was that by 1959 and 1960 the BNSPs included provisions that reflected both the pro- and the anti-sharing point of view—that is, phrases that each side could cite as a warrant for its own policy position.[160]

---

[156] The point was understood by the more perceptive American officials at the time. See, for example, Kohler to Herter, November 9, 1960, Records Relating to State Department Participation in the National Security Council, 1947–61, box 107, NSC 6017 memorandums, RG 59, USNA. For the text of the Herter statement, see FRUS 1958–60, 7(1):674–682.

[157] Neither Eisenhower nor Dulles had been enthusiastic about the prospect of Herter taking over as secretary of state, but they felt that he would be acceptable given that the administration did not have many months left in office. See Dulles-Eisenhower meeting, April 13, 1959, DP/WHM/7/DDEL.

[158] Eisenhower-Norstad meeting, August 3, 1960, FRUS 1950–60, 7(1):609–610.

[159] Thus the State Department–backed proposal for the 1959 BNSP paper had said that the United States should try to "prevent" additional countries from developing "national nuclear weapons capabilities"; after discussion in the NSC, this was softened to a passage simply calling upon the government to "discourage" efforts in this direction, with exceptions to be determined by the president. NSC meetings, July 16 and 30, 1959, and NSC 5906/1, August 5, 1959, FRUS 1958–60, 3:259–261, 288–290, 298. For another example, note how the majority proposal for putting off a study of bilateral nuclear cooperation with France was defeated after a discussion at the NSC level in which Eisenhower laid out his basic pro-sharing philosophy. Briefing note for, and notes of, October 29, 1959, NSC meeting, ibid., 7(2):290 n, 290–295.

[160] The 1959 BNSP paper, NSC 5906/1, reaffirmed nonproliferation as a fundamental policy objective—the importance of preventing the spread of "national nuclear capabilities" had initially been

It was as though there was no longer a strong hand on the rudder. Even America's friends in Europe were shaken by certain clear signs that Secretary Herter, in particular, was out of his depth.[161] People wondered whether the U.S. government was fit to lead the western bloc. The French, especially, had their doubts.[162] The whole "tripartism" affair of 1959–60, in particular, raised serious questions in their minds about American competence in the whole foreign policy area. This episode is in fact quite extraordinary, and is worth examining in some detail for the light it sheds on the way the American government was conducting its affairs in the late Eisenhower period. It also helps explain why de Gaulle dealt with America the way he did later on, especially in January 1963.[163]

The story begins with de Gaulle's famous memorandum of September 1958, which proposed that America, Britain and France set up an organization to make "joint decisions on political questions affecting world security." That tripartite body, he said, would not just work out common military plans, but would also oversee their implementation.[164] The basic concept was not new. Beginning in the late 1940s, the French had from time to time called for setting up some kind of tripartite body to deal with these basic issues of policy, and in particular to deal with military and especially nuclear issues.[165] But for de Gaulle, the idea was a centerpiece of his policy, and in spite of a series of disappointments, he remained interested in it well into the Kennedy period.[166]

---

recognized in the 1958 BNSP—but it also called for giving the president the authority to "enhance the nuclear weapons capability of selected allies" by turning over nuclear information, materials, or even weapons, under control arrangements "to be determined." This provision was very far-reaching; a similar provision had been considered too extreme for inclusion in the 1957 BNSP. The BNSPs are published in Trachtenberg, *Development of American Strategic Thought,* vol. 1; for the relevant passage in NSC 5906/1, see FRUS 1958–60, 3:298. For the point about this provision being considered too radical two years earlier, see NSC meeting, May 27, 1957, FRUS 1955–57 19:495–499.

[161] At one point, for example, Herter stated that he could not imagine the president involving the country in general war unless America was about to suffer a devastating nuclear attack. This was shocking because it showed that he did not understand what America's basic policy for the defense of Europe actually was. The key sentence is quoted in a State Department circular telegram of July 10, 1959, FRUS 1958–60, 7(1):466.

[162] See, for example, the de Gaulle remark quoted in Alphand, *L'étonnement d'être,* p. 318.

[163] It is also worth noting that the true story does not appear in the background memoranda on the tripartism question that the State Department prepared for the new Kennedy administration in 1961. See, for example, the State Department memorandum on tripartism, January 24, 1961, FRUS 1961–63, 13:641–644, and another such memorandum, dated May 22, 1961, in "De Gaulle, Book 2," box 153, Ball Papers, ML. The full story is also missing from the Tyler memorandum on the issue, February 3, 1964, DDRS 1991/2543.

[164] For the original text, see DDF 1958, 2:377. For an English translation, see FRUS 1958–60, 7(2):82–83. The French text in de Gaulle, LNC 1958–60, pp. 83–84, is somewhat inaccurate: the reference in the original text to an organization consisting of "the United States, Great Britain, and France" was deleted here, as though even the Gaullists who had published this version of the document were embarrassed by a direct reference to the three powers by name. The memorandum is discussed in detail in Maurice Vaïsse, "Aux origines du mémorandum de septembre 1958," *Relations internationales,* no. 58 (Summer 1989): 253–268, and also in Vaïsse, "Indépendance et solidarité."

[165] See, for example, Irwin Wall, *The United States and the Making of Postwar France,* p. 133; and Dulles-Mendès meeting, November 20, 1954, SSMC, no. 800.

[166] Alphand, *L'étonnement d'être,* pp. 333, 353, 355. See also draft instructions for French ambassador in Washington, late January 1961; de Gaulle to Debré and Couve, June 13, 1961; de Gaulle to

The U.S. government disliked the idea of a formal organization. A formal body would embitter the allies who were not included. But this did not mean that Eisenhower shut the door completely on the de Gaulle proposal. As he wrote Dulles at the end of 1958, he was against doing "this 3 power business *unless* we *have* to."[167]

A year later, Eisenhower felt the time had come to make a formal proposal. He met with de Gaulle and Macmillan at Rambouillet in December 1959. At the very start of their first session, he called for "the establishment of a tripartite machinery to operate on a clandestine basis with the object of discussing questions of common interest to the three Governments." His idea was "that each country should supply one or two men who should not only be competent but also of specially good judgment and of reasonably high rank. There might perhaps be someone on the political side, a military figure and an economist." De Gaulle was pleased with the proposal, which seemed to have come out of the blue. Macmillan, although astonished, was also happy to go along, and thought he could capitalize on his support for the proposal by getting de Gaulle to be more accommodating on trade issues, a fundamental concern for the British at this point. "We should not be obstructive about establishing the Tripartite group in London," the prime minister said, "tiresome though this may be for us in some ways."[168]

All of this, however, came as a big surprise to the State Department. Herter had been left entirely in the dark. The British, in fact, had to show him their record of the meeting where Eisenhower had made his proposal. It was always hard for the State Department, Herter complained, "to find out what had taken place at meetings where the President had only been accompanied by an interpreter." And the secretary of state was not pleased by what he had learned. Eisenhower had suggested setting up the secret "tripartite machinery" on December 20; on December 21, Selwyn Lloyd, the British foreign secretary, got the impression, after telling Herter what had been proposed, that his American counterpart "clearly felt that continuation of the present system should be our aim and should suffice."[169]

Soon the State Department began to backpedal. Instead of "tripartite machinery," Herter proposed informal talks over dinner; the main U.S. representative would be a diplomat in the London embassy, not even the ambassador.[170] The

---

Kennedy, January 11, 1962; in Charles de Gaulle, *Letters, notes et carnets (1961–1963)* (Paris: Plon, 1986) [LNC 1961–63], pp. 30, 96, 194.

[167] Dulles to Eisenhower, October 15, 1958, FRUS 1958–60, 7(2):100; emphasis in original. Dulles himself was not fundamentally opposed to the idea, and seemed willing to go along with the three-power plan provided that the arrangements were kept relatively informal. When he met with de Gaulle in July, Dulles told the French leader that "formalization of groupings for directing the free world would be resented, but there was no reason why this should not exist in fact." He took the same line in November. Ibid., pp. 57, 118. Professionals like Chauvel were more than willing to proceed on that basis, but they could not convince de Gaulle that the reality was more important than the form. See Chauvel, *Commentaire*, 3:265.

[168] De Gaulle–Eisenhower-Macmillan meeting, December 20, 1959, Prem 11/2991, PRO, and DDF 1959, 2:765. Macmillan to Lloyd, December 22 and 23, 1959, FO 371/152095; Macmillan to chancellor of the Exchequer, December 22, 1959, Prem 11/2996; all PRO.

[169] Herter-Lloyd meeting, December 20, 1959, Prem 11/2987, and extract from record of Herter-Lloyd meeting, December 21, 1959, FO 371/152095; both PRO.

[170] Macmillan to Lloyd, December 23, 1959, and Herter to Lloyd, December 30, 1959, FO 371/152095, PRO.

British Foreign Office took a similar view.[171] When the French responded by pressing for the establishment of the sort of "tripartite machinery" de Gaulle had called for in September 1958, Herter sought to "sidestep" that proposal.[172] Not only that, but in his reply to the French foreign minister, he actually claimed that it had been de Gaulle and not Eisenhower who at Rambouillet had raised the idea of holding "private tripartite talks," even though the British record, the best evidence he had, shows quite clearly that this indeed had been Eisenhower's proposal. Basically all that Herter was willing to accept was a continuation of the tripartite talks that were already taking place in Washington: "we for our part are only too happy to leave matters as they now stand." The Americans, as a British diplomat happily pointed out, were pouring "as much water as possible into the rather heady wine of the Eisenhower proposals of last December."[173]

The French were clearly disappointed. The French ambassador in London discussed the matter with de Gaulle and "had formed the distinct impression that de Gaulle had now rather lost interest in this matter."[174] But Eisenhower could not understand the French reaction. He was "quite astonished" by the French attitude, especially by their interest in formal structures. His plan at Rambouillet, he said, had been to bring together "one or two junior but capable staff officers" from each country to keep on top of issues of common concern, and it had seemed then that de Gaulle had been happy to go along. "Just where it jumped the track," he wrote Macmillan, "I do not know."[175]

Not only had Eisenhower allowed the State Department to sabotage his proposal, but he was not even aware of what had happened. It is not hard to imagine how de Gaulle must have reacted. The episode tended to confirm many of his prejudices about America. The Americans did not know how to pursue an effective foreign policy. The president was not quite in control. The U.S. government, it seemed, was like a congeries of semiautonomous fiefdoms. De Gaulle himself would not tolerate for a minute in France the sort of independent action that was evidently par for the course in the American policymaking system[176] The United States was obviously a very strong country, but did American leaders really know how to manage the enormous power they possessed? It was the moral authority of the United States, America's fitness to lead the West, that was brought into question by episodes of this sort.

Indeed, by the end of the Eisenhower period, the world in general had the sense of an administration at loose ends, soft and flaccid and incapable of steering a clear

[171] Hoyer Millar to Jebb and to Caccia, both January 10, 1960, both in FO 371/152095, PRO.

[172] Couve to Herter, January 23, 1960, and Herter to Lloyd, February 3, 1960, both FO 371/152095, PRO.

[173] Herter to Couve, February 3, 1960, FO 371/152095; Roberts to Dean, February 12, 1960, FO 371/152096, PRO.

[174] Hoyer Millar note, February 19, 1960, and draft of letter from Lloyd to Herter, February 18, 1960, both in FO 371/152096, PRO.

[175] Eisenhower to Macmillan, February 18, 1960, FO 371/152096, PRO.

[176] For de Gaulle's iron control within the French government, see, for example, Chauvel, *Commentaire,* 3:273. Note also de Gaulle's rather understated comment in a meeting with Macmillan: "It seemed that the United States was a very difficult country to govern." De Gaulle–Macmillan meeting, December 21, 1959, p. 10, Prem 11/2996, PRO.

Figure 8. *Top left:* President-Elect Eisenhower in Korea, December 1952 (Eisenhower Library). *Top right:* President Eisenhower in his last year in office (Eisenhower Library). *Bottom:* Secretary of State Christian Herter, with British Foreign Secretary Selwyn Lloyd (*left*) and French Foreign Minister Maurice Couve de Murville (*right*), in Geneva, May 1959 (Archive Photos).

course. This impression played a key role during the American presidential election campaign in 1960, and many Europeans also felt that something was amiss. On September 9, Norstad met with Adenauer and two other west European leaders. The sense of the discussion was that the Eisenhower policy of "leadership by generosity" had failed, and that the U.S. needed to take a stronger and clearer line.[177] A year earlier, NATO Secretary General Paul-Henri Spaak had told Eisenhower directly "that the United States is too kind, too indulgent," and that "sometimes it is necessary to speak out with full strength."[178] And Adenauer, in his first meeting with President Kennedy in early 1961, also stressed the importance of America playing a stronger role in the alliance.[179] When the gods wish to punish us, they answer our prayers: the policy of "leadership by generosity" would end in 1961, and under Kennedy America would become far more assertive in her dealings with the NATO allies. But the Europeans—and Adenauer above all—would not be too happy with what they were about to get.

In the late Eisenhower period, however, it was not at all clear how things would develop. Everything was very much up in the air. The great issues of the defense of the West, the control of nuclear weapons, and Germany's place in the international system were all still unresolved. The whole idea of a German nuclear force, and thus of a strong Germany with a truly independent foreign policy, was by no means out of the question. There might be no way to prevent the Germans from building such a force. Europe could not depend so completely on America; an integrated NATO, or even European, force might not be viable or meaningful as an alternative; national forces might be the only answer. Britain and France were going to have forces of this sort. How could Germany, more exposed than they were, accept a permanent non-nuclear status?

A system based on the control of German power, the sort of system that the Paris accords had been designed to establish, had not really taken root. Germany was in the process of getting effective control over nuclear weapons, and no one could tell how far that process would actually go. For the USSR, this question of a German nuclear capability was of fundamental importance. A non-nuclear Federal Republic, dependent on the western powers for protection, was no problem, but a nuclearized Germany, able to play her own hand in international politics, was another matter entirely. And the Americans, it now seemed, were moving ahead with a policy that might well lead to a real German nuclear capability. They were arming the Germans with nuclear weapons, and by 1960 Eisenhower was publicly calling for a change in the law to make a more liberal sharing policy possible. "I have always believed," he told the press, "that we should not deny to our allies what our enemies or potential enemies already have. Allies should be treated as allies, not as junior members of a firm who are to be seen but not heard."[180]

This, in fact, had been the president's view for many years. In 1957 and 1958, the Soviets saw what the United States was doing in Europe. They saw an Ameri-

---

[177] Thurston to Herter, September 10, 1960, SS/ITM/5/NATO (4) [1959–1960]/DDEL.

[178] Eisenhower-Spaak meeting, November 24, 1959, DDRS 1987/291.

[179] Adenauer-Kennedy meeting, April 12, 1961, FRUS 1961–63, 13:274.

[180] Eisenhower's February 3, 1960, press conference, *Public Papers of the Presidents* [PPP]: *Eisenhower* (1960), pp. 148, 152.

can policy which they had every reason to fear was leading directly to a German nuclear capability. From their point of view, events could not simply be allowed to run their course. They had earlier tried to deal with this problem through diplomacy, but that effort had failed. Of the western powers, only Britain had been interested in the Soviet-backed idea of a nuclear-free zone in central Europe. So tougher measures might now be necessary.

Berlin was the obvious lever, since the vulnerability of West Berlin made it easy for the Soviets to exert pressure. The "Berlin question," Khrushchev bluntly told the American ambassador in Moscow, Llewellyn Thompson, "was one of geography that he intended [to] make use of." Thompson thought he knew what the Soviet leader's real goal was. "Khrushchev," he cabled Washington in November 1958, "is a man in a hurry and considers that time is against him," especially on the German nuclear issue. The western powers, he advised, had better get ready for a "major showdown" with Russia.[181]

That showdown was not long in coming. The great Berlin crisis of 1958 to 1962, the central episode of the Cold War, began that very month.

[181] See Trachtenberg, *History and Strategy,* pp. 171, 191.

PART III

The Cold War Peace

The Politics of the Berlin Crisis, 1958–1960

IN NOVEMBER 1958, the Soviet leader Nikita Khrushchev announced that his government was going to sign a peace treaty with East Germany. When it did so, he said, western rights in Berlin would be ended. He would give the western powers six months to negotiate a settlement that would transform West Berlin into a "free city." If, however, the western powers refused to work out a settlement on that basis and sought instead to maintain their position through military force, the USSR would "rise in defense" of her East German ally. The Soviet Union was thus threatening war if her demands were not met, and this led to a great crisis which lasted with varying degrees of intensity until the end of 1962.

What exactly was the crisis about? The Soviets were making threats, but what were they really trying to achieve? How far were they willing to go in their confrontation with the West if they were unable to achieve their objectives peacefully? And how would the western side react to Soviet pressure? What were the NATO governments willing to do to resolve the crisis, and in particular what arrangements relating to Germany as a whole would they prepared to accept? When, if at all, would they be willing to use force rather than capitulate in the crisis? The answers to these questions would determine not just the meaning of this episode but also the basic structure of great power politics during the Berlin Crisis period.[1]

SOVIET POLICY AND THE GERMAN NUCLEAR QUESTION

Soviet pressure on Berlin was rooted in the USSR's concern with Germany as a whole, and above all with what was going on in West Germany.[2] Berlin itself was not the problem. The Soviet goal was not to drive the western powers out and

---

[1] For an account of the crisis, see Trachtenberg, *History and Strategy*, chap. 5. The basic flaw in the account there is the assumption that the crisis was over by late 1961; the 1962 phase, which I now view as crucial, was totally ignored. Otherwise, that account is still essentially valid. See also Robert Slusser, "The Berlin Crises of 1958–59 and 1961," in *Force Without War*, ed. Barry Blechman et al (Washington D.C.: Brookings, 1978); Jack Schick, *The Berlin Crisis, 1958–1962* (Philadelphia: University of Pennsylvania Press, 1971); and Walther Stützle, *Kennedy und Adenauer in der Berlin-Krise 1961–1962* (Bonn: Verlag Neue Gesellschaft, 1973). There are no satisfactory archivally based book-length accounts of the crisis. For an important microfiche collection of documents on the crisis, together with a printed guide and index, see National Security Archive, *The Berlin Crisis, 1958–1962* (Alexandria, Va.: Chadwyck-Healey, 1991); the guide includes a useful chronology of the crisis.

[2] Trachtenberg, *History and Strategy*, pp. 171–172. For some additional evidence corroborating the point that Khrushchev was concerned not with Berlin primarily but rather with the German question as a whole, see Vladislav Zubok, "Khrushchev's Motives and Soviet Diplomacy in the Berlin Crisis, 1958–1962," (unpublished paper, 1994), p. 11.

eventually take over the city. If that had been the aim, the obvious strategy would have been the much less risky one of undermining the economic life of the city by cutting off civilian ground traffic with West Germany. It was clear that force would not be used in such a case.[3]

Nor was the crisis essentially about East Germany—about stabilizing the situation there, or getting the West to accept the status quo in central Europe. Any purely internal problem in East Germany could be dealt with through police measures, backed up ultimately by Soviet military power. If the flow of refugees out of East Germany via West Berlin was a problem, the Communist authorities could deal with it by sealing the border. Anything of this sort, which involved action taken in their own sphere, would be a good deal less risky than an attempt to "liquidate" unilaterally the rights of the western powers in West Berlin. The East German leaders, in fact, asked in early 1961 to be allowed to close the border, but the Soviets held back. They made it clear that their real concerns lay elsewhere—that they had bigger fish to fry and wanted to go on using the Berlin problem as a lever.[4]

Indeed, it was because the Soviets' real concern was with the German question as a whole, and not just with Berlin or the internal situation in East Germany, that western rights and thus the western powers were being targeted. The USSR wanted something from her former allies: she wanted them to keep West Germany from becoming too powerful. The western powers themselves were clearly willing to live with the status quo in central Europe, and would not use force as long as the Soviets stayed on their side of the line of demarcation. A relatively weak Federal Republic, dependent on her allies for protection, would have little choice but to pursue a purely defensive policy. But if West Germany became strong and independent, she would, as one Soviet leader told Dulles, be able to "speak in a different tone."[5] The West Germans, if they developed their power, would be more able to intervene in the event of an uprising in the east. The East Germans perhaps would be more likely to rise up in the first place if they sensed that their brothers in the west would not leave them in the lurch. And a West German intervention could have very grave consequences. It might lead to the collapse of the Communist regime in East Germany, and could conceivably lead even to general war.

A strong West German state was above all a state with a respectable nuclear force under its own control. That force did not have to be all that large for the Soviets

---

[3] See Trachtenberg, *History and Strategy*, pp. 171–172.

[4] See, especially, Soviet Ambassador in East Germany Pervukhin to Gromyko, May 19, 1961, published in Harrison, *Ulbricht and the Concrete "Rose"* appendix D. Pervukhin here referred to the "impatience" of the East German authorities in calling for a sealing of the border. This, he said, reflected their "one-sided approach to the problem," and their failure to understand the present international situation and the interests of the "socialist camp" as a whole. See also Harrison's analysis of East German pressure on pp. 23–42. Note also the recollection of one former Soviet official that the idea of a closing of the border had been ruled out, even in early 1961, because (among other things) it "would have discredited the idea of the transformation of West Berlin into a free city." Julij Kwizinskij, *Vor dem Sturm: Erinnerungen eines Diplomaten* (Berlin: Siedler, 1993), p. 161, quoted in Zubok, "Khrushchev's Motives," p. 17.

[5] Anastas Mikoyan, first deputy chairman of the Soviet Council of Ministers, in a meeting with Dulles, January 16, 1959, Merchant Papers/5/ML, for the full document; FRUS 1958–60, 8:273, for an extract containing the passage quoted. According to the full document, the Soviet leader asked Dulles directly later that day whether the U.S. government intended "to provide West Germany with atomic weapons."

to feel menaced; thermonuclear weapons are so powerful that beyond a certain point the numbers do not matter much. Given enough time, a country like West Germany certainly had the industrial and technological base to build a force capable of destroying the Soviet Union, even if the Soviets were to strike first. If Germany were to develop such a force, she could engage in the poker game of controlled—or really semicontrolled—escalation. There was no telling how a military confrontation, if one ever did develop, would run its course, but from the Soviet standpoint the risks were real: a strong Germany—and that meant a nuclearized Germany—was a danger; the present situation of a relatively weak Federal Republic, dependent on her more status quo–oriented partners, was obviously to be preferred. And since the nuclear status of West Germany would be determined, in large part, by the attitude of the western powers, it was their policy that now needed to be targeted. The western governments needed to be made to feel the brunt of Soviet displeasure. So the Soviet leadership decided to put pressure on the western powers where they were most vulnerable, and where the level of tension was easiest for the Russians to control—and that, of course, meant Berlin.

The German nuclear question thus lay at the heart of Soviet policy during the Berlin Crisis.[6] The Soviets often emphasized the importance of this issue. Anastas Mikoyan, a top Soviet leader, brought it up repeatedly in meetings with key western figures—with Adenauer in April 1958, with Eisenhower and Dulles in January 1959, and with the British foreign secretary, Lord Home, in January 1963.[7] And indeed Soviet concerns had been building up for some time. When the Soviet ambassador, for example, raised the issue on April 25, 1957, the German leaders did not even bother to conceal their nuclear ambitions. Adenauer "did not deny that the FRG might become a nuclear power," and Foreign Minister Brentano added that "if England and other powers have atomic weapons, why should the FRG not have them?" The chancellor had in fact just made a similar point in public at a press conference.[8] In 1958, the Soviets were increasingly concerned with the problem.[9] And it was certainly no mere coincidence that the Soviets provoked the crisis just as a key threshold was about to be crossed—that is, at precisely the point when the German Air Force was about to acquire a certain atomic capability. The "Wagon Train" project—the training of a German fighter-bomber unit so that "it might have a nuclear capability" and the construction of a nuclear storage facility to serve that unit—was "successfully completed" in late 1958.[10]

The German nuclear issue, in fact, played a major role in the diplomacy of the

---

[6] For some evidence from former Communist sources that supports this general interpretation, see Harrison, "Bargaining Power of Weaker Allies in Bipolarity and Crisis," pp. 169–171, 229, 244, and Zubok, "Khrushchev and the Berlin Crisis," pp. 3–5.

[7] See Bruce to Dulles, December 23, 1958, NSA, for an extract from the German account of the April 26, 1958, meeting with Adenauer; Schwarz, *Adenauer,* 2:434; Adenauer, *Erinnerungen,* 3:385, 391; Couve to Pineau, May 1, 1958, DDF 1958, 1:542; Dulles-Mikoyan meeting, January 16, 1959, Merchant Papers/5/ML; Mikoyan-Eisenhower meeting, January 17, 1959, FRUS 1958–60, 8:279; and Home-Mikoyan talk, January 26, 1963, Prem 11/4227, PRO.

[8] The Soviet document is quoted in Zubok and Pleshakov, *Inside the Kremlin's Cold War,* pp. 195–196; the relevant extract from the Adenauer press conference of April 5, 1957, is quoted in Adenauer, *Erinnerungen,* 3:296.

[9] See the evidence in Parrish, "The USSR and the Security Dilemma," pp. 334–335.

[10] Houghton to Dulles, December 20, 1958, AWF/DH/8/DDEL.

crisis from beginning to end. The Soviets raised the issue as early as November 1958, and during the Kennedy period they repeatedly stressed its importance. In July 1961, for example, their ambassador in Washington declared that a peace treaty—that is, a settlement of the German question—was "essential because things were going on in Germany which must be stopped. There was a revanchist group in Germany which was arming Germany and seeking thermonuclear weapons."[11] In October of that year, Soviet Foreign Minister Gromyko met with President Kennedy to discuss the Berlin question. What the Soviet government had in mind was the legalization of the German borders as they presently existed, and the outlawing of a nuclear capability in both parts of Germany; the USSR, he said, "placed utmost emphasis" on this latter question.[12] And these are not just isolated examples. From the mid-1950s on, the issue of "European security"—the term referred to the idea that Germany, perhaps together with certain adjacent areas, should have a special military status, above all in the nuclear area—was high on the Soviet diplomatic agenda.[13]

Western leaders took it for granted at this time that the USSR had a "real fear" of Germany and were genuinely concerned about what would happen if the Federal Republic became strong and independent.[14] They generally assumed that the issue of a German nuclear capability was a fundamental Soviet concern, and occasionally—although by no means invariably—conjectured that the Berlin Crisis was rooted, at least to a considerable extent, in Soviet anxieties about what the nuclearization of Germany might mean. Herter, for example, met with the top permanent official in the French Foreign Ministry shortly after the Soviets had provoked the crisis. The acting secretary "thought the question of preventing German possession of nuclear weapons was a key to the present Soviet attitude." The French official "agreed this was the most important single reason, probably, for present Soviet actions."[15] Ambassador Thompson thought at the beginning of the crisis that Khrushchev's view was that "with the completion in the next few years of West German rearmament, including the stationing of atomic weapons there, the position of the East German regime will become even more precarious." The

[11] Nitze-Menshikov meeting, July 15, 1961, FRUS 1961–63, 14:204.

[12] Kennedy-Gromyko meeting, October 6, 1961, FRUS 1961–63, 14:471. See also Rusk-Gromyko meeting, October 2, 1961, ibid., p. 459.

[13] The Soviets, more than anyone else, used the term "European security" to refer to the idea of a special status for Germany. Note in this context Gromyko's remarks in a meeting with Rusk, September 27, 1961, FRUS 1961–63, 14:439. Things, in fact, eventually reached the point where, whenever the Soviets brought up the issue of "European security," Couve—in that wonderfully cynical way only the French can get away with—responded by saying, in effect, "oh, you mean the German question." François Puaux, "La France, L'Allemagne et l'atome: Discorde improbable, accord impossible," *Défense nationale* 41 (December 1985): 9. The term had begun to acquire this connotation in the 1950s, which was why the Germans—and Adenauer above all—disliked the concept throughout this period. See, for example, German Foreign Minister Schröder's remarks in a meeting with the other western foreign ministers in late 1961, Schröder-Rusk-Couve-Home meeting, December 11, 1961, FO 371/160567, PRO.

[14] See, for example, Eisenhower, in a meeting with Macmillan, March 28, 1960, FRUS 1958–60, 9:258–259. For similar views from the Kennedy period, see FRUS 1961–63, 13:497, and 14:103, 204, 208, 464.

[15] Herter-Joxe meeting, November 20, 1958, DSP/80/72411/ML.

Soviet leader, he speculated, was afraid that "West German intervention in an East German revolt under such circumstances might face Khrushchev with the choice of almost certain world war or the loss of East Germany and subsequently of most or all of his satellite empire."[16] The British were also worried about the risk of war "if there was rioting in East Germany, and West Germany, having nuclear weapons, could not be restrained from going to the rescue."[17] Secretary of State Dean Rusk's view in July 1962 reflected what had by that point become the conventional wisdom. "We must remind ourselves," he said, "that the Russians really hate and fear the Germans. They are concerned about the revival of the Federal Republic and about its possible claim to nuclear weapons."[18]

Would the Soviets have been justified in thinking that there would be a greater risk of war if West Germany did acquire a nuclear capability of her own? Close observers like Thompson took it for granted that "a people as strong and as virile" as the Germans would not for long accept the division of their country, "particularly when they are well armed," and that given Soviet policy, it was hard to see "how Germany could ever be put together again except by force."[19] And there were in fact indications that the Germans themselves were not happy with a policy that forced them to remain passive in the event of an uprising in the east. Strauss, for example, thought even in 1956 that it would be almost impossible in such an event to prevent the "West German people from trying to help their brothers across the border."[20] In July 1961, he told his American counterpart that German troops could at present take no action if an uprising in the east was being crushed by the Russians because "the West was not yet ready for a showdown," but the western countries needed to prepare for a more active policy.[21] And Strauss was viewed as a possible successor to Adenauer. In the mid-1950s, the chancellor himself evidently felt a certain pressure of this sort.[22] In August 1961, furthermore, the German foreign minister, von Brentano, suggested to his western colleagues that in the event of an uprising in East Germany, some real action might be necessary. A formal protest would scarcely suffice; West German opinion, he said, would not "acquiesce" if German troops and the border police remained "quietly in their barracks" while the uprising was put down.[23] All this underscored the importance of the German nuclear question: if the Germans were saying these things while they were weak, what might they be tempted to do when they became strong?

So if the Soviets took the problem of German power seriously, they were not simply being paranoid. From their point of view, the problem was very real. The

---

[16] Thompson to Dulles, November 11, 1958, 762.00/11–1158, RG 59, USNA.

[17] Note to Macmillan, November 12, 1958, Prem 11/2929, PRO.

[18] Sulzberger, *Last of the Giants,* entry for July 24, 1962, p. 909.

[19] Thompson to Dulles, March 9, 1959, SS/I/6/Berlin—vol. 1 (4)/DDEL.

[20] Sulzberger, *Last of the Giants,* entry for December 14, 1956, p. 349.

[21] Strauss-McNamara meeting, July 14, 1961, appended to Nitze to Rusk et al, July 21, 1961, RG 200 (McNamara)/133/Memcons with Germans/USNA.

[22] See Adenauer's reference to the problem of holding "his own boys" back, in Gruenther to Goodpaster, November 19, 1956, FRUS 1955–57, 26:175.

[23] Western foreign ministers' meeting, August 5, 1961, FRUS 1961–63, 14:282. This remark caused some concern at the time. See Ball to Paris embassy, August 8, 1961, National Security Archive Berlin File [NSABF], Washington.

USSR's most basic interests in Europe were at stake. In the long run, if nothing were done, a resurgence of German power could threaten their whole position in Europe, and might even lead to war. Some action had to be taken before it was too late. The Soviets wanted to see if they and the western powers could reach an understanding that would stabilize the situation in central Europe and in particular that would keep West Germany from acquiring a nuclear capability under her own control. But first the Soviets needed to make the western powers take their concerns seriously, and Berlin was the obvious lever.

U.S. POLICY IN THE CRISIS

The Soviets were threatening western rights in Berlin. How far would the western powers go to defend those rights? What kinds of concessions would they be willing to make to settle the crisis? What they were prepared to accept would depend in part on how they felt about the German question as a whole—about the basic idea of a system that would limit German power and stabilize the status quo.

The United States was by far the most important western power, and the fundamental point to note about American policy in the crisis is that the U.S. government was in the final analysis far more willing than any other western power to fight a general nuclear war rather than capitulate over Berlin. This was a terribly difficult issue and it should not be surprising that Eisenhower's basic attitude was marked by a certain degree of ambivalence. He often took a tough line on the question. A few months before the crisis began, when Dulles said that America's pledge to go to war if necessary over Berlin was something that he himself did not quite believe, the president "expressed surprise." Of course America would have to go to war if the Soviets attacked the city. If she failed to do so, he said, soon all of Europe would be lost and the United States would run the risk of being overwhelmed by the power of the new Communist colossus.[24] And during the crisis, the president often seemed to take it for granted that if the United States were pushed far enough, a full-scale nuclear war would be unavoidable. America, he knew, was stronger than the USSR, and the Soviets would in all likelihood not push things to the point of war. But if they did, the U.S. government would have little choice but to launch a full-scale nuclear attack. As he explained to congressional leaders in March 1959, "the actual decision to go to all-out war will not come, but if it does come, we must have the crust to follow through." When the "acute crisis period" was reached, the United States, he said, would have to "engage in general war to protect our rights." His "basic philosophy" was that America had to be prepared to push her "whole stack of chips into the pot" when that became necessary.[25] On the other hand, he often seemed to shy away from that

---

[24] NSC meeting, May 1, 1958, FRUS 1958–60, 3:89. See also NSC meetings, December 10, 1953, and January 22, 1954, DDRS 1996/2796 and 2764.

[25] Eisenhower meeting with congressional leadership, March 6, 1959, FRUS 1958–60, 8:433, and meeting with a group of congressmen, March 6, 1959, DDRS 1996/3493; see also the extract from the Bruce diary entry for March 31, 1959, quoted in FRUS 1958–60, 8:550 n. A week before those meetings with congressional leaders, the president noted his concern about the problem of getting support

strategy, to the point where he sometimes appeared to favor the alternative of a major ground war in Europe; on one occasion, he had to be reminded rather forcefully by the JCS chairman of what America's strategy in fact was.[26]

But whatever his misgivings, the president went along with the prevailing view that force might have to be used and that a certain risk of general war would therefore in the final analysis have to be accepted. West Berlin was not militarily defensible in any normal way, the argument ran, so the freedom of the city depended on America's ultimate willingness to escalate up to the level of general nuclear war. It was not as though the United States intended to launch an all-out nuclear attack as soon as the first convoy to the city was stopped. The plan was first to probe Soviet intentions through the use of limited military force. If that failed, the next step would be a major military operation, involving perhaps a single division. If the USSR chose to attack a force of that size, it would be crossing the critical threshold: the "fat" would be "in the fire." The United States would not commit any additional forces to the Berlin operation, but instead, in the words of the key policy documents, "resort would have to be made to general war."[27]

This had been America's basic strategy for the defense of the city since the end of the Truman administration, and the coming of the crisis changed very little. The military authorities in particular still strongly supported this kind of strategy. Indeed, both Norstad and the JCS favored a more rapid use of force than Dulles thought prudent.[28] The American military leaders in general—as the British summed up their thinking—believed "that the time for a show-down with the Russians was at hand, and they were prepared to go the lengths of a real test of strength, up to the point of 'losing a division or two,' to show their determination. They were hardly prepared to discuss whether their plans made military sense, but were obsessed by the need to maintain their right of access by road, no matter the cost."[29] General Twining's views were particularly extreme. The JCS chairman

from Congress if the crisis came to a head and the government felt compelled "to act quickly so as to avoid any unnecessary damage to ourselves." Eisenhower memorandum, February 27, 1959, ACW/A/7/Berlin Paper/DDEL.

[26] Eisenhower meeting with key advisers, January 29, 1959, and special NSC meetings, March 5 and April 23, 1959, FRUS 1958–60, 8:302, 424–425, 626, 629. The alternatives discussed in this last meeting were laid out in a document that the editors of FRUS were not able to get declassified (ibid., p. 261); the alternatives are, however, outlined briefly in the agenda for the meeting included in the slightly fuller version of the minutes found in DDRS 1997/2689.

[27] Eisenhower meetings with top State and Defense department officials, January 29 and March 17, 1959; Dulles-Adenauer meeting, February 8, 1959; special NSC meeting, April 23, 1959; FRUS 1958–60, 8:301–303, 346–347, 499, 625–626. See also DOS Berlin History, pt. 1, chap. 3, and esp. p. 110, and the general discussion in Trachtenberg, *History and Strategy*, pp. 130–131, 209–212. For the formal Berlin policy documents, see NSC 5404/1, January 25, 1954, NSA; NSC 5727, December 13, 1957, supplement 1, FRUS 1955–57, 26:521–525; NSC 5803, February 7, 1958, Supplement 1, is almost exactly the same—see FRUS 1958–60, 9:631 n.

[28] Thurston to Dulles, November 16, 1958, 762.00/11–1758; Norstad to Twining, November 23, 1958, and Dulles-Eisenhower telephone conversations, November 18 and 24, 1958; FRUS 1958–60, 8:115–117, 119, and DDRS 1985/2544. For JCS views, see State-JCS meeting, January 14, 1959, FRUS 1958–60, 8:259–265.

[29] For British accounts of U.S. thinking, see confidential annexes to COS(60)59th meeting, and COS(61)38th, 42nd, and 65th meetings, September 27, 1960, and June 20, July 4, and September 27, 1961, Defe 4/129, 136 and 139, PRO. The passage quoted is from the July 4 document.

wanted a confrontation with Russia over the issue. "We certainly have to stop this somewhere," he said in December 1958. "We must ignore the fear of general war. It is coming anyway. Therefore we should force the issue on a point we think is right and stand on it."[30] But the consensus view at this point, shared by both military and civilian leaders, was that America's whole position in Europe depended on her willingness to defend her rights, and that the country therefore had to be prepared in the final analysis to risk general nuclear war over the issue.[31] Top American officials therefore reached the conclusion that the United States "should be prepared to resort to force if necessary to maintain access to Berlin—even at the risk of general war."[32] Dulles's view at this point was typical. The Soviet demand to liquidate western rights, he said, was "outrageous both in tone and substance," and to give way "would be a disaster."[33] The western position in Berlin was "legally and morally unassailable."[34] The Soviets, moreover, were also relatively weak in military terms. If the West stood firm, he thought that there was not one chance in a thousand that the Soviets would "push it to the point of war."[35]

This did not mean, however, that the Eisenhower administration was simply going to dig in its heels and take an intransigent line in the crisis. It preferred for two reasons to take a more moderate stance. To begin with, the United States was the leader of an alliance and could not set policy on a purely unilateral basis. The western alliance had to be kept together, the views of the major European countries had to be taken into account, and the fact was that those countries were leery of military action. In December 1958, for example, the U.S. government had tried to get the two other western powers with responsibilities in Berlin to accept the principle that force would be used if necessary to maintain land access to Berlin, and that contingency planning would proceed on that basis.[36] But the British were unwilling to make that sort of commitment; the French were also quite cautious. If the allies were to be brought along, the U.S. government needed to tread more softly. In that way the alliance would remain intact, and the Europeans would probably accept tough measures when the time came, even if they were unwilling to commit themselves to particular military plans in advance.[37]

And allied support was of considerable importance. To be sure, America was physically capable of taking action on a unilateral basis, and indeed plans had been

[30] State-Defense meeting, December 13, 1958, FRUS 1958–60, 8:195.

[31] See, for example, the views of Clay and McCloy, in McCloy to Merchant, December 10, 1958, and Ambassador Bruce's view in his diary entry for December 10, 1958, FRUS 1958–60, 8:165–166, 171.

[32] McElroy and Herter to Eisenhower, March 17, 1959, FRUS 1958–60, 8:501.

[33] State-Defense meeting, December 13, 1958, ibid., pp. 193, 195.

[34] Dulles-Herter-Merchant meeting, March 14, 1959, ibid., p. 487.

[35] Dulles-Couve meeting, December 17, 1958, and Dulles-Herter telephone conversation, March 6, 1959, ibid., pp. 219, 438.

[36] This principle was embodied in paragraph D of the December 11, 1958, U.S. proposal for joint action, ibid., pp. 179–180, which Dulles discussed with the British and French foreign ministers on December 15, ibid., pp. 200–203. For the U.S. reaction to the position taken by those two allies, see State-Defense meeting, January 14, 1959, ibid., pp. 259–265. The two sentences deleted from the version published here are in the full version, released under the FOIA, and available in the NSABF.

[37] Secretary's staff meeting, November 18, 1958; Eisenhower-Dulles meeting, November 18, 1958; Eisenhower-Dulles-McElroy meeting, January 29, 1959; in FRUS 1958–60, 8:84, 85, 301–302.

worked out for the eventuality that she might have to act alone. The goal of the contingency planning was to conduct operations that would ultimately force the Soviets to accept the fact that general war was imminent, and thus oblige them to back down. The United States had the forces needed for this purpose, and also the legal right to deploy those forces from German territory as this strategy required. But the American government disliked the idea of carrying the entire burden. It felt that the responsibility needed to be shared: it was very important that Germany at least, and probably one other major ally as well, go along with what the United States proposed to do.[38]

There was a more fundamental reason for American moderation in the crisis, and this had to do with the U.S. government's basic approach to the German problem. American policy was essentially defensive in nature. The United States was willing to live with things as they were and felt that the Soviet Union should do likewise. A formal acceptance of the status quo might be out of the question: Soviet control of eastern Europe, and especially of eastern Germany, could not be recognized as legitimate.[39] But both sides understood what the fundamental political realities were, and if conflict was to be avoided, they needed to find some way of dealing with each other on the basis of those realities.

With regard to Berlin in particular, Eisenhower felt that there were very real problems here that needed to be dealt with on a practical basis. Berlin was over a hundred miles behind Soviet lines. The western allies had only gone there in the first place because they had assumed Germany would be run on a unified basis. But as the Cold War set in, as the two German states were established, the city became a kind of albatross. At the end of the war, Eisenhower, as he now recalled, had foreseen "what a trouble the thing was going to be." But Roosevelt and Churchill had just dismissed those concerns out of hand: "Oh, we can get along with Uncle Joe." Even "at the time he knew better," and now "everything he had feared had come to pass."[40]

---

[38] On the existence of unilateral plans, see JSC 1907/137, April 19, 1956, CCS 381 (8-20-43), RG 218, USNA. A number of unilateral plans are listed in Live Oak Status Report, September 15, 1961, COS(61)332, Defe 5/117, PRO. In the 1958–59 discussions, the issue of whether the U.S. could act on its own came up repeatedly. Everyone agreed that allied support was highly desirable; the question was whether America could go ahead even if the allies were opposed to the use of force. Some officials said that the United States, in the final analysis, should be prepared to act unilaterally rather than capitulate on this issue. See, for example, McElroy in Berlin planning group, March 14, 1959, FRUS 1958–60, 8:478. But the president strongly disliked the idea of independent action. At one point, he supported this view with the argument that the military operations would lead to a traditional ground war; in such circumstances, allied cooperation was obviously necessary. This comes across as very odd: the heart of American policy, as General Twining pointed out on this occasion, was that the West was not going "to fight the USSR on the ground conventionally," and that the only way to defend Berlin was to "risk general war." The president did not press the point, and in the end left the issue of unilateral action open: if this problem developed, the United States, he thought, would just have to play it by ear. Eisenhower meeting with top advisers, January 29, 1959, and special NSC meetings, March 5 and April 23, 1959, ibid., pp. 302–303, 424, 629.

[39] There might be a great deal "to be said in favor of the status quo," Dulles noted, but this was not "a position which we could take publicly." Dulles to Eisenhower, February 6, 1959, FRUS 1958–60, 8:335.

[40] Eisenhower-Dulles telephone conversation, November 27, 1958, AWF/DDED/37/DDEL.

But what could be done now? The problem was not just that for military reasons, an outpost like Berlin might not be tenable over the long run.[41] Even if one
assumed that the West could maintain its presence there indefinitely through sheer
resolve—that is, through an ultimate willingness to risk nuclear escalation—that
in itself might not be enough to save the Berliners. As Eisenhower pointed out over
and over again, the Communists could undermine the economic life of the city by
effectively cutting off trade between Berlin and West Germany, even if allied military convoys remained free to move through the corridors. The movement of
goods into and out of the city was in practice subject to Communist control. "The
East Germans," he said, could therefore "stop all economic connection with West
Berlin. They could make West Berlin a dead weight on us." He in fact "did not see
how a city like West Berlin, surrounded by hostile elements who could hamper
and harass at will, could long survive."[42]

The United States was certainly not going to capitulate to the Communists or
abandon the Berliners, but the whole situation was a mess—a "can of worms,"
Eisenhower called it—and he very much wanted to find a way out. The United
States had stumbled into this situation because of mistakes made at the end of the
war; it had clearly been an "error," he thought, to try "to control Germany from
Berlin, so far behind the Russian lines."[43] America had ended up, for political reasons, assuming a military position that was "wholly illogical."[44] The West, he said,
had "made a mistake in 1944 and 1945 and must now find a way to pay for it."[45]
Some arrangement had to be worked out to normalize the situation without sacrificing the interests of the Berliners. "We will not," he said, "abandon our rights
and responsibilities—unless there is a way made for us to do so"—that is, unless
acceptable alternative arrangements were worked out.[46] And that alternative
might involve giving West Berlin a special status, making it "somehow a part of
West Germany," or bringing in the United Nations to help guarantee the freedom
and security of the city. But it would not necessarily include the continuing presence of western troops. Indeed, Eisenhower thought that "the time was coming
and perhaps soon when we would simply have to get our forces out."[47]

In his dealings with the allies, Eisenhower never actually proposed a settlement
involving the withdrawal of western forces from Berlin. But he very much wanted
to work out some sort of practical arrangement that would protect everyone's basic
interests. If that arrangement involved dealing with the East Germans on the ac-

[41] Eisenhower-Dulles meeting, November 18, 1958, FRUS 1958–60, 8:85.
[42] Eisenhower-Herter meeting, October 16, 1959, and Eisenhower-Macmillan meeting, March 28,
1960, ibid., 9:70, 260–261. See also below, note 123.
[43] Eisenhower meeting with top officials, December 11, 1958, FRUS 1958–60, 8:173.
[44] Eisenhower-Dulles meeting, November 30, 1958, ibid., p. 143.
[45] Eisenhower-Herter meeting, October 16, 1959, ibid., 9:70.
[46] Eisenhower-Kozlov meeting, July 1, 1959, DDRS 1983/633.
[47] Eisenhower-Gray meeting, September 30, 1959, FRUS 1958–60, 9:55. Dulles, however, did
not see things that way at all. In his view, the western military presence was the "only thing" that kept
Berlin "from being engulfed," and mere paper agreements were "no good" as a substitute. Dulles-Eisenhower telephone conversation, January 13, 1959, DP/TC/13/DDEL and ML. A few weeks later Dulles
told Lloyd that once the western troops left Berlin, the "game would be up"—or at least that this was
the way the Berliners felt. Dulles-Lloyd meeting, February 5, 1959, FRUS 1958–60, 8:319.

cess routes, his inclination (and Dulles's as well) was to work things out on that basis: "I suppose in this kind of low level business we would have to go along if we were going to keep things straightened out."[48] Some things were worth fighting for. The freedom of West Berlin could not be sacrificed. America would not allow herself to be humiliated, would not capitulate to Soviet threats, and would not accept the collapse of her whole political position in Europe. These things were real. But the whole question of whether it was the Soviets or the East Germans who exercised the controls on the access routes, with whatever that implied about the recognition of the East German regime by the western powers, was more metaphysical. One could hardly imagine going to war over such issues. So if they had to, and as long as access to Berlin remained open, Eisenhower and Dulles were prepared to deal with East German officials.[49]

This by no means meant that the West would be accepting the legitimacy of the East German state or giving up on German reunification as a long-term goal. The West Germans might claim that to deal with East German officials and allow them to stamp documents on the access routes was a step toward diplomatic recognition and acceptance of a divided Germany and thus had to be ruled out. But this was just a theory, and one could just as well argue that to treat the East Germans as agents of the USSR, regardless of what the Soviets said, was to underscore the western claim that East Germany was still under effective Soviet occupation, and that the regime there was just a puppet state, with no legitimate authority of its own.

The basic feeling was that the theoretical issue of what constituted "recognition" and what "recognition" meant was not of overwhelming importance. The American government was therefore not opposed in principle to increased contacts with East Germany. Dulles himself "doubted the practicality of total non-recognition of the existence of something which is a fact." One had to recognize facts, he told the German ambassador, even if one does not like them: "To pretend the enemy does not exist is not a very realistic or practical policy."[50] And one basic fact, as Eisenhower put it, was that "East and West Germany were not going to be reunified for a long time," that reunification was not a realistic answer to the Berlin problem, and that one had to work out some sort of modus vivendi.[51] If the solution involved dealings with the East Germans, even movement toward de facto acceptance of that regime and toward stabilization of the status quo in central Europe, the Americans themselves could easily live with that.

But if the Berlin Crisis was not really about the status of East Germany, if the real Soviet concern related to West Germany, then this sort of flexibility did not go to the heart of the problem. And on that core issue, the Eisenhower administration was not willing to go very far. The president himself did not believe that West German power needed to be kept limited, or in particular that the Federal Republic had to be prevented from getting a nuclear force under her own control. If the burden of defense in Europe was to be shifted to the Europeans, if the Eu-

---

[48] Eisenhower-Dulles telephone conversations, November 24, 1958, FRUS 1958–60, 8:118, 119.

[49] Dulles to Bruce, November 14, 1958; Dulles-Grewe meeting, November 17, 1958; Dulles to Adenauer, November 24, 1958; in ibid., pp. 66, 78–79, 120.

[50] Dulles-Grewe meeting, November 17, 1958, ibid., p. 79.

[51] Eisenhower-Segni meeting, September 30, 1959, ibid., 7(2):541.

ropeans were to be weaned from excessive dependence on the United States, if nuclear weapons were the ultimate basis of the defense of the NATO area, then obviously the Europeans needed to be armed with nuclear weapons and to have much greater say over their use. He understood why the Europeans would want a nuclear capability of their own and felt America should treat her allies generously in this area. And when he spoke along these lines, he was referring not just to Britain and France; he put Germany in the same category.[52] Indeed, from the start, he was relatively relaxed about the prospect of a buildup of German power. In the past, he thought, this might have been a problem, but that was only because Russia had been weak. But now with Russia so strong, he would "take a strong Germany." The implication was that a German nuclear capability was no cause for alarm.[53]

Dulles's views were in theory somewhat different. He and his top lieutenants in the State Department did think that there was a real problem of German power. Dulles in fact thought that the United States and the Soviet Union had a common interest in keeping Germany under "some measure of external control." But his mind was focused on the risk that a strong and reunified Germany would pose if she were not tied to the western bloc. The Germans, he said, could not be allowed to do "a third time what they had done in 1914 and 1939." A reunified Germany could not be "turned loose" and allowed to "exercise its tremendous potentialities in Central Europe."[54] Soviet fears about Germany, he and his main advisers felt, were legitimate, and, if the country were reunified, certain "military restraints on Germany" were appropriate. The USSR was "entitled to a sense of security," and the Soviet Union had the right, as part of a general settlement, to guarantees against a "rebirth of German militarism."[55] Indeed, this was the price they felt the West would have to pay if the Soviets were ever to agree to German reunification.[56]

If, however, Germany were to remain divided, none of these considerations really applied. Dulles may not have fully agreed with Eisenhower's basic thinking on issues relating to the defense of Europe. He certainly wanted more in the way of "flexibility," and hoped to rely less on strategic nuclear forces. He also disagreed with Eisenhower on the related question of the size and permanence of the American military presence in Europe. And he was a good deal less inclined than the president to think that the Europeans had to take over primary responsibility for their own defense.[57] He was therefore somewhat less inclined to think that the Eu-

[52] See especially Eisenhower-Norstad meeting, August 3, 1960, ibid., 7(1):610.

[53] Eisenhower-Macmillan meeting, March 28, 1960, ibid., 9:260.

[54] NSC meeting, February 6, 1958, AWF/NSC/9/DDEL. For a similar Dulles remark, see Willy Brandt, *People and Politics: The Years 1960–1975* (Boston: Little, Brown, 1976), p. 79. Indeed, Dulles sometimes implied that a Germany not tied in to either bloc might actually be worse than a reunified Germany integrated into the Soviet system. See his remarks to a U.S. ambassadors' meeting, May 9, 1958, DSP/77/70464/ML, and in a meeting with de Gaulle, July 5, 1958, DDF 1958, 2:25.

[55] Livingstone Merchant, "Thoughts on the Presentation of the Western Position at the Prospective Conference this Spring with the Soviets," February 6, 1959, Merchant Papers/5/ML; Dulles-Gromyko meeting, October 5, 1957, pp. 2–3, DDRS 1991/925; Dulles-Mikoyan meeting, January 16, 1959, FRUS 1958–60, 8:272.

[56] See Trachtenberg, *History and Strategy,* pp. 175–176.

[57] See especially NSC meeting, May 1, 1958, FRUS 1958–60, 3:85–89. Eisenhower referred re-

ropeans needed nuclear forces under their own control. But he agreed with the basic philosophy behind the sharing policy, and if he did have any misgivings about a German nuclear capability, he took care not to express them: he did not directly oppose the idea of a West German nuclear force.

So neither Eisenhower nor Dulles was prepared to give the Russians what they wanted. If Germany were to remain divided, they would not agree that West Germany should be kept non-nuclear. American policy during the Eisenhower period was thus not open to the idea of a settlement with Russia based on maintaining the status quo—on accepting the division of Germany and keeping the Federal Republic dependent on her allies.

Britain and the Berlin Crisis

British leaders were fundamentally opposed to the basic thrust of American policy during the Berlin Crisis. The United States was ultimately willing to use force rather than capitulate to Soviet demands, but for Britain Berlin was not worth a war. Could the United States, Macmillan asked, really expect Britain to go to war for the sake of the Germans in West Berlin, "for two million of the people we twice fought wars against and who almost destroyed us?"[58] The western powers, the British further believed, could not bluff their way through the crisis. The British simply did not accept the idea that Berlin could be saved by nuclear threats. As their foreign secretary, Lord Home, put it in July 1961: "our position was very weak on the ground and only tenable on the assumption, which he did not believe for a moment was realistic, that nuclear weapons would be used to defend our position."[59] A tough line might well lead to the incineration of the British Isles, or more probably to a humiliating capitulation at the last moment. Macmillan and other top British officials wanted to do what they could to make sure that the crisis did not reach the point where either outcome was likely. They felt that a military confrontation of any sort had to be ruled out. Nuclear escalation was out of the question; it therefore made little sense to contemplate more limited forms of military action, which could always be easily countered by the Communist side. To send in a battalion in the event Berlin was cut off would be "militarily unsound." To send in a division with orders to fight would lead to a major military disaster. To send in an army corps would be even worse.[60] British Defense Minister Harold

---

peatedly to his differences with Dulles on this issue. See Gordon Gray–Eisenhower meeting, July 27, 1959, OSANSA/SA/P/4/DDEL; FRUS 1958–60, 7(1):499, 511, 517, 653, for various comments in this vein from 1959 and 1960; and above all the Allen Dulles–Eisenhower meeting, August 22, 1961, NSF/82/JFKL, quoted in Trachtenberg, *History and Strategy*, p. 185.

[58] NSC meeting, May 24, 1960, FRUS 1958–60, 9:510. See also de Zulueta to Macmillan, December 19, 1961, Prem 11/3782, PRO.

[59] Rusk-Home meeting, July 21, 1962, FO 371/163575, PRO.

[60] For British military thinking, and British differences with the Americans on these issues, see confidential annexes to COS(60)50th, 52nd, 59th and 66th meetings, August 9, August 23, September 27, and October 25, 1960, and C.O.S.(61)38th, 42nd, and 65th meetings, June 20, July 4, and September 27, 1961, Defe 4/128–130, 136, and 139, PRO. See also Harold Macmillan, *Riding the Storm, 1956–1959* (New York: Harper, 1971), p. 634.

Watkinson in fact characterized such measures in late 1961 as "conventional aggression by the West," and told his American counterpart that under no circumstances would Britain agree that the western powers should put themselves "in the position of being the aggressors."[61] Macmillan himself considered the contingency plans "absurd."[62]

But the British were reluctant to lock horns directly with the Americans over this issue, and therefore from the start sought to evade the fundamental question of whether, in the final analysis, force would be used to maintain allied access rights. They agreed to allow Norstad to direct a planning effort code-named "Live Oak," and in December 1959 even agreed to allow him to plan for "any likely contingency." But they were always careful to stress that the plans his group came up with had no official government sanction, that the British government was in no sense committed to the Live Oak plans, and that the plans could not be implemented until the governments gave their consent. In 1961, for example, when the new Kennedy administration sought to develop a posture that would allow the West to draw out and intensify the phase of limited military operations before a full-scale nuclear attack was launched, Macmillan was willing to allow planning to proceed on the basis of the new American thinking, even though the British were even more out of sympathy with that strategy than they had been with the Eisenhower approach. For Macmillan, military planning was simply an "academic exercise," and he again emphasized that "specific political approval" had to be given before even the most limited military operation could begin.[63]

If the military option was effectively ruled out, it was obvious to the British that the western powers had no choice but to negotiate. The best strategy was to settle the crisis quickly, before the bankruptcy of a policy of maintaining the status quo through force if necessary became too obvious. "The premises of our position in Berlin," Macmillan told Eisenhower and Dulles, "and particularly the premise of our presence by right of conquest, are fast fading away." The Soviets, "with their control of the GDR," had the "upper hand." Hence, he said, "we should try to salvage something by negotiation."[64] As one of his principal advisers pointed out in August 1959: "We *must* negotiate some sort of settlement with the Russians and so recognise the realities of the situation because otherwise our position in Berlin will be destroyed anyway."[65] This meant movement toward the de facto recognition of the East German regime, acceptance of the Oder-Neisse line, and also a special military status for an area in central Europe that would include both parts of Germany.[66]

[61] Watkinson-McNamara meeting, December 11, 1961, Defe 13/254, PRO.

[62] Macmillan, *Pointing the Way*, p. 389.

[63] For British unwillingness to commit themselves on the use of force, see, for example, Dulles-Lloyd-Couve meeting, December 15, 1958, and Merchant-Hood meeting, January 2, 1959, FRUS 1958–60, 8:201, 227. For Macmillan's playing down of the significance of the allied military planning, see his handwritten note on Ormsby Gore to Foreign Office, January 11, 1962, Prem 11/3804, PRO. See also Irwin's characterization of the British position in a meeting of the Berlin Coordinating Group, May 23, 1960, FRUS 1958–60, 9:529.

[64] Macmillan-Dulles-Eisenhower meeting, March 20, 1959, FRUS 1958–60, 7(2):835–836.

[65] De Zulueta to Macmillan, August 18, 1959, Prem 11/2703, PRO.

[66] This policy was laid out explicitly in a paper Foreign Secretary Home wrote for the Cabinet on Berlin, C(61)116, July 26, 1961, Cab 129/106, PRO.

None of this was at all to the liking of the three other main allied governments. The German reaction was particularly strong. For Adenauer, the British were simply "traitors."[67] Macmillan, of course, deeply resented being "howled at" for taking what he thought was the only realistic line, especially by governments like Adenauer's that themselves were unwilling to face the terrible prospect of general nuclear war.[68]

But while Macmillan was ready to part company with Germany over these issues, his attitude toward America was rather different. The Americans were more serious about risking general war, and the hostile U.S. reaction could not be taken in stride, given especially the fact that cooperation with the United States was a cardinal principle of British policy. And it was clear from the start that the Americans were disturbed by the obvious thrust of British policy. The British were "wobbly," U.S. leaders complained.[69] The British foreign secretary, Selwyn Lloyd, sent Dulles a short essay on the Berlin question in January 1959. There was a tendency in Europe, Lloyd argued, to think that the Americans wanted a showdown with Russia, and indeed wanted to provoke a war from which they themselves "would be relatively immune"; Lloyd added that he was "not criticizing such a view if it has been expressed." The essay was "very disturbing," Dulles told Eisenhower. If that sort of thinking prevailed, he said, the West was "in a bad fix. It indicates a Chamberlain attitude."[70]

Macmillan, in fact, was soon flying off to Russia to meet with Khrushchev. Dulles did not like the idea. He thought the Soviets would interpret what he referred to sarcastically as "Harold's solitary pilgrimage to Moscow" as a sign of weakness.[71] These British efforts at peacemaking were generally interpreted in terms of British domestic politics. Macmillan, Dulles said, was "running pretty hard for election."[72] And Adenauer, when he was told of the planned visit, asked the British ambassador point blank: "Was this an election manoeuvre?"[73] Such suspicions were not off the mark. As Lloyd himself wrote, "no Prime Minister could face an election without having made a personal effort to ease tensions, i.e., by a meeting with Khrushchev."[74] In substantive terms, Britain's allies did not have much respect for the line of policy Macmillan was following.

The issue came to a head when Macmillan returned from Russia and then flew off again for America. In his meetings with U.S. leaders, he called for compromise

---

[67] Steel to Hoyer Millar, March 31, 1959, FO 371/145774, PRO. See also Macmillan, *Pointing the Way*, p. 64, and Trachtenberg, *History and Strategy*, p. 201.

[68] See Macmillan, *Riding the Storm*, pp. 581, 637; and Macmillan, *Pointing the Way*, pp. 63–64.

[69] Herter-Eisenhower telephone conversation, November 22, 1958, DDRS 1984/227; Dulles-Eisenhower telephone conversation, January 13, 1959, 12:06 P.M., DP/TC/13/DDEL; Herter to Eisenhower, July 30, 1959, AWF/DH/9/DDEL.

[70] Dulles-Eisenhower telephone conversation, January 25, 1959, DP/TC/13/DDEL; Dulles, "Thinking Out Loud," FRUS 1958–60, 8:292–294.

[71] Dulles-Eisenhower telephone conversation, January 20, 1959, DP/TC/13/DDEL; Dulles to Eisenhower, February 5, 1959, FRUS 1958–60, 8:324.

[72] Dulles-Eisenhower telephone conversations, January 20, 21, and 25, 1959, DP/TC/13/DDEL. Eisenhower, however, thought that Macmillan was making a mistake, even from a domestic political point of view. See Eisenhower-Herter meeting, March 17, 1959, FRUS 1958–60, 8:494.

[73] Steel to Foreign Office, February 3, 1959, FO 371/145773, PRO.

[74] Selwyn Lloyd, "Reflections, written August 1960," on the February 1959 "approach" to the USSR, Lloyd Papers, Churchill Archives Centre, Churchill College, Cambridge.

and defended Soviet policy as not aggressive. Eisenhower said the United States "would absolutely refuse 'to throw the West Berliners to the wolves.'" Macmillan became emotional. The smell of war was in the air. There had to be a summit meeting, he said, to head off a war. But Eisenhower would not be "dragooned to a Summit meeting." Macmillan claimed that the First World War could have been averted if a summit conference had been held. Eisenhower "countered by saying that prior to World War II Neville Chamberlain went to such a meeting and it is not the kind of meeting with which he intends to be associated." He would not surrender to blackmail. One could not avoid war, he said, "by surrendering on the installment plan."[75]

Dulles also clashed sharply with Macmillan. What was the use, he asked, of maintaining a powerful deterrent force "if whenever the Soviets threaten us and want to take something from our present positions we feel that we have to buy peace by compromise"?[76] From Dulles's point of view, Britain was weak, not just militarily but morally as well. Relations with Britain, he now thought, were going to be difficult. The British had apparently decided to chart their own course. The period of close Anglo-American collaboration seemed to be over.[77]

The following year, with Dulles dead and buried, Macmillan returned to the charge. He now told Eisenhower explicitly that Britain did not intend to use force in a Berlin crisis, and he assumed the U.S. government "felt likewise." That was not the case at all, Eisenhower replied. If the Soviets tried to put "an end to our rights, then we do intend to go through to Berlin with armed forces."[78] The United States and Britain were deeply divided on this fundamental issue. The two countries, more generally, seemed to be drifting apart.

Macmillan was aware of the problem; in early 1960 one of his advisers ticked off for him a whole list of examples of the new coolness in America's attitude toward Britain.[79] This was a disturbing trend, which the British felt they needed to counteract. They therefore now began to trim their sails. They would not press so overtly for a radical shift in western policy on fundamental political issues, but rather would follow the American lead in this area.[80] And they would play down their opposition to the Berlin contingency plans: their goal now was to avoid provoking renewed criticism of their "infirmity of purpose."[81] A modicum of cooperation, they felt, was necessary to avoid losing whatever influence the British government had left.[82]

[75] Anglo-American meetings, March 20, 1959, FRUS 1958–60, 7(2):832–837, 844–847; Goodpaster memorandum of 7 P.M., Eisenhower-Macmillan meeting, SS/ITM/6/Macmillan Talks/DDEL.

[76] Anglo-American meeting, March 20, 1959, FRUS 1958–60, 7(2):835.

[77] Dulles-Herter meeting, April 24, 1959, with attached Dulles outline on "British and United States Views on Dealing with the Soviet Union," April 21, 1959, DP/SACS/14/DDEL.

[78] Eisenhower-Macmillan meeting, March 28, 1960, FRUS 1958–60, 9:260.

[79] De Zulueta to Macmillan, March 8, 1960, and de Zulueta memorandum, "The Future of Anglo-American Relations," March 8, 1960, Prem 11/2986, PRO.

[80] See, for example, draft Foreign Office letter to Hood, February 24, 1960, FO 371/154085, PRO.

[81] Confidential Annex to COS(60)52nd meeting, August 23, 1960, Defe 4/128, PRO. Note also Mountbatten's comment in mid-1961 that the British Chiefs of Staff "had always taken the view that land operations on a large scale were militarily unsound," but had been "restrained by Ministers from making their views known in full to General Norstad lest he gain the impression that we were dragging our feet." Confidential Annex to COS(61)38th meeting, June 20, 1961, Defe 4/136, PRO.

[82] This was the view of both military and political leaders. For the military view, see Confidential

In reality, Britain had little control over the situation. For American leaders, British softness was regrettable, but was in itself by no means catastrophic. The Americans could pursue their policy even without British support. As Dulles explained to Adenauer in February 1959, "final decision" would rest "with the nation which holds the greatest power." If the British wanted to make "dangerous" concessions, the U.S. government "would express its views very clearly, and he was certain they would prevail."[83] And he made the point even more bluntly in a short piece on Anglo-American relations written in the hospital at the very end of his tenure as secretary of state. Macmillan and his government had "not been candid" with the Americans that year, but ultimately Britain would play only a minor role: "Ours is the 'king-pin' of power; therefore our views are in the last analysis compelling on the UK and our other allies."[84]

DE GAULLE, GERMANY, AND BERLIN

Neither Eisenhower nor Dulles, however, really felt that the United States should simply call the tune, and that the European allies would just have to follow the American lead. British misgivings could perhaps be swept aside; the Germans could in theory be virtually forced to toe the American line. But the American government was not comfortable with a policy of simply dictating to the allies. There was a vague sense that the whole western system might collapse if the Europeans came to feel that the United States was blind to their concerns and was arrogantly dragging them to the brink of war, or, alternatively, was unilaterally forcing distasteful concessions down their throats. The enormous responsibilities relating to the great issues of war and peace had to be shared. It was therefore important, especially given the British attitude, to find some real political support in Europe.

This was why French policy mattered as much as it did. If the French were also ultimately willing to risk war over Berlin, that would give a certain legitimacy to the American position that would otherwise be missing. And if the French took a tough line on that issue, but also supported the general idea of a negotiated settlement with Russia, then a policy that aimed at some kind of settlement would be much easier to implement. In German eyes, the British might be dismissed as appeasers, and even the Americans, especially after Dulles left the scene, could be tarred with the same brush. But if France sought a negotiated settlement, it would

---

Annex to COS(61)56th meeting, August 28, 1961, Defe 4/138, PRO. It was pointed out in this discussion of Berlin contingency planning that "the United States military staff and General Norstad, in his United States capacity, were already examining unilaterally the question of more extensive operations, including the use of nuclear weapons. There was therefore every advantage in the United Kingdom agreeing to take part in such planning or we should otherwise be unable to influence its course." Foreign Office officials felt much the same way. There was a "real danger," one official wrote, "of the Americans saying 'to hell with the Allies' and going it alone over Berlin. It is all very well for us to insist that nothing is done over Berlin except on the basis of tripartite agreement, but if we withhold our agreement all the time to the nasty things . . . we shall only encourage a mood of desperation in the Pentagon or even chez Norstad." Killick to Shuckburgh, September 25, 1961, FO 371/160553, PRO.

[83] Dulles-Adenauer meeting, February 7, 1959, DSP/80/72722/ML.

[84] Dulles outline on "British and United States Views on Dealing with the Soviet Union," April 21, 1959, DP/SACF/14/DDEL.

be harder to condemn such a policy as the product of Anglo-Saxon weakness, and there would be greater pressure on Germany to go along. On the other hand, if the French opposed a policy of negotiation, the German government would find it easier to resist what the Americans wanted to do in this area.

It was thus of considerable importance that French and American policy ran along parallel lines from the beginning of the crisis until late 1961. Both countries felt that the status quo of a divided Germany was something they could live with and sought mainly to safeguard the status quo where it was threatened—that is, in Berlin. And indeed in spite of all their complaints about American "immobilism"—Gaullist mythology held that the Americans were intent on maintaining the division of Europe that they and the Soviets had supposedly agreed upon at Yalta—the French were even stronger defenders of the status quo of a divided Germany and thus of a divided Europe than the Americans were.[85]

Dulles and Eisenhower took the ultimate goal of German reunification seriously. The Germans, in Eisenhower's view, were a single people who wanted to come together in a single state, and he took it for granted that "we should do everything we can to let nature take its course."[86] But de Gaulle made it quite clear to his allies, and even to the Soviets, that he was perfectly happy to live with the status quo in central Europe indefinitely. "France," he said, "was not in a hurry for the reunification of Germany."[87] A few months later he reiterated the point. "For understandable reasons," he noted, France was "not unduly anxious for German reunification or to see Germany grow larger."[88] As far as Berlin was concerned, the present situation was perfectly acceptable: "All that the West really wanted from Mr. Khrushchev was that he should not start a war and would agree to work out some sort of a *modus vivendi*."[89] De Gaulle did not even agree with Eisenhower in principle that western policy should be based on the theme of "self-determination of peoples." When Eisenhower said the West "should stress that we believe in this" and that this belief should be the basis for western policy in Berlin and East Germany, de Gaulle replied with characteristic bluntness that the Americans "did believe in this but he did not."[90] In keeping with a long-standing French tradition, de Gaulle did not view German unity as wholly natural in any case. The East Germans, whom he often referred to as "the Prussians and the Saxons," were not quite the same people as the West Germans, and part of the reason he liked Adenauer

[85] See, for example, Maurice Couve de Murville, *Une politique étrangère, 1958–1968* (Paris: Plon, 1971), p. 30; De Gaulle, *Mémoires d'espoir: Le renouveau*, pp. 211, 239.

[86] Eisenhower-Herter telephone conversation, April 4, 1959, HP/10/DDEL.

[87] De Gaulle–Macmillan–Eisenhower meeting, December 20, 1959, p. 8, Prem 11/2991, PRO. Note also Prime Minister Debré's comments, ibid., pp. 5–6. See also de Gaulle's comments in this vein in his meetings with Eisenhower, September 2–4, 1959, DDF 1959, 2:276, 284.

[88] De Gaulle–Eisenhower meeting, April 22, 1960, FRUS 1958–60, 7(2):346. De Gaulle and his associates frequently expressed views of this sort. See, for example, de Gaulle–Dulles meeting, February 6, 1959, FRUS 1958–60, 8:332–333; Sulzberger, *Last of the Giants,* p. 884; Groepper to Foreign Office, December 4, 1963, AAPBD 1963, 3:1543; and Ernst Weisenfeld, *Quelle Allemagne pour la France?* (Paris: Colin, 1989), pp. 104–105. Note also Couve de Murville, *Le monde en face,* p. 49, to be compared with Couve's comments in Institut Charles de Gaulle, *De Gaulle et son siècle,* vol. 5 (Paris: Plon, 1991), p. 425.

[89] De Gaulle–Macmillan meeting, December 21, 1959, p. 6, Prem 11/2996, PRO.

[90] Eisenhower–de Gaulle meeting, April 25, 1960, FRUS 1958–60, 7(2):355–356.

so much was that the German chancellor saw things much the same way. "Adenauer," he said, "does not believe in German reunification, in the return of Prussia to Germany. *Il se moque de Berlin*—he doesn't care about Berlin at all."[91] Adenauer was the best of all the Germans, a Rhenish Catholic, a bourgeois democrat but a strong leader, pro-western and pro-French—and a skillful politician who knew to how steer his fundamentally unstable nation along the proper course.[92]

It followed that the western powers in general, and France especially, had to conduct their policy with great care. On the one hand, as Prime Minister Michel Debré put it, France wanted coexistence with the east and "could accept the existence of two Germanies." The goal therefore was a modus vivendi on that basis. The problem was that for the Germans this policy was anathema. If the West pursued those goals too openly, there was no telling how the Germans would react. If they felt betrayed and turned away from the western alliance, the results could be disastrous. The West therefore had to go on pretending that it favored reunification. This was a theme the western governments were stuck with, but the "practical problem was how in practice to accept the division of Germany."[93]

French policy during the crisis was shaped with an eye to these two conflicting goals. In principle, the French government took a tough line. If the allies were cut off from Berlin, the western powers would not capitulate. Force, in the final analysis, would have to be used. "If that means war," de Gaulle told Macmillan, "well then, there will be a war."[94] But if the allies stood firm, the Soviets would not block access to the city. Thus the overriding need was to demonstrate resolve, so as to minimize the risk of a Soviet miscalculation. The allies should avoid initiatives that would be taken as signs of weakness. And it is often said that for this reason de Gaulle from the start opposed the very idea of negotiations with the USSR.

In reality French policy was not nearly so unambiguous. On the vital issue of whether force, in the final analysis, would be used, French officials were surprisingly cautious. The Soviets in November 1958 had given their former allies a six-month grace period before their rights were to be liquidated, and the U.S. government wanted to take advantage of the delay to work out military contingency plans with the other two powers with responsibilities in West Berlin. The Americans therefore proposed in December 1958 that this planning be based on the principle that force would be used if access were cut off. But the French, in spite of all of de Gaulle's talk about the importance of tripartite cooperation in the working out of common military plans, sought to evade this vital question. They were "weaseling," the U.S. representative in these talks told top American military leaders. Like the British, they finally agreed that military planning would take place under Norstad's supervision, but Norstad would not be allowed to implement

[91] Alphand, *L'étonnement d'être*, entry for August 23, 1961, p. 363. See also de Gaulle's comments in his December 21, 1959, meeting with Macmillan, DDF 1959, 2:781, and a remark along the same lines he made in late 1962, quoted in Peyrefitte, *C'était de Gaulle*, p. 161.

[92] De Gaulle, *Mémoires d'espoir: Le renouveau*, pp. 183–187.

[93] Debré-Macmillan meetings, March 9 and April 13, 1959, and De Gaulle–Macmillan meeting, March 10, 1959, DDF 1959, 1:315, 318, 320, 492–493; Debré in de Gaulle–Macmillan-Eisenhower meeting, December 20, 1959, pp. 5–6, Prem 11/2991, PRO. Note also Couve's remarks in a meeting with Rusk and Home, August 5, 1961, FRUS 1961–63, 14:270.

[94] De Gaulle–Macmillan meeting, March 10, 1959, DDF 1959, 1:317.

these plans on his own authority.[95] De Gaulle took an ostensibly tough line because he thought the Soviets were bluffing, but if his own bluff were called, it was by no means clear that he was ready to face nuclear war over Berlin.

Indeed, French officials sometimes even suggested that West Berlin might have to be sacrificed in the end. De Gaulle himself told Eisenhower in April 1960 that he "felt we should not allow ourselves to be pushed out of Berlin, but that we should not use the word never, never, never."[96] Prime Minister Debré was even more explicit. In May he told Macmillan that there should be no war over access to Berlin—at least if West Berlin itself was not overrun—and that if the Soviets cut the city off there could be no military action. The most the West could do was to set up a "sort of economic counter-blockade."[97] The foreign minister, Maurice Couve de Murville, suggested much the same thing, even in late 1961 when the French were taking what to the world seemed a very tough line on the Berlin question. Khrushchev, he told his British and American counterparts in August, thought the West would not fight and would ultimately accept his terms. Perhaps in the final analysis, Couve thought, Khrushchev was right about that; what was wrong was to "give him the immediate impression that he is right."[98] The implication was that the West might have to capitulate in the end, but should not do so prematurely. It was for this reason that he thought the Americans were committing themselves too strongly to the defense of Berlin. De Gaulle himself made a similar point to Adenauer in December. The French, it seemed, had resigned themselves to the eventual loss of the city, and were now worried mainly about the effect this would have on the Federal Republic. "The main problem now," Couve noted, "was to safeguard Western Germany. The fate and freedom of 2,000,000 splendid West Berliners was of course important, 'but after all,' he said, with a shrug of the shoulders. He felt that in staking so much prestige on Berlin the Americans were taking Western Germany far too much for granted. We could all see the state the West Germans were in now. That was where the real problem lay."[99]

The basic idea was that if concessions had to be made, even if Berlin itself had to be abandoned, it was vital that West Germany not be lost in the process. That

[95] See DOS Berlin History, 1:25, 98; NAC delegation to State Department, December 15, 1958, and tripartite meeting, January 13, 1959, FRUS 1958–60, 8:201, 250–253. Ambassador Alphand found this position hard to defend; *L'étonnement d'être,* entry for January 12, 1959, p. 297. For the reference to the French as "weaseling," see State-JCS meeting, January 14, 1959, p. 4, NSABF. Note also Clay's remark that "neither British nor French will ever react in Berlin," in Clay to Rusk, January 11, 1962, FRUS 1961–63, 14:746. The French position remained somewhat "evasive" even at the very end of the crisis. See Kennedy-Couve meeting, October 9, 1962, ibid., 15:354–355.

[96] Eisenhower–de Gaulle meeting, April 22, 1960, FRUS 1958–60, 7(2):346.

[97] Debré–Macmillan meeting, May 19, 1960, FO 371/152097, PRO. Debré said here that he was supporting a view Eisenhower had expressed at a meeting held the previous day, but it is clear from the record of that meeting that the president had said nothing of the sort. This misrepresentation should therefore be seen as a device Debré was using to lay out the French view without taking full responsibility for it. Eisenhower–de Gaulle–Macmillan meeting, May 18, 1960, FRUS 1958–60, 9:491.

[98] Couve-Rusk-Home meeting, August 5, 1961, FRUS 1961–63, 14:272.

[99] Couve-Heath meeting, November 9, 1961, FO 371/160563, PRO. See also Heinrich Krone, "Aufzeichnungen zur Deutschland- und Ostpolitik 1954–1960" [Krone diary], ed. Klaus Gotto, in *Adenauer-Studien,* vol. 3, ed. Rudolf Morsey and Konrad Repgen (Mainz: Matthias-Brünewald-Verlag, 1974), entry for December 15, 1961, p. 165.

meant that France had to take a tough line—or more precisely, that France had to appear to take a tough line. The Germans must not come to feel that the West had broken faith with them. They needed to be carried along: they themselves had to agree that the West had little choice but to make concessions if war was to be avoided. What the French objected to was what they saw as the British policy of giving away too much too quickly. As Couve put it in early 1959, Berlin was an albatross, and it would perhaps have been better never to have gone into the city in the first place. But a withdrawal now would mean the collapse of western policy. It was clear, he said, that the western powers were about to enter into "a very long negotiation" with the Russians, and all hope for a relatively successful outcome depended on allied firmness at the outset. "We can be flexible in the course of the negotiations," he said, but it would be a grave mistake, he thought, to start out from a "position of weakness."[100]

The French government was thus not opposed to talks with the USSR. "With regard to the German question," de Gaulle himself said in early 1959, "one must accept a negotiation." He was "not opposed to a summit conference." He in fact "hoped that there would be a conference" on the German question as a whole. In October, he was calling for a summit conference to be held about seven months later.[101] De Gaulle's main subordinates were more explicit about what the French had in mind. Debré thought just after the collapse of the Paris summit conference in May 1960 that since force was out of the question, and economic countermeasures would not be very effective, the West should "as soon as we could without a great loss of face" resume negotiations, perhaps at the foreign minister or ambassadorial level.[102] Couve in August 1961 said that deciding what the West was prepared to do in these talks was a "disagreeable responsibility which had to be faced."[103] The French view, as he bluntly pointed out to his British and American counterparts (but in the absence of the Germans, as he observed), was that "we obviously had to try to make a deal and this involved giving something away." The problem was how to bring the Germans along. At present, there was a gap between what the Germans could accept and what the three western powers "might wish to propose." As the crisis set in, the German position might change. But no one could tell what the German attitude would be "when it came to the real trial."[104] Even in September 1961, when Secretary of State Rusk was about to begin talks with Gromyko, Couve noted that those talks "would constitute real negotiations." He believed in the idea of direct, bilateral talks that would deal with substantive issues, and said that Rusk could proceed "with the general support of all."[105]

As for de Gaulle himself, in his own meeting with Rusk on August 8, he took what was at first glance a much tougher line. The western powers, he pointed out,

[100] Couve-Lloyd meeting, March 10, 1959, and Debré-Couve-Adenauer meeting, May 6, 1959, DDF 1959, 1:326, 613. Couve-Herter meeting, March 31, 1959, FRUS 1958–60, 8:541.

[101] Dulles-Alphand meeting, February 3, 1959, FRUS 1958–60, 8:312; De Gaulle–Macmillan meeting, March 10, 1959, DDF 1959, 1:317–318, 320; De Gaulle to Eisenhower, March 11 and October 20, 1959, LNC 1958–1960, pp. 204, 272.

[102] Debré-Macmillan meeting, May 19, 1960, FO 371/152097, PRO.

[103] Western foreign ministers' meeting, August 6, 1961, FRUS 1961–63, 14:296.

[104] Rusk-Couve-Home meeting, August 5, 1961, ibid., pp. 269, 274, 277.

[105] Western foreign ministers' meeting, September 15, 1961, ibid., pp. 418–419.

could have said simply that they were in Berlin by right, and that they would maintain their position in Berlin, by force if necessary. If the Americans had taken that course, "we would have been with you." The policy of pressing for negotiations was "not our way." But in practically the same breath, he told Rusk that France did not object to what America was doing. "Please go on with your probing," he said, "we have nothing against it. Tell us if you find some substance in these negotiations and we shall join you."[106] To British and American officials, it seemed increasingly that de Gaulle wanted to have it both ways: to allow the search for a settlement to proceed, but to avoid taking responsibility for the sacrifices that would have to be made.

The French government was thus thinking in terms of a negotiated settlement, and in fact in terms of concessions that the West might eventually have to make. De Gaulle differed with his allies—first with the British, and then, from late 1961 on, with the Americans as well—on tactics. To appear too eager for talks was counterproductive. The western powers should be hard bargainers. The French were concerned about the effect of a soft line both on Russia and on Germany. But sooner or later a settlement would have to be worked out and concessions of as yet indeterminate size would be unavoidable.

What sort of arrangement did the French have in mind? Their basic aim was to preserve the status quo. The present situation might not be perfect, but people had lived with it since the end of the war, and there was no reason why one could not go on living with it indefinitely. The Soviets said that realities had to be accepted. The division of Germany, the Communist regime in the east, and the Oder-Neisse line, they argued, were all facts of life that the West needed to recognize. From the French point of view, there was no problem with that in principle. The French were not dogmatic on questions relating to the status of the East German regime. Like the Americans, they had no real problem with allowing the East Germans to stamp documents or to take over Soviet responsibilities on the access routes.[107] De Gaulle, again like the Americans, favored increased contacts between the two parts of Germany.[108] On the general issue of dealings with the Communist authorities, he agreed with Dulles that the West Germans had behaved "rather stuffily."[109] Full de jure recognition was out of the question, but the French president thought in early 1959 that it might be possible to work out a modus vivendi involving "de facto relations between the Federal Republic and the Western Powers on the one hand and the GDR on the other."[110] Indeed, as part of a Berlin settlement, de Gaulle in 1959 could (like Eisenhower) imagine a peace treaty, presumably with both parts of Germany, after the West German elections in 1961.[111]

[106] Rusk–de Gaulle meeting, August 8, 1961, ibid., pp. 313–315.

[107] De Gaulle–Macmillan meeting, March 10, 1959, DDF 1959, 1:320–322; Couve in western foreign ministers' meeting, August 5, 1961, FRUS 1961–63, 14:289.

[108] See, for example, de Gaulle–Macmillan meeting, March 10, 1959, DDF 1959, 1:318, 320.

[109] De Gaulle–Dulles meeting, February 6, 1959, FRUS 1958–60, 8:333.

[110] Dulles-Alphand meeting, February 3, 1959, ibid., p. 312.

[111] Alphand, *L'étonnement d'être*, p. 318; for Eisenhower, see Trachtenberg, *History and Strategy*, p. 197.

As far as the Oder-Neisse line was concerned, de Gaulle made it clear that he accepted that border as final. A western guarantee of the Oder-Neisse line, he and Eisenhower both felt, might be a "valuable card to play" in negotiations with the USSR if they could get the Germans, even tacitly, to go along with it.[112] There were thus certain realities that the West should ultimately be prepared to accept, and indeed he hoped that an agreement reflecting these "facts" might "be reached with the Russians." But the West had to get something in return. The Communists for their part also had to accept the status quo in Berlin.[113]

The French would have regarded a settlement of this sort as a very successful outcome of the crisis, and in reality were prepared to accept a good deal less. Even in 1959, they were willing to make certain concessions to meet Soviet wishes on Berlin. The Russians had certain complaints about West Berlin—about the city as a base for western propaganda and espionage, and as an escape hatch for East German refugees. Couve was prepared to go a long way toward meeting Soviet concerns in all these areas; he was also willing to limit the political ties linking West Berlin to the Federal Republic.[114] By late 1961 the French were ready to go further still. For Couve in August 1961, a deal was necessary and it would inevitably involve making concessions. It was, he said, the use of allied "military rights as a camouflage for essential German traffic," and especially the movement of East German refugees by air from West Berlin to West Germany, that caused problems. Allied protection of that German traffic was therefore one of the things that might have to be sacrificed if a settlement was to be reached. West German political ties with West Berlin might also have to be discontinued. The Soviets would insist on it, and this was a fact that had to be faced "if there was to be any agreement with the Soviets."[115] And finally there was the question of Germany's nuclear status. Here too the French were willing to make major concessions as part of a settlement with the USSR—or really half-concessions, since these were things that the French themselves were not fundamentally opposed to. A reunified Germany, in their view, should be subject to the same constraints in this area as the Federal Republic. The regime established by the Paris accords would be applied to Germany as a whole. This in fact was the American view as well. The more important question was whether limitations of this sort could be made part of an agreement with Russia that would settle the Berlin Crisis even if Germany remained divided, and it is important to note that the French in 1959 would not rule this out. Although de Gaulle, of course, took exactly the opposite line in his meetings with Adenauer, the real French view (at least until 1962 or so, when their attitude became more ambivalent) was that a "certain inequality of status" with Germany in this area had

---

[112] Eisenhower–de Gaulle meeting, April 22, 1960, FRUS 1958–60, 7(2):346. For Eisenhower's views, see also Eisenhower-Macmillan meeting, March 28, 1960, ibid., 9:259. De Gaulle accepted the Oder-Neisse line as final in a March 25, 1959, press conference.

[113] Macmillan to Ormsby Gore, November 27, 1961, Prem 11/3338, PRO. See also Couve in western foreign ministers' meeting, December 11, 1961, FRUS 1961–63, 14:655.

[114] De Gaulle–Macmillan meeting, March 10, 1959, and Macmillan-Debré-Couve meeting, April 13, 1959, DDF 1959, 1:320, 494, 496.

[115] Rusk-Home-Couve meeting, August 5, 1961, FRUS 1961–63, 14:272–273, 277.

to be maintained.[116] Indeed, their assumption was that restrictions on West Germany's nuclear status might well emerge in the course of the negotiations.[117]

Thus the French, practically from the start of the crisis, were thinking in terms of a negotiated settlement, and they knew where they were ready to make concessions. On fundamentals, France and the United States were not far apart.[118] Both governments were comfortable with the status quo, although the United States, under Eisenhower at least, was more interested than France in seeing Germany reunified. Both governments were willing to give the status quo a degree of formal acceptance as part of a modus vivendi that would save Berlin and avoid a war. Both were held back, the French more than the Americans, by concerns about the German reaction. And both countries took a tough line on the fundamental issue of the use of force if no agreement were reached and the Communists actually followed through on their threats—although here the Americans were clearly more willing in the final analysis to resort to military action.

But whatever the French really felt about the use of force, de Gaulle's standard line was that the risk of war would have to be accepted. What this meant was that the Americans could feel that they were not simply imposing a tough stance on Europe. The iron in the western position would not depend on the United States alone. And the fact that France supported the idea of negotiations, at least until late 1961, meant that a policy that aimed at a negotiated settlement might also be easier to implement. The Germans would probably be more willing to make certain sacrifices and go along with a negotiated settlement if all three of the other major western governments thought those arrangements were necessary.

GERMAN POLICY IN THE CRISIS

In principle German policy was fundamentally different from that of the three western allies. The goal for Britain, France and the United States was essentially defensive. They wanted the Soviets to accept the status quo, in particular around Berlin. Neither force nor the threat of force should be used to try to effect change. The western powers were willing to coexist with the Russians on this basis, and they were not fundamentally averse to a policy aimed at stabilizing the status quo. But the Germans were basically opposed to a policy of that sort. Efforts in that direction, they argued, would lead to a hardening of the division of their country. For Adenauer in particular, the very idea of détente was suspect. It was associated in his mind with the notion of America and Russia together running the world,

---

[116] Debré, in his meeting with Lloyd, November 12, 1959, DDF 1959, 2:565, to be compared with de Gaulle's comment the next month in a meeting with Adenauer, Macmillan, and Eisenhower, December 20, 1959, ibid., p. 775.

[117] Debré in meeting with Macmillan, March 9, 1959, ibid., 1:315. Note also de Gaulle's account of his March 1960 meeting with Khrushchev in which he outlined the sort of settlement he had in mind, one of whose elements was that Germany—or, more precisely, the two Germanies—not have a nuclear capability. De Gaulle, *Mémoires d'espoir: Le renouveau*, p. 241.

[118] This point was frequently noted at the time. See, for example, Dulles-Alphand meeting, February 3, 1959, FRUS 1958–60, 8:314; Alphand to Couve, March 14, 1959, DDF 1959, 1:355; Alphand, *L'étonnement d'être*, p. 301.

with the political eclipse of Europe, with permanent constraints on German power and independence, perhaps even with an eventual American withdrawal from Europe and a neutralization of Germany—in short, with a sellout of the most basic German interests.

The great question was which view would prevail. Would the Germans go along with a policy of stabilization, or would the western allies, worried about a possible loss of Germany, end up deferring to Adenauer on all the key issues? The United States might be by far the strongest power in the western alliance, but during the Eisenhower period U.S. leaders were reluctant to simply lay down the law. Eisenhower himself strongly disliked the idea of moving ahead without the allies. A remark he made in October 1959 typifies his general approach: "he thought that he could strike a bargain of his own with Khrushchev if he were to try to do so, but he knew our allies would not accept his acting unilaterally."[119] The German government in particular could not be ignored. Adenauer had violently opposed the idea of dealing with the East Germans as "agents" of the Soviet Union: he insisted that they not be allowed to exercise the controls on the access routes that the Soviets were already exercising. The Americans then officially abandoned that idea. Even if East Germany promised "to carry out the responsibilities heretofore exercised by the Soviets," Eisenhower said, "we could not, even though tempted to accept, give it consideration, because it would be death to Adenauer."[120]

But Adenauer's victory was more apparent than real. The U.S. government had no intention of beginning military operations before access was cut off, and something close to the agent theory was in effect adopted as policy.[121] The Americans were not going to allow Adenauer to set policy for the West as a whole. They had a whole series of complaints about the line Adenauer wanted the western powers to follow. The West Germans themselves had no problem dealing with the East German authorities when it suited them—on interzonal trade, most notably. What then gave them the right to object so violently to any dealings between the western powers and East Germany?[122] The whole point of a firm stand in the crisis was to save the Berliners, but Adenauer had no answer for Eisenhower's argument, which the president made over and over again, that the Soviets could, without violating the rights of the western powers, cut off Berlin's trade with West Germany, that the city's economy would die—that for the sake of the city, a modus vivendi with the Communists was a practical necessity, and that for this reason alone a degree of flexibility was essential.[123]

---

[119] Eisenhower-Herter meeting, October 16, 1959, DDRS 1982/2219.

[120] Eisenhower-Herter meeting, March 17, 1959, FRUS 1958–60, 8:493. See also Trachtenberg, *History and Strategy,* pp. 196–198, and FRUS 1958–60, 8:172, 305–306, 477, 493, 498, for various documents bearing on this question.

[121] See appendix 5, "The Question of East German Control of Access to Berlin" (IS).

[122] This was a common argument at the time, and the British in particular often raised this point. See, for example, State-JCS meeting, January 14, 1959, FRUS 1958–60, 8:264, and Steel to Foreign Office, February 16, 1959, FO 371/148773, PRO.

[123] Eisenhower pressed the chancellor repeatedly on this point at the western summit meeting at Rambouillet in December 1959, and again at the Paris summit in May 1960, but as he later complained, he could never get a straight answer. "Adenauer always says we must preserve our juridical position," Eisenhower told the NSC in mid-1960. "The President felt we might end up preserving our juridical

There was an even more basic problem with Adenauer's position. He took a rigid line on the political issues, but at the same time he made it clear that he felt that armed conflict absolutely had to be avoided. Berlin, he felt, was not worth a war. He took it as fundamental, he told Dulles in February 1959, that "under no circumstances should atomic weapons be used." Dulles responded by laying out the American position. Nuclear weapons, he said, would not be used at the outset, but the western powers had to be prepared to escalate. If they were, the Soviets would almost certainly back down. If, on the other hand, the use of nuclear weapons was to be ruled out from the start, the West would "suffer defeat after defeat" because of Communist superiority in conventional forces. If the Federal Republic would not back America's "strong policy," the U.S. government should "know this from the outset so that it would not commit itself and its prestige." Adenauer then tried to cover his tracks. He had been misunderstood, he said. Germany would of course support the tough American line. But the cat was out of the bag, and Adenauer's real feelings were clear enough.[124] When he met with Eisenhower in August, he again insisted that "no one could or should carry on a nuclear war over these questions." He nevertheless thought the three western powers had to stand on their rights in Berlin. He did not think the Soviets "would let it come to war," but if the USSR did not back down, he was prepared to give way. "For the most extreme emergency," he said, the Soviet proposal to make Berlin a "free city" might be accepted.[125]

The Americans were not happy with Adenauer's position. It seemed that the Germans wanted the West to bluff its way through the crisis, but this was just not an acceptable way of managing the situation. The bluff might not work. A more serious policy had to be worked out. If the NATO powers simply relied on words

position while losing Berlin." See Eisenhower-Adenauer–de Gaulle–Macmillan meetings, December 19, 1959, pp. 27–30, Prem 11/2991, PRO, and May 15, 1960, FRUS 1958–60, 9:419–420; Eisenhower-Herter meetings, February 8 and March 14, 1960, Eisenhower-Macmillan meeting, March 28, 1960, and NSC meetings, May 24 and September 21, 1960, ibid., pp. 190, 219–220, 260, 509 (for the quotation), 576–577. When the president complained to de Gaulle that he had not been able to get a direct answer from the chancellor, the French leader simply shrugged his shoulders: "What answer could he give?" Eisenhower–de Gaulle–Macmillan meeting, May 15, 1960, ibid., p. 434. In fact, de Gaulle himself did have an answer: the allies would preserve their rights, and the Berliners could leave if they could not deal with Soviet economic pressure on the city. But Adenauer never said that, ignored the point Eisenhower had been making, and insisted on taking the Eisenhower argument as evidence of American weakness. For both points, see Adenauer, *Erinnerungen*, 4:24, 124.

[124] Dulles-Adenauer meeting, February 8, 1959, DSP/80/72720–72728/ML. For a shorter account, see FRUS 1958–60, 8:346. See also Trachtenberg, *History and Strategy*, p. 198, and Schwarz, *Adenauer*, 2:493–494.

[125] Eisenhower-Adenauer meeting, August 27, 1959, FRUS 1958–60, 9:19–23. This feeling that military force, and especially nuclear force, should under no circumstances be used in connection with the Berlin crisis was the consensus view of the German leadership throughout the Berlin Crisis period. See Hans-Peter Schwarz, *Die Ära Adenauer, 1957–1963* (Stuttgart: Deutsche Verlags-Anstalt, 1983), pp. 132, 136, 241; Schwarz, *Adenauer*, 2:663, 694; and Arnulf Baring, *Sehr verehrter Herr Bundeskanzler! Heinrich von Brentano im Briefwechsel mit Konrad Adenauer, 1949–1964* (Hamburg: Hoffmann und Campe, 1974), p. 328. Strauss, even as early as 1956, ruled out the nuclear option in this context, and this remained his view for the entire crisis period. See Radford-Strauss meeting, December 10, 1956, DSP/52/57412/ML, and Strauss-Nitze meetings, July 29–30, 1961, AP/85/SDWHA/HSTL.

and did nothing in the military area to show that they were ready for a showdown, then the Soviets would see through their bluff and bring the crisis to a head. If they did, and if at the climax of the crisis "everybody backs down and puts pressure on us to accept the free city proposal"—the line Adenauer had taken with the president in August—"this would obviously be a fiasco." American leaders often argued along these lines with German officials.[126] And when they did, the Germans always gave way and conceded the fundamental point. The Federal Republic would support the Americans and agree to military action when the time came. But it was clear that the Germans were in their hearts opposed to military action, and that they remained opposed to it for the entire crisis period.

The Americans in 1959 were coming to have little patience with the basic German position. The western powers had to stand on their rights and could accept no change in the status quo—but the use of force had to be ruled out? There was a sense that the Germans were clinging to theories that were increasingly remote from reality. They seemed caught up in a theology of their own making. The western powers could not deal with the East Germans, they argued, because that would be a step toward formal recognition of the East German regime, and recognition would mean that all hope of reunification was being abandoned and that the status quo was being accepted as final. But why was this more compelling than the counterargument that reunification could only come about after political tensions had eased, and that détente implied better relations with the East German regime? The American view, in fact, was that if Germany was ever to be reunified, it could not be through force. The "only way" it could be achieved, Eisenhower thought, was through a "peaceful agreement" with the East German authorities. It therefore did not make sense for Adenauer to be so opposed to a policy of détente in central Europe. The hard line was supposed to keep the hope of reunification alive, but Dulles and Eisenhower both thought that a softer line was more likely in the long run to lead to a fusion of the two German states.[127]

Couldn't the German government be brought to see this? Privately, Adenauer agreed with Eisenhower that reunification "would have to be achieved in a step-by-step process in which the two sides of Germany would themselves have to exhibit a clear readiness to be conciliatory and reasonable."[128] But if he conceded the principle, why did he cling so rigidly in practice to the opposite kind of policy, which rejected the idea of anything like a "normalization" of relations between the two German states? Maybe Adenauer did not really care about reunification. Could it be that he had adopted a hard line in the past for domestic political purposes—that he in fact had never taken the "policy of strength" seriously, that its

[126] Kohler-Grewe meeting, February 24, 1960, and Kohler-Carstens meeting, March 15, 1960, FRUS 1958–60, 9:201–202, 233–234.

[127] Eisenhower-Dulles telephone conversation, November 24, 1958, ibid., 8:118. See also Trachtenberg, *History and Strategy,* pp. 196–197. Dulles also frequently argued for a more flexible German policy on dealings with the east. See, for example, Dulles-Grewe meeting, January 15, 1959; de Gaulle-Dulles meeting, February 6, 1959; Dulles-Adenauer meeting, February 7, 1959, FRUS 1958–60, 8:267, 333, 339.

[128] Eisenhower-Adenauer conversation, May 27, 1959, AWF/DDED/39/DDEL.

real purpose had been to outflank his nationalistic opponents at home from the right, that his real but unavowed aim was to neutralize the pressure for a deal with Russia that would reunify Germany but would at the same time take the country out of the western bloc?[129]

American and other western leaders had assumed for some time that reunification was not a matter of high priority for Adenauer. In the east, the SPD was much stronger than the CDU. Reunification would quite possibly tip the political balance within the country and bring the socialists to power; the assumption was that Adenauer therefore was not particularly eager to see East Germany brought into the Federal Republic. Herter, for example, thought that Adenauer for this reason "does not want a reunified Germany, even though he continues to call for reunification publicly, as he must."[130]

This was not just pure speculation: the German leaders had made it quite clear that they were not terribly interested in reunification. The western countries were wrong, Adenauer complained in early 1959, to place so much emphasis on this issue.[131] He and other German leaders intimated that their coolness toward reunification really did have a lot to do with likely SPD voting strength in the east. In April, Brentano admitted to Herter that the German position on the Berlin question was essentially negative, but he argued that his government had to protect the interests of the fifty million people in the Federal Republic. "A great part of the opposition in the Federal Republic favored 'undemocratic socialism,'" he said, and a coalition between the SPD and "Communist elements in the GDR might result in a loss of control of developments in Germany." He did not disagree when Herter pointed out that this seemed to mean that "the Federal Republic did not appear to want reunification."[132]

Even more amazingly, Adenauer himself made it clear to Herter a year later "that he had no interest in bringing East Germany into reunification with West Germany at all. He said that reunification is not practicable, and referred to the Socialist voting strength in East Germany."[133] But given all this, how could the Americans be expected to support a policy that despite official claims was not rooted in any genuine concern with reunification? Eisenhower especially was very much out of sympathy with a policy based on parochial domestic political calculations. If the Ger-

[129] Note also Adenauer's comment to the Soviet ambassador in November 1958 that the "policy of strength" was just a cliché, and was not to be taken seriously. Adenauer, *Erinnerungen,* 3:453.

[130] Herter-Eisenhower meeting, August 21, 1959, FRUS 1958–60, 9:4. See also the April 4, 1959, Herter-Eisenhower telephone conversation quoted in Trachtenberg, *History and Strategy,* p. 176. Such views were in fact quite common at the time. Even Khrushchev thought that Adenauer did not want Germany united because he feared it would bring the SPD to power. See Eisenhower-Khrushchev meeting, September 26, 1959, FRUS 1958–60, 9:37. Note also, in this context, the series of comments from former American officials quoted in Rupieper, *Der besetzte Verbündete,* p. 248.

[131] Adenauer memorandum, January 30, 1959, para. 11, Adenauer, *Erinnerungen,* 3:466–467; DOS Berlin History, 1:46. When Dulles told Lloyd about Adenauer's complaint, the British foreign secretary noted that it was only "out of loyalty to Adenauer" that the western powers, "somewhat tongue in cheek," had been arguing that the division of Germany was a basic cause of international tension. Dulles to State Department, February 5, 1959, FRUS 1958–60, 8:318.

[132] Brentano-Herter meeting, April 4, 1959, FRUS 1958–60, 8:581–583, and (for the paraphrase quoted of the passage deleted from this version of the document), DOS Berlin History, 1:83.

[133] Eisenhower-Herter meeting, March 17, 1960, FRUS 1958–60, 9:239.

mans, he felt, could get a "true free reunification," then they would "have to take their chances on politics."[134]

So the Americans were increasingly unhappy with what they saw as Adenauer's rigidity, and in mid-1959 they began to make their displeasure felt. The president told Adenauer in August that "he was getting tired of standing pat," and Herter told Brentano "that the United States was tired of a negative attitude."[135] The Germans were repeatedly "needled" about their inflexibility and urged to "come up with some new ideas."[136] In March 1960, the president was thinking of telling Adenauer directly that the American people were not going to "subordinate themselves and their objectives to those of the Chancellor."[137] His view was that the West "could not really afford to stand on a dime for the next fifty years."[138]

This pressure could not easily be ignored, and the German attitude did become more flexible in the course of 1959. On the whole cluster of issues relating to the division of Germany, dealings with the East German regime, and the recognition of the Oder-Neisse line—in short, on the general question of the stabilization of the status quo—Adenauer was in principle inclined to shift course and take a more "realistic" line. Reunification, he now recognized, was not a serious goal; the maintenance of the status quo was the most one could hope for.[139] The objective now was to get the Soviets to make life more bearable for the Germans in the east; this theme now became a leitmotif of German policy. The whole question, Adenauer told the American president in August 1959, "was really a human and not a national problem. He would like to see the people in the Soviet Zone lead a freer life." For him, he said, "it was a matter of human beings and not one of frontiers." Of course, he said, he could not come out in public and talk realistically about such things as the Oder-Neisse line because there were "refugees and other groups" in Germany who put "nationalistic feelings above human problems."[140] But he personally, as Eisenhower later reported, "accepted the present frontiers of Germany as a fait accompli."[141] As far as dealings with the East German authorities were concerned, he was again prepared to be realistic. De jure recognition was out of the question, he told the other western leaders at Rambouillet in December 1959, but whether "some de facto arrangement for treating with them should be worked out was another matter which would have to be examined in the light of developments."[142] Brentano argued along similar lines when he met with Herter in Au-

---

[134] Eisenhower-Herter telephone conversation, April 4, 1959, quoted in Trachtenberg, *History and Strategy*, p. 176.

[135] Eisenhower-Macmillan meeting, August 29, 1959, FRUS 1958–60, 9:27.

[136] Herter-Stone meeting, November 13, 1959, ibid., p. 111.

[137] Eisenhower-Herter meeting, March 14, 1960, ibid., p. 218.

[138] Eisenhower-Macmillan meeting, March 28, 1960, ibid., p. 259.

[139] Krone diary, entry for March 16, 1959, *Adenauer-Studien*, 3:152; Schwarz, *Adenauer*, 2:480–482; and Seydoux to Couve, February 12, 1959, DDF 1959, 1:200–201.

[140] Eisenhower-Adenauer meeting, August 27, 1959, FRUS 1958–60, 9:19. See also Brentano's views, reported in Seydoux to Couve, November 16, 1959, and Adenauer in a meeting with de Gaulle, December 2, 1959, DDF 1959, 2:577, 660.

[141] Eisenhower–de Gaulle–Macmillan meeting, December 20, 1959, p. 5, Prem 11/2991, PRO.

[142] Eisenhower-Adenauer–de Gaulle–Macmillan meeting, December 19, 1959, p. 25, Prem 11/2991, PRO.

gust. There were political problems having to do with the ten million refugees from the east now in the Federal Republic. "He was very frank in saying," Herter wrote, "that he believed the relationship between West Germany and East Germany could be settled if it were not for the emotional problems involved in a settlement of the Berlin question." Once the German government had gotten through the 1961 elections, he implied, it could take a less "emotional" and more realistic line. And that meant making concessions, even on Berlin. The occupation regime might be ended; West Berlin could become "some kind of free or guaranteed city with U.N. responsibility."[143]

But this flexibility related entirely to Berlin and East Germany. There could be no Berlin settlement, Brentano told Herter, "which in any way weakened *West* Germany or involved moves tending toward neutralization of *West* Germany."[144] The Adenauer government was afraid that the western powers—especially the British, but perhaps even the United States—would agree to a special status for West Germany as a way out of the Berlin crisis. The great fear was that they would agree to a settlement that would perpetuate West Germany's non-nuclear status. An agreement on "European security"—the code term for an arrangement to limit German power, above all in the nuclear area—was widely viewed as one of the key elements of a possible German settlement. Adenauer strongly opposed not just a formal treaty of that kind, but anything that pointed in this general direction. In April 1959, an allied working group had developed a four-phase "Plan for German Reunification, European Security and a German Peace Settlement." German representatives had been in on the drafting of the plan, but now Adenauer refused to go along with it. His main objection was "in the field of security." According to the plan, the ban on nuclear production already accepted by West Germany "would be extended to cover" a security area including the whole of a reunified German state, plus Poland and Czechoslovakia. IRBMs would also not be deployed in that area, even in the first phase of the plan when reunification was simply being discussed. Adenauer was personally putting his foot down. At his instruction, German representatives, to the astonishment of their allies, now "vigorously opposed" these "discriminatory provisions." The restrictions, targeted so obviously on Germany, were too high a price to pay for reunification—indeed, even for reunification within the NATO framework. This, of course, was a complete reversal of the line Adenauer had taken in 1953 and 1955.[145]

[143] Herter-Brentano meeting, August 27, 1959, FRUS 1958–60, 9:18.

[144] Ibid.; emphasis added. See also Schwarz, *Adenauer,* 2:481, 658.

[145] This new line was laid down by Adenauer personally. Brentano made it clear that "these objections" to the working group's plan represented the chancellor's views. It was certainly not the Bonn Foreign Office that was putting its foot down. In fact, after an earlier working group report presented in March had been repudiated by Brentano, the German representatives on that body became "extremely cautious" and cleared everything—and, in particular, everything in the April report that was now being attacked—with the Foreign Office in Bonn. DOS Berlin History, 1:68–94, esp. pp. 76, 84–87, 92–93. On this incident, see also de Leusse to Couve, April 27, 1959, DDF 1959, 1:556–557. For Adenauer's opposition to "European security" arrangements and the more flexible line taken by the German Foreign Office, see Adenauer memorandum, January 30, 1959, para. 12, in Adenauer, *Erinnerungen,* 3:467; Seydoux to Couve, July 13, 1959, DDF 1959, 2:45; Lloyd–van Scherpenberg meeting, January 29, 1959 (reporting the views of the top permanent official in the German foreign ministry), DSP/80/72679/ML.

This episode typified the German position during the whole period of the Berlin crisis. There was little chance that the Soviets would accept a reunification deal that would allow Germany to remain in NATO, but Adenauer was now not willing to accept even the principle of non-nuclear status under any circumstances. The Federal Republic's nuclear status was the one area where concessions would not be made. Defense Minister Strauss, for example, in August 1959 strongly opposed the idea of allowing the question of whether the Bundeswehr should, as planned, be armed with American nuclear weapons "to become a bargaining point in the east-west negotiations."[146] And in March 1960, Adenauer himself "reacted violently" when Herter brought up the idea of a military inspection zone in Europe.[147] This was just a step away from the idea of a security zone and a special status for Germany: one had to avoid being pulled onto the slippery slope. This remained the German view in the Kennedy period as well. A "special status" for Germany was "unacceptable," Adenauer wrote President Kennedy on October 1961. "To our mind zones of a special military status—no matter of what kind— would be disastrous, if not impossible, in Europe."[148]

By then, the German nuclear question had emerged as the great sticking point. This had now become the fundamental issue for Adenauer. The chancellor, as one key German diplomat put it, understood that the Federal Republic "would have to make sacrifices to avoid the very real danger of war and to save the freedom of West Berlin." But there was one area where he "refused to contemplate any concessions," and that had to do with "the armament of the Bundeswehr."[149] It was indeed clear to British and American officials at this point that German resistance to concessions in this area would be very strong.[150]

The question of a German nuclear capability was thus fundamental, both for the USSR and for the Federal Republic. Under Eisenhower, the U.S. government was not prepared to push for concessions in this area. The Berlin Crisis brought no change in Eisenhower's nuclear sharing policy. In December 1958, when the weapons were about to be introduced into Germany in accordance with the stockpile plan, Norstad checked with Washington to make sure that he should "move ahead in this matter." Dulles replied immediately that "he saw no objection on political grounds" to Norstad proceeding as he saw fit."[151] The coming of the crisis was, in fact, a major reason for *not* drawing back. The "development of an atomic capability by German forces" was not only essential for military reasons, but, in the State Department view, it was also "an indication of the West's firmness and resolve, particularly with respect to the Berlin situation."[152] The basic American

[146] Herter to State Department, August 29, 1959, FRUS 1958–60, 9:15.

[147] Adenauer-Herter meeting, March 16, 1960, ibid., p. 237.

[148] Adenauer to Kennedy, October 4, 1961, DDRS Retrospective/326F.

[149] Remarks of the German ambassador in Moscow, quoted in Roberts to Foreign Office, September 5, 1961, FO 371/160548, PRO.

[150] Kohler-Rusk-Shuckburgh meeting, September 17, 1961, FO 371/160552, PRO.

[151] Thurston to Dulles, December 20, 1958, and Murphy to Thurston, December 22, 1958, AWF/DH/8/DDEL.

[152] Murphy to Eisenhower, December 24, 1958, AWF/DH/8/DDEL; also DDRS 1989/1474. Dulles, especially, felt that the country was "entering a test of nerve and will with the Soviets," and was therefore very interested "in going ahead with the quiet moves of increased military preparedness in Europe

attitude under Eisenhower was that limits on German military power could be made part of a general settlement with Russia, but only as part of a deal that would provide for German reunification. If the country was to remain divided, the feeling was that the West should not commit itself on the "security" issue. An agreement in this area—that is, essentially a promise to keep the Federal Republic from acquiring an independent nuclear capability—was too high a price to pay for a Berlin settlement alone.

What this meant was that there was no chance for a general settlement during the late Eisenhower period. The issue of German power—and above all the question of a German nuclear capability—was fundamental for Russia. But on this issue the Federal Republic was determined not to give way, and the Eisenhower administration was not going to make her. A general settlement was thus not in the cards, and from the Soviet point of view there was therefore little point to pressing the issue. The USSR certainly did not want to come anywhere near the point where war was a real possibility. On the other hand, the Soviets did not want to liquidate the crisis either—for example, by working out an arrangement stabilizing the situation around Berlin.

So the Berlin question was put on hold during the last year of the Eisenhower period. The crisis atmosphere faded. Even the collapse of the east-west summit conference in May 1960 did not lead to a sharpening of tension. But soon a new administration took office in Washington, and by early 1961 the Soviet Union was again threatening western rights in Berlin. A new and more dangerous phase of the crisis was about to begin.

---

along the lines he had discussed with General Norstad." In particular, "he was anxious to have atomic weapons moved into Germany as promptly as possible, believing that this would be picked up by Soviet intelligence but not by the general public." Merchant-Dulles meeting, February 27, 1959, 611.61/2–2759, RG 59, USNA.

Kennedy, NATO, and Berlin

IN EARLY 1961, soon after John Kennedy was sworn in as president of the United States, it became clear that the Soviets were again going to press the western powers on Berlin. Khrushchev met with Kennedy at Vienna in June and issued a new "ultimatum." The Soviet leader now explicitly threatened to "liquidate" western rights in the city if a settlement was not worked out by the end of the year.

Kennedy knew what was at stake and was determined not to cave in to these threats. But he was not simply going to dig in his heels and prepare for a showdown. A negotiated settlement would be the best solution. Like Eisenhower before him, he thought that an intransigent position made little sense. The status quo, in his view, was "as undesirable for the United States and the West as it is for the Russians in a good many particulars." The whole Berlin problem, he said, was a "dangerous mess" which he had inherited and which he now sought to clean up by reaching an understanding with the USSR.[1]

Kennedy hoped the two major powers could find some way to live with each other in peace. America and Russia, he felt, were both very great powers. They should deal with each other on that basis and in particular should respect each other's most fundamental interests. The U.S. government, he told Khrushchev at Vienna, did not "wish to act in a way that would deprive the Soviet Union of its ties in Eastern Europe"—that is, the Americans would in effect accept that area as a Soviet sphere of influence. The U.S. government would also make sure that German power remained limited. The United States, Kennedy told the Soviet leader, was "opposed to a buildup in West Germany that would constitute a threat to the Soviet Union"—and, given military realities, that could only mean the development of an independent German nuclear capability. But in return the USSR would have to respect American interests in Europe, and in particular would have to accept the status quo in Berlin. The city itself might not be of fundamental importance. But if America were to capitulate on Berlin, if she were to allow the Soviets to trample on her rights and to treat her most solemn commitments as though they were of no account, then her whole political position in Europe would collapse. The effect on the global balance of power would be profound. Khrushchev, the president said, would not accept a "similar loss and we cannot accept it either."[2]

The basic goal was thus to stabilize the status quo in central Europe. Both sides would agree to leave things as they were. If a general settlement of this sort were reached, Berlin would no longer be a problem for the West and Germany would no longer be a problem for the USSR. But a system based on keeping German power limited meant that the United States would have to remain in Europe in-

[1] Krock-Kennedy meeting, October 11, 1961, KP/1, vol. 3, item 343, ML.
[2] Kennedy-Khrushchev meetings, June 4, 1961, FRUS 1961–63, 14:87–98. The sentence about eastern Europe (p. 95) was deleted from the version of the document declassified in 1990.

definitely. The limitations on German power—above all, West Germany's non-nuclear status—and the maintenance of a sizeable American force on West German soil were two sides to a coin. There had to be some effective counterweight to Soviet military power in central Europe. If Germany was to remain non-nuclear, only American power could play that role, and to play it effectively, American forces had to be physically present on German territory. The Germans were being asked to make major sacrifices—to accept a non-nuclear status and thus to remain totally dependent on America for their security—and they were entitled to something in exchange: the United States would have to protect the Federal Republic by maintaining a military force there on a more or less permanent basis.

This, of course, was very different from the Eisenhower policy. Eisenhower had hoped that the unification of Europe would make it possible for the Europeans to defend themselves, and would thus pave the way for an American withdrawal. A unified western Europe, with a nuclear force under its own control, could effectively counterbalance Soviet power without direct American involvement. But under Kennedy all this was considered quite unrealistic. Whatever the long-term prospects, it was clear that a genuine pooling of sovereignty in western Europe was not imminent. Under present political conditions, any so-called European force would be a simple knitting together of forces under ultimate national control, and would thus not solve the fundamental problem of how to balance Soviet power without allowing the Germans to get a nuclear force of their own. A European force that included a German contingent was out of the question, because it meant in the final analysis a German finger on the nuclear trigger, and a force built up from British and French contingents alone would scarcely solve Germany's security problem, or lead the Germans to accept a permanent non-nuclear status. So from the point of view of the new administration, there was no purely European solution to the security problem. The American military commitment to Europe was therefore inescapable.

This whole approach was rooted in the premise that the Germans could not be allowed a nuclear capability of their own, and indeed that premise was a very basic part of the Kennedy policy. The new administration felt from the outset that some "mechanism must be provided to make it impossible for the Germans to develop an independent nuclear capacity."[3] It was a "fixed point" of American policy, as McGeorge Bundy, Kennedy's national security adviser, later wrote, "that Germany should not have independent control of nuclear weapons."[4] The assumption was

[3] Acheson's views, paraphrased by Kennedy, in Anglo-American meeting, April 5, 1961, 3:15 P.M., p. 2, Cab 133/244, PRO.

[4] Bundy to Kennedy, "The U.S. and de Gaulle—The Past and the Future," January 30, 1963, p. 8, President's Office Files [POF]/116/JFKL. Bundy identified himself as the author of this document in a meeting on the Nassau conference held at the Woodrow Wilson Center in Washington on February 11, 1992. The basic assumption that a German nuclear capability would be quite dangerous and therefore had to be avoided is reflected in many U.S. documents from the period. Note, for example, Rusk's comment that "national ownership of MRBM's by Germany might be considered *casus belli* by the Soviets" and "might also have serious repercussions within the Alliance itself" (Rusk-Stikker meeting, February 7, 1962, DDRS 1996/2056, and also his remarks in a meeting with the Senate Foreign Relations Committee on August 28, 1963, *Executive Sessions of the Senate Foreign Relations Committee (Historical Series)*, vol. 15 (Washington, D.C.: GPO, 1987), pp. 520–521.

that the development of a German nuclear force would be a source of instability both in itself and because of the likely Soviet reaction. But if a German force was to be ruled out, that meant that the United States would also have to oppose the French nuclear force and even the British nuclear force. The Federal Republic could not be singled out as the one major ally that would not be allowed to have nuclear weapons. To keep Germany non-nuclear, the United States would therefore have to oppose nuclear forces under national control as a matter of general policy. And that general policy implied that the U.S. government would have to tighten control over American nuclear weapons with the NATO forces in Europe. The deployment of American strategic missiles on European soil would also have to be opposed, because these weapons might fall too easily into the hands of host country forces.

U.S. policy on the nuclear sharing question was thus now utterly transformed. Eisenhower had wanted the Europeans to be able to defend themselves. Since they had to confront a nuclear-armed superpower, that had meant that they needed nuclear forces under their own control. But under Kennedy nuclear sharing was no longer a goal of American policy. The term itself now fell into disfavor, and people were beginning to talk instead about the great problem of nuclear "proliferation." The allies were now encouraged to leave the "nuclear deterrent business" in American hands.

Would the Germans go along with the new U.S. policy? Would they agree to remain non-nuclear in exchange for an American security guarantee, a permanent American troop presence, and a Soviet promise to respect the status quo in Berlin? The other allies, Britain and France in particular, were also being asked to make sacrifices, especially in the nuclear area. Could the U.S. government get them to cooperate? And above all, would the Soviets accept a settlement of the sort Kennedy had in mind? Their most basic security interests would be accommodated. But it was by no means clear that they would pay the price Kennedy insisted on. Would they be willing to respect the status quo in central Europe and leave things as they were in Berlin?

So Kennedy had to conduct a struggle on two fronts: with the Soviet Union, but also with his own allies. With Russia, the goal was to avoid both war and a disastrous capitulation over Berlin. That meant that there had to be some iron in the western position, and the president therefore had to think in terms of how force might be used if America were pushed far enough. But he also needed to see whether a negotiated settlement along the lines he had in mind could be worked out. At the same time, he had to get the allies to accept what he was trying to accomplish—that is, a stabilization of the status quo. Positions that the Federal Republic had defended for many years might have to be abandoned. Could the Germans be made to accept such a far-reaching change of policy? Their attitude would depend to a certain extent on the position that the other allies, and France above all, took on these issues. But could de Gaulle be brought along? And all these issues were tightly bound up with the question of the control of nuclear forces within the Atlantic alliance. An arrangement keeping Germany non-nuclear might be an important part of a settlement with Russia; but to keep Germany from building a nuclear force of her own, the United States might also have to oppose the idea of

British and French nuclear forces. What would this imply about NATO strategy? What sort of NATO structure might meet the Europeans' concerns about the declining credibility of the American nuclear deterrent, if they were to have no nuclear forces of their own? These were all very difficult questions, and ultimately the president himself needed to decide on the answers.

Nuclear Weapons and the Defense of Berlin

What would the United States do if the Berlin Crisis came to a head—if the Soviets actually carried out their threat to "liquidate" western rights in Berlin and cut off western access to the city? In principle, the Kennedy administration adopted a new defense policy in 1961. The old Eisenhower strategy of "massive retaliation" was to be replaced by a new strategy of "flexible response." A president, the argument ran, should never be forced to choose between "holocaust and capitulation." It was vital that he have a broader range of options. The Soviets were building up their nuclear forces, and a full-scale American nuclear attack on Russia would probably be suicidal—if not now then certainly in the very near future. In such circumstances, the USSR would not take American nuclear threats seriously. America therefore could not rely so heavily on her nuclear capability; instead, NATO's conventional forces needed to be built up.

The basic idea behind flexible response, at least officially, was to "enhance the credibility" of the nuclear deterrent, and not to phase out all reliance on nuclear weapons. By being able to engage in non-nuclear operations on a fairly major scale, the argument ran, the western powers might be able to convince the Russians that "political aggression" on their part was too risky. There would "inevitably" be a "substantial risk" that a non-nuclear conflict in Europe would rapidly develop into a full-scale nuclear war. By being able to use conventional force in a major way, the western powers might be able to get the Soviets to draw back before it was late. This approach, the top civilians in the Defense Department argued, was obviously better than relying on simple nuclear threats that were no longer credible.[5]

Berlin was the main case in point. The Eisenhower strategy for the defense of Berlin clearly had to be changed. The United States, Secretary of State Dean Rusk explained, "no longer anticipated a situation in which interruption of our access rights would be immediately followed by 'the big bang' of nuclear warfare." The old strategy of launching a full-scale nuclear attack as soon as a few jeeps were turned back on the autobahn was no longer acceptable. Instead, one had to start with nonmilitary actions and then take military measures in "ascending order of violence."[6]

The new administration had thus opted for a Berlin strategy of "mounting pressures"—that is, for a strategy of controlled escalation, or, more precisely, of semi-controlled escalation, because the pressure would result from the growing risk that

---

[5] McNamara to Kennedy, September 18, 1961, p. 4, FRUS 1961–63, vols. 13–15, mic. supp., no. 177.

[6] Rusk meeting with European ambassadors, August 9, 1961, and Rusk to Bruce, August 26, 1961, ibid., 14:321, 372.

the conflict would become uncontrollable as the fighting became more intense. The fundamental objective was to make "nuclear deterrence more credible." The assumption was that the nuclear deterrent would not be credible to the Soviets "unless they are convinced of NATO's readiness to become engaged on a lesser level of violence and are thereby made to realize the great risks of escalation to nuclear war."[7] This would be done by creating a "chain of plausible U.S. response in which each stage would believably lead to the next higher chain of force."[8] One could begin with a small probe. If that failed, the allies could take various non-military actions and at the same time mobilize and prepare themselves for major military operations. If access remained blocked, the allies could then take non-nuclear action, beginning perhaps with a battalion-size operation, then using a full division, and perhaps eventually a three- or four-division force. If the Soviets still did not back down, nuclear weapons would have to be used, perhaps initially in a limited way in the theater of operations in central Europe, but ultimately, if necessary, a full-scale nuclear attack on the USSR would be launched.[9] The plan was thus to "provide for a number of measures involving a progressive degree of force, thereby compelling the Russians to take a series of decisions, each more dangerous than the last."[10] The West would in this way be able to drive home to the Soviets the extraordinary risks they would be running if they persisted with their policy.

American officials at the time often spoke as though this new strategy represented a total break with what had come before, but the shift in strategy was not nearly as radical as the rhetoric implied. Under Eisenhower, the plan for Berlin had never been to order a full-scale nuclear attack as soon as a few jeeps were stopped on the autobahn. Instead, various non-nuclear measures would be undertaken, culminating in a division-size operation. If the division were attacked, the "fat would be in the fire," and at that point an all-out nuclear attack would be launched.[11] With regard to NATO strategy in general, the importance of a degree

[7] Kennedy to Norstad, October 20, 1961, and NSAM 109, "U.S. Policy on Military Actions in a Berlin Conflict," October 20, 1961, ibid., pp. 520–523. The basic U.S. philosophy of controlled escalation was portrayed in some detail in the British documents. See especially Confidential Annex to COS(61)38th meeting, June 20, 1961, on Berlin contingency planning, pp. 3–4, and Confidential Annex to COS(61) 42nd meeting, July 4, 1961, p. 2, both in Defe 4/136, PRO, and Joint Planning Staff, "Brief on Plans to Restore Access to Berlin," July 14, 1961, JP(61)82 (Final), p. 2, Defe 6/71, PRO. Another British document presents American thinking at a slighter later point, and gives the British critique; it also outlines the various Berlin contingency plans—the "Bercons"—that had been worked out by this point. Joint Planning Staff, "Berlin Contingency Planning—Phasing of Military Operations," January 19, 1962, JP(62)6(Final), appended to C.O.S.(62) 7th meeting, January 23, 1962, Defe 4/142, PRO. See also Paul Nitze, From Hiroshima to Glasnost (New York: Grove Weidenfeld, 1989), pp. 203–205.

[8] NSC meeting, July 19, 1961, FRUS 1961–63, 14:221.

[9] See the sources cited in above, note 7. The biggest ground operations described in the January 19, 1962, document cited there, Bercons Charlie 3 and 4, called for the use of three divisions. By July of that year, these plans had evidently been revised to provide for a four-division force. See Nitze to Mc-Namara, July 20, 1962, FRUS 1961–63, vols. 13–15, mic. supp., no. 363.

[10] Shuckburgh paraphrase of U.S. thinking, Confidential Annex to COS(61) 38th meeting, June 20, 1961, Defe 4/136, PRO.

[11] See the discussion in chapter 7 above, pp. 257–258, and in Trachtenberg, History and Strategy, pp. 209–212.

of "flexibility" had often been recognized during the Eisenhower period. At the NATO Council meeting in December 1960, Secretaries Gates and Herter, for example, had each stressed the importance of "flexibility of response."[12] And Norstad had been quite outspoken about the need for forces with a strong conventional capability. In September 1960, for example, he told Gates that "we should be very careful not to go overboard in our reliance on the use of nuclear weapons," that it was "necessary to raise the level of conventional response," that nuclear use should "not be considered as the normal immediate response," and that "we should be very careful not to organize ourselves into a position where we *must* respond at once with nuclear weapons."[13]

Under Eisenhower, the threat of nuclear escalation was of course the ultimate basis of U.S. defense policy. But under Kennedy as well, the defense of NATO Europe continued to rest on America's ultimate willingness to accept a full-scale nuclear confrontation with the USSR. People like Secretary of Defense Robert McNamara might have been inclined to think that nuclear escalation would for all intents and purposes be suicidal, that nuclear weapons were therefore good only for deterring their use by others, and that the West ultimately needed conventional forces strong enough to balance Soviet conventional power on their own.[14] But Kennedy never saw things this way. In his view, a sizeable nuclear force could keep the Soviets from attacking western Europe no matter what the conventional balance was, and it was the Berlin problem alone that had created the need for substantial conventional capabilities. "Absent the problem of Berlin," Kennedy thought, nuclear forces by themselves would be enough to stabilize the situation in Europe: in that case, aggression across the line of demarcation in Europe "would in fact lead promptly to nuclear warfare"; "for that reason," he thought, "the nuclear deterrent would be effective."[15] This was very much in line with the way his

[12] For Herter's remarks, see U.S. Delegation to State Department, December 17, 1960, FRUS 1958–60, 7(1):678; for the Gates statement, see DDRS 1987/1141.

[13] Gates Norstad meeting, September 16, 1960, NP/91/US Support of NATO 1958 60 (2)/DDEL. Emphasis his. Norstad in fact often argued along these lines. On February 2, 1961, for example, he told the NATO Military Committee that "we must be able to deter incidents by having a graduated capability cover the full range of threats from minor incursion to a situation approaching general war." The NATO command, he said, would use whatever force was necessary, but a "substantial conventional capability" would "add to the credibility of the deterrent." Token forces, he argued, "would simply invite piecemeal attacks and gradual erosion." Norstad meeting with the Military Committee, February 2, 1961, NP/105/Memos for the Record II: 1960–61 (4)/DDEL. See also the extracts from NATO documents (including a top secret letter of September 13, 1960, from Norstad to the NATO commander in central Europe) quoted at some length in Stikker to Acheson, January 9, 1961, pp. 7–9, AP/WHSDA/HSTL.

[14] McNamara much later argued quite explicitly that nuclear forces serve no purpose beyond deterring their use by others. See, for example, his article, "The Military Role of Nuclear Weapons: Perceptions and Misperceptions," *Foreign Affairs* 62 (Fall 1983): 79. He says this was his view when he was secretary of defense, even in 1961, and a document that David Rosenberg found seems to support him on this point. See McNamara to JCS Chairman, February 10, 1961, appendix A, enclosed in JCS 2101/408, CCS 3001 Basic National Security Policy (10 February 1961), RG 218, USNA.

[15] Kennedy-Bundy-Rusk-McNamara meeting, December 10, 1962 (notes dated December 13), p. 3, FRUS 1961–63, vols. 13–15, mic. supp., no. 27. Kennedy frequently argued along these lines. See, for example, Kennedy-Strauss meeting, June 8, 1962, ibid., no. 350; Kennedy-Adenauer meeting, November 14, 1962, and Kennedy-Macmillan meeting, December 19, 1962, ibid., 13:452, 1098; and

predecessor had viewed the problem: a war in Europe, Eisenhower had thought, could not be fought without nuclear weapons; a conflict over Berlin was the only exception.[16]

The real difference between the Kennedy and the Eisenhower strategy was one of degree. How far should the western side go—how far would the western side be able to go—before nuclear weapons would have to be used? How hard should the western side try to slow down the escalatory process? The whole thrust of the new thinking in 1961 was that the process needed to be drawn out in order to allow the terrible threat of nuclear escalation time to sink in. The aim, once the crisis had moved into its military phase, was "to produce non-nuclear combat, on a substantial scale, over as extended a period as possible." The Soviet political leadership needed to be forced to make a very serious decision, and "Allied interests appear to be best served by giving the Soviet leaders both motive and opportunity for changing their course. To do this, the Allied objective must be the ability to prolong, not abbreviate, the non-nuclear phase."[17] The goal was to avoid both nuclear war and a massive political defeat; and while there could be no guarantees, the assumption was that this strategy gave the western side its best chance of achieving that objective.

Military leaders disliked this kind of thinking, and Norstad was particularly critical. The NATO commander thought that the new political leadership was just kidding itself about how much control would be possible. The idea of moving "easily and by prepared steps" from one stage of a military confrontation to another—the idea that the development of the crisis would be "within our own control"—struck him as unrealistic. Escalation, he told the president, was "apt to be explosive."[18] The western allies could not afford to wait too long before acting, in part because NATO nuclear strike capabilities would be degraded during a period of conventional fighting.[19] A degree of flexibility was of course essential, but the new administration wanted to go too far. Norstad was sorry, he told Kennedy, that he had ever introduced concepts like "pause" and "threshold" into strategic discourse, given the "rigid and misleading" way they were now being used.[20]

Norstad's critique was by no means limited to an argument about the dynamics of escalation. He attacked the new thinking at an even more basic level.

---

briefing on Berlin, August 9, 1962, ibid., 15:269. For another document reflecting Kennedy's inclination to accept a nuclear-based strategy, see Kennedy-McNamara-JCS meeting, December 27, 1962, ibid., 8:449.

[16] Eisenhower-Spaak meeting, October 4, 1960, p. 3, SS/ITM/5/NATO(6)[1959–1960]/DDEL. The relevant sentence, which appeared in the version of the document declassified in 1979, was sanitized out of the version released in 1987 (DDRS 1987/2101) and published in FRUS 1958–60, 7(1):641, in 1993.

[17] Rusk and McNamara to Kennedy, December 5, 1961, NP/104/Kennedy, J.F. (3)/DDEL.

[18] Norstad-Kennedy meeting, October 3, 1961, FRUS 1961–63, vols. 13–15, mic. supp., no. 191. See also Legere and Smith to Taylor, "General Norstad's Views," September 28, 1961, NSABF.

[19] "General Norstad's General Comments on the Secretary of Defense's Answers to the Ten Questions," September 16, 1961, para. 6, DDRS 1989/91. On this point, see also Legere to Taylor, September 28, 1961, para. 2, NSABF, and LeMay in Kennedy-JCS meeting, September 20, 1961, DDRS 1993/2309.

[20] Kennedy-Norstad meeting, October 3, 1961, p. 2, FRUS 1961–63, vols. 13–15, mic. supp., no. 191.

Kennedy's top civilian advisers, most notably McNamara and Rusk, were willing to accept "some unbalanced losses," including losses of nuclear capability, while the fighting was going on at the non-nuclear level. They were even willing to discontinue military operations, at least for a certain period of time, after the Soviets had "destroyed" an allied probe force. The whole philosophy was to avoid escalation unless the Soviets insisted on it. Norstad was deeply opposed to this whole approach. "Once major forces were engaged," he told the president, "the United States must be in a position to use whatever forces were necessary." He would not use nuclear weapons if there were any alternative, but "when you have started a serious ground action, you cannot afford to get thrown back." The defense of Europe rested ultimately on nuclear deterrence, but "the deterrent has no meaning except in the context of the readiness to use atomic weapons." And the West had to be ready to escalate quickly, as soon as a major force got into serious trouble. The plan to use limited force, possibly eventually involving the use of a relatively small number of nuclear weapons, had a political and not a military objective. The aim was to test the Soviet response. These actions, in Norstad's view, would serve their purpose very quickly, "probably within hours." Either the crisis would be settled quickly, or a full-scale nuclear war would break out.[21]

Norstad's basic argument here was that nuclear deterrence was the heart of western strategy, and it was therefore vital that nothing be done to reduce the risk that the USSR would be running if the crisis came to a head. The Soviets could not be given a free ride; they could not be given control over the escalatory process. "The credibility of the deterrent," he argued, "can be destroyed by emphasizing a policy that could be construed by the Soviets as permitting them to become involved, and then, if they decide the risks are too great, to disengage." The Soviets had to be "forced to act and move at all times in full awareness that if they use force they risk general war with nuclear weapons." More generally, the whole strategy that the civilians were calling for, especially the increased emphasis they placed on conventional capabilities, however cleverly this was rationalized, was bound to come across as reflecting a growing reluctance on America's part to use nuclear weapons, no matter what happened in Europe. The United States, whatever its real motives, would be seen, not just by the Soviets but by the Europeans as well, as running away from nuclear deterrence. The results, Norstad thought, might well be disastrous.[22]

In this dispute Kennedy's instinct was to side with his civilian advisers and to put more distance between himself and the terrifying prospect of nuclear war. But

[21] Rusk and McNamara to Kennedy, December 5, 1961, NP/104/Kennedy, J.F. (3)/DDEL; Norstad-Kennedy meeting, October 3, 1961, pp. 1–4, FRUS 1961–63, vols. 13–15, mic. supp., no. 191; Norstad to Kennedy, November 16, 1961, with SACEUR's "Instructions to SHAPE Planners," NP/104/Kennedy, J.F.(4)/DDEL. Note also Bundy to Kennedy, October 20, 1961 (for his reference to the question of "delay" vs. "prompt action" as "the issue which divides the soldiers and the civilians"), FRUS 1961–63, vols. 13–15, mic. supp., no. 208, and the account of Norstad's meeting with Rusk and McNamara in Paris on December 15, 1961, in Thurston to Fessenden, December 18, 1961, 740.5/12-1861.

[22] Norstad's comments on McNamara's answers to the "Ten Questions," September 16, 1961, DDRS 1989/91. For Norstad's thinking, see also Norstad to Kennedy, November 16, 1961, with SACEUR's "Instructions to SHAPE Planners," and Rusk and McNamara to Kennedy, December 5, 1961 (commenting on the November 16 letter), NP/104/Kennedy, J.F. (3) and (4)/DDEL.

he was anything but doctrinaire on these issues, and he certainly did not dismiss the military view out of hand. As the president saw it, there obviously was something to what Norstad now argued. It was, for example, by no means evident that a conventional buildup would "convince Khrushchev of our readiness to fight to a finish for West Berlin." The president wondered whether it might in fact "have the opposite effect."[23] His mind was open. And he had to think these extremely serious issues out for himself—not on an abstract level, but in as concrete a context as possible. He and his top advisers therefore pressed hard for information. What was likely to happen once military operations began? Why exactly did military leaders think that escalation was "apt to be explosive"? If escalation was virtually inevitable after a certain point, should the United States try to limit damage to herself and to her allies by striking first? How effective would such an attack be in eliminating the USSR's ability to retaliate?

Kennedy discussed these issues repeatedly and in considerable detail with top military leaders. The basic conclusion to emerge was that once serious fighting had begun, the pressure to escalate really would be enormous. It might be possible for the enemy to prevent a relatively small force from moving, and if that force got into trouble it might be possible to send in a larger force to bail it out. But if an American force, especially a relatively large force, was attacked and was in danger of being wiped out, the president could hardly stand by and allow that force to be destroyed. He would probably have little choice but to authorize the use of nuclear weapons locally to save that force. And indeed the main plans for large-scale ground operations in connection with the Berlin Crisis provided for possible nuclear support.[24]

The whole point of a major ground operation, in fact, was to create a situation that would force the enemy to see "that if the fighting continues, nuclear weapons will be used."[25] The idea was in effect to burn America's bridges, to sacrifice a degree of control, to make escalation almost automatic as soon as the Soviets attacked the American force. The ball would be in their court; it would be they and not the Americans who would have to make the terrible decision to start what would almost certainly end up being a full-scale nuclear war; the hope was that they would draw back and agree to settle the crisis on terms the U.S. government could accept.

[23] Kennedy to Rusk and McNamara, September 8, 1961, NSAM 92, FRUS 1961–63, 14:398–399. Note also his later comment that it had perhaps been a mistake to press so hard for a conventional buildup. Carstens to Schröder, February 6, 1963, AAPBD 1963, 1:274.

[24] See especially British Joint Planning Staff, "Brief on Plans to Restore Access to Berlin," July 14, 1961, JP(61)82(Final), pp. 3, 7, Defe 6/71, PRO. Another British document pointed out that some of the key Berlin contingency plans had nuclear annexes, and that military operations could thus, "if necessary, be conducted as nuclear operations." British Joint Planning Staff, "Berlin Contingency Planning—Phasing of Military Operations," January 19, 1962, JP(62)6(Final), appended to COS(62)7th meeting, Defe 4/142, PRO. On the issue of nuclear use if the Berlin Crisis came to a head, see also Stoessel to Kohler, August 11, 1961, and Rusk in meeting with Alphand and Hood, October 6, 1961, p. 3, both in NSABF.

[25] Acheson report on Berlin, June 28, 1961, FRUS 1961–63, 14:155–156; Acheson remarks in Berlin Coordinating Group, June 16, 1961, at NSC meeting, June 19, 1961, and in Berlin steering group, September 7, 1961, ibid., pp. 119–121, 161, 397; McNamara to Kennedy, September 18, 1961, p. 4, ibid., vols. 13–15, mic. supp., no. 177.

And Kennedy basically accepted this view. He agreed that once the battle was joined and the Soviets began to kill Americans on a major scale, the president could no longer hold back. "I suppose if we get involved in a war in Europe," he remarked during an August 1962 briefing on Berlin contingency plans, "we will have no choice but to use nuclear weapons."[26] And as soon as nuclear weapons started to be used, the level of violence would almost certainly escalate very rapidly, as each side sought to destroy the enemy's nuclear forces as rapidly as possible. The president had been advised, as he himself noted, "that if I ever released a nuclear weapon on the battlefield I should start a pre-emptive attack on the Soviet Union as the use of nuclear weapons was bound to escalate and we might as well get the advantage by going first."[27] As he told de Gaulle in June 1961: "in nuclear warfare, the advantage of striking first with nuclear weapons is so great that if Soviets were to attack even without using such weapons, the U.S. could not afford to wait to use them." If war broke out and the Soviets "threatened to overrun Europe," America, he said, would have to "strike first with nuclear weapons."[28]

The assumption was thus that if a sizeable American force were attacked and threatened with destruction, the fighting would probably escalate rapidly, and that from that point on a full-scale war was very likely. It followed that major military operations should be undertaken only if the United States was prepared to accept the risk of nuclear escalation, and indeed, if necessary, to engage in general nuclear war. Acheson, now back in power as a top Kennedy adviser, argued in June 1961 that if the American government were to undertake any military action at all, it had to be prepared ultimately to go to war with Russia. He had earlier felt that the West might be able to bluff its way through the crisis, but that if the Soviets forced the issue, the western powers would ultimately have to give way. Nuclear weapons, he had argued in April, should under no circumstances be used, and indeed he had thought the United States "should make plain by its preparations that it did not intend to initiate the use of nuclear weapons." But by June he had concluded that a strategy of bluff could not work. Military operations should only be begun if the United States was willing, in the final analysis, to go to war rather than to capitulate in the crisis. "If we were not prepared to go all the way," he said, "we should not start."[29]

[26] Quoted in John Ausland, "A Nuclear War to Keep Berlin Open?" *International Herald Tribune,* June 19, 1991. Note also Kennedy's comment that as soon as "someone gets killed, the danger of major involvement is very great," in his October 3, 1961, meeting with Norstad, p. 5, FRUS 1961–63, vols. 13–15, mic. supp., no. 191. Note finally his comment in an NSC meeting on May 9, 1963, that "if we were overrun in Korea, in Formosa, or in Western Europe, we would obviously use nuclear weapons." Ibid., 19:588.

[27] NSC meeting on NESC report, September 12, 1963, ibid., 8:507.

[28] Kennedy-de Gaulle meeting, June 1, 1961, DDRS 1994/2586.

[29] For Acheson's position, see Anglo-American talks, April 5, 1961, FRUS 1961–63, 14:37, and Acheson to Kennedy, April 3, 1961 (preliminary report on Berlin), NSABF, which has the first passage quoted. See also Dean Acheson, "Wishing Won't Hold Berlin," *Saturday Evening Post,* March 7, 1959, and the discussion in McGeorge Bundy, *Danger and Survival: Choices about the Bomb in the First Fifty Years* (New York: Random House, 1988), pp. 375–376. Note also Nitze's similar views at this point: Nitze to Lippmann, October 26, 1959, Acheson Papers, box 23, folder 295, Sterling Library, Yale University, New Haven, Conn. Nitze and Acheson were very close throughout this period. For Acheson's later, more tough-minded, views, see his report on Berlin, June 28, 1961, FRUS 1961–63, 14:141,

The key factor, therefore, was whether the United States could indeed contemplate going all the way. Would it make sense for America, in extreme circumstances, to launch a major nuclear attack? If the United States could essentially wipe out the Soviet retaliatory force—that is, if the attack the Soviets would be capable of mounting with whatever they had left would not cause really heavy destruction—then a preemptive attack would in the final analysis be a possible option. It was an option that would be considered only if America had her back to the wall, only if the alternative was a massive American military and political defeat in central Europe; but if the Americans did have such a capability, that fact would condition both sides' behavior at every stage of the crisis. The USSR would be more likely to back off in the end, and the Americans would know it. They would therefore be in a position to take a relatively tough line, and indeed, if necessary, to escalate the conflict; the Soviets would in such circumstances be reluctant to push things too far. From the U.S. point of view, the risks would be relatively low: American strategic superiority could support the western position in Berlin.

But was the United States in a position to execute a preemptive attack of this sort? Even among Kennedy's top civilian advisers opinions on this issue varied.[30] The president therefore had to decide the issue for himself, so he pressed hard for information about war plans, alert procedures, and so on. He wanted to make sure, for example, that if he had to order a nuclear attack, the effectiveness of the action would not be compromised by measures that would tip off the Soviets about what was being prepared and allow them to take countermeasures. In a July 1961 meeting with the JCS, he "talked about the difficulty in Central Europe with a conventional war and stated that he felt that the critical point is to be able to use nuclear weapons at a crucial moment before they use them. He inquired as to our capabilities of making such a decision without letting the enemy know what we are about to do it." What did his government know about the "Soviet capability to detect and to react" to an American attack once it had been launched? The effectiveness of the attack might depend on how quickly the Soviets were able to respond and launch their own missiles before they were destroyed, so he wanted to learn what he could about the "reaction time required by the Soviets to launch an attack with currently available medium and intercontinental range ballistic missiles."[31]

Kennedy succeeded in educating himself on these issues, and by the end of his first year in office he had reached a number of very important conclusions. The

---

155–156, 159, and his remarks in the Berlin Coordinating Group, June 16, 1961, and at the NSC meeting of June 19, 1961, ibid., pp. 119–121, 161; the last passage quoted is on p. 121.

[30] McNamara and Nitze, for example, took very different positions on this question. See White House meeting, October 10, 1961, FRUS 1961–63, 14:489.

[31] See Kennedy-JCS meeting, July 27, 1961, and Lemnitzer to Kennedy, September 27, 1961, ibid., 8:123, 152. Note also JCS Chairman Lemnitzer's reference in a letter to Norstad to a long meeting with Kennedy on January 17, 1962. "Last evening," Lemnitzer wrote, "I and several members of the Joint staff had a two-hour conference with the President and several specially selected members of the White House staff on the subject of alert procedures, SIOP, employment of nuclear weapons in Europe, etc." He warned Norstad to be prepared for a "thorough discussion of the subject" when he met with the president the following week. Lemnitzer to Norstad, January 18, 1962, NP/Policy File, Berlin–Live Oak 1962 (3)/DDEL.

first was that a preemptive strike was, for the time being at least, still a viable option. Kennedy obviously had no wish to start a nuclear war, but if the alternative was a massive American defeat in Europe and thus the collapse of America's whole position in the world, a preemptive attack might be his best—or, more precisely, his least bad—option.[32]

By January 1962 he had in fact come to the conclusion that a preemptive strike might indeed at some point be necessary, and he wanted to be certain that if he had to order an attack, that order would be executed without delay. On January 18, he told the NSC that the Berlin Crisis was probably going to become more acute, that military plans had to be studied carefully, and that in particular it was important "to think hard about the ways and means of making decisions that might lead to nuclear war."[33] He had just met with top military officers to discuss these matters in some detail. A recently declassified document gives some sense for the sort of question he wanted answered:

Question Number 1.
Assuming that information from a closely guarded source causes me to conclude that the U.S. should launch an immediate nuclear strike against the Communist Bloc, does the JCS Emergency Actions File permit me to initiate such an attack without first consulting with the Secretary of Defense and/or the Joint Chiefs of Staff?

Question Number 2.
I know that the red button on my desk phone will connect me with the White House Army Signal Agency (WHASA) switchboard and that the WHASA switchboard can connect me immediately to the Joint War Room. If I called the Joint War Room without giving them advance notice, to whom would I be speaking?

Question Number 3.
What would I say to the Joint War Room to launch an immediate nuclear strike?

Question Number 4.
How would the person who received my instructions verify them?

And on it went. Another document referred to this meeting on "Emergency Alerting Procedures" and noted that it was clear "that the President expects to be able to initiate, as well as to participate in, an emergency conference with the Secretary of Defense and the Joint Chiefs of Staff."[34] Kennedy was clearly taking the possibility of an American preemptive attack very seriously indeed.

All this was based on the premise that the United States still had the upper hand in strategic terms, and this in fact was Kennedy's assumption. "As of now," he

[32] Note especially a report of Kennedy's visit to SAC headquarters in December 1962. The assumption at SAC was that if the issue ever really came to a head, the United States would have to strike first, and Bundy made it clear to the White House staff that the president felt the same way. Legere memorandum, December 10, 1962, quoted in FRUS 1961–63, 8:436. The record of the president's September 12, 1963, discussion of these issues with the NESC strongly suggests that prior to that point he had considered strategic preemption to be a real option; see ibid., pp. 499–507.

[33] NSC meeting, January 18, 1962, ibid., 14:762, 8:242.

[34] Bundy to McNamara, January 17, 1962, with "Alert Procedures and JCS Emergency Actions File," NSF/281/JCS 1/62—12/62/JFKL. The meeting in question was the one Lemnitzer referred to in his letter to Norstad quoted above, note 31.

pointed out in January 1962, "the credibility of our nuclear deterrent is sufficient to hold our present positions throughout the world," even in places "where our strength on the ground does not match what the Communists can bring to bear."[35] America, in other words, was still strong enough to maintain her position in Berlin. This was not just his personal view: many key U.S. policymakers shared this basic belief. Charles Bohlen, for example, now special assistant to the secretary of state, thought in October 1961 that since the USSR's strategic position was so weak, there had to be "a large area of bluff" in the Russian political position, and that therefore there was a "very large area of Soviet give which must be fully exploited."[36] Paul Nitze, at that point a top Defense Department official, also felt that the strategic balance made it possible to take a tough line in the Berlin conflict.[37] And indeed, as the British noted, U.S. officials involved in Berlin Crisis planning generally believed "that their nuclear superiority allowed them to adopt a forceful position on Berlin."[38]

So the basic conclusion was that the U.S. government really could in the final analysis go all the way over Berlin. Given this assumption, the frequent expressions of American willingness to go to war if necessary over Berlin should probably be taken at face value, a point underscored by the fact that American leaders, and in particular Kennedy himself, took this kind of line not just in public speeches and in meetings with allied leaders but also in internal discussions.[39]

But Kennedy understood that this posture could not be sustained indefinitely. From the start, he had been very interested in the question of how the strategic

---

[35] NSC meeting, January 18, 1962, FRUS 1961–63, 8:239.

[36] Bohlen to Rusk, October 3, 1961, ibid., 14:466.

[37] Ormsby Gore to Foreign Office, January 26, 1962, Prem 11/3804, PRO.

[38] Confidential Annex to COS(62)7th meeting, January 23, 1962, Defe 4/142, PRO. For a discussion of the strategic balance and how it was changing over time, see above, pp. 179–183.

[39] Note especially Kennedy's statement that "it is central to our policy that we shall have to use nuclear weapons in the end, if all else fails, in order to save Berlin"; Kennedy to Clay, October 8, 1961, FRUS 1961–63, 14:485. See also his comments to German officials, including the chancellor, that the U.S. was prepared to go to the "brink of nuclear war," and that nuclear weapons would be used if the West was losing the conventional battle. Kennedy-Grewe meeting, August 30, 1961, and Kennedy-Adenauer meeting, November 20, 1961, ibid., pp. 382, 595 n. Note finally Kennedy's comments at the end of his October 3, 1961, meeting with Norstad, ibid., vols. 13–15, mic. supp., no. 191, and the basic strategy outlined in the key policy document NSAM 109 of October 23, 1961, ibid., 14:523. It should be noted, however, that the evidence is mixed and that this is a difficult issue to assess. For many years, I leaned toward the idea that the president had at bottom opted for a strategy of bluff, and that if forced to choose, he would have sacrificed Berlin rather than start a nuclear war. Even documents like NSAM 109 could be interpreted in terms of a deterrent strategy: the plans would be briefed to the allies; the Soviets would learn about those plans through agents in NATO and in the European governments; finding out about the plans in this clandestine way, they would believe that this was what the Americans would actually do, and hence would draw back from really serious action. As Dean Rusk wrote in 1984: "For reasons which I cannot specify, we assumed that the Soviet Union would become fully informed of these [contingency plans] and would take such possibilities into full account." Rusk to the author, January 25, 1984; see also May et al., "History of the Strategic Arms Competition," p. 682. (Georges Pâques was the Soviet agent most frequently cited in this context.) What this implied was that the plans and related documents were not necessarily to be taken at face value, and that the American government might have been bluffing. I now lean in the opposite direction. What struck me as decisive in this regard was Kennedy's behavior immediately before the Cuban missile crisis; this will be discussed at the end of the chapter.

balance was changing over time and how those changes were likely to affect the behavior of both sides in the crisis.[40] It quickly became evident that America's strategic superiority would soon be a thing of the past. The United States, as Bundy put it in January 1962, was "headed for a nuclear stalemate."[41] The president himself had pointed out the previous month that in two or three years "the possibilities of devastation would be so equal that neither side would be prepared to use nuclear weapons."[42] It was clear that America's window of strategic advantage was closing, probably forever.

This very important conclusion had a number of major implications as far as the Berlin Crisis was concerned. In 1961 and 1962, the United States might still be in a strong position in strategic terms and could therefore in the final analysis feel relatively free to use force if the crisis came to a head. But since this situation was not going to last much longer, it made sense to try to settle the crisis while America was still in a relatively strong position, rather than to put things off to a time, just a year or two away, when nuclear escalation would be far more difficult and nuclear threats could be discounted far more readily.[43] There was nothing particularly new about these conclusions: when the CIA and the JCS had analyzed the issue in 1959, the same basic points had emerged.[44] The only difference now was that since the end of American strategic superiority was so clearly in sight, the basic argument was somewhat more compelling than it had been in 1959.

The closing of the window had a second major implication, which in a sense pointed in the opposite direction: perhaps the United States should try hard to bring about a negotiated settlement, but if the Soviets turned out to be totally intransigent, if they refused to accept the very moderate terms the Americans were

[40] See especially NSC meeting, July 20, 1961, DDRS 1994/406, and Kennedy-JCS meeting, September 20, 1961, DDRS 1993/2309. In July 1962, he had asked for an interagency study of the impact on Soviet foreign policy of the impending end of American nuclear superiority, but the study he got was a typical bureaucratic product and argued both sides of the issue. On the one hand, it was likely that the Soviets would "not abandon caution in Soviet-American confrontations, including Berlin," a view that implied that the shift in the strategic balance would not have a major impact on their behavior. On the other hand, the study pointed out that "as Soviet strategic capabilities grow the USSR may well judge that it can press more aggressively toward limited objectives without running serious risks of general war," a view that suggested that a major change was quite possible. Editorial note and McCone notes of July 10, 1962, NSC meeting, and report for Kennedy, n.d., FRUS 1961–63, 8:343–344, 355–367; the passages quoted are on pp. 356 and 366. It is not hard to imagine how Kennedy must have reacted to studies of this sort: he probably realized that the bureaucracy could provide him with information, but that he would have to do the real thinking essentially on his own.

[41] Bundy outline for Kennedy NSC talk, January 17, 1962, DDRS 1991/3578.

[42] Kennedy-Macmillan meeting, December 21, 1961, 5:15 P.M., p. 3, Prem 11/3782, PRO. Note also the president's comments on basic military policy in NSC meeting, January 18, 1962, FRUS 1961–63, 8:239.

[43] Kennedy-Adenauer meeting, November 20, 1961, FRUS 1961–63, 14:592.

[44] CIA memorandum, "U.S. Negotiating Position on Berlin, 1959–62," July 13, 1959, SS/S/DoD/4/Joint Chiefs of Staff (7)/DDEL. Burke to Secretary of Defense, "Relative Military Capabilities in the 1959–1961/62 Time Period," July 13, 1959, JCSM 269–59, JCS Chairman's Files for 1959, 9172 Berlin/9105 (13 July 1959), RG 218, USNA. See also Gray memo of meeting with Eisenhower, July 13, 1959 (memo dated July 16), OSANSA/SP/P/4/DDEL. Here Gray reported these findings to Eisenhower, saying in fact that they were the findings of "an ad hoc committee consisting of State, Defense, JCS and CIA," but the president found these conclusions "hard to believe."

prepared to offer, then it might make sense to bring matters to a head with them before it was too late—while America still had the upper hand, and while a nuclear war was in the final analysis still fightable. By October 1962, as will be seen, the president had come to view the situation quite explicitly in these terms—and this, in fact, is a key to understanding the Cuban Missile Crisis, the great climax of the confrontation over Berlin.

THE CENTRALIZATION OF CONTROL: THE U.S. SIDE

It was clear from the start that Kennedy was going to have to deal with a whole complex of difficult issues centering on the Berlin problem. There was the military question of what action should be taken if access to Berlin were cut off, and this involved a series of issues relating to the dynamics of escalation, the effectiveness of an American preemptive strike, and the value (and cost) of large conventional forces. There was also the political problem of the sort of settlement the West should try to work out, and the tactical issue of whether a turn toward a more flexible political position would be taken as a sign of weakness and thus might actually make a political settlement harder to reach. And then there were the problems resulting from the fact that this was not simply a U.S.–Soviet confrontation. America's three main European allies all played important roles. Could they be brought along on both the political and the military issues? Should America ultimately be prepared to act alone, if the allies were unwilling to go along with U.S. policy? The real issue here was how much power the United States should exercise within the western alliance, and this issue was intimately related to the question of the control and possession of nuclear weapons. Should America insist on retaining full control of the West's nuclear forces in her own hands—if only as a way of keeping the Germans from getting nuclear weapons of their own, something which might be particularly important as a key part of a general understanding with the USSR?

These issues were all tightly intertwined. They therefore could not be parceled out to the executive departments; the various organs of government each saw only part of the picture, and the policies they advocated often had a certain parochial quality. So policy, Kennedy and his main advisers came to feel, had to be worked out at the center. The president personally needed to play a very active role—to take hold of the reins, to absorb as much information as he could, and to set policy for the government as a whole. The Berlin problem was the central issue and thus the main case in point: it was vital, Bundy wrote Kennedy, that the president put himself "in immediate, personal, and continuous command of this enormous question"—and that applied to both its military and its political aspects.[45]

And Kennedy gradually did take control of policy. In early 1961, he had asked Acheson—then not a government official, but just an adviser—to take the lead in setting Berlin policy. But by July the president himself had taken charge. At no

---

[45] Bundy to Kennedy, June 10, 1961, FRUS 1961–63, 14:108. See also John Mapother's comments, Nuclear History Program Berlin Crisis Oral History Project, session no. 1, October 9, 1990, p. 60 (at NSA).

point did the State Department play a fundamental role. On basic political issues relating to Berlin, policy was set at the top. On NATO questions—and that meant above all questions relating to the control and possession of nuclear weapons within the alliance—the president was slower to impose his views. Here again the basic policy was initially worked out by Acheson, and the line he set was supported by an energetic group of officials based in the State Department. Kennedy went along with that policy in 1961, but in 1962 became increasingly disenchanted, finally breaking with the Acheson line at the very end of the year. By early 1963, on the whole cluster of issues relating to NATO and the control of nuclear weapons, the president had taken direct control of policy making.

On military issues, it was a rather different story. Here the clash was more fundamental: this was a period of great strain in civil-military relations. The president made it clear that he wanted to be deeply involved in war planning, especially on issues relating to the Berlin Crisis and general nuclear war. He and his civilian advisers felt that control of military operations—not at a very detailed level of course, but when major issues were involved—had to rest with the political authorities in Washington. They were thinking above all in terms of the Berlin Crisis, where the key decisions were political at their core, not least because they involved a judgment about how the political authorities on the other side would respond, and so could not be made on the basis of narrow military criteria.

What this implied, in particular, was that the predelegation arrangements that had taken shape under Eisenhower were much too loose. As Bundy explained to Kennedy very early on, under the arrangements they had inherited, "a subordinate commander faced with a substantial Russian military action could start the thermonuclear holocaust on his own initiative if he could not reach you (by failure of communication at either end of the line)."[46] This system was not at all to the liking of the new leadership, and in 1961 the control problem received a great deal of attention. As one official study put it, "no subject consumed more time and effort in the highest levels of the government, within the DOD, USAF and SAC during 1961 than command and control of US nuclear forces."[47] The administration very much wanted to tighten up on command and control. The letters delegating authority over nuclear use to top military commanders were not withdrawn, but civilian officials became more involved in war planning and in the details of military, and especially nuclear, operations.[48]

[46] Bundy to Kennedy, January 30, 1961, FRUS 1961–63, 8:18. An official OSD history outlined the problem as the civilian leadership saw it at this point: "Given the vulnerability of the command links and the impressive complexity of the preprogrammed attacks, SIOP-62 made the often-lamented dilemma of the massive retaliation threat all too real: faced with any serious nuclear provocation, a President would have to retaliate massively or not at all. Moreover, *it was by no means certain that the choice would not quickly slip from his grasp, given the degree of control over the forces which the operational commanders actually possessed.*" Given the weak command and control system, this study pointed out, "it appeared possible that a battle over Berlin could precipitate a nuclear reaction from NATO forces *without authorization from the U.S. Government and even against its wishes.*" May, et al., "History of the Strategic Arms Competition," pp. 589, 596. Emphasis added.

[47] *History of Headquarters Strategic Air Command 1961*, p. 24, and *Strategic Command Control Communications (1959–1964)*, p. 3, SAC Historical Studies nos. 69 and 98, Office of Air Force History, Bolling Air Force Base, Washington, D.C.

[48] Kaysen interview, August 1988; Rosenberg, "Nuclear War Planning," in *The Laws of War: Constraints on Warfare in the Western World*, ed. Michael Howard, George Andreopoulos and Mark Shul-

All this was deeply resented in military circles. The civilians did not respect the authority of the military leadership in what was traditionally its own domain. They had no business, it was felt, getting involved in what were considered purely military matters. General Lyman Lemnitzer, the JCS chairman, complained, for example, about the "constant hounding and harassment" to which the military authorities were now subjected.[49] The new strategic thinking that had taken hold among the civilians in the Pentagon cut against the grain of certain basic military values. Military leaders disliked an approach which "tended to over-emphasize control of military forces, avoidance of casualties and damage, defense, survival, without comparable concern for combat effectiveness, the offensive, or the will to succeed." They disliked a philosophy which would lead to the disappearance of the "all-important will to win."[50]

They also disliked what they saw as the arrogance of civilians—McNamara above all—who sought to impose policies rooted in abstract and academic theorizing, and who showed little regard for or understanding of operational realities. Here was this new secretary of defense, without any real background in strategic issues, simply telling the military professionals how to do their job—ordering them, for example, on March 1, 1961, to "prepare a 'doctrine' which, if accepted, would permit controlled response and negotiating pauses in the event of thermonuclear attack," without even consulting with them, before the instruction was issued, to see whether such a strategy was within reach from an operational point of view.[51] McNamara had been briefed on a strategy of that sort on February 10—that is, very soon after taking office—and had adopted it at once.[52] Military officers were appalled that amateurs like McNamara thought they could deal in this way with the most vital issues the nation might had to face.

Incidents of this sort simply confirmed military officers in their more general belief that the civilians had no right to tell the military how to conduct its affairs. Carl Kaysen, Bundy's deputy in the White House, remembers going out to SAC headquarters in the summer of 1961 and asking questions about war plans, predelegation, and so on. The military attitude, as Kaysen recalled it, was "very unpleasant, very hostile. It was as though they were practically going to clap us in irons and never let us get out. We spent two days there and their whole attitude— you know, it was sort of, 'You bastards, it's none of your business.'"[53] Kennedy himself clashed directly with the top military commanders over these issues. In October 1961, Lemnitzer briefed the president on the Single Integrated Opera-

---

man (New Haven, Conn.: Yale University Press, 1994), p. 172; Rosenberg, "Origins of Overkill," pp. 48–49. For the special interest in the command and control problem in NATO Europe, see McNamara to Kennedy, October 7, 1961, DDRS 1992/1866, and NSC Action, "NATO and the Atlantic Nations," March 10, 1962, DDRS 1994/3463.

[49] Lemnitzer to Norstad, January 18, 1962, NSABF.

[50] JSSC talking paper, August 5, 1961, cited in FRUS 1961–63, 8:121–122.

[51] McNamara memorandum, March 1, 1961, POF/77/DoD, Defense Budget/JFKL, quoted in Kaplan, *Wizards of Armageddon*, p. 273. For the JCS response (which amounted to a refusal to prepare such a "doctrine"), see Lemnitzer to McNamara, April 18, 1961 (with attachment), FRUS 1961–63, 8:74–78. Note also the Hickey report of December 1, 1961, ibid., p. 196 n.

[52] Deborah Shapley, *Promise and Power: The Life and Times of Robert McNamara* (Boston: Little, Brown, 1993), pp. 139–140.

[53] Kaysen interview, August 1988.

tional Plan [SIOP], the nation's basic plan for general nuclear war. Under Eisenhower, briefings of this sort had become rather pat and formulaic, but Kennedy took these matters quite seriously and began asking Lemnitzer some basic questions. Why, he wanted to know, would the United States be "hitting all those targets in China?" They would be attacked, Lemnitzer replied, because they were "in the *plan,* Mr. President." This answer infuriated Kennedy. He took the JCS chairman aside after the briefing and made it clear to Lemnitzer that he was not going to have another briefing like that inflicted on him again.[54]

Civil-military relations in general were thus not good at all, and the growing dispute with Norstad has to be seen in this context. The dispute was not just about Berlin policy, although the issue of how rapidly the United States should escalate the fighting if the crisis came to a head was certainly an important element in the conflict. Nor was it fundamentally about the other main issue where the two sides clashed, especially in 1962: the Kennedy administration opposed the deployment of land-based MRBMs in Europe, while Norstad continued to regard their deployment as essential. The more basic problem had to do with SACEUR's relationship with the American government, and ultimately with SACEUR's place in the whole western system.

SACEUR, as Norstad saw it, could not be a mere puppet of the American president. He represented the alliance in its entirety, and his independent authority was linked to his supranational status. That authority had been rooted in the idea that SACEUR would exercise his discretion on the basis of essentially military considerations, and that he would in particular do whatever was necessary to protect NATO Europe. He might therefore have to act very quickly in an emergency and thus could not rely on external forces like SAC or the Polaris missile force. The external forces, as programmed, would not provide timely coverage of targets whose immediate destruction was vital to the defense of Europe.[55] Norstad therefore insisted on the importance of a land-based MRBM force under the direct control of SACEUR: NATO needed a certain degree of autonomy, and the NATO commander therefore needed an adequate nuclear force of his own. Norstad's opposition to the Kennedy Berlin strategy in late 1961 had also been based partly on this kind of reasoning: SACEUR's ability to carry out his mission of defending Europe would, in Norstad's view, be compromised by the way his atomic strike force would be degraded during the phase of conventional fighting. The new administration, Norstad felt, did not understand the importance of military considerations of this sort, and it did not understand that the military authorities, and above all SACEUR himself, needed to play the leading role in shaping strategy in this area.[56]

Norstad was determined not to bend to the will of the new political leadership in Washington, or at any rate not to give way without a struggle. On Berlin planning, he refused to accept as binding the fundamental policy document, NSAM

---

[54] Ibid. For the text of the briefing and an analysis, see Scott Sagan, "SIOP-62: The Nuclear War Plan Briefing to President Kennedy," *International Security* 12 (Summer 1987): 22–51.

[55] See Nitze, *From Hiroshima to Glasnost,* p. 201, and Finletter to McNamara, Nitze, and Rowen, October 17, 1962, an account of the briefing Norstad gave the North Atlantic Council on the MRBM issue that same day, NSF/216/MLF, General, Stikker Paper/JFKL.

[56] For Norstad's views, see especially Stoessel to Fessenden, April 12, 1962, NSABF.

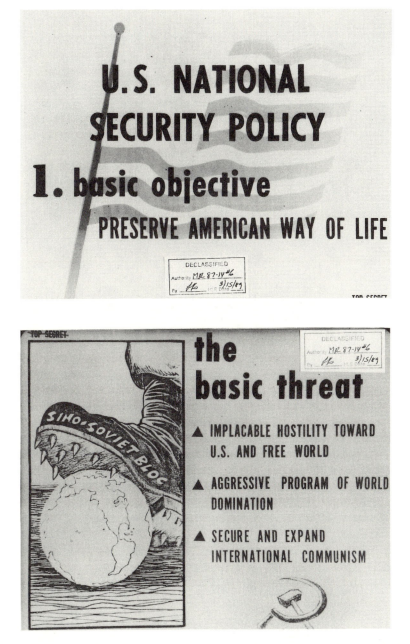

Figure 9. Two pages from the top secret briefing book for a briefing by the Joint Chiefs of Staff chairman on the U.S.–Soviet strategic balance. Undated, but from the late Eisenhower period. Office of the Staff Secretary, Subject Series, Department of Defense Subseries, box 4, JCS (10), Dwight D. Eisenhower Library.

109, which the president had approved in October 1961. The American government, he said, was free to give him advice, but he was responsible to the alliance as a whole and could not "receive directives" from any one country.[57] He also refused to toe the official line on the MRBM question. Here again Norstad was not going to take orders from the U.S. government, especially orders that he felt were based on a fundamentally misguided policy.

To the Kennedy administration, all this was simply unacceptable. Norstad, it was felt in Washington, was the senior U.S. commander in Europe and his job was to champion American policy.[58] "How could Norstad," Rusk wondered, "have a policy that was a NATO policy? What is a NATO policy? In the end, he has to speak as an American. There is only one American policy."[59] The issue came to a head in mid-1962. SACEUR's independence, the president and his chief advisers now felt, had to be curtailed: Norstad could not be allowed to pursue a policy of his own, at odds with what the political leadership wanted. When the question was put to him in June 1962, Norstad insisted on his autonomy. He was summoned back to Washington in July. McNamara and Kennedy told him how much they regretted the fact that he was going to have to retire for reasons of health. He objected, but to no avail. When he returned to Paris, he told his friend General Pierre Gallois what had happened. "Pete," he said, "I've been fired."[60]

Soon Norstad was in fact retired. General Lemnitzer was sent over to replace him, and General Maxwell Taylor, the president's military adviser, replaced Lemnitzer as JCS chairman. SACEUR's wings had been clipped. He had been "racked back" essentially to the role of a field commander, and his orders would come directly from Washington. The whole concept of a strong and independent SACEUR, and the whole cluster of political ideas with which it had been linked, had finally been swept away—a point which did not go unnoticed in Europe.[61]

THE CENTRALIZATION OF CONTROL: AMERICA AND THE ALLIES

Kennedy and his chief advisers felt that they needed to play a very active role, not just within the U.S. government but within the western alliance as well. The power to make war, the power to control military operations, the power to set both military and foreign policy—all this was to be concentrated at the top political level in Washington.

The American government, in their view, had the right to become far more assertive with the allies and play this kind of role. There was no viable purely European solution to the problem of European security, so the United States was more

---

[57] Stoessel to Fessenden, December 18, 1961, 740.5/12-1861, RG 59, USNA. See also Pedlow, "Norstad and the Second Berlin Crisis," p. 47.

[58] Draft letter from Kennedy to Norstad, October 10, 1961, NSA Berlin file.

[59] Sulzberger, entry for July 24, 1962, *Last of the Giants,* p. 908.

[60] Pedlow, "Norstad," pp. 54–55. I heard Gallois tell the same story at a conference in Paris in 1992.

[61] For de Gaulle's reaction, see Lemnitzer–de Gaulle meeting, July 23, 1962, NSF/71a/France: General/JFKL. See also French Council of Ministers meeting, July 25, 1962, in Peyrefitte, *C'était de Gaulle,* pp. 290–292.

or less forced to remain involved. But if America was to carry this burden—if the United States was to maintain a large and costly military force in Europe, and put its own cities at risk as part of the policy of committing American power to the defense of Europe—then the Americans could legitimately ask for certain things in return. "We are bound to pay the price of leadership," Bundy wrote. "We may as well have some of its advantages." That meant that the United States should play the key role in setting policy. De Gaulle and Adenauer seemed to think that they could chart their own course politically, but that no matter what they did, America would always be there to protect them. Such an attitude was simply unacceptable: U.S. forces, as Rusk put it, were not "gendarmes" for use "at the whim of any member of the alliance." America, Bundy said, was not going to allow herself to be "pushed around" by the Europeans. If the defense of Europe was going to rest so heavily on America power, the Europeans could not expect to set their own course politically. They could not have it both ways. "A Europe beyond our influence— yet counting on us—in which we should have to bear the burden of defense without the power to affect events"—this was what Kennedy now saw as intolerable.[62]

So the allies were now expected to follow the American lead. The British, for example, might hope that their "special relationship" with the United States would enable them to play a real role in international politics, but the Americans were not thinking in terms of genuine cooperation and compromise. They were willing to go through the motions and engage in consultations, as long as the British fell in behind the United States on really important matters. Bundy's attitude was typical. In April 1961, Macmillan was coming over to meet with Kennedy, and Bundy outlined the position he thought the president should take with the British leader. "We should of course be willing to look at any new schemes they may dream up," he said, "but in return we should press very hard for British firmness at the moment of truth."[63] As for the French, Rusk took it for granted, even in September 1961, that they would also have little choice but to fall in with American policy. If the United States and Britain were determined to go ahead with the Berlin negotiations, the French, he thought, would ultimately "have to toe the line."[64] The

[62] Bundy outline for Kennedy's talk to the NSC, January 17, 1962, DDRS 1991/3578. The passage about not being pushed around was deleted from the version of the document released in 1981, and was released only in 1991. For the quotation about the Europeans counting on American military support but expecting the United States to give them a free hand in the political area, see the notes of Kennedy's remarkable meeting with André Malraux, May 11, 1962, FRUS 1961–63, 13:696. This is an extraordinary document; Kennedy had decided to open up and lay out his most basic feelings about U.S.–European relations. Note also Kennedy's remarks in his meeting with Krock a few months earlier. "The President spoke impatiently," Krock wrote, "of the obstacles to this effort"—his attempt to reach a settlement with the Russians—"constantly being set up by the West German and French governments." People like Adenauer and de Gaulle "seemed to want to operate as makers of United States policy and not as allies." Krock-Kennedy meeting, October 11, 1961, Krock Papers, box 1, vol. 3, item 343, ML. See also Gavin to State Department, May 16, 1962, giving de Gaulle's view that America should stay out of European affairs and only bring her power to bear "in case of necessity," and Kennedy to Gavin, May 18, 1962, giving the president's sharp reaction, in FRUS 1961–63, 13:702–704. For Rusk's remark about "gendarmes," see Rusk-Segni meeting, December 12, 1961, NSABF.

[63] Bundy to Kennedy, April 4, 1961, DDRS 1986/2903.

[64] Rusk-Home meeting, September 15, 1961, FO 371/160551, PRO.

same point applied to Germany. "The West Germans," Rusk said in August 1961, "were going to have to swallow a lot of things that they had hitherto maintained were entirely unacceptable to them."[65]

On the Berlin issue in particular, the American government now intended to set policy for the West as a whole. Eisenhower had felt that the United States could not simply impose its views on the allies, and indeed had thought of America almost as a kind of broker, whose aim was to work out a common line of action acceptable both to the British and to Adenauer.[66] But in 1961 the U.S. government became far more assertive. In August of that year, Kennedy approved a plan for negotiations on Berlin. He wrote Rusk that America should "make it plain to our three Allies [Britain, France and West Germany] that this is what we mean to do and that they must come along or stay behind."[67] Acheson also thought the United States should simply set policy for the West as a whole. In June, for example, he had argued that the question "was essentially one of U.S. will, and we had to make up our minds and begin to act regardless of the opinions of our allies."[68] And at a very important meeting on October 20 he took the same line. The United States, he said, was wasting too much time consulting with the allies. America did not "need to coordinate with our allies. *We need to tell them.*" It was U.S. policy that mattered, and the Europeans would be pulled along in America's wake.[69] America, he thought—and this view was accepted by the administration as a whole—should become a kind of "executive agent" for the NATO alliance, responsible for managing the western side of a military crisis in Europe.[70]

On the NATO nuclear question, it was much the same story. Again the key concept was the centralization of control in American hands. This basic objective was in turn reflected in a whole series of specific U.S. policies: on French and British nuclear weapons, on the physical control of American nuclear weapons in Europe, on land-based MRBMs, and on a sea-based multilateral MRBM force. The general policy of concentrating control in U.S. hands was also reflected in formal strategic doctrine: the goal of centralizing control was rationalized by a new strategy which held that the United States and NATO in general had to be prepared to fight a controlled nuclear war.

This new policy on NATO nuclear issues was adopted at the very start of the Kennedy administration. At the beginning of 1961, Acheson was asked to look into the whole complex of issues relating to NATO and nuclear weapons. The re-

[65] Rusk-Home meeting, August 5, 1961, FO 371/160541, PRO.

[66] See especially the president's references to "walking a rickety fence," and to the difficulty of pleasing both Adenauer and the British, in Eisenhower-Herter meeting, March 17, 1959, p. 3, SS/I/6/Berlin, vol. II (1)/DDEL.

[67] Kennedy to Rusk, August 21, 1961, FRUS 1961–63, 14:359.

[68] Berlin coordinating group, June 16, 1961, ibid., p. 119.

[69] Meeting between Kennedy, Acheson, Rusk, McNamara, et al., October 20, 1961, ibid., pp. 518–519. Emphasis in original text.

[70] Acheson Berlin report, c. July 31, 1961, ibid., p. 255, and Rusk's remarks in allied foreign ministers' meeting, August 6, 1961, ibid., p. 300. See also Stoessel to Kohler, August 11, 1961 (for Norstad's view that the allies would accept the "executive agent" plan), NSABF. Rusk brought up the "executive agent" idea again in a meeting with British and French diplomats, October 6, 1961, NSABF.

port he presented in March contained a whole series of specific policy recommendations. On April 21, after some minor changes, Kennedy approved the policy directive Acheson had proposed in the report. America's NATO policy was now set, and the U.S. government would continue along the course Acheson had laid out until the end of 1962.

The thrust of the new policy was hard to miss. National nuclear forces were to be avoided and control was to be concentrated in American hands. It was "most important to the U.S.," Acheson wrote, "that use of nuclear weapons by the forces of other powers in Europe should be subject to U.S. veto and control." The French attempt to develop an independent nuclear capability was to be opposed. Even the British should be encouraged to get out of the "nuclear deterrent business." Control over American nuclear weapons needed to be tightened up, and MRBMs were not to be deployed on European soil.[71]

These various policies had one fundamental objective: to prevent the Germans from acquiring a nuclear force under their own control. It was taken for granted that a German move to develop such a force would be very dangerous. The Soviets, as Rusk put it, had "an overriding fear that the Germans will somehow manage to obtain control of nuclear weapons which they can fire on their own decision."[72] They might take some kind of preventive action as soon as it was clear that Germany was moving in this direction. If Germany was about to acquire a strategic missile force under her own control, this, he thought, "might be considered *casus belli* by the Soviets."[73] So a nuclear force under German national control had to be ruled out. Kennedy himself was personally "very anxious to prevent nuclear weapons from coming into the hands of the Germans." It was, in fact, a fixed and very basic tenet of American policy throughout the Kennedy period that a German nuclear force would have to be blocked.[74]

The various components of America's new NATO policy were rooted in this fundamental concern. The Kennedy administration was not opposed to national nuclear forces as a matter of principle. Neither a British nor even a French nuclear force was a real problem in itself. It was only because of the effect on Germany that the British and French forces posed problems. If France developed a nuclear force, and especially if she did so with America's blessing, how could one prevent the Germans from following suit? The United States therefore had to oppose the French effort to build an independent nuclear force. The German factor was decisive. As Kennedy himself pointed out in mid-1962, "the chief argument against the French having nuclear information has been the effect it would have on the Germans, encouraging them to do the same." He made the same point in December. The United States, he said, "had not supported the French in the nuclear field

[71] Policy Directive, April 20, 1961, FRUS 1961–63, 13:288–290; and "A Review of North Atlantic Problems for the Future" (Acheson Report), March 1961, pp. 43–46, 53–62, Records relating to State Department participation in the NSC, box 107, NATO—NSC 6017—Acheson Report, RG 59, USNA.

[72] NSC Executive Committee meeting, February 12, 1963, FRUS 1961–63, 13:497.

[73] Rusk-Stikker meeting, February 7, 1962, p. 3, DDRS 1996/2056.

[74] Kennedy-Macmillan meeting, April 28, 1962, Prem 11/3783, PRO; Bundy paper for Kennedy, "The U.S. and de Gaulle—The Past and the Future," January 30, 1963, POF/116/JFKL.

and the result of this policy had been to sour American relations with France. Rightly or wrongly they [the Americans] had taken this attitude because of Germany."[75]

The problem was that the French were obviously determined to build a nuclear force of their own, regardless of what the Americans said. To oppose their aspirations would not only place a burden on American relations with them in general, but it might also lead them to turn to the Germans for help in the nuclear area, and this inevitably would bring the Germans closer to acquiring a nuclear capability. The "dilemma," as Acheson put it in April 1961, "was that, if we helped the French, the Germans would insist on equal treatment. If we did not and the French persisted, they could only succeed by calling in the Germans. This would lead to the Germans acquiring nuclear power."[76] Kennedy himself also wondered whether the policy of refusing to help the French would "encourage them to go to the Germans—thus making German possession more likely." Perhaps the opposite policy was worth considering. Maybe one could make an "arrangement with the French that would limit the Germans in their demands," or at least one that would prevent the French from cooperating with the Germans in the nuclear area.[77]

Kennedy was in fact reluctant to rule out the possibility of some kind of deal with France. Relations with de Gaulle had deteriorated sharply in the course of 1961. The French president disliked Kennedy's Berlin policy as well as his policy on NATO nuclear issues. But in 1962 Kennedy did not think the gap was unbridgeable and he wanted to see if de Gaulle could be brought back on board. Perhaps a liberalization of America's policy on nuclear aid to France might help solve the problem. In March 1962, Kennedy seemed to be "casting about for areas of cooperation with France in the nuclear weapons field." He wanted to find "some mechanism for bringing France back into the community of western nations." These efforts were supported by the JCS and by the top civilian officials in the Defense Department, who thought that nuclear assistance would free up funds for the conventional buildup the civilians especially considered so important. McNa-

---

[75] Kennedy's "Eight Questions" to Ball, with Ball's answers, attached to Ball to Kennedy, June 17, 1962, NSF/226/JFKL, and Kennedy quoted in the British record of the Anglo-American meetings at Nassau, December 19, 1962, morning session, p. 9, Prem 11/4229, PRO. The U.S. record is essentially the same; see FRUS 1961–63, 13:1094. Many documents reflect the same basic assumption. See, for example, Rusk to Stoessel (personal), May 5, 1961: "Key question throughout, in my view, is not so much whether France will achieve some sort nuclear weapons capability but effect on German aspirations and thus on NATO of US posture of encouraging French nuclear effort." NSF/70/France—General/JFKL. See also Kennedy to de Gaulle, December 31, 1961, FRUS 1961–63, 14:718; for de Gaulle's response, see LNC 1961–1963, p. 193.

[76] Anglo-American meetings in Washington, April 5–8, 1961, second meeting, p. 1, Cab 133/244, PRO.

[77] Kennedy's "Eight Questions" to Ball, questions 1 and 2, May 25, 1962, NSF/226/JFKL. The Defense Department was thinking along similar lines. See Nitze-Norstad meeting, April 4, 1962, 711.5611/4-462. Note also McNamara's comment that same month that "before the French could be helped in their nuclear programme they would certainly have to promise to give very comprehensive safeguards and guarantees that they would not pass on knowledge to the West Germans," McNamara-Macmillan meeting, April 29, 1962, p. 28, Prem 11/3783, PRO.

mara even argued that "missile aid to France would be justified on balance of payments grounds alone."[78]

But the effort failed. "Basic NATO policy," as outlined in the April 1961 policy directive, was reaffirmed. There would for the time being be no nuclear aid for France. In the final analysis, this decision turned on a judgment about de Gaulle. The general, it was thought, was probably unappeasable. He would take what was offered, but give nothing in return. He was not the type to cut a deal with the Americans. His policy derived from fundamental convictions and would not change significantly even if American policy on nuclear assistance became a good deal more liberal. Yet in Kennedy's mind this remained something of an open issue. The president was not opposed in principle to the idea of nuclear cooperation with France and thought the question needed to be dealt with pragmatically. The important thing was to make sure that whatever was done with France, the Germans did not come closer to acquiring a nuclear force under national control.[79]

What was true of France was even more true of Britain. The official American policy in 1961 and 1962 was to get the British "out of the nuclear business," but this goal was purely derivative in nature. After the administration had turned so sharply against the idea of nuclear cooperation with France, how could it go on supporting the British nuclear program? "We must try to eliminate the privileged British status," one official wrote. This was essential if American views were to carry any weight with the French: "in matters nuclear, the road to Paris may well be

---

[78] Fessenden to Kohler, March 7, 1962, 751.5611/3-262, Ball to McNamara, March 10, 1962, 751.5611/3-1062, and Kohler to Rusk, April 12, 1962, 740.5611/4-1262, all in RG 59, USNA. Note also the information (which came from McNamara's staff) about a "new turn" in the defense secretary's thinking, in Tyler to Rusk and Ball, July 26, 1962, 740.5611/7-2662, RG 59, USNA. McNamara was thinking about abandoning the MLF "in favor of a multilateral MRBM force geared more directly to US financial needs." The idea was to create a large, all-European force, probably made up largely of missiles deployed on the continent. Tyler, a top State Department official, was against the plan, but he opposed it in part because of what he saw as "the possible need to save such nuclear concessions as US sale or provision of warheads to a European nuclear force until we can see whether these concessions will be needed to balance off concessions we may be seeking in the economic field."

[79] For the debate on nuclear sharing with France and related issues, see Neustadt, "Skybolt and Nassau," pp. 29–30, and Bundy to Kennedy, May 7, 1962, POF/116a/France—Security/JFKL. For some important documents bearing on this debate, see Gavin to Kennedy, March 9, 1962, White House meeting, March 15, 1962; Taylor to Kennedy, April 3, 1962, and enclosure 2; Kennedy-Rusk-McNamara-Bundy meeting, April 16, 1962; and NSAM 147, April 18, 1962; in FRUS 1961–63, 13:687–688, 366–370, 377–380, 384–387. For Ambassador Gavin's efforts in this area three months earlier and the response at that time of other officials, see ibid., pp. 678–679, 678n. For the judgment about de Gaulle's unappeasability as the decisive factor and the fundamentally pragmatic approach of the Kennedy administration, see Bundy to Kennedy, "The U.S. and de Gaulle—the Past and the Future," January 30, 1963, p. 7, POF/116/JFKL. When Kennedy met with Malraux on May 11, he noted explicitly that "as for the atomic difficulty, that came because on every other matter there was trouble" (ibid., p. 698), implying that the United States would have taken, and indeed would take, a much more liberal attitude on nuclear sharing if France were more cooperative in other key areas. The idea that de Gaulle would simply take what was offered without changing his basic policy was fairly common at the time: see, for example, Norstad's views in Nitze-Norstad meeting, April 4, 1962, 711.5611/4-462, RG59, USNA. Finally, note that the Kennedy approach was attacked as too pragmatic by certain key policymakers, who thought the U.S. should oppose the French nuclear force as a matter of principle. See, for example, Gerard Smith and Bowie to Kohler, May 4, 1962, FRUS 1961–63, 13:691n.

through London."[80] The hope was that if the British gave up trying to maintain an independent nuclear force, then the French—perhaps after de Gaulle left the scene—might go the same route, and it would then be easier to keep the Germans in line. Within the British government, some high officials, including certain Cabinet ministers, were in fact ready to cooperate with this policy and leave the "nuclear business" in American hands.[81] So the basic American objective here did not seem totally beyond reach.

The new U.S. policy in this area implied, first of all, that the American government would have to phase out the special nuclear relationship with the British that had developed during the late Eisenhower period. The original decision to enter into such a relationship was now regarded as a "mistake." That relationship had developed, as Bundy pointed out, "at a time when thinking on these matters was very different from what it is now." If the U.S. government "had it to do over again," it would not have helped the British with their nuclear effort. "The correct line of our policy now" was to move away gradually "from an intermittent partnership with the British and to use our own influence in the direction of a gradual phasing down of the British nuclear commitment." Rusk took essentially the same line.[82]

The general Kennedy administration view was that the arrangements with the British worked out during the Eisenhower period needed to be scaled back. The bomber-based deterrent was obsolescent, so the way to get the British out of

[80] "A New Approach to France," n.a., April 21, 1961, NSF/70/France—General/JFKL.

[81] See the Neustadt, "Skybolt and Nassau," pp. 23–26, 71 (for the basic U.S. policy on the British nuclear force in 1961 and 1962), and pp. 46–47 (for the willingness of certain British officials to cooperate with this American policy). On the politics of this issue within Britain, see especially Andrew Pierre, *Nuclear Politics: The British Experience with an Independent Strategic Force, 1939–1970* (London: Oxford University Press, 1972), pp. 202–210. Note also an important document written by Sir Norman Brook, the Cabinet secretary, "Some Aspects of our Relations with the United States and Europe," January 18, 1961, Cab 133/244. Macmillan had written President-Elect Kennedy on December 19, 1960, to suggest joint talks that would deal with the most basic policy issues facing the two countries, and in conjunction with this he asked Brook to set up a group to draft a report on the whole complex of issues relating to NATO, Anglo-American relations, and Britain's relations with Europe. See especially the material in FO 371/159671, PRO. Brook argued in the January 18 report that there was "no great need for an independent British contribution to the strategic nuclear deterrent of the West," that it was declining in value in any case, and that by relinquishing at least a certain degree of independence now, while the British force still counted for something, the U.K. might be able to achieve important political goals. France might be kept from building an independent force, and it was crucial to do so, because if France went nuclear, countries like Germany were sure to follow. Other top officials were thinking along similar lines. See Baylis, *Ambiguity and Deterrence,* pp. 278, 307. Such views were very much in line with the thinking of the new Kennedy administration, but a bit too much for Macmillan. For Foreign Office views on this complex of issues, and some insight into how they differed from the prime minister's views, see Ramsbotham memo, "The Prime Minister's Visit to General de Gaulle," January 17, 1961, with Schuckburgh minute, FO 371/159671, PRO. For the policy that emerged, and the cool American reaction, see especially the documents in Prem 11/3311, PRO.

[82] Rusk in White House meeting, April 16, 1962, FRUS 1961–63, 13:378; Bundy to Aron, May 24, 1962, NSF/71a/France—General/ JFKL; Kennedy to Gavin (draft, probably written by Bundy), n.d., NSF/71a/France, General, 4/1—4/12/61/JFKL. This last document was probably misfiled, and almost certainly dates from the spring of 1962. It contains a reference to Gavin's March 9 letter to Kennedy, and a letter dated March 9, 1962 to the president dealing with this subject was published in FRUS 1961–63, 13:687–688.

the "nuclear business" was to keep them from acquiring ballistic missiles. The existing program of cooperation went back to a December 1957 Eisenhower-Macmillan agreement. This now involved "extensive and frequent interchange" of ballistic missile information, in spite of the fact that the British did not have an MRBM program and the United States did not now "wish them to start one."[83] Obviously, this had to change. In the American view, there was no real point to the British deterrent force. "We would much rather have British efforts go into conventional weapons," Bundy wrote Kennedy, "and have the British join with the rest of NATO in accepting a single U.S.–dominated force."[84]

Control over NATO nuclear weapons was thus to be concentrated in American hands. This implied, among other things, that the weapons now in Europe needed to be placed under effective American control. The present situation was clearly unsatisfactory. Acheson understood that under current arrangements U.S. "custody"—he placed the word in quotation marks—was often more theoretical than real. "Many of the European Allies," he pointed out in April, "were in fact holding nuclear weapons." "There was no way at present," he noted, "of guaranteeing that those Allies who held nuclear weapons would in fact get the President's agreement before using them."[85] The Acheson Report therefore called for a study of how "nuclear weapons in NATO Europe could be made more secure against unauthorized use."[86] This recommendation was accepted on April 6, and the administration soon took steps to place the weapons under effective American control.[87]

The most important of these measures was the introduction of the Permissive Action Link, a device that would secure the weapons against unauthorized use. In June 1962, it was decided that PALs would be put on all American-owned nuclear weapons in Europe. Weapons outside of Europe—those, for example, on American naval vessels—were not affected. The basic goal was to make sure that the European allies could not use those American weapons on their own. But the weapons assigned to the American forces in Europe were also to be fitted with PALs. This was in part because Norstad had warned about the "allied reaction if U.S. and [European] NATO nuclear weapons were to be treated differently." But it also to a certain extent reflected the administration's interest in limiting SACEUR's autonomy and downgrading the NATO command as a whole.[88]

[83] Rusk to McNamara, September 8, 1962, 741.5611/5-1862, RG 59, USNA. This passage was deleted from the version of the document in FRUS 1961–63, 13:1080.

[84] Bundy to Kennedy, April 24, 1962, FRUS 1961–63, 13:1068.

[85] Anglo-American talks, April 5–8, 1961, second meeting, p. 1, Cab 133/244, PRO; Acheson Report, p. 31, NSF/220/JFKL.

[86] Policy Directive, April 20, 1961, FRUS 1961–63, 13:288; Acheson Report, pp. 54–55, NSF/220/JFKL.

[87] Bundy to McNamara, "Improving the Security of Nuclear Weapons in NATO Europe against Unauthorized Use," NSAM 36, April 6, 1961, NSAM files, JFKL. See also Acheson Berlin Report, June 28, 1962, FRUS 1961–63, 14:145.

[88] Feaver, *Guarding the Guardians*, pp. 183–198; Stein and Feaver, *Assuring Control of Nuclear Weapons*, pp. 38–39; Scott Sagan, *The Limits of Safety: Organizations, Accidents, and Nuclear Weapons* (Princeton, N.J.: Princeton University Press, 1993), p. 106. In March 1963, the PAL development and production program was put in the "highest national priority category." NSAM 230, March 22, 1963, NSF/340/JFKL. For further background, see May et al., "History of the Strategic Arms Competition," pp. 589–590. According to this study, based on many still highly classified documents, it became clear

American policy on the MRBM issue was cut from the same cloth. Once again, the aim was to avoid the development of European nuclear forces under national control, and to keep the war-making power fully in American hands. In October 1959, NATO headquarters had called for the deployment in Europe of a ballistic missile with a range of up to fifteen hundred miles. Norstad wanted three hundred such missiles, with yields of up to a single megaton, to be deployed by 1963.[89] He wanted those missiles to be based in Europe, not at sea. Land-based missiles were more accurate; this meant that warheads with smaller yields could be used, and collateral damage could be kept down. Land-based missiles were also easier to control than seaborne weapons and had a shorter reaction time.[90] Norstad also had certain political objectives in mind. An MRBM force under the direct control of SACEUR could have a powerful deterrent effect, over and above the effect produced by the external forces under American national control. With such a force, NATO in his view could become a "fourth nuclear power."[91]

This was in line with the old Eisenhower policy, but the new Kennedy administration did not find this concept the least bit attractive, and it very much disliked the idea of deploying MRBMs on European soil. Land-based missiles, it was frequently argued, "would be subject to seizure or use in an emergency by the national Governments in whose territory they were deployed." Even if these missiles were assigned to NATO and the warheads remained officially in American custody, there was a serious risk that the MRBMs would fall under de facto national control. "Since the warheads would be contained in the missiles," it was argued, "each country could fire off at will missiles which were capable of striking the USSR," and "nominal commitment of the missiles to SACEUR would not prevent this." U.S. custody would consist of American technicians "whose 'second key' was required to fire those missiles," but those technicians could easily be overpowered. "A nation that had reached the stage of desperation in which it contemplated national use of nuclear weapons," Gerard Smith wrote, "would hardly boggle at re-

---

in the course of Berlin planning in 1961 that because of the weakness and ambiguity of arrangements for command and control a "battle over Berlin could precipitate a nuclear reaction from NATO forces without authorization from the U.S. Government and even against its wishes." A task force under General Earle Partridge was then set up to look into the problem of the control of nuclear forces, and the Partridge Committee reported that with the installation of the PALs, the NATO weapons could be made secure against unauthorized use, but that the other side of the coin was that with this system, the vulnerability of the command and control system meant that "positive control"—that is, the assurance that the weapons would actually be used when use was authorized—could not be assured. It was for this reason, moreover, that the PALs could not be installed on the main American strategic forces. This implied a certain downgrading of the NATO force in comparison with the "external forces" like SAC and the Polaris submarine force. And in fact the value of the forces controlled by SACEUR had already been downgraded by "operational rules that gave overriding priority to SIOP execution and precluded attack" on strategic targets by theater commanders. Ibid., p. 468a.

[89] "Mid-Range Ballistic Missiles," n.d., but probably from around September 1960, and "MRBMs in Allied Command Europe," with annex, March 24, 1960, both in Defe 11/312, PRO; British Joint Planning Staff, "NATO Strategy and the Role of NATO Forces," February 23, 1962, JP(62)22(Final), annex, paragraph 26, attached to COS(62)16th meeting, March 1, 1962, Defe 4/143, PRO.

[90] Herter-Norstad meeting, November 4, 1959, 740.5/11-459, RG 59, USNA; Norstad-NAC meeting, June 30, 1961, NP/91/US Support of NATO/DDEL.

[91] See Pedlow, "Norstad," p. 5.

voking a paper commitment to SACEUR or seizing a key from the US technician." It was therefore clear, as Henry Owen, another key U.S. official, argued in a memorandum to Acheson, that "we don't want these missiles deployed in Europe." A deployment there would amount to "placing these strategic missiles (with mated warheads) in European hands."[92]

Acheson did not need much convincing. His March report on NATO made the same sort of argument about the danger of MRBMs in Europe, even if they were officially committed to NATO, being diverted "to national purposes," and it came down hard against any policy that would lead to effective "national [i.e., European] ownership or control of MRBM forces," or which would weaken "centralized [i.e., American] command and control over these forces." This language was carried over into the April 21 policy directive.[93] But the issue remained unsettled, so in July Acheson returned to the charge. In a long memorandum to McNamara, he developed the case against land-based MRBMs. Again, the key argument was that the European national forces, especially German forces, would be able to get control of the weapons. There were "physical gadgets," he said (meaning the PALs), which could "help maintain centralized SACEUR control." But he thought the Europeans would be able to devise countermeasures, and indeed that was the first thing the French, and probably the Germans as well, would do if the MRBMs were deployed on their territory.[94] This soon became the official State Department view.[95]

So the American government began to back away from the idea of land-based MRBMs. Owen thought that U.S. representatives needed to engage "in a certain amount of soft-talk, in order to explain our position to the Europeans in a way that will not appear a direct repudiation of SACEUR." But the purpose of the soft talk was "to let the MRBM proposition down easily," not to leave it alive "as a topic for further inter-agency haggling within the U.S. Government."[96] And in fact the American line in 1961 was that the issue of a land-based MRBM force was being put on the back burner—that there were more important things to worry about in the military area, and that the military requirement, such as it was, could be met on an interim basis by the assignment of a number of U.S. Polaris missile submarines to SACEUR.[97] The goal here was clear enough. U.S. leaders wanted to avoid an MRBM deployment in Europe, but they did not want to appear "to completely overthrow the actions of their predecessors." So they simply adopted the tactic of saying that they gave this issue "very low priority."[98]

[92] "MRBM's for Europe?" July 6, 1961, n.a., but probably by Owen; Smith to Rusk, January 17, 1961; and Owen to Acheson, March 9, 1961; all in PPS 1957-61/183/Owen, RG 59, USNA. See also Kohler and McGhee to Rusk, October 27, 1961, NSF/216/Multilateral Force—General/JFKL. Eisenhower of course understood all this, but for him it was not so much a problem as a selling point. See above, p. 209.

[93] FRUS 1961–63, 13:290; Acheson Report, pp.44–45, NSF/220/JFKL.

[94] Acheson to McNamara, July 19, 1961, PPS 1957–61/183/Owen, RG 59, USNA.

[95] Rusk to McNamara, October 29, 1961, FRUS 1961–63, 13:334–335.

[96] Owen to Acheson, March 9, 1961, PPS 1957-61/183/Owen, RG 59, USNA.

[97] Rusk to Finletter, April 25, 1961, giving text of presentation Finletter was to make the next day to the NATO Council, NP/91/US Support of NATO/DDEL.

[98] Watkinson meeting with McNamara et al., March 21, 1961, Defe 13/211, PRO; Kennedy to Norstad, July 21, 1961, DDRS 1997/1738.

Instead of a land-based MRBM force, American officials pushed the idea of a seaborne MRBM force, owned and operated on a thoroughly multinational basis. The idea of a multilateral force had originally emerged at the end of the Eisenhower administration, but the goal at that point had been to create a NATO force, not subject to American veto, as a bridge to a truly independent European nuclear force.[99] Under Kennedy, however, the fundamental goal was radically altered. The United States was now determined to retain a veto over use of the force.[100] The American government did not openly insist on the maintenance of the veto until 1963.[101] The line in 1961 and 1962 was that other arrangements might be considered, and that it was up to the Europeans to propose them.[102] But this was just a tactic, a "debating trick," as Bundy later called it.[103] The Europeans, Rusk and McNamara agreed, "would not be able to settle on any other controlling agent than the President." The State Department thought, however, that it was "most important" that the Europeans reach this conclusion on their own. That was why it was considered very unwise to state flatly at the outset "that we insist on unilateral U.S. control." If the Europeans reached that conclusion themselves, they could not then say that America was dictating to them and deliberately trying to keep them down.[104]

The military authorities disliked the MLF and would have preferred to deploy land-based missiles in Europe. Norstad was particularly outspoken on these matters. "All this talk about a multilateral force," he said in December 1962, "is meaningless and confusing," and indeed America's whole "nuclear policy toward Europe had been silly."[105] But Norstad's views were ignored. He was not even

---

[99] See above, pp. 213–215.

[100] Political Directive, April 21, 1961, FRUS 1961–63, 13:289. This particular policy remained intact throughout the Kennedy period. See especially the president's remarks in a meeting on the MLF question held on February 18, 1963, ibid., pp. 503, 505.

[101] See, for example, Kennedy to Adenauer, March 29, 1963, ibid., p. 545.

[102] See, for example, Acheson to Kennedy and Rusk, April 20, 1961, Finletter-Adenauer meeting, July 5, 1961; NSC Executive Committee meeting, February 12, 1963; ibid., pp. 294–295, 325, 494.

[103] Bundy to Kennedy, June 15, 1963, ibid., p. 593. Compare this with Bundy's discussion in *Danger and Survival*, p. 497, which implies that the U.S. government was serious about the idea of a European nuclear force free of an American veto. Evidence showing that this was not the case, incidentally, is sometimes suppressed, even today. The State Department tried to convince a skeptical Kennedy in mid-1962 that the MLF was still feasible by arguing the Europeans might go along if the United States continued "to avoid explicitly foreclosing the possibility that such an approach might eventually lead to a force over whose use the US did not exercise a clear and unfettered veto"—that is, if the American government deliberately misled the Europeans on the veto question. This was the one passage deleted from the version of the document released by the Kennedy Library in 1997; it had been left in the version found in the Ball Papers at Princeton a couple of years earlier. Ball to Kennedy, June 17, 1962, with attached memorandum on the president's eight questions, (answer to question no. 4), NSF/226/NATO: Weapons, Cables, France/JFKL; and Ball Papers, box 153, ML.

[104] "NATO and the Atlantic Community," State Department briefing paper, attached to Bundy to Kennedy, April 24, 1961, para. 3, and "MRBM's for Europe?" July 6, 1961, para. 6, both in PPS 1957-61/183/Owen, RG 59, USNA. "Control over Multilateral MRBM Force: NAC Tactics," April 9, 1962, NSF/216/MLF—General/JFKL. Kennedy-Rusk-McNamara-Bundy meeting, April 16, 1962, and Kohler comments in meeting with British officials, June 26, 1962, FRUS 1961–63, 13:379, 424.

[105] Sulzberger, entry for December 5, 1961, *Last of the Giants*, p. 936.

consulted before the American ambassador to NATO made a major statement in June 1962 laying out U.S. views on the MRBM question.[106]

JCS misgivings were also swept aside. In April 1962, the Chiefs denied the claim that "there was no military requirement for MRBMs."[107] But McNamara dismissed the idea that there was a military need for these missiles. Those who said there was—and that included the JCS—did not understand the "nuclear control problem," and this "was in itself dangerous."[108] What he meant was that the real issue was political, that there was an overriding need to make sure that the host countries did not get control of these strategic nuclear weapons. This was also what Rusk had in mind when he later noted that SACEUR's MRBM "requirement" had been "downgraded for political reasons."[109] Since land-based MRBMs were politically undesirable, the line had to be that they were militarily unnecessary. McNamara therefore claimed that the Chiefs had agreed with the official line that MRBMs were not urgently needed. But, as General Taylor pointed out, this simply was not true.[110]

Taylor soon took over from Lemnitzer as JCS chairman. But the Chiefs' position on the MRBM question did not change—that is, until McNamara forced them to change it. On May 1, 1963, the JCS met and reached certain conclusions. They could not state that it was "militarily advisable" to go ahead with the MLF. A "more prudent" course of action, in their view, was to proceed with arrangements involving national MRBM forces committed to NATO. McNamara and his deputy, Roswell Gilpatric, got wind of what was being decided. They met with the Chiefs the next day and a very different JCS position emerged. The JCS, taking political considerations into account, now agreed that the MLF was feasible and would be "militarily effective."[111] The Chiefs had thus been

[106] Memorandum for the President, n.a., n.d., FRUS 1961–63, 13:431, and Taylor to Kennedy, July 2, 1962, Taylor Papers [TP], box 35, 6B NATO, National Defense University [NDU], Washington, D.C. See also Stoessel to Fessenden, April 10, 1962, DDRS 1991/1912, for more information on Norstad's conflict with the civilians in Washington. Among other things, Norstad felt that the U.S. government was "misleading" its allies on many "matters connected with nuclear forces," and in particular on questions related to external forces like SAC.

[107] Kennedy-Rusk-McNamara-Bundy meeting, April 16, 1962, FRUS 1961–63, 13:380.

[108] Meeting with Kennedy, Bundy, et al., March 15, 1962, ibiid., p. 368.

[109] Rusk-Home meeting, May 23, 1963, ibid., p. 581. In November 1961, the Pentagon was considering the development of a fast-reacting, highly mobile, and very accurate MRBM, to be deployed in Europe, but at a high-level meeting held to discuss funding for the project, it was "vigorously attacked by Bundy on political grounds." Meeting between McNamara, Bundy, Sorensen, et al., on defense budget, November 3, 1961, from the TP/NDU, provided by Reynolds Salerno of Yale University. In 1963, Bundy admitted that a sea-based force made little sense in military terms, and that in fact "ships look silly when you consider the alternatives." Anglo-American meeting, June 28, 1963, p. 6, DOD-FOIA 91-03459.

[110] Memorandum for the Record, June 13, 1962, TP/35/NATO 1961/NDU; Memorandum for the President, June 13, 1962, TP/35/MRBMS/NDU, both quoted from and cited in an unpublished paper by Reynolds Salerno on the MRBM question.

[111] Memorandum for General Taylor, June 1, 1963, TP/39/MLF/NDU. Salerno, in the paper mentioned in the previous note, tells the whole story and quotes at length from this document. The British, incidentally, according to the account in the June 1 memorandum, were now told by supporters of the MLF that the JCS finding proved that the scheme made military sense. This was in spite of the fact that

made to give their formal approval to a policy that McNamara himself saw as foolish.[112]

Once again, the German nuclear question played the key role in shaping American policy in this area. The whole point of the MLF was to absorb and deflect the pressure for national nuclear forces, which, if unchecked, would lead sooner or later to a German nuclear capability. As Nitze put it, it was "in the main" to deal with the problem of eventual German nuclear ambitions that the MLF had been proposed.[113] The MLF had been designed in particular as an alternative to a land-based MRBM force, and the land-based MRBMs had been opposed mainly because it was felt that they could fall too easily into the hands of host country, and especially German, forces. The problem Kennedy faced here had to do with the American veto. Under Eisenhower, the assumption had been that the MLF would eventually devolve into an independent European force; the Kennedy administration, however, was dead set against the idea of a force not subject to American control. But if the use of the force would be subject to an American veto, it was hard to see how such a force would do more for Europe than the much larger forces under direct American control. Top U.S. officials were quite clear in their own minds that the MLF was therefore of no real value—that, as Kennedy himself put it, it was "not a real force but merely a façade."[114] If the MLF had no real strategic value, how then could it ultimately serve any real political function? Were the Europeans so much stupider than their American counterparts that they would be unable to see through all the talk and grasp what was actually going on? Kennedy certainly did not think so, and was therefore strongly tempted to junk the whole project.

What held him back in 1962 was a sense that if the MLF were abandoned, the United States would probably have to face the issue of a German nuclear capability head on—and this he was reluctant to do. In the long run, the Germans would be more likely to accept a non-nuclear status if they were not being discriminated against too overtly. Non-nuclear status, with all that it implied about the allies' continuing distrust of Germany, the Federal Republic's dependence on her allies, and the limits on her political freedom of action, was a bitter pill for any German government to swallow, and it was therefore important that it be packaged the right way. It had to be presented as part of a more general policy that, on the surface at least, had little to do with the German problem as such. The MLF might be

---

McNamara himself had told the British defense minister that the plan had little military utility. McNamara's views were cited by Thorneycroft in a meeting with Rusk on May 23, 1963, FRUS 1961–63, 13:580.

[112] For McNamara's views, see high-level meetings, November 30 and December 16, 1962, FRUS 1961–63, 13:446–447 and 1088–1089; and especially McNamara–von Hassel meeting, February 28, 1963, McNamara Papers, box 133, Memcons with Germans, RG 200, USNA.

[113] Nitze-Laloy meeting, September 25, 1962, 740.5/9-2562, RG 59, USNA. See also Neustadt, "Skybolt and Nassau," pp. 23, 26, 28, 71, 76. In 1963, Rusk noted that "the real genesis" of the MLF project "was an effort to keep 600 MRBM's out of Germany"—which was not quite accurate, but which nonetheless reflects the basic thinking behind the proposal. Anglo-American meeting, June 28, 1963, DOS FOIA 91–03459.

[114] NSC Executive Committee meeting, February 12, 1963, FRUS 1961–63, 13:499. For Kennedy's skepticism, see the notes of three high-level meetings, March 15, 1962, and February 5 and 18, 1963, ibid., pp. 173–174, 367, 502–503. Note also Bohlen's characterization of the scheme as a "fraud" in a letter to Kennedy of February 16, 1963, ibid., p. 760.

useful in this context; the State Department seemed convinced that this was the case. So whatever his misgivings, Kennedy was willing to give the MLF lobby a chance, but always in his mind with the proviso that if the policy turned out to be bankrupt, he might have to try another approach.

There is one final element in this picture of the U.S. government's new NATO policy, and this has to do with the Kennedy administration's new strategy for general nuclear war. If one were to believe the rhetoric, it seemed that the new administration believed that a controlled nuclear war might actually be possible. The official claim now was that with a new strategy, a strategy of "controlled and discriminate general nuclear war," nuclear deterrence would get a new lease on life. Even with the growth of Soviet nuclear capabilities, the United States, thanks to this strategy, could rationally take the initiative and launch a major nuclear strike on the USSR in the event of a massive Soviet attack on western Europe. The European allies could therefore continue to rely on the American nuclear deterrent and need not build nuclear forces of their own.

This new doctrine differed fundamentally from the Eisenhower strategy. During the Eisenhower period, there had been no attempt to create a force that could fight a controlled or protracted nuclear war. Quite the contrary: the goal had been to work out a single, precise, and well-rehearsed operational plan "that could be implemented with a simple unambiguous decision, almost without further command intervention." As JCS Chairman Twining had put it, operations would be "pre-planned for automatic execution to the maximum extent possible and with minimum reliance on post-H-hour communications." The SIOP—the basic plan for general nuclear war—had been designed at the end of the Eisenhower period with these goals in mind. This plan "incorporated a comprehensive set of individual strategic strikes, prescribing tasks, targets, tactics, timing, and other operational particulars in minute detail, and demanding utmost precision in execution by earmarked forces." The procedure was to transmit a single "go code" to the strike forces "giving them the signal to carry out previously designated assignments to deliver prescribed weapons in a specified manner against preselected targets, all in quasi-automatic fashion that reduced communications and other command requirements to the barest human and technical minimums." Once the go code had been received, there was in fact "no way to stop" the attack from running its course. Indeed, the targets assigned to each carrier were the same "whether our strike is preventive or retaliatory."[115]

Top officials in the Kennedy administration intensely disliked this strategy and sought to introduce more flexibility into the plan for general nuclear war. The issue was discussed at great length, and by the spring of 1962 it seemed that a new formal strategy had officially been adopted. McNamara laid out the new doctrine in a top secret speech to the NATO Council at Athens in April and then in a public address at Ann Arbor in June. The American nuclear guarantee of Europe, he in-

[115] L. Wainstein et al., "The Evolution of U.S. Strategic Command and Control and Warning, 1945–1972," pp. 283–284, Institute for Defense Analyses, June 1975, DOD-FOIA and also NSA. David Rosenberg gave me a copy of this study and also opened my eyes to its importance. On the point about targeting being the same for a first as for a second strike, see Kistiakowsky to Eisenhower, FRUS 1958–60, 3:492, and also Admiral Burke's comments in Rosenberg, "Origins of Overkill," pp. 7–8.

sisted in the Athens speech, remained intact: McNamara explicitly noted here that if NATO's defenses were overwhelmed, the West would have to escalate the war and "initiate the use of nuclear weapons." It was extremely important in such circumstances—and indeed crucial to the credibility and thus to the effectiveness of the new strategy—that the Soviets not retaliate with whatever survived the attack. They therefore had to be given a very strong incentive—the desire to preserve the bulk of their own society intact—for holding their remaining forces back. Soviet cities were to be spared, the Soviet population kept alive for its hostage value. The United States would focus instead on military targets, and especially on the Soviet nuclear force; urban-industrial targets would be avoided. The western attack would be discriminate. Yields would be matched to targets. Accuracy would be improved so that yields could be reduced. There would be greater reliance on airbursts than on groundbursts so as to limit the amount of fallout. The aim was to "reduce damage to civilians": "the more discriminating the attack, the less the damage."[116]

The goal, in other words, was to be able, in the event of war, to "engage in a controlled and flexible nuclear response": the "counterforce-no-cities" strategy, as it was called, was thus a strategy for controlled nuclear war. To operate such a strategy, McNamara pointed out, a survivable command and control system was essential. But there was more to such a system than underground bunkers, airborne control centers, and the like. What was vital, McNamara said, was "unity of planning, executive authority, and central direction." Control within the alliance had to be "indivisible":

> There must not be competing and conflicting strategies in the conduct of nuclear war. We are convinced that a general nuclear war target system is indivisible and if nuclear war should occur, our best hope lies in conducting a centrally controlled campaign against all of the enemy's vital nuclear capabilities. Doing this means carefully choosing targets, pre-planning strikes, coordinating attacks, and assessing results, as well as allocating and directing follow-on attacks from the center. These call, in our view, for a greater degree of Alliance participation in formulating nuclear policies and consulting on the appropriate occasions for using these weapons. Beyond this, *it is essential that we centralize the decision to use our nuclear weapons to the greatest extent possible. We would all find it intolerable to contemplate having only a part of the strategic force launched in isolation from our main striking power.*[117]

So there it was. Independent use of European forces was "intolerable." Indeed, McNamara went on to argue that "relatively weak nuclear forces," targeted on cities, were not "likely to be adequate to perform the function of deterrence." A small force would invite preemptive attack; to launch it "would be tantamount to suicide."[118] A force of that sort would not be a credible deterrent.

American spokesmen, both official and semiofficial, now repeatedly argued along these lines. Rusk, for example, developed these points with top German leaders in June 1962. The idea that a "relatively small national nuclear force" might

---

[116] McNamara remarks, NATO ministerial meeting, May 5, 1962, pp. 3–4, DOD-FOIA 79-481.

[117] Ibid., pp. 9–10. Emphasis added.

[118] Ibid., pp. 11–12.

be used independently of the alliance was "frightening." Deterrence, he and other U.S. officials declared over and over again, was "indivisible": an attack on Europe would warrant the same response as an attack on the United States; the Europeans could therefore safely leave the burden of nuclear deterrence in American hands; indeed, it was somewhat insulting for them even to suggest that America might abandon them in the end rather than see her own cities destroyed. The term "indivisibility" was used so frequently in the American attack on national nuclear forces that Bohlen, now ambassador to France, finally urged the U.S. government to drop it. "To any European," he wrote, it was simply a "euphemism for absolute American control."[119]

How is all this to be taken? Was the policy of opposing nuclear forces under European control rooted, to any important extent, in the sort of thinking McNamara laid out in the Athens speech? Or is the strategic doctrine to be understood primarily in instrumental terms, as a way of getting the Europeans to accept arrangements the Americans wanted for essentially political reasons? Was the strategy, in other words, driving the policy, or vice versa?

The first point to note in this context is that American leaders at this point did not really believe that the United States would be able to launch a first strike under any circumstances—not for more than a year or two at any rate. McNamara's argument at Athens was that the American nuclear deterrent was still effective because if the Soviets attacked Europe, the United States, under the new strategy, could still rationally launch a first strike; the claim that European nuclear forces were pointless and indeed dangerous was based on this fundamental contention. But McNamara himself did not think that the United States could rationally strike first with nuclear weapons, even if Europe was being overrun. Indeed, he insisted in an important memorandum for the president in late 1962 that the "coercive strategy"—that is, the sort of strategy he had outlined in the Athens speech—was not an option, unless the Soviets had already launched a nuclear attack on America and the United States was "trying to make the best of a bad situation." The United States, he thought, should under no circumstances be the first to launch a major nuclear attack. And the views laid out in this November 21, 1962, memorandum had not suddenly popped into his head on November 20; he had been thinking along these lines for some time—probably even as early as February 1961.[120]

---

[119] U.S.–German meeting, June 22, 1962, and Bohlen paper, July 2, 1962, FRUS 1961–63, 13:420, 430. See also Albert Wohlstetter, "Nuclear Sharing: NATO and the N + 1 Country," *Foreign Affairs* 39 (April 1961): 355–387. Wohlstetter was not in the government, but he had close ties with key Defense Department officials, and had played a major role in developing the policy outlined in the Acheson NATO report. The "Nuclear Sharing" article was a powerful argument against nuclear forces under European national control, and it is important to note that Wohlstetter had favored such capabilities just a couple of years earlier. In his most famous article, "The Delicate Balance of Terror," which appeared in *Foreign Affairs* in January 1959, he had considered the development of independent capabilities in Europe to be in principle "a useful thing" (p. 227). This shift on his part is one measure of how radically and how quickly thinking on the nuclear sharing issue had been transformed by the beginning of 1961.

[120] Draft Presidential Memorandum, "Recommended FY 1964–FY 1968 Strategic Retaliatory Forces," November 21, 1962, pp. 5–9; OSD-FOIA. On the DPMs, which were quite important during

Kennedy, however, did not see things exactly the same way, and it was only in September 1963 that he concluded that a first strike would no longer be possible.[121] The president had not ruled out a preemptive attack in 1961 or 1962. At that time, a limited nuclear strike aimed simply at destroying the Soviet nuclear force had been viewed as a serious option. An attack of this sort, it was thought, could destroy the great bulk of the Soviet retaliatory force—the Soviets, that is, would not be able to do really heavy damage (to America at least) with whatever survived the attack—and a certain amount of planning for such a strike actually took place at the time. But this was not a strategy for controlled or protracted nuclear war. A limited strike was conceivable only because it was felt that there was a very good chance that the attack would essentially wipe out the USSR's strategic nuclear capability, and that the war would then end very quickly.[122]

If, however, substantial Soviet forces were to survive the attack—and this, of course, was the situation that the leaders of the Kennedy administration knew was just a year or two away—an American first strike, it was assumed, would not be a viable option. Once the Soviets had survivable forces, an attack would become too risky; there was too great a chance that the war would become uncontrollable. The rhetoric was one thing, but neither Kennedy nor his closest advisers ever really believed in the strategy of "controlled and discriminate general war." And in fact by early 1962 they had learned that such a strategy was not feasible for technical reasons. The command and control system in place in 1961 could not support this sort of strategy—that is, it could not survive a nuclear attack and function in a nuclear environment—and the kind of system that could support the strategy was for all practical purposes beyond reach.[123] There was also the related question of whether the Soviets would be able to control their surviving forces and keep them from attacking western cities, even if they wanted to, after the Americans had launched their attack.

For these and other reasons, the political leadership did not insist on a really fundamental reworking of operational strategy or on a radical rebuilding of the American nuclear arsenal in line with the thinking laid out in the Athens speech—that is, with the goal of minimizing collateral damage. And, as noted above, the impact of the new thinking on the nation's basic plan for general nuclear war was evidently a good deal more limited than the rhetoric implied.[124]

---

the McNamara period, see, for example, Kaplan, *Wizards of Armageddon*, p. 281, and Alain Enthoven and K. Wayne Smith, *How Much is Enough? Shaping the Defense Program, 1961–1969* (New York: Harper and Row, 1971), pp. 53–58. For his views in early 1961, see above, note 14.

[121] NSC meeting, September 12, 1963 (discussion of NESC report), FRUS 1961–63, 8:499–507.

[122] Rosenberg, "Nuclear War Planning," p. 178; Kaplan, *Wizards of Armageddon*, pp. 296–301; Taylor to Kennedy, September 19, 1961, FRUS 1961–63, 8:126–129; Kaysen interview, August 1988; Taylor to Lemnitzer, September 19, 1961 (for Kennedy's evident interest in the idea), FRUS 1961–63, vols. 7–9, mic. supp., no. 242; and above all, for a detailed description of the proposal, Smith to Taylor, September 7, 1961, DDRS 1996/2496.

[123] Wainstein, "Evolution of U.S. Strategic Command and Control," pp. 285–294, 326, 336–337, 346–347, 431.

[124] For a brief description of how the basic war plan was changed, see Rosenberg, "Nuclear War Planning," pp. 178–179; on the new guidance introduced in early 1962, see Wainstein, "Evolution of U.S. Strategic Command and Control," pp. 290–291. On the relative superficiality of the changes introduced during the McNamara period, see Rosenberg, "Reality and Responsibility," pp. 46, 48. Gen-

What all this means is that the strategy laid out in the Athens speech is not to be taken at face value.[125] It simply did not reflect the real thinking of the leaders of the Kennedy administration. Kennedy and his closest advisers knew that the United States would soon no longer be in a position to launch a first strike, and that NATO strategy could therefore not permanently be built on the premise that the United States in the final analysis could rationally launch a first strike if Europe were attacked; and yet the strategy laid out in the Athens speech was supposed to provide the basis for a permanent change in policy. This was a strategy that assumed that the United States would retain a meaningful strategic edge even after the Soviets had developed a survivable force; and yet the real feeling of top U.S. officials from Kennedy on down was that as soon as the Soviets had acquired a such a force, the United States would not have a politically meaningful strategic advantage no matter what strategy was adopted—and that, in particular, the "coercive strategy" would not give U.S. strategic superiority a new lease on life.

Kennedy and his main advisers leaned toward what was later called the "finite deterrence" or "existential deterrence" approach to nuclear issues—toward the idea that relative numbers, beyond a certain point, are not terribly important, and that relatively small forces could deter much larger ones. Kennedy understood, for

---

eral Bruce Holloway, director of the Joint Strategic Target Planning Staff at the time—the SAC-dominated unit that worked out the SIOP, the basic plan for general nuclear war—noted in an oral history interview that the military officers under his command were relatively free to work out the war plan as they saw fit: McNamara never overruled them on the SIOP while Holloway headed the JSTPS. Holloway oral history, p. 359, Office of Air Force History, Bolling Air Force Base, Washington, D.C. There is also a NATO aspect to this story. One of the reasons SACEUR wanted land-based MRBMs was that they were a good deal more accurate than sea-based weapons, thus making it possible to use warheads with much smaller yields; this was in line with Norstad's "constraints policy"—i.e., his policy for limiting collateral damage. If the U.S. government had been serious about the strategy of "controlled and discriminate nuclear war," this would have been an important consideration in favor of the MRBM deployment, but in reality this factor evidently did not count for much. For SACEUR's argument about the MRBMs and the "constraints policy," see Finletter to Rusk, October 17, 1962 (report of Norstad's briefing that day to North Atlantic Council), NSF/216/MLF—General—Stikker Paper/JFKL; for more information on the "constraints policy" (also called the "restraints policy"), see above, chapter 5, note 176.

[125] The most compelling piece of evidence in support of this interpretation is an excerpt from the tape of a July 30, 1963, meeting between Kennedy, McNamara, and Bundy. McNamara informed the president here that a "very controversial force proposal" was in the making, and that counterforce was going to be abandoned as a goal, at least for force sizing purposes. The reason was that counterforce would not substantially reduce casualties in the event of war. For Kennedy, that point was self-evident, but he wondered what this shift in doctrine would do to what he called the "McNamara thesis." McNamara's attachment to the no-cities/counterforce doctrine was so weak that the president had to explain that he was referring to the "idea that we were just going to attack their means of delivery"—that is, the line laid out in the Athens speech. Kennedy then went on to add: "That was just that. . ."—but his voice trailed off, as though a point had registered in his mind and he saw no need to verbalize it fully. The use of the word "just" implies clearly enough that the McNamara doctrine, as outlined at Athens, is not to be taken at face value and that its real purpose lay elsewhere. It is also quite clear from this conversation that the coming and going of the "no-cities" doctrine was not taken too seriously: it was a source of some amusement to these top officials that these strategies had a short shelf-life and tended to get used up rather rapidly. This particular one, Bundy jokingly remarked here, "was only good for about a year," and McNamara, in the same spirit, added: "we're running out of them, Mr. President." White House meeting, July 30, 1963, tape 102/A38, cassette 1, side 2 (discussion begins after first excision), POF, JFKL.

example, that even a small Chinese nuclear force would largely neutralize America's enormous nuclear power. The old idea that the Communists had to be prevented from taking over countries like Laos and Vietnam because of the domino effect no longer had much point, he said, because "the Chinese Communists are bound to get nuclear weapons in time, and from that moment on they will dominate South East Asia."[126] The assumption here was that as soon as the Chinese developed a nuclear force, no matter how small, American nuclear power would no longer be able to keep China at bay. As long as the risk of nuclear escalation was real, that risk was bound to affect political behavior. Even a relatively small risk, even the prospect of having to absorb a relatively limited number of nuclear attacks, would have a major deterrent effect. The twenty missiles that the Soviets had in Cuba, as Kennedy noted after the missile crisis, "had had a deterrent effect on us," and this, he pointed out, meant that small nuclear forces were not without real deterrent value.[127]

But by the same token, countries like France and Germany—in particular if they cooperated with each other, and especially if they received help from the United States—would be able to build nuclear forces that could in theory counterbalance the Soviet nuclear threat. If a relatively small Soviet nuclear force was able to balance off a much larger American force, then, by the same logic, the Europeans would, given enough time, be able to build forces that could serve as effective counterweights to Soviet nuclear power. Relative size was not the crucial factor. All the European countries had to do was to build a survivable force of a certain absolute size, and to Kennedy it was clearly not beyond their ability to do so. "If the French and other European powers acquire a nuclear capability," he said in January 1963, "they would be in a position to be entirely independent and we might be on the outside looking in."[128]

So if U.S. leaders claimed that European nuclear forces had no deterrent value, this was not because such claims reflected their real thinking. If they pressed arguments of this sort, it therefore must have been for political reasons. If they argued for a strategy of controlled nuclear war that they did not really believe in, this must have been because that strategy served an important political purpose. The Europeans were to be convinced or pressured or cajoled into getting out of the "nuclear business" and accepting a system in which power was concentrated in Americans hands: this, by 1962 at any rate, was the real purpose of the new American strategic doctrine.[129]

[126] Kennedy-Krock meeting, October 11, 1961, KP/1/3/343/ML. Note also his comment in an NSC meeting in January 1963 that "we will have a difficult time protecting the free areas of Asia if the Chinese get nuclear weapons." NSC meeting, January 22, 1963, FRUS 1961–63, 8:462.

[127] Anglo-American meeting, December 19, 1962, FRUS 1961–63, 13:1094. For the impact that the presence of Soviet missiles in Cuba had on America's ability to escalate during the missile crisis, see Trachtenberg, *History and Strategy*, pp. 250–253.

[128] NSC meeting, January 22, 1963, FRUS 1961–63, 8:460, 13:486. Note also the president's assumption that Europe was becoming less dependent on the United States as the French built up their own nuclear force, a point that ran counter to the official position that the French force had no value whatsoever. NSC Executive Committee meeting, January 25, 1963, ibid., p. 487.

[129] Denigrating European nuclear forces was a tactic that the U.S. government deliberately adopted for political reasons. McNamara, for example, noted at one point that "disparaging French nuclear ca-

This policy of centralizing control in American hands, however, had not been adopted because the United States wanted to dominate NATO Europe as a kind of end in itself. Nor had it been adopted because people like Kennedy and McNamara were opposed in principle to the idea of nuclear forces under national control—and most notably under British or French control. The real issue had to do with Germany: the fundamental goal, as Kennedy himself said, was "to prevent nuclear weapons from coming into the hands of the Germans."[130] The Germans, however, could not be discriminated against too directly. Hence the great premium placed on achieving that goal by means of more general policies, by policies that applied to Britain and France as well as to Germany and which had a formal and plausible strategic rationale.

But the fact that the U.S. government now felt so strongly about that fundamental goal—so strongly that it had adopted a whole series of basic policies rooted in that fundamental objective—meant that a basic settlement with the USSR might now be possible. The Soviets were deeply interested in keeping Germany non-nuclear, and now the idea that nuclear weapons needed to be kept out of German hands was also a central element of American policy. A reaffirmation of Germany's non-nuclear status might therefore be an important element of a Berlin settlement. But if Germany was to be kept non-nuclear, U.S. forces would have to remain on German soil. American power would continue to balance Soviet power in central Europe; the Germans could then accept their non-nuclear status because their security would be guaranteed by the United States. A non-nuclear Federal Republic and a permanent American troop presence in Europe would thus be the twin pillars on which a settlement might be built. If in addition everyone made it clear, in one way or another, that they were willing to live with the status quo in central Europe—with a divided Germany and with West Berlin under the military protection of the western allies—then the threat of war would disappear. A stable peace might thus be within reach.

This was the vision that was taking shape during the early Kennedy period. It remained to be seen, however, whether the Soviets, and the European allies as well, would accept the kind of arrangement the U.S. government now had in mind.

---

pabilities" was something that could be done for political purposes. NSC Executive Committee meeting, January 25, 1963, ibid., p. 490. The assumption was that even small nuclear capabilities would have major (but, from the U.S. point of view, undesirable) political effects; it was therefore important to dissuade other countries from going nuclear; and to do that one had to deny that relatively small nuclear forces were of much value. The Gilpatric Committee report on the nuclear proliferation problem, although prepared a bit later, provides a good illustration of this kind of thinking. The report recognized that new nuclear capabilities would affect the distribution of power in the world, and noted that as more countries went nuclear, American "diplomatic and military influence would wane." It then argued that in order to "minimize the incentives for others to acquire nuclear weapons," the Americans had to "avoid giving an exaggerated impression of their importance and utility," and that the United States needed to "stress the current and future important role of conventional armaments"—which is yet another example of how the flexible response doctrine is to be understood, to a certain extent, in instrumental terms. Report to the President by the Committee on Nuclear Proliferation, January 21, 1965, pp. 2, 20, DDRS 1991/2928.

[130] Kennedy-Macmillan meeting, April 28, 1962, Prem 11/3783, PRO.

CRISIS WITH RUSSIA, CRISIS IN NATO

When Kennedy met with Khrushchev at Vienna in June 1961, he in effect laid out the terms of a general east-west settlement. Both sides would live with things as they were. The Soviets would respect western rights in Berlin, and the United States in return would respect the USSR's most vital interests. The American government, the president said, was not interested in challenging Soviet hegemony in Russia's own sphere of influence in eastern Europe, and he also understood Soviet concerns about Germany. The United States, he told the Soviet leader, was against a buildup of German power that would threaten the USSR. The implication here was that as part of a general settlement the U.S. government would keep the Federal Republic from developing a nuclear force under national control.[131]

But Khrushchev was not interested in a deal of this sort. Instead, using the most violent language that a Soviet leader had ever used with an American president, he threatened war over Berlin. Unless the western powers agreed by the end of the year to make West Berlin a "free city," the USSR would sign a "peace treaty" with East Germany. Western rights in Berlin would be "annulled" and "eliminated." The Communists would then block access to the city. Indeed, the USSR considered "all of Berlin to be GDR territory." If the western powers tried to maintain their rights through military action, "force would be met by force." If the United States wanted war, he said, "that was its problem." The USSR had made an "irrevocable" decision and if the West used force, she would have no choice but "to accept the challenge."[132] It was as though the Berlin Crisis had taken on a life of its own, as though Khrushchev was no longer mainly interested in getting an agreement that would protect basic Soviet security interests.

The Soviet leader, it seemed, was out to humiliate the United States, but how was the American government to react? On the one hand, Kennedy made it clear that the United States was not going to surrender to the Soviets on this issue. On July 25, he outlined America's Berlin policy in a major televised speech. West Berlin, he said, was the "great testing place of Western courage and will," and it would not be abandoned. If necessary, the United States would fight to defend it. A series of steps would be taken to strengthen the U.S. military position, and America's civil defense program would be beefed up significantly. The message was that war—general nuclear war—was a real possibility. Negotiations were of course possible, but they could not be one-sided. The "legitimate security interests of all nations" had to be taken into account. "We cannot negotiate," he said, "with those who say 'What's mine is mine and what's yours is negotiable.'"[133]

---

[131] Kennedy-Khrushchev meetings, June 4, 1961, FRUS 1961–63, 14:87–98. For another example of Kennedy's tendency to think in spheres of influence terms, see the report of his meeting with Adzhubei in January 1962. When the Soviets had problems with Hungary, the president noted, they felt free to use force; the U.S., he implied, should be able to deal with the Cuban problem the same way. See Aleksandr Fursenko and Timothy Naftali, *"One Hell of a Gamble": Khrushchev, Castro, and Kennedy, 1958–1964* (New York: Norton, 1997), pp. 152–153.

[132] Kennedy-Khrushchev meetings, June 4, 1961, FRUS 1961–63, 14:87–98.

[133] Radio and Television Report to the American People on the Berlin Crisis, July 25, 1961, PPP Kennedy, 1961, pp. 534–538. The phrase had been suggested by the famous television journalist Edward R. Murrow, then head of the United States Information Agency.

Khrushchev had perhaps thought at Vienna that his bluster would intimidate Kennedy, but if that had been his assumption, it now appeared that he had miscalculated. The Soviets were alarmed. Events, it seemed, might be spinning out of control. Their reaction to the Kennedy speech was anything but belligerent. The last thing they wanted was to see the crisis develop into a full-blown military confrontation. So Khrushchev soon shifted course. The change was not immediate. When he met with Italian Prime Minister Fanfani at the beginning of August, the Soviet leader was still trying to bluff his way through the crisis. Khrushchev, Fanfani told Rusk, had said "that he would not fire first if the Western powers attempted physical access to Berlin, but that they would have to pass 'over his dead body' and that if they fired first he would retaliate. . . ." Khrushchev had also told the Italian leader that if the West attempted an airlift, "he would resist this as 'spying overflights,' and would then fire first using nuclear weapons." When Rusk asked whether this meant that those weapons would be used "in the area of Berlin or in general war," Fanfani replied "that it was his understanding that it would be in the framework of general war."[134]

But just a few days later there was a dramatic change in the Soviet line. Khrushchev now declared that he wanted to ease what he saw as a growing "war psychosis." "War hysteria," he said, would "lead to nothing good. There must be a sense of proportion and military passions must not be fanned. If the feelings are let loose and they predominate over reason, then the flywheel of war preparations can start revolving at high speed. Even when reason prompts that a brake should be put on, the flywheel of war preparations may have acquired such speed and momentum that even those who had set it revolving will be unable to stop it." He would take no new military measures of his own, at least not for the time being. And the substantive Soviet position also became more moderate. At Vienna, in direct response to a question from Kennedy, he said that the signing of a peace treaty with East Germany would "block access to Berlin," but now on August 7 he declared: "we do not intend to infringe upon the lawful interests of the Western Powers. Any barring of access to West Berlin, any blockade of West Berlin, is entirely out of the question." And that same day, the top Soviet commander in the area, Marshal Konev, reiterated the point in a meeting with the western military authorities in Berlin: "Gentlemen, you may be reassured, whatever is going to happen in the near future, your rights will not be touched."[135]

Just a few days later, East Berlin's border with West Berlin was sealed off. On August 13, the East German authorities began to construct what would eventually become a wall dividing the two parts of the city. The refugee flow, which had been draining East Germany of many of its most skilled inhabitants, was now suddenly

---

[134] Rusk-Fanfani meeting, August 9, 1961, NSABF.

[135] Khrushchev speeches on August 7 and August 11, 1961, *New York Times,* August 8, 1961, p. 8, and U.S. Senate, Foreign Relations Committee, *Documents on Germany, 1944–1961* (New York: Greenwood, 1968), pp. 718–720. For the Konev quotation (which I have put into English slightly differently), see Helmut Trotnow, "Who Actually Built the Berlin Wall? The SED Leadership and the 13th of August 1961," paper presented at OSD and U.S. Army Center of Military History Conference on Cold War Military Records and History, Washington, D.C., March 1994, p. 6. For Khrushchev's original threat at Vienna to block access, see Kennedy-Khrushchev meeting, June 4, 1961, FRUS 1961–63, 14:91.

cut off. Khrushchev had previously resisted East German pleas to seal the border. The ending of the refugee exodus and even the internal stabilization of the East German state were not his most fundamental goals. He had had more far-reaching objectives, having to do with the German question as a whole, and in particular with West German policy and West German power. He had therefore wanted to keep the Berlin question alive. But now, confronted with the specter of war, he put these broader goals on the back burner.[136]

The sealing of the border took the western countries by surprise, but the events of August 13 did not lead to a crisis in east-west relations. It was out of the question that force would be used to prevent the Communists from doing whatever they wanted on their side of the line of demarcation. The use of force was only conceivable for purely defensive purposes, to hold onto what the western side already had. What, then, was the point of making a fuss? Why put the prestige of the western powers on the line if everyone knew they would have to back down in the end and acquiesce in what the Communists were doing in the part of Berlin they controlled? Macmillan decided not to interrupt his holiday in Scotland. Couve de Murville also saw no reason to get excited about what the Communists had done. There was no need, he said, for immediate consultations with the Americans: "a note would be prepared, and that would be it." Adenauer, worried about the possibility of an uprising in the east, and about the horrible prospect of the western countries standing by helplessly as the Communists crushed it, deliberately took a very mild line. As for the Americans, their view all along had been that force would be used for the defense of West Berlin only, and American officials immediately agreed that the "closing of the border was not a shooting issue." For the U.S. government, "the problem was essentially one of propaganda." And in substantive political terms, the Communist move was not viewed in a purely negative light. The ending of the refugee flow meant that the Soviets would find it easier to live with the status quo, and that they would be more ready to accept an arrangement that would safeguard the West's basic interests. As Rusk put it at the time, while "the border closing was a most serious matter, the probability was that in realistic terms it would make a Berlin settlement easier."[137]

[136] Hope Harrison has shown that the East German regime pressed for Soviet action, and in particular for a closing of the "door to the West," but that the USSR resisted these demands. For the Soviets, the refugee problem was never the central issue, and they made it clear that they had bigger fish to fry. The most important document here is a letter from the Soviet ambassador in East Germany, Pervukhin, to Gromyko of May 19, 1961. The East German "friends" were pressing for the sealing of the border in Berlin, Pervukhin wrote, but this reflected "a somewhat one-sided approach to this problem," and they did not take adequate account of "the interests of the entire socialist camp." See Harrison, "Ulbricht and the Concrete 'Rose,'" appendix D.

[137] See, for example, Schwarz, *Adenauer,* 2:660–665; Alphand, *L'étonnement d'être,* p. 361 (for Couve's remark); western foreign ministers' meeting, December 11, 1961, FRUS 1961–63, 14:652 (for another example of Couve's very accepting attitude). For U.S. views: Kennedy remarks in NSC meeting, July 13, 1961; Rusk comments in western foreign ministers' meeting, August 5, 1961, and in a meeting of the Berlin steering group, August 15, 1961, ibid., pp. 194, 286, 334. Ambassador Thompson had earlier argued that the border would have to be sealed if the Communists were to accept the status quo in West Berlin. See Thompson to Rusk, March 16, 1961, ibid., p. 32.

It is often argued that the Kennedy administration's emphasis on *West* Berlin marked a shift in U.S. policy. See, for example, Schwarz, *Adenauer,* 2:654; for an even more extreme claim (blaming the Wall

It would be a mistake, however, to say that western leaders were relieved by what the Soviets had done. The Americans in particular were afraid that unilateral action of this sort might foreshadow a more aggressive Soviet policy on the Berlin question as a whole. Kennedy and McNamara therefore sought to speed up military preparations. But at the same time, the episode also underscored the importance of efforts to reach a negotiated settlement. The Americans were worried that if nothing were "put into the works," the Soviets might well soon sign their "peace treaty" with East Germany and force a showdown with the West.[138]

Kennedy had in fact already decided to see whether some sort of agreement to settle the crisis could be worked out with the USSR. Acheson had opposed the idea of serious talks with the Russians on Berlin. To press for negotiations, he thought, would be taken as a sign of weakness; if the Soviets were to be made to back down, the West would have to take a very tough line.[139] But even before Acheson presented his report on Berlin, this view was coming to be seen as too dogmatic. Bundy, for example, spoke with the political columnist Walter Lippmann about the Berlin problem, and then wrote a memo to the president outlining the differences between the Acheson and the Lippmann approach. Those differences, he said, turned "on whether there is any legitimate Soviet interest to which we can give some reassurance." Acheson did not think so, but in Lippmann's view there might be "ways of meeting what he thinks may be the fundamental Soviet impulse—a need for security in Eastern Europe and the fear of what the post-Adenauer Germany might be like." Bundy was laying out for Kennedy what he saw as the range of responsible opinion. His own view lay between the two extremes he described. Firmness on access to Berlin was fundamental, but that did not mean a negotiated settlement was out of the question: "What we might later be willing to consider with respect to such items as the Oder-Neisse line and a de facto acceptance of a divided Germany is matter for further discussion, and we ourselves might indeed have new proposals at a later time."[140]

This turned out to be the president's view as well. He had no great interest in German reunification, nor was he fundamentally opposed to dealing with the East German authorities. When Rusk on July 17 brought up the question of America's "eventual position toward the DDR," Kennedy "made plain his belief that since we shall have to talk with representatives of that regime at some stage, we should not now take so strong a line that these later talks will look like a defeat."[141] By mid-July, the administration intended to "lean forward on negotiation."[142] What really

---

on the "erosion of Anglo-Saxon firmness"), see Schwarz's "Adenauer, le nucléaire et la France," p. 307. But this is a myth: under Eisenhower, the defense of West Berlin was seen as vital, but no one in authority thought that force would have to be used if the border between the two parts of the city were closed. See the DOS Berlin History, 2:110–111.

[138] Kennedy to McNamara, August 14, 1961, NSF/82/Germany—Berlin—General/JFKL; Bundy to Kennedy, August 14, 1961, and McNamara in Berlin steering group, August 17, 1961, FRUS 1961–63, 14:330–331, 347; Rusk-Alphand meeting, August 26, 1961, NSABF.

[139] Acheson in Berlin coordinating group, June 16, 1961, and Acheson report, June 28, 1961, FRUS 1961–63, 14:119, 139, 148, 151.

[140] Bundy to Kennedy, May 29, 1961, POF/126/Vienna documents (A)/JFKL.

[141] Meeting on Berlin, July 17, 1961, FRUS 1961–63, 14:210.

[142] Bundy to Sorensen, July 22, 1961, NSF/81/German—Berlin—General/JFKL.

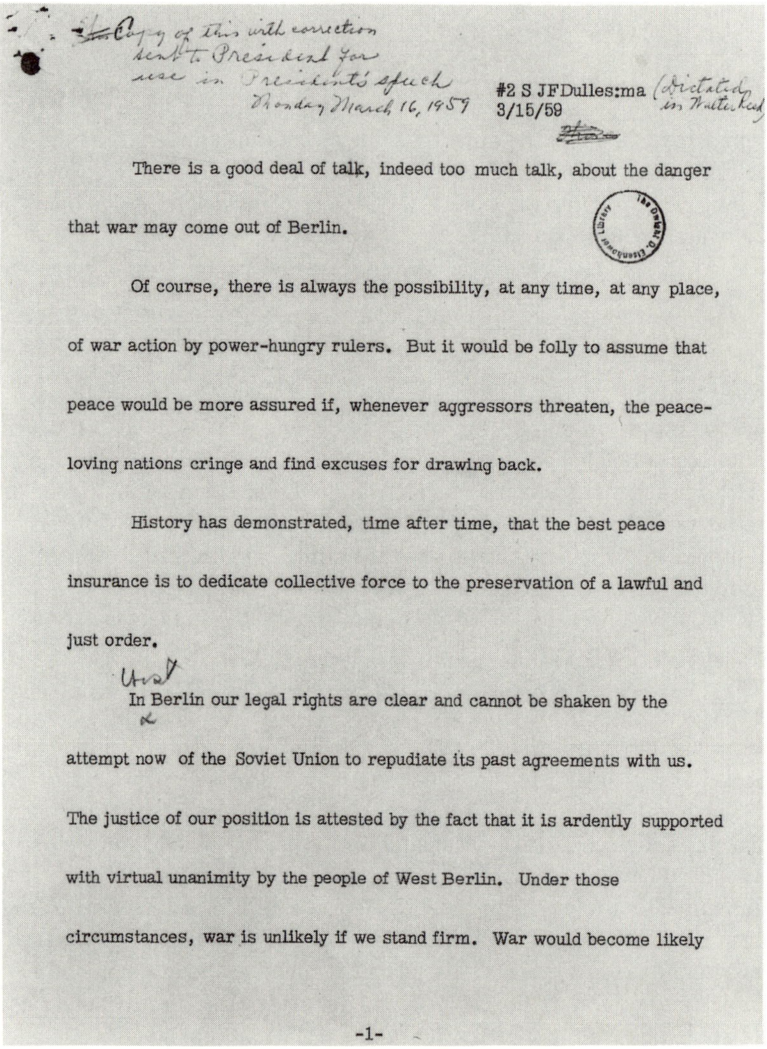

*Copy of this with correction
sent to President for
use in President's speech
Monday, March 16, 1959*

#2 S JFDulles:ma *(Dictated
in Walter Reed)*
3/15/59

There is a good deal of talk, indeed too much talk, about the danger

that war may come out of Berlin.

Of course, there is always the possibility, at any time, at any place,

of war action by power-hungry rulers. But it would be folly to assume that

peace would be more assured if, whenever aggressors threaten, the peace-

loving nations cringe and find excuses for drawing back.

History has demonstrated, time after time, that the best peace

insurance is to dedicate collective force to the preservation of a lawful and

just order.

Our

In Berlin our legal rights are clear and cannot be shaken by the

attempt now of the Soviet Union to repudiate its past agreements with us.

The justice of our position is attested by the fact that it is ardently supported

with virtual unanimity by the people of West Berlin. Under those

circumstances, war is unlikely if we stand firm. War would become likely

-1-

Figure 10. Dulles amends a draft of Eisenhower's speech to the nation on the Berlin crisis to emphasize America's commitment to the defense of the *western* part of the city. From Dulles Papers, White House Memoranda Series, box 7, White House Correspondence—General 1959, Eisenhower Library.

mattered, Kennedy thought, was "our presence in Berlin, and our access to Berlin."[143] Other issues were not nearly so important. What would the West actually be giving away if it moved toward a more formal acceptance of the status quo in central Europe? If the Oder-Neisse line was given some kind of official recognition, would the West be sacrificing anything of substance? Everyone knew it was more or less permanent in any case. As even Acheson recognized, a recog-

[143] NSC meeting, July 13, 1961, FRUS 1961–63, 14:194.

nition of the border "would probably be in the West's interest in any event, as a potential means of eventually weakening Soviet-Polish ties."[144]

And how important was it to maintain the fiction that the East German state did not exist? The division of Germany did not result from anything the western powers had said. A refusal to deal with East German officials on the access routes or elsewhere would not bring reunification any closer. There was a certain aura of unreality surrounding this whole complex of problems. These were not the kinds of issues that one could imagine fighting a nuclear war over. This had been true under Eisenhower, and it was even more true under Kennedy. If "concessions" in this area—concessions of an essentially theoretical nature in any case—could be traded for Soviet acceptance of the status quo in Berlin, wouldn't such an arrangement be very much to the interest of the West as a whole?

So Kennedy had by now parted company with Acheson. The president now had to take charge of policy himself. His advisers were divided on the fundamental issue of how far America should go, and he was the only one who could determine the substance of the negotiating position.[145] And he decided on a very active policy. To Kennedy, the whole Berlin situation was not satisfactory, even for America. He wanted to clean up this "mess" if he could. There was no point to just standing on the status quo or simply rehashing old proposals about reunifying Germany through free elections—proposals that would obviously lead nowhere.

Instead, Kennedy now pressed for the development of a negotiating position based on the idea of a stabilization of the status quo in central Europe. On August 21, he laid out some basic guidelines. America, he said, should make a fresh start. The new policy should "protect our support for the *idea* of self-determination, the *idea* of all-Germany, and the *fact* of viable, protected freedom in West Berlin." The "option of proposing parallel peace treaties" with the two German states should be considered carefully; with regard to Berlin itself, occupation rights were not essential "if other strong guarantees can be found." It was clear that the president was thinking in terms of a recognition of the Oder-Neisse line and "*de facto* acceptance of the GDR." As Bundy pointed out, "the main line of thought among those who are now at work on the substance of our negotiating position is that we can and should shift substantially toward acceptance of the GDR, the Oder-Neisse line, a non-aggression pact, and even the idea of two peace treaties."[146]

Kennedy wanted a "real reconstruction of our negotiating proposals."[147] In particular, the goal of reunification would be put on the back burner, as a mere "idea" which one would have to continue to support. But the freedom and viability of West Berlin were of fundamental importance. A more secure West Berlin was what the West would be getting in exchange for the concessions it would be willing to make. The president was determined to push forward with this policy, on a unilateral basis if necessary. America, he wrote, could "not accept a veto from

---

[144] Acheson Report, June 28, 1961, ibid., p. 151.

[145] Bundy to Kennedy, August 28, 1961, ibid., pp. 379n.

[146] Kennedy to Rusk, August 21, 1961, ibid., pp. 359–360; Rusk-Alphand meeting, August 26, 1961, NSABF; Bundy to Kennedy, August 28, 1961, NSF/82/Germany—Berlin—General/JFKL. Emphasis in original text.

[147] Kennedy to Rusk, September 12, 1961, FRUS 1961–63, 14:403.

any other power." The three main European allies "must come along or stay behind."[148]

The new U.S. policy had another major component. As part of a Berlin settlement, the Federal Republic would be kept from acquiring an independent nuclear capability. Under Eisenhower, the American government had not been willing to make a concession of this sort. Only as part of a deal providing for German reunification would the Soviet Union be given security guarantees in this area. But now the Federal Republic's non-nuclear status would be part of an arrangement that would settle the crisis and secure the status quo in Berlin and in central Europe as a whole—that is, an arrangement based on the division of Germany. The USSR, it was felt, might have legitimate concerns about a resurgence of German power. If so, the "general security situation in central Europe" could be discussed, and it might be possible in the Berlin talks to make "some headway" in this area. In other words, the American government was ready to include some limitation on West Germany's nuclear status in an agreement that would end the crisis.[149]

It seemed in fact that a deal of the sort Kennedy had in mind might be within reach. In talks between Soviet Foreign Minister Andrei Gromyko and American leaders in late September and early October, Gromyko made it clear that the German nuclear weapons issue would be a central part of an agreement. This, he told the president, was a matter of fundamental importance for the USSR.[150] It seemed to some high-ranking U.S. officials that western concessions on "certain all-German matters," including an arrangement preventing West Germany from getting control of nuclear weapons, might be traded for a "Soviet agreement on Berlin."[151] This was exactly what Kennedy wanted. For him, a Berlin settlement would be tantamount to a settlement of the German question as a whole, and if that issue were settled, any other problems the two sides had would prove manageable. An agreement on Berlin would therefore lay the basis for a fairly stable international system.

The emergence of this new U.S. policy scarcely went unnoticed in Europe. Indeed, it seemed that American thinking had been utterly transformed. Even the British foreign secretary, Lord Home, thought as early as August 6 that the Americans were "almost too keen" on negotiations.[152] "One continues to be staggered," one of his chief subordinates noted in late September, by the lengths to which the Americans seemed prepared to go on such matters as the "Oder-Neisse line, *de*

[148] Kennedy to Rusk, August 21, 1961, ibid., p. 359.

[149] On September 5, Kennedy had asked the State Department to consider including a "limitation or prohibition of nuclear arms in either part of Germany" as part of a Berlin settlement, and Rusk did in fact make it clear that the United States was willing to discuss the issue when he met with Gromyko later that month. Kennedy-Rusk meeting, September 5, 1961, and Rusk-Gromyko meetings, September 28 and 30, 1961, FRUS 1961–63, 14:393, 439–441, 459. See also Kennedy-Adzhubei interview, November 25, 1961, PPP Kennedy, 1961, p. 751.

[150] Kennedy-Gromyko meeting, October 6, 1961, FRUS 1961–63, 14:471, 472, 474. See also Nitze-Menshikov meeting, July 15, 1961, and Rusk-Gromyko meeting, September 30, 1961, ibid., pp. 204, 459.

[151] Bohlen to Rusk, October 3, 1961, ibid., p. 465. See also Rusk-Bruce meeting, October 2, 1961, and Bundy to Kennedy, October 2, 1961, ibid., pp. 460 n, 460–461.

[152] Home to Macmillan, August 6, 1961, FO 371/160541, PRO.

facto dealings with the DDR," and also on "security measures in Europe," a term that referred above all to the question of nuclear weapons in German hands.[153] The French were also "astounded" by the new American policy, and their misgivings ran a good deal deeper. Kennedy seemed ready to accept the East German regime. How would the West Germans react? Was the U.S. government really prepared to move ahead without them?[154]

The Germans, of course, were deeply upset by the new thrust of American policy. By early October, the new U.S. line had become clear from press leaks. The German ambassador came to see Acheson on October 11. He was "disturbed and depressed" by the recent shift in U.S. thinking. The German government, he said, was being told that it was a "waste of time even for negotiating purposes to talk about reunification." The Americans seemed ready to accept the Oder-Neisse line and "were moving toward something which was indistinguishable from de facto recognition of East Germany." In all his years of working with the U.S. government, he had never "felt so depressed about its policy."[155] To Adenauer, it seemed that the Americans were willing to give away practically everything.[156]

And in fact Kennedy was out to demolish what a British diplomat later called that "edifice of illusions and shibboleths which the German politicians have erected around their hopes of reunification."[157] If the goal was to save Berlin without a war, then one could not allow oneself to be locked into positions that had little basis in reality. The division of Germany was a fact of life. If the freedom of Berlin could be preserved by recognizing things for what they were, how could there be any real justification for holding back? But the German government found it hard to break away from the "illusions and shibboleths" of the past. That meant that the United States had to carry on the struggle on two fronts. The Soviets had to be made to accept the fundamental American condition: that the settlement effectively guarantee the freedom of West Berlin. And the Federal Republic would also have to accept the arrangement Kennedy had in mind.

But could the German government be brought into line? It was evident, as one of Kennedy's closest advisers told the British, that a degree of "arm-twisting was in fact required."[158] The Americans made it clear that they found the basic German posture unacceptable. The Germans were not only unwilling to risk war but they were even unwilling to take the sort of vigorous military measures that might convince the Russians that the West would go to war rather than capitulate over Berlin. At the same time, however, they would not agree to the sort of political concessions that might make a negotiated settlement possible. As Acheson told their ambassador when he came to complain about the new American policy, they "could not have it both ways." Kennedy himself disliked the German attitude and was not

---

[153] Killick to Schuckburgh, September 25, 1961, FO 371/160553, PRO.

[154] Kohler-Winckler meeting, August 22, 1961 (for a report of Couve's views), FRUS 1961–63, 14:368 n; Alphand-Rusk meeting, August 26, 1961, NSABF.

[155] Acheson-Grewe meeting, October 11, 1961, FRUS 1961–63, 14:490–491.

[156] Schwarz, *Adenauer.* 2:684.

[157] Steel to Foreign Office, October 30, 1962, FO 371/163583, PRO.

[158] Sorensen remark at dinner in mid-October, reported in Thomson to Killick, October 20, 1961, FO 371/160559.

going to defer to the German government in these matters. Although unwilling themselves to accept a real showdown with the USSR, the Germans had the nerve to claim that the American government was too weak. Kennedy resented the charge that he was an appeaser, and resented the carping of the West German government, which felt free to attack American ideas, but had nothing serious of its own to offer as a possible basis for negotiation.[159]

In late 1961, German policy did shift in the direction favored in Washington. In early September, according to the German ambassador in Moscow, Adenauer now "realised that Germany would have to make sacrifices to avoid the very real danger of war and to save the freedom of West Berlin." The one area where he "refused to contemplate any concessions" had to do with "the armament of the Bundeswehr"—that is, with German access to nuclear weapons.[160] On September 17, Rusk and Foy Kohler, a high State Department official, told a British diplomat that the Germans had "come along very nicely so far." They expected even greater flexibility after the German elections, which were being held that same day. The one point on which the Germans "would probably remain very stiff," Kohler and the British official agreed, was on the issue of "discrimination against German forces in the matter of arms." But "even on this point," Kohler thought, the Germans might be susceptible to American pressure.[161]

The nuclear issue was thus emerging as the sticking point. On every other issue, Adenauer was prepared to be flexible. Even on the question of dealings with the GDR, it seemed that "the Chancellor was fully open to persuasion." The one point Adenauer was stressing was that "there was to be no nonsense about atom-free zones" and so on. "All the fire is concentrated on this," the British ambassador in Bonn reported, "and not a word is reported to have been said about recognition, *de facto* or *de jure*."[162]

In November Adenauer came to Washington for an important series of meetings with American leaders. He was "very gloomy"—"more discouraged," U.S. officials felt, "than we had expected." The use of nuclear weapons, he argued, was out of the question, and in a conventional war the West would be crushed. A military confrontation thus had to be ruled out. "Therefore," he concluded, "we must negotiate."[163]

---

[159] Acheson-Grewe meeting, October 11, 1961 (for the quotation), FRUS 1961–63, 14:492; Kohler to Rusk, October 4, 1961, with Kohler-Grewe meeting, September 29, 1961, 611.62a/10-461, RG 59, USNA. Note the president's reference to "hesitation and delay" in the military area "on the part of some who talk as if they were firm and resolute"; Kennedy to Clay, October 8, 1961, FRUS 1961–63, 14:484. Kennedy's feelings came out very clearly in a talk with Ormsby Gore, which the British ambassador reported to Home on February 19, 1962; FO 371/163567, PRO. On German unwillingness to face the risk of nuclear war, or even to make a serious military effort of any kind, see, in general, Schwarz, *Adenauer,* 2:493–494, 654–659, 663, 694, and Clay to Kennedy, October 18, 1961, FRUS 1961–63, 14:512. Even today, some leading German authorities, while recognizing that Adenauer was against the use of force under any circumstances, nonetheless insist on applauding Adenauer for his toughness and on characterizing Kennedy as an appeaser. Note especially Schwarz's frequent references to Kennedy's "appeasement" policy: Schwarz, *Adenauer,* 2:732, 733, 743, 745, 750.

[160] Roberts to Foreign Office, September 5, 1961, FO 371/160548, PRO.

[161] Shuckburgh-Kohler-Rusk meeting, September 17, 1961, FO 371/160552, PRO.

[162] Steel to Shuckburgh, October 7, 1961, FO 371/160555, PRO.

[163] Acheson-Adenauer meeting, November 21, 1961, and Acheson to Shulman, November 23,

German hardliners were upset by the weakening of Adenauer's position, and de Gaulle by now considered him a broken man. But Kennedy was delighted by Adenauer's newfound flexibility, and he considered the chancellor's visit his best meeting with a foreign leader since taking office.[164] Adenauer told him that if the negotiations with the USSR resulted in "improved living conditions for the people of Berlin, along with the maintenance of their freedom, then the U.S. need not fear any difficulties from the German side."[165] It was true that on many points Adenauer defended the standard German positions. But Kennedy came away from the talks with the impression that if an agreement strengthened western rights of access to Berlin, the Germans would be "quite forthcoming on other points."[166]

From Kennedy's point of view, the main problem now on the NATO side had to do with the French. Adenauer might have given way, but this did not mean that the German people would ultimately accept what was going on, and de Gaulle's main concern at this point was with the effect of the new American policy on Germany as a whole. The French government, it is important to remember, did not object on fundamental grounds to the substance of the American position. French officials from de Gaulle on down were quite comfortable with the situation as it existed, and in itself (as noted above) a deal to stabilize the status quo would have been perfectly acceptable to them. As part of a Berlin settlement, Couve said, the West might even recognize the sovereignty of the GDR; in return, the Soviets might agree to respect western rights in Berlin. He felt, in fact, that this was the best arrangement the West could hope for.[167] As for the other "broader questions," as they were called, the French were not in principle opposed to concessions. De Gaulle had been the first western leader to openly accept the Oder-Neisse line. The French would in principle have liked to head off a German nuclear capability. Even the issue of the western powers' legal right to be in Berlin, and whether it could be formally based on something other than their rights as occupying powers, was for Couve an "academic question" that his government did not take too seriously.[168] So a negotiated settlement was by no means out of the question. "We obviously had to try to make a deal," Couve bluntly told his American and British colleagues on August 5, "and this involved giving something away."[169] The American talks with Gromyko "would constitute real negotiations," he said, and Rusk would be engaging in those discussions "with the general support" of all the main western governments.[170]

1961, AP/65/SDWHA/HSTL; Rusk meeting with Ormsby Gore, November 24, 1961, NSABF; Kennedy-Adenauer meeting, November 21, 1961, FRUS 1961–63, vols. 13–15, mic. supp., no. 247.

[164] Krone diary, November 19, 1961, *Adenauer-Studien,* 3:164; Horst Osterheld, *"Ich gehe nicht leichten Herzens. . ." Adenauers letzte Kanzlerjahre: Ein dokumentarisches Bericht* (Mainz: Matthias Grünewald, 1986), pp. 85–88; Alphand, *L'étonnement d'être,* p. 367; Robert d'Harcourt, *L'Allemagne d'Adenauer à Erhard* (Paris: Flammarion, 1964), p. 99; Anglo-American meetings, December 21–22, 1961, FRUS 1961–63, 14:701–703.

[165] Adenauer-Kennedy meeting, November 21, 1961, FRUS 1961–63, 14:615.

[166] Kennedy to Macmillan, November 22, 1961, ibid., p. 633.

[167] Western foreign ministers' meeting, September 15, 1961, p. 2, FO 371/160551, PRO.

[168] Western foreign ministers' meeting, September 15, 1961, FRUS 1961–63, 14:419.

[169] Couve-Home-Rusk meeting, August 5, 1961, ibid., p. 277.

[170] Western foreign ministers' meeting, September 15, 1961, ibid., pp. 418–419.

But de Gaulle had come to dislike certain aspects of the new American policy. The Americans were thinking in terms of an arrangement that would prevent the Germans from getting nuclear weapons. The French might not have been too happy about the thought of a nuclearized Germany, but they now viewed this aspect of U.S. policy in the context of America's new NATO policy—the increased emphasis on conventional forces, the opposition to nuclear forces under national control, the refusal to base MRBMs on the continent, and so on. All of these things, in the French view, pointed in one very clear direction. America, with her own cities increasingly at risk, was withdrawing from the nuclear defense of Europe, and indeed was aiming at a kind of denuclearization of the continent, which de Gaulle, of course, considered extremely dangerous. Denuclearization ultimately meant the neutralization of western Europe. The denuclearization of Germany was a major step in this direction; it certainly was a step toward the neutralization of the Federal Republic. But if West Germany were neutralized, what then would be the fate of France? And if the Americans were so unreliable, so unwilling to commit their power to the nuclear defense of Europe, wasn't it important for the Europeans to have a degree of independence, and to have the kind of military force that could sustain an independent policy? Maybe the continentals needed to get together and develop a nuclear capability of their own; the door could not be shut on a German nuclear option or on the possibility of Franco-German nuclear collaboration.[171]

Substantive considerations aside, the French had also come to dislike the way the United States was playing the western hand. The crisis, Couve said, was "essentially a test of strength between the Soviet Union and the United States." To press for negotiations would "merely show what was really at the bottom of our hearts—fear of war." It would be taken as a sign of American weakness. It would only encourage the Russians to dig in their heels.[172] The Americans had the power, and it was therefore natural for them to take the lead. But the French government

[171] See, for example, de Gaulle remarks, December 21, 1961, in Alphand, *L'étonnement d'être,* p. 367. This, incidentally, was the way American analysts came to interpret French policy. In their view, the French had looked at the various components of the new U.S. policy on NATO issues, put two and two together, and reached the conclusion that America was out to denuclearize and perhaps neutralize Europe. Such suspicions had probably begun to take shape in 1961. By July 1962, what de Gaulle delicately referred to as the "departure of General Norstad" was added to the list of indicators, and after the Cuban Missile Crisis, the American decision to withdraw the Jupiter missiles from Turkey was also cited in this context. Draft airgram, n.a. and n.d. but probably from late June 1962, reporting meetings Bowie and Rowen had with French officials on NATO nuclear issues, pp. 6–7, DDRS 1990/1372; Lemnitzer–de Gaulle meeting, July 23, 1962, NSF/71a/France—General/JFKL; Kissinger meeting with French officials, May 23, 1963, DDRS 1996/2000. The French interpretation was shared by Taylor's assistants Legere and Ewell, who criticized the "anti-nuclear wrecking crew" within the government, a group that they thought was out to "denuclearize Europe." Legere to Taylor, May 3, 1962, and Ewell to Taylor, April 16, 1962, quoted in FRUS 1961–63, 8:300 n. There are many other memoranda in the Taylor Papers, especially from Legere, developing similar arguments. And in fact there was some talk at high levels within the administration about denuclearizing central Europe. See, for example, Carl Kaysen, "Thoughts on Berlin," August 22, 1961, p. 10, and Harriman to Kennedy, September 1, 1961, both NSF/82/Germany—Berlin—General/JFKL. But the fundamental tendency of the Kennedy administration was to keep Europe nuclearized by maintaining a strong, American-controlled nuclear force there.

[172] Rusk-Home-Couve meeting, August 5, 1961, and western foreign ministers' meetings, September 15 and December 12, 1961, FRUS 1961–63, 14:272, 416, 675, 677.

did not want to identify itself too closely with U.S. policy. The Americans could move forward if they wanted to, but it had to be clear where the real responsibility lay. "Go on with your probing," de Gaulle told Rusk on August 8, "we have nothing against it." But France, he said, would not have chosen that route, and France would not be held liable for the consequences: "you really are doing it on your own account."[173]

In October, as the details of the new American thinking about a Berlin settlement became more widely known, the French attitude hardened. On October 9, de Gaulle still "approved warmly" of Rusk's and Kennedy's discussions with Gromyko.[174] But just five days later, the French ambassador in Washington, Hervé Alphand, made what a high U.S. official called a "very serious communication." Whereas Couve had said on September 15 that Rusk would be negotiating "with the general support" of the four major western governments, now France announced that she could "give no mandate" for continued exploratory talks in Moscow. The French government, Alphand said, was in fact now against further talks and "wished explorations to stop." The French government wanted a modus vivendi, but the proposed talks would not lead to one. The French view was that the USSR was being rewarded for her outrageous behavior. The implication was that with the Americans so eager to negotiate, the West could only expect more of the same from the Soviets. "If we wanted a *modus vivendi*," Alphand said, "a showdown was necessary."[175]

But the French did not want a real showdown with Russia. Berlin itself, in their view, might well have to be abandoned in the end. What was crucial was that West Germany not be lost in the process. The American insistence on negotiations, at a time when the Soviets were continuing to take an intransigent line, was a sure sign of weakness; indeed, de Gaulle now thought that the "hour of Munich" was at hand. Whatever the Adenauer government now agreed to, de Gaulle was certain that the German people would eventually feel betrayed by America. There would then be a sharp nationalistic reaction and Germany would turn away from the NATO system, possibly toward a kind of weak neutralism, possibly toward a strong independent policy. In either case, the consequences would be disastrous. The "Anglo-Saxons," de Gaulle felt, did not quite grasp the seriousness of the problem, and were not sufficiently attuned to the risk of losing Germany. But because of their geographic position, the French were able to see things more clearly: the fate of Germany was a "vital" interest for France, but merely an "important" interest for America and Britain.[176]

So if the Americans ultimately capitulated over Berlin and the whole NATO structure collapsed, France would have to do what she could to save the situation. If Berlin were lost, it was crucial that the Germans not blame the West as a whole. The "Anglo-Saxons" were pressing for negotiations, and really for concessions at

[173] Rusk–de Gaulle meeting, August 8, 1961, ibid., pp. 313–314.

[174] Dixon to Foreign Office, October 9, 1961, FO 371/160555, PRO.

[175] Hood to Foreign Office, October 13, 1961, FO 371/160555, PRO; Alphand-Bohlen-Kohler meeting, October 14, 1961, NSABF.

[176] Alphand, *L'étonnement d'être*, entries for August 23 and December 21, 1961, pp. 363, 367; Rusk-Home-Couve meeting, August 5, 1961, and western foreign ministers' meeting, December 11, 1961, FRUS 1961–63, 14:270, 273, 650, 652. On this general issue, see also above, pp. 270–272 above.

Germany's expense. France alone could not prevent them from acting in this way, but she could openly disassociate herself from that policy. "Perhaps we shall end up with a new Western retreat," de Gaulle said in late September. "If so France will not take part in it. France will remain firm on the position which she has never ceased to defend and for the future this is a very important thing."[177]

De Gaulle now repeatedly argued along these lines. In a meeting with Macmillan in late November, he laid out his views with characteristic bluntness. France, he said, "was concerned above all, and perhaps even more than her British and American Allies, to ensure that Germany was tied in to the West." Berlin was simply "one part of this problem, and not in itself of capital importance." Adenauer might now be willing to accept negotiations with the Russians about Berlin, but even if his government "accepted the concessions which would be asked of them," what really mattered was that "the German people would be left with a sense of betrayal." So whatever Britain and America did, France "would not be a party to such an arrangement. The Germans would then in the future feel that at least they had one friend left in the West."[178]

In opposing the United States, the French leader was not being perverse or nationalistic. His Berlin policy was rooted in his most basic assumptions about international politics in the nuclear age. In his view, the American nuclear guarantee would sooner or later be exposed as fraudulent, and indeed it was natural that the United States would not wish to commit suicide for the sake of Europe. But that meant that some alternative had to be worked out. When the NATO system collapsed, there had to be something else that could be put in its place. Berlin itself might be indefensible and might well have to be written off, and he was ultimately prepared to take the loss of the city philosophically.[179] The key thing was to make sure that it did not lead to the loss of West Germany as well. France, therefore, had to lay the basis for an independent European policy—a policy that necessarily would pivot on a close understanding between France and Germany. If British policy had been different, Britain too might have played a fundamental role in building an independent Europe. But Britain was too dependent on America, and even less inclined than the Americans had been to worry about how the Germans would react to what was going on. So an independent Europe had to be a continental Europe, a Franco-German Europe.

Ideas of this sort had played a certain role in French policy even during the early Gaullist period. In March 1959, for example, less than a year after his return to power, de Gaulle told Adenauer that the NATO alliance would not survive a western defeat over Berlin. For the time being, there was not much that could be done to affect what might happen. The Americans had the power and the policy of the

---

[177] Account of de Gaulle remarks to MRP representatives, quoted in Rumbold to Shuckburgh, September 27, 1961, FO 371/160554, PRO. See also Couve-Heath meeting, November 9, 1961, FO 371/160563, PRO.

[178] De Gaulle–Macmillan talks, in Foreign Office to Washington, November 27, 1961, FO 371/160565; also in Prem 11/3338; both PRO. See also the prime minister's reflections on this meeting, in Macmillan, *Pointing the Way*, p. 426.

[179] Couve-Heath meeting, November 9, 1961, FO 371/160563, PRO; Krone diary, December 15, 1961, *Adenauer-Studien*, 3:165.

West would thus be set in Washington. But even if the West were defeated and NATO collapsed, France and Germany had to remain together. Their power was rising; soon they would be able to control their own destiny.[180]

But until late 1961, this strand of French thinking, the "European" or "continental" strand, coexisted uneasily with two other and somewhat contradictory strands of policy. There was first of all a certain tendency for France to think of herself along with Britain and America as one of the three western powers. Germany, in this conception, was an ally to be sure, but not quite a full member of the club. This was reflected, for example, in de Gaulle's concept of a tripartite "directorate" for the West. But it also came out in little ways. There were certain things, French leaders sometimes said, that they could discuss freely with the British and the Americans, but could not talk about if the Germans were present.[181] And then, of course, there was a third element in French policy, a certain tendency to think more parochially in terms of French national interests and French sovereignty strictly defined.

These three strands of policy—"European," "western," and "nationalistic"— were all rooted in de Gaulle's conviction that French policy had to be active, that France could not just be a follower country. But they pulled in different directions. Sometimes, for example, de Gaulle and his followers argued that the main function of the armed forces was the defense of French territory, that in the event of war there would be a "battle for Germany" in which France was not fully engaged, followed by a "battle for France." But this nationalistic conception was at variance with the idea that the defense of Germany was as important as the defense of France herself, and that idea lay at the heart of the concept that France and Germany could act as a bloc, that continental western Europe could become a third force, independent of America and able to withstand Soviet pressure on its own.[182]

[180] De Gaulle–Adenauer meeting, March 4, 1959, DDF 1959, 1:278–279. See also de Gaulle's comments to two Italian leaders, March 20, 1959, ibid, p. 400; de Gaulle–Adenauer meeting, September 14, 1958, and especially de Gaulle–Spaak meeting, September 24, 1958, ibid., 1958, 2:344, 430.

[181] See, for example, Rusk-Home-Couve meeting, August 5, 1961, FRUS 1961–63, 14:269.

[182] On de Gaulle's general strategic concept, see above, chapter 6, note 98. For specific references by de Gaulle to two distinct and successive battles in a European war—a "battle for Germany" to be followed by a "battle for France"—see de Gaulle–Eisenhower-Macmillan meeting, December 20, 1959, DDF 1959, 2:770; de Gaulle–Macmillan meeting, June 3, 1962, Prem 11/3712, PRO; and de Gaulle–Alphand meeting, June 26, 1962, Alphand, L'étonnement d'être, p. 379. De Gaulle was talking along these lines even in early 1963; see Peyrefitte, C'était de Gaulle, p. 345. For various comments in the opposite vein, reflecting a conception of France and Germany, or of continental western Europe, as a strategic unit, see de Gaulle's remarks at the German military academy, Hamburg, September 7, 1962, Discours et messages, vol. 4: Août 1962–décembre 1965 (Paris: Plon, 1970), p. 13; de Gaulle–Segni-Pella meeting, March 20, 1959, DDF 1959, 1:400, and above all the de Gaulle–Adenauer meeting, January 21, 1963, AAPBD 1963, 1:117. See in addition Soutou, L'alliance incertaine, pp. 161–162, 248–249, who also notes this basic contradiction in French policy. The Americans, for obvious reasons, made a point of attacking de Gaulle's "two battles" idea when talking with the Germans, and many Germans were in fact put off by the idea; this was to have a certain bearing on German behavior in 1963, somewhat diminishing the attractiveness of the French option in German eyes and tarnishing German Gaullism in the process. Note, for example, General Speidel's comments in this context in January 1963, and also Chancellor Erhard's complaint about the "two battles" concept in a meeting with de Gaulle in November of that year. De Gaulle at that point tried to cover his tracks and explicitly rejected the concept, but the damage had already been done. Kennedy-Adenauer meeting, November 14,

By late 1961, in reaction to Kennedy's handling of the Berlin crisis, French policy was becoming less ambiguous. De Gaulle was leaning increasingly toward the "European" approach. France was taking her distance from the United States, and thus, increasingly, from Britain as well. She was identifying her interests with those of Germany and portraying herself as Germany's one true friend in the West. If the Germans came to feel that the United States had sold them down the river, they would at least still have France to turn to. The Germans would thus be less inclined to turn in on themselves, after the great betrayal, after the collapse of NATO. Instead of a parochial nationalism of the 1920s variety, they could embrace a kind of European "nationalism," with a distinct anti-American flavor to be sure, but not nearly as dangerous as the other options that would remain open to them. France and West Germany should therefore think of themselves as countries with identical strategic interests. They should bind themselves together, develop their own power, and operate as a unit politically and indeed ultimately militarily as well.

As French policy moved in this direction, there was (as noted above) a certain shift in the French position on the German nuclear question. Although he had sometimes taken the line that a German nuclear force was inevitable (and indeed, in an important meeting with Adenauer in July 1960, had actually encouraged the Germans to build such a force),[183] de Gaulle in that early period was generally opposed to the idea of nuclear weapons in German hands. This was still his attitude, for example, when he met with Kennedy in June 1961.[184] Even as late as November 6, a French diplomat was still saying that an arrangement confirming the Federal Republic's non-nuclear status was "definitely" an item "in the concessions column."[185]

1962, FRUS 1961–63, 13:452; Soutou, *L'alliance incertaine*, pp. 162, 255–256 (for Speidel); Erhard–de Gaulle meeting, November 21, 1963, AAPBD 1963, 3:1471, 1474. These contradictions, to my mind, reflect de Gaulle's basic uncertainty about the German question—about whether to treat the Germans as full partners or as something less—an uncertainty also reflected in his ambivalent attitude on the German nuclear question. Indeed, according to the top permanent official at the Quai d'Orsay, de Gaulle recognized these difficulties and was "more uncertain" about the German problem than about any other problem on the European scene. Bohlen to Kennedy, February 23, 1963, State Department Central Files [DOSCF] for 1963, POL 15-1 FR, RG 59, USNA.

[183] The key document is quoted in Soutou, "De Gaulle, Adenauer und die gemeinsame Front," pp. 498–499.

[184] Kennedy–de Gaulle meeting, June 1, 1961, DDRS 1994/2586.

[185] Thomson to Killick, November 6, 1961, FO 371/160563, PRO. The impression that French policy was shifting is based on the evidence to be discussed below, but it should be noted at this point that this evidence is by no means unambiguous. French officials, from de Gaulle on down, continued to deny in 1962 and 1963 that they intended to help Germany acquire a nuclear capability. See, for example, Sulzberger's conversation with Burin des Roziers, "de Gaulle's right hand in the Elysée," March 10, 1962, and Sulzberger-Pompidou meeting, February 1, 1963, in Sulzberger, *Last of the Giants*, pp. 859, 960. Note also the Couve-Home meeting, April 8, 1963, Prem 11/4221, PRO. "The French found this whole problem worrying," Couve told his British counterpart. "They were far from believing the Germans should be given something in the atomic field. On the contrary the German appetite for nuclear weapons was something which must be carefully watched and to which we must not give way." The following month Couve told Kennedy that France "would never help the Germans to make nuclear weapons." He had in fact told Rusk in late 1962 that if Germany acquired nuclear weapons, "this could be a cause for a world war." Kennedy-Couve meeting, May 25, 1963, FRUS 1961–63, 13:772; Rusk-Couve meeting, October 7, 1962, 700.5611/10–762, RG59, USNA. These comments were not simply for external consumption. De Gaulle took essentially the same line in internal discussions. See,

But at the end of the month, in a meeting with Macmillan, de Gaulle took the opposite line. "The idea of an agreement about nuclear weapons for Germany," he said, "was a gratuitous present to the Russians." France had no "present intention" of helping the Germans develop a nuclear capability, but this, he said, might not always be the case.[186] Couve made a similar point to Rusk in February 1962. In five or ten years, he said, France and Germany might get together to produce nuclear weapons, "but not now."[187]

The Americans sensed what was going on and were angered by de Gaulle's new attitude. It was not just that the French leader had begun to toy with the idea of Franco-German nuclear collaboration. This was bad enough in itself. But de Gaulle was now attacking American policy down the line. What was really resented was the way de Gaulle was trying to make America into a "fall guy" in the eyes of the Germans. If concessions had to be made as part of a Berlin settlement, the Germans might eventually complain that their interests had been sold out. De Gaulle wanted to be able to say that his hands were clean, that only the "Anglo-Saxons" had been to blame. The Germans were apparently also trying to pin responsibility on the United States.[188] What was outrageous here was that these two governments were themselves not prepared to face a military confrontation with the USSR. They might "talk as if they were firm and resolute." But in reality, as had become clear in the discussions on Berlin contingency planning, the German government especially "was prepared to take no risk at all." As for the French, although they might talk tough, their real attitude was more ambivalent. Even as late as October 1962, right before the Cuban Missile Crisis, Couve simply evaded the fundamental issue of whether force would be used if Berlin were cut off—although de Gaulle himself, one should note, did take a very firm line when the issue came to a head during the missile crisis.[189]

---

for example, the de Gaulle–Alphand meeting, June 26, 1962, in Alphand, *L'étonnement d'être*, p.380, and a de Gaulle–Peyrefitte conversation, January 1963, in Peyrefitte, *C'était de Gaulle,* p. 346.

[186] De Gaulle–Macmillan meetings, November 24–25, 1961 (account dated November 27), Prem 11/3338, PRO; also in FO 371/160565, and quoted in Macmillan, *Pointing the Way,* p. 421.

[187] Couve-Rusk meeting, February 14, 1962, 375/2-1462, RG 59, USNA. There were a number of other indications of this developing French attitude. One key French official (François de Rose) told an American diplomat that the "Germans are going to want nuclear weapons sooner or later, probably sooner than we think," that de Gaulle's goal was to "weld" Germany to France, and that the French leader was "not quite ready to give nuclear information to the Germans now, but he will be later." Paris embassy to Rusk, December 27, 1961, 375/12–2761, RG 59, USNA.

[188] Rusk-Kohler-Shuckburgh meeting, September 17, 1961, FO 371/160552; Kennedy-Macmillan phone conversation, October 6, 1961, FO 371/160555; Kennedy-Macmillan meeting, April 28, 1962, Prem 11/3783; and, for the "fall guy" reference, Rusk-Home meeting, December 10, 1961, FO 371/160567; all PRO.

[189] Kennedy to Clay, October 8, 1961; Acheson-Grewe meeting, October 11, 1961; Clay to Kennedy, October 18, 1961; all in FRUS 1961–63, 14:484, 491, 512. Note also Rusk's remarks in a meeting with Sulzberger, December 16, 1961, Sulzberger, *Last of the Giants,* p. 826, and the discussion following the Ausland Berlin briefing, August 9, 1962, in audiocassette no. 9, POF/JFKL. On the French attitude in late 1962, see Bundy to Kennedy, October 9, 1962, NSABF, and especially Kennedy-Couve meeting, October 9, 1962, FRUS 1961–63, 15:354–355. This is to be compared with de Gaulle's attitude when he was briefed by Acheson during the missile crisis: Lyon to Rusk, October 22, 1962, FRUS 1961–63, 11:166. If the Soviets retaliated to the blockade of Cuba by threatening Berlin, the western powers, de Gaulle said, would have to take the countersteps that had been prepared.

But that was still in the future, and the American view in late 1961 and through most of 1962 was that France and Germany could not be allowed to get away with their phony displays of "toughness." They would have to face up to their responsibilities. The U.S. government, Rusk said in December 1961, "was determined not to be cast into the role of the 'fall guy' for the French and the Germans—in other words to be the ones who made concessions which were afterwards described as betrayals."[190] France and Germany had to be made to sign on to the common policy. Rusk was therefore furious that de Gaulle at that time simply refused to go along with the American policy on talks with the USSR. He had come to think of the French leader as practically "a devil with horns and a tail."[191] Kennedy was only a shade less hostile. In April 1962, he surprised Macmillan "by the bitterness of his feeling" toward the French.[192] Relations now were about as bad as they ever get between allied powers.[193]

De Gaulle had by this point decided to tell the Americans directly that they should keep out of European politics and let the Europeans run their own affairs. America should limit herself to giving a general security guarantee. The U.S. government, he said, "should not be mixed up in Western European difficulties and should keep itself apart only bringing its weight to bear in case of necessity."[194] He had occasionally expressed similar views in the past. In September 1958, for example, he had told the NATO secretary general that France, Germany, and Italy should set NATO policy.[195] But now he was telling America to her face that she "should stay out of the affairs of Europe." Ambassador Gavin was "almost startled" by the "cold harshness" of that "unqualified statement."[196]

Kennedy was outraged by the line de Gaulle was now taking. It was absurd that Europe should be able to draw freely on American power and conceivably pull the

[190] Rusk-Home meeting, December 10, 1961, FO 371/160567, PRO.

[191] Gavin's view, cited in Sulzberger, *Last of the Giants,* entry for January 5, 1962, p. 833. See also an Italian diplomat's comments on Rusk's attitude toward de Gaulle, ibid., p. 876.

[192] Kennedy-Macmillan meeting, April 28, 1962, Prem 11/3783, PRO.

[193] One measure of how bad relations had become is that Rusk at one point even threatened the French with an American nuclear attack if they dared to act independently in a crisis. In late 1961, he told the French defense minister, Pierre Messmer, that the United States "could not allow" her "smaller allies" to "use or threaten to use nuclear weapons" independently against the USSR. "This would be a direct menace to U.S. security," and if France intended to build her own force, he warned Messmer, "they had better think of supplying themselves with inter-continental missiles directed across the Atlantic." Rusk's account in a meeting with Lord Home, December 10, 1961, FO 371/160567; see also Alphand, *L'étonnement d'être,* p. 368n; Rusk also touched on this issue in a meeting with top British officials, June 28, 1963, p. 7, DOSCF for 1963, POL 7 US/Kennedy, RG 59, USNA. It is hard to think of any other case in the history of international politics of a great power making this sort of threat to a major ally, and I wondered how the French had reacted. So I asked Messmer about this episode when I met him at a conference in Paris in February 1996. He did not take it very seriously. Rusk, he said, had been worried that the French intended to use their small nuclear force as a kind of "detonator" that could set off a general U.S.–Soviet nuclear war, but the French, he said, had never thought of their force in such terms. It turns out, however, that they in fact were thinking in terms of the "detonator" strategy. See Soutou, *L'alliance incertaine,* pp. 88, 223. The "detonator" concept, incidentally, also played a certain role in British thinking on these questions. See Pierre, *Nuclear Politics,* p. 175.

[194] Gavin to State Department, May 16, 1962, FRUS 1961–63, 13:702.

[195] De Gaulle–Spaak meeting, September 24, 1958, DDF 1958, 2:430.

[196] Gavin to State Department, May 16, 1962, FRUS 1961–63, 13:703.

United States into a war, but that the U.S. government should have no control over the policies that could lead to conflict. The Americans could not accept the idea, the president wrote, that "we should stay out of all of Europe's affairs while remaining ready to defend her if war should come." The United States could not give "this kind of blank check." Since American power was engaged, the U.S. government in his view had to concern itself with the "problem of Germany," the central issue in international politics. Indeed, America had to take the lead in dealing with that problem, since no one else was going to confront it realistically. But de Gaulle rejected the idea that Europe should follow the American lead. The U.S. government, as the French leader saw it, acted as though the European states were mere "protectorates" with no right to challenge American policy. They had to resist American domination, especially when they felt U.S. policy was deeply misguided, and de Gaulle made it clear to Gavin that he put America's German policy in this category.[197]

The gulf between France and America was now profound, but for Adenauer this meant that Germany now had a certain room for maneuver. De Gaulle's game was to make the "Anglo-Saxons" take the blame for whatever concessions needed to be made to prevent the Berlin crisis from escalating into an armed conflict. U.S. leaders wanted to frustrate that strategy; that meant that German support was more important than it would otherwise have been. This was an important consideration for the Americans even in late 1961. Rusk and Kohler, for example, agreed with a British diplomat in September of that year that de Gaulle was probably "thinking ahead to the time when the Germans were confronted with the fact that negotiations had resulted in a substantial deterioration in their position and that a myth might develop that Germany had been let down by her allies. He might then want to claim that it was the Anglo-Saxons alone who were responsible." The two Americans then went on to point out "that this made it extremely necessary 'to keep the Germans on board' at every stage."[198]

It followed that the Germans could not simply be forced to toe the line. If the United States mishandled the situation, the Germans might "pick up their French option," as Henry Kissinger, then a White House consultant, put it in February 1962.[199] It was much easier for Germany to resist American pressure if she had France on her side than if she had to act entirely on her own. A "European" policy, based on Franco-German cooperation, was always more acceptable, even in the eyes of the German people themselves, than a policy that could be labeled "nationalistic."

So by early 1962, Adenauer was starting to take what the U.S. government saw as a more defiant line. He knew that his position had become stronger now that he had a "French card" to play. The German chancellor was certainly encouraged by what de Gaulle was doing, and, like de Gaulle, he was increasingly determined to resist the policy the Americans were now pursuing.

The nuclear question lay at the heart of Adenauer's growing conflict with the

---

[197] Kennedy to Gavin, May 18, 1962, and Gavin to Rusk, May 28, 1962, ibid., pp. 704–706.

[198] Rusk-Kohler-Shuckburgh meeting, September 17, 1961, FO 371/160552, PRO.

[199] Kissinger memorandum, "Summary of Conversations in Germany about Negotiations," February 21, 1962, p. 5, Mandatory Declassification Review release NLK 89-67, JFKL.

United States. The Kennedy administration wanted to prevent the Federal Republic from acquiring a nuclear capability and in its view a Berlin settlement might include an arrangement guaranteeing Germany's non-nuclear status. But the Adenauer government strongly disliked this aspect of American policy. Already in September and October 1961 it was becoming clear that this was the one area where German resistance to concessions would be very strong, no matter how flexible the Germans were on other questions relating to a settlement.[200] And indeed the German position on this point began to harden toward the end of the year. In June, the Germans had taken the line that they were not opposed as a matter of principle to promising not to seek an "independent nuclear capability," or to including such a promise in a Berlin settlement. They did not want to give anything away for free, but they would consider such a promise if they got something substantial from the Soviets in exchange.[201] In November, however, they took a tougher line. The Federal Republic was now opposed on more fundamental grounds to arrangements that would prevent her from ever becoming a nuclear power. The German ambassador in Washington, the same man who had made the earlier comment in June, now made it clear that the German government was opposed to "freezing" the military status quo—that is, to perpetuating Germany's non-nuclear status through international agreement. "There might be a change in the basic situation in a few years," he said, "and we should therefore keep flexibility in common Western defence arrangements." When Bohlen asked him pointedly what this meant, the ambassador said that "his Government had no present interest in altering their undertaking not to manufacture ABC [atomic, biological and chemical] weapons, but they would like to keep the possibility open."[202]

When Adenauer met with Kennedy later in the month, he took much the same line. The United States pressed for German "flexibility" in this area, but Adenauer now resisted even the idea that the Federal Republic might reiterate its 1954 non-production pledge as part of a Berlin settlement. When the two leaders met privately and Kennedy again raised the issue, Adenauer told his old story about Dulles coming up to him at the time the pledge was made and saying that "this declaration was of course valid only as long as circumstances remain unchanged." Nevertheless, he said, "Germany had not undertaken anything in this respect as yet." He also played down the extent of Germany's commitment at a formal meeting of the two delegations. The 1954 declaration, he noted, spoke of "not *producing* ABC weapons." It did not say Germany could not *have* them if her allies gave them to her. He also resisted the idea of including a reaffirmation of that pledge in any deal with Russia. "If this matter were now brought into the Soviet negotiations," he warned, "it could have very serious consequences."[203]

The German position on this issue did not change in 1962, in spite of the fact that the U.S. government made it clear, in all sorts of ways, how strongly it felt

[200] Rusk-Kohler-Shuckburgh meeting, September 17, 1961, FO 371/160552, PRO.

[201] Ambassador Grewe's views, cited in State Department to embassy in Germany, June 17, 1961, FRUS 1961–63, 14:127.

[202] Gore to Foreign Office, November 1, 1961, FO 371/160559, PRO.

[203] Kennedy-Adenauer meetings, November 21–22, 1961, FRUS 1961–63, 14:616–618, 620, 625–626.

about the issue. Right after Adenauer left Washington, Kennedy gave an important interview to Alexei Adzhubei, editor of *Izvestia* and Khrushchev's son-in-law. The president did not mince words on the German nuclear issue. He "would be extremely reluctant," he told Adzhubei, "to see West Germany acquire a nuclear capacity of its own." He could understand the Soviet concern about the prospect of the Germans developing a nuclear capability of their own, and indeed he "would share it." But a non-nuclear West Germany, integrated into NATO, would pose no threat. NATO was under American command; in this system, he said, there was "security for all." Kennedy also took the division of Germany as a fact of life. As long as Soviet policy remained as it was, he told Adzhubei, "Germany will not be reunified." To say this was to state the obvious, but it did not go down well in the Federal Republic.[204]

Indeed, the Adzhubei interview was widely resented in Germany. Kennedy had told Adzhubei that he could understand Soviet concerns about Germany, and agreed that the Germans had to be kept from getting nuclear weapons. Just who, many Germans thought, was America's ally, and who was the enemy? The American president obviously thought the division of Germany was a simple political reality. Did this mean that America was getting ready to renege on her formal commitment to support German reunification? For some German leaders, this simply underscored the importance of being able to pursue a somewhat independent policy. The Federal Republic was utterly dependent on the United States, and this was how the Americans now treated her. She therefore needed to become more independent and thus had to develop the sort of military power that a truly independent policy could be based on: she needed, in other words, a nuclear force of her own.

Thanks to de Gaulle the German government now felt somewhat freer to move ahead in this direction. The French had cleared the way. They had openly defied America, both on Berlin policy and on the nuclear question. A more assertive German policy was now less likely to come across as parochial and nationalistic. If it were pursued in collaboration with France, it would even have a certain attractive "European" flavor.

So Adenauer now felt able to dig in his heels, especially on the nuclear issue. In June 1962, he met with Rusk and again told his story about the 1954 pledge and how Dulles had supposedly said that the "*rebus sic stantibus* doctrine would of course apply." To Rusk—and this fact shows how poor American intelligence was on the issue—this came as something of a revelation. The Germans, he was surprised to discover, would not agree to abandon their nuclear option. He therefore reached the conclusion that the problem was not purely theoretical, but that German nuclear aspirations were to be taken seriously. Other high officials had reached similar conclusions by mid-1962. Kohler, for example, was also struck by the fact that the Germans had been careful to say there were no pressures for a national nuclear program "as of now." Nitze told the president in July that in Germany the pressure for a "nuclear capability was very great." And McNamara told Macmillan in March that he was "much concerned about the drive for mili-

[204] Kennedy-Adzhubei interview, November 25, 1961, PPP: Kennedy, 1961:751.

tary power, including nuclear power, which the Germans were beginning to make."[205]

How far would Kennedy go in pushing the Germans into line? Initially, in November and December 1961, the U.S. government had held back from a far-reaching policy in the Berlin talks. The agreement with Adenauer had been to focus the talks, at least at first, on narrow issues relating to the problem of Berlin itself. The aim would be to see if access to the city could be put on a more solid basis. But even at the time it was taken for granted that the Soviets would never settle the Berlin issue in a narrow negotiation on terms the West could accept. They were not in the habit of making love-presents to the West, so why should they now agree to arrangements that would improve the situation in Berlin without getting anything in return? It was taken for granted that the Soviets would "almost inevitably" raise the "broader questions"—the status of East Germany, the frontier issue, the German nuclear question, and the idea of a NATO-Warsaw Pact nonaggression pact.[206]

But the Americans felt they had to proceed cautiously at this point. For the time being, as a State Department official noted, it was "not wise" to press the Germans on the broader issues. This was for "tactical reasons" and did not relate to the substance of the American position.[207] "At the present moment," Rusk himself pointed out in early January 1962, it was important not to "frighten" the Germans by pressing for concessions in those areas. Too assertive a policy, he said, might lead the Germans "to line up once more with the French against the Anglo-Saxons."[208] The Germans had to be kept on board and be made to accept their share of the responsibility for whatever concessions ultimately needed to be made.

But in early 1962 Kennedy's attitude began to shift. The present approach—informal "exploratory talks" with the Soviets, based on common positions worked out with the British and the Germans—was unsatisfactory. The Americans were unable to "to talk frankly to the Russians"—that is, the Germans were holding the U.S. government back—but at the same time "we cannot really pull our Allies into a position of responsible participation."[209]

The president laid out his basic thinking in a February 1962 talk with his close friend David Ormsby Gore, the British ambassador in Washington. He was by this point fed up with the French and the Germans. Their game, he said, "was to make the Americans carry the main responsibility for the whole problem." They ex-

---

[205] Adenauer-Rusk meeting, June 22, 1962, FRUS 1961–63, 13:422; Rusk-Home meeting, June 25, 1962, Prem 11/3715, PRO; Bruce to State Department, June 26, 1962 (for another account of this meeting and Kohler's remarks), FRUS 1961–63, 13:423–424. Bohlen also seemed to think that Adenauer's reference to Dulles's alleged "rebus sic stantibus" was new and important; Bohlen paper, July 2, 1962, ibid., p. 428. For the Nitze quotation: Kennedy-Nitze meeting, July 30, 1962, FRUS 1961–63, 7:521. For McNamara's comment, see Macmillan-McNamara meeting, April 29, 1962, p. 28, Prem 11/3783, PRO. For the U.S. assessment of German nuclear aspirations, see appendix 6 (IS).

[206] Rusk remarks in western foreign ministers' meeting, December 11, 1961, FRUS 1961–63, 14:656–657.

[207] Hillenbrand-Thomson meeting, November 24, 1961, FO 371/160564, PRO.

[208] Ormsby Gore to Foreign Office, January 5, 1962, FO 371/163564, PRO.

[209] Kennedy to Rusk, January 15, 1962, FRUS 1961–63, 14:760.

pected him "either to threaten nuclear war to preserve the present *status quo* in Berlin with the fairly clear indication that if Khrushchev called his bluff he would in fact be asked not to start the war he had been threatening" or "to make concessions in order to reach an agreement with the Russians which the French and the Germans could then blame him for if the result turned out to be unsatisfactory." France and Germany were not making the kind of serious military effort that might back up the tough policy, nor were they willing to work out a "sensible negotiating position" that might safeguard basic western interests without a war. He thought their policy was irresponsible, and indeed he was coming to the conclusion that none of the European countries "cared enough about West Berlin to take any of the unpopular steps which would be required in order to bring about some solution to the problem." The time had come to change this whole state of affairs. The present approaches to Moscow were a "waste of time," since the West had put nothing on the table that had "any attraction for the Russians." He was "not prepared to allow this situation to continue." He had told the State Department that he was going to take personal charge of U.S. policy in this area. Adenauer's attitude was "the key to the whole situation." He was not sure how he would approach Adenauer, but he was thinking in terms of confronting him "with the blunt alternative of deciding against serious negotiations and preparing in the final analysis to fight a war, or of deciding in favour of negotiations which have some hope of a successful outcome. Put like this, he would hope and expect that Adenauer would exert himself in favour of the second alternative."[210]

Adenauer was not directly confronted with such a choice, but it soon became clear that Kennedy was determined to move ahead on a more unilateral basis in the talks with the Russians. In early March the president made a fundamental decision. He was going to "throw off" the "Franco-German shackles and talk freely to the Russians, although without commitment."[211]

Kennedy had now decided to move ahead and engage in "informal bilateral" talks with the Russians on the broader issues. A proposal for a modus vivendi was being prepared. The written draft, he said, did not go very far "mainly because we must not put on paper things which might shock our Allies if presented without prior consultation." But it was to be intimated to the Soviets verbally that the United States would be quite accommodating on the broader issues if a satisfactory Berlin arrangement could be worked out. He recognized that secret, unilateral initiatives would pose a threat to the alliance. The Germans would therefore be given "appropriate oral indications" of what the United States was doing. But the policy was no longer to do nothing which they did not consent to in advance, and in fact the Germans did not approve of the broadening of the talks. Kennedy was nonetheless determined to move ahead.[212]

Soon Rusk was off to Switzerland for a round of meetings with the British and German foreign ministers, and then with Gromyko. "We must not spare any effort

---

[210] Ormsby Gore to Home, February 19, 1962, FO 371/163567, PRO.

[211] Ledwidge to Shuckburgh, memo on Berlin, March 8, 1962, FO 371/163568, PRO.

[212] Kennedy to Khrushchev, February 15, 1962; Kennedy-Grewe meeting, February 19, 1962; Rusk to Thompson, March 1, 1962, FRUS 1961–63, 14:821, 832–833, 852. Kennedy to Rusk, March 9, 1962, ibid., 15:2–3.

to find a modus vivendi," Kennedy cabled him.[213] The president was prepared, in the final analysis, to accept a military confrontation over Berlin, but before the crisis became acute, he felt he had to make sure that no stone had been left unturned and that it was only because of Soviet intransigence that a reasonable settlement could not be reached.[214]

On March 12, Rusk laid out the basic lines of the new American approach in a long meeting with Gromyko. The American plan was for the two sides to reach agreement on certain principles, and then to agree on a "procedure for negotiations on the basis of those principles." The two sides would also accept certain interim arrangements which would hold until those talks resulted in more definitive agreements.[215] The plan would cover both Berlin and the broader issues. The "Principles" paper, the document in which the Americans laid out the new approach, was handed to Gromyko on March 22.[216] This the Americans had done on their own. The German foreign minister, Gerhard Schröder, was not shown the paper until after it had been given to the Soviets. It was only after Gromyko had seen it that Schröder gave the Americans his okay.[217]

The U.S. government made it clear that it was presenting a package. If the Soviets were willing to respect the vital interests of the West on Berlin, everything else, it said, would "fall into place."[218] Agreement on the "broader issues"—German borders, a nonaggression pact, the nuclear status of Germany, and so on—could then be reached quickly. If the Soviets wished to "stabilize the situation on the basis of existing facts," Rusk told Gromyko, "we had considerable understanding for this." The United States, he stressed, was not a "prisoner" of West Germany, but was rather concerned with vital American interests.[219] The U.S. goal was peace on the basis of the status quo, with America and Russia relating to each other as great powers, and respecting each others' most vital interests.[220]

The Soviets showed "considerable interest" in what the Americans were now putting on the table. The German nuclear question was for them a matter of fundamental importance. As Gromyko had told Rusk in October 1961, the Soviet government "placed utmost emphasis on this question." In his March 1962 meetings with the secretary of state, Gromyko again showed great interest in this issue. To be sure, he had certain reservations about the American plan. The arrangement outlined in the "Principles" paper was not targeted sufficiently on Germany for Gromyko's taste, and placed excessive emphasis on the two major powers' more general interest in nonproliferation. He also noted that the American plan did not

[213] Kennedy to Rusk, March 11, 1962, ibid., p. 15.

[214] See, for example, Kennedy-Grewe meeting, February 19, 1962, ibid., 14:832–833.

[215] Rusk-Gromyko meeting, March 12, 1962, ibid., 15:28.

[216] Rusk-Gromyko meeting, March 22, 1962, ibid., p. 67; for the text of the paper, see ibid., pp. 69–71.

[217] Dowling to Rusk, April 27, 1962, POF/117/Germany—Security/JFKL.

[218] Rusk-Gromyko meeting, March 13, 1962; Rusk to Kennedy, March 19, 1962; Rusk to Dowling, April 28, 1962; Rusk-Dobrynin meeting, May 30, 1962; in FRUS 1961–63, 15:35, 50n., 121, 162.

[219] Rusk-Gromyko meeting, March 20, 1962, and Rusk-Mikoyan meeting, November 30, 1962, ibid., pp. 54, 452.

[220] See, for example, Kohler-Semenov meeting, December 3, 1962, ibid., pp. 456–457.

adequately cover the possibility of the Germans getting control of nuclear weapons through some kind of NATO multilateral force.[221]

But these were not fundamental problems. The American document had been deliberately framed in general terms for tactical reasons. It was best to play down the fact that Germany was the target. The U.S. government naturally preferred to take the line, as Kennedy himself put it in a meeting with Brentano, "that our policy was a general one not directed against Germany."[222]

The same point applied to the other issue Gromyko raised. The Soviets were afraid the Germans would get their hands on nuclear weapons through the MLF. Rusk repeatedly made the American position quite clear to Soviet officials. "Whatever multilateral arrangements come out of NATO," he told Ambassador Dobrynin in August, "we did not intend they would involve transfer of national control."[223] The U.S. government was in effect saying that as part of a deal that would settle the Berlin Crisis and stabilize the political situation in central Europe, it would see to it that Germany would remain non-nuclear, and in particular that the MLF would not serve as a vehicle that would allow Germany to get effective control over nuclear weapons. Indeed, it intended to make sure that no one in the West, not even "Europe" as a whole, could use nuclear forces without American consent. But again U.S. officials preferred not to be too explicit about these matters in writing. A settlement would have to be sold to the Germans. Many Germans wanted the door to be left open to the possibility of at least a European nuclear force, independent of the United States. Why rub their noses in the fact that the Americans were determined to rule out anything of the sort, except perhaps in the very distant future after a truly unified and fully sovereign federal European state had emerged? What harm was there in dangling the carrot—in suggesting that some sort of European nuclear force might be possible just a few years down the road— so the Germans could be kept on board?

From the Soviet standpoint, the Americans were offering something real, indeed something of truly fundamental importance. Preventing the Germans from getting control of nuclear weapons was a vital Soviet interest. The other issues in the Berlin talks were not nearly so important. The Soviets did not insist, for example, on formal recognition of the GDR. Gromyko, in fact, said that the western powers already recognized the East German state de facto. Rusk reported Gromyko's remark to the other western foreign ministers and noted that "if existing Western practice was enough for the Russians, there was really no problem here."[224] The Soviets, moreover, spoke only of the need for the western powers to "respect the sovereignty" of the GDR, and refused repeatedly to explain exactly what they meant by this phrase.[225] This implied that the issue was not vital in itself, but rather was de-

[221] Kennedy-Gromyko meeting, October 6, 1961, FRUS 1961–63, 14:471, 474; Rusk to Kennedy, March 25, 1962, and Rusk-Gromyko meeting, March 26, 1962, ibid., 15:75, 81.

[222] Kennedy-Brentano meeting, April 30, 1962, ibid., p. 127.

[223] Rusk-Dobrynin meeting, August 8, 1962, p. 3, 700.5611/8-862, RG 59, USNA; see also the account in FRUS 1961–63, 7:541–547. Note also Rusk's comments in his March 26 meeting with Gromyko, ibid., 15:85.

[224] Western foreign ministers' meeting, May 3, 1962, FO 371/163572, PRO.

[225] See, for example, Kohler-Semenov meeting, March 18, 1962, FRUS 1961–63, 15:48.

liberately being kept open only for bargaining purposes. Other issues were also of relatively limited importance. "On the face of it," as Couve told the other western foreign ministers, "non-aggression declarations seemed harmless." And German Foreign Minister Schröder noted that he had long "been inclined to accept a non-aggression agreement." Declarations that no one would change existing frontiers through force would simply reiterate existing policy. The whole issue of the inviolability of existing borders, Rusk noted, referring to both the Oder-Neisse line and the intra-German border, "did not have high priority in his talks with Dobrynin."[226]

It thus seemed that a settlement might be within reach. The Soviets liked what the Americans were now offering and signaled their interest in a very tangible way. Western flights in the air corridors to Berlin were being harassed by Soviet aircraft, but after the Rusk-Gromyko meeting in March the harassment was "suspended." This was understood by both sides as a political signal.[227] Even more important, it seemed for a time that the hardline Soviet stance on Berlin proper might be softening. In April, Dobrynin suggested to Rusk that the "present position" of the USSR on the key issue of a western troop presence in the city might be about to shift. "As of now," Dobrynin stressed, the USSR wanted the western forces out as part of an access agreement, but added: "What the future attitude of my Government might be, I would not be in a position to say."[228]

Adenauer, however, did not at all like the sort of settlement that seemed to be taking shape. He was "shocked" by the "Principles" paper, and evidently leaked the substance of the new American proposal to the press.[229] He complained that he had been given only two days to respond to the paper, and the claim is still often made that Adenauer had been presented with something like an ultimatum. The Americans were infuriated by the leak. As for the alleged "ultimatum," they pointed out that the version of the "Principles" paper that Adenauer had seen was almost identical to another draft that had already been cleared with Foreign Minister Schröder.[230] "Astonished" in April by the intensity of the official German reaction, U.S. leaders were also angered by a "stream" of anti-American comments coming from the chancellor himself later that spring. Adenauer had in fact decided to rise up in opposition to American policy. Germany had to be ready, he thought, to go through a certain period of tension in her relations with the United States, and to form a kind of bloc with France. He made little secret of his views, which the press was now reporting on in detail. And in a press conference in early May, he openly attacked America's whole Berlin policy.[231]

[226] Western foreign ministers' meeting, May 3, 1962, FO 371/163572, PRO.

[227] Rusk-Dobrynin meeting, April 16, 1962; Rusk to Kennedy, July 24, 1962; and Rusk-Gromyko meeting, July 24, 1962; in FRUS 1961–63, 15:118, 241, 246.

[228] Rusk-Dobrynin meeting, April 16, 1962, ibid., p. 116.

[229] Nitze-Adenauer meeting, April 13, 1962, ibid., p. 102. See also Schwarz, *Adenauer*, 2:743–749.

[230] Kohler-Grewe meetings and telephone conversation, April 13–14, 1962; Kohler draft of letter to Adenauer, April 14, 1962; Rusk to Dowling, April 25, 1962; FRUS 1961–63, 15:107, 109n, 111, 112n, 120.

[231] Dowling to State Department, May 9, 1962, and Rusk to Dowling, May 12, 1962, ibid., pp. 140, 143. Note also Bundy to Dowling, May 9, 1962, giving text of Daniel Schorr broadcast reporting what Adenauer was saying about the Americans in private conversations, and Salinger to Kennedy, May 10,

Once again, the German nuclear question was fundamental. Adenauer's criticism of the American plan focused on the nuclear issue and the proposal for a Berlin access authority.[232] If that proposal was adopted, neutral powers like Sweden and Switzerland would cast the deciding votes in resolving any disputes over access that arose. According to Adenauer, this meant that power would pass into the hands of relatively weak neutrals, allied rights would be weakened, and Berlin would be even less secure. But this objection to the access authority idea was not valid, and was probably trumped up to obscure the fact that the nuclear issue was Adenauer's only real concern. In fact, the goal of the access authority proposal had been precisely to make access to the city more secure. Under the current regime, the East Germans fully controlled nonmilitary traffic between Berlin and the Federal Republic. That power, it was felt, might be diluted by setting up an authority in which neutral countries played a decisive role. Indeed, the plan for an access authority had been rooted in the idea that the other American proposals had all amounted to concessions to the USSR, and that unless the West insisted on something in return, it would be on a "dangerous slope of appeasement." That quid pro quo might come in the form of an access agreement on Berlin, based on the idea of moving away from full East German control.[233]

All of this was obvious to American officials, and they bitterly resented Adenauer's attack on the proposal. In October, for example, Kennedy told Willy Brandt, the mayor of West Berlin, that since the earlier U.S. plan for an access authority had been rejected, the United States "would make no more proposals on the subject." It was now up to the Germans to come up with a plan of their own, if they wanted to. America had been burned, the president obviously felt, and was not going to make the same kind of effort a second time. When the German ambassador came to complain about this, saying that the president must have been misinformed, and that the German government had been "in basic agreement" with the earlier U.S. plan, American officials did not mince words, so great was their continuing bitterness about what had happened five months earlier. The Germans certainly had publicly "shot down" the U.S. plan for an access authority. The U.S. government still resented "the great public hullaballoo" which had resulted from Adenauer's "public denunciation last Spring of the international access proposal."[234]

Adenauer was in revolt against America, and the nuclear issue and not the access plan was the real bone of contention. But what effect did Adenauer's actions actually have? The key point here is that even his open opposition to the Kennedy policy did not lead the Americans to shift course. In the talks with Russia, the U.S. proposals remained on the table. If the Soviets had been willing to accept a settle-

---

1962, suggesting that Clay was one of Schorr's sources, 762.00/5-962, and 611.62a/5-1062, RG 59, USNA. On Adenauer's willingness to accept a period of tension with the Americans, see Osterheld, *Adenauers letzte Kanzlerjahre*, pp. 111–112.

[232] Adenauer-Nitze meeting, April 13, 1962, FRUS 1961–63, 15:102. Note also Couve's comment in June that as he understood it the "two main problems with the Germans had arisen over the International Access Authority and nuclear non-diffusion"; Couve-Rusk meeting, June 20, 1962, NSABF.

[233] Bundy to Kennedy, October 2, 1961, FRUS 1961–63, 14:460–461.

[234] Knappstein-Tyler-Hillenbrand meeting, October 10, 1962, ibid., 15:355–357.

ment along the lines the Americans had in mind, the United States would have been prepared to force the Germans into line. Indeed, Kennedy made it clear to the Russians that German obstructionism would not be a problem. If the United States and the USSR reached an understanding, he told the Soviet ambassador in July, there were "issues on which we would be willing to press the Germans quite hard." But things never reached that point in 1962, and it was not Adenauer who deserves the blame, or the credit, for sabotaging an agreement.[235]

The problem had to do with Soviet intransigence on the question of a western military presence in Berlin—that is, with West Berlin's status as a territory under the military protection of the western powers. This was the key to the continued freedom of West Berlin, and the U.S. government made it abundantly clear that the Soviets would have to give way on this point if they were to get the kind of settlement the United States was offering them. But this, for reasons that remain hard to understand, the USSR simply would not do. The United States was ready to give the Russians everything they could legitimately ask for, but the USSR was unwilling to give America the one thing she insisted on: a free West Berlin, securely tied to the West, with western military forces, and western forces alone, in the city as guarantors of its extraordinary status.

This Soviet attitude was increasingly resented. Initially the assumption had been that the Soviets had perhaps staked out an extreme position for bargaining purposes, and that as the talks proceeded they might well become more reasonable. But this was turning out not to be the case. The Soviets seemed to think they could simply take everything the United States was prepared to offer and, as Rusk said, store it "away in the refrigerator."[236] They were just putting the U.S. concessions "in a bag," and giving nothing in return.[237] The basic issue was reciprocity. The United States was not going to accept a purely one-sided arrangement, but rather sought an agreement negotiated "on the basis of equality." What the Soviets proposed, Kennedy told Gromyko in October 1961, amounted to "trading an apple for an orchard."[238] The Soviets said the western powers had to accept facts, that the East German regime was a reality and its authority had to be accepted. Very well, the Americans replied, a settlement could indeed be based on the "factual situation." But all the facts had to be taken into account, not just those that the Soviets found it convenient to recognize. The western presence in Berlin was a reality that the Soviets, for their part, had to respect.[239] But this was something that the USSR simply refused to accept, and in the talks they were never able to deal effectively with this argument.[240]

[235] Rusk-Dobrynin meetings, April 16 and 27, 1962; Kennedy-Dobrynin meeting, July 17, 1962; and Rusk-Gromyko meeting, August 6, 1963; ibid., pp. 116, 121, 223, 560. This paragraph takes issue with Schwarz's argument that Adenauer successfully sabotaged Kennedy's "appeasement" policy (he uses the English word) and should thus be considered the "saviour" of Berlin. See his *Adenauer*, 2:743–749, esp. p. 749.

[236] Rusk-Dobrynin meeting, May 30, 1962, FRUS 1961–63, 15:162.

[237] Rusk-Dobrynin meetings, June 18 and July 12, 1962, ibid., pp. 184, 221.

[238] Kennedy-Gromyko meeting, October 6, 1961, ibid., 14:476–477; Rusk-Dobrynin meetings, May 30 and June 18, 1962, ibid., 15:163, 182.

[239] Rusk-Gromyko meeting, March 12, 1962, and Rusk-Dobrynin meeting, May 30, 1962, ibid., pp. 32, 163.

[240] For the records of the most important high-level U.S.–Soviet discussions of the issue from May

From the U.S. point of view, the whole Soviet attitude was outrageous. The American government had gone very far, but what the USSR was now demanding was totally unreasonable. The Russians were asking the United States to capitulate on what was for the Americans a core issue, the freedom of West Berlin. The Soviets wanted the western forces removed from the city. As an alternative, they suggested that the western powers accept a Soviet military contingent, so that troops from all four powers would be present there. The Soviet claim was that in neither case would the political and social system in place in the city be affected. But few believed that these assurances were anything more than an invitation for the West to surrender "on the installment plan." If the Soviets really intended to respect the status quo in the city, why were they so determined to put an end to the situation where West Berlin was under the protection of the western powers, and the western powers alone? Their argument that West Berlin was a NATO military base was absurd. It was ludicrous to think that the small allied contingents in the city posed any military threat to the eastern bloc. And yet in their talks with the Americans, the same arguments were trotted out over and over again. It was as though they were impervious to reason, deaf to what the Americans were saying. In 1962, their core position on Berlin was absolutely rigid. It was all take and no give with these people. The Americans had tried to be as reasonable and as understanding as they could, but the Soviets would not reciprocate and remained intransigent on what was for the United States an absolutely vital issue.

It was becoming quite clear that the Soviets were not interested in negotiating the sort of settlement the U.S. government could accept. Instead, it seemed they were out to humiliate the United States. The American attitude now hardened. De Gaulle, Rusk was forced to admit, had been right after all: the negotiations were proving fruitless. The United States had gone a good way toward meeting Soviet wishes, in the process putting relations with America's own allies in jeopardy, but had gotten nothing in return. Had the Soviets, as the hardliners had predicted, taken the American interest in an accommodation as a sign of weakness? Did they think that if they remained intransigent long enough the United States would give way in the end?

American leaders were becoming increasingly bitter. In his July 23 meeting with Gromyko, Rusk, for example, now openly referred to the East German regime as a Soviet "puppet," a "ventriloquist's dummy."[241] By this point it was obvious, as Khrushchev himself noted, that the effort to reach a negotiated settlement was coming to an end.[242] Bundy, for example, wrote in late August that the crisis had recently heated up and "looks as if it is getting worse."[243] In early September, Rusk told the French ambassador that "he had a hunch we are in for a serious time."[244] Another U.S. document from mid-September saw Khrushchev moving toward a

---

30 to October 18, 1962, see ibid., pp. 161–172, 177–189, 215–222, 243–252, 370–387. For the record of the one important meeting from this period not published in this volume, the July 22, 1962, Rusk-Gromyko dinner conversation, see 110.11-RU/7-2362, RG 59, USNA.

[241] Rusk to Kennedy, July 23, 1962, FRUS 1961–63, 15:237 and Rusk to State Department, July 23, 1962 (section 5 of six), 110.11-RU/7-2362, RG 59, USNA.

[242] Thompson to State Department, July 26, 1962, FRUS 1961–63, 15:253.

[243] Bundy to Sorensen, August 23, 1962, ibid., p. 284.

[244] Rusk-Alphand meeting, September 7, 1962, ibid., p. 312.

"Berlin showdown."[245] In early October, top American officials made it clear both in public and in private meetings with foreign officials that they thought a real confrontation was coming soon.[246]

On October 18, Gromyko met with Rusk and then Kennedy in Washington. The Soviet foreign minister took a line that the president later characterized as "completely unreasonable and downright insulting."[247] The USSR would do nothing, he told Kennedy, until after the U.S. midterm elections in November; Khrushchev had already made this clear the previous month. But then, right after the elections, Gromyko said, talks would have to be held, and if they were not successful the Soviet government would be "compelled" to sign its peace treaty with East Germany, with the results that had been spelled out many times. The United States had threatened to engage in military action in such a case, but those threats he dismissed out of hand: they would have "no effect on the USSR whatsoever." As Khrushchev had said, "the NATO military base and the occupation regime in West Berlin represented a rotten tooth which must be pulled out."[248]

In his meeting with Rusk, Gromyko took much the same line. The secretary of state reviewed the American position. The Americans, he said, had sought to accommodate the Soviet Union on a whole series of issues. They had prevented West Berlin from becoming a *Land* of the Federal Republic. They had pursued a policy in the nuclear area which should have eased Soviet concerns. And Rusk reminded Gromyko that he had privately indicated to him "that the Eastern boundaries were not a problem in a de facto and practical sense." But it had all been to no avail because the USSR could not accept the one point the United States insisted on, the "presence of Western forces in West Berlin." So it had all come down to a simple test of will. The Soviet Union, he said, had to "decide whether it wanted to go to war to remove those forces."[249] The implication of Gromyko's remarks, as both U.S. and British diplomats were quick to point out, was that "the next round of conversations would be the last."[250]

Kennedy had already reached the conclusion that a showdown with Russia was probably inevitable; he felt that since this was the case, it was better for matters to come to a head sooner rather than later. In early October, he wanted to be able to react instantly on Berlin—that is, to take action as soon as access was cut off. He told Couve on October 9 that "we ought to have forces ready to go within one or two hours on the Autobahn."[251] On October 2, he met with Rusk and the British foreign secretary, Lord Home. He ruled out the idea of talks with Khrushchev in late November, after the U.S. elections, unless of course the Soviet attitude had

[245] Burris to Johnson, September 18, 1962, ibid., p. 324.

[246] "Kennedy Warning Nation and Allies on Berlin Crisis," *New York Times,* October 12, 1962. Note especially the reference here to Robert Kennedy's Las Vegas speech of October 9, in which the president's brother predicted a "great crisis."

[247] Kennedy-Adenauer meeting, November 14, 1962, FRUS 1961–63, 15:432.

[248] Kennedy-Gromyko meeting, October 18, 1962, ibid., pp. 371–372; Khrushchev to Kennedy, September 28, 1962, ibid., 6:157.

[249] Rusk-Gromyko meeting, October 18, 1962, ibid., 379–380.

[250] Ormsby Gore to Foreign Office, October 19, 1962 (no. 2621), and Roberts to Foreign Office, October 22, 1962, FO 371/163582, PRO.

[251] Kennedy-Couve meeting, October 9, 1962, FRUS 1961–63, 15:353.

changed by then and there was some evidence that the talks might be productive. He disagreed with the two foreign ministers about the desirability of further diplomatic action. Home and Rusk thought that some formula—a deputy foreign ministers' meeting, for example—might "provide Khrushchev with another excuse to postpone signature of a treaty." But Kennedy was no longer interested in tactics of this sort. The reason he gave was that "the military balance was more favourable to us now than it would be later on."[252]

Kennedy knew that while the United States still had the upper hand in strategic terms, American nuclear superiority would soon be a thing of the past. A year earlier, in late 1961, this had been a major argument for a negotiated settlement. The terms the West could get would be better now, the argument ran, while the United States still had an important strategic edge, than they would be a couple of years down the road, after that advantage had disappeared and the Soviets had achieved nuclear parity.[253] But by October 1962 the argument had been turned on its head. American nuclear superiority would soon disappear. The Soviets were intent on humiliating the United States and bringing about a radical shift in the global balance of power. If that was their attitude, a confrontation was inevitable; and that being the case, it made sense to have it out with them now, while the strategic balance still favored the United States.

Kennedy was thus prepared by this point to accept a showdown with the USSR over Berlin. As it turned out, however, the confrontation was not precipitated by any specific move the Soviets made in central Europe. It was set off instead by the deployment of Soviet missiles in Cuba.

[252] Home to Foreign Office, October 2, 1962, FO 371/163581.

[253] See, for example, the president's remarks in a meeting with Adenauer, November 20, 1961, FRUS 1961–63, 14:592.

A Settlement Takes Shape

IN THE HISTORY of the Cold War, 1963 was a watershed year. It was at that point that east-west relations took a decisive turn for the better. Problems remained, but the Cold War became a different kind of conflict. Its focus moved away from Europe and toward areas of secondary or even tertiary importance; the basic interests of each side were no longer seriously threatened; the conflict lost its apocalyptic edge.

This happened in spite of the fact that 1963 also marked the end of American nuclear superiority. The coming of parity, so long awaited, was bound to dilute the deterrent value of the U.S. nuclear force: the USSR would now have a freer hand to challenge the United States. But the loss of America's nuclear edge did not lead to a more aggressive Soviet policy; instead, political relations between the two sides became more relaxed.

The reason was that in 1963 the elements of a political system finally fell into place. At the core of this system was a set of understandings about Berlin and West Germany, about the American presence in Europe, and about the structure of power within the western alliance. This system would provide the basis for a relatively stable peace for the balance of the Cold War period, and beyond.

THE CRISIS OF OCTOBER 1962

The Cuban Missile Crisis played a key role in this story: its course and resolution set the stage for what was to come in the following year. The crisis began when the American government discovered that the USSR was secretly building missile bases in Cuba. After a week of deliberation, President Kennedy and his top advisers worked out a strategy for dealing with the problem. Kennedy laid out the U.S. position in a televised speech to the nation on October 22, 1962. The United States, he said, would not tolerate the deployment in Cuba of nuclear-tipped missiles. A naval blockade was being instituted as a way of underscoring America's determination to see this matter through.[1]

---

[1] There is a large literature on the missile crisis, but still no comprehensive study based on archival materials. The two most important books to appear recently are Fursenko and Naftali, *"One Hell of a Gamble,"* and May and Zelikow, *The Kennedy Tapes.* I myself published a number of articles dealing with certain aspects of the crisis: "The Influence of Nuclear Weapons in the Cuban Missile Crisis" (with some major documents and an introduction to those documents), *International Security* 10 (Summer 1985); "New Light on the Cuban Missile Crisis?" *Diplomatic History* 14 (1990); and "L'ouverture des archives américaines: vers de nouvelles perspectives," in *L'Europe et la Crise de Cuba,* ed. Maurice Vaïsse (Paris: Colin, 1993). A mass of new material has recently become available, and much of it is readily available on microfiche: National Security Archive, *The Cuban Missile Crisis, 1962,* over fifteen thousand pages on microfiche with two-volume printed guide.

The Americans had now thrown down the gauntlet. It was clear that the Soviets might respond by establishing a counterblockade around Berlin, that matters might escalate, and that a third world war was now a real possibility.[2] But Kennedy felt that the showdown with Russia had to be accepted. The Russians, he noted repeatedly during the missile crisis, were getting ready to move on Berlin anyway.[3] Indeed, it seemed that the point of the missile deployment was to improve the Soviet strategic position quickly and cheaply, and thus to put the USSR in a better position to bring the Berlin Crisis to a head.[4] But if a showdown over Berlin was inevitable, it was best to accept the confrontation while the United States still had an important strategic edge. If the Soviets were getting ready to move, he said just before the missiles were discussed in Cuba, it "might be better to allow a confrontation to develop over Berlin now rather than later."[5]

This is not to say that Kennedy was out to humiliate the Soviets, or that he took an intransigent line in the crisis. The U.S. government could certainly not just sit on its hands and allow work on the missile sites to continue indefinitely, if only because military action would become increasingly problematic as more and more missiles became operational. If the Soviets did not stop work on the sites and agree to talks, it was taken for granted that the United States would have to attack the missile bases and invade the island. But Kennedy was worried about escalation and especially about the possibility of Soviet counteraction around Berlin.[6] He therefore preferred the blockade to direct military action—an air strike or even an invasion—and wanted to see if some sort of negotiated arrangement could be worked out. Perhaps the Soviets would agree to withdraw their missiles from Cuba, and the United States in exchange would dismantle the Jupiter IRBMs deployed in Italy and Turkey. Kennedy considered a trade of this sort the only alternative to an invasion.[7] The Jupiters, in his view, had little military value in any case, and from early 1961 on the U.S. government had in fact wanted to pull them out. America would be in a "bad position," he thought, "if we appear to be attacking Cuba for the purpose of keeping useless missiles in Turkey"; the United States therefore had to "face up to the possibility of some kind of trade over missiles."[8]

His main advisers, however, all strongly objected to the idea. The very notion of a trade was "anathema" to the Turks. The weapons had been deployed in accordance with a NATO decision, and it would take a NATO decision to get Turkey to agree to their withdrawal. The Cuban business was one thing; the "NATO–Warsaw Pact arms problem," Rusk said, "was a separate problem." If the notion of a trade were now accepted, in Bundy's view, America's position would "come apart very fast." The Europeans would view it as a sellout. It would perhaps be seen,

---

[2] Kennedy-Macmillan phone conversation, October 22, 1962, FRUS 1961–63, 11:164. See also meetings of Kennedy with key advisers, October 18 and 21, 1962, ibid., pp. 109, 133, 146.

[3] See May and Zelikow, *Kennedy Tapes,* pp. 143, 172, 176, 237, 284.

[4] Ibid., pp. 90, 172, 179, 286; Kennedy-Macmillan phone conversation, October 22, 1962, FRUS 1961–63, 11:164.

[5] Home to Foreign Office, October 2, 1962, FO 371/163581, PRO.

[6] See, for example, Kennedy in phone conversation with Macmillan, October 22, 1962, in May and Zelikow, *Kennedy Tapes,* pp. 285–286.

[7] NSC Executive Committee Meeting no. 6, October 26, 1962, FRUS 1961–63, 11:225.

[8] NSC Executive Committee Meeting no. 7, October 27, 1962, ibid., pp. 255–256.

Nitze suggested, as a step toward denuclearizing NATO. But Kennedy was not convinced. He wanted a standstill agreement. Once work on the sites had been suspended, the pressure for military action would subside, and negotiations—both with the Soviets and with the NATO allies—would be possible.[9]

But how should he proceed? The United States might hold off from proposing a trade right away, in the hope that the Soviets would agree to withdraw their missiles from Cuba without a corresponding American concession relating to the Jupiters. But so favorable an outcome did not seem very likely. If the issue were put off, the odds were that the Soviets would come back a day or two later and raise the question of the missiles in Turkey. In that case, precious time would have been lost: more missiles would have become operational, and military action would become more perilous.[10]

On the other hand, if the U.S. government pressed for the withdrawal of the Jupiters right away, the NATO allies would be angered. If the United States went to NATO and the allies objected to a trade, Kennedy might find his hands tied. But perhaps the allies could be made to agree. If they were against a trade now, the president believed, this was probably because they had not thought the matter through. The Americans could explain to them that this kind of intransigence would foreclose a political settlement, that Cuba would therefore have to be attacked in "two or three days," and that the Soviets would then probably respond by seizing Berlin or with a strike on Turkey. When they understood this, he argued, their attitude would change. But the answer here was that if the allies were convinced of all this, they might well try to veto an American attack on Cuba, and that once again the president's hands would be tied. In any event, the prospect of America having to frighten the allies in this way was hardly appealing. The United States would come across as the great champion of what could easily be portrayed as a policy of appeasement, with incalculable long-term effects on both Soviet and allied behavior.[11]

Whichever way Kennedy turned, the problems were daunting. It seemed that there was only one way out. Kennedy decided to cut the Gordian knot by going behind the backs of the NATO allies, and indeed behind the backs of all but his closest advisers. He sent his brother Robert to see the Soviet ambassador and deliver an important message. The Soviets were told that the United States was about to attack Cuba. If they wished to prevent this, they would have to promise within twenty-four hours to withdraw their missiles. If the weapons were taken out, the United States would promise not to invade Cuba. As for the Jupiters, the Soviets were told (inaccurately, to obscure the fact that a concession was being made) that the president "had ordered their removal some time ago," and that they would in fact be withdrawn within four or five months. This, the Soviets were informed, was not to be seen as a quid pro quo for the removal of the missiles from Cuba, and

---

[9] NSC Executive Committee meetings nos. 6, 7 and 8, October 26–27, 1962, ibiid., pp. 225–226, 252–255, 264–267; October 27, 1962, White House meetings, May and Zelikow, *Kennedy Tapes*, pp. 496, 500, 523–528.

[10] October 27 White House meetings, May and Zelikow, *Kennedy Tapes*, pp. 496–531, 552–554.

[11] Ibid., 541–549, 564, 579.

they were asked to keep this assurance secret. If they referred to it in public, it would become null and void. "This is not a deal," they were in effect told, "and if you breathe a word of it in public, the deal's off."[12]

The very next day the USSR announced that the missiles would be withdrawn. The key decision to give way had evidently been made even before word of Robert Kennedy's meeting with Ambassador Dobrynin had reached Moscow. Khrushchev had decided very early on not to risk a real confrontation with the United States: on October 23, he had dismissed the idea of a counterblockade of West Berlin out of hand.[13]

The Cuban Missile Crisis was now over. From Kennedy's point of view, the crisis had not ended with a Soviet capitulation pure and simple. The United States, for its part, had made a concession of sorts involving the Jupiters. But the fact remained that the U.S. government had laid down an ultimatum, and the USSR had acceded to America's terms.

KENNEDY'S NEW NATO POLICY

The whole tenor of east-west relations now changed dramatically. The Soviets, it was clear, were not made of steel. The United States did not have to worry so much about them, and indeed might do well to take a tougher line in dealing with them. On Cuban issues, the American position now hardened. The U.S. government, for example, now insisted that the Soviets withdraw their Il-28 bombers from Cuba, something Kennedy had earlier thought was not very important.[14] And the president was inclined to take a harder line with the Soviets in general. He now thought that the earlier policy of trying so hard to reach an accommodation with the USSR had been misguided, and he even wondered now whether it was a mistake to always treat the Soviet leaders "with consideration and courtesy."[15]

But he still wanted a settlement, and on the same basic terms as in 1961 and 1962. If the two sides accepted the status quo in central Europe—if they agreed not to use force to change it—they could live together in peace.[16] If the United States and the Soviet Union could agree on something of the sort, the NATO allies could be made to cooperate, and indeed Kennedy thought that now, after the missile crisis, the United States "could push its Allies" even harder than before.[17]

[12] Robert Kennedy, *Thirteen Days* (New York: Norton, 1969), pp. 106–109; Arthur Schlesinger, *Robert Kennedy and His Times* (Boston: Houghton Mifflin, 1978), pp. 520–523; Bundy, *Danger and Survival*, pp. 432–434.

[13] May and Zelikow, *Kennedy Tapes*, pp. 683, 689.

[14] During the crisis, Kennedy had felt the United States could live with the threat posed by IL-28s in Cuba. NSC minutes, October 20, 1962, FRUS 1961–63, 11:131, 133. But in the post-crisis talks, the U.S. government took a much tougher line. See ibid., p. 350 n, 359.

[15] Kennedy-Macmillan meeting, December 19, 1962, and meeting between Kennedy, Rusk, et al., February 15, 1963, ibid., 15:469, 487; Kennedy-Harriman meeting, July 10, 1963, ibid., 7:789.

[16] Rusk-Mikoyan meeting, November 30, 1962, and Kohler-Semenov meeting, December 3, 1962, ibid., 15:451, 456–457.

[17] Thompson to Rusk, October 29, 1962, ibid., p. 15:406 n.

If a settlement was in sight, he was "willing to press the French and the Germans very hard to go along."[18] America had her own policy and was not beholden to Germany. It was made clear to the Soviets on a number of occasions that if the two major powers reached an agreement, West Germany would not be allowed to "stand in the way."[19]

If, however, an agreement was not within reach—that is, if the Russians were not willing to accept the status quo in West Berlin—then there was no sense going through the charade of a negotiation. If the Soviets were not prepared to be forthcoming on that key issue, there was little point, Kennedy said, "in continuing a dialogue bound to arouse the suspicion, even the antagonism, of our Allies."[20] The earlier attempt in late 1961 and early 1962 to reach a negotiated settlement, he now thought, had been "foolish." France and Germany had been alienated by these American efforts, but no real progress had been made with the Russians.[21]

The whole course of action his government had pursued on European issues since April 1961 Kennedy now regarded as bankrupt. The policy laid out in the Acheson report had had a profoundly corrosive effect on the alliance. De Gaulle was openly hostile to America, and even relations with Britain had been strained. The MLF, as Kennedy had long suspected, was not a solution to anything, but was rather turning into a problem in its own right. The time had come for a fundamental reappraisal of the whole Acheson strategy. America could now contemplate a more liberal policy on NATO nuclear questions. This was the key to restoring decent relations with the French and possibly to avoiding a rift with the British as well.

Britain and France might be helped in the nuclear area, but this did not mean that the Germans would be allowed to come any closer toward acquiring a nuclear capability. In this very fundamental area, Kennedy's views remained unchanged. Acheson and his supporters had long argued that the Germans would not accept this type of discrimination indefinitely, and that if they were to be kept from going nuclear, the United States would have to oppose British and French nuclear forces as well. To help France, and even to go on helping Britain, was to open the floodgates: in the long run, the German problem would become unmanageable.

But Kennedy by now had come to question that basic premise. Even if Britain and France were helped, the Germans could still be told that they could not have their own nuclear weapons. They would not like it, but they were dependent on the United States and could be made to swallow the pill. If they defied America, where else could they go for protection? It was a question of who needed whom, and the Germans would have to give way in the end.

Responsible opinion had, of course, long warned against this kind of thinking,

---

[18] Foreign Office background note for talks with Kennedy, December 10, 1962, FO 371/163585, PRO. This note presented information that had come from Kennedy's close friend, David Ormsby Gore, the British ambassador in Washington.

[19] Rusk-Mikoyan meeting, November 30, 1962, FRUS 1961–63, 15:452; Rusk-Gromyko meeting, October 2, 1963, pp. 10, 12, NSF/187/USSR; Gromyko Talks (Rusk)/JFKL.

[20] Meeting of Kennedy, Rusk, et al., February 15, 1963, FRUS 1961–63, 15:487.

[21] Kennedy's remarks at Macmillan's dinner party, December 19, 1962, quoted in the British record of the Nassau conference, p. 26, in Prem 11/4229, PRO.

and Kennedy had long deferred to the views of the experts in the State Department and elsewhere.[22] But the policies he had adopted on their advice were clearly not working. In April 1961, he had been relatively inexperienced in these matters, and had accepted Acheson's views without giving the matter much thought. But now, after dealing with these issues intensively for almost two years, and after having taken his measure of people like Acheson, he was inclined to give greater weight to his own judgment—especially after his experience during the missile crisis, when his advisers had all told him that anything like a deal involving the Jupiters would wreck the alliance, and he had gone ahead with it anyway and had ended the crisis on quite acceptable terms. America, it was now clear to him, was strong enough to act unilaterally—strong enough, in the final analysis, to lay down the law to the Germans.

This did not mean, however, that Kennedy was looking for a confrontation. If possible, a softer course of action was obviously preferable. His tactic was to create a situation that would lead the Germans to fall into line more naturally. His aim now was to rebuild the bloc of the three western powers—Britain, France, and the United States—and thus to isolate the Germans, leaving them with little choice but to accept a non-nuclear status.

Britain would certainly cooperate if the Americans moved in this direction. Macmillan thought that Britain, France, and America should be the only three nuclear powers in the West—or as he put it, nuclear "trustees" for the West as a whole. Their nuclear forces would be coordinated within the NATO structure but would remain in the final analysis under national control. Within that general framework, America and Britain would help France develop her nuclear capability. There would in particular be direct Anglo-French nuclear collaboration—but only if the United States went along with the idea; this was part of Macmillan's more general policy of bringing Britain into Europe, and was thus closely linked to the idea that Britain should join the Common Market. Throughout 1961 and 1962 he pressed repeatedly for such a policy and made a number of overtures to the French along these lines. And de Gaulle was by no means averse to an arrangement of this sort.[23]

From Macmillan's standpoint, the problem lay with the Americans. The British leader's idea was that after France was helped and the French force was somehow tied into the western defense system, "no other countries would bother to build a

[22] See, for example, Kissinger to Bundy, August 18, 1961, p. 2, DDRS 1993/2331.

[23] See the dossier on the question in Prem 11/3712, PRO, and the following documents: Anglo-American talks, April 5–8, 1961, notes of first meeting, p. 8, Cab 133/244, PRO; Macmillan to Kennedy, April 28, 1961 (with enclosures), NSABF; de Zulueta to Macmillan, "The Nuclear," n.d. but around May 5, 1961, Prem 11/3311, PRO; Macmillan-Chauvel meeting, April 19, 1962, Prem 11/3792, PRO; and Note for the Record, October 9, 1962, Prem 11/3772, PRO. See also Alistair Horne, *Harold Macmillan*, vol. 2 (New York: Viking, 1989), pp. 328, 445. Macmillan's views were by no means universally accepted within the British government. For some insight into the internal British debate, see Ramsbotham, "The Prime Minister's Visit to General de Gaulle," January 17, 1961, FO 371/159671, PRO. For de Gaulle's views, see Macmillan–de Gaulle meeting at Champs, June 3, 1962, Prem 11/3712, and Zuckerman note on "Anglo/French Co-operation," May 25, 1962, Prem 11/3712, both PRO. See also Finletter to Rusk, August 9, 1961, 740.5/8-961, and Nitze–de Rose meeting, August 5, 1961, 740.5611/8-661, both RG 59, USNA. See finally Soutou, *L'Alliance incertaine*, pp. 193, 225.

nuclear force."[24] Key U.S. officials, however, thought that Macmillan was "dead wrong" in this regard, and Kennedy in 1961 simply refused to go along with Macmillan's plan.[25] Macmillan, for his part, was not willing to pursue the project if the United States was against it. But he continued in 1962 to press for a green light. The State Department was still strongly opposed to nuclear cooperation with France, but already in the spring of that year the president's views were more nuanced. He did not "take up an attitude of doctrinaire opposition" to the Macmillan plan, but would go along only it would "buy something really spectacular like full French co-operation in NATO and elsewhere plus British entry into the European Economic Community." The right moment for such a deal might come eventually, but now was not the time to move in that direction.[26]

As Kennedy saw it, the general French attitude was the key to the whole problem. Was there any way that de Gaulle could be brought back on board? The puzzle here was that in spite of all the signs of conflict, France and America did not really differ much on the most basic issues of policy. Both were happy to leave things as they were in central Europe—that is, both favored détente with Russia on the basis of the status quo—and neither really wanted to see Germany develop a nuclear capability of her own. So why were the two nations at odds? There was of course the nuclear problem, but the U.S. government opposed France in this area only because of fears about the effect of a French force on Germany. So maybe a deal was possible. If the United States helped France in the nuclear area, would de Gaulle cooperate more with America's German policy? Would he be content to work within the NATO framework? American nuclear assistance would save the French a good deal of money. Would he be willing to plow those savings back into the kind of conventional buildup people like McNamara thought was so important? Or was he so set in his anti-American ways that he would refuse even to consider an arrangement along these lines?

The British, of course, wanted Kennedy to see whether some sort of understanding could be worked out with de Gaulle. From their standpoint, it would be most unpleasant if they were forced to choose between America and "Europe." It would be much better if Macmillan could negotiate with de Gaulle with America's blessing. And the policy of trying to reach an understanding with de Gaulle had important sources of support within the American government as well. In military circles especially, the course of action laid down in the April 1961 policy directive was thoroughly disliked—and on essentially political grounds. Norstad, for example, thought that "Washington's arrogance was turning all Europe against us."[27] And Colonel Lawrence Legere, General Taylor's right-hand man, thought it absurd that the Europeans would ever accept a policy which, "stripped of camouflage and

[24] Kennedy-Macmillan meeting, December 19, 1962, 9:50 A.M., Nassau conference records, p. 10, Prem 11/4229, PRO.
[25] Owen to Bundy, May 3, 1961, PPS 1957–61/183/Owen, RG 59, USNA; Kennedy to Macmillan, May 8, 1961, Prem 11/3311, PRO.
[26] For the State Department view, see Rusk's comments, "Note of a Conversation at Luncheon at the State Department on 28th April, 1962," Prem 11/3712, PRO. Kennedy's views are summarized in a top secret personal letter from Ormsby Gore to Macmillan, May 17, 1962, Prem 11/3712, PRO.
[27] Sulzberger, *Last of the Giants*, entry for December 16, 1962, p. 942.

verbiage," was based on the idea that they should be "rational enough to see" that total dependence on the United States "for the defense of their existence" was their only real option—and absurd also that midlevel officials like Henry Owen had found it so easy to get official sanction for this "arrogant policy."[28] The top civilians at the Pentagon, on the other hand, tended to emphasize military considerations, especially the importance of getting the French to contribute to the conventional buildup and the key role that nuclear assistance could play in this regard.[29] This was the fundamental consideration for McNamara, but he was also out of sympathy with the State Department line for political reasons. Not only did an MLF subject to an American veto have no military value in his view, but he could not see how it served any major political purpose either.[30]

So the Acheson policy never had universal support in the government, and Kennedy himself, with his essentially pragmatic approach to these issues, was becoming increasingly disenchanted with it. The critics, in fact, had been strong enough to mount a major attack on the policy in the spring of 1962. But the Acheson line had prevailed, at least temporarily, and the policy laid out in the April 1961 directive was reaffirmed. This "process of reaffirmation," as Richard Neustadt says, produced a whole series of fundamental policy documents, the most important of which was McNamara's Athens speech in May. "Essentially the choices had been negative," Neustadt writes. Fundamental policy was not going to be changed, and "by action or inaction three decisions followed: *not* to base MRBMs in central Europe, *not* to aid the French, and *not* to back Bowie's idea of MLF in any form which might confer substance on European nuclear status—or divert funds from conventional goals."[31] But even at this point Kennedy wanted to keep the door somewhat open: the U.S. government approved the sale to the French of twelve tanker aircraft which would enable the French Mirage IV planes to refuel in the air, thus giving them for the first time the ability to launch a nuclear attack on the Soviet Union.[32]

By the end of the year, Kennedy was ready to abandon the April 1961 strategy in its entirety and to try to work out some kind of arrangement with France. One early sign of this was a "directive" he issued during the missile crisis to "reverse our policy on nuclear assistance to France"; his goal, he said, was to make sure that the French sided with America in the crisis.[33] Nothing much, however, came of this; and it was only in December that the president was able to engineer a real shift in American policy in this area.

The Skybolt affair provided the occasion for this change of course. Skybolt was an air-to-ground missile which the U.S. had been developing, and which the Eisenhower administration had promised to provide to the British if the development

[28] Legere to Taylor, June 18, June 22, and August 1, 1962, TP/36/1 and 3/NDU.

[29] See especially McNamara's remarks in the Secretary of Defense Staff Meeting, January 7, 1963, p. 5, CJCS Taylor/23/Secretary of Defense Staff Meetings, RG 218, USNA. See also McNamara-Rusk-Bundy meeting, December 28, 1962, FRUS 1961–63, 13:1116.

[30] McNamara-von Hassel meeting, February 28, 1963, p. 8, McNamara Papers, 133/Memcons with Germans, RG 200, USNA.

[31] Neustadt, "Skybolt and Nassau," pp. 29–30. See above, p. 307.

[32] Soutou, *L'alliance incertaine*, p. 226.

[33] NSC meetings, October 20 and 21, 1962, FRUS 1961–63, 11:135, 148.

process was successful. That promise had been loosely tied to a British agreement to allow the United States to build a submarine base in Scotland. Now in late 1962 the American government had reached the conclusion that for technical reasons Skybolt was not worth producing. This raised the question of what, if anything, the British would be offered as a replacement. The obvious alternative was the Polaris submarine-launched missile. But the State Department objected. Skybolt, as an air-launched weapon, would only prolong the life of the British bomber-based deterrent a few more years, but Polaris would allow Britain to move into the missile age. To provide Polaris was therefore inconsistent with the existing policy of trying to "get the British out of the nuclear business." If the British were helped, then the French and eventually the Germans would also have to be helped; a German force was out of the question; therefore the British had to be made to bite the bullet. They could not be given Polaris.[34]

According to the standard interpretation of the Skybolt affair, the American government accepted the State Department line. McNamara was responsible for working out the issue with his British counterpart Peter Thorneycroft; he supposedly agreed not to offer Polaris, but instead decided to wait for the British to "press Polaris on him." The British defense minister "had the same notion in reverse." He could not "step out" on Polaris until the Americans offered it; he was "immobilized" by McNamara's failure to make the offer. The American and British governments thus faced each other like frightened rabbits, each unable to utter the magic word "Polaris," each hoping and waiting for the other to make the first move. The British, the argument runs, did not want to appear to be coming to the Americans hat in hand, and American representatives, bound by the State Department line, did not want to offer Polaris until every alternative had been explored. The result was that the British, frustrated by America's unwillingness to offer an acceptable substitute for Skybolt, and suspecting that the Americans were using the technical problems as a device to force them to give up their independent deterrent, angrily brought the issue to a head when Kennedy and Macmillan met at Nassau just before Christmas. Macmillan, in an impassioned plea to Kennedy, demanded Polaris and threatened an "agonizing reappraisal" of British policy if he did not get it. Kennedy, the argument continues, valuing America's "special relationship" with Britain, seeing a fellow politician in trouble, and not fully realizing the broader implications of what he was doing, improvised a deal—the Nassau agreement— which essentially gave the British Polaris under ultimate national control. The Nassau agreement is thus not to be interpreted as resulting from, or even as marking, a truly fundamental shift in basic American policy on the NATO nuclear issue.[35]

This interpretation, however, does not stand up in the light of the evidence that has become available in recent years. The first problem is that from the start nei-

[34] Neustadt, "Skybolt and Nassau," is the basic source on the Skybolt affair. See also Rusk to McNamara, September 8 and November 24, 1962, ibid., 13:1078–1080, 1086–1088.

[35] This was basically Neustadt's interpretation in "Skybolt and Nassau"; for the quotations, see pp. 34–35, 42, and 61. Many other scholars have followed his lead. See, for example, Arthur Schlesinger, Jr., *A Thousand Days: John F. Kennedy in the White House* (Boston: Houghton Mifflin, 1965), pp. 856–866, esp. p. 861; Horne, *Macmillan*, 2:432–443; Shapley, *Promise and Power*, pp. 241–244. See also Theodore Sorensen, *Kennedy* (New York: Harper and Row, 1965), pp. 564–568.

ther Thorneycroft nor McNamara had any trouble bringing up the idea of Polaris as an alternative to Skybolt. The two men first discussed the issue on the telephone on November 9; Thorneycroft, in that conversation, actually "used the word 'Polaris.'"[36] McNamara, for his part, told Thorneycroft that the United States was willing to supply Polaris "without political strings."[37] President Kennedy himself told the British ambassador in early December—that is, well before the crisis came to a head—that "if we all came to the conclusion" that Skybolt was no good, "then the Americans ought to provide us [the British] with whatever weapons system suited us, and he mentioned both Polaris and Minuteman."[38] And when McNamara came over to London to discuss the problem with Thorneycroft on December 11, he hinted broadly that the United States would be willing to sell Polaris to the British. "Would you buy POLARIS systems if we could make them available?" he asked Thorneycroft. Would the U.K. consider "the possibility of utilizing a POLARIS-type fleet that would be set up in coordination with other forces, such as U.S. forces"?[39]

And Thorneycroft wanted to pursue the Polaris proposal. The problem was not that the Americans were unwilling, but that Macmillan vetoed the idea. "The Prime Minister," one of his secretaries noted at the time, "thought the right course would be to take a very cagey line." Even though the British had been warned that the U.S. government was about to drop development of the missile, Macmillan thought as late as December 9 it would be best "to try and play Skybolt along for another year to eighteen months in order to avoid political difficulties at home. It was clearly in our interests to get on to a Polaris deterrent at some stage but we had made a number of statements about Skybolt and it would be a little easier if that continued for the time being."[40]

So when McNamara came over to London and hinted broadly that the British could have Polaris, they seemed determined to reject the offer. What was odd about this was that the British took this position even after McNamara had made it clear in public that he no longer thought much of Skybolt and that the U.S. government would probably not continue to develop the weapon. The Skybolt option was thus no longer viable, and McNamara, in his meeting with Thorneycroft, now suggested an alternative arrangement: the British would get Polaris missiles, and these weapons would be part of the western defense system. This corresponded quite closely to what Macmillan had often said he wanted, but when McNamara put it on the table, the British did not seem at all interested in closing the deal. Yes, Thorneycroft told McNamara, Polaris was a possibility, but only if it were built in Britain. And an arrangement linking the British force to American and perhaps other forces might be possible in the future, but only if the British freely chose to accept an arrangement of this sort. It could not be imposed as a condition; Britain's

[36] Neustadt, "Skybolt and Nassau," p. 20. Emphasis in original.
[37] Unsigned memo, "Skybolt," November 19, 1962, Prem 11/3716, PRO.
[38] Ormsby Gore to Home, December 8, 1962, pp. 5–6, Prem 11/4229, PRO.
[39] Rubel transcript of McNamara-Thorneycroft meeting, December 11, 1962, pp. 5–6, Neustadt Papers/19/Skybolt-Nassau (classified)/ JFKL. Rubel is identified as the author in the Neustadt, "Skybolt and Nassau," p. 63.
[40] Bligh note for the record, December 9, 1962, Prem 11/3716, PRO.

nuclear independence first had to be guaranteed.[41] That very evening the British newspapers carried a distorted account of the McNamara-Thorneycroft conversation. The secretary of defense "was featured in them all as a man who had assaulted British interests but had been stood off by Thorneycroft in a 'tempestuous' meeting" in which the British minister had threatened a "complete reappraisal of British policy and defence commitments."[42] So from the start the Skybolt affair was a little odd. As a U.S. official later noted, "the thing was whipped up into a crisis on purpose by Thorneycroft and Macmillan."[43]

And indeed, appearances to the contrary, there was no real confrontation at Nassau. Kennedy, in fact, conceded the fundamental point at issue at the very beginning of the conference. Although he went through the standard State Department arguments, he wasted no time in making it clear that a "Polaris arrangement" would be possible. The Polaris missiles to be sold to Britain would be part of some kind of multinational force, possibly including France as well as Britain and America; the purpose of this multinational packaging was to avoid upsetting "other members of the alliance." But the missiles would be under ultimate national control: "Of course, in extremes they could be taken out." These statements, it is important to note, were made well before Macmillan made his impassioned plea to Kennedy at the end of that first meeting for precisely this sort of an arrangement, and a full day before Macmillan threatened an "agonizing reappraisal" of British policy in the event agreement was not reached.[44]

It was as though a kind of charade was being acted out—for the benefit of the British public, who were being shown that a strong British prime minister, willing to lay everything on the line, was able to bring about a major change in American policy, that he was able to do battle with and defeat those who sought to get Britain "out of the nuclear business" or thought the U.K. was played out as a world power and could be treated as an American satellite; for the benefit of the Royal Air Force and its supporters who might have resented a simple, behind-the-scenes deal to substitute Polaris for Skybolt without any fuss; and for the benefit of people like George Ball, Henry Owen, and the whole MLF clique in the State Department and elsewhere, who could be told that it was the intensity of British feeling and the need to save America's relationship with her only remaining friend among the major European countries that had made the change of course necessary.[45]

[41] Rubel transcript of McNamara-Thorneycroft meeting, December 11, 1962, pp. 5–9, Neustadt Papers/19/Skybolt-Nassau (classified) (2)/JFKL.

[42] Neustadt, "Skybolt and Nassau," p. 68.

[43] David Nunnerley, *President Kennedy and Britain* (New York: St. Martin's, 1972), p. 148.

[44] Anglo-American meetings, December 19 and 20, 1962, FRUS 1961–63, 13:1095–1100, 1112 (for the "agonizing reappraisal" threat). It is worth noting that shortly after Kennedy had stated that "of course, in extremes they could be taken out" (p. 1095), Ball, as though deaf to what the president had just said, said point blank that "the right of withdrawal would not be envisaged" (p. 1096). The part of Macmillan's plea deleted from this account (p. 1100) is available in Neustadt, "Skybolt and Nassau," p. 90.

[45] For the point that the Nassau encounter was being stage-managed, see especially Bundy to Kennedy of December 18. Bundy reported the conclusions a number of top U.S. officials had reached about what should go on at the first Kennedy-Macmillan talk: "We assume that you will want to let him [Macmillan] give his full speech on Skybolt, and we assume it may be quite fervent." Ball Papers, box 154, ML.

In reality, a basic and far-reaching shift in American policy had taken place. This, certainly, was how McNamara understood the Skybolt/Nassau episode. As he pointed out soon after returning to Washington from the Bahamas, the Skybolt affair had made it possible to "cast off the old program and to begin the new."[46] Indeed, he thought that "if 'Skybolt' hadn't happened, it should have been invented to get us set on this new track of viable policy."[47] The line laid out in the April 1961 policy directive was bankrupt; he had in fact thought for some time that the MLF made no military and little political sense—and he made a point of saying so to both the British and the Germans at a time when the U.S. government was officially still pressing for that project.[48]

Kennedy saw things much the same way. He was certainly well aware of the fact that far more was at stake in the Skybolt affair than the Anglo-American "special relationship" or Macmillan's political position in Britain. It was the whole policy laid out in the Acheson report that was on the line. Given Kennedy's prior involvement in these fundamental issues, especially the key role he had played in deciding the issue when that policy had been challenged in the spring of 1962, there was no way he could not have understood this. Under Secretary of State George Ball, the highest-ranking champion of the April 1961 line, had spelled out for Kennedy what the real issue was at a White House meeting held a few days before U.S. leaders were scheduled to fly off to the Bahamas. At this December 16 meeting, when McNamara called for selling Polaris to the British as a straight substitute for Skybolt, Ball "expressed his grave concern." He pointed out that "any arrangement which appeared to give the British a national capability in this field would lead us at once to the question of what we would do to the French, and so, inexorably, to the question of the role of the Germans. A decision in favor of a national force in this range of weapons would change our entire policy and would represent a major political decision." He told the president "that this might be the biggest decision he was called upon to make." But Kennedy was dismissive: "That we get every week, George."[49]

Kennedy did not, however, want to set policy by simple presidential fiat—that is, to make it clear that he was shifting course and that dissidents in the State Department and elsewhere would either have to follow his lead or resign. He preferred to take a more indirect approach. The "true believers" in the State Depart-

[46] Secretary of Defense Staff Meeting, January 7, 1963, p. 5, CJCS Taylor/23/Secretary of Defense Staff Meetings, RG 218, USNA.

[47] Neustadt, "Skybolt and Nassau," pp. 2, 100, 114.

[48] Thorneycroft, for example, said that McNamara had told him that the MLF had no military utility; Rusk meeting with Home and Thorneycroft, May 23, 1963, FRUS 1961–63, 13:580. This rings true, given what McNamara told German Defense Minister von Hassel on February 26, 1963. In that meeting, McNamara developed the argument against the MLF: "In arguing against it, he would raise three questions. The first was how can one say there is a military purpose for the MLF? The U.S. has said it is providing enough nuclear power to take care of the Soviet target system. It is trebling its alert forces between '63 and '68. The second question would be, since the U.S. is providing this force, at its expense, why should we Germans or we Belgians pay for what the U.S. will pay for anyway? A third question is how does this force fulfill any political purpose? The U.S. will still have a veto over its use." McNamara–von Hassel meeting of February 26, 1963 (memo dated February 28, 1963), McNamara Papers, 133/Memcons with Germans, RG 200, USNA.

[49] White House meeting, December 16, 1962, FRUS 1961–63, 13:1089–1090.

ment could be kept at arm's length. Important messages revealing American flexibility on all these NATO nuclear issues could be sent through military channels or CIA channels, so that State Department officers would not know what was going on until it was too late to do anything about it.[50] Kennedy might support the State Department line in Rusk's presence, and especially when Rusk's subordinates were in attendance; but he could express his real views when he was talking with the officials (like Bohlen and Harriman) who would be doing the actual negotiating.[51] McNamara even used the very simple technique of lying—for example, about what went on in his December 11 meeting with Thorneycroft. When the British defense minister had asked him whether the U.S. government would state publicly that it would do all it could to help Britain maintain an independent nuclear deterrent, McNamara's answer had been unambiguous: "Yes, I would." But a few days later, at the White House meeting with Ball, he gave a very misleading account of his encounter with Thorneycroft. He noted "the insistent desire of the British to obtain a categorical assurance that the United States was in favor of the independent British nuclear deterrent, and his own refusal to give such an assurance."[52] He obviously had no intention of allowing Ball to see how far he had gone in London. But McNamara was not conducting policy on his own; the position he took was thoroughly in line with what the president wanted.

Kennedy himself fully agreed that this issue had to be dealt with in this indirect way. He thus thought it was important to muddy the waters a bit, by continuing, for example, to use the term "multilateral force." Thus under the Nassau agreement, the British would get American Polaris missiles to be deployed on British submarines and armed with British warheads. This British force would be assigned to NATO and would become part of a "NATO multilateral nuclear force." Since the British force would be under national control and would be available for independent use when the British government decided that "supreme national interests" were at stake, the "multilateral" force in question was not the kind of multilateral force that the State Department had had in mind. But the use of the term was a sort of bone thrown to the MLF clique in the State Department; its continued use would also help obscure the embarrassing fact that the policy the Kennedy administration had been pursuing for almost two years was bankrupt and needed to be abandoned. And vague and somewhat confusing language would also help

---

[50] On the use of military channels, see Neustadt, "Skybolt and Nassau," pp. 21, 55. Note the use of CIA channels for Bundy to Kaysen, June 29, 1963, which advised the two key officials who were to conduct negotiations in Moscow not to take the rigid State Department line too seriously; ibid., 7:751n.

[51] Compare Kennedy's support for Rusk's view that in the Moscow talks the U.S. delegation should not abandon the MLF, with the president's comment to the principal negotiator the next morning that the U.S. should take a more flexible line on this issue. NSC meeting, July 9, 1963, and Kennedy-Harriman meeting, July 10, 1963, FRUS 1961–63, 7:780–781, 790. Note also the way Kennedy dealt directly with Ambassador Bohlen in late December 1962, instructing him to take a line on the French nuclear weapons issue that was considerably more liberal than what the State Department was ready to countenance. Neustadt, "Skybolt and Nassau," pp. 103–107.

[52] Rubel transcript of McNamara-Thorneycroft meeting, December 11, 1962, p. 4, Neustadt Papers/19/Skybolt-Nassau (Classified) (2)/ JFKL; also quoted in Neustadt, "Skybolt and Nassau," p. 65. White House meeting, December 16, 1962, FRUS 1961–63, 13:1088.

Kennedy deal with the problem he knew he would have with the major European allies. The Germans wanted "assignment to NATO" to mean as tight a commitment as possible, to play down the fact that the other major European countries would have forces ultimately under national control, and that Germany was therefore being discriminated against. The British and the French (assuming they too were brought in) would, on the other hand, want the term to be defined as loosely as possible, to underscore their nuclear independence.[53] A certain degree of ambiguity therefore had to be built into the agreement. But Kennedy was quite clear in his own mind about what was going on. As he told Macmillan at Nassau, the two governments had the same objectives, but for "the next few weeks they might be saying different things. The United States had for some years been declaring their opposition to national deterrents and it was difficult to abandon this position."[54]

So although Kennedy was covering his tracks a bit, it is clear that he had decided to break with the policy adopted in April 1961. He was no longer really behind the MLF. McNamara had argued in the December 16 meeting with Ball that the MLF was bankrupt, that "our current position with respect to a multilateral force simply will not work."[55] And after Nassau, McNamara's goal was to move to a system based on British and French national forces: he wanted to make sure that Britain obtained "a Polaris capability as quickly and *economically* as possible," and sought to "bring France up to parity with Britain by 1970," again, "as economically as possible."[56] Kennedy agreed with this basic approach. At his first meeting with Macmillan at Nassau, he laid out his basic thinking. "There was," he said, "more logic in the present arrangements"—that is, forces under ultimate national control—"than in a multilateral force."[57] He told Macmillan that "it might be necessary to abandon the multilateral concept and for the United States and the United Kingdom to make an approach to President de Gaulle to see if France would be prepared to join with their two Governments as joint defenders of Europe"—precisely the sort of arrangement Macmillan had long sought, and which he continued to call for at Nassau.[58]

The point about France is fundamental. It again shows that Kennedy was aware of the broader implications of what he was doing—that he was trying to engineer a fundamental change in American policy, and was not just attempting to deal with a relatively narrow problem in Anglo-American relations. If the British were given Polaris, he understood that the French would be angered—unless they were given Polaris as well. He therefore raised the issue of nuclear aid to France repeatedly at Nassau, and there is no doubt that he favored the idea: "The President said that if

---

[53] See Kennedy's comment in the Anglo-American meeting, December 19, 1962, ibid., pp. 1102–1103.

[54] Anglo-American meeting, December 20, 1962 (12 noon), records of Nassau meeting, p. 34, Prem 11/4229, PRO.

[55] FRUS 1961–63, 13:1089–1090.

[56] Kitchen to Rusk, January 9, 1963, 740.5611/1-963, RG 59, USNA. Emphasis in original.

[57] Anglo-American meeting, December 19, 1962, FRUS 1961–63, 13:1097.

[58] Anglo-American meeting, December 19, 1962, Records of the Nassau Conference, p. 13 (for the quotation), pp. 10–11 (for Macmillan's and Lord Home's general views), Prem 11/4229, PRO. See also Anglo-American meetings, December 19 and 20, 1962, FRUS 1961–63, 13:1095, 1110–1111.

de Gaulle were to ask whether the US was prepared to make the same offer to him as to the UK we should say 'yes.'"[59]

Saying "yes" to Britain meant saying "yes" to France. The standard U.S. view up to that point was that you could not do either of these things because of the effect on Germany. Kennedy was of course quite familiar with that argument, but he had his own answer, very different from the State Department view, but in line with the way the British were thinking. Up to now, he told Macmillan at Nassau, the Americans "had not supported the French in the nuclear field and the result of this policy had been to sour American relations with France. Rightly or wrongly they [the Americans] had taken this attitude because of Germany."[60] To change course now, to offer Polaris to Britain and maybe to France as well, would generate problems, especially with Germany. "Pressure in Germany for similar help would rise," he said. Earlier, the Americans had hoped to finesse the issue. The whole point of the MLF had been to deflect and absorb the pressure for national, and especially German, nuclear forces. But that policy had not been successful. The issue perhaps needed to be dealt with directly. "It might be possible to overcome these pressures," the president said, "and it might be necessary to face them."[61]

This was a very important remark. It meant that Kennedy was now ready in principle to draw the line after France. The three western powers would come together as "joint defenders of Europe," but Germany would not be admitted into that charmed circle. If the Federal Republic objected, the president was now willing to face that problem head on: if the Germans wanted American protection, they would have to accept a non-nuclear status, even if Britain and France had nuclear forces under their own control. In this new concept, the three western powers, Britain, France, and the United States, would be acting as a bloc; faced with that unified front, Germany would have little choice but to fall into line. But if this policy was to be implemented, it was important now to rebuild bridges with de Gaulle, and the key to bringing him back on board was a far-reaching liberalization of American policy on nuclear assistance to France. The president had made his views on this point quite clear at Nassau. He had repeatedly raised the issue of what would have to be done with France. It was obvious that he thought France would have to be helped—not unconditionally, but only as part of a general understanding on basic political and military issues. This meant that the French would have to be told that the door was now open, that nuclear assistance was now possible, but that fundamental and far-reaching negotiations were now necessary.[62]

Kennedy saw the French ambassador, Hervé Alphand, in Palm Beach right after Christmas. The British ambassador, Kennedy's friend David Ormsby Gore, remembers Alphand emerging from his meeting with the president "like a 'cock-of-the-walk.'" "He could smell warheads at the end of the road"—maybe British war-

[59] Anglo-American meetings, December 19 and 20, 1962, FRUS 1961–63, 13:1096, 1098, 1111 (for the quotation).

[60] Anglo-American meeting, December 19, 1962, Records of Nassau conference, p. 9, Prem 11/4229, PRO.

[61] Ibid., p. 10.

[62] See Neustadt, "Skybolt and Nassau," esp. pp. 100, 103–104; Soutou, *L'Alliance incertaine,* pp. 236–237.

heads, Gore went on, "which would have been all right" from the British point of view.[63] And indeed Macmillan, now that he had in effect received America's blessing, felt free at this point to move ahead with a policy of nuclear cooperation with France as part of his general policy of taking Britain into Europe. There would be talks with France on the issue. The French were to be asked what nuclear assistance from Britain "would in fact be helpful to them."[64] Kennedy, for his part, explained the new thinking in person to Charles Bohlen, now ambassador to France. According to Bohlen's formal instructions from Rusk, nuclear assistance to France would depend on de Gaulle's acceptance of the "multilateral principle." But Bohlen knew what Kennedy wanted, and when he met with de Gaulle on January 4, he took the presidential and not the State Department line. He made it clear that the door was open, that American policy had undergone a "major shift," that Nassau was just a beginning, that the U.S. government was now "prepared to discuss any aspect of the atomic question." Under the Nassau agreement, of course, the British Polaris force was to be part of a NATO multilateral force, but the "multilateral principle" had no precise meaning and exactly how it would be applied, Bohlen told the French leader, "was a matter for further discussion."[65]

De Gaulle seemed interested. Perhaps a bilateral arrangement with the Americans, perhaps a deal involving the British as well, could somehow be worked out. He certainly very much wanted nuclear assistance from the United States. But France needed to remain independent; the weapons had to remain under French control. De Gaulle therefore needed to find out what the U.S. government meant when it referred to the "multilateral principle." Were the Americans still pushing their old idea of a mixed-manned force that would make independent use on a national basis impossible, or had they really abandoned that policy, and were they now willing to accept as "multilateral" some sort of knitting together of national forces within the NATO framework—arrangements for consultation on use, for coordinated planning and targeting, and so on? If American policy had really changed, and "multilateral" now meant simply "multinational," then maybe something could be worked out.

THE CLIMAX OF THE NATO CRISIS

For Kennedy and McNamara at Nassau, "multilateral" did in fact mean "multinational." In their view, a system of national forces assigned to NATO qualified as "multilateral," and this was obvious even from the text of the Nassau agreement.

---

[63] Neustadt, "Skybolt and Nassau," p. 103.

[64] De Zulueta to Macmillan, January 9, 1963 (and enclosure), Prem 11/4148, PRO.

[65] Rusk to Bohlen, January 1, 1963, and Bohlen to Kennedy and Rusk, January 4, 1963, FRUS 1961–63, 13:743, 745–747; Neustadt, "Skybolt and Nassau," p. 105. Note also Kennedy's later references to this episode. On January 31, 1963, he "recalled that a sizeable part of the Nassau arrangements was designed to please the French"; in a meeting with Couve de Murville in May, he referred to the "open door held out to France at the time of the Nassau meeting," and how this could have led to real "cooperation in the nuclear field." NSC Executive Committee meeting No. 39, January 31, 1963, and Kennedy-Couve meeting, May 25, 1963, FRUS 1961–63, 13:160, 772. See also Soutou, L'alliance incertaine, pp. 236–237.

But the MLF lobby in Washington refused to accept the hijacking of the concept. Indeed, these officials refused to accept the legitimacy of what the president had done at Nassau. For people like Henry Owen, missile help for France and Britain was simply not an option; the mixed-manned multilateral force still had to be the fundamental goal of American policy. And although they considered Nassau a disaster, their basic tactic was to pretend that the Nassau agreement had changed nothing of substance—that Kennedy could not possibly have meant to alter fundamental policy in such an offhand way, that he must have gotten carried away by immediate concerns, that American policy needed to be saved from such impetuous actions. The use of the term "multilateral" in that agreement gave these people the opening they needed, and although they knew better, they now claimed that the United States still supported the "multilateral concept" as they interpreted it.[66]

George Ball, the highest-ranking official in the MLF group, now set out to undo the damage the president had supposedly done at Nassau. Ball initially supported the idea of talks with the French, but for purely tactical reasons. In his view (as Neustadt paraphrased it), a negotiation with the French "might entangle them in such a way as to assure complaisance toward the British at the coming round of talks on EEC." "But once the British had got into 'Europe,'" Ball thought, "we should modify that formula as fast as possible, and work our way back to the safe ground of a 'truly' multilateral solution—MLF." On reflection, however, he evidently considered this tactic too risky, and decided that the MLF and the "attack on national forces" could not be abandoned, even momentarily. In early January, he flew to Europe and told Adenauer and Couve, in separate meetings, that "the whole emphasis of Nassau's multilateral arrangements was on the mixed-manned force." Couve was surprised. The president had opened the door, but now Ball was slamming it shut. De Gaulle would obviously have no interest in the arrangement as Ball described it.[67]

Ball had effectively sabotaged the president's policy.[68] As far as de Gaulle was

---

[66] See Neustadt, "Skybolt and Nassau," pp. 93, 106.

[67] Neustadt, "Skybolt and Nassau," pp. 101, 107.

[68] This was Bohlen's view. See Neustadt, "Skybolt and Nassau," p. 107; Bohlen to State Department, January 24, 1963, and Bohlen to Bundy, March 2, 1963, FRUS 1961–63, 13:753–754, 765; Bohlen to State Department, February 2, 1963, enclosing memorandum of Bohlen-Malraux meeting, January 23, 1963, DOSCF for 1963, POL France-US, RG 59, USNA. Note also Kissinger-Stehlin meeting, May 25, 1963, DDRS 1996/1999; General Stehlin also thought that Ball's visit had played a decisive role in January. There is, however, a certain amount of evidence to the effect that what Ball did was not crucial—that de Gaulle had made his mind up even before the Nassau conference to veto Britain's admission to the Common Market at his January 14 press conference, that he never varied from this course, and that he was not for a moment interested in anything the Americans were proposing. See especially the notes Alain Peyrefitte took of his meetings with de Gaulle; Peyrefitte, *C'était de Gaulle*, pp. 334–350. But this evidence is not necessarily to be taken at face value, since the image of de Gaulle that comes across in the Peyrefitte notes is more extreme and more hardline than the image that emerges from the documents. Compare, for example, de Gaulle's account of what he told Bohlen ibid., pp. 354–355, with Bohlen's account in FRUS 1961–63, 13:745–748, and in Neustadt, "Skybolt and Nassau," p. 105. Note also Malraux's comment, in the January 23 meeting with Bohlen cited above, that when he saw de Gaulle on January 7, the general had told him that he wanted to keep the door open

concerned, the carrot had been dangled and was now being yanked away. It is not hard to imagine his reaction. Did the Americans even know what they were doing? Was he dealing with a government that actually had a policy, in any real sense of the term? How could the Europeans put their fate so totally in the hands of such people? This, of course, was not a view that had emerged overnight. De Gaulle had spent many years taking his measure of America, and his experience with Eisenhower on the tripartism issue in 1959–60 undoubtedly played a certain role in shaping his opinion.[69] But this was the final straw. He had now had it with the United States, and on January 14, 1963, he rose up in open revolt.

On that day, the French president announced at a memorable press conference that France was vetoing Britain's admission to the Common Market. The move was aimed as much at America as at Britain. De Gaulle wanted to create a "European Europe" with a policy of its own, a Europe that was something more than an American protectorate. To let Britain in would prevent that kind of Europe from coming into being. If Britain were admitted, the whole nature of the EEC would be utterly transformed. The continental countries, he declared, would eventually be absorbed into a "colossal Atlantic community dependent on America and under American control," and this France would not permit.[70]

Indeed, in de Gaulle's view, the Americans had wanted to prevent the kind of Europe the six continental countries had been trying to create from ever taking shape, and this was why they were now such fervent supporters of British entry into the Common Market. Britain was an American "satellite," "stuffed" with American nuclear weapons, but incapable of using them independently. If admitted into Europe, Britain would be a kind of Trojan horse, an instrument through which America could prevent a unified Europe from acting independently. The British had shown their true colors. The nuclear issue was the ultimate test of how "European" they were. They could have joined with France in revolt against the American policy of getting the European nations "out of the nuclear business," a policy which if successful would have made Europe utterly dependent on America. British Gaullists like Thorneycroft had in fact been attracted to the idea of joining hands with France in the nuclear area, defying America, and building Europe on the basis of a new Anglo-French entente; indeed, some Americans had wanted to slam the door on the British during the Skybolt affair—that is, to give them nothing as a substitute—in order to push them in that direction. But Macmillan had refused to take the anti-American road. The "special relationship" with the United States still lay at the heart of British policy.[71]

for talks with the Americans. My basic assumption, in sorting out this conflicting evidence, is that de Gaulle would not have slammed the door on the Anglo-Saxons if he had thought there was a chance that something real was being offered—and given what Alphand was reporting, as well as what de Gaulle himself was able to learn from his meeting with Bohlen, there was no way it could not have been clear to him that there might be some substance in what Kennedy was now proposing. See Soutou, *L'alliance incertaine,* pp. 235–237. In other words, only a fool would have been as dismissive of the American offer as Peyrefitte portrays de Gaulle as being, and de Gaulle, whatever his faults, was no fool.

[69] See above, pp. 242–244.

[70] January 14, 1963, press conference, in de Gaulle, *Discours et messages,* 4:69.

[71] De Gaulle, *Mémoires d'espoir: Le renouveau,* p. 182; Alphand, *L'étonnement d'être,* p. 343; Blanken-

Did this mean, however, that an Anglo-French arrangement was entirely out of the question? It seemed for a few days after Nassau that the issue might not have to be so sharply drawn, that the British might be able to share their nuclear know-how with France with America's blessing, that Britain might not have to choose between the United States and Europe, and that France therefore could work out some kind of arrangement with the "Anglo-Saxons." But after Ball's visit, it was quite clear to de Gaulle that this had been a mirage. At Nassau, as he now saw it, the British had accepted the MLF in its original form—that is, they had agreed to place their nuclear force under effective American control. That meant that Britain really was an American satellite, and thus had no place in the kind of Europe de Gaulle intended to build.[72]

The Kennedy administration wanted Britain to join the EEC. In purely economic terms, Kennedy believed that America would have to pay a certain price if Britain went in; by definition, the members of a customs union discriminate in favor of each other and thus against all outsiders. But the political benefits would, in the American view, greatly outweigh the economic disadvantages.[73] Britain would be able to help "steer" Europe in the right direction. (This, of course, was the Trojan horse argument in reverse.) A Europe that included the U.K. would be less parochial, more open, more "Atlantic," and friendlier toward the United States than one built on a Franco-German axis.[74] But now de Gaulle was saying that Europe could not include Britain, that Europe had to be independent of America, and therefore had to be constructed on a purely continental basis.

American leaders were livid. Kennedy had tried to mend fences with France. In fact, as he himself pointed out, "a sizeable part of the Nassau arrangement was designed to please the French."[75] And now, without the slightest attempt to engage the Americans in a dialogue, there was this sudden, unexpected slap in the face. The assumption was that de Gaulle's anti-Americanism was so deep-seated that with him evidently anything was possible. De Gaulle might be acting in accordance with a long-term, step-by-step plan; he might soon try to organize the six continental countries in the EEC into a grouping with its own nuclear force; Kennedy thought he might even be "trying to run us out of Europe by means of a deal with the Russians."[76]

The great question now was whether the Germans would go along with de Gaulle. Adenauer seemed to be throwing in his lot with the French leader more clearly than ever before. He agreed with de Gaulle that Britain was to be kept out of the Common Market, and the U.S. government was quite aware of his views on

---

horn memorandum, February 15, 1963, p. 320, AAPBD 1963, 1:320; Peyrefitte, *C'était de Gaulle,* passim, esp. pp. 282, 346, 348, 350, 374. Sulzberger-Pompidou conversation, February 1, 1963, in Sulzberger, *Last of the Giants,* p. 959.

[72] De Gaulle-Adenauer talks, January 21–22, 1963, AAPBD 1963, 1:116, 141–143.

[73] Kennedy to Macmillan, May 23, 1961, Kennedy to Ball, August 21, 1961, Anglo-American meeting, April 28, 1962, FRUS 1961–63, 13:20, 32, 85.

[74] Note for Macmillan on a conversation with Kennedy, April 6, 1961, Prem 11/3311, PRO.

[75] NSC Executive Committee meeting no. 39, January 31, 1963, FRUS 1961–63, 13:160.

[76] NSC Executive Committee meetings nos. 38 and 39, January 25 and 31, 1963, ibid., pp. 158, 160, 487. On February 14, Kennedy asked Bohlen whether de Gaulle was "planning a systematic campaign to reduce American influence and presence on the continent." Ibid., p. 758 n.

the subject.[77] And just eight days after de Gaulle's January 14 press conference, Adenauer came to Paris to sign a treaty of friendship with France, an event the chancellor viewed as his crowning achievement.[78] It seemed that a Franco-German entente, an alignment with a distinct anti-American coloration, was on the verge of taking shape.

The Americans, already angered by de Gaulle's veto of British admission into the Common Market, were enraged by the Franco-German treaty.[79] The political meaning of the treaty, especially coming when it did, was clear enough. Adenauer was falling in with the Gaullist policy of creating a strong continental bloc, independent of America and able to chart its own course in world affairs. That general goal implied that the continental countries would develop a nuclear force of their own, since there could be no political independence in the nuclear age without such a force. That in turn implied that France and Germany would collaborate in this area, and thus that the Federal Republic would be able to acquire a nuclear force under her own control.

French officials often denied that France would ever help Germany build a nuclear force. But they sometimes qualified this by pointing out that unless the United States cooperated with France in the nuclear area, the French might be forced to work together with the Germans.[80] The Americans took this possibility quite seriously, and indeed in the spring 1962 nuclear sharing debate, one of the strongest arguments for nuclear assistance to France was that unless the U.S. government liberalized its policy, the French would end up cooperating with Germany on a joint program, whereas U.S. help for France could be made conditional on a French promise not to cooperate with the Federal Republic.[81]

These arguments in turn had been inspired by indications in February 1962 that France and Germany were about to begin working together in this area. Throughout 1962 there were signs that a joint Franco-German nuclear program, or a program undertaken by the six EEC countries, had by no means been ruled out. There was a good deal of talk about the possibility of a European nuclear force under the

---

[77] Schwarz, *Adenauer,* 2:753, 825; Ball to Kennedy, November 15, 1962, and Kennedy-Spaak meeting, May 28, 1963, FRUS 1961–63, 13:123, 586.

[78] Schwarz, *Adenauer,* 2:822. On the origins of the treaty, see Jacques Bariéty, "De Gaulle, Adenauer, et la genèse du traité de l'Elysée du 22 janvier 1963," and Hans-Peter Schwarz, "Le président de Gaulle, le chancelier fédéral Adenauer et la genèse du traité de l'Elysée," both in Institut Charles de Gaulle, *De Gaulle et son siècle,* vol. 5 (Paris: Plon, 1992), pp. 352–373.

[79] See Knappstein to Schröder, January 23, 1963, AAPBD 1963, 1:163–164; NSC Executive Committee meetings nos. 38 and 39, January 25 and 31, 1963, FRUS 1961–63, 13:156–163, 487–491.

[80] In January 1962, for example, the French diplomat François de Rose, who specialized in nuclear issues, told Norstad that if the United States did not help France with her nuclear program, the French might "have to assist proliferation." When Norstad asked him if that meant France would help the Germans attain a nuclear capability, de Rose was evasive. Stoessel to Rusk, January 12, 1962, 611.51/1-1262, RG 59, USNA. Over the next few months, de Rose's warnings became more explicit. In May he told a British official that if it turned out that France was unable "for economical and technological reasons" to build a nuclear force on her own, she might have to turn to Germany—a course of action which he considered "highly dangerous." This British official inferred from that that the matter was obviously being discussed. Zuckerman memo, "Anglo/French Co-operation," May 25, 1962, Prem 11/3712, PRO.

[81] See above, pp. 305–307.

Figure 11. *Top:* De Gaulle at his January 14, 1963, press conference (Hulton Getty). *Bottom:* De Gaulle and Adenauer embrace eight days later following the signing of the Franco-German treaty (Archive Photos). The juxtaposition of these two images made a profound impression on American opinion.

control of the Six, about Europe needing to become a strategic and not just an economic entity, and about the importance of France and Germany coming together to form a political and military unit.[82] De Gaulle himself, in a speech he gave in Hamburg on September 7, called for a policy of "organic cooperation" between the two countries on defense issues.[83] It was not perfectly clear what he had in mind, but at the end of the year U.S. officials had learned from Blankenhorn that the German government "had offered to bear some of the cost" of developing the French nuclear force, and Bundy, in January 1963, referred to "secret French feelers for nuclear cooperation" with Germany.[84]

By this time de Gaulle was coming to talk about a German nuclear capability as "inevitable" in the long run.[85] Germany, he declared at his January 14 press conference, had the same right as any other country to decide whether to have a nuclear force.[86] And when he met with Adenauer on January 21, he made it clear that in his view Germany would sooner or later build such a force, that he sympathized with German nuclear aspirations, that he knew that this development would have far-reaching consequences, but that France would do nothing to prevent Germany from developing a nuclear capability.[87]

The U.S. government probably had no way of knowing what de Gaulle had told Adenauer, but the meaning of the Franco-German treaty seemed clear enough. Perhaps the two countries would begin working together in the nuclear area.

[82] See Soutou, *L'alliance incertaine*, p. 250; Gavin to Rusk, August 1, 1962, 740.5611/8-162, and Nitze-Norstad meeting, April 4, 1962, 711.5611/4-462, both RG 59, USNA; and Sulzberger, *Last of the Giants*, p. 913. When pressed to explain what all this talk meant, French leaders were often evasive. See, for example, the exchange between Raymond Aron and former Prime Minister Michel Debré, in Raymond Aron, *Les articles du Figaro*, ed. Georges-Henri Soutou, vol. 2: *La coexistence, 1955–1965* (Paris: Fallois, 1993), p. 1268, and Aron's comment on Debré's remarks, p. 1280.

[83] De Gaulle, *Discours et messages*, 4:13.

[84] Dowling to Rusk, December 10, 1962, 751.5611/12-1062, RG 59, USNA; Bundy memo for Kennedy, "The U.S. and de Gaulle—The Past and the Future," p. 8, POF/116/JFKL. For Adenauer at this point, this was at the very least an open question. See Schwarz, *Adenauer*, 2:819. The Americans, above all Kennedy himself, remained very interested in what was going on in this area, especially in May and June 1963. The U.S. government learned from German officials that "discussions concerning German financial participation" in the Pierrelatte gaseous diffusion plant had been held at French initiative; Pierrelatte was the "principal producer of weapons grade enriched uranium for the French nuclear weapons program." Kaplan to Foley, June 12, 1963 (for the quotations), and Kaufman memorandum, "Pierrelatte Gaseous Diffusion Plant," May 29, 1963 (for the president's interest), both in Bureau of European Affairs, Office of Atlantic Political and Economic Affairs, records relating to atomic energy [MLR 3104], box 2, France, RG 59, USNA, a file containing a number of other documents bearing on this issue. For these matters in general, see also DOSCF for 1963, POL 4 France–West Germany and DEF 4 France–West Germany, especially Tyler to Rusk, May 27 and May 29, 1963. General Stehlin, the head of the French Air Force, told Kissinger in May that in November 1962 he had "sounded out his friend General Speidel" about the possibility of a "Franco-German nuclear effort," but that de Gaulle had then given strict orders "that there was to be no collaboration with Germany in the nuclear field." Kissinger-Stehlin meeting, May 25, 1963, p. 4, DDRS 1996/1999.

[85] Bohlen–de Gaulle meeting, January 4, 1963, FRUS 1961–63, 13:745; Sulzberger, *Last of the Giants*, p. 961. De Gaulle made the same point to Rusk a few months later; these remarks were in line with what he had told Adenauer in July 1960. See Rusk–de Gaulle meeting, April 8, 1963, NSF/72/France-General/JFKL; Schwarz, *Adenauer*, 2:566.

[86] De Gaulle, *Discours et messages*, 4:78.

[87] De Gaulle–Adenauer meeting, January 21, 1963, AAPBD 1963, 1:117–118.

Something of that sort seemed quite possible, and to Kennedy this prospect underscored the seriousness of what was now going on.[88]

And the president was not going to just sit back and take it. The Franco-German treaty was aimed at the United States, he said, and if the Europeans were no longer interested in working with America, the time had come for a fundamental reappraisal of American policy. The United States had to take a "cold, hard attitude." If the Europeans wanted to go their own way, it had to be made clear that the United States could also turn away from them. The Americans, after all, could "take care of ourselves" and were "not dependent on European support." America, he said, should begin to think now about how to use her "existing position to put pressure on the Europeans if the situation so demands." De Gaulle might be about to propose "a European defense system in which we would have no part." The United States would have to be prepared to fight back: "we should get ready with actions to squeeze Europe." The U.S. government had to be ready to reduce its commitment to Europe, and especially to scale back on its troop presence there. If the Europeans were "getting ready to throw us out of Europe," he said, "we want to be in a position to march out." The "threat of withdrawal" in his view was in fact "about the only sanction we had."[89]

This was no mere fit of pique. These feelings had, in fact, been building up for some time. In May 1962, for example, during an earlier quarrel with de Gaulle and Adenauer, Kennedy had cabled the ambassador in Paris that "if Europe were ever to be organized so as to leave us outside, from the point of view of these great issues of policy and defense, it would become most difficult for us to sustain our present guarantee against Soviet aggression. We shall not hesitate to make this point to the Germans if they show signs of accepting any idea of a Bonn-Paris axis."[90]

The Americans thus understood that their efforts needed to focus on Germany. There was "not much we can do about France," Kennedy said in January 1963, "but we can exert considerable pressure on the Germans." (One look at the map and one could see why.) The Germans had to be told that "they can't have it both ways." They had to choose between France and America. If they chose to align themselves with de Gaulle and if they backed the policy of an independent Europe, they could not count on the United States to defend them. If they wanted American protection, they would have to follow the American lead on political and nuclear questions.[91]

So a line was being drawn in the sand. The Americans did not disguise their anger over the Franco-German treaty, and made it clear to the Germans that if they ratified the treaty in its present form, they would be putting their relations with the United States at risk. "Unless we make clear our opposition to the Franco-

---

[88] See, for example, NSC Executive Committee meeting no. 39, January 31, 1963, FRUS 1961–63, 13:157.

[89] NSC Executive Committee meetings nos. 38, 39 and 40, January 25, January 31, and February 5, 1963, ibid., pp. 156, 162–163, 178, 488–490.

[90] Kennedy to Gavin, May 18, 1962, ibid., p. 704.

[91] NSC Executive Committee meetings nos. 38 and 39, January 25 and 31, 1963, ibid., pp. 163, 489.

German treaty," Kennedy said, "we would not be able to make clear to the Germans that they faced a choice between working with the French or working with us." The ambassador to West Germany then outlined how this could be done. The Germans should be kept "nervous about our relations with them," "uncertain as to how we would react" if they did not do what the Americans wanted. Vice Chancellor Ludwig Erhard should be "discreetly" encouraged to insist that the treaty could only be ratified with reservations that would reflect the Federal Republic's continuing loyalty to America and to NATO.[92]

This in fact was the policy which the U.S. government now followed. In a multitude of ways, the Germans were made to feel American displeasure and made to understand that they had to make a choice. The campaign began even before the Franco-German treaty was signed. On January 21, the well-known columnist James Reston published a widely noted article in the *New York Times,* which obviously reflected the way U.S. leaders were now thinking. What kind of people, Reston asked, do they think we are? How could de Gaulle and Adenauer possibly think that America would defend them while they pursued an anti-American policy? "If they are asking us," he said, "to defend a Europe which questions American good faith; to cooperate in the spread of national nuclear weapons first to France and inevitably, on de Gaulle's thesis, to Germany; if they expect that we will cooperate with a Gaullist Europe that rejects and humiliates Britain and is contemptuous of all 'maritime powers'; if they believe we will cooperate with a protectionist, inward-looking Europe which puts the continent before the Atlantic— then they are asking and expecting things that have never been and never will be." Adenauer in particular had to choose not just between the Common Market as it was and a wider community that included Britain. He had to choose "in the end between France and the United States."

The Germans were left in no doubt whatsoever about how American leaders felt. Kennedy was angry, Rusk told the German ambassador. "We have to know where you stand." He pointed out that given Germany's geographical position, it was absurd to think she could choose France with her fifty atomic bombs over America with her fifty thousand [sic] nuclear weapons. Clay warned that if the treaty were ratified unchanged, it would mean "the end of Berlin." Acheson's reaction was the sharpest of all. He decided "not to mince words with the ambassador." The German argument that the treaty was simply aimed at promoting Franco-German reconciliation, and did not have anything like the meaning the Americans read into it, was, Acheson said, "an insult to my intelligence." The German government was not run by fools. They certainly knew exactly what they were doing.[93]

U.S. representatives made it quite clear that the kind of anti-American policy de

[92] NSC Executive Committee meeting no. 40, February 5, 1963, ibid., pp. 175–176. See also Dean Acheson, "Reflections on the January Debacle," January 31, 1963, esp. pp. 3–5, NSF/316/Ex Comm Meetings 38–42/JFKL.

[93] Knappstein to Schröder, January 23, 28, and 30, 1963; Adenauer-Dowling meeting, January 24, 1963; Knappstein to Bonn Foreign Office, January 28, 1963; Carstens memo, February 9, 1963; AAPBD 1963, vol. 1, documents 49, 50, 52, 58, 65 and 88. Kennedy to Adenauer, February 1, 1963, FRUS 1961–63, 13:164. Acheson-Knappstein meeting, January 30, 1963, AP/SDWHA/HSTL (NLT 92–13). The basic story was clear enough at the time. See, for example, d'Harcourt, *L'Allemagne d'Adenauer à Erhard,* pp. 173, 176, 179.

Gaulle and now Adenauer had embraced would, if unchanged, lead the American people to turn against Europe and end the U.S. military presence there. The ingratitude of the Europeans was galling. Given all the United States had done for western Europe since 1945, the "hostility of certain European leaders," Adenauer was warned, was bound to cause deep resentment in Congress and in the public and would lead many Americans to feel that a more isolationist policy was in order.[94] Other American leaders argued along similar lines. The danger of the de Gaulle press conference, Rusk told Brentano in March, was that the American people might get the idea that the "American connection" was no longer wanted in Europe, and this "would make it impossible" to keep U.S. troops there.[95] If Europe was to be independent, he told the allied leaders at Ottawa in May, then "the United States would be independent too."[96] The message was that the Europeans, and above all the Germans, had to choose between independence and cooperation with America.[97]

If they chose cooperation, moreover, it would have to be on American terms. The Americans had made it clear, even in 1962, that they intended to lead Europe, but the two major events of January 1963, the de Gaulle veto and the Franco-German treaty, led to an even more assertive American policy.[98] The time had come for the United States to play hardball with the Europeans. "We have been very generous to Europe," the president told the NSC on January 22, the very day the Franco-German treaty was signed, "and it is now time for us to look out for ourselves, knowing full well that the Europeans will not do anything for us simply because we have in the past helped them."[99] Top American officials made it clear that they intended to take the lead and that Europe, and especially Germany, would have to follow. In particular, if Soviet policy softened to the point where there was a real chance of a general settlement, the United States would not be held back by the allies. As Bundy told Sulzberger in June, "if we thought we could get a major settlement, we would not be deterred from bilateral discussions with Rus-

[94] Kennedy to Adenauer, February 1, 1963, FRUS 1961–63, 13:164; Krone diary, January 25, 1963, *Adenauer-Studien* 3:173; Schwarz, *Adenauer,* 2:823.

[95] Rusk-Brentano meeting, March 22, 1963, FRUS 1961–63, 13:191.

[96] Anglo-American meetings, June 27–30, 1963, pp. 9, 10, Prem 11/4586, PRO. This was a common theme in Rusk's meetings with foreign leaders. See, for example, Rusk-Schröder meeting, September 20, 1963, AAPBD 1963, 2:1165.

[97] See also Gilpatric-Adenauer meeting, February 13, 1963, AAPBD 1963, 1:303, 307.

[98] On October 2, 1962, Bundy had told Adenauer that none of the three major European allies would lead Europe, but that Europe would instead by led by America; the chancellor was quite irritated by their remark. Osterheld, *Adenauers letzte Kanzlerjahre,* pp. 147–148; Adenauer–de Margerie meeting, June 11, 1963, AAPBD 1963, 2:621; Hermann Kusterer, *Der Kanzler und der General* (Stuttgart: Neske, 1995), p. 293. This new American attitude was clear even to the public at the time. See especially Sulzberger's columns in the *New York Times,* October 20–24, 1962. Kennedy's remarks to the press in a background interview after the Nassau conference were taken as indicating a hardening of the American attitude in this area. See Partial Transcript of a Background Press Interview at Palm Beach, December 31, 1962, PPP Kennedy, 1962:915, and the report this gave rise to in *Le Monde* of January 3, 1963, "President Kennedy Has Decided to Direct the Western Alliance without Bothering Himself Too Much with Possible Objections of His Allies," cited in Newhouse, *De Gaulle and the Anglo-Saxons,* pp. 229–230.

[99] NSC meeting, January 22, 1963, FRUS 1961–63, 13:486.

sia. We would not make allied representation a precondition to such talks." This, Sulzberger noted, was "a *most* important statement."[100]

The new tough line led to a major American intervention in internal German politics. Key political figures in Germany were urged to oppose Adenauer's foreign policy, and to insist that the treaty with France not be ratified without reservations or changes. In accordance with Ambassador Dowling's suggestion, Erhard was encouraged to act by American and British officials, and on February 5 he openly attacked the Adenauer policy. The SPD also asked the Americans for advice about the line they should take on the treaty.[101] The issue became tied up with the question of how long Adenauer would continue in office and who would succeed him as chancellor. Germany was now divided into two camps, the German Gaullists headed by Adenauer and the Atlanticists headed by Erhard. The Atlanticists were clearly in the majority, even within Adenauer's own party. Forced to choose, the Germans chose America—and that meant following the American line in return for American protection. The Franco-German treaty was ratified, but only after it had been altered by the Bundestag. Mere reservations would no longer suffice. Instead, a new preamble was added unilaterally, affirming the Federal Republic's continuing loyalty to NATO. And Adenauer was removed from office—in effect (as he himself said) dismissed by his own party. The key decisions were made by the CDU in April, and Erhard replaced him as chancellor six months later.[102]

Adenauer had grossly misjudged the whole political situation. In the early years of the Federal Republic, he had benefited enormously from allied anxieties about Germany. He had been the indispensable man. If he ever lost power in Bonn, who could tell how German policy would evolve? For the western powers, the goal was to make sure that Germany would remain more or less voluntarily in their bloc, and it was therefore vital that Adenauer remain at the helm. Adenauer fully agreed with this analysis, and indeed did what he could to make sure that the allies continued thinking along these lines. Only his strong and steady hand, he encouraged them to think, could keep his people from going off in the wrong direction. His policy was under attack from powerful forces within Germany. It would be a disaster, he argued in the early 1950s, if someone like the SPD leader Kurt Schumacher replaced him as chancellor. His ability to master the situation was by no means guaranteed. The allied governments therefore had to do everything they could to support him. They had to give him the concessions he needed to maintain his political position within Germany. And in fact the allies gave him what he needed: Germany's international position was very different in 1955 from what it had been in 1949. To the German electorate, Adenauer had thus accomplished a great deal. He was the man the western powers trusted, the man who had brought Germany into the West and had won for the Federal Republic the protection and

[100] Sulzberger, entry for June 6, 1963, *Last of the Giants,* p. 985. Emphasis his.

[101] Schwarz, *Adenauer* 2:826, 836; Daniel Koerfer, *Kampf ums Kanzleramt: Erhard und Adenauer* (Stuttgart: Deutsche Verlags-Anstalt, 1988), p. 723; "Erhard Challenges Paris Pact after Moving to Oust Adenauer," *New York Times,* February 6, 1963. On the SPD, see Bahr-Hillenbrand-Creel meeting, February 21, 1963, DOSCF for 1963, POL 4 France-West Germany.

[102] Schwarz, *Adenauer,* 2:810–839; Koerfer, *Kampf ums Kanzleramt,* pp. 707–751; d'Harcourt, *L'Allemagne d'Adenauer à Erhard,* pp. 161–194.

support of the western powers—the man who therefore had to be kept in power.

But allied support for Adenauer, as reflected in Dulles's extraordinary intervention in the 1953 German elections, led in the course of the 1950s to a fundamental change in the structure of German politics. The SPD, the main opposition party, came to the conclusion that it could not hope to gain power as long as the allies, and especially the Americans, were so strongly in Adenauer's camp—so long as the CDU/CSU was the party of the western alliance and the SPD was hostile to the NATO system.[103]

These political considerations provided the framework for a fundamental rethinking of SPD policy on alliance and strategic issues. By 1961, when the SPD fought the national elections with Willy Brandt as their chancellor-designate, the party had become perfectly acceptable to the Americans as an alternative to Adenauer. The policy of the Schumacher period was dead and buried. The SPD was now a moderate, pro-western party, committed to NATO and to the American alliance. Adenauer therefore could no longer tell the western countries that if he fell from power they would have to deal with someone like Schumacher. Indeed, from the U.S. point of view, the new SPD was in many ways better than Adenauer. It was pro-NATO, but a good deal more moderate than Adenauer and Strauss on the nuclear issue. It was thus more likely to fall in with the Kennedy policy on NATO and east-west questions. Adenauer was no longer the indispensable man, and among other things this weakened the chancellor's position vis-à-vis the other leaders of his own governing coalition.[104]

In fact, quite apart from the question of his relations with the Americans, Adenauer's hold on the levers of power within Germany was weakening. The sense was growing that the old man had outlived his usefulness—that his policy was stale, out of touch with new political realities. The old "policy of strength" had not brought German reunification any closer. To many, the Berlin Wall symbolized the bankruptcy of the Adenauer policy. When West Berlin was sealed off in August 1961, the chancellor did not seem up to the occasion, and many Germans were put off by his partisan and indeed personal attacks on Brandt at that time. If the policy had failed, if the hard line had gotten Germany nowhere, wasn't the alternative policy worth considering? A policy of détente might eventually lead to something different, perhaps in the very long run to the reunification of the divided country. This was what the Americans had been preaching, even under Dulles.[105] Now Kennedy was going to move ahead, with or without Germany. The Federal Republic had to

[103] The best study in English is Stephen J. Artner, *A Change of Course: The West German Social Democrats and NATO, 1957–1961* (Westport, Conn.: Greenwood Press, 1985); see esp. pp. 165, 167, 174–182.

[104] Adenauer was very bitter about these developments, and his reaction was a measure of the importance of these changes. He considered the shift in the SPD line to be fraudulent; but many people, he felt, had been taken in by it, and this he considered extremely dangerous. He and Strauss were particularly disturbed, especially right before the 1961 elections, by the new American ties with the SPD. Adenauer and Strauss in CDU Bundesvorstand, September 22, 1960, and August 25, 1961, Günter Buchstab, ed., *Adenauer: ". . . um den Frieden zu gewinnen": Die Protokolle des CDU-Bundesvorstands, 1957–1961* (Düsseldorf: Droste, 1994), pp. 850, 1017–1018.

[105] For some examples, see Dulles-Eisenhower meeting, August 11, 1955, FRUS 1955–57, 5:546; Dulles-Grewe-Dittmann meeting, January 14, 1959, Dulles–de Gaulle meeting, February 6, 1959, and

be realistic. She could not afford to alienate her most powerful ally. If Adenauer did not understand all this, then maybe it was time for him to go.[106]

With this sort of thinking on the rise, there was little chance that the Adenauer policy could survive the kind of attack the U.S. government mounted in early 1963. If the Germans had to choose between France and America, that choice was relatively easy to make: the Federal Republic would follow the American lead.

THE NEAR-SETTLEMENT OF 1963

For Kennedy, these events were of fundamental importance, but only half the problem had been solved. The other half had to do with the Soviet Union. As noted above, America's basic policy in this area had not changed: the goal was still the stabilization of the status quo in central Europe. The Soviet Union and the western powers could get along by "recognizing existing facts, of which there are three important elements—the existence of East Germany, West Germany and West Berlin." The U.S. government would accept the status quo in eastern Germany, and indeed in eastern Europe as a whole. The one thing it asked in exchange was that the Soviets, for their part, also respect the status quo, and in particular that the USSR respect western rights in West Berlin. It was "almost a waste of time to go on," Rusk told Gromyko, "if this is not accepted."[107] But if the Soviets accepted the "fact of our presence in West Berlin," just as the Americans accepted "the fact of theirs in East Germany and East Berlin," the two sides, Soviet officials were told, could live together in peace in central Europe.[108]

Thus the policy laid out in the March 1962 "Principles" document was still in effect—and the Soviets were in fact told that this was the case.[109] The American aim, as Rusk explained to Khrushchev, was to bring about "more normal relations," not just between the two Germanies, but also between West Germany and what he now called (having been chided by Khrushchev on this point) the "socialist countries to the east."[110] The United States, moreover, agreed with the USSR

Dulles-Adenauer meeting, February 7, 1959, all in FRUS 1958–60, 8:267, 333, 339. For the use of the argument in late 1962 and 1963, see for example the Rusk-Brandt meeting, September 29, 1962, and the Rusk-Schröder meeting, September 24, 1963, FRUS 1961–63, 15:343, 582.

[106] On these matters in general, see Schwarz, *Adenauer*, 2:660–666, 822–823 (for the views of the chancellor's former right-hand man Blankenhorn), 841 (for the views of foreign minister Schröder). Krone diary, August 18, 1961, *Adenauer-Studien*, 3:162; and d'Harcourt, *L'Allemagne d'Adenauer à Erhard*, pp. 70–71, 211, 217–218. For an interesting American analysis of the internal political situation in Germany and its relation to American policy, see Carl Kaysen, "Thoughts on Berlin," August 22, 1961, esp. pp. 1–2, 6, NSF/82/Kaysen Memo/JFKL. Kaysen noted the important changes that had taken place within Germany since the official American position on the German question had taken shape under Eisenhower; he stressed the major shift that had taken place within the SPD; and all this, he argued, increased America's freedom of action vis-à-vis Germany.

[107] Rusk-Gromyko meeting, August 6, 1963, FRUS 1961–63, 15:561.

[108] Rusk in Rusk-Mikoyan meeting, November 30, 1962, and Kohler in Kohler-Semenov meeting, December 3, 1962, ibid., pp. 451, 456–457.

[109] Rusk-Gromyko meeting, August 6, 1963, ibid., p. 560.

[110] Khrushchev-Rusk meetings, August 5 and 9, 1963, ibid., pp. 553 (for Khrushchev's chiding of Rusk), 567 (for the quotations).

"that the Germans should not have a national nuclear capability."[111] If the two sides were to reach an agreement on the basis of these principles, the German government would not be allowed to block it. U.S. policy was based on America's own vital interests. "The United States," Rusk said in October, was "no monkey on the stick manipulated by West Germany."[112]

The Americans had thus laid out the terms on which they were ready to settle what everyone knew was the central problem of the Cold War, and there was a good deal in that American offer that the USSR found attractive. The German nuclear question, as Soviet officials often pointed out, was the USSR's "number one" problem,[113] and the Americans were apparently still offering what by any reasonable standard was a quite acceptable solution. Even in 1961 and 1962 many high Soviet officials had disliked the Khrushchev policy, and now that it had failed so miserably the grumbling became more intense: Khrushchev should not have embarked upon such a provocative course of action, especially given that the Americans still had the upper hand in strategic terms. Perhaps they even felt that because of his ineptness and amateurishness, he might have squandered a major opportunity to solve the USSR's most important foreign policy problem.[114]

If nothing were done, the situation, from the Soviet point of view, might deteriorate very rapidly. The Germans, for example, might get a nuclear capability of their own, perhaps through the MLF. When the Soviets brought up this issue, which they often did, the standard American reply was that this simply could not happen, that the whole point of the MLF, in fact, was to absorb pressures for nuclear forces under national control. But Soviet leaders were not convinced. As one Soviet diplomat remarked in March, his government was getting "rather tired" of these arguments about how the MLF would satisfy the Germans and thus head off a real German nuclear force. Similar assurances given in the past about limits on German military power had turned out not to be worth much, and he took it for granted that if the Germans participated in the MLF and paid for the weapons, "they would of course in time demand greater control over them."[115] This sort of argument was by no means viewed as unreasonable, even within the U.S. govern-

[111] Rusk-Khrushchev meeting, August 9, 1963, ibid., p. 567.

[112] Rusk-Gromyko meeting, October 2, 1963, pp. 10–12, DOSCF for 1963, POL-GER, RG 59, USNA; Rusk-Mikoyan meeting, November 30, 1962, FRUS 1961–63, 15:452.

[113] Rusk-Dobrynin meeting, August 8, 1962, ibid., 7:546. See also Dobrynin's remarks in a meeting with his German colleague Knappstein, February 17, 1963, and Khrushchev's comments in a meeting with German Ambassador Groepper, March 9, 1963, AAPBD 1963, 1:330, 381–382. Western officials generally recognized that this Soviet concern was very real. Kohler, for example, referred to the prospect of a German nuclear capability as "a very sensitive Soviet nerve"; Kohler to Bruce, February 8, 1963, HP/540/Test Ban Treaty/LOC.

[114] For the criticism of Khrushchev in 1961, see Zubok and Pleshakov, *Inside the Kremlin's Cold War*, p. 261. For the disapproval of Khrushchev's actions in 1962 and the sharp attack on his adventuristic policy at the time of his fall in 1964, see Fursenko and Naftali, *"One Hell of a Gamble,"* pp. 125, 180, 353–354.

[115] Meeting between Romanov and a high British official, March 21, 1963, Prem 11/4495, PRO. See also Rusk-Dobrynin meeting, April 12, 1963, NSF/185/Rusk-Dobrynin Talks/JFKL, and Rusk-Mikoyan meeting, November 30, 1963, p. 4, DOS-FOIA 91-03439 (the relevant section of the document was not published in FRUS). For various documents giving the standard U.S. response, see FRUS 1961–63, 7:503 n, 543, 546, 673, 704.

ment.[116] And the MLF, of course, was not the only way the Germans could get their hands on nuclear weapons. Now, after the Franco-German treaty, there was a good deal of talk about a continental bloc and especially about a German force being built in cooperation with France. The USSR, in fact, violently attacked the treaty, precisely because it raised the specter of Franco-German nuclear collaboration.[117]

A strong case could therefore be made within the Soviet leadership for moving ahead with the United States and working out a settlement on the basis of the American plan. After all, a deal with America might be the only way to solve the problem. The Americans had in effect won the great test of strength in October 1962: it was obvious that the hard line, based ultimately on the threat of war, was no longer viable. The USSR's growing conflict with China also underscored the importance of some sort of understanding with the United States. But Khrushchev was stubborn. He still would not give way on Berlin, not formally at any rate. Using another one of the anatomical metaphors of which he was so fond, he now told the Americans that the West had "corns" in Berlin, and that from time to time he would step on the president's foot "so he could realize he should cut off his corns."[118] American leaders were not quite sure how to take this threat, but it was clear that the Soviet leader was not going to give the Americans what they wanted on Berlin. A formal settlement was therefore simply not in the cards.

But this did not mean that a more informal understanding could not be worked out: if the front door was locked, maybe the back door was still open. And, indeed, from Kennedy's point of view, there were certain advantages to dealing with these matters in a somewhat indirect way. Anything formal was bound to irritate the Germans. It would be like putting an official seal of approval on the division of Germany. And the Europeans in general would certainly resent the idea of America and Russia deciding the fate of their continent over their heads.

The nuclear question was fundamental, and here especially the Kennedy administration understood that it was not a good idea to focus too explicitly on West Germany. Wouldn't it be better to frame the formal arrangements in quite general terms, and support what was being done with the argument that the world as a whole had a vital interest in halting the spread of nuclear weapons? As Rusk once pointed out, it was precisely in order to avoid dealing with the issue in the con-

[116] A leading State Department analyst, Raymond Garthoff, thought the Soviet reaction was quite understandable. The basic lines of the story, he wrote, were clear to the Russians: first assurances, as late as 1950, that "West Germany should never be rearmed," then the 1954 agreements establishing a framework for a limited German rearmament, and finally "the nuclear-armed German fighter-bombers on strip alert today." "Soviet Reactions to NATO Developments," January 4, 1963, pp. 2–3, Ball Papers/154/ML. The French, like the Russians, thought the Germans viewed the MLF as a stepping-stone to a full nuclear capability. See, for example, Bohlen-Couve meeting, March 23, 1963, in Bohlen to Rusk, March 26, 1963, NSF/72/France—General/JFKL.

[117] The Soviet view was clear at the time. See, for example, "Moscow Assails Paris-Bonn Pact as Peace Threat: Notes Reported to Discuss Possibility of Germans' Getting Atom Arms," *New York Times,* February 6, 1963.

[118] Khrushchev-Harriman meeting, July 27, 1963, and Khrushchev-Rusk meeting, August 9, 1963, FRUS 1961–63, 15:543–544, 568–569. The Soviet leader had earlier referred to West Berlin variously as an "ulcer," a "running sore," a "rotten tooth," the "balls" of the West, and as a thorn in his side.

text of the German question "that we proposed to take up non-proliferation in a wider framework."[119] Even if the Germans knew what was going on—and some officials in Bonn certainly understood that the nonproliferation policy was in large measure directed at the Federal Republic—still, this general approach was more palatable than one that singled out Germany explicitly for discriminatory treatment.[120]

The German nuclear question could thus be dealt with by means of a relatively broad arms control agreement. But this could be an element of a general settlement only if there were some link—perhaps simply a tacit or structural link—with the other parts of the German question, and in particular with the Berlin problem. Perhaps there could be no explicit quid pro quo: the Soviets might not formally accept the status quo in Berlin in exchange for an American promise to keep West Germany non-nuclear. But the linkage could be established in other ways. It could be a by-product of the process that gave rise to the arms control agreement in the first place. And in this indirect way, the basic elements of a settlement could fall into place.

That, in fact, was essentially what happened in 1963. In that year, a settlement of sorts took shape. The Limited Nuclear Test Ban Treaty of July 1963 was the central event in this process, not because arms control was in itself a fundamental element of the system now coming into being, but rather because major political understandings could be reached in the guise of arms control agreements.[121]

It was because a test ban could play this central political role that that issue had become so important. Nuclear arms control, of course, had been on the international agenda since 1945, but under Eisenhower policy in this area had been largely an exercise in public relations. The U.S. government in the 1950s knew that its main arms control proposals were one-sided, and that the USSR would never accept them; but the western governments, in its view, had to at least appear to make a certain effort because public opinion expected it. Thus it was understood that the Americans would "gain greatly" from the Open Skies plan that Eisenhower proposed at the Geneva summit conference in 1955, and would gain even more if the U.S. plan for a cutoff in the production of fissionable material were put into effect. The Open Skies arrangement would allow the United States to gather the target intelligence it needed to mount an effective attack, and would do little to solve the surprise attack problem, its ostensible goal. And a cutoff in the production of fissionable material would "freeze our superiority," and would thus be very much to the advantage of the United States. These proposals were in fact so one-sided that American officials understood that there was no chance the Soviets would accept them. But the U.S. government had to at least appear to be taking arms control seriously; it was important that the world not come to view America as a militaristic nation.[122]

---

[119] Rusk-Alphand meeting, February 28, 1963, FRUS 1961–63, 7:652. See also Rusk-Dobrynin meeting, August 8, 1962, and Rusk-Adenauer meeting, August 10, 1963, ibid., pp. 544–546, 874.

[120] See Soutou, "De Gaulle, Adenauer und die gemeinsame Front," p. 505.

[121] For an elaboration of the point, see Marc Trachtenberg, "The Past and Future of Arms Control," *Daedalus,* Winter 1991, esp. p. 213. Note also Couve's comment along these lines quoted below, p. 391.

[122] For the evidence and a brief discussion, see appendix 7, "U.S. Arms Control Policy under Eisen-

But even at that time, there was one area of arms control that the U.S. government did take seriously. America and Russia, as Dulles told Gromyko in 1957, had a common interest in preventing the spread of nuclear weapons. Neither country, he said, would use its weapons "irresponsibly," but smaller countries might behave differently. It was "frightening to think of a world "where anybody could have a bomb."[123] This did not mean that the Eisenhower administration thought it could freeze the status quo and make sure that there were no new nuclear powers; indeed, for Eisenhower it was natural that the major allies would sooner or later have nuclear forces of their own. But the line obviously had to be drawn somewhere, and America and Russia might be able to cooperate in this area.

Under Kennedy, these concerns became more intense, and the idea that the two major powers had a common interest in preventing what was now coming to be called "nuclear proliferation" was brought up again and again in high-level U.S.–Soviet meetings during the Kennedy period. Rusk, for example, stressed that on the proliferation issue, the existing nuclear powers had "identical" interests, and that "it was almost in the nature of nuclear weapons that if someone had them, he did not want others to have them."[124]

The new administration thus tried hard to reach a test ban agreement with the Soviets, and this effort climaxed with the signing of the Limited Test Ban Treaty in mid-1963. The test ban was the centerpiece of the Kennedy administration's nonproliferation policy. A ban on testing would not have a major effect on the strategic balance one way or the other. As Kennedy told Khrushchev in June 1961, it would not reduce the American or the Soviet nuclear stockpile, nor would it affect the production of nuclear weapons. It would, however, make proliferation less likely. If there were no test ban agreement, then other countries besides the four that had already tested nuclear devices would "undoubtedly launch a nuclear weapons program," and "in a few years there might be ten or even fifteen nuclear powers."[125] But even a limited test ban, the Soviets were later told, would be a "big

hower" (IS). Note especially Dulles's remarks in a meeting with Adenauer, May 28, 1957, FRUS 1955–57, 26:272, 274–275.

[123] Dulles-Gromyko meeting, October 5, 1957, p. 3, DDRS 1991/925.

[124] Rusk to State Department, August 7, 1963 (sec. 5), NSF/187/USSR—Gromyko Talks—Rusk/JFKL.

[125] Kennedy-Khrushchev meeting, June 4, 1961, FRUS 1961–63, 7:88. On the limited impact of a test ban on the strategic balance, see Harold Brown, "Questions Bearing upon the Resumption of Atomic Weapons Testing," in McNamara to NSC, May 15, 1961; Kaysen to Kennedy, January 15, 1962; Foster in NSC, July 9, 1963; ibid., pp. 63–64, 297–303, 784. On nonproliferation as the key argument for a test ban treaty: Kennedy in meeting with Rusk et al., July 27, 1962; Kennedy to Khrushchev, September 15, 1962; and especially Nitze's remarks in a top-level meeting, June 14, 1963; ibid., pp. 512, 569, 725. The British saw things much the same way. See for example Macmillan's views in a meeting with Rusk, June 24, 1962, ibid., p. 471. The French also understood that the main effect of a test ban would be to prevent new nuclear powers from emerging, and it was for this reason that in 1958 they opposed the idea. See, for example, Couve's remarks to Brentano, September 14, 1958, DDF 1958 2:348–349. But in 1961, after France had become a nuclear power, the French defense minister told his British counterpart that he was aware that the Germans "might well wish to be a member of the nuclear club when the French had their own deterrent," but he was "confident that with the help of a nuclear test agreement the Germans could be kept out." Watkinson-Messmer meeting, April 13, 1961, Defe 13/211, PRO.

step forward" toward nonproliferation, "since countries could not produce weapons without tests in the atmosphere."[126]

Nonproliferation, however, was not just a general goal that applied to all prospective nuclear powers in a more or less undifferentiated way. The policy was directed above all at two countries, the Federal Republic of Germany and the People's Republic of China, and a fundamental aim of American policy on the test ban issue was to prevent both of them from developing nuclear forces of their own. The test ban treaty was thus not a mere arms control measure, only marginally related to the core issues that lay at the heart of international political life. It was important because it related directly to two great political issues: the German question and the problem of China.

Originally, the hope was that there could be some sort of arrangement dealing with both Germany and China. The Americans had by late 1962 become quite concerned with the China problem. The prospect of a Chinese nuclear force, Bundy wrote in November, was "the greatest single threat to the status quo over the next few years."[127] Even small nuclear forces in the hands of people like the Chinese Communists, Kennedy thought, "could be very dangerous to us all," to Russia as well as to America; the assumption was that even a limited test ban might be an effective way to deal with this problem.[128] The president in fact went so far as to say that the problem of China was "the whole reason for having a test ban."[129] The Soviets, on the other hand, were mainly interested in keeping nuclear weapons out of German hands. As Kennedy himself pointed out in June 1963, a non-nuclear Germany was one of the main things the Soviets could hope to get from a test ban treaty.[130]

But even if China was America's main concern and the Russians were concerned mainly with Germany, it was also true that both major powers wanted to prevent both China and Germany from going nuclear. It thus seemed possible that some sort of arrangement could be worked out: the United States would keep Germany non-nuclear, and in exchange the Soviets would make sure that China did not develop a nuclear capability. Rusk hinted at an understanding of this sort when he met with Mikoyan in November 1962. A nonproliferation arrangement, he pointed out, would have little meaning if countries who wanted to get into the nuclear club refused to sign the agreements: "For instance, we assume the Soviet Union would be greatly concerned if Germany refused to sign. On our part, we would be greatly concerned if China, or indeed any one of twenty other countries capable of developing atomic weapons, refused to sign."[131]

It was assumed that an arrangement of this sort—one that would prevent both Germany and China from becoming nuclear powers—might be worked out in the

---

[126] Harriman quoted in Hailsham to Macmillan, July 18, 1963, FO 371/171223, PRO.

[127] Bundy to Kennedy, November 8, 1962, FRUS 1961–63, 7:598.

[128] Kennedy to Harriman, July 15, 1963, ibid., p. 801.

[129] Seaborg diary, entry for February 8, 1963, quoted ibid., p. 646. See also Kennedy's remarks in the NSC meeting of January 22, 1963, quoted in Gordon Chang, *Friends and Enemies: The United States, China, and the Soviet Union, 1948–1972* (Stanford, Calif.: Stanford University Press, 1990), p. 237.

[130] Anglo-American meetings, June 27–30, 1963, p. 16, Prem 11/4586, PRO.

[131] Rusk-Mikoyan meeting, November 30, 1962, DOS FOIA 91–03439.

context of the test ban negotiations. A test ban, the Soviets would be told, would mean that "there would be no additional nuclear powers in our camp."[132] The Russians, for their part, would prevent their allies from building nuclear forces. And these commitments would be linked: the United States would "take responsibility in respect to nondissemination with relation to those powers associated with it, if the Soviet Union is willing to take a corresponding obligation for the powers with which it is associated."[133] Germany and China were the real targets here; the Kennedy administration's policy toward other incipient or potential "proliferators," especially France and Israel, was considerably more liberal.[134]

But could an arrangement of the sort the U.S. government had in mind actually be worked out? The Soviet Union, embroiled in an increasingly nasty conflict with China, might want to keep nuclear weapons away from that country, but did the Russians have it within their power to make the Chinese accept a non-nuclear status? There was, after all, a basic difference between Germany and China. Germany was far more dependent on America than China was on the USSR. There was a good chance that the Germans could be made to toe the line, but it would be much harder to make China sign the test ban agreement.

The Americans, however, had given some thought to the problem. If the Chinese insisted on pursuing their nuclear program, the problem might be dealt with by means of direct military action. The Chinese nuclear facilities could be attacked and destroyed—perhaps by the Americans themselves, perhaps by the Soviets, but in either case with the other's tacit or open support.[135] In November 1962, Bundy evidently raised the issue with Kennedy.[136] The military leadership at about this time was also beginning to think about how "military means can be brought to bear on Red China in the coming years to assure a behavior favorable to U.S. national objectives."[137] In February 1962, Nitze asked the Chiefs to outline their views on how China could be persuaded or compelled to accept a test ban agreement, and in April General LeMay listed a number of military actions which could

[132] From a paper by the deputy director of the Arms Control and Disarmament agency, June 20, 1963, FRUS 1961–63, 7:732. This paper presented the "line of thought" that had evolved from discussions among key U.S. officials. Kaysen to Kennedy, June 20, 1963, ibid., p. 728n.

[133] From the draft instructions to the U.S. negotiators, quoted in Kaysen, "Non-diffusion of Nuclear Weapons," July 9, 1963, HP/541/Test Ban Treaty (8)/LOC. The language in the final draft was more guarded, but the passage quoted shows what the real thinking was at the time.

[134] The French case will be discussed later in this chapter. It is interesting to note that McNamara put France and Israel on the same plane, as two countries whose acceptance of a test ban agreement would require a mix of incentives and disincentives; the "sharing of weapons information" (meaning nuclear weapons information) was the main incentive he had in mind. McNamara to Kennedy, February 12, 1963 (draft), Vice President Security File, box 7, Disarmament Proposals, February 1963, Lyndon B. Johnson Library, Austin. For a discussion of the Israeli case, see appendix 8, "Kennedy and the Israeli Nuclear Program" (IS).

[135] Chang, *Friends and Enemies,* pp. 241, 243, 244; William Foster Oral History, p. 37, DDRS 1995/1874. See also FRUS 1961–63, 22:339, 341, 370, and National Security Archive Electronic Briefing Book no. 1, "The United States, China, and the Bomb," http://www.seas.gwu.edu/nsarchive/NSAEBB/NSAEBB1/nsaebb1.htm.

[136] Bundy to Kennedy, November 8, 1962, FRUS 1961–63, 7:598, especially the sanitized paragraph E.

[137] Taylor memo for Joint Strategic Survey Council, December 6, 1962, CJCS Taylor/ CM File, RG 218, USNA.

be used to force the Chinese into line.[138] American officials had not excluded the possibility of direct Soviet military action against the Chinese nuclear facilities, "perhaps in the context of our assuming obligations to prevent West Germany's obtaining nuclear weapons."[139] If the Chinese moved ahead with their nuclear program and the USSR "did nothing," Kennedy said on June 29, "it would be very hard for the United States to continue with a test-ban treaty."[140] And during the Moscow test ban negotiation in July, Kennedy personally instructed the U.S. representative to find out if Khrushchev was willing "either to take Soviet action or to accept U.S. action" aimed at "limiting or preventing Chinese nuclear development."[141]

A test ban treaty, even one that China did not sign, would help the U.S. government achieve its goal of keeping China non-nuclear. The treaty would establish a kind of international norm that would provide a degree of legitimacy for military action of the sort the U.S. government had in mind. The more countries that signed the treaty, the stronger the norm, and the firmer the basis for international action. This, incidentally, was one of the reasons why it was so important that France sign the treaty, and why the U.S. government went to such lengths to bring de Gaulle on board. If France came in, it would make China more of a pariah, more a legitimate target for military action.

But the project could only be implemented if the USSR agreed to cooperate. And although the Soviets were concerned with the prospect of China developing a nuclear capability within a year or two, they simply were not ready for the sort of policy the U.S. government had in mind. Military measures were considered too extreme. As a result, China in fact did proceed with her nuclear program, and nothing was done to prevent her from doing so.

But the fact that China was not included was bound to affect what was done with Germany. Part of the reason the United States had originally been so interested in including China in the arrangement was that if she were not a party, "the undertakings would in fact be directed against the West Germans alone."[142] Now that China would not be included, the Federal Republic would thus be left as the only real target. The treaty therefore would mean that the United States would be guaranteeing West Germany's non-nuclear status. For this not to be a simple gift to the USSR, the United States had to be given a certain quid pro quo, and what the Americans wanted from Russia was an acceptance of the status quo in Berlin.

The Berlin issue was in fact linked to the German nuclear question and thus to the test ban, and that linkage was an essential part of the structure that was taking shape in 1963. These issues were not tied together in any formal way: there was no secret deal whereby the Soviets agreed to respect western rights in Berlin in return for an American commitment to keep Germany non-nuclear. But by mid-1963 the two sides had come to understand that these issues were in fact related.

---

[138] LeMay to McNamara, April 29, 1963, FRUS 1961–63, 7:689–690.

[139] Rice to Harriman, June 21, 1963, HP/539/Test Ban Treaty (1)/LOC.

[140] Anglo-American meetings, June 27–30, 1963, p. 15, Prem 11/4586, PRO.

[141] Kennedy to Harriman, July 15, 1963, FRUS 1961–63, 7:801.

[142] Foreign Office brief, "U.S. Attitude on Collateral Measures and Non-dissemination," December 13, 1962, Cab 133/245, PRO.

Indeed, it had become clear, as Macmillan put it at the time, that a test ban, coupled with a nondissemination agreement, was "the real key to the German problem" as a whole.[143]

This understanding was a product of the political process that culminated in the test ban agreement. From the late 1950s on, the Soviets had made their feelings about the prospect of a German nuclear capability quite clear. The Kennedy plan for a settlement of the Berlin Crisis had taken those feelings into account. The March 1962 "Principles" paper laid out the sort of arrangement the Americans had in mind. The Soviets would respect the status quo in Berlin, and the two countries would cooperate in preventing "further diffusion of nuclear weapons."[144] When the plan was initially presented, the Soviets objected to the very general way in which the nondiffusion provision was framed. As Gromyko told Rusk, earlier U.S.–Soviet talks "had dealt with this problem with specific reference to the two Germanies," and he still wanted the understanding to apply specifically to Germany.[145] But the Americans refused to give way on this point. It was important to be able to tell German leaders, as Kennedy himself did in April 1962, that "our policy was a general one not directed at Germany."[146] By August, the Soviets had come to accept the American approach.[147] Both sides had come to understand that the German nuclear problem could be dealt with by means of a general arms control agreement.

It was also understood that that agreement did not have to be a formal nonproliferation treaty. A test ban treaty would serve the same purpose. The U.S. negotiators in the talks with Russia were instructed to stress the importance of the test ban in preventing proliferation. It was quite clear to U.S. officials, moreover, that current policy on the test ban question was rooted in the earlier U.S.–Soviet exchanges, beginning with the Rusk-Gromyko meeting in March 1962—that is, in the efforts to deal with the Berlin Crisis by working in the issue of a German nuclear capability.[148]

So all these problems were related, and this was reflected in the way they were discussed. When, for example, Khrushchev met with Harriman in April 1963, the American brought up the test ban issue; the Soviet leader replied that the German question was more important. "He was not saying these two subjects were linked"— although in fact, as Harriman noted, "he linked them twice." Khrushchev then said flatly that Berlin was no longer a problem, and proposed an arrangement which

[143] Macmillan to Kennedy, March 16, 1963, in C(63)61, Cab 129/113, PRO.

[144] Rusk-Gromyko meeting, March 22, 1962, and "Draft Principles" paper, FRUS 1961–63, 15:67, 69–71. There were other aspects to the plan, but Berlin and the "nuclear diffusion" question were the two most important issues, a point which Carstens, for example, recognized on May 22. Dowling telegram, May 22, 1962, ibid., p. 155n.

[145] Rusk-Gromyko meeting, March 26, 1962, FRUS 1961–63, 15:81, 85.

[146] Kennedy-Brentano meeting, April 30, 1962, ibid., p. 127. Note also Rusk's remarks in Rusk-Schröder meeting, p. 2, June 22, 1962, NSA Berlin File.

[147] Rusk-Gromyko meeting, July 24, 1962, Rusk-Dobrynin meeting, August 8, 1962, and oral message from Gromyko to Rusk, August 23, 1962, FRUS 1961–63, 7:503n, 544–546, 557–559. See also Rusk to Kennedy, November 27, 1962, 700.5611/11-2762, RG 59, USNA.

[148] Instructions to Harriman, July 10, 1963, FRUS 1961–63, 7:786; Kaysen memorandum, July 9, 1963, HP/541/Test Ban Treaty (8)/LOC.

directly tied the two issues together. "I will give my word that I will find a basis for a test ban agreeable to both sides provided you agree to work out the basis of a German settlement which would recognize the two Germanies as they now exist."[149] And when Kennedy endorsed the idea of a test ban treaty in his June 10 American University speech—"the best statement," Khrushchev thought, "made by any President since Roosevelt"—the Soviet leader responded positively, adding, however, that the test ban should be linked to a nonaggression pact between NATO and the Soviet bloc. This new proposal automatically raised a whole series of issues related to Berlin and the German question—would a cutoff of access to Berlin constitute aggression? would a western attempt to maintain their rights through force be considered aggression?—showing once again how the test ban was being tied to fundamental political questions.[150]

Kennedy and his main advisers also understood that the test ban was not just a simple arms control measure, but rather was closely linked to the most central political problems. The State Department wanted to move cautiously on these political questions, but a number of high officials thought the test ban talks would provide an opportunity for seeing whether some sort of "package deal with Moscow" could be worked out.[151] Harriman, who was going to the Soviet capital to negotiate the test ban, sought to explore the prospects for a fundamental agreement. He and Kaysen, who was accompanying him to Moscow, objected to what they saw as the State Department's overly cautious line. If the State Department view reflected official policy, Kaysen wrote Bundy, he and Harriman "might as well stay home," and a less senior official could be sent to negotiate with the Russians. McNamara also favored a "serious and wide-ranging" discussion of a whole range of political issues.[152]

Kennedy basically agreed that such an attempt should be made, and to maximize his leverage, he was now prepared to use the MLF as a bargaining chip. The State Department fought the idea that the MLF might be an item in the concessions column—that it could conceivably be negotiated away as part of a settlement with Russia—and in the NSC on July 9 Kennedy supported Rusk on this point. But that did not prevent the president from telling Harriman in a private meeting the very next morning that he could take a more flexible line in the Moscow talks. The MLF might be dropped if the two sides could reach agreement on the China problem or on some other issue. Harriman should make no definite promises, but he could use his judgment in deciding how far to go.[153] And in fact a few days ear-

---

[149] Khrushchev-Harriman meetings, April 26 and July 27, 1963, and Harriman telegram, April 28, 1963, FRUS 1961–63, 15:510–511, 510n, 540, 543.

[150] Khrushchev-Harriman meeting, July 27, 1963, ibid., 7:862; "Draft Scope Paper of Harriman-Hailsham Mission with Reference to Non-aggression Pact," July 7, 1963, probably by W. R. Tyler, HP/539/Test Ban Treaty (1)/LOC.

[151] "Elements for a Package Deal with Moscow," n.a., July 3, 1963, NSF/365/ACDA—Disarmament—Harriman Trip (3)/JFKL. The term had been used earlier. See, for example, Thompson memo, "Possible Berlin Solutions," c. November 9, 1962, FRUS 1961–63, 15:423–424. Note also Klein to Bundy, May 17, 1962, ibid., p. 152.

[152] Kaysen to Bundy, June 28, 1963, ibid., 7:751; the State Department line was laid out in Bruce to Harriman and Foster, June 27, 1963, ibid., pp. 744–746.

[153] Seaborg diary, June 21, 1963; NSC meeting, July 9, 1963; Kennedy-Harriman meeting, July 10,

lier Kennedy had told British leaders (this time with Rusk present) that the "West might want to trade the idea off" in the Moscow talks.[154]

The president clearly wanted to move ahead, and at the Moscow meetings the two sides cautiously broached the issue of a general political settlement. The Soviets had brought up the question of a nonaggression pact; this was negotiable, Harriman suggested, if the USSR was willing to agree that interference with access to Berlin would be considered aggression. The Berlin issue was now on the table. It was a central part of the "package." Harriman went on to point out that the United States did not simply expect the Soviets to accept the status quo in Berlin without getting anything in return: "we desired no one-way arrangement, the interests of all are involved, and we came prepared also to include language on boundary lines and demarcation lines which would be of interest to the USSR's allies, if the USSR so desired."[155] So now the Oder-Neisse line and the question of the inner-German border were also being introduced into the talks.

The Soviets, however, could not quite bring themselves to accept the sort of arrangement the Americans had in mind. They hinted at times that they were willing to give the Americans a certain degree of satisfaction in this area—to put the Berlin issue on ice as part of an arrangement to stabilize the status quo in central Europe. When Rusk, for example, argued that if a nonaggression pact were followed by a sharp Berlin crisis, "we should all look like fools," the Soviet ambassador replied ("with some significance," Rusk thought) "that such a pact would make such a crisis far less likely."[156] And when the issue came up in October, Gromyko read Kennedy a statement on Berlin that might be issued in conjunction with a nonaggression pact. The statement was somewhat ambiguous, but the Soviets seemed to be accepting the principle that the use of force would be ruled out in connection with the "situation in West Berlin."[157] Indeed, when Khrushchev discussed these issues with Harriman, he stressed that Berlin was no longer a problem, and that he felt quite comfortable with the present situation there.[158]

All of this had a certain significance, even if the Soviets were not willing to go all the way and guarantee the status quo in Berlin. No formal settlement might have been possible in 1963, but the fact that these discussions had taken place was of considerable importance. Linkages had been established; there was a general sense of connectedness; the test ban was tied to the German nuclear question, which in turn was tied to the Berlin problem.

1963; in ibid., pp. 735, 780–781, 790. Note also Merchant to Ball, June 17, 1963, and Harriman to Merchant, June 20, 1963, HP/537/Test Ban Treaty (1)/LOC. Merchant opposed the idea of weakening on the MLF in the talks with Russia, and Harriman reassured him: "Don't worry—I am not going to be negotiating in areas that need bother you."

[154] Anglo-American talks, June 27–30, 1963, p. 19, Prem 11/4586, PRO.

[155] Harriman-Gromyko meeting, July 17, 1963, FRUS 1961–63, 7:806.

[156] Rusk-Dobrynin meeting, May 18, 1963, p. 5, DOSCF for 1963, POL US-USSR, RG 59, USNA.

[157] Kennedy-Gromyko meeting, October 10, 1963, in State Department to Finletter, October 22, 1963, DOSCF for 1963, Pol US-USSR, RG 59, USNA.

[158] Khrushchev-Harriman meetings, April 26 and July 27, 1963, FRUS 1961–63, 15:510, 543. Note also Semenov-Tyler meeting, October 10, 1963, and Semenov-Scott meeting, October 3, 1963, in which the "senior Soviet expert on Germany" took a very moderate line on Berlin, ibid., vols. 13–15, mic. supp., no. 432.

It was the Berlin Crisis that had pulled these issues together. An American guarantee of Germany's nonnuclear status was the most attractive carrot the U.S. government had dangled in front of the Soviets in its attempt to reach a negotiated settlement of the crisis in late 1961 and early 1962. The Americans had also made this issue work the other way: Soviet pressure on Berlin, U.S. leaders suggested, might well lead to a German nuclear capability; the Soviets should therefore settle the crisis by accepting the status quo in Berlin. Kennedy himself made the point in a meeting with Adzhubei on January 31, then in a letter to Khrushchev on February 15, and again in a meeting with Dobrynin on July 17.[159] A variant of this argument was used with the Germans: if they were interested in saving Berlin, they should not go nuclear. The threat of doing so could have a powerful deterrent effect on the Soviets, but the threat value would vanish as soon as the Germans built a nuclear force. Linking nonproliferation to a Berlin arrangement would thus serve to "hold the Russians" to the agreement. When the point was made to a top German official in March 1962, that official had to admit that he was "impressed by this argument."[160]

A web of linkages had thus come into being during the Kennedy period, and the Soviets could hardly act in Berlin as though these linkages did not exist. To threaten the status quo in Berlin would put Germany's non-nuclear status at risk. The same point applied to the Germans, but in reverse: they could not move ahead in the nuclear area without creating tension around Berlin. The existence of a connection—not formal, but tacit and structural—thus tended to tie both Germany and Russia into the status quo. There was no overt "deal," but a system was taking shape. And at the heart of that system was the link that had established itself, both objectively and in people's minds, between Berlin and Germany's non-nuclear status.

The test ban treaty, the one formal agreement that was worked out, thus came to have a certain symbolic value: it had come to represent a whole web of understandings that lay just below the surface. The treaty, in other words, is not to be understood—and was not understood at the time—as a simple arms control agreement, devoid of broader political significance. The three powers involved in the Moscow talks—the United States, the Soviet Union, and Great Britain—were aware of what was going on. But so were the opponents of the treaty—above all,

---

[159] The idea of using this threat had been around for some time. See, for example, Komer to Bundy, July 20, 1961, in ibid., no. 361. Bundy took up the argument in January 1962. He thought that the dangers the Soviets were running had to be brought home to them. Those dangers, he said, were "not hard to spell out." They related among other things to "German revanchism" and to the "diffusion of nuclear weapons." Draft memorandum for the president, January 15, 1962, enclosed in Bundy to Rusk, January 15, 1962, 762.00/1-1562, RG 59, USNA. For Kennedy's use of the argument, see Kennedy-Adzhubei meeting, January 31, 1962, and Kennedy to Khrushchev, February 15, 1962, FRUS 1961–63, 14:782, 821, and Kennedy-Dobrynin meeting, July 17, 1962, ibid., 15:224. See also Rusk's comment in a meeting with the British and French on February 13 that by "pressing on Berlin too hard," the Russians "might force the Western Powers to allow Germany to acquire a national nuclear capability and thus cause a major change in Power relationships." Ormsby Gore to Foreign Office, February 14, 1962, FO 371/163567. For the U.S. account, see FRUS 1961–63, 14:809.

[160] Carstens-Kohler meeting and Schröder-Rusk-Carstens-Kohler meeting, both March 11, 1962, NSABF.

Adenauer and de Gaulle. As Couve pointed out at the time, the arms control measures then on the international agenda were not to be taken at face value. "In the guise of formal disarmament," he noted, "the subject of all of them is Germany, her status, her future." De Gaulle was more direct: the test ban treaty, he said, was "another Yalta," a new division of Europe between Russia and the Anglo-Saxons, and he would have no part of it.[161]

Kennedy found de Gaulle's attitude difficult to understand. The president very much wanted to bring France into the system, and in particular into the test ban regime. If France agreed to stop testing in the atmosphere, it would be harder for potential nuclear powers like China and Germany to break what would in that case be an almost universal ban and to move forward with their own nuclear programs—and easier for America and Russia to prevent them from doing so. And the way to bring France into the test bar regime was to help her with her atomic program—to help her test underground, and to assist her in other ways as well. "President Kennedy," Harriman told the British, "was ready to consider very seriously giving nuclear weapons or information to the French as the price of getting them in to this agreement."[162] Kennedy, in fact, made a major effort to work out some kind of arrangement with the French, but de Gaulle was simply not interested: there would be no deal with America, and France would not sign the treaty.[163]

It was not just a question of getting the French to accept a nuclear test ban. What Kennedy really wanted was a political understanding with de Gaulle. If France supported the structure he was trying to build, it would be harder for the Germans to challenge it. The "Gaullists" in the Federal Republic would no longer have a "French card" to play, so mending fences with de Gaulle would help stabilize the system. The United States and France, Kennedy felt, had had their differences, but this was now just history. De Gaulle had objected to the American push for negotiations with Russia in late 1961 and early 1962. But Kennedy, looking back, had come to agree that the earlier policy had been a mistake.[164] American opposition to France's nuclear program had been another source of tension. But by now, he told Couve in May 1963, this issue had been settled. The United States accepted the fact that France had become a nuclear power, and indeed the door to nuclear cooperation had been opened right after the Nassau meeting.[165]

So where was the problem? It was hard for Kennedy to see what the conflict with France was really about. Couve outlined French policy for the president at

[161] Couve de Murville speech to French National Assembly, October 29, 1963, quoted in U.S. embassy Paris to State Department, October 30, 1963, NSF/73/France—General/JFKL. The de Gaulle remark is quoted in David Schoenbrun, *The Three Lives of Charles de Gaulle* (New York: Atheneum, 1966), p. 323.

[162] Home-Harriman meeting, July 12, 1963, FO 371/171222, PRO.

[163] For various documents showing Kennedy's attempt to work out an arrangement with the French, and de Gaulle's cold response, see FRUS 1961–63, 7:646, 727, 781, 797n, 801n, 828n, 851–853, 868, 868n, and AAPBD 2:805–806. See also Bohlen to Bundy and Rusk (eyes only), August 5, 1963, 7 P.M., DOSCF for 1963, POL Fr-US, RG 59, USNA, reporting a discussion of the issue with Couve, who was obviously a little exasperated by de Gaulle's attitude.

[164] See, for example, Kennedy-Harriman meeting, July 10, 1963, FRUS 1961–63, 7:789.

[165] Kennedy-Couve meeting, May 25, 1963, ibid., 13:772.

the May meeting and again at another White House meeting in October. France, he said, wanted détente in Europe. She wanted a continuing American military presence there, since Europe could not provide for her own security without American military support. She wanted a Europe that would include the British. And France, he insisted, was dead set against the idea of a German nuclear force. The Franco-German pact had "added nothing substantive to the relations between the two countries." France "would never help the Germans to make nuclear weapons." When Kennedy asked whether the French would cooperate with the Germans in this field if the United States "gave up on the MLF," Couve replied "certainly not." Indeed, he opposed the MLF in part because he thought it would "whet" the German nuclear appetite. To Kennedy all this sounded quite reasonable. Why, then, were the two countries so much at odds?[166]

The conflict did not seem to be rooted in any real clash of policy. De Gaulle, to be sure, had certain very general aims, which seemed to be at variance with what the Americans wanted. He wanted Europe to be "a going concern with her own policy, including her own means of defense"; he called for a "European Europe," for a far-reaching transformation of NATO, and for a Europe stretching from the "Atlantic to the Urals."[167] But these were rather vague goals and did not really put him on a collision course with the Americans. Indeed, it was not entirely clear what these phrases were supposed to mean. What did this sort of rhetoric translate into, in real political terms?[168]

The German nuclear question was the ultimate touchstone. The idea of a "European Europe," a Europe of nation-states charting its own course, a Europe built on close collaboration between France and Germany, a Europe with "her own means of defense"—all this implied that Germany, like France, would have a nuclear capability of her own. But did de Gaulle really want Germany to have a nuclear force? If he was against the idea, then what exactly was he calling for? If Germany was to remain non-nuclear, wouldn't the United States have to continue playing the key role in defending Europe? De Gaulle seemed to think there was a viable alternative to a system based on American power, but with a non-nuclear Germany, what kind of alternative could there possibly be? These were the real problems, but was de Gaulle facing up to them? In May, Couve said that France was against a German nuclear force; in October 1962 he had said that the building of such a force might well lead to a third world war. But how did France propose to deal with the problem? The French nuclear program, and the Gaullist rhetoric that justified it, would not help keep Germany non-nuclear. In fact, the Americans argued, it would obviously have the opposite effect. Couve did not dispute the point. The only solution, in his view, was a genuine political unification of Europe, which would make it possible to have a European nuclear force whose elements would not be subject to national control. But this was hardly an answer. Under the best of circumstances, Couve admitted, European unification was a long way off, and in fact, as the Americans went on to point out, it would never hap-

---

[166] Kennedy-Couve meetings, May 25 and October 7, 1963, FRUS 1961–63, 13:771–773, 782–786.

[167] Kennedy-Couve meeting, October 7, 1963, ibid., p. 782.

[168] See Bohlen to Bundy, March 2, 1963, ibid., pp. 763–765.

pen as long as Gaullist policies, which placed such emphasis on national sovereignty, remained in effect.[169]

So the French, in Kennedy's view, had no real solution to this fundamental problem. The United States had at least tried to deal with it in 1961 and 1962, by opposing national nuclear capabilities in general and by backing the MLF as an alternative. By 1963, however, Kennedy had come to the conclusion that these policies were bankrupt, and was now prepared to try something new. The United States had tried to finesse the issue of a German nuclear force, but he now recognized that the question had to be faced head on. Since the French agreed with the United States on fundamentals, why couldn't they cooperate with this policy of keeping Germany non-nuclear and of stabilizing the status quo in Europe? Britain, France, and the United States should come together politically; the Americans, for their part, would help the French with their nuclear program. Why, if their fundamental policy was as Couve had outlined it, would they refuse to go along with a plan of that sort?

The Americans were thus coming to the conclusion that de Gaulle was not fully rational. If the French leader had spurned these American overtures, it was not because he was pursuing a policy that made sense in substantive terms. His policy was rooted instead in resentment, most recently over the way Germany had been forced to chose between American and France in early 1963.[170] Indeed, by September, the White House had come to take it for granted that de Gaulle's policy was "largely animated by anti-American prejudice."[171] De Gaulle, it seemed, was nursing a grudge against America. He and his followers were cultivating a series of myths that had little to do with reality—like the myth that the Americans had never responded to de Gaulle's September 1958 proposal for a tripartite "directorate," or the myth that France had never asked for American nuclear assistance, or the myth that Russia and the Anglo-Saxons had divided up Europe at Yalta and that France had stood for a very different kind of policy.[172] The view was therefore taking hold in Washington that one could not deal with de Gaulle on a busi-

[169] Kennedy-Couve meetings, May 25 and October 7, 1963, ibid., pp. 773, 786; Ball-Couve meeting, May 25, 1963, NSF/72/France—General/JFKL; Couve-Home meeting, April 8, 1963, Prem 11/4221, PRO; Couve-Rusk meeting, October 7, 1962, 700.5611/10-762, RG 59, USNA.

[170] See, for example, Tyler memo, "De Gaulle and Atlantic Nuclear Matters," November 2, 1964, p. 6, AP/SDWHA/HSTL; Couve-Bohlen meeting, September 15, 1963, FRUS 1961–63, 13:780; Couve-Rusk meeting, October 7, 1963, ibid., 15:589–590.

[171] Ball to Bohlen, giving "highest level guidance" from the White House, September 25, 1963, p. 2, NSF/72/JFKL.

[172] On the issue of America's alleged failure to respond to the September 1958 memorandum, see Debré's claim and Raymond Aron's (and Soutou's) comment in Aron, Articles du Figaro, 2:1281; Bohlen to Rusk, March 6, 1963, DOSCF for 1963, POL Fr-US, RG 59, USNA (for the leak of the documents to Sulzberger), and Sulzberger entry for March 6, 1963, Last of the Giants, p. 965. On France as a "demandeur" in the nuclear area, note Debré's own use of the term, in meeting with Herter, May 1, 1959, DDF 1959, 1:590. As for the standard Gaullist myth about Yalta and the Anglo-Saxons' acceptance of a divided Europe (see, for example, Peyrefitte, C'était de Gaulle, pp. 380–381), it is worth noting that the French provisional government, headed by de Gaulle, was, if anything, quicker to accept the Soviet domination of Poland than the British and the Americans were, and that de Gaulle was happy that France was not invited to Yalta and did not have to take political responsibility for what was going to be done there. See Soutou, "Le Général de Gaulle et l'URSS, 1943–1945," esp. pp. 339–343.

nesslike basis. Kennedy had made a great effort to do so, but it was quite clear, by late 1963, that that attempt had not been successful.

In the final analysis, however, the French attitude was not of fundamental importance. It might be useful to mend fences with de Gaulle, but the fate of Germany was the central concern. And if, to paraphrase de Gaulle himself, the "battle for Germany" could be won, the "battle for France" would be of secondary importance. But in a sense the battle for Germany had been won in advance. The Germans had made their choice earlier in the year. The Bundestag had added a preamble of its own to the Franco-German treaty, reaffirming Germany's loyalty to the alliance with America. It had repudiated Adenauer's "Gaullist" policy. Indeed, Adenauer had been forced to resign the chancellorship, although he remained in office for a few months as a lame duck. The alignment with the United States, moreover, was supported by the great mass of the German people. When Kennedy visited their country in June, the reception, in Berlin especially, was enthusiastic and "triumphal"—or "almost hysterical," as Adenauer characterized it.[173] And Kennedy was "willing to draw on this feeling," he told Harriman in early July, "if there was something to be achieved by it."[174] If something reasonable could be worked out with the Russians, it seemed that there was an excellent chance that the Germans would follow the American lead.

As it turned out, the Moscow negotiations in July did not lead to a formal east-west settlement. The test ban treaty was the only formal agreement to emerge from the talks. The Germans were now asked to sign the treaty, but their accession was far from automatic. The American request, in fact, came as a rather unpleasant surprise. There had been no prior consultations with the Americans on the issue. The German assumption had been that the test ban question was not their concern because it involved only the nuclear powers. But now the Americans made it plain that they expected the Federal Republic to sign the treaty. The effect, which Adenauer clearly understood, would be to yet further lock in Germany's non-nuclear status.[175]

So Adenauer opposed the treaty, which he called "senseless and pointless."[176] His key argument against it was that the treaty, which East Germany would also sign, would enhance the status of that regime. The Americans warned that making a big fuss over this issue would backfire. If the Germans harped on this question, people would think that the treaty really would improve East Germany's international status, whereas in reality its significance in terms of international law

---

[173] Adenauer-Rusk meeting, August 10, 1963, AAPBD 1963, 2:974.

[174] Kennedy-Harriman meeting, July 10, 1963, FRUS 1961–63, 7:789.

[175] Ilse Dorothee Pautsch, "Im Sog der Entspannungspolitik: Die USA, das Teststopp-Abkommen und die Deutschland-Frage," in *Von Adenauer zu Erhard: Studien zur auswärtigen Politik der Bundesrepublik Deutschland 1963*, ed. Rainer Blasius (Munich: Oldenbourg, 1994), p. 124; Adenauer-McNamara meeting, July 31, 1963, Schröder-McGhee meeting, August 3, 1963, and Schröder-Bundy meeting, September 20, 1963, all in AAPBD 1963, 2:860, 905–909, 1151. For the point about the treaty confirming Germany's non-nuclear status, see Schwarz, *Adenauer*, 2:847.

[176] Adenauer-de Gaulle meeting, September 21, 1963, AAPBD 1963, 2:1201; Schwarz, *Adenauer* 2:846–848.

Berlin

ish FROYA mish	I am proud
in daim FRY-en bear-LEAN tsu zine,	to be in free Berlin,
dair SHTAT,	the city
dee ine LOISH-tendess zim-BOWL IST,	which is a shining symbol,
nisht NOOR fear oy-RO-pah,	not only for Europe
zondarn fear dee GANTSA VELT.	but for the whole world.
ear MOOT	Your courage
oont ee-ra OUSE-dow-ar	and your perseverance
hab dee VORTA	have made the words
"ish bin ine bear-LEAN-ar"	"I am a Berliner"
tsu inem SHTOLT-sen be-KENT-niss	a proud declaration.
VAIR-den lassn	(the rest of the verb)

These translations are somewhat literal. The German is a very good free
translation of what the President wrote on Tuesday, June 18.

Figure 12. A small memento of a great moment in U.S.–German relations: some
notes prepared for President Kennedy's use during his visit to Berlin. President's
Office Files, box 117, Germany—JFK Visit, John F. Kennedy Library.

was negligible. U.S. officials also warned that dwelling on this issue would make
people suspect that the Germans were looking for an excuse to avoid signing the
treaty in order to keep their nuclear options from being closed off completely.[177]

In any case, Adenauer no longer had the political strength to resist this American pressure. The prevailing view within the country—within his party, and even
within his government—was that the Germans had little choice but to follow the

[177] Schröder-McGhee meeting, August 3, 1963, and Knappstein to Foreign Office, August 8, 1963,
AAPBD 1963, 2:907–908, 958–959.

American lead.[178] Where else could Germany go? It was absurd to think she could align herself with France and turn her back on America. France, in fact, had little of substance to offer Germany, in either political or military terms. On the nuclear issue in particular, France had turned out to be rather reluctant to engage in a full partnership with her neighbor across the Rhine.[179] Nor could Germany really turn toward Russia, although the specter of a new "Rapallo" was sometimes brandished by German diplomats and politicians.[180] A "Rapallo" policy would get her nowhere. The Russians had no interest in a strong Germany, and Germany would have to be strong if she burned her bridges with the West and tried to stand between the two blocs.

So there was no viable alternative to the alliance with America. The Germans had to be realistic. Their dependence on America placed limits on how far they could go and on how independent their policy could really be. They could not assume that America's hands were tied, that U.S. leaders knew that they had no choice but to defend Germany because of the decisive effect the loss of that country would have on the global balance of power, and that the Federal Republic therefore had a relatively free hand.[181] There was no guarantee that American policy would be shaped in such a cool and unemotional way by power political considerations of that sort. Indeed, the Americans might be tempted to pull out of Europe. Even someone as committed to the alliance as Eisenhower, the Germans noted, was now talking in public about a radical scaling down of the American military presence in Europe.[182] In addition, there was the obvious fact that the U.S. government was increasingly concerned with America's balance of payments problem. Overseas military spending placed a considerable burden on the balance of payments; that burden was of the same order of magnitude as the payments deficit itself. Since military spending was the one major component of the balance of payments under direct government control, there was a standing temptation to deal with the problem by cutting back on America's military presence abroad—or by using the implied threat of a withdrawal to get the allied governments in general, and Germany above all, to assist America on international economic issues.[183]

[178] Note, for example, the Carstens memorandum of August 7, 1963 (with the foreign minister's marginal comments), ibid., pp. 947–948.

[179] Carstens memorandum, August 7, 1963, and Schröder-Rusk meeting, September 20, 1963, ibid., pp. 948, 1163–66.

[180] See, for example, Strauss's remarks summarized in Soutou, L'Alliance incertaine, p. 205.

[181] This point is suggested in a Carstens memorandum of August 16, 1963, AAPBD 1963, 2:1035.

[182] Eisenhower interview of October 18, 1963, cited by the new chancellor, Ludwig Erhard, in a meeting with U.S. Ambassador McGhee, October 22, 1963, and by Schröder in a meeting with Rusk, October 26, 1963, ibid., 3:1365, 1391.

[183] For various documents giving the figures on the payments loss resulting from the American troop presence overseas, and figures for the overall payments deficit during the early 1960s, see FRUS 1961–63, 9:30, 60, 68, 149–150. McNamara himself told Adenauer on July 31, 1963, that the cost of stationing troops abroad was about equal to the total balance of payments deficit. AAPBD 1963, 2:863. Note also McNamara's top secret speech to the NATO ministerial meeting in Paris, December 17, 1963, in FRUS 1961–63, vols. 13–15, mic. supp., no. 51. The linkage between the U.S. troop presence overseas (and above all in Germany) and the balance of payments problem is reflected in many documents in FRUS 1961–1963, vol. 9, especially in the first two sections (pp. 1–188). My understanding of the

An American withdrawal was thus not entirely out of the question. Germany could not take the American security guarantee for granted, and hence her freedom of action was a good deal more limited than it would otherwise have been. If the Americans now wanted détente, how could the Federal Republic resist? If the Americans insisted that Germany remain non-nuclear as part of the détente policy, the Federal Republic had little choice but to accept that status.

This was now the dominant view within Germany. Adenauer did not agree with it, but he was on the way out, in large part because he had stood for a very different kind of policy. Gerhard Schröder's views were more in line with mainstream German opinion. Schröder had been foreign minister since late 1961. Adenauer had been forced to accept him as part of the process of coalition building after the September 1961 elections, and Schröder's appointment reflected the weakening of Adenauer's hold on power, itself the result of the growing gap between the old chancellor's thinking and opinion in the country at large. Schröder's policy was more nuanced and more balanced than Adenauer's. On the one hand, he understood that Germany could not move too far from the American line, and in particular felt that the Federal Republic had little choice but to sign the test ban treaty.[184] But this did not mean that Germany would be a mere puppet of the United States. The Federal Republic needed a policy of her own, one that ultimately might lead to reunification. The Adenauer line had not brought reunification any closer, and it was perhaps time to try a fresh approach. The Americans wanted a policy of détente, and Germany could accept that, but the goal of that policy, Schröder insisted, could not be to "bury" the German question or to put it in the "icebox." The ultimate goal was to change the status quo. The new policy, which Schröder called the "policy of movement," was thus in line with fundamental long-term German national goals.[185]

So it was not as though the Germans were simply forced, against their better judgment, to toe the American line; it was not that the Germans, as Adenauer's followers complained, were simply "victims of America's détente policy."[186] The situation was a good deal more complex. The American attitude was certainly a major factor in German political calculations, but the new policy was not out of line with what one could reasonably argue were basic German national interests. The Germans were of course making major concessions, above all in the nuclear area, but none of this was purely one-sided. In particular, the Americans were under a certain obligation to give the Federal Republic an effective security guarantee; if Germany was to remain non-nuclear, the United States more or less had to agree to provide for German security. And the commitment was not long in coming: the U.S. government now promised (in Rusk's Frankfurt speech of

---

issue is based in large part on discussions with and written work done by Frank Gavin and Hubert Zimmermann, both of whom have recently completed dissertations in this general area.

[184] Schwarz, *Adenauer*, 2:721, 746, 841.

[185] Schröder-Bundy and Schröder-Rusk meetings, September 20, 1963; Schröder-Sorensen meeting, September 24, 1963; Schröder-Rusk-Home meeting, September 27, 1963; all in AAPBD 1963, 2:1152–1154, 1156, 1159–62, 1170, 1226–1227, 1240–1246.

[186] Krone diary, August 5, 1963, *Adenauer-Studien*, 3:178; see Schwarz, *Adenauer*, 2:840–853.

October 27, 1963) to maintain a sizeable force in Germany on a more or less permanent basis.[187]

THE COLD WAR POLITICAL SYSTEM

By 1963 it seemed that the period of great danger had ended. Things had settled down. The risk of a Soviet attack on western Europe, Kennedy thought, was now "minimal." "Europe was quite secure militarily now," he said. That continent was "probably about eighth on our list of dangers." Even West Berlin was now relatively secure.[188] Other key figures had the same impression. Couve, for example, agreed in May that the Berlin problem was "more or less liquidated."[189] Indeed, Khrushchev himself assured Harriman that Berlin was "no longer a source of any trouble."[190]

It was not that a final settlement had been reached or that the Cold War was completely over. It took a while before the structure that had taken shape by 1963 was accepted as definitive. The whole question of the American troop presence in Europe remained on the international agenda, certainly throughout the 1960s; the commitment made in the Rusk Frankfurt speech was not taken as sacrosanct; the issue was kept alive by the ongoing balance of payments problem. Even the question of a German nuclear force did not vanish entirely: Ludwig Erhard, Adenauer's successor as chancellor, told President Johnson in late 1965 that it was "impossible to assume that Germany will go forever without a nuclear deterrent."[191] And Berlin, of course, did not immediately disappear as a problem; it was only in 1971 that this issue was settled by a four-power treaty.[192] But although there were incidents on the access routes after 1963, there was no new Berlin crisis. The sense people had that year that a major threshold had been crossed turned out to be justified. The period of high drama, of truly heroic decision making, had come to an end. The threat of general nuclear war, which had loomed so large in 1961 and 1962, now faded into the background. The Cold War had become a different kind of conflict, more subdued, more modulated, more artificial, and, above all, less terrifying.

A relatively stable system had, in fact, come into being. This system was built

[187] NSAM 270, October 29, 1963, FRUS 1961–63, 9:99; Rusk-Erhard meeting, October 25, 1963, AAPBD 1963, 3:1385. Note also Kennedy's discussion of this issue with Rusk and Bundy, October 24, 1963, audiotape 117/A53, POF/JFKL.

[188] Kennedy-JCS meeting, February 28, 1963; Kennedy-Spaak meeting, May 28, 1963; Kennedy-Couve meeting, May 25, 1963; in FRUS 1961–63, 13:517, 587, 772.

[189] Rusk-Home-Couve-Schröder meeting, May 21, 1963, ibid., 15:515.

[190] Khrushchev-Harriman meeting, April 26, 1963, ibid., p. 510.

[191] Johnson-Erhard meeting, December 20, 1965, FRUS 1964–68, 13:291. On America's German policy during the Johnson period, and in particular U.S. policy on the German nuclear question at this time, see Frank Costigliola, "Lyndon B. Johnson, Germany and the 'End of the Cold War,'" in *Lyndon B. Johnson Confronts the World*, ed. Warren Cohen and Nancy Tucker (New York: Cambridge University Press, 1994).

[192] For some later problems, see, for example, John Ausland, "Six Berlin Incidents, 1961–1964: A Case Study in the Management of U.S. Policy regarding a Critical National Security Problem," NSABF.

on three main pillars: a general respect for the status quo in central Europe, especially in Berlin; the non-nuclear status of West Germany; and a continuing, large-scale American military presence on German soil. All these things were closely bound up with each other; in particular, the American presence and the non-nuclear status of Germany were two sides to a coin. If Germany was to remain non-nuclear, the Americans would have to remain in central Europe to provide the necessary counterweight to Soviet power. Indeed, if the Germans were to accept their non-nuclear status, they were entitled to something substantial in return: they had the right to expect the Americans to provide for their security. The existence of this web of linkages tended to tie everyone into the status quo. If the Soviets wanted to keep Germany non-nuclear, they had to accept the NATO system—the system based on American power, and on the American military presence in Europe. The status quo in Berlin was tied to the NATO system and to West Germany's non-nuclear status. If the Soviets pressed too hard on Berlin, even if there were no war, the result might be quite unpleasant from their point of view. The NATO structure might collapse; they might end up having to deal with a nuclearized Germany; it was better, therefore, to accept things as they were. The same sort linkage also tied the western countries to the status quo. If the West wanted to protect Berlin, the Federal Republic needed to be kept non-nuclear, so as to avoid provoking the Russians, and so that the threat of Germany going nuclear could be maintained intact as a means of deterring the Russians from putting pressure on the city. In other words, the stability of the system did not result from a simple balance of military power in central Europe. It was not simply a question of the presence of American forces having a certain deterrent effect, even on Soviet behavior around Berlin. The political effects were more subtle and wide-ranging, and were of fundamental importance; by the end of 1963, a political system had come into being, and this system was not based on nuclear deterrence alone.

This basic structure was rounded out and reinforced by developments in other areas. Certain financial arrangements, for example, were worked out between the United States and Germany. If American forces were to guarantee German security, it seemed only fair that the Germans should help offset the foreign exchange costs the United States incurred by deploying a large force in Europe; indeed, it was essential that this be done, given the severity of America's balance of payments problem and the nature of the international monetary system in place at the time. The arrangements in this area thus helped make it possible for the United States to maintain a sizeable army in Europe. The mutual hostage relationship that had developed between Cuba and Berlin also tended to tie both America and Russia into the status quo, and was thus another—albeit relatively minor—girder in the structure.[193] The shift in American nuclear doctrine—the move away from counterforce, the acceptance of the view that nuclear superiority was neither a feasible nor (more importantly in this context) even a desirable objective—was another important element in the picture.[194] And the emergence of China as a serious

---

[193] Note in this context Kennedy's remarks in the NSC, January 22, 1963, FRUS 1961–63, 8:458, 458n. See also White House meeting, October 24, 1962, May and Zelikow, *Kennedy Tapes*, p. 382.

[194] Note especially McNamara's then shocking remark, in an interview in late 1962, that it was good that the United States was losing its ability to destroy the Soviet retaliatory force, and thus its ability to

problem for both Russia and America tended to bring those two powers together, and thus helped in a general way to stabilize their relations with each other. But the heart of the system was the series of arrangements and understandings that related to the situation in central Europe: the non-nuclear status of Germany, the continuing American military presence in Europe, and respect for the political status quo in this area, especially in Berlin.

This was a system that could work because it safeguarded everyone's most basic interests. For the USSR, it meant that German power was contained in a structure dominated by the United States—that is, the Federal Republic was dependent on a country which was determined not to use force to change the status quo. As Rusk told Gromyko in July 1962, the presence of both America and Russia in central Europe was a "stabilizing factor," and would keep both Germanies from indulging in "adventures."[195] In August 1963, he told Khrushchev much the same thing: a U.S.–Soviet presence in Germany, and the acceptance by those two major powers of "substantial responsibility" for handling the German question, was at present "an element of stability and not instability."[196] The Soviets did not fundamentally disagree: their goal was not to eject the United States from Europe, but to make sure that the Federal Republic did not pose a threat to their control of the east.[197]

As for the Germans, their most basic interests would also be protected in a system of this sort. First and foremost, their own territory would be defended, and West Berlin would remain free, even after American nuclear superiority had vanished. Germany, moreover, would be part of the West, with all that implied in terms of the political transformation and moral rehabilitation of the country. And, for increasing numbers of Germans, détente also implied that fundamental change in Europe, perhaps even reunification, might be possible in the long run.

Finally, the system was in line with America's most fundamental interests. It was not that the United States wanted to dominate western Europe as a kind of end in itself: the U.S. government had never sought to make the NATO area into a kind of American empire. The United States, in fact, was paying a price for its involve-

---

take the initiative in a general nuclear war. See Shapley, *Promise and Power*, p. 191. This was of considerable symbolic importance, and it also had certain far-reaching material implications. The Americans were saying that they would not press hard for strategic advantage; the Soviets would have a certain interest in not placing that aspect of American policy at risk; this gave them a certain interest in maintaining the great power status quo. The issue of strategic parity also evidently came up in connection with the test ban treaty in 1963. Rusk and Thompson had apparently told Dobrynin that the United States "was ahead in tactical nuclear weapons," that the Soviets could "catch up by accepting" a limited test ban, and that there could be a "tacit understanding" that the U.S. "would not go ahead with underground tests unless we decided the Soviets had overdone theirs." This, one well-informed observer noted, might explain the pressure "to go slow on underground testing." William Y. Smith memorandum, August 21, 1963, on "events leading up to the Harriman Moscow Mission," FRUS 1961–63, vols. 7–9, mic. supp., no. 220.

[195] Rusk-Gromyko meeting, July 24, 1962, FRUS 1961–63, 15:243, 249, 251; Rusk-Dobrynin meeting, March 26, 1963, ibid., p. 501. The next day Kohler followed up on Rusk's remarks by presenting Gromyko with the texts outlining America's reserved powers with regard to Germany and Berlin. Kohler-Gromyko meeting, July 25, 1962, 110.11-RU/7-2562, RG 59, USNA.

[196] Rusk-Khrushchev meeting, August 9, 1963, FRUS 1961–63, 15:566–568.

[197] See, for example, Soutou, *L'Alliance incertaine*, p. 264. On this point in general, see above, pp. 80 and 141–142.

ment in Europe, and one that was not to be measured simply in economic terms: the fact that U.S. power was engaged meant that the Americans were in the final analysis willing to put their own cities at risk for the sake of western Europe. But what they were buying was a stable political order in Europe, a system in which free nations could live in peace.

It was by no means inevitable that a system of this sort would eventually take shape. Things could have developed in many different ways; even general war was not entirely out of the question. It certainly was not obvious in 1945 or 1949 that the world would end up with the kind of arrangements that had come into being by 1963. Even as late as 1959, Eisenhower could scarcely conceive of a situation where American forces were permanently stationed in Berlin: "Clearly we did not contemplate 50 years in occupation there." But American troops ended up remaining in Berlin for almost exactly fifty years, and left only after the Cold War had ended and Germany had been reunified.[198]

The fact that a particular path was followed had to do with the specific policy choices that were made. Those choices were not easy, and the process that led to a more or less stable system was not one that anybody would want to go through a second time. That simple fact should have a certain bearing on how we think about basic foreign policy issues today.

In 1998, Soviet armies are no longer on the Elbe; indeed, the Soviet Union no longer exists. West Berlin is not an isolated outpost in the middle of communist East Germany. That state has been absorbed into the Federal Republic, the communist system there has been swept away, and the western troops have left Berlin for good.

But the other half of the Cold War system remains in place. American troops are still in Europe, and Germany still has no nuclear weapons of her own. Germany's non-nuclear status was reaffirmed in the September 1990 Treaty of Moscow, which established the legal framework for German reunification. NATO still exists, and in fact the final settlement with the Soviet Union provided for the unified Germany's continuing membership in NATO. Even in 1990 the Americans took it for granted that both Russia and the western countries had a common interest in making sure that German power would be contained within the western system—that inclusion in NATO would keep Germany from ever posing a threat, and that greater risk would "come from a neutral Germany that becomes militaristic."[199] The Russians saw things much the same way. When Secretary of State James Baker asked the Soviet leader, Mikhail Gorbachev, whether he would really prefer "an independent Germany outside of NATO, with no U.S. forces on German soil," Gorbachev made it clear that he understood the advantages of the present system: "We don't really want to see a replay of Versailles, where the Germans were able to arm themselves. . . . The best way to constrain that process is to ensure that Germany is contained within European structures. What you have said

---

[198] Eisenhower-Khrushchev meeting, September 27, 1959, FRUS 1958–60, 9:46. The U.S. troops arrived at the beginning of July 1945 and left on September 8, 1994.

[199] Secretary of State James Baker, in a talk with Soviet Foreign Minister Shevardnadze in February 1990, quoted in Philip Zelikow and Condoleezza Rice, *Germany Unified and Europe Transformed: A Study in Statecraft* (Cambridge, Mass.: Harvard University Press, 1995), p. 181.

to me about your approach and your preference is very realistic."[200] The assumption was that America and Russia had a common interest in the maintenance of the fundamental structure that had come into being during the Cold War period. Neither wanted Germany to reemerge as a fully independent great power; both understood that a continuing American troop presence in Germany, and the maintenance of the NATO system, went hand in hand with that basic objective.

The Cold War may have ended, but the Cold War political system remains largely intact. Whether it can, or should, be kept intact is bound to be one of the great political issues of the twenty-first century.

[200] Gorbachev-Baker meeting, February 9, 1990, quoted in Zelikow and Rice, *Germany Unified,* p. 184.

SOURCES AND BIBLIOGRAPHY

THE BIBLIOGRAPHY does not include every work cited in the footnotes. It is meant to serve mainly as a finding aid for those books and articles cited there in abbreviated form—that is, for works cited more than once. For both published and unpublished sources, abbreviations were used extensively in the footnotes. Those abbreviations were given, in brackets, the first time a source was cited; they are again given, also in brackets, with the sources listed below; and they also appear in the list of source abbreviations, above, pp. xv–xvi.

Archival references contain at least some of the following information, but always in the following order: description of document, date, collection, series, subseries, box or volume, folder, record group, repository, and location of repository. The description is sometimes the title found on the document, but it is more often a description I give it ("briefing paper on NATO strategy") whether it is found on the document or not. In the case of records of meetings or memoranda of conversations, a reference to the most important participants in the discussion is generally all that is given (e.g., "Kennedy-Adenauer meeting," even when other people took part); terms like "notes of" or "record of" are not used. The date is the date of the meeting itself, not the date when the record was made. Certain information is deleted when it is easy to find a document without it: it is obvious, for example, to anyone working in the Kennedy Library that the documents in the President's Office Files there are in the Kennedy Papers, so there was no need to note the collection in any of the references. The same point applies to folder titles: sometimes the particular folder a document is in will be so obvious to anyone using the box that no folder title need be given; sometimes only an abbreviated folder title is all that is necessary.

Some of the unpublished documents cited here—that is, documents that have been neither printed nor published on microfilm or microfiche—are included in an Internet Supplement (IS), which I intend to maintain for at least ten years following the publication of the book. The Internet Supplement can be found at the following location: http://www.history.upenn.edu/trachtenberg. The documents included there were selected to illustrate an important method I used in developing the argument laid out in the book. Before documents are released to the public, they often get "sanitized"; certain documents are sanitized differently at different times or in different repositories. It is thus possible to study what gets deleted when documents are declassified; this gives the researcher some insight into what was really important—that is, some insight into what is considered so sensitive that it has to be kept from the public. The analysis of those documents, moreover, gives the researcher some sense for the nature of the bias introduced into the corpus of available evidence by the fact that declassification is a highly politicized process; once that bias is identified, one can control for it when an interpretation is being worked out.

The Internet Supplement also includes a number of appendices, which deal with detailed subjects or with issues only marginally related to the main thrust of the argument in the book. Those appendices are cited at appropriate points in the footnotes.

Appendix 1: The Potsdam Agreement and Reparations from Current Production
Appendix 2: The German Threat as a Pretext for Defense against Russia
Appendix 3: The United States, France and the German Question, 1953–1954
Appendix 4: The Politics of the Nuclear Sharing Question
Appendix 5: The Question of East German Control of Access to Berlin
Appendix 6: The U.S. Assessment of German Nuclear Aspirations

Appendix 7: U.S. Arms Control Policy under Eisenhower
Appendix 8: Kennedy and the Israeli Nuclear Program

The Internet Supplement also includes an informal guide to doing research on Cold War history.

Archival Sources

United States

Harry S Truman Library [HSTL], Independence, Missouri
  President's Secretary's Files [PSF]
  Dean Acheson Papers [AP]
    State Department and White House Advisor [SDWHA]
Dwight D. Eisenhower Library [DDEL], Abilene, Kansas
  Papers of Dwight D. Eisenhower as President (Ann Whitman File) [AWF]
    Administration Series [A]
    Ann Whitman Diary Series [AWD]
    Dwight D. Eisenhower Diary Series [DDED]
    International Series [I]
    National Security Council Series [NSC]
    Dulles-Herter Series [DH]
  White House Office. Office of the Staff Secretary Files [SS]
    International Series [I]
    International Trips and Meetings Series [ITM]
    Subject Series [S]
      Alphabetical subseries [A]
      Department of Defense subseries [DoD]
      Department of State subseries [DoS]
      White House subseries [WH]
  Office of the Special Assistant for National Security Affairs Files [OSANSA]
    National Security Council Series [NSC]
      Policy Papers subseries [PP]
      Subject subseries [S]
    Special Assistants Series [SA]
      Presidential subseries [P]
      Subject subseries [S]
  John Foster Dulles Papers [DP]. (A copy is at the Seeley Mudd Library in Princeton.)
    General Correspondence and Memoranda Series [GCM]
    Subject Series [S]
    Telephone Conversations Series [TC]
    White House Memoranda Series [WHM]
    Special Assistant's Chronological Series [SACS]
  Lauris Norstad Papers [NP]
John F. Kennedy Library [JKFL], Boston, Massachusetts
  National Security Files [NSF]
  President's Office Files [POF]
United States National Archives [USNA], College Park, Maryland
  Record Group [RG] 59: Department of State
    Central Files
      Decimal Files (1945–62)
      Subject-Numeric Files (1963) [DOSCF for 1963]

Lot Files
    Policy Planning Staff [PPS] records
    Conference Files (cited by CF number)
    Files relating to disarmament
    Records relating to atomic energy
    Records relating to State Department participation in the National Security
        Council, 1947–61
  Record Group 200
    Robert McNamara Papers
  Record Group 218: Joint Chiefs of Staff
    Central Files
    Chairman's Files [CJCS]
  Record Group 273: National Security Council
  Record Group 319: Army Staff
Library of Congress [LOC], Washington, D.C.
  Averell Harriman Papers [HP]
Seeley Mudd Library [ML], Princeton University, Princeton, New Jersey
  George Ball Papers
  John Foster Dulles Papers [DP] (Copy of the collection at the Eisenhower Library)
  Dulles State Papers [DSP]. Classified documents, on microfilm, cited by frame number;
    the documents cited have been declassified and can be consulted without a clearance.
  James Forrestal Papers [FP]
    Forrestal Diaries [FD]
  Arthur Krock Papers [KP]
  Livingstone Merchant Papers
Sterling Memorial Library, Yale University, New Haven, Connecticut
  Dean Acheson Papers
  Henry Stimson Papers
Rand Corporation, Santa Monica, California
  Rand Corporation archives
Office of Air Force History, Bolling Air Force Base, Washington, D.C.
National Security Archive [NSA], Washington, D.C.
  Berlin Crisis File [NSABF]
National Defense University [NDU], Washington, D.C.
  Maxwell Taylor Papers [TP]
Department of Defense, Freedom of Information Office, Washington [DOD-FOIA]. A
  small library of Defense Department material released under the Freedom of
  Information Act [FOIA]
Department of State, Freedom of Information Office, Washington [DOS-FOIA]. State
  Department material released under the FOIA, and available on microfiche.

Great Britain

Public Record Office [PRO], Kew
  FO 371: Foreign Office, Political Correspondence
  FO 800: For Ernest Bevin Papers
  Prem 11: Prime Minister's Office files
  Defe 4, 5 and 6: Chiefs of Staff files
  Cab 128 and 129: Cabinet meetings and memoranda
  Cab 133: International meetings
Liddell Hart Centre for Military Archives [LHCMA], King's College, London
  Ismay Papers

Imperial War Museum, London
  Montgomery Papers
Churchill Archives Centre, Churchill College, Cambridge University
  Winston Churchill Papers
  Selwyn Lloyd Papers

France

French Foreign Ministry Archives [FFMA], Paris
  Y: International, 1944–49
  Z: Europe, 1944–49
  Europe, 1949–55
  René Massigli Papers [MP]
  Henri Bonnet Papers [BP]
Service Historique de l'Armée de Terre [SHAT], Vincennes
  Etat-Major de la Défense Nationale (4Q)
  Clément Blanc Papers (1K145)
Institut Mendès France, Paris
  Mendès France Papers

MAJOR UNPUBLISHED REPORTS, STUDIES, AND DECLASSIFIED HISTORIES

Bowie, Robert. "The North Atlantic Nations: Tasks for the 1960's" [Bowie Report]. August 21, 1960. A full copy was made available through the Nuclear History Program in 1991.
Lumpkin, H. H. "The SACEUR/USCINCEUR Concept." U.S. European Command, August 1957. DOD-FOIA.
"History of the Custody and Deployment of Nuclear Weapons, July 1945 through September 1977." Office of the Assistant to the Secretary of Defense (Atomic Energy), February 1978.
May, Ernest, John Steinbruner, and Thomas Wolfe. "History of the Strategic Arms Competition, 1945–1972," Part I. Office of the Secretary of Defense, Historical Office, March 1981. DOD-FOIA.
Neustadt, Richard. "Skybolt and Nassau: American Policy-Making and Anglo-American Relations" [Neustadt Report], November 1963. NSF, box 322, Staff Memoranda: Neustadt, JFKL. Also available from the Kennedy School of Government Case Program, Harvard University, Cambridge, Mass.
U.S. Congress, Joint Committee on Atomic Energy. Report of Ad Hoc Subcommittee on the Assignment of Nuclear Weapons to NATO [Holifield Report]. February 15, 1961. Available at the NSA.
U.S. Department of State, Historical Office. "Crisis over Berlin: American Policy Concerning the Soviet Threats to Berlin, November 1958 - December 1962" [DOS Berlin History]. Parts 1–6, covering November 1958 through September 1961. October 1966–April 1970. Available at the NSA.
Wainstein, L., et al. "The Evolution of U.S. Strategic Command and Control and Warning, 1945–1972." Institute for Defense Analyses, June 1975. DOD-FOIA.

UNPUBLISHED ORAL HISTORIES

Interview with Carl Kaysen. August 3, 1988: Marc Trachtenberg and David Rosenberg, interviewers. October 17, 1988: Marc Trachtenberg and Stephen Van Evera, interviewers. Tapes and a transcript are in the author's possession.

Nuclear History Program. Transcript of Berlin Crisis Oral History Project Oral History Sessions Nos. 1–8. Conducted October 1990–October 1992. Principal interviewer: David Rosenberg. On deposit at NSA.

Office of Air Force History, Bolling Air Force Base, Washington, D.C.. Oral history interviews with General David Burchinal (April 1975), General Truman Landon (May-June 1977), and General David Holloway (August 1977).

PUBLISHED SOURCES

Diplomatic Documents

United States. Department of State. *Foreign Relations of the United States* [FRUS].
  The Conferences at Malta and Yalta, 1945. Washington, D.C.: GPO, 1955.
  The Conference of Berlin (The Potsdam Conference), 1945. 2 vols. Washington, D.C.: GPO, 1960.
  1945:
    Vol. 2: *General: Political and Economic Matters.* Washington, D.C.: GPO, 1967.
    Vol. 3: *European Advisory Commission; Austria; Germany.* Washington, D.C.: GPO, 1968.
    Vol. 4: *Europe.* Washington, D.C.: GPO, 1968.
    Vol. 5: *Europe.* Washington, D.C.: GPO, 1967.
  1946:
    Vol. 1: *General.* Washington, D.C.: GPO, 1972.
    Vol. 2: *Council of Foreign Ministers.* Washington, D.C.: GPO, 1970.
    Vol. 3: *Paris Peace Conference.* Washington, D.C.: GPO, 1970.
    Vol. 5: *The British Commonwealth; Western and Central Europe.* Washington, D.C.: GPO, 1969.
  1947:
    Vol. 1: *General.* Washington, D.C.: GPO, 1973.
    Vol. 2: *Council of Foreign Ministers; Germany and Austria.* Washington, D.C.: GPO, 1972.
    Vol. 3: *The British Commonwealth; Europe.* Washington, D.C.: GPO, 1972.
  1948:
    Vol. 1 (2 parts): *General.* Washington, D.C.: GPO, 1975.
    Vol. 2: *Germany and Austria.* Washington, D.C.: GPO, 1973.
    Vol. 3: *Western Europe.* Washington, D.C.: GPO, 1974.
  1949:
    Vol. 1: *National Security Affairs.* Washington, D.C.: GPO, 1976.
    Vol. 3: *Council of Foreign Ministers; Germany and Austria.* Washington, D.C.: GPO, 1974.
  1950:
    Vol. 1: *National Security Affairs.* Washington, D.C.: GPO, 1977.
    Vol. 3: *Western Europe.* Washington, D.C.: GPO, 1977.
    Vol. 4: *Central and Eastern Europe; The Soviet Union.* Washington, D.C.: GPO, 1980.
  1951:
    Vol. 1: *National Security Affairs.* Washington, D.C.: GPO, 1979.
    Vol. 3 (2 parts): *European Security and the German Question.* Washington, D.C.: GPO, 1981.
  1952–54:
    Vol. 2 (2 parts): *National Security Affairs.* Washington, D.C.: GPO, 1984.

Vol. 5 (2 parts): *Western European Security*. Washington, D.C.: GPO, 1983.

Vol. 7 (2 parts): *Germany and Austria*. Washington, D.C.: GPO, 1986.

1955–57:

Vol. 4: *Western European Security and Integration*. Washington, D.C.: GPO, 1986.

Vol. 5: *Austrian State Treaty; Summit and Foreign Ministers Meetings, 1955*. Washington, D.C.: GPO, 1988.

Vol. 19: *National Security Policy*. Washington, D.C.: GPO, 1990.

Vol. 26: *Central and Southeastern Europe*. Washington, D.C.: GPO, 1992.

Vol. 27: *Western Europe and Canada*. Washington, D.C.: GPO, 1992.

1958–60:

Vol. 3: *National Security Policy; Arms Control and Disarmament*. Washington, D.C.: GPO, 1996.

Vol. 7, pt. 1: *Western European Integration and Security; Canada*. Washington, D.C.: GPO, 1993.

Vol. 7, pt. 2: *Western Europe*. Washington, D.C.: GPO, 1993.

Vol. 8: *Berlin Crisis, 1958–1959*. Washington, D.C.: GPO, 1993.

Vol. 9: *Berlin Crisis, 1959–1960; Germany; Austria*. Washington, D.C.: GPO, 1993.

1961–63:

Vol. 6: *Kennedy-Khrushchev Exchanges*. Washington, D.C.: GPO, 1996.

Vol. 7: *Arms Control and Disarmament*. Washington, D.C.: GPO, 1995.

Vol. 8: *National Security Policy*. Washington, D.C.: GPO, 1996.

Vol. 9: *Foreign Economic Policy*. Washington, D.C.: GPO, 1995.

Vol. 11: *Cuban Missile Crisis and Aftermath*. Washington, D.C.: GPO, 1996.

Vol. 13: *West Europe and Canada*. Washington, D.C.: GPO, 1994.

Vol. 14: *Berlin Crisis, 1961–62*. Washington, GPO, 1993.

Vol. 15: *Berlin Crisis, 1962–1963*. Washington, D.C.: GPO, 1994.

Documents on British Policy Overseas [DBPO]

Series I

Vol. 1: *The Conference at Potsdam, July–August 1945* (with microfiche supplement). London: HMSO, 1984.

Vol. 5: *Germany and Western Europe, 11 August–31 December 1945*. London: HMSO: 1990.

Vol. 6: *Eastern Europe, August 1945–April 1946*. London: HMSO, 1991.

Series II

Vol. 2: *The London Conferences: Anglo-American Relations and Cold War Strategy, January–June 1950*. London: HMSO, 1987.

Vol. 3: *German Rearmament, September–December 1950*. London: HMSO, 1989.

France. Ministère des Affaires Etrangères. Commission de Publication des Documents Diplomatiques Français. *Documents Diplomatiques Français* [DDF]

1954. (July 21–December 31). Paris: Imprimerie Nationale, 1987.

1955. 2 vols. Paris: Imprimerie Nationale, 1987–88.

1956. 3 vols. Paris: Imprimerie Nationale, 1988–90.

1957. 2 vols. Paris: Imprimerie Nationale, 1990–91.

1958. 2 vols. Paris: Imprimerie Nationale, 1992–93.

1959. 2 vols. Paris: Imprimerie Nationale, 1994–95.

Federal Republic of Germany. Auswärtiges Amt. *Akten zur auswärtigen Politik der Bundesrepublik Deutschland* [AAPBD]

Vol. 1: *Adenauer und die Hohen Kommissare, 1949–1951*. Munich: Oldenbourg, 1989.

1963. 3 vols. Munich: Oldenbourg, 1994.

Other Printed Material, Including Memoirs

Acheson, Dean. *Present at the Creation: My Years at the State Department.* New York: Norton, 1969.

Adenauer, Konrad. *Erinnerungen.*

　　Vol. 1: *1945–1953.* Stuttgart: Deutsche Verlags-Anstalt, 1965.

　　Vol. 3: *1955–1959.* Stuttgart: Deutsche Verlags-Anstalt, 1967.

　　Vol. 4: *1959–1963 (Fragmente).* Stuttgart: Deutsche Verlags-Anstalt, 1968.

　　———. *Memoirs 1945–1953.* Chicago: Regnery, 1966.

Alphand, Hervé. *L'étonnement d'être.* Paris: Fayard, 1977.

Aron, Raymond. *Les articles du Figaro,* ed. Georges-Henri Soutou. Vol. 2: *La coexistence, 1955–1965.* Paris: Fallois, 1993.

Ayers, Eben. *Truman in the White House: The Diary of Eben A. Ayers,* ed. Robert Ferrell. Columbia: University of Missouri Press, 1991.

Billotte, Pierre. *Le passé au futur.* Paris: Stock, 1979.

Buchstab, Günter, ed. *Adenauer: "Wir haben wirklich etwas geschaffen": Die Protokolle des CDU-Bundesvorstands, 1953–1957.* Düsseldorf: Droste, 1990.

　　———, ed. *Adenauer: ". . . um den Frieden zu gewinnen": Die Protokolle des CDU-Bundesvorstands 1957–1961.* Düsseldorf: Droste, 1994.

Central Intelligence Agency, Center for the Study of Intelligence. *Selected Estimates on the Soviet Union, 1950–1959,* ed. Scott Koch. Washington, D.C.: CIA Center for the Study of Intelligence, 1993.

Chauvel, Jean. *Commentaire,* vol. 3: *De Berne à Paris (1952–1962).* Paris: Fayard, 1973.

Chuev, Felix. *Molotov Remembers: Inside Kremlin Politics, Conversations with Felix Chuev,* ed. Albert Resis. Chicago: Dee, 1993.

Clay, Lucius. *The Papers of General Lucius D. Clay: Germany 1945–1949,* ed. Jean Smith. 2 vols. Bloomington: Indiana University Press, 1974.

Couve de Murville, Maurice. *Une politique étrangère, 1958–1968.* Paris: Plon, 1971.

　　———. *Le monde en face: Entretiens avec Maurice Delarue.* Paris: Plon, 1989.

De Gaulle, Charles. *Mémoires d'espoir: le Renouveau.* Paris: Plon, 1970.

De Gaulle, Charles. *Discours et messages.* vol. 4: *Août 1962–décembre 1965.* Paris: Plon, 1970.

　　———. *Lettres, notes et carnets* [LNC]

　　Juin 1958–décembre 1960. Paris: Plon, 1985.

　　1961–1963. Paris: Plon, 1986.

Djilas, Milovan. *Conversations with Stalin.* New York: Harcourt Brace, 1962.

Eisenhower, Dwight. *Papers of Dwight David Eisenhower,* ed. Louis Galambos et al. vols. 9–17. Baltimore: Johns Hopkins University Press, 1978–1996.

　　———. *The Eisenhower Diaries,* ed. Robert Ferrell. New York: Norton, 1981.

Forrestal, James. *The Forrestal Diaries,* ed. Walter Millis. New York: Viking, 1951.

Kohn, Richard, and Joseph Harahan, eds. *Strategic Air Warfare: An Interview with Generals Curtis E. LeMay, Leon Johnson, David A. Burchinal and Jack J. Catton.* Washington, D.C.: Office of Air Force History, 1988.

Krone, Heinrich. "Aufzeichnungen zur Deutschland- und Ostpolitik 1954–1969" [Krone Diary], ed. Klaus Gotto. *Adenauer-Studien,* vol. 3, Rudolf Morsey and Konrad Repgen. Mainz: Matthias Grünewald, 1974.

Lane, Arthur Bliss. *I Saw Poland Betrayed: An American Ambassador Reports to the American People.* Indianapolis: Bobbs-Merrill, 1948.

Loewenheim, Francis, Harold Langley, and Manfred Jonas. eds. *Roosevelt and Churchill: Their Secret Wartime Correspondence.* New York: Dutton, 1975.

McClellan, Woodford. "Molotov Remembers," Cold War International History Project *Bulletin*, no. 1 (Spring 1992): 17–20.

Macmillan, Harold. *Riding the Storm, 1956–1959.* New York: Harper, 1971.

———. *Pointing the Way, 1959–1961.* London: Macmillan, 1972.

Massigli, René. *Une comédie des erreurs: Souvenirs et réflexions sur une étape de la construction européenne.* Paris: Plon, 1978.

May, Ernest, and Philip Zelikow. *The Kennedy Tapes: Inside the White House during the Cuban Missile Crisis.* Cambridge, Mass.: Harvard University Press, 1997.

Mendès France, Pierre. *Oeuvres complètes,* vol. 3: *Gouverner, c'est choisir.* Paris: Gallimard, 1986.

Murphy, Robert. *Diplomat Among Warriors.* Garden City, N.Y.: Doubleday, 1964.

Nitze, Paul. *From Hiroshima to Glasnost.* New York: Grove Weidenfeld, 1989.

Osterheld, Horst. *"Ich gehe nicht leichten Herzens . . . ": Adenauers letzte Kanzlerjahre, ein dokumentarisches Bericht.* Mainz: Matthias Grünewald, 1986.

Peyrefitte, Alain. *C'était de Gaulle.* Paris: Fayard, 1994.

Pieck, Wilhelm. *Wilhelm Pieck: Aufzeichnungen zur Deutschlandpolitik, 1945–1963,* ed. Rolf Badstübner and Wilfried Loth. Berlin: Akademie Verlag, 1994).

Public Papers of the Presidents [PPP], for Eisenhower and Kennedy periods.

Radford, Arthur. *From Pearl Harbor to Vietnam: The Memoirs of Admiral Arthur W. Radford,* ed. Stephen Jurika, Jr. Stanford, Calif.: Hoover Institution Press, 1980.

Ratchford, B. U., and Ross, W. D. *Berlin Reparations Assignment: Round One of the German Peace Settlement.* Chapel Hill: University of North Carolina Press, 1947.

Ruhm von Oppen, Beate. *Documents on Germany under Occupation.* London: Oxford University Press, 1955.

Sulzberger, Cyrus. *The Last of the Giants.* New York: Macmillan, 1970.

Trachtenberg, Marc, ed. *The Development of American Strategic Thought, 1945–1969.* 6 vols. New York: Garland, 1988.

Truman, Harry. *Memoirs: Year of Decisions.* Garden City, N.Y.: Doubleday, 1955

———. *Dear Bess: The Letters from Harry to Bess Truman, 1910–1959,* ed. Robert Ferrell. New York: Norton, 1983.

Truman, Harry. *Strictly Personal and Confidential: The Letters Harry Truman Never Mailed,* ed. Monte Poen. Boston: Little Brown, 1982.

United States. Senate. *Executive Sessions of the Senate Foreign Relations Committee (Historical Series)*
　　Vol. 14: *1962.* Washington, D.C.: GPO, 1986.
　　Vol. 15: *1963.* Washington, D.C.: GPO, 1986.

Walters, Vernon. *Silent Missions.* Garden City, N.Y.: Doubleday, 1978.

Microform Sources

Declassified Documents Reference System [DDRS]. Documents on microfiche, with printed index, compiled periodically. Washington, D.C.: Carollton Press.

National Security Archive. *The Cuban Missile Crisis, 1962* (microfiche, with printed index and guide). Alexandria, Va.: Chadwyck-Healey, 1990.

———. *The Berlin Crisis, 1958–1962* (microfiche, with printed index and guide). Alexandria, Va.: Chadwyck-Healey, 1992.

National Security Council: Documents (with supplements; microfilm with printed indexes). Bethesda, Md.: University Publications of America, 1980–95.

National Security Council: Minutes of Meetings (with supplements; microfilm with printed indexes). Bethesda, Md.: University Publications of America, 1982–1995.

United States Department of State. *Secretary of State's Memoranda of Conversation, November*

1952–December 1954 [SSMC]. Microfiche supplement to FRUS. Washington, D.C.: GPO, 1992.

———. *Foreign Relations of the United States, 1961–63.* Microfiche supplements. Vols. 7–9. Washington, D.C.: Department of State, 1997. Vols. 13–15. Washington, D.C.: Department of State, 1995.

SCHOLARLY BOOKS, ARTICLES, AND DISSERTATIONS

Adamthwaite, Anthony. "Britain and the World, 1945–9: The View from the Foreign Office." *International Affairs* 61, no. 2 (Spring 1985): 223–235.

Ahonen, Pertti. "Franz-Josef Strauss and the German Nuclear Question, 1956–1962." *Journal of Strategic Studies* 18, no. 2: (June 19995): 25–51.

Alperovitz, Gar. *Atomic Diplomacy: Hiroshima and Potsdam.* New York: Simon and Schuster, 1965.

Ambrose, Stephen. *Eisenhower,* vol. 2. New York: Simon and Schuster, 1984.

Appleby, Charles, Jr. "Eisenhower and Arms Control, 1953–1961: A Balance of Risks." Ph.D. diss., Johns Hopkins University, 1987.

Artner, Stephen. *A Change of Course: The West German Social Democrats and NATO, 1957–1961.* Westport, Conn.: Greenwood Press, 1985.

Backer, John. *Winds of History: The German Years of Lucius DuBignon Clay.* New York: Van Nostrand, 1983.

Baylis, John. *Anglo-American Defense Relations 1939–1984: The Special Relationship.* 2d ed. New York: St. Martin's, 1984.

———. *The Diplomacy of Pragmatism: Britain and the Formation of NATO, 1942–1949.* Kent, Ohio: Kent State University Press, 1993.

———. *Ambiguity and Deterrence: British Nuclear Strategy, 1945–1964.* Oxford: Clarendon, 1995.

Bédarida, François, and Jean-Pierre Rioux. *Pierre Mendès France et le mendésisme.* Paris: Fayard, 1985.

Botti, Timothy. *The Long Wait: The Forging of the Anglo-American Nuclear Alliance, 1945–1958.* New York: Greenwood, 1987.

Buffet, Cyril. "Le Blocus de Berlin: Les Alliés, l'Allemagne et Berlin, 1945–1949." Doctoral thesis, University of Paris IV, 1987.

———. "La politique nucléaire de la France et la seconde crise de Berlin, 1958–1962." *Relations internationales,* no. 59 (Fall 1989): 347–358.

———. *Mourir pour Berlin: La France et l'Allemagne, 1945–1949.* Paris: Colin, 1991.

Bullock, Alan. *Ernest Bevin: Foreign Secretary, 1945–1951.* New York: Norton, 1983.

Bundy, McGeorge. *Danger and Survival: Choices about the Bomb in the First Fifty Years.* New York: Random House, 1988.

Burr, William. "Avoiding the Slippery Slope: The Eisenhower Administration and the Berlin Crisis, November 1958–January 1959." *Diplomatic History,* 18, no. 3 (Spring 1994): 177–205.

Chang, Gordon. *Friends and Enemies: The United States, China, and the Soviet Union, 1948–1972.* Stanford, Calif.: Stanford University Press, 1990.

Clark, Ian. *Nuclear Diplomacy and the Special Relationship: Britain's Deterrent and America, 1957–1962.* Oxford: Clarendon, 1994.

Clemens, Diane. *Yalta.* New York: Oxford University Press, 1970.

Cohen, Avner. "Stumbling into Opacity: The United States, Israel, and the Atom, 1960–63," *Security Studies* 4, no. 2 (Winter 1994–95): 195–241.

412   · *SOURCES AND BIBLIOGRAPHY* ·

Cold War International History Project [CWIHP]
  Bulletin.
  Working Paper series.
Coutrot, Aline. "La politique atomique sous le gouvernement de Mendès France." In François Bédarida and Jean-Pierre Rioux, *Pierre Mendès France et le mendésisme.* Paris: Fayard, 1985.
Dallek, Robert. *Franklin D. Roosevelt and American Foreign Policy, 1932–1945.* Oxford: Oxford University Press, 1979.
Davis, Lynn. *The Cold War Begins: Soviet-American Conflict over Eastern Europe.* Princeton, N.J.: Princeton University Press, 1974.
Deighton, Anne. *The Impossible Peace: Britain, the Division of Germany and the Origins of the Cold War.* Oxford: Clarendon, 1990.
Dilks, David. "Britain and Europe, 1948–1950: The Prime Minister, the Foreign Secretary and the Cabinet." In *Histoire des débuts de la construction européenne (mars 1948–mai 1950),* ed. Raymond Poidevin. Brussels: Bruylant, 1986.
Doise, Jean, and Maurice Vaïsse. *Diplomatie et outil militaire, 1871–1969.* Paris: Imprimerie Nationale, 1987.
Douglas, Roy. *From War to Cold War, 1942–1948.* New York: St. Martin's, 1981.
Eisenberg, Carolyn. *Drawing the Line: The American Decision to Divide Germany, 1944–1949.* Cambridge: Cambridge University Press, 1996.
Feaver, Peter. *Guarding the Guardians: Civilian Control of Nuclear Weapons in the United States.* Ithaca, N.Y.: Cornell University Press, 1992.
Fischer, Peter. "Das Projekt einer trilateralen Nuklearkooperation." *Historisches Jahrbuch* 112 (1992): 143–156.
———. "Die Reaktion der Bundesregierung auf die Nuklearisierung der westlichen Verteidigung." *Militärgeschichtliche Mitteilungen* 52, no. 1 (1993): 105–132.
Foschepoth, Josef. "Britische Deutschlandpolitik zwischen Jalta und Potsdam," *Vierteljahrshefte für Zeitgeschichte* 30, no. 4 (1982): 675–714.
——— ed. *Adenauer und die deutsche Frage,* 2d ed. Göttingen: Vandenhoeck and Ruprecht, 1990.
Franklin, William. "Zonal Boundaries and Access to Berlin," *World Politics* 16 (1963): 1–31.
Gaddis, John Lewis. *The United States and the Origins of the Cold War, 1941–1947.* New York: Columbia University Press, 1972.
———. *Strategies of Containment: A Critical Appraisal of Postwar American National Security Policy.* New York: Oxford University Press, 1982.
———. "Spheres of Influence; The United States and Europe, 1948–1949," In his *The Long Peace: Inquiries into the History of the Cold War.* New York: Oxford University Press, 1987.
———. *We Now Know: Rethinking Cold War History.* Oxford: Clarendon, 1997.
Gardner, Lloyd. *Spheres of Influence: The Great Powers Partition Europe from Munich to Yalta.* Chicago: Ivan Dee, 1993.
Gerbet, Pierre. "Les origines du Plan Schuman: Le choix de la méthode communautaire par le gouvernement français," in *Histoire des débuts de la construction européenne (9 mars 1948–mai 1950),* ed. Raymond Poidevin. Brussels: Bruylant, 1986.
Gillingham, John. *Coal, Steel, and the Rebirth of Europe, 1945–1955: The Germans and French from Ruhr Conflict to Economic Community.* New York: Cambridge University Press, 1991.
Greenwood, Sean. "Bevin, the Ruhr and the Division of Germany: August 1945–December 1946." *Historical Journal* 29, no. 1 (1986): 203–212.
Greiner, Christian. "Zwischen Integration und Nation: Die militärische Eingliederung der Bundesrepublik Deutschland in die NATO, 1954 bis 1957." In *Westdeutschland 1945–1955: Unterwerfung, Kontrolle, Integration,* ed. L. Herbst. Munich: Oldenbourg, 1986.

Guillen, Pierre. "Les chefs militaires français, le réarmement de l'Allemagne et la CED (1950–1954)." *Revue d'histoire de la deuxième guerre mondiale,* no. 129 (January 1983): 3–33.

———. "Les militaires français et la création de l'OTAN." In *La France et l'OTAN, 1949–1996,* ed. Maurice Vaïsse et al. Paris: Editions Complexe, 1996.

Harbutt, Fraser. *The Iron Curtain: Churchill, America, and the Origins of the Cold War.* New York: Oxford University Press, 1986.

Robert d'Harcourt. *L'Allemagne d'Adenauer à Erhard.* Paris: Flammarion, 1964.

Harrison, Hope. "The Bargaining Power of Weaker Allies in Bipolarity and Crisis: The Dynamics of Soviet–East German Relations, 1953–1961," Ph.D. diss., Columbia University, 1993.

———. Ulbricht and the Concrete 'Rose': New Archival Evidence on the Dynamics of Soviet-East German Relations and the Berlin Crisis, 1958–1961. Cold War International History Project Working Paper No. 5. Woodrow Wilson Center, Washington, D.C.: 1993.

Heuser, Beatrice. *Western Containment Policies in the Cold War: The Yugoslav Case, 1948–1953.* London: Routledge, 1988.

Hogan, Michael. *The Marshall Plan: America, Britain, and the Reconstruction of Western Europe, 1947–1952.* Cambridge: Cambridge University Press, 1987.

Horne, Alistair. *Harold Macmillan,* vol. 2. New York: Viking, 1989.

Hüser, Dietmar. "Charles de Gaulle, Georges Bidault, Robert Schuman et l'Allemagne." *Francia* 23 (1996): 49–73.

Institut Charles de Gaulle. *De Gaulle et son siècle,* vol. 5. Paris: Plon, 1991.

Ireland, Timothy. *Creating the Entangling Alliance: The Origins of the North Atlantic Treaty Organization.* Westport, Conn.: Greenwood, 1981.

Joint Chiefs of Staff, Historical Office. *History of the Joint Chiefs of Staff* [JCS History]
   Vol. 2: Kenneth Condit, *The Joint Chiefs of Staff and National Policy, 1947–49.* Wilmington, Del.: Glazier, 1979.
   Vol. 3: James Schnabel and Robert Watson, *The Korean War,* part 1. Wilmington, Del.: Glazier, 1979.
   Vol. 4: Walter Poole, *The Joint Chiefs of Staff and National Policy, 1950–1952.* Wilmington, Del.: Glazier, 1979.
   Vol. 5: Robert J. Watson, *The Joint Chiefs of Staff and National Policy, 1953–54.* Washington, D.C.: GPO, 1986.
   Vol. 6: Kenneth Condit, *The Joint Chiefs of Staff and National Policy, 1955–1956.* Washington, D.C.: GPO, 1992.

Kaplan, Fred. *The Wizards of Armageddon.* New York: Simon and Schuster, 1983.

Kaplan, Karel. *Dans les archives du Comité Central.* Paris: Albin Michel, 1978.

———. *The Short March: The Communist Takeover in Czechoslovakia, 1945–1948.* New York: St. Martin's, 1987.

Kaplan, Lawrence. *The United States and NATO: The Formative Years.* Lexington: University of Kentucky Press, 1984.

Kimball, Warren. *The Juggler: Franklin Roosevelt as Wartime Statesman.* Princeton, N.J.: Princeton University Press, 1991.

———, ed. *Swords or Ploughshares? The Morgenthau Plan for Defeated Nazi Germany, 1943–1946.* Philadelphia: Lippincott, 1976.

Koerfer, Daniel. *Kampf ums Kanzleramt: Erhard und Adenauer.* Stuttgart: Deutsche Verlags-Anstalt, 1988.

Kosthorst, Daniel. *Brentano und die deutsche Einheit: Die Deutschland- und Ostpolitik des Aussenministers im Kabinett Adenauer 1955–1961.* Düsseldorf: Droste, 1993.

Krieger, Wolfgang. *General Lucius D. Clay und die amerikanische Deutschlandpolitik, 1945–1949.* 2d ed. Stuttgart: Klett-Cotta, 1988.

Küsters, Hanns Jürgen. "Souveränität und ABC-Waffen-Verzicht: Deutsche Diplomatie auf der Londoner Neunmächte-Konferenz 1954." *Vierteljahrshefte für Zeitgeschichte* 42, no. 4 (October 1994): 499–536.

Kuklick, Bruce. *American Policy and the Division of Germany: The Clash with Russia over Reparations.* Ithaca, N.Y.: Cornell University Press, 1962.

Kuniholm, Bruce. *The Origins of the Cold War in the Near East and Greece.* Princeton, N.J.: Princeton University Press, 1980.

Large, David. *Germans to the Front: West German Rearmament in the Adenauer Era.* Chapel Hill: University of North Carolina Press, 1996.

Laufer, Jochen. "Konfrontation oder Kooperation? Zur sowjetischen Politik in Deutschland und im Alliierten Kontrollrat 1945–1948," In *Studien zur Geschichte der SBZ/DDR*, ed. Alexander Fischer. Berlin: Duncker and Humblot, 1993.

Leffler, Melvyn. *A Preponderance of Power: National Security, the Truman Administration, and the Cold War.* Stanford, Calif.: Stanford University Press, 1992.

Loth, Wilfried. "Adenauers Ort in der deutschen Geschichte." In *Adenauer und die Deutsche Frage*, ed. Josef Foschepoth. 2d ed. Göttingen: Vandenhoeck and Ruprecht, 1990.

Lundestad, Geir. *The American Non-Policy towards Eastern Europe, 1943–1947: Universalism in an Area not of Essential Interest to the United States.* New York: Humanities Press, 1975.

Mai, Gunter. *Der Alliierte Kontrollrat in Deutschland 1945–1948: Alliierte Einheit–deutsche Teilung?* Munich: Oldenbourg, 1995.

Mark, Eduard. "American Policy toward Eastern Europe and the Origins of the Cold War, 1941–1946: An Alternative Interpretation." *Journal of American History* 68, no. 2 (September 1981): 313–336.

Mastny, Vojtech. *The Cold War and Soviet Insecurity: The Stalin Years.* New York: Oxford University Press, 1996.

Mélandri, Pierre. *Les Etats-Unis face à l'unification de l'Europe.* Paris: A. Pedone, 1980.

Messer, Robert. *The End of an Alliance: James F. Byrnes, Roosevelt, Truman, and the Origins of the Cold War.* Chapel Hill: University of North Carolina Press, 1982.

Militärgeschichtliches Forschungsamt. *Anfänge westdeutscher Sicherheitspolitik, 1945–1956.*
    Vol. 1: Roland G. Foerster, Christian Greiner, Georg Meyer, Hans-Jürgen Rautenberg, and Norbert Wiggershaus, *Von der Kapitulation bis zum Pleven-Plan.* Munich: Oldenbourg, 1982.
    Vol. 2: Lutz Köllner, Klaus Maier, Wilhelm Meier-Dörnberg, and Hans-Erich Volkmann, *Die EVG-Phase.* Munich: Oldenbourg, 1990.
    Vol. 3: Hans Ehlert, Christian Greiner, Georg Meyer, and Bruno Thoss, *Die NATO-Option.* Munich: Oldenbourg, 1993.

Miscamble, Wilson. *George F. Kennan and the Making of American Foreign Policy.* Princeton, N.J.: Princeton University Press, 1992.

Mosely, Philip E. "The Occupation of Germany: New Light on How the Zones were Drawn." *Foreign Affairs* 28 (1949–50): 580–604.

Naimark, Norman. *The Russians in Germany: A History of the Soviet Zone of Occupation, 1945–1949.* Cambridge, Mass.: Belknap Press, 1995.

Nash, Philip. *The Other Missiles of October: Eisenhower, Kennedy, and the Jupiters, 1957–1963.* Chapel Hill: University of North Carolina Press, 1997.

Newhouse, John. *De Gaulle and the Anglo-Saxons.* London: Andre Deutsch, 1970.

Nunnerley, David. *President Kennedy and Britain.* New York: St. Martin's, 1972.

Nuti, Leopoldo. "Le rôle de l'Italie dans les négociations trilatérales, 1957–1958," *Revue d'histoire diplomatique* 104, nos. 1–2 (1990): 133–156.

————. "'Me Too, Please': Italy and the Politics of Nuclear Weapons, 1945–1975." *Diplomacy and Statecraft* 4, no. 1 (March 1993): 114–148.

Parrish, Scott. "The USSR and the Security Dilemma: Explaining Soviet Self-Encirclement, 1945–1985." Ph.D. diss., Columbia University, 1993.

Pautsch, Ilse Dorothee. "Im Sog der Entspannungspolitik: Die USA, das Teststopp-Abkommen und die Deutschland-Frage." In *Von Adenauer zu Erhard: Studien zur auswärtigen Politik der Bundesrepublik Deutschland 1963,* ed. Rainer Blasius. Munich: Oldenbourg, 1994.

Pechatnov, Vladimir. "The Big Three after World War II: New Documents on Soviet Thinking about Post War Relations with the United States and Great Britain," Cold War International History Project Working Paper no. 13. Woodrow Wilson Center, Washington, D.C. 1995.

Pedlow, Gregory. "General Lauris Norstad and the Second Berlin Crisis." Unpublished paper.

Pierre, Andrew. *Nuclear Politics: The British Experience with an Independent Strategic Force, 1939–1970.* London: Oxford University Press, 1972.

Poidevin, Raymond. "Le facteur Europe dans la politique allemande de Robert Schuman." In *Histoire des débuts de la construction européenne (9 mars 1948–mai 1950),* ed. Raymond Poidevin. Brussels: Bruylant, 1986.

————. *Robert Schuman, homme d'état: 1886–1963.* Paris: Imprimerie Nationale, 1986.

Pruessen, Ronald. *John Foster Dulles: The Road to Power.* New York: Free Press, 1982.

Rearden, Steven. *History of the Office of the Secretary of Defense,* vol. 1: *The Formative Years, 1947–1950.* Washington, D.C.: Office of the Secretary of Defense Historical Office, 1984.

Richter, James. "Reexamining Soviet Policy towards Germany during the Beria Interregnum." Cold War International History Project Working Paper no. 3. Woodrow Wilson Center, Washington, D.C., 1992.

Riste, Olav, ed. *Western Security: The Formative Years.* New York: Columbia University Press, 1985.

Rosecrance, Richard. *Defense of the Realm: British Strategy in the Nuclear Epoch.* New York: Columbia University Press, 1968.

Rosenberg, David. "American Atomic Strategy and the Hydrogen Bomb Decision." *Journal of American History* 66, no. 1 (June 1979): 62–87.

————. "Toward Armageddon: The Foundations of U.S. Nuclear Strategy." Ph.D. diss., University of Chicago, 1983.

————. "The Origins of Overkill: Nuclear Weapons and American Strategy, 1945–1960." *International Security* 7, no. 4 (Spring 1983): 3–71.

————. "Reality and Responsibility: Power and Process in the Making of United States Nuclear Strategy, 1945–1968." *Journal of Strategic Studies* 9, no. 1 (March 1986): 35–52.

————. "Nuclear War Planning." In *The Laws of War: Constraints on Warfare in the Western World,* ed. Michael Howard, George Andreopoulos and Mark Shulman. New Haven, Conn.: Yale University Press, 1994.

Rothwell, Victor. *Britain and the Cold War, 1941–1947.* London: Jonathan Cape, 1982.

Rowe, Richard. "American Nuclear Strategy and the Korean War," M.A. thesis, University of Pennsylvania, 1984.

Rupieper, Hermann-Josef. *Der besetzte Verbündete: Die amerikanische Deutschlandpolitik 1949–1955.* Opladen: Westdeutscher Verlag, 1991.

Sagan, Scott. *The Limits of Safety: Organizations, Accidents and Nuclear Weapons.* Princeton, N.J.: Princeton University Press, 1993.

Schlesinger, Arthur. *A Thousand Days: John F. Kennedy in the White House.* Boston: Houghton Mifflin, 1965.

————. *Robert Kennedy and His Times.* Boston: Houghton Mifflin, 1978.

Schwabe, Klaus, ed. *Die Anfänge des Schuman-Plans, 1950–51.* Baden-Baden: Nomos, 1988.

Schwartz, Thomas. *America's Germany: John J. McCloy and the Federal Republic of Germany.* Cambridge, Mass.: Harvard University Press, 1991.

Schwarz, Hans-Peter. *Vom Reich zur Bundesrepublik.* Neuwied: Luchterhand, 1966.

———. *Die Ära Adenauer, 1957–1963.* Stuttgart: Deutsche Verlags-Anstalt, 1983.

Schwarz, Hans-Peter. *Adenauer.*

Vol. 1: *Der Aufstieg, 1876–1952.* Stuttgart: Deutsche Verlags-Anstalt, 1986.

Vol. 2: *Der Staatsmann, 1952–1967.* Stuttgart: Deutsche Verlags-Anstalt, 1991.

———. "Adenauer und die Kernwaffen." *Vierteljahrshefte für Zeitgeschichte* 37, no. 4 (October 1989): 567–593

———. "Adenauer, le nucléaire, et la France." *Revue d'histoire diplomatique* 106, no. 4 (1992): 297–311.

Shapley, Deborah. *Promise and Power: The Life and Times of Robert McNamara.* Boston: Little Brown, 1993.

Sherwood, Robert. *Roosevelt and Hopkins: An Intimate History.* New York: Harper, 1950.

Shlaim, Avi. *The United States and the Berlin Blockade, 1948–1949: A Study in Crisis Decision-Making.* Berkeley: University of California Press, 1983.

Smirnov, Yuri, and Vladislav Zubok. "Nuclear Weapons after Stalin's Death: Moscow Enters the H-Bomb Age." Cold War International History Project *Bulletin,* no. 4 (Fall 1994): 1, 14–18.

Smith, Jean. *Lucius D. Clay: An American Life.* New York: Holt, 1990.

Soutou, Georges-Henri. "La France, l'Allemagne et les accords de Paris." *Relations internationales,* no. 52 (Winter 1987): 451–470.

———. "La France et les notes soviétiques de 1952 sur l'Allemagne." *Revue d'Allemagne* 20, no. 3 (July-September 1988): 261–273.

———. "La politique française à l'égard de la Rhénanie 1944–1947." In *Franzosen und Deutschen am Rhein: 1789, 1918, 1945,* ed. Peter Huttenberger and Hans-Georg Molitor. Essen: Klartext, 1989.

———. "Les problèmes de sécurité dans les rapports franco-allemands de 1956 à 1963." *Relations internationales,* no. 58 (Summer 1989): 227–251.

———. *The French Military Program for Nuclear Energy, 1945–1981.* Nuclear History Program Occasional Paper no. 3. College Park: Center for International Security Studies at Maryland, 1989.

———. "La politique nucléaire de Pierre Mendès France." *Relations internationales,* no. 59 (Fall 1989): 317–330. Also in *La France et l'atome,* ed. Maurice Vaïsse. Brussels: Bruylant, 1994.

———. "Georges Bidault et la construction europeénne, 1944–1954." In *Le MRP et la construction européenne,* ed. Serge Bernstein et al. Brussels: Complexe, 1993.

———. "Le Général de Gaulle et l'URSS, 1943–1945: Idéologie ou équilibre européen?" *Revue d'histoire diplomatique* 108, no. 4 (1994): 303–355.

———. "Les accords de 1957 et 1958: Vers une communauté stratégique et nucléaire entre la France, l'Allemagne et l'Italie?" In *La France et l'atome: Etudes d'histoire nucléaire,* ed. Maurice Vaïsse. Brussels: Bruylant, 1994.

———. "De Gaulle, Adenauer und die gemeinsame Front gegen die amerikanische Nuklearstrategie." In *Politischer Wandel, organisierte Gewalt und nationale Sicherheit: Beiträge zur neueren Geschichte Deutschlands und Frankreichs,* ed. Ernst Hansen et al. Munich: Oldenbourg, 1995.

———. *L'alliance incertaine: Les rapports politico-stratégiques franco-allemands, 1954–1996.* Paris: Fayard, 1996.

———. "La sécurité de la France dans l'après-guerre." In *La France et l'OTAN, 1949–1996,* ed. Maurice Vaïsse et al. Paris: Editions Complexe, 1996.

Stares, Paul. *Allied Rights and Legal Constraints on German Military Power.* Washington, D.C.: Brookings, 1990.

Staritz, Dietrich. "Das ganze oder das halbe Deutschland? Zur Deutschlandpolitik der Sowjetunion und der KPD/SED (1945–1955)." In *Die Republik der fünfziger Jahre: Adenauers Deutschlandpolitik auf dem Prüfstand,* ed. Jürgen Weber. Munich: Olzog, 1989.

Stein, Peter, and Peter Feaver. *Assuring Control of Nuclear Weapons: The Evolution of Permissive Action Links.* Harvard Center for Science and International Affairs Occasional Paper no. 2. Boston: University Press of America, 1987.

Steininger, Rolf. *Eine vertane Chance: Die Stalin-Note vom 10. März 1952 und die Weidervereinigung.* Bonn: Dietz, 1985. English translation: *The German Question: The Stalin Note of 1952 and the Problem of Reunification.* New York: Columbia University Press, 1990.

Stueck, William. *The Road to Confrontation: American Policy toward China and Korea, 1947–1950.* Chapel Hill: University of North Carolina Press, 1981.

Taubman, William. *Stalin's American Policy: From Entente to Détente to Cold War.* New York: Norton, 1982.

Theoharis, Athan. "Roosevelt and Truman on Yalta: The Origins of the Cold War," *Political Science Quarterly* 87, no. 2 (June 1972): 210–241.

Trachtenberg, Marc. "New Light on the Cuban Missile Crisis?" *Diplomatic History* 14, no. 2 (Spring 1990): 241–247.

———. *History and Strategy.* Princeton, N.J.: Princeton University Press, 1991.

———. "L'ouverture des archives américaines: Vers de nouvelles perspectives." In *L'Europe et la Crise de Cuba,* ed. Maurice Vaïsse. Paris: Colin, 1993.

———. "La formation du système de défense occidentale: les Etats-Unis, la France et MC 48," in *La France et l'OTAN, 1949–1996,* ed. Maurice Vaïsse et al. (Paris: Editions Complexe, 1996).

Tusa, Ann and John. *The Berlin Blockade.* London: Hodder and Stoughton, 1988.

Vaïsse, Maurice. "L'echec d'une Europe franco-britannique, ou comment le pacte de Bruxelles fut créé et délaissé." In *Histoire des débuts de la construction européenne,* ed. Raymond Poidevin. Brussels: Bruylant, 1986.

———. "Aux origines du mémorandum de septembre 1958." *Relations internationales,* no. 58 (Summer 1989): 253–268.

———. "Un dialogue de sourds: Les relations nucléaires franco-américaines de 1957 à 1960." *Relations internationales,* no. 68 (Winter 1991): 407–423.

———. "La France et le Traité de Moscou (1957–1963)." *Revue d'histoire diplomatique* 107 (1993): 41–53.

———. "Indépendance et solidarité, 1958–1963." In Vaïsse et al., *La France et l'OTAN,* pp. 219–245.

———, ed. *L'Europe et la Crise de Cuba.* Paris: Colin, 1993.

Vaïsse, Maurice, Pierre Mélandri, and Frédéric Bozo, eds. *La France et l'OTAN, 1949–1996.* Paris: Editions Complexe, 1996.

Wall, Irwin. *The United States and the Making of Postwar France, 1945–1954.* New York: Cambridge University Press, 1991.

Wampler, Robert. *NATO Strategic Planning and Nuclear Weapons, 1950–1957.* Nuclear History Program Occasional Paper 6. University of Maryland: Center for International Security Studies at Maryland, 1990.

———. "Ambiguous Legacy: The United States, Great Britain, and the Foundations of NATO Strategy, 1948–1957." Ph.D. diss., Harvard University, 1991.

———. "Conventional Goals and Nuclear Promises: The Truman Administration and the Roots of the NATO New Look." In *NATO: The Founding of the Atlantic Alliance and the Integration of Europe,* ed. Francis Heller and John Gillingham. New York: St. Martin's, 1992.

———. "Eisenhower, NATO, and Nuclear Weapons: The Strategy and Political Economy of Alliance Security." in *Eisenhower: A Centenary Assessment,* ed. Günter Bischof and Stephen Ambrose. Baton Rouge: Louisiana State University Press, 1995.

————. "The Die is Cast: The United States and NATO Nuclear Planning." Unpublished paper.

Weathersby, Kathryn. "Soviet Aims in Korea and the Origins of the Korean War, 1945–1950: New Evidence from Russian Archives." Cold War International History Project Working Paper no. 8. Woodrow Wilson Center, Washington, D.C., 1993.

Weil, Martin. *A Pretty Good Club: The Founding Fathers of the U.S. Foreign Service.* New York: Norton, 1978.

Weisenfeld, Ernst. *Quelle Allemagne pour la France?* Paris: Colin, 1989.

Wiggershaus, Norbert. "Bedrohungsvorstellungen Bundeskanzler Adenauers nach Ausbruch des Korea-Krieges." *Militärgeschichtliche Mitteilungen* no. 1 (1979): 79–122.

————. "The German Question and the Foundation of the Atlantic Pact." In *The Origins of NATO,* ed. Joseph Smith. Exeter: University of Exeter Press, 1990.

Williamson, Samuel, and Steven Rearden, eds. *The Origins of U.S. Nuclear Strategy, 1945–1953.* New York: St. Martin's, 1993.

Wohlstetter, Albert. "The Delicate Balance of Terror." *Foreign Affairs* 37, no. 2 (January 1959): 211–234.

————. "Nuclear Sharing: NATO and the N + 1 Country," *Foreign Affairs* 39, no. 2 (April 1961): 355–387.

Woodward, E. L. *British Foreign Policy in the Second World War,* vol. 3. London: HMSO, 1971.

Yergin, Daniel. *Shattered Peace: The Origins of the Cold War and the National Security State.* Boston: Houghton Mifflin, 1978.

Young, John W. *France, the Cold War and the Western Alliance, 1944–49: French Foreign Policy and Post-War Europe.* New York: St. Martin's Press, 1990.

Zelikow, Philip. "George C. Marshall and the Moscow CFM Meeting of 1947," *Diplomacy and Statecraft* 8, no. 2 (July 1997): 97–124.

Zelikow, Philip, and Condoleezza Rice. *Germany Unified and Europe Transformed: A Study in Statecraft.* Cambridge, Mass.: Harvard University Press, 1995.

Zubok, Vladislav. "Soviet Intelligence and the Cold War: The 'Small' Committee of Information, 1952–53." Cold War International History Project Working Paper no. 4. Woodrow Wilson Center, Washington, D.C., 1992.

————. "Khrushchev and the Berlin Crisis (1958–1962)." Cold War International History Project Working Paper no. 6. Woodrow Wilson Center, Washington, D.C., 1993.

————. "Khrushchev's Motives and Soviet Diplomacy in the Berlin Crisis, 1958–1962." Unpublished paper, 1994.

Zubok, Vladislav, and Constantine Pleshakov. *Inside the Kremlin's Cold War: From Stalin to Khrushchev.* Cambridge, Mass.: Harvard University Press, 1996.

German Democratic Republic (East Germany),
86; possible uprising in, 252, 254–255; dealings with, 260–261, 272, 275, 327
German nuclear question: and USSR, 146,
246–247, 252–256, 344–345, 380–381; and
U.S., 209–210, 234, 261–263, 281–285,
305–306, 314, 321, 328, 340–342, 344–345,
373–374, 379–382; and NATO or European
nuclear force, 202–203; and U.S. NATO
policy (1961–62), 305–306, 314, 321; and
Britain, 219–221; and France, 205–206, 225,
273–274, 336–337, 371–374, 381, 392–393,
396; and Adenauer, 232–238, 253, 280–281,
330, 339–342, 347; and Berlin settlement,
280–282, 328, 340–342, 344–347, 386–390;
and test ban, 381–387. See also FIG agreements
German question: during World War II and at
Potsdam, 15–33; from late 1945 to December
1947, 34, 41–65, 69–77; in 1948–49, 66,
73–85; in 1950–55, 101–114, 123–145. See
also Berlin Crisis; German nuclear question;
Germany, Federal Republic of
Germany, Federal Republic of (West Germany):
establishment of West German state, 78, 86;
rearmament of, 73, 95, 101–103, 106–113,
121–125, 127–128; political status of,
102–103, 105–106, 112–114, 125–128; policy of (1955–60), 231–238; and Berlin Crisis,
274–281, 329–331, 339–342, 346–348; and
U.S., 133, 138, 231–238, 275–281, 329–331,
339–341, 346–348, 394–398; and France,
133, 235, 238, 339, 341, 346, 370–371; internal politics, 377–379, 394–396; and U.S.
arms control policy, 394–395. See also Adenauer, Konrad; Berlin; Berlin Crisis; German
nuclear question; German question
Gorbachev, Mikhail, 401–402
Gray, Gordon, 198
Great Britain: and spheres of influence, 5–6,
35–36; at Potsdam, 32–33; and German
question (1945–48), 51–52, 60–61, 68–71;
and German reunification, 103, 102n.22,
129–130, 130n.117, 220; and German rearmament, 107–108, 110, 111; and German
nuclear question, 219–221; and Europe as
"third force," 67–68, 115–117; and European
unification, 115–117; and the United States,
115–117, 216–219, 265–267; nuclear relations with U.S., 195, 198, 207–208,
216–219, 307–309; and NATO nuclear force,
218–219; defense policy, 83–84, 168,
174–175, 186–187, 216–222, 308n.81; and
disengagement, 221; and Berlin Crisis,
263–267, 328–329; and nuclear cooperation

with France, 357, 366–367. See also Bevin,
Ernest; Macmillan, Harold
Greece, 5–6, 64, 88
Gromyko, Andrei (Soviet foreign minister,
1957–85), 254, 344–345, 350
Gruenther, Alfred (SACEUR, 1953–56), 127,
137n.147, 160, 163, 165–167, 170,
174–176, 180, 188

Harriman, Averell, 20, 28, 387–389
Herter, Christian (U.S. secretary of state,
1959–61), 189, 212, 217, 240–244, 254,
278–280
Home, Lord (British foreign secretary,
1960–63), 220, 263, 350–351
Hopkins, Harry, 13

Intermediate Range Ballistic Missiles (IRBMs):
production of, in Europe, 207, 210–211,
218; control of, by allies, 195–196, 198–199,
207–209
Iran, 36–37, 38, 40
Israel, 385
Italy, 64, 88

Japan, 36, 40
Joint Chiefs of Staff (JCS), 81, 90, 107, 111,
118n.76, 152, 167, 172, 174, 257, 296, 306,
313–314
Joint Committee on Atomic Energy, 194–196,
198
Jupiter missiles, 195–196, 353–354

Kaysen, Carl, 299, 388
Kennan, George, 41, 104–105
Kennedy, John: basic policy of, 283–285, 322;
and military issues, 290–296, 318–320; and
Berlin Crisis, 283–297, 304, 322, 325–331,
337–351; and Germany, 283, 322, 325–328,
373–376; and German nuclear question,
283–285, 321, 328n.149, 366, 373–374; and
France, 306–307, 337–339, 358, 359,
365–367, 370, 391–394; and Britain,
357–358; and MLF, 314, 356, 365, 388–389;
and Cuban Missile Crisis, 352–355; and new
NATO policy, 355–367; and terms of settlement in Europe, 355, 379; attitude toward
the allies, 302–304, 355–356, 376–377;
American University speech, 388; trip to
Berlin, 394
Khrushchev, Nikita, 140, 142; and Berlin, 247,
283, 322–324, 349–350, 381, 387, 389, 398;
and Cuban Missile Crisis, 355
Kohler, Foy, 330, 341
Korea, 36, 87